Cambridge
O Level
Mathematics

Audrey Simpson

CAMBRIDGE
UNIVERSITY PRESS

CAMBRIDGE
UNIVERSITY PRESS

University Printing House, Cambridge CB2 8BS, United Kingdom

One Liberty Plaza, 20th Floor, New York, NY 10006, USA

477 Williamstown Road, Port Melbourne, VIC 3207, Australia

314–321, 3rd Floor, Plot 3, Splendor Forum, Jasola District Centre, New Delhi – 110025, India

79 Anson Road, #06-04/06, Singapore 079906

Cambridge University Press is part of the University of Cambridge.

It furthers the University's mission by disseminating knowledge in the pursuit of education, learning and research at the highest international levels of excellence.

Information on this title: education.cambridge.org

First published 2012
Second edition 2016
20 19 18 17 16 15 14 13 12 11 10 9 8 7 6 5

Printed in Great Britain by CPI Group (UK) Ltd, Croydon CR0 4YY

A catalogue record for this publication is available from the British Library

ISBN 978-1-316-50644-8 Paperback

Additional resources for this publication at www.cambridge.org/9781316506448

Cambridge University Press has no responsibility for the persistence or accuracy of URLs for external or third-party internet websites referred to in this publication, and does not guarantee that any content on such websites is, or will remain, accurate or appropriate. Information regarding prices, travel timetables, and other factual information given in this work is correct at the time of first printing but Cambridge University Press does not guarantee the accuracy of such information thereafter.

....

....

IGCSE® is the registered trademark of Cambridge International Examinations.

Past question papers through-out are reproduced by permission of Cambridge International Examinations.

Cambridge International Examinations bears no responsibility for the example answers to questions taken from its past question papers which are contained in this publication.

The exam-style questions, answers and commentary in this title are written by the author and have not been produced by Cambridge International Examinations.

Contents

Introduction

This book covers the entire syllabus for the Cambridge O Level Mathematics from Cambridge International Examinations.

Students will find that the structure of the book allows them to proceed at their own pace through each chapter by:

- working through the essential skills exercise

- reading the explanatory text

- following and understanding the worked examples

- working through each exercise with frequent checking of the answers at the back of the book

- and finally working through the mixed exercise at the end of the chapter.

The book is designed to be worked through sequentially as the required skills and knowledge are built up chapter by chapter and the questions in each chapter only refer to work already covered.

The mixed exercises contain original questions and also carefully chosen questions from past examination papers. These are taken from the O Level examination papers but some appropriate examples are also taken from Cambridge IGCSE papers.

The mixed exercise should consolidate the work covered in the chapter and the past examination questions help students to prepare for examination.

The Cambridge O Level Examination consists of two papers. Calculators are not allowed in Paper One, but may be used in Paper Two. This book provides plenty of practice in, and methods for, working without a calculator. Students are encouraged to work without a calculator where possible.

A final section provides suggestions for revision and support as students prepare for examination.

Note to students

- The text in each chapter introduces you to essential mathematical tools.

- The exercises help you gain confidence in using these tools.

- To make the best progress you should ensure that you understand the worked examples. When you have read through each of these examples it can be very helpful to cover up the working and try to reproduce it yourself.

- You should check your answers as you go along. It is important to practise working correctly, and you will not help yourself if you work through a lot of questions incorrectly before you realise that you have been in error. Of course you will be helping no one if you look up the answer *before* you try the question!

- If you work through the whole of this book you will have covered every topic in the O Level syllabus and will have built up a bank of skills to help you be successful in the future and feel prepared for examination.

Acknowledgements

I would like to thank Professor Gordon Kirby for his invaluable advice and encouragement. I am also grateful for his efforts to check my work patiently for errors, both mathematical and stylistic.

I am also indebted to my sister, Pat Victor, for the times she sorted out frustrating problems with both my computer and the software needed for the production of the manuscript.

Audrey Simpson

Understanding Number

Learning Objectives (Syllabus sections 1, 3, 4, 7, 8)

In this chapter you will learn to:
- identify and use different types of number
- express numbers as products of prime numbers
- find the lowest common multiple and highest common factor of two or more numbers
- understand operations and inverses
- recognise common mathematical symbols
- understand and order integers
- convert numbers to and from standard form
- use the recognised order of working in calculations.

1.1 Introduction

By the end of this chapter, you should know more about the different types of numbers that you need to study for the rest of the course. You may feel that you know most of it already, but please work through it as there are plenty of things in it that will help you build the skills you need to be successful in your course. Treat it as revision if you like.

1.2 Essential Skills   NO CALCULATOR IN THIS EXERCISE

To get the most from this course, you should know the multiplication tables from 2 to 10 and be able to recall them without hesitation. It is also important to know the facts about addition and subtraction.

Try the following mini-test and see how quickly you can answer the questions without using a calculator.

a 4×6	**b** 3×7	**c** 8×5	**d** 9×8	**e** 2×7
f 6×9	**g** 8×8	**h** 9×5	**i** 7×7	**j** 3×6
k $6 + 7$	**l** $5 + 8$	**m** $9 + 7$	**n** $3 + 5 + 9$	**o** $8 + 9$
p $11 + 9$	**q** $13 + 6$	**r** $3 + 4 + 5$	**s** $16 + 5$	**t** $4 + 17$
u $9 - 4$	**v** $11 - 7$	**w** $15 - 9$	**x** $7 - 4$	**y** $16 \div 8$
z $24 \div 6$				

1.3 Sets of Numbers

The numbers that we use today have developed over a period of time as the need arose. At first, humans needed numbers just to count things, so the simplest set of numbers was the set of **natural** or **counting** numbers. We use the symbol $\mathbb{N}$ to represent the counting numbers, and we use curly brackets to list some of these numbers.

$$\mathbb{N} = \{1, 2, 3, 4, \ldots\}$$

The dots at the end mean 'and so on' because the list goes on forever. (Lists like these are often shown in curly brackets. However, this is not essential.)

When addition and subtraction were introduced, a new set of numbers was needed.

For example, I had three goats. Three were stolen. How many goats do I have now?

We know that the answer is none or zero, which does not appear in the counting numbers.

Subtraction also meant that negative numbers were needed, as we will see later in this chapter.

Our next set of numbers is the set of **integers**, which have the symbol $\mathbb{Z}$, and include negative whole numbers, zero and the natural numbers.

$$\mathbb{Z} = \{\ldots, -3, -2, -1, 0, 1, 2, 3, \ldots\}$$

Key terms

Natural (or Counting) numbers ($\mathbb{N}$) are the whole numbers you need to count individual items, for example 1, 5, 72, 1000.

Integers ($\mathbb{Z}$) are the counting numbers and also zero and negative whole numbers, for example $-50, -2, 0, 11, 251$.

Practical work

- Make yourself an integer number line on a long strip of paper, like in Figure 1.1.
- Mark on it the integers from -20 through zero to $+20$. Make sure they are evenly spaced.
- Fold the strip and stick it on the inside cover of your exercise book so that you can unfold it whenever you need it later in the course.

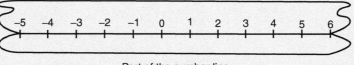

Part of the number line

Figure 1.1

Key term

Rational numbers ($\mathbb{Q}$) are the counting numbers, integers and also numbers which can be written as fractions (or ratios), for example $-20, -\frac{3}{4}, 0, 1, 50\frac{1}{2}$.

After addition and subtraction came division and multiplication. What happens when we divide two by three?

The answer is that we get the fraction $\frac{2}{3}$. But where does that fit in with our latest set of numbers? We need another set which includes all the fractions or **rational numbers**. This is the set $\mathbb{Q}$.

Rational numbers can all be expressed as fractions or ratios made up of one integer over another. Remember, for example, that 5 can be written as $\frac{5}{1}$, so integers themselves are included in the set of rational numbers. We can only list some examples of this set because there is an infinite number of members belonging to $\mathbb{Q}$.

Some examples of rational numbers are:

$$\frac{2}{3}, \frac{5}{2}, -2\frac{1}{2}, \frac{3}{100}, 5, 0, 29, -500, \text{ and so on.}$$

The last set we need for our number sets is the set of **real numbers**, $\mathbb{R}$. This includes all the previous sets and also the irrational numbers. **Irrational numbers** are numbers which *cannot* be written as fractions (or ratios) made up of one integer over another.

The Greek letter π (which is spelled and pronounced as pi) is used to represent what is perhaps the most famous irrational number. Pi is the number you get when you divide the length of the circumference of a circle by its diameter. *You can never find the value of π exactly.* We will do some experiments later in the course to see how close we can get to the calculated value of π.

Irrational numbers include square roots of numbers that are not perfect squares themselves, and as we find in the case of π, irrational numbers are decimals that go on and on forever, and never repeat any pattern.

The number π ($= \mathbf{3.141592653589793238462664\ldots}$) has been calculated to billions of places of decimal by high-powered computers, using a more advanced method than measuring the circumference and diameter of a circle. However, no recurring pattern has been found.

Recurring decimals are not irrational numbers because they can always be written as fractions.

For example, $0.66666666666\ldots = \frac{2}{3}$, and $0.285714285714285714\ldots = \frac{2}{7}$.

Recurring decimals do, of course, have a repeating pattern, unlike irrational numbers.

Write down the sequence of numbers that recur in the decimal equivalent of $\frac{2}{7}$.

Figure 1.2 will help you to see how these sets of numbers build up.

Each number type has been drawn with two or three examples in it.

Another way to show these sets is on number lines like in Figure 1.3. Some examples of each set are shown below. The arrows show that the sets go on forever in that direction.

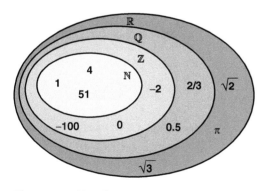

Figure 1.2 Number sets

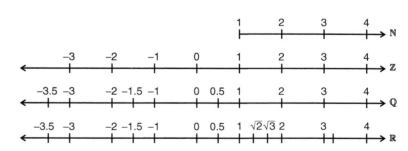

Figure 1.3 Number lines

Example 1

| 2 | $\sqrt{3}$ | $\frac{1}{1000}$ | -99 | $2\frac{1}{2}$ | $-\frac{1}{4}$ | π | 0.3 | 0 | 2005 |

From the list given above, select:

a the natural numbers   **b** the integers   **c** the rational numbers

d the irrational numbers   **e** the real numbers.

Answer 1

a   The natural numbers ($\mathbb{N}$) are: 2 and 2005.

b   The integers ($\mathbb{Z}$) are: −99, 0, 2 and 2005 (because each larger set includes the set before it).

c   The rational numbers ($\mathbb{Q}$) are: −99, $-\frac{1}{4}$, 0, $\frac{1}{1000}$, 0.3, $2\frac{1}{2}$, 2, 2005.

d   The irrational numbers are: $\sqrt{3}$ and π (because these are decimals that go on forever with no repeating pattern).

e   The real numbers ($\mathbb{R}$) are: 2, $\sqrt{3}$, $\frac{1}{1000}$, −99, $2\frac{1}{2}$, $-\frac{1}{4}$, π, 0.3, 0, 2005.

Within the above sets of numbers there are other, smaller sets. Some of these sets are discussed below.

1.4 Prime Numbers, Factors and Multiples

In this section we will use natural numbers only.

Prime numbers are natural numbers that are only **divisible** by themselves or by 1.

Some examples of prime numbers are:

$$2, 3, 5, 7, 11, 13, 17, \ldots$$

Notice that 1 is *not* counted as a prime number, and 2 is the only *even* prime number.

Example 2

Write a list of all the prime numbers between 20 and 35.

Answer 2

23, 29, 31

(All the other numbers between 20 and 35 are divisible by numbers other than just themselves or 1.)

The **factors** of a number are the natural numbers that can be multiplied together to make the number.

For example, 2 and 3 are factors of 6 because $2 \times 3 = 6$.

The **multiples** of a number are obtained by multiplying the number by other natural numbers.

For example, the multiples of 12 would include 12, 24, 36, 48 and so on.

The factors of 12 in Figure 1.4 are shown multiplied together. This is called a **product of factors**. So numbers that are multiplied together are called **factors**, and the result of multiplying them together is called the **product**. There are other factors of 12.

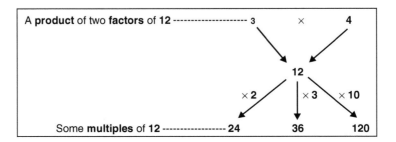

Figure 1.4 Factors and multiples of 12

Altogether the factors of 12 are: 1, 2, 3, 4, 6 and 12 (all the numbers that will divide into 12 without leaving a remainder).

Of particular interest are the prime factors. The prime numbers among the factors of 12 are 2 and 3. We can write 12 as a **product** of its **prime factors**:

$$12 = 2 \times 2 \times 3$$

or we can **list** the prime factors of 12: {2, 3}.

A factor tree is a neat method for finding prime factors of larger numbers. The following example will show you how to make a factor tree.

Example 3

Write 200 as a product of its prime factors.

Answer 3

First make a list of the smaller prime numbers:
2, 3, 5, 7, …
Start by dividing by 2, and repeat until
the number will no longer divide by 2.
Then work through your list in order,
trying 3, then 5 and so on.
The answer is: $200 = 2 \times 2 \times 2 \times 5 \times 5$.
(Check this by multiplying out.)

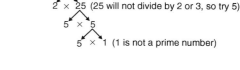

Example 4

a List all the factors of 18. **b** List the prime factors of 18.
c Write 18 as a product of its prime factors. **d** List three multiples of 18.

Answer 4

a {1, 2, 3, 6, 9, 18} **b** {2, 3} **c** $18 = 2 \times 3 \times 3$
d For example, 36 (18 × 2), 54 (18 × 3), 90 (18 × 5).

Exercise 1.1

NO CALCULATOR IN THIS EXERCISE

1 5, −100, −3.67, π, 0, 1507, $\dfrac{99}{7}$, $\dfrac{6}{1}$

From the list above:
a Write down all the real numbers. **b** Write down all the rational numbers.
c Write down all the integers. **d** Write down all the natural numbers.
e One of the numbers is irrational. Which is it?

2 a List all the factors of 30. **b** List the prime factors of 30.
c Write 30 as a product of its prime factors. (Multiply out to check your answer.)
d Write down three multiples of 30.

3 1, 4, 30, 45, 5, 15, 9, 1500, 3, 10

From this list choose:
a the multiples of 15 **b** the factors of 15.

4 Use a factor tree to find the prime factors of 240. Write your answer:
a as a list of prime factors **b** as a product of prime factors.

5 Write down all the prime numbers between 20 and 40.

6 Which of the following numbers are prime numbers?

37, 49, 53, 81, 87, 93, 101

7 Write down a list of numbers between 80 and 90, including 80 and 90. From your list find:

a two prime numbers   **b** three multiples of 5   **c** a factor of 348.

1.5 Highest Common Factor (HCF) and Lowest Common Multiple (LCM)

'Common' in this case means 'belonging to all'.

We often need to find the factors or multiples of two (or more) numbers that belong to both (or all) the numbers. One way to do this is to list all the factors or multiples of both numbers and see which factors or multiples occur in both lists.

The following example shows how this is done.

Key terms

The Highest Common Factor (HCF) of two or more given numbers is the highest number which will divide into both or all of the given numbers without leaving a remainder, for example 3 is the HCF of 9, 12 and 15.

The Lowest Common Multiple (LCM) of two or more given numbers is the lowest number which is a multiple of both or all of the given numbers, for example 18 is the LCM of 2, 6 and 9.

Example 5

a   **i**   List all the factors of 30.   **ii**   List all the factors of 20.

     iii   From your two lists find the common factors of 20 and 30 (not including 1).

b   **i**   List the first four multiples of 30 (not including 30 itself).

     ii   List the first five multiples of 20 (not including 20 itself).

     iii   From your two lists, find any common multiples.

c   Find the HCF of 30 and 20.   **d**   Find the LCM of 30 and 20.

Answer 5

a   **i**   {1, 2, 3, 5, 6, 10, 15, 30}   **ii**   {1, 2, 4, 5, 10, 20}   **iii**   {2, 5, 10}

b   **i**   {60, 90, 120, 150}   **ii**   {40, 60, 80, 100, 120}   **iii**   {60, 120}

c   10   **d**   60

Using the above example you should see that finding the highest common factor (HCF) of 20 and 30 is simple. It is the highest number that appears in both lists of factors of both the numbers. The HCF of 20 and 30 is 10.

Similarly, the lowest common multiple of 20 and 30 is the smallest number that appears in both lists of multiples. The LCM of 20 and 30 is 60.

An alternative method for finding the HCF of two or more numbers is first to write them as products of their prime factors, and then pick out the factors common to both lists. The example shows this.

Example 6

a   Write

     i   360   and   **ii**   980

     as products of their prime factors.

b   Find the highest common factor of 360 and 980

Answer 6

a   **i** $360 = 2 \times 2 \times 2 \times 3 \times 3 \times 5$ **ii** $980 = 2 \times 2 \times 5 \times 7 \times 7$

b $HCF = 2 \times 2 \times 5 = 20$

1.6 Tests of Divisibility without Using a Calculator

Before you go any further you might like to try some tests of divisibility which can help you save time in these questions. These tests show what will divide into a number without leaving a remainder.

- **Divisibility by 2:** All even numbers divide by 2. (All even numbers end in 2, 4, 6, 8 or 0.)
- **Divisibility by 3:** This is a rather surprising test, but it does work!

Add all the digits (individual numbers) of the entire number together. If the result is 3, 6 or 9 then the number will divide by 3. If the result is 10 or more, keep adding the digits until you get to a single digit. This is called finding the **digital root** of the number. If the digital root is 3, 6 or 9 then the number will divide by 3.

For example, the digital root of 2115 is $2 + 1 + 1 + 5 = 9$, so 2115 will divide by 3 (check it on your calculator).

Of course, it does not matter what order the digits of the number appear or if any zeroes appear in the number, so 5121, 2511, 12510, 105120 (and so on) will all divide by 3.

To find the digital root of 3672:

$$3 + 6 + 7 + 2 = 18$$
$$1 + 8 = 9$$

So the digital root of 3672 is 9. Hence, 3672 will divide by 3.

- **Divisibility by 5:** All numbers ending in 5 or 0 will divide by 5. Therefore, 3672 will not divide by 5 whereas 3670 will.
- **Divisibility by 6:** All *even* numbers with a digital root of 3, 6 or 9 will divide by 6. 3672 will divide by 6.
- **Divisibility by 9:** All numbers with a digital root of 9 will divide by 9. 3672 will divide by 9.

Example 7

a Test 552 for divisibility by 2, 3, 5, 6 and 9.

b Test 6165 for divisibility by 2, 3, 5, 6 and 9.

Answer 7

a 552 is even, so it will divide by 2.

$5 + 5 + 2 = 12 \rightarrow 1 + 2 = 3$, so it will divide by 3.

552 does not end in 5 or 0, so it will not divide by 5.

552 is even *and* it will divide by 3, so it will also divide by 6.

The digital root of 552 is 3, not 9, so it will not divide by 9.

b 6165 is not even, so it will not divide by 2.

$6 + 1 + 6 + 5 = 18 \rightarrow 1 + 8 = 9$, so it will divide by 3.

6165 ends in 5, so it will divide by 5.

Although 6165 will divide by 3 it is not even, so it will not divide by 6.

The digital root of 6165 is 9, so it will divide by 9.

Exercise 1.2 **NO CALCULATOR IN THIS EXERCISE**

1 a List all the factors of 8. Then list all the factors of 12.
   b Find the highest common factor of 8 and 12.

2 Find the highest common factor of 21 and 42.

3 a List all the factors of:
     i 15   **ii** 35   **iii** 20
   b Write down the highest common factor of 15, 35 and 20.

4 a List the first six multiples of 12 and of 8.
   b Write down the lowest common multiple of 12 and 8.

5 Find the lowest common multiple of 3, 5 and 12.

6 Test 21603 for divisibility by 2, 3, 5 and 9. Explain your reasoning (see Example 6).

7 Test 515196 for divisibility by 2, 3, 5, 6 and 9. Explain your reasoning.

1.7 Operations and Inverses

Mathematical operations like addition, or division, have inverses which 'undo' the operation.

For example, $2 \times 3 = 6$, and $6 \div 3 = 2$.

Division is the inverse of multiplication because it 'undoes' multiplication.

Also, multiplication is the inverse of division, as you can see in Figure 1.5.

What do you think is the inverse of addition? Look at Figure 1.6.

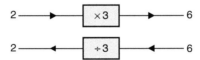

Figure 1.5 Multiplication and division are inverses

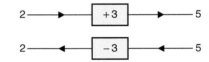

Figure 1.6 Addition and subtraction are inverses

1.8 Squares and Square Roots, Cubes and Cube Roots

The square of a number is the result of multiplying a number by itself.

For example, the square of 9 is $9 \times 9 = 81$, the square of 11 is $11 \times 11 = 121$, and the square of 35 is $35 \times 35 = 1225$.

The compact way of showing that the number is to be squared is to write it to the power of 2.

So the square of 9 is written as $9^2 = 81$. Similarly, $11^2 = 121$ and $35^2 = 1225$.

Finding the square root of a number *undoes* the squaring, so for example, the square root of 81 is 9, the square root of 121 is 11, and the square root of 1225 is 35.

The compact way of showing that the square root of a number is to be found is to use the square root sign: $\sqrt{\ }$.

So the square root of 81 is written as $\sqrt{81} = 9$; also, $\sqrt{121} = 11$ and $\sqrt{1225} = 35$.

You should be able to see that squaring and finding the square root undo each other.

As we have seen above, operations which 'undo' each other are inverses of each other.

Hence, squaring and finding the square root are **inverse operations** (see Figure 1.7).

We will come across more inverse operations later in the course.

We can find the square of any number. My calculator tells me that the square of 2.41 is 5.8081. It also tells me that $\sqrt{468.2896} = 21.64$.

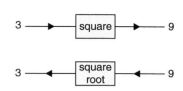

Figure 1.7 Square and square root are inverses

However, not all numbers have exact square roots. For example, $\sqrt{2}, \sqrt{3}$ or $\sqrt{5}$ are numbers with decimals that 'go on forever' without any repeating pattern; they are irrational numbers.

$\sqrt{49} = 7$ exactly, so $\sqrt{49}$ is a rational number. As we see above, $\sqrt{468.2896} = 21.64$, so $\sqrt{468.2896}$ is a rational number.

My calculator tells me that $\sqrt{7.2} = 2.683\,281\,573$ before it runs out of space on its display, so $\sqrt{7.2}$ *looks* as if it could be an irrational number, although we cannot tell for certain by this method alone.

The numbers that you get when you square the natural numbers are called **perfect squares**.

They are called perfect squares because on being square rooted they give whole numbers.

The first four perfect squares are 1, 4, 9, 16. Write down the next three square numbers.

The **cube** of a number is the result of multiplying that number by itself twice.

The cube of $4 = 4 \times 4 \times 4 = 16 \times 4 = 64$.

The compact way of writing the cube of a number is to write it to the power 3, so the cube of 4 is: $4^3 = 4 \times 4 \times 4 = 64$.

The cubes of the first four numbers are 1, 8, 27, 64. What is the cube of the next number?

Cube numbers are also often called **cubic numbers**.

The inverse of cubing a number is finding the cube root, and you may find that your calculator has a cube root button if you look carefully.

The cube root sign is $\sqrt[3]{}$, so $\sqrt[3]{27} = 3$ (because $3 \times 3 \times 3 = 27$).

Example 8

a 12, 6, 7, 36, 125, 5, 15, 4

From the list of numbers choose:
  i a perfect square **ii** the square root of 49 **iii** 6^2
  iv $\sqrt{25}$ **v** 5^3

b **Use your calculator** to find:
  i 42.3^2 **ii** $\sqrt{9.61}$ **iii** 1.6^3 **iv** $\sqrt[3]{64}$

Answer 8

a **i** 36 or 4 **ii** 7 **iii** 36
  iv 5 **v** 125

b **i** 1789.29 **ii** 3.1
  iii 4.096 **iv** 4

Exercise 1.3   NO CALCULATOR UNLESS SPECIFIED

1 For each of the operations below state the inverse.

   a multiply   **b** subtract   **c** square   **d** cube root

2 Write down:

   a the square of 6   **b** the square root of 9

   c 2^3 **d** $\sqrt{25}$ **e** 10^2 **f** 10^3

3 **Use your calculator** to find:

   a 5.2^2 **b** $\sqrt{82.81}$ **c** $\sqrt{100}$ **d** $\sqrt[3]{1000}$

4 $\sqrt{256}$ $\sqrt{6.1}$ $\sqrt{841}$ $\sqrt{7}$ $\sqrt{449.44}$

   Use your calculator to choose from the above list:

   a three numbers that you think are rational

   b two numbers that you think are irrational.

   In each case write down all the figures on your calculator display.

5 Write a list of the first seven square numbers.

6 Fill in the gaps in this list of cube numbers.

   1, 8, …, 64, …, 216.

7 Using your answers to questions 5 and 6, write down a number which is both a perfect square and a perfect cube.

8 **Using your calculator**, find another number which is both a perfect square and a perfect cube.

9   1   2   3   4   5   6   7   8   9   10   11

   Copy Table 1.1. Enter each of the numbers in the list above in the correct rows in your table. (Some numbers may fit in more than one row.)

Natural numbers	
Prime numbers	
Even numbers	
Multiples of 3	
Square numbers	
Cube numbers	
Factors of 20	

Table 1.1 Number types

1.9 Directed Numbers

We have looked at integers, which are positive (with a plus sign) or negative (with a minus sign) whole numbers, or zero, which has no sign.

Directed numbers are also positive or negative but include the whole set of real numbers, hence they also include rational and irrational numbers, as well as integers.

They are called **directed numbers** because they indicate a direction along a number line.

Think of a thermometer that measures temperatures above and below zero.

Key term

Directed numbers are numbers that can be positive as well as negative. The sign indicates a direction, for example −10 °C is 10 °C *below* freezing.

If the temperature starts at 4 °C and *falls* by 5 °C, it will end at −1 °C. This can be written as 4 − 5 = −1.

The minus sign in front of the 5 shows the direction in which the temperature has moved from 4.

The minus sign in front of the 1 shows that it is 1 degree *below* zero. If the temperature starts at 4 °C and *rises* by 5 °C, it will end at +9 °C. This can be written as 4 + 5 = +9.

The plus sign shows that the temperature is 9 degrees *above* zero. In practice we do not usually write in the plus sign. If a number is written without a sign it is assumed that it is positive. We are not restricted to whole numbers, so 4 − 5.5 = −1.5.

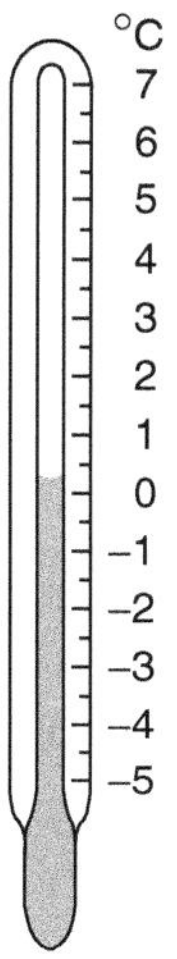

°C
7
6
5
4
3
2
1
0
−1
−2
−3
−4
−5

Figure 1.8

Example 9

a Use the thermometer shown in Figure 1.8 to find the new temperature in each case below.
  i The temperature starts at −5 °C and rises by 4 °C.
  ii The temperature starts at −1 °C and falls by 2 °C.
  iii The temperature starts at −2.5 °C and rises by 5.5 °C.

b Use the thermometer to work out the following:
  i 3 − 6   **ii** −5 + 9   **iii** −1 − 3.5
  iv 3 − 5 + 6   **v** the difference between 4 °C and 7 °C
  vi the difference between −2 °C and −4 °C
  vii the difference between −2 °C and 4 °C.

c Which is warmer, 2 °C or −5 °C?

Answer 9

a **i** −5 + 4 = −1, so the new temperature is −1 °C.
  ii −1 − 2 = −3, so the new temperature is −3 °C.
  iii −2.5 + 5.5 = +3, so the new temperature is +3 °C, (or just 3 °C).

b **i** 3 − 6 = −3   **ii** −5 + 9 = +4 (or just 4)   **iii** −1 − 3.5 = −4.5
  iv 3 − 5 + 6 = −2 + 6 = 4   **v** 3 °C (look at the thermometer)
  vi 2 °C   **vii** 6 °C

c 2 °C is warmer than −5 °C.

Exercise 1.4   **NO CALCULATOR IN THIS EXERCISE**

1 Draw a thermometer, with temperatures between −10 °C and +10 °C.
Use it to complete the following statements.
  a −10 + 5 =   **b** −2 − 3 =   **c** 5 − 8 =
  d 0 − 7 =   **e** 6 + 2 − 3 =

2 Figure 1.9 shows a marker in a reservoir which is used to show the level (in metres) of the water. Copy the diagram and use it to answer the following questions.
  a Overnight the water level sinks from the level shown in the diagram to −1.5 metres. By how many metres has the water level in the reservoir fallen?
  b The water level falls another 2.1 metres. What is the new level?
  c By how much does the water have to rise to bring the level up to 2 metres?

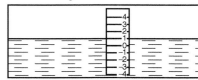

Figure 1.9 Water level

3 Figure 1.10 shows the cross-section of a mountain region. Sea level is 0 metres. A climber starts at 15 metres *below* sea level and climbs 100 metres. How high is he above sea level now?

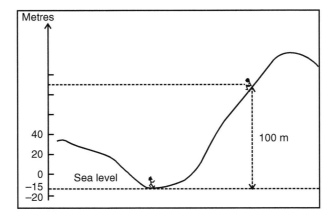

Figure 1.10

4

	Bank Account		
Start	Money in	Money out	Balance
–$216			–$216
	$503		(a)
		$290	(b)
	(c)		$0.00

Table 1.2 Bank statement

My bank account is overdrawn by $216. The balance (the amount of money I have in the bank) is shown in the first line in Table 1.2 as –$216. This means that I owe the bank $216.

a I pay in $503. What should my account balance show now?
b I write a cheque for $290 to pay for my electricity. Am I still overdrawn?
c If so, how much would I need to pay in to clear my debt?

We will learn more about directed numbers in Chapter 3.

1.10 Important Mathematical Symbols

You are already familiar with some mathematical symbols.

For example, $+, -, \times, \div, \pi, \sqrt{}$ and $=$.

Another symbol which is sometimes used is $\neq$, which means 'is not equal to'.

For example, $4 \neq 7$, or 'four is not equal to seven'.

We also need to be able to use symbols to mean 'is greater (or larger) than', or 'is less (or smaller) than'.

For example, we need a mathematical way of writing 'four is less (or smaller) than seven'.

This is written as $4 < 7$.

We can also write $7 > 4$. This means that 'seven is greater than four'.

Suppose we wanted to say that the number of days in February is greater than or equal to 28? This would be written as: Number of days in February $\geqslant$ 28.

So $\geqslant$ means greater than *or equal to* and $>$ means *strictly* greater than. What do you think $\leqslant$ means?

The signs $>$ and $<$ are called **inequality signs**.

1.11 Ordering Integers

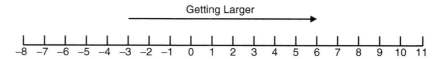

Figure 1.11 The number line

The number line in Figure 1.11 shows the integers from −8 to 11. The rest of the real numbers fit in their correct places along the line, so −2.5 would be halfway between −3 and −2.

The numbers get *larger* as you go from *left* to *right*.

For example, $8 > 3$ (as we know).

Also, $1 > -2$, $-4 < 0$ and so on.

This is also true for all the positive and negative real numbers, so $-6.25 < 3.5$.

Example 10
Use the number line you made earlier to insert the correct symbol between the following pairs of numbers:

a $7 \ldots 20$	**b** $-5 \ldots 10$	**c** $2 \ldots -1$
d $-8 \ldots -19$	**e** $4.5 \ldots -6.5$	**f** $-\frac{1}{2} \ldots -4$

Answer 10

a $7 < 20$	**b** $-5 < 10$	**c** $2 > -1$
d $-8 > -19$	**e** $4.5 > -6.5$	**f** $-\frac{1}{2} > -4$

Exercise 1.5

NO CALCULATOR IN THIS EXERCISE

1 Write down the symbol for:
   a pi
   b square root
   c cube root
   d is not equal to
   e is less than
   f is greater than or equal to

2 Fill in the correct inequality sign between each of the following pairs of numbers.
   a $2 \ldots 4$
   b $-2 \ldots -5$
   c $-10 \ldots 4$
   d $-1 \ldots 0$

3 Arrange the following integers in the correct order, starting with the smallest.
   100,   −1,   −100,   0,   −89,   −76,   75,   101,   61,   −62

1.12 Standard Form

Sometimes we have to work with very large numbers (the distance from earth to the moon is approximately 384 400 000 metres), or very small numbers (the thickness of a page in one of my books is approximately 0.000 021 3 metres).

There is a neater way of writing these numbers without having to use so many zeroes.

It is called **standard form**. Using standard form we write numbers in the form $a \times 10^n$, where a is a number greater than or equal to 1 and less than 10 ($1 \leqslant a < 10$) and n is an integer.

To write 230 000 (two hundred and thirty thousand) in standard form:

- First identify the place where the decimal point belongs (since it is not shown). We know that if the decimal point is not shown, it actually comes after the last digit.
  So 230 000 could be written as 230 000.0.
- Next count how many places the decimal point would have to be moved back until it is between the 2 and the 3. You will see that it is 5 places.
- So $230\,000 = 2.3 \times 10^5$. This is read as 'two hundred and thirty thousand is equal to two point three times ten to the power five'.

You will learn more about powers and working with standard form in a later chapter. For the moment, you just have to understand how to write numbers in standard form.

To write 0.000 003 546 in standard form:

- Count how many places the decimal point would have to be moved forward to lie between 3 and 5. It is 6 places.
- So $0.000\,003\,546 = 3.546 \times 10^{-6}$ (this is ten to the power of **negative** six).

> **NOTE:**
> If it is a problem to remember which power to use, you should notice that numbers less than one have a negative power and numbers greater than 10 have a positive power in standard form.

Example 11

a Write in standard form:

  i   20 015   **ii**   175   **iii**   3 200 000

  iv   0.127   **v**   0.005 06

b Write in the normal way:

  i 9.013×10^{-3} **ii** 1.0007×10^7

Answer 11

a **i** 2.0015×10^4 **ii** 1.75×10^2 **iii** 3.2×10^6

  iv 1.27×10^{-1} **v** 5.06×10^{-3}

b **i**   0.009 013   **ii**   10 007 000

1.13 Order of Working in Calculations

Ram was asked to calculate $5 + 2 \times 3$, without using a calculator. His answer was 21.

He checked his answer with a calculator. The calculator answer was 11.

What has happened?

Both Ram and the calculator were correct in different ways.

Ram first added 5 and 2 and then multiplied by 3 ($5 + 2 = 7$ then $7 \times 3 = 21$).

The calculator multiplied 2 and 3 first and then added 5 ($2 \times 3 = 6$ then $6 + 5 = 11$).

It is clearly not satisfactory to get two different answers to the same question, so an order of working had to be decided to ensure that all calculations yield the same answer.

The accepted order is:

- First **B**rackets.
- Next **D**ivision and **M**ultiplication (in either order).
- Lastly **A**ddition and **S**ubtraction (in either order).

Try to follow this example.

To calculate $7 + 3 \times 2 - (6 - 2) \div 2$,

B (brackets)	$= 7 + 3 \times 2 - \mathbf{4} \div 2$	$[(6 - 2) = \mathbf{4}]$
D (division)	$= 7 + 3 \times 2 - \mathbf{2}$	$[4 \div 2 = \mathbf{2}]$
M (multiplication)	$= 7 + \mathbf{6} - 2$	$[3 \times 2 = \mathbf{6}]$
A (addition)	$= \mathbf{13} - 2$	$[7 + 6 = \mathbf{13}]$
S (subtraction)	$= \mathbf{11}$	$[13 - 2 = \mathbf{11}]$

Answer: $7 + 3 \times 2 - (6 - 2) \div 2 = 11$

Try putting this in your calculator in exactly the same order as it is written and see if your calculator arrives at the same answer when you press the 'equals' button. Most calculators now use this form of logic (order of working), but you need to be sure about your own.

There will be more about this in Chapter 4.

Work out $4 \times 6 \div 2$ by doing the multiplication first.

$$4 \times 6 \div 2 = 24 \div 2 = 12$$

Now do the same sum but do the division first.

$$4 \times 6 \div 2 = 4 \times 3 = 12$$

You should note that multiplication and division can be done in either order. Can you find a rule for addition and subtraction?

It is very important that you learn this order of working, and know how to use it.

NOTE:
There are different ways of remembering this order. For example, the made-up word BoDMAS is often used. You could say that the 'o' stands for 'of', which usually means multiply, as in $\frac{1}{7}$ of $35 = \frac{1}{7} \times 35$.

Example 12

Work out the following, showing your working:

a $4 + 3 \times 10 - 6 \div 2$ **b** $(4 + 3) \times 10 - 6 \div 2$ **c** $4 + (3 \times 10) - 6 \div 2$

d $4 + 3 \times (10 - 6) \div 2$ **e** $(4 + 3) \times (10 - 6) \div 2$ **f** $4 + (3 \times 10 - 6) \div 2$

Answer 12

a $4 + 3 \times 10 - 6 \div 2$
$= 4 + 30 - 3 = 31$

b $(4 + 3) \times 10 - 6 \div 2$
$= 7 \times 10 - 3$
$= 70 - 3 = 67$

c $4 + (3 \times 10) - 6 \div 2$ (This is the same as **(a)** because the multiplication is done
$= 4 + 30 - 3 = 31$ first anyway, and so does not need brackets.)

d $4 + 3 \times (10 - 6) \div 2$
$= 4 + 3 \times 4 \div 2$ (Notice that $3 \times 4 \div 2 = 12 \div 2 = 6$ or $3 \times 4 \div 2 = 3 \times 2 = 6$)
$= 4 + 6 = 10$

e $(4 + 3) \times (10 - 6) \div 2$
$= 7 \times 4 \div 2 = 14$

f $4 + (3 \times 10 - 6) \div 2$ (The working inside the brackets also follows BoDMAS, so
$= 4 + (30 - 6) \div 2$ 3×10 first, then -6)
$= 4 + 24 \div 2$
$= 4 + 12$
$= 16$

Setting Out Your Working

It is important to be able to communicate in mathematics. You have to be able to explain to another person how you have arrived at your answer in a mathematical and concise way.

If you write an equals sign, the things that come before and after that sign must be equal to each other.

Look at how two students answer the same question, showing their working.

Rita writes: $(10 + 2) \div 4 = 10 + 2 = 12 \div 4 = 3$ *Sara writes:* $(10 + 2) \div 4$
$= 12 \div 4$
$= 3$

Which is the easier to follow?

In the first case, Rita has written $10 + 2 = 12 \div 4$. But this is not true!

Sara has set out her work so that the equals sign means exactly that. She has also used a new line between each bit of working, which makes it easier to read.

The examples throughout this book will show you how to set out your work, so do practise this right from the beginning. In general, writing one equals sign per line is good practice. However, please note that in this book, for reasons of economy and space, it has not always been possible to restrict working to one equals sign per line.

Exercise 1.6

NO CALCULATOR UNLESS SPECIFIED

1 Write in standard form:
   a 12 000   **b** 365   **c** 59 103   **d** 6000   **e** 7 010 400

2 Write in standard form:
   a 0.0035   **b** 0.156   **c** 0.0005   **d** 0.000 0043   **e** 0.0102

3 Write in standard form:
   a 0.003 45   **b** 520 160   **c** 112
   d 0.001   **e** 0.1001   **f** 2 million

4 Write as a normal number:
   a 5.6×10^3 **b** 2.7×10^{-4} **c** 1.16×10^{-2} **d** 6×10^5 **e** 2×10^{-3}

5 Calculate the following, **without using a calculator**:
   a $4 + 7 \times 2$ **b** $12 \div 3 \times 2 + 6$
   c $1 + 2 + 3 - (2 \times 3)$ **d** $(4 + 5) \div (4 - 1)$

   Check your answers with a calculator.

6 **Use your calculator** to work out the following:
   a $(5 + 7 - 2) \div (6 - 4)$ **b** $2 \times 3 + 5 \times 7$ **c** $3 \times (14 - 7) - 2$

   Check your answers by calculating without the calculator.

7 Put brackets in the right places to make each of these sums correct:
   a $5 - 3 \times 4 = 8$ **b** $9 + 50 - 24 + 2 = 22$ **c** $31 - 15 \div 10 - 2 = 2$

Exercise 1.7

NO CALCULATOR IN THIS EXERCISE

Mixed exercise

1 a $\{-5, -4, -3, -2, -1, 0, 1, 2, 3, 4, 5, 6, 7, 8, 9, 10, 11, 12, 13, 14, 15, 16, 17\}$
   Using the set of numbers above, answer true or false to the following:
   i All the numbers come from the set of real numbers.
   ii All the numbers come from the set of rational numbers.
   iii All the numbers come from the set of natural numbers.
   iv All the numbers come from the set of integers.

   b Insert an inequality sign to make the following true:
   i $-4 \ldots 3$ **ii** $0 \ldots -2$ **iii** $5 \ldots -5$ **iv** $3 \ldots -2$

   c List (in curly brackets):
   i the set of prime numbers less than 10
   ii the set of factors of 45
   iii the set of multiples of 3 less than 20.

2 Find the LCM of:
   a 12 and 20   **b** 5 and 15 and 90

3 Find the HCF of:
   a 16 and 12   **b** 20 and 8 and 12

4 Calculate the following:
   a 2.1^2 **b** 3^3 **c** $\sqrt{81}$ **d** $\sqrt{8100}$ **e** $\sqrt[3]{125}$

5 Write 600 as a product of its prime factors.
6 List all the factors of 160.

Exam-style questions

7 Tasnim records the temperature, in °C, at 6 a.m. every day for 10 days:
$-6, -3, 0, -2, -1, -7, -5, 2, -1, -3$
  a Find the difference between the highest and the lowest temperatures.
  b Find the median temperature.   (4024 paper 12 Q2 June 2012)

8 Add brackets to the expression to make it correct.
$1 + 72 \div 4 \times 2 = 10$ (4024 paper 01 Q3b June 2012)

9 Work out $4^3 - 5^2$.   (0580 paper 01 Q1 June 2004)

10 The Dead Sea shore is 395 metres **below** sea level. Hebron is 447 metres **above** sea level. Find the difference in height.   (0580 paper 01 Q2 June 2004)

11 a Express 154 as the product of its prime factors.
    b Find the lowest common multiple of 154 and 49.   (4024 paper 01 Q6 June 2007)

12 Place brackets in the following calculation to make it a correct statement.
$10 - 5 \times 9 + 3 = 60$ (0580 paper 01 Q2 November 2004)

13 Write down a multiple of 4 and 14 which is less than 30.
        (0580 paper 01 Q1 November 2008)

14 Write 0.003 62 in standard form.   (0580 paper 01 Q7 June 2008)

15 Written as the product of its prime factors, $360 = 2^3 \times 3^2 \times 5$.
  a Write 108 as the product of its prime factors.
  b Find the lowest common multiple of 108 and 360.
     Give your answer as the product of its prime factors.
  c Find the smallest positive integer k such that $360k$
     is a cube number.   (4024 paper 01 Q8 November 2006)

16 a Write down the two cube numbers between 10 and 100.
    b Write down the two prime numbers between 30 and 40.   (4024 paper 01 Q3 June 2009)

17 a Write down all the factors of 18.
    b Write 392 as the product of its prime factors.   (4024 paper 01 Q6 June 2009)

18 The numbers 294 and 784, written as the product of their prime factors, are
$294 = 2 \times 3 \times 7^2$ $784 = 2^4 \times 7^2$

Find
  a the largest integer which is a factor of both 294 and 784
  b $\sqrt{784}$.   (4024 paper 01 Q4 November 2009)

Fractions, Decimals and Percentages

Learning Objectives (Syllabus sections 5, 6, 8, 12)

In this chapter you will:
- revise and learn more about fractions, decimals and percentages and, without using a calculator,
- convert between fractions, decimals and percentages

- work with fractions, decimals and percentages
- order quantities expressed as fractions, decimals and percentages.

2.1 Introduction

This chapter should give you the basic skills for working with fractions, decimals and percentages that you will need later in the course. You may already have a good grasp of the basic ideas, but misunderstandings and errors in the handling of fractions are often the cause of difficulties in arithmetic and algebra. Make sure you can complete the examples and exercises confidently.

You should **not** use a calculator when working through this chapter. It is important that you first understand the principles so that you will be able to work more easily with algebra. We will go on to more difficult work requiring a calculator in a later chapter.

Remember: no calculator in this chapter!

2.2 Essential Skills NO CALCULATOR IN THIS EXERCISE

Make sure you can calculate the following. Look back to the previous chapter if you need a reminder.

1 Find the LCM of the following numbers:

   a 2, 5   **b** 7, 14   **c** 3, 8, 12   **d** 3, 5, 12, 60

2 Find the HCF of the following numbers:

   a 12, 36   **b** 18, 24   **c** 50, 150, 200   **d** 40, 24, 56

2.3 Understanding Common Fractions

When we use the word fraction we normally think of numbers like $\frac{7}{8}$, $\frac{2}{3}$ or $\frac{1}{2}$.

These are actually *common* or *vulgar* fractions.

In your O Level course the word fraction will normally mean common fraction, but sometimes it will help you to understand your work if you remember that decimals (decimal fractions) and percentages are also fractions. Percentages are fractions with a denominator of a hundred. For example, 21% is the same as $\frac{21}{100}$.

As you know, common fractions have a number above the fraction line, and another number below the fraction line. These numbers are called the **numerator** and the **denominator** respectively. So in the fraction $\frac{2}{3}$, 2 is the numerator and 3 is the denominator.

You can think of the denominator as the name of the fraction with the numerator showing the number of fractions with this name. Figure 2.1 should help you to see this.

one third	one third	one third

Figure 2.1 Two thirds

The strip in Figure 2.1 has been divided into three equal parts.

Each part is one third $\left(\frac{1}{3}\right)$ of the whole strip.

Three thirds $\left(\frac{3}{3}\right)$ make up the whole strip.

Two thirds $\left(\frac{2}{3}\right)$ are shaded.

The **numerator** is the top number in a common fraction.

The **denominator** is the bottom number in a common fraction.

The denominator shows into how many equal parts the whole strip has been divided. The denominator tells us the name of the fraction, in this case 'thirds'.

The numerator shows the number of these fractions, in the case 2 'thirds' have been shaded. Look at Figure 2.2 to see this drawn out.

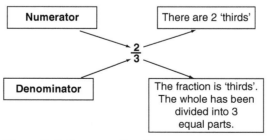

Figure 2.2 Common fraction

Mixed Numbers and Improper Fractions

Mixed numbers have a whole part and a fraction part. The mixed number $1\frac{2}{3}$ means there is one whole part and 2 thirds. Figure 2.3 shows two strips, each divided into three equal parts.

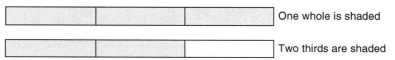

Figure 2.3 One and two thirds

Key term

Common or vulgar fractions are ordinary fractions, for example $\frac{2}{3}$, usually just abbreviated to 'fractions'. Here, 2 is the **numerator**, 3 is the **denominator**.

Key term

Mixed numbers combine integers and fractions, for example $3\frac{2}{5}$. Here, 3 is the whole number part and $\frac{2}{5}$ is the fraction part.

NOTE:
An improper fraction is often referred to as a 'top heavy' fraction, which describes it well because the top number is larger than the lower number.

Key terms

Improper fractions are 'top heavy' fractions, for example $\frac{9}{5}$.

Equivalent fractions represent the same number, for example $\frac{3}{5}, \frac{6}{10}, \frac{90}{150}$ all represent $\frac{3}{5}$ of the whole.

Figure 2.3 also shows how we can write a mixed number as an improper fraction. An **improper** fraction is a mixed number written entirely in fractions, so the numerator is larger than the denominator. The diagram shows the shaded parts of the two strips as either $1\frac{2}{3}$ or $\frac{5}{3}$ (or 5 thirds).

Equivalent Fractions

Fractions can be given different names, and if the rules for doing this are followed, the resulting fraction is of the same size as the original.

Equivalent fractions are fractions of the same size, but with different denominators (names) and numerators. Look at Figure 2.4.

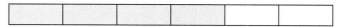

Figure 2.4 Two thirds

Figure 2.4 shows the strip divided into three equal parts with the fraction $\frac{2}{3}$ shaded as before. If we divide *each* third into two equal parts you should see that there are now six equal parts, and four of these are equivalent in size to 2 thirds. Figure 2.5 shows this.

Figure 2.5 Four sixths

This shows that $\frac{2}{3} = \frac{4}{6}$. These two fractions are called equivalent fractions because they represent the same amount of the whole strip. The rule for finding equivalent fractions is that the denominator *and* numerator have to be multiplied (or divided) by the same number. In this case the first fraction has had the numerator and denominator multiplied by 2. You will find out more about this later.

More Examples of Fractions

We can work with things other than strips of paper to understand fractions. Imagine a bag containing 20 sweets. You want to share these sweets equally among four people. The 20 sweets would have to be divided into 4 equal parts. There would be 5 sweets in each part. Each part would be one quarter of the whole.

This could be written as $\frac{1}{4} \times 20 = 5$, as shown in Figure 2.6.

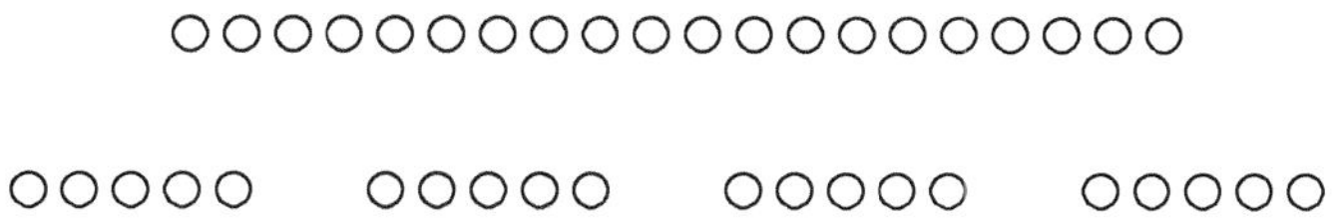

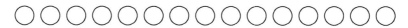

Figure 2.6 Twenty sweets

How many counters would there be in $\frac{2}{3}$ of 15 counters?

You can use the diagram of 15 counters in Figure 2.7 to help.

Figure 2.7 Fifteen counters

Look at the clock face in Figure 2.8.

We know that 15 minutes is a quarter of an hour, and that there are 60 minutes in one hour. The hour is divided into sixty equal parts. So each minute is 1 sixtieth $\left(\frac{1}{60}\right)$ of an hour. Therefore, fifteen minutes is fifteen sixtieths of one hour.

Figure 2.8 Fractions of an hour

Simplifying shows that $\frac{15}{60} = \frac{1}{4}$ (divide numerator and denominator by 15).

How do we work out what fraction of an hour is ten minutes?

Write ten sixtieths and simplify.

$\frac{10}{60} = \frac{1}{6}$ (divide numerator and denominator by 10).

So ten minutes is one sixth of an hour.

Other shapes can be divided into equal parts.

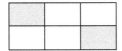

Figure 2.9 Other representations

The rectangle in Figure 2.9 has been divided into six equal areas, and so each is $\frac{1}{6}$th of the rectangle.

Two of these are shaded. This means that $\frac{2}{6}$, which is equivalent to $\frac{1}{3}$ of the rectangle, is shaded. The circle has been divided into 8 equal parts, and 3 are shaded, so $\frac{3}{8}$ of the circle is shaded.

2.4 Working with Common Fractions

Changing a Mixed Number to an Improper Fraction

As an example, the steps to be followed to change $3\frac{1}{5}$ to an improper fraction are given below:

- multiply: $3 \times 5 = 15$ (there are 15 fifths in three wholes, so $3\frac{1}{5} = \frac{15}{5} + \frac{1}{5}$)
- add: $15 + 1 = 16$ (add the extra 1 fifth)
- answer: $\frac{16}{5}$ (16 fifths).

Changing an Improper Fraction to a Mixed Number

As an example, the steps to be followed to change $\frac{23}{4}$ to a mixed number are given below:

- divide: $23 \div 4 = 5$ remainder 3 (23 quarters = 5 wholes with 3 quarters left over)
- answer: $5\frac{3}{4}$.

Equivalent Fractions

As an example, to change $\frac{4}{10}$ to equivalent fractions:

- either multiply numerator and denominator by the same number: $\frac{4 \times 2}{10 \times 2} = \frac{8}{20}$
- or divide numerator and denominator by the same number: $\frac{4 \div 2}{10 \div 2} = \frac{2}{5}$.

Addition and Subtraction of Fractions

Before fractions are added or subtracted, we have to make sure they have the same name. For example, look at Figure 2.10, which represents the addition sum $\frac{3}{4} + \frac{1}{8}$. The only way we can add these two is to write them with the same name (denominator).

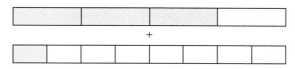

Figure 2.10 Three quarters plus one eighth

To do this we divide *each* of the quarters into two equal parts, to make eighths. The three quarters has become six eighths and can now be added to the one eighth, as in Figure 2.11.

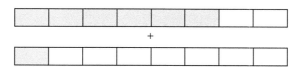

Figure 2.11 Six eighths plus one eighth

It is now easy to see that $\frac{3}{4} + \frac{1}{8} = \frac{6}{8} + \frac{1}{8} = \frac{7}{8}$.

The answer is seven eighths.

It can be easier to add or subtract mixed numbers by changing them to top heavy (improper) fractions first, as you will see in Example 1, part **f iv**.

You may have to change both fractions to equivalent fractions with the same denominator.

For example, consider $\frac{2}{3} + \frac{4}{5}$.

Follow these steps to see how to work this out:

- Change any mixed numbers to improper fractions.
- Find the lowest common multiple of both denominators (LCM of 3 and 5 is 15).
- Change both fractions to equivalent fractions with the same denominator $\left(\frac{2 \times 5}{3 \times 5} + \frac{4 \times 3}{5 \times 3} = \frac{10}{15} + \frac{12}{15}\right)$.
- Add or subtract the fractions in the usual way $\left(\frac{10}{15} + \frac{12}{15} = \frac{22}{15}\right)$.
- Simplify and change to a mixed number if necessary $\left(\frac{22}{15} = 1\frac{7}{15}\right)$.
- Answer: $\frac{2}{3} + \frac{4}{5} = 1\frac{7}{15}$.

Simplifying Fractions

Simplifying fractions refers to writing them in the simplest equivalent form. For example, $\frac{4}{10}$ can be simplified by dividing both the numerator *and* denominator by 2. This means that $\frac{4}{10} = \frac{2}{5}$.

This is often called **'cancelling down'** the fraction.

For example, the steps to be followed to simplify $\frac{42}{162}$ are given below.

Either:

- Find any common factor and divide the numerator and denominator by this number:

$$\frac{42 \div 2}{162 \div 2} = \frac{21}{81}$$

- Repeat if possible: $\frac{21 \div 3}{81 \div 3} = \frac{7}{27}$.
- Stop when there are no more common factors.
- Answer: $\frac{7}{27}$.

Or:

- Find the HCF of the numerator and denominator to simplify in one step:

$$\frac{42 \div 6}{162 \div 6} = \frac{7}{27}$$

Example 1

a Change the top heavy (improper) fraction $\frac{7}{2}$ to a mixed number.

b Change the mixed number $4\frac{3}{5}$ to an improper fraction.

c Which of these fractions are equivalent?

$\frac{20}{50}, \frac{2}{5}, \frac{3}{10}, \frac{4}{10}, \frac{3}{5}, \frac{8}{20}$

d Change $\frac{4}{5}$ to twentieths.

e Fill in the blank spaces to give equivalent fractions.

$\frac{}{16} = \frac{3}{8} = \frac{30}{} = \frac{15}{}$

f Calculate, simplifying and writing the answers as mixed numbers if necessary:

   i $3 + \frac{5}{6}$ **ii** $\frac{5}{8} + \frac{1}{2}$ **iii** $\frac{3}{4} - \frac{2}{3}$

   iv $2\frac{1}{3} + 4\frac{5}{6}$ **v** $1 - \frac{7}{9}$

g Write each of the following fractions in their simplest forms:

   i $\frac{5}{40}$ **ii** $\frac{6}{48}$ **iii** $\frac{18}{72}$

h How many sheep are there in 3 fifths of a flock of 25 sheep?

i How many students are there in $\frac{2}{7}$ of a class of 35?

Answer 1

a $\frac{7}{2} = 3\frac{1}{2}$ **b** $4\frac{3}{5} = \frac{23}{5}$ **c** $\frac{20}{50} = \frac{2}{5} = \frac{4}{10} = \frac{8}{20}$

d $\frac{4}{5} = \frac{4 \times 4}{5 \times 4} = \frac{16}{20}$ **e** $\frac{6}{16} = \frac{3}{8} = \frac{30}{80} = \frac{15}{40}$

f **i** $3 + \frac{5}{6} = 3\frac{5}{6}$ **ii** $\frac{5}{8} + \frac{1}{2} = \frac{5}{8} + \frac{4}{8} = \frac{9}{8} = 1\frac{1}{8}$

    iii $\frac{3}{4} - \frac{2}{3} = \frac{3 \times 3}{4 \times 3} - \frac{2 \times 4}{3 \times 4} = \frac{9}{12} - \frac{8}{12} = \frac{1}{12}$ **iv** $2\frac{1}{3} + 4\frac{5}{6} = \frac{7}{3} + \frac{29}{6} = \frac{14}{6} + \frac{29}{6} = \frac{43}{6} = 7\frac{1}{6}$

    v $1 - \frac{7}{9} = \frac{9}{9} - \frac{7}{9} = \frac{2}{9}$

g **i** $\frac{5}{40} = \frac{5 \div 5}{40 \div 5} = \frac{1}{8}$ **ii** $\frac{6}{48} = \frac{1}{8}$ **iii** $\frac{18}{72} = \frac{18 \div 2}{72 \div 2} = \frac{9}{36} = \frac{1}{4}$

h One fifth of the flock is 5 sheep, so 3 fifths is 15 sheep.

i $\frac{1}{7}$ of 35 = 5, so $\frac{2}{7}$ of 35 = 10. Answer: 10 students.

Exercise 2.1   **NO CALCULATOR IN THIS EXERCISE**

1 Change to mixed numbers:

   a $\frac{19}{5}$ **b** $\frac{201}{10}$ **c** $\frac{33}{2}$

2 Change to improper fractions:

   a $3\frac{7}{8}$ **b** $100\frac{1}{2}$ **c** $3\frac{11}{12}$

3 Fill in the blank spaces to give equivalent fractions:

$\frac{5}{} = \frac{10}{30} = \frac{}{3} = \frac{7}{} = \frac{21}{}$

4 Write the following as hundredths (denominator = 100):

   a $\frac{7}{10}$ **b** $\frac{4}{25}$ **c** $\frac{19}{20}$

   d $\frac{52}{200}$ **e** $\frac{81}{900}$

5 Calculate the following, simplifying and writing your answers as mixed numbers if necessary:

   a $\frac{3}{7} + \frac{2}{7}$ **b** $\frac{4}{5} - \frac{3}{5}$ **c** $\frac{7}{12} - \frac{1}{6}$ **d** $\frac{2}{9} + \frac{3}{4}$

   e $2\frac{1}{5} + 1\frac{3}{4}$ **f** $3\frac{2}{5} - 1\frac{1}{2}$ **g** $1 - \frac{6}{7}$ **h** $1 - \frac{5}{12}$

6 Simplify:

   a $\frac{22}{77}$ **b** $\frac{60}{72}$ **c** $\frac{45}{60}$ **d** $\frac{45}{360}$

7 How many sweets would be in a bag of 28 sweets after $\frac{1}{4}$ of them had been eaten?

8 One third of a class of 45 students has gone away on a field trip. How many students have gone on the trip?

Multiplying and Dividing Fractions

The first part of Figure 2.12 shows a strip divided into thirds, with one third shaded.

We can use this figure to work out $\frac{1}{2} \times \frac{1}{3}$, which means $\frac{1}{2}$ **of** $\frac{1}{3}$.

The second part of Figure 2.12 shows the same strip with the shaded third divided into two equal parts. Each of these is one half of a third of the strip.

You should see that each of these is equal to one sixth of the whole strip.

So $\frac{1}{2} \times \frac{1}{3} = \frac{1}{6}$, which means $\frac{1}{2}$ of $\frac{1}{3} = \frac{1}{6}$.

Figure 2.12 Multiplying fractions

You will probably find multiplying and dividing fractions easier than adding and subtracting.

The rules for multiplying fractions are:

- Change any mixed numbers to top heavy (improper) fractions.
- Write any whole numbers over one.
- Multiply the numerators together, and multiply the denominators together.
- Simplify the answer if necessary, and change to a mixed number if necessary.

Applying these rules to our example above:

$$\frac{1}{2} \times \frac{1}{3} = \frac{1 \times 1}{2 \times 3} = \frac{1}{6}$$

Example 2

a Multiply the following fractions, simplifying and writing your answers as mixed numbers if necessary:

   i $3 \times \frac{3}{4}$ **ii** $\frac{5}{6} \times \frac{2}{3}$ **iii** $\frac{6}{7} \times 2\frac{1}{3}$ **iv** $1\frac{2}{3} \times 2\frac{1}{5}$

b Calculate the following:

   i $\left(\frac{3}{5}\right)^2$ **ii** $\left(\frac{2}{3}\right)^3$

Answer 2

a **i** $3 \times \frac{3}{4} = \frac{3}{1} \times \frac{3}{4} = \frac{9}{4} = 2\frac{1}{4}$ **ii** $\frac{5}{6} \times \frac{2}{3} = \frac{10}{18} = \frac{5}{9}$

   iii $\frac{6}{7} \times 2\frac{1}{3} = \frac{6}{7} \times \frac{7}{3} = \frac{42}{21} = \frac{2}{1} = 2$ **iv** $1\frac{2}{3} \times 2\frac{1}{5} = \frac{5}{3} \times \frac{11}{5} = \frac{55}{15} = \frac{11}{3} = 3\frac{2}{3}$

b **i** $\left(\frac{3}{5}\right)^2 = \frac{3}{5} \times \frac{3}{5} = \frac{9}{25}$ **ii** $\left(\frac{2}{3}\right)^3 = \frac{2}{3} \times \frac{2}{3} \times \frac{2}{3} = \frac{8}{27}$

You have probably noticed that in Example 2**a** parts **ii**, **iii** and **iv** the working could have been shortened considerably by simplifying earlier. We will look at this now.

In Example 2**a ii**:

$$\frac{5}{6} \times \frac{2}{3} = \frac{5 \times 2}{6 \times 3} = \frac{5 \times 2 \div 2}{6 \times 3 \div 2} = \frac{5}{9}$$

So we could have simplified before doing the multiplication:

$\frac{5}{6} \times \frac{2}{3} = \frac{5}{3 \times 3} = \frac{5}{9}$ (dividing the top and bottom of the fraction by 2)

In Example 2**a iii**:

$\frac{6}{7} \times 2\frac{1}{3} = \frac{6}{7} \times \frac{7}{3} = \frac{6}{3} = 2$ (divide top and bottom by 7 first, and then by 3)

Try Example 2(a) (iv) yourself.

Warning: This only works for multiplication, so do not use it in addition or subtraction!

How can we visualise division? Remember that if you do the division $10 \div 2$ you are finding how many twos there are in ten. The answer of course is 5.

Think about $\frac{3}{4} \div \frac{1}{8}$. This means 'how many eighths are there in three quarters?'

Figure 2.13 shows one strip with $\frac{3}{4}$ shaded, and another divided into eight equal parts and shaded to show that 6 eighths will go exactly into $\frac{3}{4}$. So the answer is 6.

i.e. $\frac{3}{4} \div \frac{1}{8} = 6$

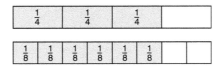

Figure 2.13 Dividing fractions

The rules for dividing fractions are:

- Change any mixed numbers to top heavy (improper) fractions.
- Write any whole numbers over one.
- Change the division sign to multiplication.
- Turn the second fraction upside down.
- Proceed as for multiplication.

Using these rules for $\frac{3}{4} \div \frac{1}{8}$, we get:

$$\frac{3}{4} \div \frac{1}{8} = \frac{3}{4} \times \frac{8}{1} = \frac{24}{4} = 6$$

Example 3

Do the following divisions:

a $\frac{5}{6} \div 3$ **b** $\frac{3}{4} \div \frac{1}{2}$ **c** $1\frac{2}{5} \div 4\frac{3}{5}$ **d** $\frac{2}{5} \div \frac{5}{8}$

Answer 3

a $\frac{5}{6} \div 3 = \frac{5}{6} \div \frac{3}{1} = \frac{5}{6} \times \frac{1}{3} = \frac{5}{18}$

b $\frac{3}{4} \div \frac{1}{2} = \frac{3}{4} \times \frac{2}{1} = \frac{6}{4} = \frac{3}{2} = 1\frac{1}{2}$ (or $\frac{3}{4} \times \frac{2}{1} = \frac{3}{2} = 1\frac{1}{2}$ by dividing top and bottom by 2)

c $1\frac{2}{5} \div 4\frac{3}{5} = \frac{7}{5} \div \frac{23}{5} = \frac{7}{5} \times \frac{5}{23} = \frac{7}{23}$ (by dividing top and bottom by 5)

d $\frac{2}{5} \div \frac{5}{8} = \frac{2}{5} \times \frac{8}{5} = \frac{16}{25}$ (Be careful! You cannot divide top and bottom by 5 here!)

Looking at these examples you should see that you can do the simplifying shortcut *only after* the second fraction has been inverted and the sign has changed from division to multiplication.

Exercise 2.2   NO CALCULATOR IN THIS EXERCISE

Calculate the following, simplifying your answers and changing to mixed numbers as necessary:

1   a $3 \times \frac{1}{5}$ b $3 \times \frac{2}{5}$ c $\frac{3}{4} \times 10$

2   a $\frac{1}{3} \times \frac{1}{6}$ b $\frac{3}{4} \times \frac{1}{7}$ c $\frac{5}{8} \times \frac{3}{4}$

3   a $\frac{5}{7} \times \frac{1}{10}$ b $\frac{7}{8} \times \frac{2}{5}$ c $\frac{4}{9} \times \frac{3}{8}$

4   a $2\frac{1}{2} \times 3\frac{1}{4}$ b $5\frac{3}{5} \times 2\frac{1}{8}$ c $1\frac{1}{3} \times 2\frac{1}{3}$

5   a $3 \div \frac{2}{5}$ b $\frac{4}{3} \div 3$ c $\frac{2}{7} \div 4$

6   a $\frac{1}{2} \div \frac{3}{7}$ b $\frac{3}{7} \div \frac{1}{2}$ c $\frac{5}{9} \div \frac{6}{7}$

7   a $\frac{2}{9} \div \frac{2}{3}$ b $\frac{2}{3} \div \frac{2}{9}$ c $\frac{5}{8} \div \frac{3}{8}$

8   a $2\frac{3}{4} \div 1\frac{1}{2}$ b $5\frac{1}{2} \div \frac{3}{4}$ c $3\frac{3}{5} \div 1\frac{2}{3}$

9   a $\frac{2}{5} \div \frac{1}{15}$ b $\frac{3}{5} \div \frac{5}{6}$ c $2\frac{1}{3} \div \frac{3}{7}$

2.5 Working with Decimals

> **Key term**
>
> **Decimal fractions** are usually abbreviated to 'decimals'.

Decimals (or decimal fractions) are usually easier to work with than (common) fractions, so the rules and a few examples should be sufficient to remind you how to do each operation. We will abbreviate to decimals and fractions because these terms are generally understood to mean decimal fractions and common fractions.

Addition and Subtraction of Decimals

As an example, to simplify $3 + 1.205 + 40.016$ follow the steps given below:

- Add '.0' to the whole number to remind you where the decimal point belongs. $(3.0 + 1.205 + 40.016)$
- Write the numbers in column form, but with the decimal points in a vertical line.

$$
\begin{array}{r}
3.0 \\
1.205\,+ \\
40.016\,+
\end{array}
$$

- Starting from the right, add (or subtract) using the normal methods of addition (or subtraction).
- Place the decimal point in the answer vertically under the other decimal points.

$$
\begin{array}{r}
3.0 \\
1.205\ + \\
\underline{40.016\ +} \\
44.221
\end{array}
$$

Multiplying Decimals

As an example, to simplify 2.16×0.002 follow the steps given below:

- At first, ignore the decimal points.
- Starting from the right multiply using the normal methods.
- Count how many digits (numbers) come after the decimal points.
- Starting from the right count back this number of places and insert the decimal point, inserting zeroes if necessary.

$$\begin{array}{r} 2.16 \\ 0.002 \times \\ \hline 0.00432 \end{array}$$

(There are 5 digits after the decimal points, so counting 5 places from the right it is necessary to insert 2 zeroes.)

- Answer: $2.16 \times 0.002 = 0.00432$.

Multiplying by 10, 100, 1000 and so on is straightforward with decimals. For example, 0.013×100:

NOTE:
Remember that *multiplying* by 10, 100 and so on will make the answer *larger*.

- Count the number of zeroes (2 in this example) in the number you are multiplying by.
- Move the decimal point to the *right* by the same number of places, inserting zeroes if necessary ($0.013 \times 100 = 1.3$).
- Answer: $0.013 \times 100 = 1.3$.

Dividing Decimals

As an example, to divide 63.6 by 0.012 follow the steps given below:

- Write the first number over the second number $\left(\frac{63.6}{0.012}\right)$.
- Multiply top and bottom by 10, 100, 1000 or 10 000 until the lower number is a whole number (in this case we need to use 1000, i.e. $\frac{63.6 \times 1000}{0.012 \times 1000} = \frac{63600}{12}$).
- Divide the new lower number into the top number ($63600 \div 12 = 5300$).
- Answer: 63.6 divided by $0.012 = 5300$.

NOTE:
Remember that dividing by 10, 100, 1000 and so on will make the number smaller.

Dividing decimals by 10, 100, 1000 and so on is also straightforward. For example, divide 0.234 by 1000:

- Count the number of zeroes (three in this case) in the number you are to divide by.
- Move the decimal point 3 places *left*, filling in zeroes if necessary ($0.234 \div 1000 = 0.000234$).
- Answer: $0.234 \div 1000 = 0.000234$.

Example 4
Calculate the following:

a $2.501 + 12.6$	**b** $45.3173 - 1.012$	**c** 3.513×100
d 0.012×10	**e** 4.12×1000	**f** 2.1×1.1
g $0.16 \div 100$	**h** $31.323 \div 0.03$	

Answer 4

a $2.501 + 12.6 = $ $\begin{array}{r} 2.501 \\ 12.6 + \\ \hline 15.101 \end{array}$

b $45.3173 - 1.012 = $ $\begin{array}{r} 45.3173 \\ 1.012 - \\ \hline 44.3053 \end{array}$

c $3.513 \times 100 = 351.3$

d $0.012 \times 10 = 0.12$

e $4.12 \times 1000 = 4120$

f $2.1 \times 1.1 = $ $\begin{array}{r} 2.1 \\ 1.1 \times \\ \hline 2.31 \end{array}$

g $0.16 \div 100 = 0.0016$

h $31.323 \div 0.03 = \frac{31.323 \times 100}{0.03 \times 100} = \frac{3132.3}{3} = 1044.1$

Exercise 2.3

NO CALCULATOR IN THIS EXERCISE

Calculate the following.

1 $3.5 + 0.16 + 10.2$ **2** $501 + 1.67 + 0.3$ **3** $17.95 - 1.4$

4 $6.119 - 2.01$ **5** 13.41×1000 **6** 0.0169×1000

7 $6.017 \div 100$ **8** 10.2×3.1 **9** $18.96 \div 1.2$

2.6 Percentages

It may help you to visualise **percentages** and compare them with fractions if you imagine a stack of, say 100 counters, as in Figure 2.14. Imagine that the counters are numbered from 1 to 100, with 1 at the bottom of the stack.

Each of the counters is $\frac{1}{100}$ of the whole stack, so each counter is 1% of the stack. The whole stack is 100% of the stack or one whole.

Now you can see that half way up is 50%, one quarter of the way up is 25%, $\frac{1}{10}$ of the way up is 10% and so on.

Copy Figure 2.14 and mark in $\frac{3}{4}$ and its corresponding percentage, 20% and any others that you can think of.

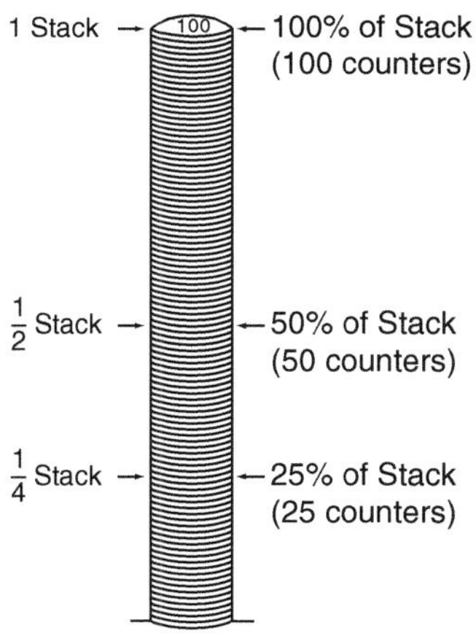

1 Stack → 100 ← 100% of Stack (100 counters)

$\frac{1}{2}$ Stack → ← 50% of Stack (50 counters)

$\frac{1}{4}$ Stack → ← 25% of Stack (25 counters)

Figure 2.14 Percentages

2.7 Conversion Between Common Fractions, Decimals and Percentages

Common fraction	Divide the numerator by the denominator	Decimal fraction
$\frac{2}{5}$	2 divided by 5	0.4
$3\frac{2}{5}$		3.4
Decimal fraction	**Multiply by 100**	**Percentage**
0.45	0.45×100	45%
0.613	0.613×100	61.3%
2.051	2.051×100	205.1%

Divide by 100 to change a percentage to decimal fraction.

Decimal fraction	Write decimal over 1, then multiply the top and bottom by 10, or 100, or 1000 until the numerator is a whole number. Simplify if necessary.	Common fraction
0.7	$\frac{0.7 \times 10}{1 \times 10}$	$\frac{7}{10}$
0.45	$\frac{0.45 \times 100}{1 \times 100} = \frac{45}{100}$	$\frac{45}{100} = \frac{9}{20}$

Exercise 2.4 NO CALCULATOR IN THIS EXERCISE

Copy and complete Table 2.1 for conversions between common fractions, decimals and percentages. It is a good idea to learn these as they occur quite frequently and you can save time if you know them. The last two have been done for you, and it is *definitely* a good idea to learn these!

The dot above a number means that the number repeats forever. For example, $0.\dot{3}$ means $0.33333333333\ldots$; it is called 'zero point three recurring'.

	Fraction	**Decimal**	**Percentage**
1	$\frac{1}{2}$		
2		0.25	
3			75%
4	$\frac{1}{10}$		
5		0.3	
6		0.2	
7			12.5%
8	$\frac{1}{3}$	$0.\dot{3}$	$33\frac{1}{3}\%$
9	$\frac{2}{3}$	$0.\dot{6}$	$66\frac{2}{3}\%$

Table 2.1 Converting between fractions, decimals and percentages

Calculating Percentages of an Amount

There are several ways to calculate percentages quickly.

The first is to know the common percentages (50%, 10%, 25% and so on) and their corresponding fractions (see part **a** of Example 5).

The second is to find 1% by dividing by 100, and then multiply by whatever percentage is required (see part **b** of Example 5).

Lastly, some percentages can be 'built up' from smaller percentages that are easy to find (see part **c** of Example 5).

Example 5

a Find:
  i 50% of 136   **ii** 10% of 34   **iii** 75% of 32

b Find:
  i 7% of 61   **ii** 21% of 400   **iii** 12% of 700

c Find:
  i 15% of 96   **ii** 65% of 140   **iii** 17.5% of 260

Answer 5

a **i** $50\% \text{ of } 136 = \frac{1}{2} \text{ of } 136 = 68$ **ii** $10\% \text{ of } 34 = \frac{1}{10} \text{ of } 34 = 3.4$

  iii $75\% \text{ of } 32 = \frac{3}{4} \text{ of } 32 = 3 \times \frac{1}{4} \text{ of } 32 = 3 \times 8 = 24$

b **i** $7\% \text{ of } 61 = 7 \times 1\% \text{ of } 61 = 7 \times \frac{1}{100} \text{ of } 61 = 7 \times 0.61 = 4.27$

  ii $21\% \text{ of } 400 = 21 \times 1\% \text{ of } 400 = 21 \times \frac{1}{100} \text{ of } 400 = 21 \times 4 = 84$

  iii $12\% \text{ of } 700 = 12 \times 7 = 84$

c **i** To find 15% of 96:

find 10% of 96 ($\frac{1}{10}$ of 96) = 9.6

find 5% of 96 ($\frac{1}{2}$ of 10%) = 4.8

Add 10% and 5%: 15% of 96 = 9.6 + 4.8 = 14.4

ii 65% of 140:

50% of 140 = 70

10% of 140 = 14 +   (one fifth of 50%)

5% of 140 = 7 +   (half of 10%)

65% of 140 = 91

Answer: 65% of 140 = 91

iii 17.5% of 260:

10% of 260 = 26

5% of 260 = 13 +   (half of 10%)

2.5% of 260 = 6.5 +   (half of 5%)

17.5% of 260 = 45.5

Answer: 17.5% of 260 = 45.5

Exercise 2.5   **NO CALCULATOR IN THIS EXERCISE**

Calculate the following, showing your method:

1 75% of 64   **2** 30% of 1550   **3** 9% of 3400

4 55.5% of 680   **5** 3% of 73

Finding One Number as a Percentage of Another

We sometimes need to express one number as a percentage of another. For example, you get 6 answers correct out of 20 in a test. What is your percentage mark?

- First make a fraction by writing the first number over the second $\left(\frac{6}{20}\right)$.
- Change the fraction to a percentage by multiplying by 100 over 1.

$$\left(\frac{6}{20} \times \frac{100}{1} = \frac{600}{20} = 30\%\right)$$

There is an alternative method that can sometimes be used, if the denominator of the fraction is a factor of 100:

- First make the fraction as before $\left(\frac{6}{20}\right)$.
- Change to the equivalent fraction with the denominator as 100.

$$\left(\frac{6 \times 5}{20 \times 5} = \frac{30}{100} = 30\%\right)$$

Example 6

a Find 25 as a percentage of 40.　　　**b** Find 15 as a percentage of 25.

Answer 6

a $\frac{25}{40} \times \frac{100}{1} = \frac{250}{4} = 62.5\%$ 　　　**b** $\frac{15 \times 4}{25 \times 4} = \frac{60}{100} = 60\%$

Exercise 2.6　　　　　　　　　　**NO CALCULATOR IN THIS EXERCISE**

Calculate the first number as a percentage of the second:

1 35, 140　　　　　　**2** 72, 600　　　　　　**3** 23, 50

4 40, 125　　　　　　**5** 17, 250　　　　　　**6** 90, 180

7 12, 6　　　　　　　**8** 29, 1000

2.8 Ordering Quantities

It is often easiest when comparing fractions, decimals and percentages to change them all to decimals. Alternatively, compare fractions by finding equivalent fractions with the same denominator.

Example 7

a Using the symbols >, < or =, insert the correct sign to make the following statements true:
  i 22 ... 21　　**ii** 0.75 ... $\frac{3}{4}$　　**iii** 0.25 ... 25　　**iv** $\frac{1}{3}$ ... 0.3

b Write the following in order of size, starting with the smallest:
  i 0.48, 0.408, 0.390, 0.399　　　　　**ii** $\frac{2}{5}, \frac{3}{5}, \frac{3}{10}, \frac{9}{20}$
  iii 33%, 0.5, $\frac{3}{10}, \frac{1}{3}$

c Rafi loves eating naan. Do you think he would rather have two thirds or three quarters of a naan? Why?

d Find a fraction which is between each of the following pairs:
  i $\frac{7}{10}$ and $\frac{9}{10}$　　**ii** $\frac{1}{2}$ and $\frac{3}{4}$　　**iii** $\frac{6}{8}$ and $\frac{7}{8}$

Answer 7

a **i** 22 > 21　　**ii** 0.75 = $\frac{3}{4}$　　**iii** 0.25 < 25　　**iv** $\frac{1}{3}$ > 0.3

b **i** 0.390 < 0.399 < 0.408 < 0.48　　**ii** Changing $\frac{2}{5}, \frac{3}{5}, \frac{3}{10}, \frac{9}{20}$ to twentieths

$$\frac{8}{20}, \frac{12}{20}, \frac{6}{20}, \frac{9}{20}$$

and putting in order,

$$\frac{6}{20}, \frac{8}{20}, \frac{9}{20}, \frac{12}{20}$$

simplifying again,

$$\frac{3}{10} < \frac{2}{5} < \frac{9}{20} < \frac{3}{5}$$

　　iii Changing 33%, 0.5, $\frac{3}{10}, \frac{1}{3}$ to decimals,
0.33, 0.5, 0.3, 0.3333...
putting in order,
0.3, 0.33, 0.3333..., 0.5,
and re-writing as before $\frac{3}{10} < 33\% < \frac{1}{3} < 0.5$

c $\frac{3}{4} = 75\%$ and $\frac{2}{3} = 66\frac{2}{3}\%$, so Rafi would rather have $\frac{3}{4}$ of the naan.

d **i** $\frac{8}{10}$ is between $\frac{7}{10}$ and $\frac{9}{10}$; $\frac{8}{10} = \frac{4}{5}$.

Answer: $\frac{4}{5}$

iii $\frac{1}{2}$ and $\frac{3}{4}$ can be changed to their equivalent fractions $\frac{4}{8}$ and $\frac{6}{8}$, so $\frac{5}{8}$ is between $\frac{1}{2}$ and $\frac{3}{4}$.

Answer: $\frac{5}{8}$

iii $\frac{6}{8}$ and $\frac{7}{8}$ are equivalent to $\frac{12}{16}$ and $\frac{14}{16}$, so

Answer: $\frac{13}{16}$

Exercise 2.7   NO CALCULATOR IN THIS EXERCISE

1 Find a fraction that lies between $\frac{3}{5}$ and $\frac{4}{5}$.

2 Place the following in order of size, starting with the smallest:

451, 4.579, 4.098, 4.105

3 Place these fractions in order of size, starting with the smallest:

$\frac{4}{3}, \frac{2}{3}, \frac{3}{4}, \frac{17}{20}$

4 Place the following in order of size, starting with the smallest:

$\frac{33}{100}, 33\frac{1}{3}\%, \frac{3}{25}, \frac{3}{50}, \frac{67}{200}$

Exercise 2.8   NO CALCULATOR IN THIS EXERCISE

Exam-style questions

NOTE:
'Evaluate' means 'work out a numerical answer'.

1 **a** Evaluate $3\frac{2}{3} - 2\frac{4}{5}$.   **b** Express $\frac{48}{84}$ in its lowest terms.

(4024 paper 11 Q2 November 2011)

2 **a** Add brackets to the equation to make it correct.
$4 + 6 \times 7 - 5 = 16$
b Find the value of 27×0.002.   (4024 paper 01 Q2 November 2009)

3 **a** Express $\frac{13}{20}$ as a decimal.

b In a test, Rose scored 56 marks out of 70.
Express this score as a percentage.   (4024 paper 01 Q1 June 2005)

4 Evaluate

a $2\frac{2}{3} \times \frac{1}{7}$,   **b** $\frac{2}{5} \div \frac{7}{12}$.   (4024 paper 01 Q2 June 2005)

5 **a** Express 0.527 as a percentage.
b Evaluate $5.6 \div 0.08$.   (4024 paper 01 Q1 June 2006)

6 Evaluate

    a $\frac{6}{7} - \frac{1}{3}$,
        b $\frac{2}{5} \times \frac{4}{9}$.
        (4024 paper 01 Q2 June 2006)

7 In an examination, Alan obtained 32 out of 40 marks. In another examination Ben obtained $\frac{5}{8}$ of the total marks.

    Express the mark of each candidate as a percentage.
    (4024 paper 01 Q4 June 2006)

8 Evaluate

    a $\frac{1}{2} - \frac{3}{7}$
        b $2\frac{2}{3} \times 1\frac{3}{4}$.
        (4024 paper 01 Q1 June 2008)

9 Evaluate

    a $25 - 18.3$
        b 1.7×0.03.
        (4024 paper 01 Q2 June 2008)

10 a Evaluate 0.5×0.007.
    b Evaluate $\frac{1}{1.25}$ as a decimal.
    (4024 paper 01 Q5 June 2009)

11 Arrange these values in order of size, starting with the smallest:

    $\frac{9}{20}$ 0.39 46% $\frac{2}{5}$
    (4024 paper 01 Q3 November 2009)

12 a Evaluate $3 + 25 \div 2$.
    b Express $17\frac{1}{2}\%$ as a decimal.

    (4024 paper 01 Q1 June 2007)

13 Evaluate

    a $\frac{1}{4} + \frac{1}{7}$,
        b $1\frac{7}{8} \div \frac{3}{16}$.
        (4021 paper 01 Q2 June 2007)

14 It is given that $\frac{2}{3}, \frac{8}{d}$ and $\frac{n}{39}$ are equivalent fractions.

    Find the value of d and the value of n.
    (4024 paper 01 Q3 June 2007)

15 a Write 3% as a fraction.
    b Work out $90 - 16 \div 2$.

    (4024 paper 11 Q3 November 2014)

16 Evaluate

    a $10 - 7.56$,
        b 0.105×0.2.
    (4024 paper 01 Q1 November 2005)

17 a Evaluate $3 + 5(3 - 1.4)$.
    b Evaluate 0.2×0.07.

    (4024 paper 11 Q1 November 2011)

18 Evaluate

    a $3 + 2(4 - 5)$
        b $1\frac{1}{3} \div 2\frac{1}{2}$.
    (4024 paper 01 Q1 November 2006)

19 a Write the following in order of size, starting with the smallest:

    $\frac{66}{100}$ $0.\dot{6}$ 0.67 $\frac{666}{1000}$

    b The distance of Saturn from the Sun is 1507 million kilometres.

    Express 1507 million in standard form.
    (4024 paper 01 Q5 June 2007)

Beginning Algebra

Learning Objectives
Syllabus sections 4, 17, 18, 19

In this chapter you will begin your study of:
- the language of algebra
- addition, subtraction, multiplication and division
- directed numbers
- indices, brackets and common factors in algebra.

3.1 Introduction

Algebra is a tool for doing arithmetical calculations when some of the numbers needed are unknown. The rules of algebra help us either to calculate the values of these numbers, or to find formulae which can be used to make calculations later when some of the numbers are known. The formulae may link two or more unknown numbers. If these unknown numbers can take different values they are called variables.

Learning to use algebra is like learning a language. We need clear rules for the language so that we can all understand each other. You have met rules like these before, in Chapter 1, when you learned that the same order of working in arithmetic is needed if we are all to get the same answer.

3.2 Essential Skills NO CALCULATOR IN THIS EXERCISE

1 Calculate:
   a $2 \times 6 + 3 \times 5$
   b $3 \times (6 - 4)$
   c $1 + 2 \times 3 - 4 \div 2 + 5 \times (6 - 3)$

2 i   What is the sum of 5 and 6?
   ii What is the product of 5 and 6?

3 i   What is the HCF of 20, 45 and 15?
   ii Rewrite 20, 45 and 15 as products of this factor and one other in each case

3.3 Using Letters and Numbers

Letters as Variables

Suppose you are going to buy 3 apples and 5 oranges. If you know the price of both fruits, you can work out what the total cost will be. Suppose the apples cost 10 cents each and the oranges cost 12 cents each, then the total cost, in cents, will be:

$$3 \times 10 + 5 \times 12$$

Using the correct order of working for arithmetic we can finish this:

$$\text{Total cost} = 3 \times 10 + 5 \times 12$$

$$= 30 + 60 = 90 \text{ cents}$$

But suppose we do not know the cost of the apples?

We can still do some of the work like this:

$$\text{Total cost (in cents)} = 3 \times \textit{cost of an apple} + 5 \times 12$$

$$= 3 \times \textit{cost of an apple} + 60$$

This would take too much time to keep writing out.

If we use a to mean the number of cents that an apple costs, then the sum becomes

$$\text{Total cost (in cents)} = 3 \times a + 5 \times 12$$

$$= 3 \times a + 60$$

We can make this look neater by using one of the rules of algebra, that $3 \times a$ can be shortened to $3a$.

Our final statement is:

$$\text{Total cost (in cents)} = 3a + 60$$

which can also be written

$$\text{Total cost} = (3a + 60) \text{ cents}$$

where a represents the *number* of cents you have to pay for an apple.

Later, when we know the cost of an apple we can finish the sum.

The number of cents is a *variable*. It could be 10 cents today and 12 cents tomorrow.

The total number of cents, or cost, is also a variable, but depends on a.

It is very important that you understand that the letter a stands for a number, not an apple or a number of apples. The statement should really be written:

$$\text{Total cost (in cents)} = 3 \times a \text{ cents} + 60 \text{ cents}$$

but it is usually sufficient to use the word cents once only, *or* to explain that the whole calculation is in cents.

Algebraic Shorthand

To get started with algebra we must start to learn a few rules. We will often use x and y as our unknown quantities, but remember that we can use any letter. When two or more letters are different, we know that they are being used for *different* numbers.

We start with some shorthand.

Had you noticed that multiplication is a shorter form of addition?

There are two ways to work out $7 + 7 + 7 + 7 + 7 + 7 + 7 + 7 + 7$.

You can either go through and add sevens as you go along, or you can see that there are 9 sevens, and quickly get the answer:

$$9 \times 7 = 63$$

You can do this with any number, not just 7, so we could call the number x.

$9 \times x$ can be shortened to $9x$ without any confusion, but 9×7 cannot be shortened to 97, which is completely different.

How Algebra is Similar to Arithmetic (and How it is Different)

When we are using letters and numbers, **simplify** is an instruction to write an answer in its simplest form. The answer will usually still contain letters.

Solve usually means to find a numerical answer to an equation.

When we are using numbers only, **calculate** is an instruction to find the solution to a numerical problem. The answer will be a number, or numbers.

We can *simplify* $y \times y \times y$ to y^3, but $2 \times 2 \times 2 = 2^3 (= 8)$ can be *calculated* to give the numerical answer 8.

Much of your algebra will involve simplifying or, later, writing things in another form.

Work through the next example, paying particular attention to the numerical questions which show the similarities between algebra and arithmetic, and the difference between simplifying and calculating.

REMEMBER:
- $x+x+x+x+x+x+x+x+x = 9 \times x$ and $y+y+y = 3 \times y$.
- $9 \times x$ can be shortened to $9x$, so $9 \times x = 9x$ and $3 \times y = 3y$.

REMEMBER ALSO:
- $x \times x = x^2$ and $y \times y \times y = y^3$.
- $1x$ can be written as just x, so $1x = x$ and $1y = y$.

These also agree with our work with numbers:

$$2 \times 2 \times 2 = 2^3 \text{ and } 1 \times 2 = 2$$

Key terms

Simplify means write in its simplest form.

Solve usually means find a numerical solution to a problem or equation.

Calculate means find a numerical answer.

Example 1

Simplify the following:

a $x+x+x+x+x$

c $y \times y$

e $4x + 2x$

g $3x + x$

i $3y - y$

k $x+x+y+y+y$

m $9x - 8x$

Calculate the following:

b $2+2+2+2+2$

d 8×8

f $4 \times 7 + 2 \times 7$

h $3 \times 5 + 5$

j $3 \times 12 - 12$

l $115 + 115 + 108 + 108 + 108$

n $9 \times 157 - 8 \times 157$

Answer 1

a $x+x+x+x+x = 5x$

c $y \times y = y^2$

e $4x + 2x = 6x$

g $3x + x = 4x$

i $3y - y = 2y$

b $2+2+2+2+2 = 5 \times 2 = 10$

d $8 \times 8 = 8^2 = 64$

f $4 \times 7 + 2 \times 7 = 6 \times 7 = 42$

h $3 \times 5 + 5 = 4 \times 5 = 20$

j $3 \times 12 - 12 = 2 \times 12 = 24$

k	$x+x+y+y+y=2x+3y$	**l** $115+115+108+108+108$
		$=2\times115+3\times108$
		$=230+324$
		$=554$
m	$9x-8x=1x=x$	**n** $9\times157-8\times157=1\times157=157$

If you feel tempted to go further with Example 1 part **k** and attempt some sort of addition of the xs and ys, try it with the numbers as well and see if it works.

For example, *if* you think that $2x+3y$ could be shortened to $5xy$ (which of course you should not!), use numbers to check it.

$$2x+3y: \qquad 2\times115+3\times108$$
$$=230+324$$
$$=554$$

but $\qquad\qquad 5xy: \qquad 5\times115\times108$
$$=62100$$

which is clearly not the same as 554!

We can only arrive at a final answer when we know what numbers will replace x and y. Until then the question has to ask you to *simplify*, rather than *solve*.

Exercise 3.1 **NO CALCULATOR IN THIS EXERCISE**

Copy and complete Table 3.1 by using algebraic shorthand to simplify, and the rules of arithmetic (BoDMAS) to calculate.

		Simplify	Answer		Calculate	Answer
a	**i**	$x+x+x$		**ii**	$30+30+30$	
b	**i**	$5y-4y$		**ii**	$5\times154-4\times154$	
c	**i**	$z\times z\times z$		**ii**	$3\times3\times3$	
d	**i**	$x+x+x-y$		**ii**	$6+6+6-10$	
e	**i**	$x+x+y+y$		**ii**	$7+7+4+4$	
f	**i**	$y-y$		**ii**	$2-2$	
g	**i**	$x\times x+y\times y$		**ii**	$3\times3+4\times4$	
h	**i**	$5x+3x-2y$		**ii**	$5\times50+3\times50-2\times4$	

Table 3.1

3.4 The Language of Algebra

Expressions, equations and terms

There are some other words that have a special meaning in algebra, and you must understand them as well. First of all, try to understand the difference between an *expression* and an *equation*. Have a look at this piece of algebra:

$$3x+5y-10z+6$$

Key terms

In algebra, **terms** are numbers and letters that are added or subtracted. For example, in $3x + 5y$, $3x$ and $5y$ are terms. $3x$ is a **term in x** and $5y$ is a **term in y**.

Expressions are groups of terms to be added or subtracted. They do not have an equals sign. They cannot be solved, but may be simplified.

The **coefficient** of a term is the number in front of it, for example the coefficient of $3x$ is 3.

Like terms have the same letters, for example $4z$ and $10z$.

An **equation** has an equals sign and can often be solved.

This is an **algebraic expression.** It is not an equation since it stands alone without an equals sign. It is made up of **terms** which are to be added or subtracted. The terms are $3x$, $5y$, $10z$ and 6.

$3x$ is a 'term in x', $5y$ is a 'term in y', $10z$ is a 'term in z', and 6 is a constant or a number term.

The 6 is a constant term because it is always 6, but $3x$ is not constant because it depends on what x stands for.

Each number in front of a term is the **coefficient** of that term.

Now look at the following expression:

$$2x + 7y - 3y + 4x$$

This is an expression that can be simplified. It has **like terms.** It has two terms in x and two terms in y. We can write:

$$2x + 7y - 3y + 4x$$
$$= 2x + 4x + 7y - 3y$$
$$= 6x + 4y$$

This is called **collecting like terms**.

Each of the two equals signs shows that the next line is equivalent to the one before, but has been written in another way. They do *not* convert the expression into an equation.

But if we are given a bit more information, for example, that our expression is actually equal to something else, we have an equation.

For example, $6x + 4y = 34$ is an **equation**.

An expression is like a phrase in English, and an equation is more like a sentence. For example, 'hot and stormy weather' is a phrase in English. It means more when it becomes a sentence such as: 'Today we are having hot and stormy weather' and we have the extra bit of information that it is today that we are talking about.

An equation may be **solved** by finding replacements for the variables which make it a true statement. For example, we can solve $10z - 3 = 17$.

This is an equation which becomes true when z is replaced by 2.

$$10 \times 2 - 3 = 17$$

So the solution to the equation is $z = 2$, and in this case it is the only solution. The equation $6x + 4y = 34$ becomes true when we replace the x by 3 and the y by 4, because

$$6 \times 3 + 4 \times 4 = 18 + 16 = 34$$

So $x = 3$ and $y = 4$ is a solution to this equation.

In this case this is not the only possible solution.

For example, $x = 2.5$ and $y = 4.75$ is also a solution. Check it for yourself!

So far we have mainly used letters to represent unknowns or numbers. But remember the example of buying apples and oranges?

We wrote: Total cost (in cents) $= 3a + 60$.

Here a represents the variable cost of one apple, in cents.

Variables can be represented by words, letters or symbols.

NOTE:

NEVER try to turn an expression into an equation, for example by making it equal to zero, unless the question asks you to. This is a common mistake made by students.

Remember that you may be able to simplify an expression, but not solve it. You may be able to simplify *and* solve an equation.

For example,

$$3 \times what = 21$$
$$3x = 21$$
$$3 \times ? = 21$$
$$3 \times \square = 21$$

In each case the unknown can be replaced by 7 to make the equation true. For simplicity it is usual to use letters.

Example 2

a $3x + 4y + y = 3x + 5y$ $\qquad$ $7x + 10y = 37$ $\qquad$ $3a - 4b$

From the above, select:

i a term in x $\qquad\qquad$ **ii** a pair of like terms

iii an equation $\qquad\qquad$ **iv** an expression which is then simplified

v another expression $\qquad$ **vi** a constant term

vii the coefficient of the term in b.

b Can you find replacements for x and y that would make $7x + 10y = 37$ true?

c I give a shopkeeper 10 cents. He gives me 4 mangoes and 4 cents change.
Write an equation to show this and so find the price of one mango.

d **i** Use the letters given to write an equation to represent the following statement:
'I buy 2 bags of crisps and 3 chocolate bars. I spend 12 cents altogether.'
Use $x =$ the cost, in cents, of a bag of crisps, and $y =$ the cost, in cents, of a chocolate bar.

ii Find one pair of possible replacements for x and y which would make your equation true.

Answer 2

a **i** $3x$ or $7x$ are both terms in x.

ii $4y$ and y are like terms.

iii $7x + 10y = 37$ is an equation.

iv $3x + 4y + y$ is an expression which is simplified
to $3x + 5y$.

v $3a - 4b$ is another expression.

vi 37 is a constant term.

vii 4 is the coefficient of the term in b.

> **NOTE:**
> Remember that $3x + 4y + y = 3x + 5y$ is not an equation.

b $7x + 10y = 37$

By trying a few numbers we find that $x = 1$ and $y = 3$ would make this equation true.

$7 \times 1 + 10 \times 3 = 7 + 30 = 37$

If you use rational numbers there are an infinite number of solutions.

For example, $x = 2$ and $y = 2.3$. Can you find some more?

c If $m =$ the cost of one mango, in cents,

$10 = 4m + 4$ $\quad$ (10 cents $= 4 \times m$ cents $+ 4$ cents change)

so $4m = 6$

so $m = 1.5$

Hence, mangoes cost 1.5 cents each.

d **i** $2x + 3y = 12$

ii $x = 3$ and $y = 2$ is one possible pair of values that would make this true.

> **NOTE:**
> We can only use counting numbers here. Why?

Formulae and Substitution

Formulae are equations that are used fairly frequently to calculate quantities and are arranged so that the required quantity is the **subject** of the formula. This makes them convenient to use. For example, in our original small problem of the cost of apples and oranges, we ended up with the formula

$$Total\ cost\ (in\ cents) = 3a + 60$$

where a represents the cost of each apple in cents.

This can be called a formula because it is arranged so that the quantity we want to find (total cost) is on its own on the left and so is the subject of the statement.

When we know the cost of an apple we will be able to substitute this in to replace a, and calculate the total cost. Suppose b is the cost of one orange, in cents, and T is the total cost, in cents; then our formula could become more useful:

$$T = 3a + 5b$$

T, a and b are the unknowns or variables because the prices may vary from day to day.

When we know the cost of an apple and an orange on the day we can **substitute** these numbers for a and b and work out the total cost on the day.

Substitution is replacing unknowns or variables by numbers, usually in formulae, so that answers may be calculated. Calculating the answer when variables in an expression are substituted by numbers is often called **evaluating** the expression.

Example 3

a I think of a number (n), multiply it by 4, add 6, then take away the number I first thought of.
Write a formula for the answer (A) in terms of n.

b Use the formula to find A when:
   i $n = 3$ **ii** $n = 100$ **iii** $n = 11$

Answer 3

a $A = n \times 4 + 6 - n$
   $A = 4n + 6 - n$
   $A = 3n + 6$

b i when $n = 3$ **ii** when $n = 100$ **iii** when $n = 11$
   $A = 3 \times 3 + 6 = 9 + 6$ $A = 3 \times 100 + 6$ $A = 3 \times 11 + 6$
   $A = 15$ $A = 306$ $A = 39$

Exercise 3.2   **NO CALCULATOR IN THIS EXERCISE**

1 Maria is m years old. Her father, Bakari, is n years *older* than Maria.
Write an expression for the sum of their ages.

2 A piece of wood is 6.5 metres long. Brian saws off and uses m metres.
Write an expression for the length of wood which is left.

3 Amir starts his journey to school by walking for 10 minutes, and then takes a bus. The time (t minutes) the bus takes to get to the school depends on the traffic.

  a Write a formula for the total journey time (T minutes) in terms of t.

  b Find T when $t = 15$.

4 Substitute $y = 3$ and $z = 5$ into each of the formulae below to find x.

  a $x = 2y + 3z$ **b** $x = yz + 2$ **c** $x = 4yz - 3z + 2y$

5 Figure 3.1 shows a triangle with two sides of length a cm, and one side of length 3 cm.

  a Write a formula for the total length (L cm) round the outside of the triangle.

  b Use the formula to find L when $a = 10$.

  c Why can a not be

   i 1.5?   **ii** 1?

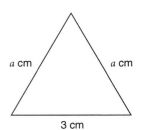

Figure 3.1

6 A recipe requires 5 eggs, 0.5 kilograms of butter and 0.5 kilograms of tomatoes.

  Eggs cost e cents per 10, butter costs b cents per half kilogram and tomatoes cost t cents per kilogram.

  a Write a formula for the total cost (C cents) of the recipe.

  b Calculate C when e = Rs. 22, b = Rs. 58 and t = Rs. 12.

7 Evaluate the following expressions when $x = 2$ and $y = 3$.

  a xy **b** $y - x$

  c $y^2 - x^2$ **d** $3x + 9y$

3.5 Addition and Subtraction of Terms in Algebra

As we have already seen, addition and subtraction of terms in algebra is also called *collecting like terms*.

We could illustrate the process by thinking of a zoo which keeps antelopes and bears.

Antelopes and bears themselves are not variables or unknown quantities, so we will not replace them with letters. This example is just to help you understand how terms can be moved within an expression as long as the sign in front of the term stays with that term.

Think: 'the sign belongs to the term that follows it'.

The zoo starts with 10 antelopes and 5 bears, and then they trade 4 of their antelopes for 2 bears with another zoo. Later on they give away 2 more antelopes. How many antelopes and bears do they now have? The situation could be written like this:

10 antelopes + 5 bears − 4 antelopes + 2 bears − 2 antelopes

which can be rearranged to:

10 antelopes − 4 antelopes − 2 antelopes + 5 bears + 2 bears

This gives us:

4 antelopes + 7 bears

So you can see that we can rearrange the sum as long as we keep the sign with the animal that follows it.

REMEMBER:
- The sign belongs to the term that follows it.
- Terms can be written in any order in the expression as long as they keep their signs.
- Only like terms can be added or subtracted.

Example 4
Simplify:

a $3x - 2y + 2x + 5y$ **b** $6x^2 + 2x + 3x + 5$

c $1 + 6xy - 5x - yx + 3$ **d** $x^2 + x^3 + 2x^2 + 3x^3$

Answer 4

a $3x - 2y + 2x + 5y = 3x + 2x + 5y - 2y$ **b** $6x^2 + 2x + 3x + 5$
   $= 5x + 3y$ $= 6x^2 + 5x + 5$

c $1 + 6xy - 5x - yx + 3$ **d** $x^2 + x^3 + 2x^2 + 3x^3$
   $= 4 + 5xy - 5x$ $= 3x^2 + 4x^3$

Exercise 3.3   **NO CALCULATOR IN THIS EXERCISE**

Simplify:

1 $3x + 10x$ **2** $5x + 7x - x$

3 $2x + 5x - 4y$ **4** $2a + 5a - 3a + 6b$

5 $6x - 3x + 2y - y$ **6** $3x + 10 - 7$

7 $4z + 2w + 2z + w - 2z$ **8** $7c - c + 6d - 3 - 6d$

9 $6 + 3a - 3 - a$ **10** $4x + y - 3x - y$

11 $8x^2 + 4y^2 - 7x^2 - 2y^2$ **12** $6x^2 + 2x - 3x^2 + x$

13 $x^2 + xy + 4x^2 + 2xy$ **14** $2x^2 + y^2 - xy + x^2$

15 $3x^2 + 2xy - xy - 4y^2$ **16** $3x^2 - 5x^3 + 2x^2y + x^2y$

17 $5x^2y^2 - 3x^2y - x^2y^2 + x^2y$

3.6 Multiplication and Division in Algebra

When you multiply or divide in algebra it is best to be systematic.

Example 5
Simplify:

a $3a \times 4b \times 6c \times a$ **b** $5x \times 6x \times 4y$ **c** $6d \times 5c \div 3d$

d $x^2y \div x^2y$ **e** $3 \div 3x^2$

Answer 5

a $3a \times 4b \times 6c \times a = 72 \times a \times b \times c \times a$ **b** $5x \times 6x \times 4y = 120 \times x \times x \times y$
   $= \mathbf{72a^2bc}$ $= 120x^2y$

c $6d \times 5c \div 3d$ **d** $x^2y \div x^2y$

   $= \dfrac{6d \times 5c}{3d} = \dfrac{30dc}{3d} = \dfrac{10dc}{d}$ $= \dfrac{x^2y}{x^2y}$

   $= 10c$

e $3 \div 3x^2$

   $= \dfrac{3}{3x^2} = \dfrac{1}{x^2}$

Exercise 3.4

NO CALCULATOR IN THIS EXERCISE

Simplify:

1 $5a \times 3b$ **2** $6y \times 4z$ **3** $3x \times 2x$

4 $10x \times 3x \times 2$ **5** $x \times y \times 3z \times 2$ **6** $5a \div 5$

7 $3d \times 4a \times d \times 5b$ **8** $8 \div 2x$ **9** $10cd \div 5c$

10 $4x \div 2$ **11** $6 \div 12d$ **12** $3ab \div 2ab$

13 $5ab \times 4cd$ **14** $2d \times 6c \div dc$

3.7 Working with Directed Numbers

We shall meet directed numbers frequently in algebra, and it is essential that you can work with them with confidence. We first met directed numbers in Chapter 1, but now we need to work with them.

Have a look at the number line in Figure 3.2.

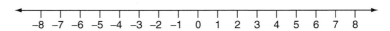

Figure 3.2 Number line

Addition and Subtraction of Directed Numbers

To **subtract** using your number line, start at the first number and move to the *left*.

You know that $9 - 4 = 5$.

On your number line start at 9 and go back 4 steps to reach the answer 5.

How about $1 - 4$?

Start at 1 on the number line and go back 4 steps to reach –3 (negative 3), so

$$1 - 4 = -3$$

For $-3 - 4$, start at negative 3 on the number line and again go back 4 steps.

You will find that negative 3 take away 4 is negative 7.

$$-3 - 4 = -7$$

The minus signs in front of the 3 and the 7 are both read as negative signs because they are directed number signs. The minus sign in front of the 4 means take away (subtract) four. So 'negative 3 take away 4 is negative 7'. In practice, many people say 'minus' instead of 'negative', but we must be careful that this does not cause confusion.

To **add**, you start at the first number and move to the *right*.

$$-6 + 15 = 9$$

Starting at –6 and moving 15 steps to the right you arrive at positive 9, (or simply 9).

There are two more ways that you will see negative numbers written in books:

−6 could be shown as ⁻6 or as (−6)

and the positive numbers could be shown in four ways:

+9 or ⁺9 or (+9) or just 9

In the examples and exercises that follow, you will find all these forms so that you get used to them.

Example 6

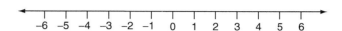

Figure 3.3 Number line

Using the number line in Figure 3.3, calculate:

a $-4+3+2-6+5-1$ **b** $-6+5-1+3-4+2$

c $3+2+5-6-1-4$ **d** Why do all these give the same answer?

Answer 6

a $-4+3+2-6+5-1$
$=-1$

b $-6+5-1+3-4+2$
$=-1$

c $3+2+5-6-1-4$
$=-1$

d You can perform addition and subtraction in any order as long as you keep the sign with the term that follows it.

Exercise 3.5   NO CALCULATOR IN THIS EXERCISE

Calculate:

1 $7-3-5+2-8$ **2** $10-2-1-3-4+7$ **3** $-2-3-4-1+10$

4 $3-3+4+2-5-1$ **5** $-8+8$ **6** $+7-7$

7 $-3-2-1$ **8** $6-4+5$ **9** $-8+9$

10 $0-5+10$

The next thing to understand is what it means when you see something like:

$$8 - {}^{-}2$$

which is read as '8 take away (or subtract or minus) negative 2'.

Taking away a negative number is the same as adding the same number.

There are many ways to try to explain this, but maybe we should just look at it as a double negative meaning a positive.

'You are *not* going to *miss* the train tonight' means that 'you *are* going to catch the train tonight'. This type of double negative is common, so it helps us to remember the rule.

If your bank balance is overdrawn, and you are in debt by, say $100, it would show as −$100. If, for some reason, someone took away the debt, you would end up with nothing in the bank, but no longer in debt. Taking away the negative amount is the same as adding it.

$$-100--100=-100+100=0$$

In the same way, adding a positive number is the same as addition, and adding a negative number is the same as subtraction.

NOTE:
Remember that two like signs (that is two signs which are the same) make a plus, and two unlike signs (different signs) make a minus.

$++=+$
$--=+$
$+-=-$
$-+=-$

Be sure that you remember these facts:

$$++10 = +10$$

$$--10 = +10$$

$$+-10 = -10$$

$$-+10 = -10$$

It is best to simplify any two signs that are together (for example, $-(-)$, $-+$ or $+-$) *before* you go on with the calculation. We could call them *double* signs, and will refer to them again later. So whenever you meet a double sign simplify it before carrying on.

REMEMBER:
- Simplify double signs before adding or subtracting.
- Addition or subtraction can be done by taking steps along the number line in the appropriate direction.

Example 7
Calculate:

a $2 - 4$

b $-19 + 7$

c $-12 - 13$

d $17 - -3$ (deal with the double sign first: a double negative is a positive)

e $21 + (-7)$ (double sign first)

f $14 - +2$ (double sign first)

g $(-5) - (-2)$ (double sign first)

Answer 7

a $2 - 4$
$= -2$

b $-19 + 7$
$= -12$

c $-12 - 13$
$= -25$

d $17 - -3$
$= 17 + 3$
$= 20$

e $21 + (-7)$
$= 21 - 7$
$= 14$

f $14 - +2$
$= 14 - 2$
$= 12$

g $(-5) - (-2)$
$= -5 + 2$
$= -3$

REMEMBER:
- If addition or subtraction of directed numbers involves double signs, deal with them *first*, applying the rules. Then go to the number line to work out the answer.
- In multiplication and division of directed numbers apply the rules while multiplying and dividing.

Multiplication and Division of Directed Numbers

The same rules described for addition and subtraction with double signs apply here. Learn these!

$+$	$\times$	$+$	$=$	$+$		$+$	$\div$	$+$	$=$	$+$
$-$	$\times$	$-$	$=$	$+$		$-$	$\div$	$-$	$=$	$+$
$+$	$\times$	$-$	$=$	$-$		$+$	$\div$	$-$	$=$	$-$
$-$	$\times$	$+$	$=$	$-$		$-$	$\div$	$+$	$=$	$-$

The rules are not so difficult to learn if you remember that two like signs make a plus, and two unlike signs make a minus.

When multiplying or dividing directed numbers it pays to work in order as before. In fact you should always be systematic in algebra to avoid unnecessary mistakes. First deal with signs, next the numbers and lastly, if there are any, the letters (see the next section).

Example 8
Calculate:

a -2×-6 **b** $-10 \div -5$

c 20×-7 **d** $55 \div -11$

> **NOTE:**
> Remember the 20 in part **c** is positive, so $+ \times - = -$

Answer 8

a -2×-6
$= +2 \times 6$
$= +12$

b $-10 \div -5$
$= +10 \div 5$
$= 2$

c 20×-7
$= -20 \times 7$
$= -140$

d $55 \div -11$
$= -55 \div 11$
$= -5$

To make this absolutely clear we will do one more mixed example.

Example 9
Calculate:

a $(-2) - (-3) + (-4)$ **b** $-3 + -5$

c -1×-6 **d** $2 \div (-3)$

e $-2 \times (-2) \times (-2)$

> **NOTE:**
> The first two negative 2s in part **e** multiplied together make positive 4. Then what happens? That positive 4 has to be multiplied by the remaining negative 2 to make a negative number in the end.

Answer 9

a $(-2) - (-3) + (-4)$
$= -2 + 3 - 4$
$= -3$

b $-3 + -5$
$= -3 - 5$
$= -8$

c -1×-6
$= +1 \times 6$
$= +6$

d $(+2) \div (-3)$
$= -2 \div 3$
$= -\frac{2}{3}$

e $-2 \times (-2) \times (-2)$
$= +4 \times (-2)$
$= -8$

Exercise 3.6

NO CALCULATOR IN THIS EXERCISE

Calculate:

1 **a** $2 + 3$ **b** $-2 + 3$ **c** $2 - 3$ **d** $-2 - 3$
      e $-2 - -3$ **f** $-2 + +3$ **g** $-2 + (-3)$ **h** $(-2) + (-3)$

2 **a** 2×3 **b** -2×3 **c** $-2 \times (-3)$ **d** 2×-3
      e $-2 \times +3$

3 **a** $6 \div 3$ **b** $-6 \div 3$ **c** $-6 \div (-3)$ **d** $6 \div -3$

4 **a** $\frac{2}{4}$ **b** $\frac{-2}{4}$ **c** $\frac{-2}{-4}$ **d** $\frac{2}{-4}$

5 $-5 - -6 + -1 + 10$

6 $4 - (-2) + (-3) - 5$

7 $10 - (+3) - (-3)$

8 $5 \times (-2) \times (-1)$

9 $6 \times 3 \div (-2)$

10 **a** -1×-1 **b** $-1 + -1$ **c** $-1 \div -1$
       d $(-1) \times (-1) \times (-1)$ **e** $(-1) \times (-1) \times (-1) \times (-1)$

11 $-7 \times -4 \div +2$

Working with Directed Numbers in Algebra

The same rules apply for working with directed numbers in algebra as we have just covered in the previous two sections where we used only numbers.

Example 10
Simplify, where possible:
a $2a + -3a - b - -6b$ **b** $-6x \times (-2y)$ **c** $-6x + (-2y)$

Answer 10
a $2a + -3a - b - -6b = 2a - 3a - b + 6b$
   $= -a + 5b$

b $-6x \times (-2y) = +6x \times 2y$ **c** $-6x + (-2y)$
   $= +12xy$ $= -6x - 2y$

Exercise 3.7

NO CALCULATOR IN THIS EXERCISE

Simplify, where possible:

1 $-x \times 2y$ **2** $-x \times -2y$ **3** $-x + (-2y)$

4 $-x - -2y$ **5** $a^2 \div 2$ **6** $3a \div (-6b)$

7 $(-2x) \times (-4y)$ **8** $(-2x) \div (-4y)$ **9** $xy \times (-3x)$

10 $xy + (-3x)$ **11** $xy \div (-3x)$ **12** $-3y \times -2x \times -x$

13 $-4z + (-2z) - (-3z^2)$ **14** $3a + 2b + (-a) - (-b)$

3.8 Working with Indices

We have already met the fact that $x + x + x$ can be shortened to $3x$, and $x \times x \times x$ can be shortened to x^3.

The 3 in x^3 is a **power** or **index**. The plural of index is indices.

Raising to a whole number power is a shorter form of multiplying something by itself many times. The number of times it is multiplied by itself is shown by the power or index.

If numbers are raised to a power the answer may be calculated, but if algebraic variables are raised to a power we can only simplify.

Two examples may help:

$$2^5 = 2 \times 2 \times 2 \times 2 \times 2 = 32$$

but

$$x \times x \times x \times x \times x = x^5$$

We can still work with powers of algebraic variables as we will see in the rest of this section.

Writing out $x^3 \times x^4$ in longhand:

$$x \times x \times x \times x \times x \times x \times x = x^7$$

In shorthand:

$$x^3 \times x^4 = x^{3+4} = x^7$$

When you **multiply** a number or a variable raised to a power by the *same* number or variable raised to another power you *add* the powers.

$$
\begin{array}{ccccccccc}
2^3 & \times & 2^2 & = & 2^{3+2} & = & 2^5 & = & 32 \\
\end{array}
$$

or $\quad 2 \times 2 \times 2 \quad \times \quad 2 \times 2 \qquad\qquad\quad = \quad 2^5 \quad = \quad 32$

or $\qquad\quad 2^3 \quad \times \quad 2^2 \quad = \quad 8 \times 4 \qquad\qquad = \quad 32$

A similar argument can be applied to division.

$$
\begin{array}{ccccccc}
2^5 & \div & 2^2 & = & 32 & \div & 4 & = & 8 \\
\end{array}
$$

or $\qquad\quad 2^5 \quad \div \quad 2^2 \quad = \quad 2^{5-2} \quad = \quad 2^3 \quad = \quad 8$

When you **divide** a number or variable raised to a power by the *same* number or variable raised to another power you *subtract* the second power from the first.

There is one more rule to learn for working with powers.

$$(2^4)^3 = (2^4) \times (2^4) \times (2^4) = 2^{4+4+4} = 2^{3 \times 4} = 2^{12}$$

So as you should see, raising to a *further* power means multiplying the powers.

Learn these three rules. The letters n and m represent natural or counting numbers.

Rule	Example
$x^n \times x^m = x^{n+m}$	$x^6 \times x^2 = x^{6+2} = x^8$
$x^n \div x^m = x^{n-m}$	$x^6 \div x^2 = x^{6-2} = x^4$
$(x^n)^m = x^{nm}$	$(x^6)^2 = x^{6 \times 2} = x^{12}$

Key term

An **index** (plural **indices**) or **power** shows how many of a certain number or variable are to be multiplied together, for example $n^4 = n \times n \times n \times n$.

NOTE:

It is very important to remember that the power *only* refers to the single variable before it, *unless* it is outside a pair of brackets.

For example,
$$2xy^2 = 2 \times x \times y \times y$$
$$= 2 \times x \times y^2$$
$$2(xy)^2 = 2 \times x^2 \times y^2$$
$$(2xy)^2 = 4 \times x^2 \times y^2$$

Example 11

a Calculate:

   i $3^2 \times 3^3$ **ii** $3^4 \div 3^3$ **iii** $(3^2)^2$ **iv** $3^2 + 3^4$

b Simplify, where possible:

   i $x^4 \times x^5$ **ii** $x^6 \div x^2$ **iii** $(x^7)^3$

   iv $x^2 + x^3$ **v** $x^3 + x^3$

> **NOTE:**
> These are unlike terms.

> **NOTE:**
> These are like terms.

Answer 11

a i $3^2 \times 3^3$ **ii** $3^4 \div 3^3$
     $= 9 \times 27 = 243$ (or 3^5) $= 81 \div 27 = 3$ (or 3^1)

  iii $(3^2)^2$ **iv** $3^2 + 3^4$
     $= 9^2 = 81$ (or 3^4) $= 9 + 81 = 90$

b i $x^4 \times x^5$ **ii** $x^6 \div x^2$ **iii** $(x^7)^3$
     $= x^{4+5} = x^9$ $= x^{6-2} = x^4$ $= x^{7 \times 3} = x^{21}$

  iv $x^2 + x^3$ No simplifying possible because *unlike* terms cannot be added.

  v $x^3 + x^3$ Like terms *can* be added.
     $= 2x^3$

Exercise 3.8   **NO CALCULATOR IN THIS EXERCISE**

1 Calculate:

  a $4^2 \times 4^3$ **b** $5^5 \div 5^3$ **c** $4^2 + 4^2$

  d $2^3 - 2^2$ **e** $(2^3)^3$

2 Simplify, where possible:

  a $x^4 \times x^5$ **b** $x^4 + x^5$ **c** $x^3 + x^3$

  d $x^3 \times x^3$ **e** $x^6 \div x^2$ **f** $2x^5 \times 3x^6$

  g $2x^5 + 3x^5$ **h** $(2x) \times (2x)$ **i** $(2x)^2$

  j $(2x^3) \times (2x^3)$ **k** $(2x^3)^2$ **l** $(x^5)^9$

3 Simplify, as far as possible:

  a $3x^4 \times x \times 2x^5$ **b** $2x^6 \times y^3 \times x^7$

  c $6x^5 \times 3x^4 \div 2x^3$ **d** $9x^3 \times 4x^2 \times 2y^3 \div 3y^2$

So far we have dealt with indices that come from the set of counting numbers. We also have to work with indices that are from the set of integers. These would include, for example, x^{-2}, x^0, x^{-1} and so on.

Look at this pattern:

$$x^2 = 1 \times x \times x$$
$$x^1 = 1 \times x$$
$$x^0 = 1$$
$$x^{-1} = \frac{1}{x}$$
$$x^{-2} = \frac{1}{x \times x} = \frac{1}{x^2}$$

You should be able to see that $x^0 = 1$.

In fact, since x can stand for anything we could say that anything raised to the power zero is one.

$$1\,000\,000^0 = 1, \qquad 0.000\,0034^0 = 1, \qquad 123\,456\,789^0 = 1,$$

$$\left(\frac{576}{0.49}\right)^0 = 1, \qquad \left(x^{24} + y^{25}\right)^0 = 1$$

This makes some of the questions you might meet rather easy!

You should also see that negative powers indicate that the term should be inverted to make the power positive.

Invert means turn upside down, so $x^{-1} = \frac{1}{x}$. (Remember that x^{-1} can be written as $\frac{x^{-1}}{1}$.)

For example,

$$x^{-2} = \frac{1}{x^2}, \qquad \frac{1}{x^{-3}} = x^3, \qquad \left(\frac{2}{3}\right)^{-1} = \frac{3}{2}, \qquad \left(\frac{2}{3}\right)^{-3} = \left(\frac{3}{2}\right)^3 = \frac{27}{8} \text{ and } \qquad x^{-n} = \frac{1}{x^n}$$

You may also meet the word **reciprocal**, which is a fraction inverted. For example, the reciprocal of $\frac{2}{5}$ is $\frac{5}{2}$.

Example 12

a Evaluate:

i 2^{-1} **ii** 2^{-4} **iii** $\frac{1}{2^{-3}}$ **iv** $2^{-1} \times 2^4$

v $2^{-1} \div 2^{-3}$ **vi** $\left(\frac{3}{5}\right)^{-1}$ **vii** $\left(1\frac{3}{5}\right)^{-2}$

b Simplify, giving the answers in a form with positive powers:

i $x^{-3} \times x^7$ **ii** $x^{10} \times x^{-3} \times x^{-1}$ **iii** $x^{-8} \div x^{-6}$ **iv** $x^5 \div x^{-1}$

v $(x^{1000})^0$ **vi** $(2x)^{-2}$ **vii** $2x^{-2}$

c In each case, find a replacement for n which will make the statement true:

i $16 = 2^n$ **ii** $\frac{1}{4} = 2^n$ **iii** $\frac{3}{4} = \left(\frac{4}{3}\right)^n$

d Find a replacement for x in each of the following:

i $27 = 3^x$ **ii** $x^3 = 64$ **iii** $\frac{1}{2^x} = 8$

Answer 12

a **i** $2^{-1} = \frac{1}{2}$ **ii** $2^{-4} = \frac{1}{2^4} = \frac{1}{16}$ **iii** $\frac{1}{2^{-3}} = 2^3 = 8$

iv $2^{-1} \times 2^4 = 2^{-1+4} = 2^3 = 8$ **v** $2^{-1} \div 2^{-3} = 2^{-1--3} = 2^{-1+3} = 2^2 = 4$

NOTE:
Remember that to divide a number with a power by the same number to another power means you subtract the powers.

(Alternative method: $2^{-1} \div 2^{-3} = \frac{1}{2} \div \frac{1}{2^3} = \frac{1}{2} \div \frac{1}{8} = \frac{1}{2} \times \frac{8}{1} = 4$)

vi $\left(\frac{3}{5}\right)^{-1} = \frac{5}{3}$ **vii** $\left(1\frac{3}{5}\right)^{-2} = \left(\frac{8}{5}\right)^{-2} = \left(\frac{5}{8}\right)^2 = \frac{25}{64}$

b **i** $x^{-3} \times x^7 = x^{-3+7} = x^4$ **ii** $x^{10} \times x^{-3} \times x^{-1} = x^{10-3-1} = x^6$

iii $x^{-8} \div x^{-6} = x^{-8--6} = x^{-8+6} = x^{-2} = \frac{1}{x^2}$ **iv** $x^5 \div x^{-1} = x^{5--1} = x^{5+1} = x^6$

v $(x^{1000})^0 = 1$ **vi** $(2x)^{-2} = \left(\frac{1}{2x}\right)^2 = \frac{1}{4x^2}$

vii $2x^{-2} = \frac{2}{x^2}$

NOTE:
Parts **c** and **d** can be answered by trying different numbers until the correct answer is found.

Exercise 3.9   NO CALCULATOR IN THIS EXERCISE

Work through this exercise carefully, checking your answers as you go.

1 Evaluate:

a 2^4 **b** 2^{-4} **c** $2^{-1} \times 2^3$

d $2^{-1} \div 2^3$ **e** $5^{-2} \times 5^0$ **f** $\left(\frac{5}{2}\right)^{-1}$

g $\frac{5^{-1}}{2}$ **h** $\left(\frac{5}{2}\right)^{-2}$ **i** $\left(\frac{1}{2}\right)^{-3}$

j $\left(2\frac{1}{2}\right)^{-2}$ **k** $\left(3\frac{1}{2}\right)^2$ **l** $\left(1\frac{3}{4}\right)^{-3}$

2 Simplify:

> **NOTE:**
> In question 2 part **e** remember Take one letter at a time: $x^4 \div x^2 = x^2$ and so on.

a $\left(\frac{x^2}{y}\right)^{-1}$ **b** $\left(\frac{x^2}{y}\right)^{-4}$ **c** $\left(\frac{x^2}{y}\right)^{-1} \div \left(\frac{x^2}{y}\right)^{-1}$

d $\left(\frac{x^2}{y}\right)^{0}$ **e** $\frac{x^4 y^2 z^3}{x^3 y^{-1} z^{-1}}$ **f** $(x^5 y^6) \div (xy)^{-2}$

3 In each question, find a replacement for n which will make the statement true.

> **NOTE:**
> In question 3 part **a** remember standard form?

a $2600 = 2.6 \times 10^n$

b $\frac{1}{10000} = 10^n$ **c** $\frac{2}{3} = \left(\frac{3}{2}\right)^n$

d $\frac{4}{9} = \left(\frac{2}{3}\right)^n$ **e** $\frac{8}{27} = \left(\frac{2}{3}\right)^n$ **f** $\frac{27}{8} = \left(\frac{2}{3}\right)^n$

> **NOTE:**
> In Question 3**q** and 3**r** k is any constant, and remember x is the same as x^1.

g $3\frac{3}{8} = \left(\frac{2}{3}\right)^n$ **h** $2^n = 2$ **i** $2^n = 1$

j $0.0015 = 1.5 \times 10^n$ **k** $x^2 = \frac{1}{x^n}$ **l** $2x = (2x)^n$

m $4x^2 = (2x)^n$ **n** $x^{-1} \times x^{-2} = \frac{1}{x^n}$ **o** $x^{-1} \div x^{-2} = x^n$

p $x^3 \times x = x^n$ **q** $x^k \times x = x^n$ **r** $x^k \div x^2 = x^n$

4 Simplify, where possible, writing your answers in a form with positive powers.

a $3x^2 + 2x^2$ **b** $3x^{-2} + 2x^{-3}$ **c** $\frac{1}{3x^{-2}}$

d $\frac{1}{(3x)^{-2}}$ **e** $\frac{1}{(3x)^{-2}} \times \left(\frac{x^2}{2}\right)^{-1}$

f $(2x^2)^3 \times 3(x^{-1})^6$

> **NOTE:**
> In 4c only the x has a power.

3.9 Brackets and Common Factors
Dealing with Brackets

In arithmetic we are told to work out brackets first (BoDMAS), but this is not so easy in algebra.

Look at the following:

$$2 \times (7 - 3)$$
$$= 2 \times 4$$
$$= 8$$

But what about $2 \times (x - y)$?

It is quite helpful to think of the pair of brackets as a bag, or bundle, containing x and $-y$.

The 2 tells us that we have two of these bags, so if we emptied them on to the table we would have two xs and two $-y$s.

This shows that $2 \times (x - y) = 2x - 2y$.

Using algebraic shorthand we can say

$$2(x - y) = 2x - 2y$$

This is called **multiplying out the brackets**, (or commonly, getting rid of the brackets).

Does this work with numbers as well?

Going back to our first example,

$$2 \times (7 - 3) = 2 \times 7 - 2 \times 3$$
$$= 14 - 6 = 8$$

This is the same answer as before, so it does work with numbers. However, with numbers it is usually quicker to work out the inside of the brackets first (remember BoDMAS).

REMEMBER:
- Multiplying out the brackets means multiplying every term inside the pair of brackets by the number (or letter) that is outside the brackets.

Once the brackets have been multiplied out we can continue with collecting like terms and so on.

Example 13
Multiply out the brackets.

a $2(c - 1)$ **b** $2(3a - 4b + c)$ **c** $5x(6x + 7y)$

Answer 13
a $2(c - 1) = 2c - 2$
b $2(3a - 4b + c) = 6a - 8b + 2c$
c $5x(6x + 7y) = 30x^2 + 35xy$

Exercise 3.10 $\qquad$ NO CALCULATOR IN THIS EXERCISE

Multiply out the brackets.

1	$2(a+b)$		**2**	$6(3+x)$		**3**	$3(x-y)$
4	$5(6-b)$		**5**	$4(3x-2)$		**6**	$7(1-3c)$
7	$5(6x+5y)$		**8**	$8(x-y+4z)$		**9**	$5(x^2+4)$
10	$7(2x^2-3y^2)$		**11**	$4(3xy+5z)$		**12**	$x(2-3y)$
13	$a(a+2)$		**14**	$x(x-y)$		**15**	$2c(c+d)$
16	$3m(2m-n)$		**17**	$4xy(2x-9y)$		**18**	$7x^2(3-2y+4z)$

All the rules for multiplication with signs also apply to multiplying out brackets, and this is one of the most common areas where mistakes occur, so make doubly sure that you work through the next example and exercise and understand it clearly.

Example 14
Multiply out the brackets and simplify where possible.
a $-4(2z-1)$

> **NOTE:**
> Remember you are multiplying by negative 4! There is a MINUS sign so take care!

b $-(a-b+c)$

> **NOTE:**
> You are taking away everything inside the pair of brackets. Taking away $-b$ is the same as adding b.

c $5(x-y)-2(x+y)$

Answer 14
a $-4(2z-1) = -8z+4$ $\qquad$ **b** $-(a-b+c) = -a+b-c$

c $5(x-y)-2(x+y) = 5x-5y-2x-2y = 3x-7y$

You should see from this example that you must be careful with minus signs, particularly in front of brackets.

Exercise 3.11 $\qquad$ NO CALCULATOR IN THIS EXERCISE

Multiply out the brackets and simplify where possible:

1	$2(3+4x)$		**2**	$-2(3+4x)$		**3**	$x(3x+4y)$
4	$-x(3x+4y)$		**5**	$-x(3x-4y)$		**6**	$-2x(7x-6)$
7	$-(x+y)$		**8**	$-(2-z)$		**9**	$6p(q+3r-s)$
10	$-6p(q+3r-s)$		**11**	$x^2y(y-5)$		**12**	$-3x^2(2y-3)$
13	$4a(-2-3a)$		**14**	$-4a(-2-3a)$		**15**	$(x+y)-(x-y)$
16	$3(a+2b)+2(a+3b)$		**17**	$-5(2x+3y)-4(3x+2y)$		**18**	$-3(-x-y)+4(x-y)$
19	$-2(x-3y)-(x-y)$		**20**	$x(x+y+z)-(x^2+y+xz)$

Common Factors

As usual, we have to be able to do the opposite to multiplying out the brackets, and this is called **taking out common factors** or **factorising**.

Remember that *common* means belonging to all, and *factors* are things that are multiplied together. We have already done some work with common factors in arithmetic when we found the HCF (highest common factor) of two or more numbers.

The following examples are designed to help you understand the process of factorising in algebra by comparing the process with the arithmetic work that you are familiar with.

Find the HCF of 20 and 35.

$$\text{factors of } 20 = \{1, 2, 4, \underline{5}, 10, 20\}$$

$$\text{factors of } 35 = \{1, \underline{5}, 7, 35\}$$

$$\text{HCF} = \mathbf{5}$$

$$\text{so } 20 = \mathbf{5} \times 4 \text{ and } 35 = \mathbf{5} \times 7$$

Find the HCF of $3ab$ and $6b^2$.

$$\text{factors of } 3ab = \{1, 3, a, b, 3a, \underline{3b}, 3ab\}$$

$$\text{factors of } 6b^2 = \{1, 2, 3, 6, b, b^2, 2b, \underline{3b}, 6b, 2b^2, 3b^2, 6b^2\}$$

$$\text{HCF} = \mathbf{3b}$$

$$\text{so } 3ab = \mathbf{3b} \times a \text{ and } 6b^2 = \mathbf{3b} \times 2b$$

In practice it is not as complicated as it looks.

If we are asked to factorise $3ab + 6b^2$, we would probably see quite easily that 3 would go into both terms, giving $3 \times (ab + 2b^2)$.

In other words,

$$3ab + 6b^2 = 3(ab + 2b^2)$$

However, this is only *partially* factorised as there is still a factor of b in both terms inside the pair of brackets, so we factorise that out as well.

$$3ab + 6b^2 = 3b(a + 2b)$$

This is now *fully* or *completely* factorised.

Example 15
Factorise completely:

a $xy - 2y^2x$ **b** $abc + 4a^2b$

c $x^2 - 3x^2y$ **d** $10mn + 5m$

Answer 15

a $xy - 2y^2x$
$= xy(1 - 2y)$

NOTE:
Do not forget the 1 at the beginning of the pair of brackets. If you leave it out you will not be able to multiply out the brackets again to get back to the original expression.

b $abc + 4a^2b$
$= ab(c + 4a)$

c $x^2 - 3x^2y$ **d** $10mn + 5m$

$= x^2(1 - 3y)$ $= 5m(2n + 1)$

Exercise 3.12

NO CALCULATOR IN THIS EXERCISE

Factorise completely:

1 $8x + 4y$ **2** $15a - 25b$ **3** $4x - 20$

4 $xy + 2x$ **5** $x^2 - 2x$ **6** $x^2 - x$

7 $3xy + 9x$ **8** $3x^3 - 9x^2 y$ **9** $3a^2 - 6ab$

10 $xyz + 4yz$ **11** $10y + 100y^2$ **12** $5fg + 6fgh$

13 $3bx - 6xy$ **14** $3b^2 x - 6bx$ **15** $4b^2 - 2b$

16 $4b^2 - b$ **17** $x^2 y^2 - xy$ **18** $7c^2 d^2 - 21cd^2$

Exercise 3.13

NO CALCULATOR IN THIS EXERCISE

Mixed exercise

1 Write down and simplify the product of these three factors: $2x$, $3x$ and $-4z$.

2 Write down and simplify the sum of these three terms: $2x$, $-5x$ and $3y$.

3 Using $x = 6$, $y = -1$ and $z = 2$, evaluate these expressions:
   a $x^2 + y$ **b** $-x - y - z$ **c** $x^2 + y^2 - z^2$
   d y^3 **e** $y(x + 4)$ **f** $x - 3z$
   g $z^2(xy + yz - xz)$ **h** xyz

4 Seema writes down an expression which has a term in x^2 which has a coefficient of 2, a term in y which has a coefficient of -1, and a constant which is -5. Write down Seema's expression.

5 Simplify the following:
   a x^0 **b** $x \div x$ **c** $\frac{x}{x}$
   d $x \times 0$ **e** $x \times 1$ **f** $x - x$
   g $x + x + x + x$ **h** $x^{-1} \times x$ **i** $(x^0)^2$
   j $x \times x \times x \times x$ **k** $x^{-2} \times x^2$ **l** $(-x)^2$
   m $(-x)^3$ **n** $-(x \times x)$

6 Find pairs of replacements for x and y which would make the following true.
   Write your answers as $x = \ldots$ and $y = \ldots$
   Take your values from the set of integers. (Part **e** has only one possible answer.)
   a $x + y = 4$ **b** $xy = -6$ **c** $\frac{x}{y} = 2$
   d $x - y = -2$ **e** $x^y = 9$ **f** $2x + y = 5$
   g $x^2 + y^2 = 25$ **h** $\sqrt{x} + \sqrt{y} = 5$ **i** $\sqrt{x + y} = 5$

7 Evaluate the following:
   a $\left(\frac{3}{4}\right)^{-2}$ **b** $\left(\frac{19}{9}\right)^{-1}$ **c** $\left(\frac{1}{2}\right)^0$
   d $2^{-1} \times \frac{1}{2}$ **e** $\left(2\frac{1}{5}\right)^2$

8 Simplify:
   a $-x + 4y - -7x$ **b** $(-x)^3 \times 3x^2$ **c** $-2x \times -3y$
   d $\frac{-x}{-x^2}$ **e** $\frac{1}{x^{-2}} \times x^2$ **f** $\left(\frac{1}{x^{-2}}\right)^3 \times \frac{1}{x}$

9 Find replacements for n:
   a $10^n = 10\,000$ **b** $3^n = \frac{1}{9}$ **c** $3^{2n} = 9$
   d $2^{2n} = 16$ **e** $6 = \frac{2}{3^n}$

10 Multiply out the brackets and simplify where possible:

a $a(ab - bc)$ **b** $2(3x + 4y) - x(1 - 2y)$

c $2a(3b + 4c - 5a) + 10a^2$ **d** $6x^2 - 3x(2 + 3x)$

11 Factorise completely:

a $ab^2 - a^2b$ **b** $2x^2 - 6xy + 4x$

c $2xyz^2 + 4x^2y^2z$ **d** $2abc - 4a^2b^2c^2$

12 Simplify:

a $x^{-1} \times x^3 \times x^0$ **b** $a^2 \times b^3 \times a^{-1} \div b^2$ **c** $x^2 \times x^3 + x^{-2} \times x^7$

d $\dfrac{a^3b^4c^6}{a^2bc}$ **e** $(a^3)^2$ **f** $(x^{-2})^{-1}$

13 Fleur can carry no more than 10 kilograms home from the market. She has bought b bags of sugar already and would also like to buy some flour. Each bag of sugar weighs 0.5 kilograms.

a Write a formula to express the amount of flour (f kilograms) she can buy in terms of b.

b If $b = 6$, use your formula to calculate f.

c If $f = 4$, how many bags of sugar has Fleur bought?

14 a Take 49 from 51.   **b** Take 49 from 40.

c Take $(2x + 3)$ from $(x + 5)$.   **d** Take $x - y$ from $x + y$.

e Divide 2 by 6.   **f** Divide $2x$ by x^2.

Exam-style questions

15 Factorise completely $4xy - 6xz$.   (0580 paper 01 Q3 June 2004)

16 $y = a + bc$

Find the value of y when $a = -3$, $b = 2$ and $c = 8$.   (0580 paper 01 Q16a June 2004)

17 When $x = 5$ find the value of:

a $4x^2$ **b** $(4x)^2$ (0580 paper 01 Q4 November 2004)

18 Simplify the following expressions.

a $a^2 \times a^5$ **b** $b^4 \div b^3$ (0580 paper 01 Q10 November 2004)

19 a Expand and simplify

i $4(2t + 3) + 5$,   **ii** $6p + 3q - 2(2p - 5q)$.

b Factorise completely

$25x^3y^2 - 15x^2y$.   (4024 paper 11 Q17 June 2014)

20 Write down the value of n in each of the following statements.

a $1500 = 1.5 \times 10^n$ **b** $0.000\,15 = 1.5 \times 10^n$

c $5^n = 1$ **d** $\dfrac{1}{36} = 6^n$ (0580 paper 01 Q17 November 2003)

21 Write down the value of $\left(1\frac{1}{2}\right)^{-2}$ as a fraction.   (0580 paper 01 Q7 June 2003)

22 a $y = 4uv - 3v$ Find the value of y when $u = -3$ and $v = 2$.

b Factorise $4uv - 3v$.   (0580 paper 01 Q8 June 2003)

23 Work out 4^{-3} as a fraction.   (0580 paper 01 Q5 June 2005)

24 When $x = -3$ find the value of $x^3 + 2x^2$.   (0580 paper 01 Q8 June 2005)

25 Simplify the following expressions:

a $9r - 4s - 6r + s$ **b** $q^4 \div q^3$ **c** $p^6 \times p^{-2}$ (0580 paper 01 Q16 November 2005)

26 Simplify:

   a $p^2 \times p^3$ **b** $q^3 \div q^{-4}$

   c $(r^2)^3$ (0580 paper 01 Q10 June 2006)

27 Factorise completely:

   a $7ac + 14a$ **b** $12ax^2 + 18xa^3$ (0580 paper 02 Q14 November 2005)

28 a $4^p \times 4^5 = 4^{15}$. Find the value of p.

   b $2^7 \div 2^q = 2^4$. Find the value of q.

   c $5^r = \frac{1}{25}$. Find the value of r.   (0580 paper 01 Q13 June 2007)

29 a Simplify $4a^3 \times a^2$.

   b Simplify fully $3x(x + 5) - 2(x - 3)$.   (4024 paper 01 Q7 June 2009)

30 Write the following numbers in order of size, starting with the smallest.

   3^1 3^{-1} $(-1)^3$ 3^0 (4024 paper 01 Q3b November 2007)

31 Simplify $(3x^3)^2$.   (4024 paper 01 Q4a June 2004)

32 Simplify $25x^2 \div 5x^{-4}$.   (4024 paper 01 Q3a November 2006)

Working with Numbers I

Learning Objectives Syllabus sections 9, 10, 11, 12, 13, 14, 15 and 16

In this chapter you will learn about:
- units of measurement and conversion between them
- simple areas and volumes
- estimation, approximation, limits of accuracy and standard form

- working with and without a calculator
- ratio and proportion
- calculations with time, speed and other rates
- personal and small business finance
- simple and compound interest

4.1 Introduction

This chapter will give you many of the skills you need for your non-calculator paper, so pay particular attention to the instructions regarding the use of calculators. You need to practise working without a calculator where possible.

4.2 Essential Skills NO CALCULATOR IN THIS EXERCISE

1 Write these numbers in standard form:
   a 12 345   **b** 0.000 34

2 Write these numbers in standard form as normal numbers:
   a 3.45×10^6 **b** 5.123×10^{-3}

3 **a** Calculate 27% of 510.
   b Find 42 as a percentage of 700.

4 Find:
   a i 0.0645×1000 **ii** $83 \times 10\,000$
   b i $0.002\,59 \times 10^4$ **ii** $7015 \div 10^6$

4.3 More Symbols

For this chapter you will need to know the following mathematical symbols:

- $\pm$ means 'plus or minus'.
- $\simeq$ and $\approx$ mean 'approximately equal to'.

4.4 Units of Measurement

You are already familiar with some units of measurement, such as centimetres, kilograms, hours, kilometres per hour and litres.

The systems of units that most of us use today are very much easier than the older systems. Most are based on powers of ten, which makes conversions much simpler. The old systems used in Britain were all different.

For example, for length:

$$12 \text{ inches} = 1 \text{ foot}$$
$$3 \text{ feet} = 1 \text{ yard}$$
$$1760 \text{ yards} = 1 \text{ mile}$$

Money, mass and capacity were just as difficult and all these conversions had to be learned for examinations.

Some of the conversions that you need to know today are:

- Length
  10 millimetres (mm) = 1 centimetre (cm)
  100 centimetres = 1 metre (m)
  1000 metres = 1 kilometre (km)
- Mass
  1000 milligrams (mg) = 1 gram (g)
  1000 grams = 1 kilogram (kg)
  1000 kilograms = 1 tonne
- Capacity (volume)
  1000 millilitres (ml) = 1 litre (*l*)

The one to watch out for is time!

Time is still measured by an old system and is not based on powers of ten. You have to be *very careful* about changing it to a decimal system.

- Time
  60 seconds (s) = 1 minute (min)
  60 minutes = 1 hour (h)
  24 hours = 1 day
  7 days = 1 week and so on.

Added to these are compound units, such as kilometres per hour (km/h). Also area (such as cm²) and volume (such as cm³) units are derived from the units of length.

Simple Areas and Volumes

In this section we shall look at the simplest examples of areas and volumes by considering squares and rectangles, and cubes and cuboids. Wherever possible the size of a shape or object is described using standard **dimensions**, like length, width and height, measured in directions at right angles to each other.

The **area** of a shape is the amount of surface it covers in *two* dimensions. This means that to calculate an area we need *two* length measurements multiplied together. Figure 4.1 shows this for a square and a rectangle.

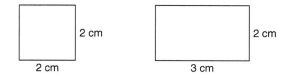

Figure 4.1 Areas

The **volume** of a solid is the amount of space it takes up in *three* dimensions. This means that to calculate a volume we need *three* length measurements multiplied together. Figure 4.2 shows this for a cube and a cuboid.

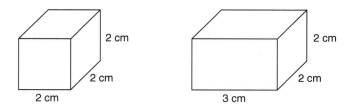

Figure 4.2 Volumes

We will look at areas and volumes in more detail in Chapter 8.

> **NOTE:**
> The words 'width' and 'breadth' are both used to mean the same thing, so you might see the formula for the area of a rectangle as $A = l \times b$ or $A = l \times w$.

The units of measurement for area and volume depend on which units of length have been used. If the lengths are in centimetres, the area will be in square centimetres, which is usually written as cm^2, and the volume will be in cubic centimetres or cm^3. Hence, the units of length must be the same in each calculation of area or volume.

Conversions for Length, Area and Volume Units

- Length
  - $1\,cm = 10\,mm$
  - $1\,m = 100\,cm$
  - $1\,km = 1000\,m$
- Area
  - $1\,cm^2 = 10\,mm \times 10\,mm = 100\,mm^2$
  - $1\,m^2 = 100\,cm \times 100\,cm = 10\,000\,cm^2$
  - $1\,km^2 = 1000\,m \times 1000\,m = 1\,000\,000\,m^2$
- Volume
  - $1\,cm^3 = 10\,mm \times 10\,mm \times 10\,mm = 1000\,mm^3$
  - $1\,m^3 = 100\,cm \times 100\,cm \times 100\,cm = 1\,000\,000\,cm^3$
  - $1\,km^3 = 1000\,m \times 1000\,m \times 1000\,m = 1\,000\,000\,000\,m^3$

You will notice how the area and volume units are much larger than the corresponding units of length. Figure 4.3 illustrates this.

Figure 4.3 shows a line segment of length 1 cm, and compares it with another of length 4 cm. (A line segment is *part* of a line. A line could, in theory, go on forever.) We know the second line segment is 4 times the length of the first.

Figure 4.3 then shows a square with a side of 1 cm (area = $1\,cm^2$) and compares it with a square of side 4 cm. You should be able to see that this square actually covers $4 \times 4 = 16$ centimetre squares. The area of this square is, therefore, $16\,cm^2$.

Subsequently, Figure 4.3 shows a cube of side 1 cm and compares it with a cube of side 4 cm.

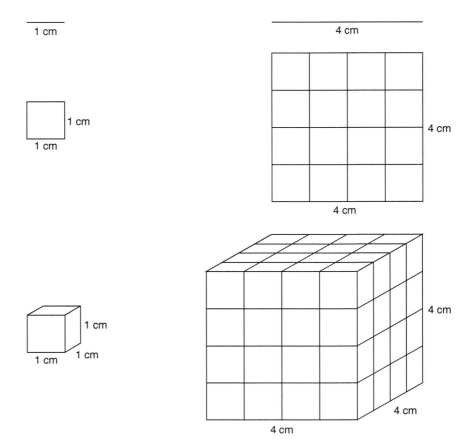

Figure 4.3 Lengths, areas and volumes

Project

Try to decide how many one centimetre cubes would fit in the 4 centimetre cube. Either get some 1 centimetre cubes and stack them up to see how many are needed, or try to visualise it in the following way.

How many 1 centimetre cubes would fit along one edge of the 4 centimetre cube to make one row? How many rows of these cubes would be needed to make one layer?

How many layers would be needed to make the whole 4 centimetre cube?

So what is the volume of the cube?

Now check using arithmetic. $4\,cm \times 4\,cm \times 4\,cm = 4^3\,cm^3 = 64\,cm^3$.

Key term

The **perimeter** of a shape is the sum of all its sides. It is a length measurement.

Area questions are often accompanied by questions about the **perimeter**. The perimeter is the measurement of the distance all round a shape, and is calculated by adding together the lengths of all the sides. Remember that the perimeter is a *length* measurement.

Example 1

a Calculate the area of a square with sides of length 6 cm.

b Calculate:

   i   the perimeter, and   **ii**   the area of a rectangle with length 3 m and width 4 m.

c Calculate the volume of a cube with sides of length 3 cm.

d   Calculate the volume of the cuboid in the diagram.

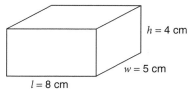

$h = 4$ cm
$w = 5$ cm
$l = 8$ cm

e   Calculate the area of the given shape.

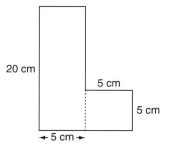

20 cm
5 cm
5 cm
5 cm

f   Calculate the volume of the given solid.

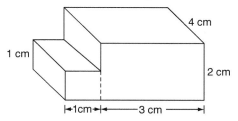

4 cm
1 cm
2 cm
1 cm
3 cm

Answer 1

a   Area of square $= 6\,\text{cm} \times 6\,\text{cm} = 36\,\text{cm}^2$

b   **i**   Perimeter of rectangle $= 3\,\text{m} + 4\,\text{m} + 3\,\text{m} + 4\,\text{m} = 14\,\text{m}$

    ii   Area of rectangle $= 3\,\text{m} \times 4\,\text{m} = 12\,\text{m}^2$

c   Volume of cube $= 3\,\text{cm} \times 3\,\text{cm} \times 3\,\text{cm} = 27\,\text{cm}^3$

d   Volume of cuboid $= 8\,\text{cm} \times 5\,\text{cm} \times 4\,\text{cm} = 160\,\text{cm}^3$

e   Area $= 5\,\text{cm} \times 5\,\text{cm} + 5\,\text{cm} \times 20\,\text{cm} = 125\,\text{cm}^2$

f   Volume $= 4\,\text{cm} \times 2\,\text{cm} \times 3\,\text{cm} + 4\,\text{cm} \times 1\,\text{cm} \times 1\,\text{cm} = 24\,\text{cm}^3 + 4\,\text{cm}^3 = 28\,\text{cm}^3$

The units (centimetres) are included in these calculations to help you understand. Normally you would not put them in until you write the answer.

Exercise 4.1

NO CALCULATOR IN THIS EXERCISE

1   Calculate the areas of the following:

a
3 km
2 km

b
500 m
90 m

c
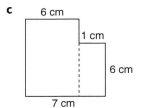
6 cm
1 cm
6 cm
7 cm

d
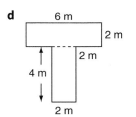
6 m
2 m
2 m
4 m
2 m

2 Calculate the volumes of the following:
 a A cube of side 7 m
 b A cube of side 10 cm
 c

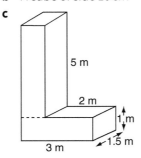

 d A cuboid measuring 2 cm by 5 cm by 20 cm

3 Calculate the perimeters of the following:

a

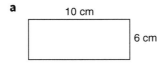

b

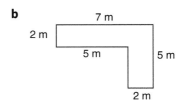

4.5 Estimation

Key term

Estimation is a method of making an informed guess at the size of a measurement or other value.

NOTE:

Remember that the ruler that you can use in your examinations will be marked in millimetres and centimetres, so you can easily see that 10 mm = 1 cm.

Before we look at the conversion of units of measurement it would be helpful for you to find your personal approximations for the sizes of the units. For example, a centimetre might be the width of your middle finger, a metre might be the length of your stride, and a kilometre the length of part of a well-known journey. These 'personal standards' should be ones that are easy for you to remember. Copy and complete Table 4.1, filling in your own personal standards.

Some examples have already been suggested, but use your own if you think of better ones. Add other measurements if you can think of any.

Unit	Personal standard
1 millimetre	
1 centimetre	
1 metre	
1 kilometre	from to
1 gram	
1 kilogram	
1 cubic millimetre	for example, a grain of sugar
1 cubic centimetre	for example, a sugar cube or a small die
1 cubic metre	

Table 4.1 Personal unit approximations

Project

Try some or all of these to improve your visualisation of size.

1 Make a metre cube by using canes each of length 1 metre, and something like modelling clay at the corners. It may be bigger than you expected. Imagine trying to fill it with sugar cubes. How many would you need?

2 If you can get a sheet of graph paper which is ruled in 1 millimetre squares, cut out a piece 10 centimetres by 10 centimetres. How many millimetre squares are on this sheet?

3 How could you put 1 million squares on your classroom wall?

4 Stand on a piece of 1 cm squared paper and draw around your foot. Use the squares to estimate the area of your foot.

5 Estimate (make a sensible guess at) the volume of your index finger.

6 Estimate the volume of your classroom.

7 Estimate the number of people you could seat round one of the tables in your classroom or at home.

8 Estimate the length of time it will take you to complete the next exercise.

9 Estimate the weight of this book. Check its weight on some scales to see how close you were.

Estimation is an important skill. You will not always be able to measure things accurately. For example, if you are catering for a large number of people you will have to estimate the amount of food and drink you need to supply.

You probably find that lengths are the easiest to estimate, followed by areas, and finally volumes.

4.6 Approximation

Key terms

Approximation is expressing a measurement or other value to a convenient or sensible degree of accuracy.

Rounding is the process of writing a number to a stated degree of accuracy according to a rule. Degrees of accuracy could be, for example, to the nearest whole number, to the nearest metre, to a stated number of decimal places, or to a stated number of significant figures.

It is a fact that measurements can never be completely accurate. You know that if your friend draws a line and says that it is exactly 15 cm long and you measure it yourself you could probably make it just a *little* more or less than 15 cm. The truth is that however accurate our measuring instruments, we can never be certain of any measurement.

So what does it mean when we say that a line is 15 cm long?

We probably mean 15 cm *to the nearest centimetre*.

Look at Figure 4.4.

In each case decide whether the line is 14 cm, 15 cm or 16 cm *to the nearest centimetre*.

You should find that **a** is nearest to 14 cm, **b** is nearest to 15 cm, **c** is nearest to 15 cm and **d** to 16 cm. But what about **e** and **f**?

There is a fairly general agreement that if a measurement is half way between two numbers then we take it to the larger number. So **e** will be 15 cm and **f** will be 16 cm to the nearest centimetre. This is the rule that will be used for your examinations.

This process is called **rounding to the nearest centimetre**. Incidentally it is also rounding **to the nearest whole number**.

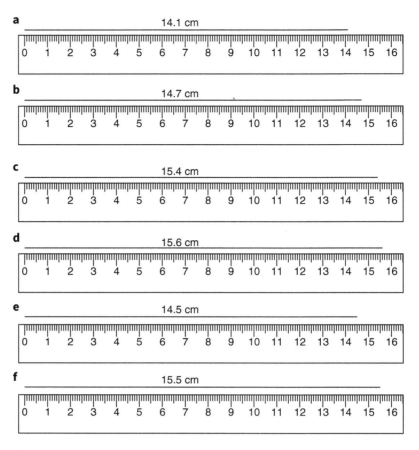

Figure 4.4 Approximating lengths

Example 2

Round to the nearest centimetre:

a 14.358 cm   **b** 14.4999 cm   **c** 15.099 cm   **d** 15.501 cm   **e** 16.5 cm

Answer 2

In each case ask yourself if the measurement is nearer to the whole number below it or the whole number above it.

a 14.358 is nearer to 14, so 14.358 cm = 14 cm to the nearest centimetre.

b 14.4999 is close to 14.5, but it *is* still less than 14.5 so it is closest to 14: 14.4999 cm = 14 cm to the nearest centimetre.

c 15.099 is closer to 15 than 16, so 15.099 cm = 15 cm to the nearest centimetre.

d 15.501 is closer to 16 than to 15, so 15.501 cm = 16 cm to the nearest centimetre.

e 16.5 is exactly half way between 16 and 17, so using the rule we round to 17: 16.5 cm = 17 cm to the nearest centimetre, by convention.

NOTE:
To avoid confusion, it may be better not to say 'round up' or 'round down' to yourself. For example, 14.3 never goes down to 13.

Exercise 4.2

Round to the nearest stated unit:

1 32.94 cm to the nearest centimetre.

2 63.49 g to the nearest gram.

3 705.501 kg to the nearest kilogram.

4 610.889 m to the nearest metre.

5 500.471 km to the nearest kilometre.

6 90.8 cm to the nearest centimetre.

7 89.793 kg to the nearest kilogram.

8 60.5 m to the nearest metre.

9 60.499 99 m to the nearest metre.

10 799.5 to the nearest whole number.

11 9.99 to the nearest whole number.

12 99.99 to the nearest whole number.

This idea of rounding need not be confined to rounding to the nearest whole number, centimetre or gram and so on.

Suppose you are asked to round 246 731 **to the nearest ten**.

The digit in the tens place is the 3. It is helpful to draw a 'squiggly line' after the 3 like this:

246 73 ⟨1

Does the 3 stay the same or does it go up to 4?

Look at the number immediately after the 3. It is 1, so 246 731 is closer to 246 730 than to 246 740. Hence, 246 731 = 246 730 to the nearest ten.

You could be asked to round 5467 to the nearest thousand.

By the same method the squiggly line goes after the 5 because this is in the thousands place.

5 ⟨467

Is this closer to 5000 or 6000?

The number after the 5 is 4, so the answer is: 5467 = 5000 to the nearest thousand.

> **NOTE:**
> Remember that you consider only the digit immediately after the squiggly line. Ignore all the rest.

> **NOTE:**
> Do remember to include the zeroes. Leaving them out is one of the commonest mistakes in rounding. In this example you do not want to say that 5467 is approximately equal to 5!

Decimal Places

You may also be asked to round to a given number of decimal places. Decimal places are counted to the right starting at the decimal point, so in the number 893.45, the 5 is in the second decimal place, and the 4 is in the first decimal place.

Example 3

Round these numbers to the stated accuracy:

a 20 056 to the nearest ten

b 20 056 to the nearest hundred

c 20 056 to the nearest thousand

d 3.4109 to 3 decimal places (dp)

e 3.4109 to 2 dp

f 20.404 to 2 dp

g 351.499 to the nearest whole number.

Answer 3

a 20 05 ⟨6 = 20 060 to the nearest ten

b 200 ⟨56 = 20 100 to the nvearest hundred

c 20 ⟨056 = 20 000 to the nearest thousand

d 3.410 ⟨9 = 3.411 to 3 dp

e 3.41 ⟨09 = 3.41 to 2 dp

f 20.40 ⟨4 = 20.40 to 2 dp

> **NOTE:**
> The zero is here to show that the number has been rounded to 2 decimal places. Although 20.4 has the same numerical value it implies that you have rounded the number to only 1 decimal place.

g 351. ⟨499 = 351 to the nearest whole number

> **NOTE:**
> Never round progressively. This means *do not* round the 4 to 5 and then the 1 to 2. This is because 0.499 is less than 0.5, so the number 351.499 is nearer to 351 than 352.

Exercise 4.3

Round to the stated accuracy:

1 239 to the nearest ten

2 520.65 to the nearest ten

3 7381.3 to the nearest hundred

4 649 to the nearest hundred

5 3985.6 to the nearest ten

6 7959 to the nearest hundred

7 1234 to the nearest thousand

8 56.1358 to 1 decimal place

9 56.1358 to 2 decimal places

10 56.1358 to 3 decimal places

11 3.098 to 1 decimal place

12 3.098 to 2 decimal places

Significant Figures

> **Key term**
>
> **Significant figures** are literally the figures in a number which are significant. For example, 5.01 has three significant figures, but 0.12 has only two.

There is one more method of approximation you need to know, and that involves the idea of *significant figures*.

To count significant figures you start at the beginning of the number and count to the right, past the decimal point if necessary. Looking at the number 25 937.065, 2 is the first significant figure, 9 is the third significant figure, 6 is the seventh significant figure and so on.

But there is one thing you have to be careful of. Zeroes at the beginning of a number do not count as significant figures, so in the number 0.005 096 the first significant figure is 5, the second is the 0 that comes after the 5, the third is 9 and the fourth is 6. The three initial zeroes are place holders only, to tell you where the decimal point belongs. An example will help you see the significance of this.

Suppose a distance is measured as 5096 millimetres to 4 significant figures, and then this length is given in kilometres. 5096 millimetres becomes 0.005096 kilometres. This length is *not* more accurate than the first, so must still be to 4 significant figures. The zeroes only tell you where the decimal point belongs, and do not count as significant figures.

Zeroes at the ends of numbers present a different problem. We do not know to what accuracy a number is given unless it is stated. For example, 2304 to 3 significant figures is 2300, and 2304 to 2 significant figures is also 2300. The zeroes are required as place holders to show that the number is two *thousand three hundred*, but they do not tell us about the accuracy.

> **NOTE:**
>
> In Example 4 part **a** remember that the two zeroes are significant figures.

> **Example 4**
>
> Round these numbers to the stated number of significant figures:
>
> **a** 10.04 to 3 significant figures
>
> **b** 0.0079 to 1 significant figure
>
> **c** 15 637 to 2 significant figures
>
> **d** 19.998 to 3 significant figures
>
> **e** 0.010 09 to 3 significant figures.
>
> **Answer 4**
>
> **a** 10.0 **b** 0.008 **c** 16 000 **d** 20.0 **e** 0.0101

Exercise 4.4

Round to the stated number of significant figures (s.f.):

1	215.67	3 s.f.	**2**	215.67	2 s.f.	**3**	350.49	3 s.f.
4	350.49	1 s.f.	**5**	6009.156	3 s.f.	**6**	6009.156	2 s.f.
7	80.964	3 s.f.	**8**	0.198 52	3 s.f.	**9**	0.198 52	2 s.f.
10	1.000 98	3 s.f.	**11**	0.000 394 6	3 s.f.	**12**	0.000 394 6	1 s.f.
13	10.149	3 s.f.	**14**	657 280	3 s.f.	**15**	657 280	1 s.f.

The general instructions on the front of your examination papers will say something like the following: If the degree of accuracy is not specified in the question, and if the answer is not exact, give the answer to three significant figures. Give answers in degrees to one decimal place.

Make sure that you understand this, and follow these instructions in all your work so that it becomes normal for you to give your answers in this way. You must be careful not to merely 'truncate' the number without correct rounding. So for example, 3.4567… should be given as 3.46 (rounded) *not* 3.45 (truncated).

Remember that if the answer works out exactly you may not need to round it.

NOTE:
If you are asked to give your answer to 'an appropriate degree of accuracy' do not give it to a higher degree of accuracy than that of the data given in the question. Answers to questions about money, for example in dollars, should not be given to more than two decimal places.

Example 5

Using your calculator:

a Calculate 34.1×47.3 giving your answer correct to 4 significant figures.

b Calculate $76.3 \div 14.2$. **c** Calculate $31.52 \div 2$.

d Calculate one third of $302°$ (302 degrees).

Answer 5

a $34.1 \times 47.3 = 1612.93 = 1613$ correct to 4 significant figures.

b $76.3 \div 14.2 = 5.373239437 = 5.37$ to 3 significant figures.

c $31.52 \div 2 = 15.76$ exactly.

d $\frac{1}{3} \times 302° = 100.6666666… = 100.7°$.

Exercise 4.5

1 Calculate 354.1×67, giving your answer to 4 significant figures.

2 Calculate $278 \div 34$.

3 Calculate one third of $16.7°$.

4 Calculate $337.38 \div 6$.

4.7 Limits of Accuracy

In mathematics, we must be able to think backward as well as forward. So we need to be able to decide exactly what is meant when a measurement is given to us as, say, 14 cm to the nearest centimetre.

You should be able to see that it could have been, for example, 13.6 cm, or 14.4 cm. In fact it must lie somewhere between 13.5 cm and 14.5 cm. Using our rule about the half way point we know that 13.5 cm would round to 14 cm, but 14.5 cm would round to 15 cm. So we can say that the length is greater than *or equal to* 13.5 cm, but less than 14.5 cm.

If the length of the line is l cm, we write:

$$13.5 \leqslant l < 14.5$$

Notice that, since the length is given as l cm, we do not put the centimetres in the answer. It is only the l we are referring to. This is as close as you can get to the original number, and 13.5 and 14.5 are known as the **limits of accuracy**, where 13.5 is the **lower limit** or bound and 14.5 is the **higher limit** or bound.

Key terms

The limits of accuracy are the smallest and largest values a measurement might take and still be within the stated accuracy.

The upper bound or **limit** is the highest value, and the **lower bound** or **limit** is the lowest value a measurement might take.

Example 6

State the limits of accuracy for the following approximations:

a   735 to the nearest whole number
b   23.56 to 2 dp (decimal places)
c   length $x = 130$ cm to 2 significant figures
d   length $y = 130$ cm to 3 significant figures.

Answer 6

a $734.5 \leqslant 735 < 735.5$ **b** $23.555 \leqslant 23.56 < 23.565$
c 125 cm $\leqslant x < 135$ cm   **d** 129.5 cm $\leqslant y < 130.5$ cm

> **NOTE:**
> It might help you to work out the limits of accuracy if you think of adding or subtracting half the smallest number of the given accuracy. This is much easier to explain by examples rather than words! So let us look back at these examples.
> **a**   Half the smallest whole number (1) is 0.5, so 735 ± 0.5 becomes 734.5 or 735.5.
> **b**   Half the smallest second decimal place (0.01) is 0.005, so 23.56 ± 0.005 becomes 23.555 or 23.565.
> **c**   130 to 2 significant figures would mean 130 ± 5 ($5 = \frac{1}{2} \times 10$) which becomes 125 and 135.
> **d**   130 to 3 significant figures would mean 130 ± 0.5 which becomes 129.5 and 130.5.

Example 7

A metal bar is measured and found to be 10.5 centimetres in length (l), correct to the nearest millimetre.

a   What is the least possible measurement for the metal bar?
b   State the upper bound of the measurement.
c   Copy and complete the statement below:

$$\text{-------} \leqslant l \text{ cm} < \text{--------}$$

Answer 7

a   The least possible measurement is 10.45 centimetres.
b   The upper bound of the measurement is 10.55 centimetres.

> **NOTE:**
> The upper bound is always given as 10.55 even though we know that it actually has to be less than 10.55, because 10.55 would round up to 10.6.

c $10.45 \leqslant l$ cm < 10.55
This is the most accurate way of stating the bounds because it clearly shows that the measurement can be greater than *or equal to* 10.45, but it actually has to be *less than* 10.55.

Exercise 4.6

1 A wooden rod is 157 cm to the nearest cm.
What is its least possible length?

2 A sheet of paper has a width of w cm and a height of h cm, both to the nearest centimetre.
If $w = 10$ and $h = 19$, copy and complete the following inequalities:

a ...... $\leqslant w <$ ......   **b** ...... $\leqslant h <$ ......

3 State the limits of accuracy for the following approximations.
In each case, copy and complete the inequalities.

a ...... $\leqslant 15$ cm $<$ ......   to the nearest centimetre
b ...... $\leqslant 23.6$ cm $<$ ......   to the nearest millimetre
c ...... $\leqslant 3060 <$ ......   to the nearest ten
d ...... $\leqslant 99.7 <$ ......   to 3 significant figures
e ...... $\leqslant 678.9 <$ ......   to 1 decimal place
f ...... $\leqslant 60\,000 <$ ......   to 1 significant figure
g ...... $\leqslant 300 <$ ......   to the nearest hundred
h ...... $\leqslant 99.9 <$ ......   to 3 significant figures.

4 A coin weighs 9 grams correct to the nearest gram.

a What is its least possible weight?   **b** State the upper bound of its weight.

4.8 Changing Units

You need to know how to change one unit of measurement to another. You may need to look back to the beginning of this chapter to remind yourself of the conversions of units of measurement.

For example, you are asked to change 0.75 km to centimetres. The first thing to ask yourself is 'would you need more or fewer centimetres?'

Remember that a centimetre is only about the width of your finger and a kilometre is an easy walking distance or whatever your personal standard distance is from the table you completed earlier. You obviously need many more centimetres, so the change will involve multiplying by a power of ten.

We know that   1 kilometre = 1000 metres

1 metre = 100 centimetres

so   1 kilometre = 1000×100 centimetres

$= 10^5$ or 100 000 centimetres

We need to change 0.75 kilometres to centimetres,

so   0.75 km = $0.75 \times 100\,000$ cm

$= 75\,000$ cm

Alternatively, make the change progressively:

0.75 km = 0.75×1000 m

$= 750$ m

$= 750 \times 100$ cm

$= 75\,000$ cm

Example 8

a Change to the units stated:

   i 0.5 m to mm   **ii** 1565 g to kg

   iii 61 m³ to cm³   **iv** 1.39 mm² to cm².

b Calculate the following, stating the units in the answer.

   i The area of a rectangle 3 metres by 4 centimetres.

   ii The volume of a cuboid with the following dimensions:

     length = 2.1 metres, breadth = 1.5 metres and height = 0.6 centimetres.

> **NOTE:**
> Before each calculation check that the units are consistent and change if necessary.

Answer 8

a **i** You need more millimetres than metres, so

       0.5 m = 50 cm = 500 mm

   ii You need fewer kilograms than grams, so

       1565 g = 1.565 kg

   iii 61 m³ = 61 × (100 × 100 × 100) cm³ = 61 000 000 or 6.1×10^7 cm³

   iv 1.39 mm² = 1.39 ÷ (10 × 10) cm²

             = 1.39 ÷ 100 cm²

             = 0.0139 cm²

b **i** 3 metres = 3 × 100 cm = 300 cm

       Area of rectangle = 300 cm × 4 cm = 1200 cm²

       or   4 cm = 4 ÷ 100 m = 0.04 m

       Area of rectangle = 3 m × 0.04 m = 0.12 m²

   ii 0.6 cm = 0.6 ÷ 100 m = 0.006 m

       Volume of cuboid = 2.1 m × 1.5 m × 0.006 m

                    = 0.0189 m³

       or 2.1 m = 2.1 × 100 cm = 210 cm

       and 1.5 m = 1.5 × 100 cm = 150 cm

       Volume of cuboid = 210 cm × 150 cm × 0.6 cm

                    = 18 900 cm³

Exercise 4.7   **NO CALCULATOR IN THIS EXERCISE**

1 Change to the stated units:

  a 3.5 m to cm   **b** 581 mm to cm   **c** 4096 cm to km

  d 0.57 km to mm   **e** 0.812 kg to g   **f** 3 cm² to mm²

  g 50 681 m² to km²   **h** 0.0067 m³ to cm³   **i** 210 ml to *l*

2 Calculate the areas of the following shapes. State the units in your answers.

a   **b**

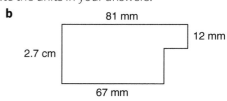

3 Calculate the volumes of the following solids. State the units in your answers.

a

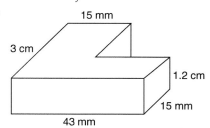

1 m

98 cm

3100 mm

b

15 mm

3 cm

1.2 cm

15 mm

43 mm

4.9 Working without a Calculator

Estimation is very useful in practical situations if you have to work without a calculator. For example, Rama arrives at Washington airport with Rs 523.5 in her pocket. She is told that Re 1 is worth $0.022 42. How can she quickly work out *approximately* how many dollars she should expect when she changes her rupees to dollars?

The best way is to round each number to 1 significant figure so that the calculation becomes easy. Re 1 is worth about $0.02, so Rs 500 are worth about Rs 500 × $0.02 = $10.

$$Rs\ 523.5 \simeq \$10$$

If you are working without a calculator you may need to *estimate* the answer by rounding to 1 significant figure, or you may need to *calculate* the answer by using your skills of addition, subtraction, multiplication and division.

Example 9

a Estimate 7951×0.578.   **b** Calculate 35×16.

c Calculate $(3.4 \times 10^6) + (5.9 \times 10^5)$.   **d** Calculate $(2.1 \times 10^3) \times (9 \times 10^2)$.

Answer 9

a $7951 \times 0.578 \simeq 8000 \times 0.6 = 800 \times 6 = 4800$

b
$$
\begin{array}{r}
35 \\
16\ \times \\
\hline
210 \\
350 \\
\hline
560 \\
\hline
\end{array}
$$

c The next answer has been written out in detail so that you can follow each step of the method.

$(3.4 \times 10^6) + (5.9 \times 10^5)$ *

$= (3.4 \times 10 \times 10^5) + (5.9 \times 10^5)$

$= (34 \times 10^5) + (5.9 \times 10^5)$ *

$= (34 + 5.9) \times 10^5$

$= 39.9 \times 10^5$ *

$= 3.99 \times 10 \times 10^5$

$= 3.99 \times 10^6$ *

Alternative method:

$(3.4 \times 10^6) + (5.9 \times 10^5)$

$= 3\,400\,000 + 590\,000$

$\begin{array}{r} 3400000 \\ 590000\,+ \\ \hline 3990000 \end{array}$

$3\,990\,000 = 3.99 \times 10^6$

d $(2.1 \times 10^3) \times (9 \times 10^2)$ *

    $= 2.1 \times 9 \times 10^3 \times 10^2$

    $= 18.9 \times 10^{3+2}$

    $= 18.9 \times 10^5$ *

    $= 1.89 \times 10 \times 10^5$

    $= 1.89 \times 10^6$ *

NOTE:

With multiplication and division the given powers of 10 may be used directly according to the normal rules of indices.

Example 10

Given that $8.95 \times 17.6 = 157.52$, work out, without using a calculator:

a 89.5×1760 **b** 0.0895×1.76 **c** $157.52 \div 8.95$

d $157.52 \div 17.6$ **e** $15.752 \div 89.5$ **f** $1575.2 \div 0.0176$

Answer 10

There are two methods you can use for (a):

a either:

    $89.5 = 8.95 \times 10$ and $1760 = 17.6 \times 100$

    so $89.5 \times 1760 = 8.95 \times 10 \times 17.6 \times 100$

                  $= 157.52 \times 10 \times 100$

                  $= 157\,520$

    or we can first approximate to 1 significant figure to estimate the size of the answer:

    $89.5 \simeq 90$ and $1760 \simeq 2000$

    so $89.5 \times 1760 \simeq 90 \times 2000 = 180\,000$

        $89.5 \times 1760 = 157\,520$

b $0.0895 \times 1.76 \simeq 0.09 \times 2 = 0.18$

    so $0.0859 \times 1.76 = 0.157\,52$

c $157.52 \div 8.95 = 17.6$

d $157.52 \div 17.6 = 8.95$

e $15.752 \div 89.5 \simeq 20 \div 90 \simeq 0.2$

    so $15.752 \div 89.5 = 0.176$

f $1575.2 \div 0.0176 \simeq 2000 \div 0.02 = 100\,000$

    so $1575.2 \div 0.0176 = 89\,500$

Example 11

Estimate the following, giving your answer correct to 1 significant figure:

a $\sqrt{170}$ **b** $\sqrt{2000}$ **c** $\sqrt[3]{67}$

Answer 11

a Think to yourself 'What number when squared would give an answer closest to 170?'

    Try some numbers:

    $10^2 = 100, 11^2 = 121, 12^2 = 144, 13^2 = 169$

    so $\sqrt{169} = 13$, and, as we only have to give the answer to 1 significant figure, we can say $\sqrt{170} \simeq 10$.

    We can do a further check by finding $20^2 = 400$, so $\sqrt{400} = 20$.

    Clearly, the answer we want to 1 significant figure is 10.

Alternatively, we can say that the possibilities, to 1 significant figure, are 10 or 20. Since $10^2 = 100$ and $20^2 = 400$, and 170 is closer to 100 than to 400, the answer is 10.

b $\sqrt{2000} = \sqrt{20 \times 100} = \sqrt{20} \times \sqrt{100} = 10 \times \sqrt{20}$

To estimate $\sqrt{20}$ try $4^2 = 16$, and $5^2 = 25$

16 is closer than 25 to 20, so, to 1 significant figure $\sqrt{20} = 4$

$10 \times \sqrt{20} \approx 10 \times 4 = 40$

c To estimate $\sqrt[3]{67}$ try some numbers:

$4^3 = 4 \times 4 \times 4 = 64$, and $5^3 = 5 \times 5 \times 5 = 125$

so $\sqrt[3]{67} \approx 4$ to 1 significant figure.

Example 12

Without using a calculator, work out the following:

a 1.5×150 **b** $2349 \div 81$ **c** 21×340 **d** 49×210

Answer 12

These answers should give you some ideas for ways in which you can simplify some calculations.

a 1.5×150 is one and a half times 150

$1 \times 150 + $ half of $150 = 150 + 75 = 225$

b $2349 \div 81 = \dfrac{2349}{81} = \dfrac{2349}{9 \times 9}$

Divide by 9 and then by 9 again

$\dfrac{2349}{9 \times 9} = \dfrac{261}{9} = 29$

c $21 \times 340 = (20 + 1) \times 340 = 20 \times 340 + 1 \times 340$

$= 6800 + 340$

$= 7140$

Alternatively,

$21 \times 340 = 3 \times 7 \times 340 = 3 \times 2380 = 7140$

d $49 \times 210 = (50 - 1) \times 210 = 50 \times 210 - 1 \times 210$

$= 10500 - 210$

$= 10290$

Alternatively,

$49 \times 210 = 49 \times 3 \times 7 \times 10 = 147 \times 7 \times 10 = 1029 \times 10 = 10290$

or

$49 \times 210 = 7 \times 7 \times 210 = 7 \times 1470 = 10290$

Exercise 4.8

NO CALCULATOR IN THIS EXERCISE

1 Hank is going to explore parts of India, but he only has a limited time.
He finds the distances between several cities by looking on the Internet.
Bengaluru to Delhi is 2039 km.
Delhi to Mumbai is 1405 km.
Mumbai to Kolkata is 1916 km.
Kolkata to Bengaluru is 1824 km.

a Estimate the total length of this round trip.

b Assuming Hank travels approximately 200 km per day, how many days travelling should he allow for this journey?

2 Estimate the answers to these calculations:

a $238582 + 496 \times 1087$ **b** $(3.987 + 1.05)^2 \div (6.93 - 1.87)$

c $\dfrac{4182}{210} + \dfrac{3944}{52.28}$

3 Calculate, giving your answers in standard form:

    a $(4.1 \times 10^5) \times (2 \times 10^3)$ **b** $(4.1 \times 10^5) \div (2 \times 10^3)$

    c $(7.12 \times 10^6) + (3.56 \times 10^7)$ **d** $(9.012 \times 10^5) - (1.1 \times 10^2)$

4 Estimate the following, giving your answers correct to 1 significant figure:

    a $\sqrt{800}$ **b** $\sqrt{66\,000}$ **c** $\sqrt{55}$

    d $\sqrt{550}$ **e** $\sqrt{5500}$

5 Calculate the following:

    a 55×24 **b** 1.25×80 **c** 42×350

    d 51×211 **e** $60 \div 25$ **f** $770 \div 22$

6 Estimate the following, giving your answers correct to 1 significant figure:

    a $\dfrac{23 \times \sqrt{70}}{63}$ **b** $9.35 \times 7.6 \times \sqrt{359}$

7 Given that $0.675 \times 2.8 = 1.89$, work out

    a 67.5×0.028 **b** $189 \div 28$

    c $0.189 \div 6.75$ **d** $0.0675 \times 28\,000$

4.10 Working with a Calculator

Carla attempts this calculation using her calculator:

$$\frac{3213 + 6156}{29 \times 52}$$

She tries three times and gets three different answers:

a $14\,251.344\,83$ **b** $16\,799.586\,21$ **c** $3217.082\,228$

Chander says none of these is right!

He has estimated the answer by rounding each number to 1 significant figure, and doing the calculation mentally.

$$\frac{3213 + 6156}{29 \times 52} \approx \frac{3000 + 6000}{30 \times 50} = \frac{9000}{1500} = 6$$

Carla tries once more. This time she puts brackets round the numerator and the denominator and gets the correct answer.

d $\dfrac{(3213 + 6156)}{(29 \times 52)} = 6.212\,864\,721 = 6.21$ to 3 s.f.

She should have remembered that the line in a fraction acts like a bracket, tying the whole of the numerator together and the whole of the denominator together. Her calculator, of course, could not see this line and so in **a**, **b** and **c** did not work out the numerator and denominator separately before doing the division.

Can you work out how Carla entered the sum into her calculator in each of her first three attempts? (She did in some of them insert brackets, but not in the best places.)

The moral of the story is that when you are asked to do this type of calculation, the first thing to do is to insert the brackets. You would be wise also to do an estimated calculation to check your answer.

Using your Calculator for Standard Form

Calculators are changing all the time, and you need to get used to your own calculator.

For example, to find the square root of 16 do you press the square root key followed by 16 or do you have to type 16 first, then press the square root key?

How do you enter standard form in your calculator?

Try typing 1.5 $\boxed{\text{EXP}}$ 3

(some of the newer calculators have a button marked $\boxed{\times 10^x}$; if yours has one use that instead of the $\boxed{\text{EXP}}$ button).

Do you get 1.5×10^3? Or do you get something like 1.5^3 or 1.5^{03}?

Find out how your calculator shows standard form, so that you recognise it.

Type in 1 234 567 891 234, until you run out of space on the screen. Press the equals sign and have another look at the screen. Your calculator should give the number in standard form. The calculator may not show the $\times 10^{12}$ on the screen, but may just show a small number (^{12}). However your calculator displays the number, when you give the answer in standard form you *must write* $\times 10^{12}$.

Example 13

Estimate the answers and then use your calculator to calculate the following:

a $\sqrt{16.23 + 8.546}$ **b** $\frac{496.3 + 35.2 \times 34}{79 \times 23}$ **c** $5.12 \times 10^2 + 6.34 \times 10^3$

Answer 13

a $\sqrt{16.23 + 8.546} \simeq \sqrt{16 + 9} = \sqrt{25} = 5$

$\sqrt{16.23 + 8.546} = \sqrt{(16.23 + 8.546)} = \sqrt{24.776} = 4.977549\ldots$

$\qquad\qquad\qquad\qquad\qquad\qquad = 4.98$ to 3 s.f.

> **NOTE:**
> The line in the square root sign also acts like a bracket. Once the brackets are in, your calculator should be able to calculate this without any intermediate steps. Start by pressing the square root key followed by the opening bracket, then the numbers followed by the closing bracket. But check this with your own calculator, because not all calculators follow the same logic. Let your calculator teach you its rules!

b $\frac{496.3 + 35.2 \times 34}{79 \times 23} \simeq \frac{500 + 40 \times 30}{80 \times 20} = \frac{1700}{1600} \simeq 1$

$\frac{496.3 + 35.2 \times 34}{79 \times 23} = \frac{(496.3 + 35.2 \times 34)}{(79 \times 23)}$

$\qquad\qquad\qquad = 0.931810\ldots$

$\qquad\qquad\qquad = 0.932$ to 3 s.f.

> **NOTE:**
> Check this calculation with your own calculator to make sure that your calculator uses BODMAS and does not need an extra pair of brackets round the 35.2×34.

c $5.12 \times 10^2 + 6.34 \times 10^3 \simeq 500 + 6000 = 5600 \simeq 6.0 \times 10^3$

$5.12 \times 10^2 + 6.34 \times 10^3 = 6852 = 6.852 \times 10^3$

Exercise 4.9

Use your calculator to work out the following, first estimating the answer.

1 $34.93 + 356.1 \times 0.029$

2 $6.598 \times 3.111 - 24.701 + 17.3 \times 28$

3 $\dfrac{34.9 + 3.005}{13.1} + 28.35$

4 $\sqrt{\dfrac{16.01 + 19.49}{15.28 - 5.82}}$

5 $1.239 \times 10^4 - 5.87 \times 10^3$

6 $(3.967 \times 10^5) \times (7.65 \times 10^3)$

Project

Use your calculator to investigate what happens when you multiply or divide a number by numbers that are larger or smaller than (or equal to) 1.

Number		1000	10	1	0.1	0.001	0.0001	0.000001
6	×	6000						
6	÷	0.006						

Table 4.2 Multiplying and dividing by large and small numbers

For example, you could copy and complete Table 4.2.

Can you summarise the results, or find a rule to remind yourself whether the answers get larger or smaller in each case?

If you use the table shown, how many zeroes are in each answer?

What happens as you divide by smaller and smaller numbers? Why is this?

What happens when you ask your calculator to divide by zero?

4.11 Ratio

Key term

A **ratio** compares the sizes of two or more quantities that are in proportion.

Calculating a **ratio** is a method for comparing the sizes of two or more quantities. For example, Hamish wishes to make basmati rice for a party. He decides to use 2 cups of water to 1 cup of rice as he normally does.

This is the ratio, water : rice = 2 : 1.

It can be used for any volumes. For example, if it was a very big party he might have to use 2 buckets of water to each 1 bucket of rice! For a more moderate party he could use 6 cups of water to 3 cups of rice. The ratio will still remain the same.

Map Scales and Scale Models

You may already be familiar with the scale of a map or model.

You may see a map with a scale of 1 : 20 000. This means that every 1 unit on the map represents 20 000 of these same units on the ground. So for example, 1 cm on the map represents 20 000 cm (200 m) on the ground.

A model may be 'half scale', or 1 : 2. It means every 1 cm on the model represents 2 cm on the real object.

The 'Toy Train' Darjeeling Himalayan Railway has a gauge of 610 mm, which means that the distance between the two parallel tracks is 610 mm. A standard, full-size train has a gauge of 1435 mm.

The ratio of: Toy Train gauge : standard gauge

$$= 610 : 1435$$

We can simplify this by dividing both numbers by the smallest number, so

Toy Train gauge : standard gauge

$$= 1 : (1435 \div 610)$$

$$= 1 : 2.35$$

If the Toy Train was a scale model, all its length measurements would be in the same ratio as those of a standard train.

An architect is designing a large building for the Olympic Games. In order to show his clients what the building will look like in three dimensions he builds a scale model. The blocks that will be used in the actual building are 450 mm long. The model blocks are 20 mm.

The scale of the model is:

model : building

$$= 20 : 450$$

$$= 1 : 22.5$$

This ratio can be used to calculate all the other measurements in either the model or the real building.

Now that we have seen how ratios are used in everyday life we will see how to simplify and calculate with them.

Simplifying Ratios

	Example
• If necessary, rewrite measurements in the same units.	200 m : 4 km
	200 m : 4000 m
• Drop the units.	200 : 4000
• Divide both (or all) parts of the ratio by any common factor.	1 : 20

Example 14

Simplify the following ratios:

a $36 \, \text{m}^2 : 120\,000 \, \text{cm}^2$ **b** $500 \, \text{g} : 1.5 \, \text{kg}$ **c** $24 : 36 : 48$

Answer 14

a $36 \, \text{m}^2 : 120\,000 \, \text{cm}^2$

$= 36 \times (100 \times 100) \, \text{cm}^2 : 120\,000 \, \text{cm}^2$

$= 360\,000 : 120\,000$ $(\div 10\,000)$

$= 36 : 12$ $(\div 12)$

$= 3 : 1$

b $500 \, \text{g} : 1.5 \, \text{kg}$ or $500 \, \text{g} : 1.5 \, \text{kg}$

$= 0.5 \, \text{kg} : 1.5 \, \text{kg}$ $= 500 \, \text{g} : 1500 \, \text{g}$

$= 0.5 : 1.5$ $(\div 0.5)$ $= 500 : 1500 \; (\div 500)$

$= 1 : 3$ $= 1 : 3$

c $24 : 36 : 48$ $(\div 12)$

$= 2 : 3 : 4$

Simplifying Ratios of Fractions

Example

- Change any mixed numbers to improper fractions.

$$1\frac{1}{2} : \frac{3}{4}$$

$$= \frac{3}{2} : \frac{3}{4}$$

- Write both fractions as equivalent fractions with the same denominators.

$$= \frac{6}{4} : \frac{3}{4}$$

- Multiply both by this common denominator to get rid of the denominator. This is now a normal ratio.

$$= 6 : 3$$

- Divide both parts of the ratio by any common factors.

$$= 2 : 1$$

Writing Ratios as $1 : n$ or $n : 1$

You may sometimes be asked to give your ratios in a specific way, particularly to have one part equal to 1. An example of this was when we changed the exchange rate from one based on American dollars to one based on Indian rupees earlier in this chapter.

- Simplify the ratio as usual.
- Divide both parts by the side you need to express as unity (one).

Example 15

a Simplify the following ratios:

   i $\frac{3}{5} : \frac{1}{2}$ **ii** $1\frac{2}{3} : \frac{5}{6}$

b Write the ratio $4 : 5$ in the form:

   i $1 : n$ **ii** $n : 1$

Answer 15

a **i** $\frac{3}{5} : \frac{1}{2} = \frac{6}{10} : \frac{5}{10} = 6 : 5$ **ii** $1\frac{2}{3} : \frac{5}{6} = \frac{5}{3} : \frac{5}{6} = \frac{10}{6} : \frac{5}{6} = 10 : 5 = 2 : 1$

b **i** $4 : 5$ in form $1 : n$ **ii** $4 : 5$ in form $n : 1$

        $= 4 \div 4 : 5 \div 4$ $(\div 4)$ $= 4 \div 5 : 5 \div 5$ $(\div 5)$

        $= 1 : 1.25$ $= 0.8 : 1$

Exercise 4.10   **NO CALCULATOR IN THIS EXERCISE**

1 Simplify the following ratios:

   a $3 : 48$ **b** $50 : 75 : 125$ **c** $45 : 360$

   d 15 litres : 3 litres   **e** $14\,000$ ml : 2.8 litres

   f 2.5 cm : 5 km   **g** $\frac{3}{7} : \frac{1}{2}$ **h** $2\frac{3}{4} : 1\frac{2}{5}$

2 A school has 25 teachers and 750 students. Write the teacher : student ratio in its simplest form.

3 A builder mixes up a mortar by mixing 3 shovels full of cement with 12 shovels full of sand. Write the cement : sand ratio in its simplest form.

4 Write the following ratios in the form $n : 1$.

   a 81 litres : $90\,000$ ml   **b** 10 km : 5 cm

5 Write the following ratios in the form $1 : n$.

   a $4 : 1$ **b** 6 kg : $72\,000$ g

6 The area of India is approximately 3 300 000 km².
The area of the whole world is approximately 510 000 000 km².
Write the ratio area of India : area of whole world in its simplest form, giving your answer to 2 significant figures.

7 An iceberg is floating in the sea. The iceberg has a mass of 900 tonnes. 810 tonnes of the iceberg lies beneath the sea. Calculate the ratio of the mass of the iceberg above the sea to the mass below the sea in the form:
   a $1 : n$ **b** $n : 1$

Using Ratios

An easy way to deal with ratios is to use columns. For example, divide **$450** between Jo and Sandy in the ratio **2 : 3**. This means dividing the $450 into **5 equal parts**, and then giving Jo 2 parts and Sandy 3 parts.

We need a column for Jo, another for Sandy, and another for the total number of parts.

	Jo	Sandy	Total	
Parts	**2**	**3**	5	450 ÷ 5 = 90, so one part is $90. Use 90 as a multiplier (5 × 90 = 450).
amounts	2 × 90	3 × 90	**450**	
	= 180	= 270		

Jo gets $180 and Sandy gets $270.

(It is also worth checking that 180 + 270 adds up to 450.)

Example 16

  a A map has a scale of 1 : 250 000. Sanjeev measures the length of his bicycle ride on the map as 5 centimetres.
      How far will he cycle? Give your answer in kilometres.

  b The ratio of boys to girls in a class is 4 : 3. If there are 20 boys, how many **students** are there in the class?
      (In all the working shown on ratios the figures given or implied in the question are shown in **bold**, to make the working clearer.)

Answer 16

> **NOTE:**
> Start by setting out your columns and rows, then enter the numbers from the question. Put a question mark where the answer will appear. There are then two ways to do the working. Either notice that in the 'Scale' row 1 has to be multiplied by 250 000, and do the same in the 'Length' row. Or notice that in the 'Map' column the 1 has to be multiplied by 5, and do the same in the 'Ground' column. The second method has been applied here, and for consistency in most of the other worked examples. You can decide later which method you prefer, but a routine is very helpful in these questions. The 5 is called the *multiplier*.

  a

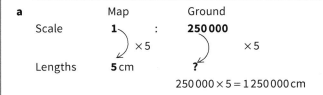

250 000 × 5 = 1 250 000 cm

$$1\,250\,000\,\text{cm} = (1\,250\,000 \div 100)\,\text{m}$$
$$= 12\,500\,\text{m}$$
$$12\,500\,\text{m} = (12\,500 \div 1000)\,\text{km}$$
$$= 12.5\,\text{km}$$

Sanjeev will cycle 12.5 kilometres.

b For this question we are asked to find the total number of students, so we need a 'Total' column.

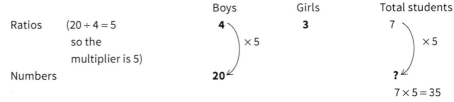

There are 35 students in the class.

Exercise 4.11   NO CALCULATOR IN THIS EXERCISE

1 The chemical formula for water is H_2O. This means that one water *molecule* is made of *atoms* of hydrogen and oxygen in the ratio $H : O = 2 : 1$.
How many atoms of hydrogen and how many atoms of oxygen are present in 42 molecules of H_2O?

2 Divide the following quantities in the stated ratios:
  a Rs 605 in the ratio 4 : 1   **b** 831.6 g in the ratio 1 : 5
  c 4.5 m in the ratio 5 : 1   **d** $300 in the ratio 2 : 5 : 13
  e 216 in the ratio 1 : 4 : 10   **f** 0.98 in the ratio 3 : 1

3 The scale of a map is 1 : 150 000. What distance on the map represents 15 km on the ground? Give your answer in suitable units.

4 A plan is drawn so that 5 cm on the plan represents 25 m on the ground. What is the scale of the plan?

5 A school has staff (teachers) and students in the ratio teachers : girls : boys = 1 : 10 : 9. How many boys are in the school if there are 700 staff and students?

6 A bag of sweets has yellow, green, red and purple sweets in the ratio yellow : green : red : purple = 2 : 3 : 5 : 1.
There are 15 red sweets.
  a How many sweets are yellow?
  b How many sweets are there all together?

7 Jane and Jill each receive some money in the ratio Jane : Jill = 3 : 5. Jane receives $15. How much does Jill receive?

8 Mortar is made in the ratio cement : sand = 1 : 4. How much of each is needed to make 5 tonnes?

9 Mina is using a map, but she does not know what the scale of the map is. She does know that the distance (in a straight line) between her home and her school is 5.5 km. She measures this distance on the map and finds it to be 2.2 cm.

NOTE:
In question 5 you will need four columns, headed 'Teachers', 'Girls', 'Boys' and 'Total'.

She measures the distance between her home and the railway station on the map. It is 4 cm. How far does she live from the railway station?

10 A classroom measures 2.5 metres high by 6 metres wide by 8 metres long.

  a Calculate the volume of the classroom.
  Nitrogen and oxygen are the main constituents of air.
  Nitrogen and oxygen are present in air in the ratio 4 : 1.

  b Calculate the volumes of (i) nitrogen and (ii) oxygen present in the classroom. Give your answers in m^3.

4.12 Proportion

Direct and Inverse Proportion

A builder uses 400 bricks to make a wall 10 metres long. How many bricks would he need to build a wall 30 metres long?

The answer is clear: the wall would be three times as long as before so he would need three times as many bricks. He would need 1200 bricks. This is called **direct proportion** because as one quantity (the length of wall) increases the other (the number of bricks) also increases in the same ratio. Notice that only two quantities are changing, the length of the wall and the number of bricks.

The builder takes three days to build his wall. How long would it take if he employed two other builders and they all worked together at the same rate?

The two quantities that are changing are now number of builders and time taken. With three builders working on the wall it should take one third of the time, so it would take only one day. This is **inverse proportion** because as one quantity (the number of builders) increases the other quantity (the time taken) decreases in the same ratio.

The words 'in the same ratio' are important, but not easy to explain. A few examples should help.

1 As children get older they get taller. This is *not* an example of proportion because they get older at an even rate, but they may grow taller over a period, and then stay the same height for a while, and then grow again. Hence, age and height are not in proportion.
2 The further you walk the longer it takes. But sooner or later you will get tired and slow down so this distance and time are not in proportion.
3 If you are driving at a *constant speed* the further you go the longer it takes in the same ratio, so this time the distance and time are in proportion. Notice that we are saying 'the further' … 'the longer', so this is *direct* proportion. In this example the quantities that are changing are the distance and time. The speed is staying the same.
4 If you drive a *fixed* distance, say 10 km, at a constant speed, the faster this speed is the less time it takes to complete the journey. Here we are saying 'the faster' … 'the less' so these two quantities are in *inverse* proportion. Here the distance stays the same and the speed and time vary.

Key term

Two items, or amounts, are in **direct proportion** when the rate at which they increase or decrease is always the same for both. They are in **inverse proportion** when while one increases the other decreases always at the same rate.

Example 17

a In 2015, in Britain, the costs for sending letters first class depended on weight. Are these quantities in proportion?

Weight	Cost
100 g	£0.95
250 g	£1.26
500 g	£1.68
750 g	£2.42

b i In one week a farmer uses 10 bales of hay for his 25 horses.
How many bales would he need in a week for 65 horses if they ate them at the same rate?

ii How long would the 10 bales last for 2 horses at the same rate?

Answer 17

a This is an example of two quantities both increasing, but not in the same ratio, so they are not in proportion.
Compare just two of the increases:

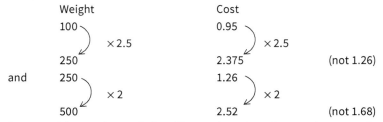

b i Quantities varying are bales of hay and number of cows. Time stays the same (1 week).

Bales of hay		Number of cows		
10		**25**		
	× 2.6		× 2.6	(65 ÷ 25 = 2.6)
26		**65**		

Hence, the farmer needs 26 bales per week for 65 cows.

> **NOTE:**
> When you are doing direct and inverse proportion questions you need to think about whether you expect the answer to be larger or smaller, and then divide or multiply by the multiplier to make this happen. Here we will definitely need more hay so we multiply by 2.6.

ii Quantities varying are time and number of cows. Number of bales (10) stays the same. Would you expect the time that the bales would last to be more or less for fewer cows?
With fewer cows to feed, the bales will last longer so you should check that your answer is longer than one week.

Time		Number of cows		
1 week		**25**		
	× 12.5		÷ 12.5	(25 ÷ 2 = 12.5)
12.5		**2**		

The farmer's 10 bales will last 12.5 weeks with only 2 cows.

Exercise 4.12   NO CALCULATOR IN THIS EXERCISE

1 State whether each of the following are examples of direct proportion, inverse proportion or neither.

   a Cost of one stamp. Cost of a number of the same stamps.

   b Age of a child. Size of the child's shoes.

   c Number of cows in a field. Length of time the grass will last (assuming that they always eat at the same rate).

   d The number of loaves of a certain type of bread and the amount of flour needed.

2 A tin of paint will cover 5.2 m². How many whole tins will have to be purchased for a wall 20 m by 2.5 m?

3 Curtain material costs $25 for 5 metres. How much will 34 m cost?

4 It takes 25 minutes to do a particular journey at a steady speed of 55 km/h. How long would it take at 45 km/h? Give your answer to the nearest minute.

5 It takes 25 minutes to travel 16 kilometres. How long would it take to cover 40 kilometres at the same speed? Give your answer to the nearest minute.

6 Three painters take four days to paint the outside of a house.

   a How long would it take six painters to paint the same house at the same rate?

   b How many painters would be needed to paint three similar houses in four days?

4.13 Time

As we mentioned above, time is not decimalised, so care is needed to work out problems involving time.

For example, to change time in hours, minutes and seconds to decimal parts of an hour or minute *without* using a calculator we need to divide by 60, as in the next example.

Example 18

Without using a calculator, change 9 hours 10 minutes to hours.

Answer 18

10 minutes $= 10 \div 60$ hours $= \dfrac{10}{60} = \dfrac{1}{6} = 0.166\,666\ldots = 0.167$ hours to 3 s.f.

9 hours and 10 minutes $= 9.167$ hours to 3 s.f.

This calculation can be done in the same way with a calculator.

Some calculators will also allow you to enter time in hours, minutes and seconds using a button marked $\boxed{\cdot \, , \, , ,}$.

The calculation will then change the hours, minutes and seconds to decimal parts of an hour. Try these:

1 To enter 9 hours, 10 minutes and 15 seconds:

Enter	**Calculator display**
9 $\boxed{\circ \, , \, , ,}$ 10 $\boxed{\circ \, , \, , ,}$ 15 $\boxed{\circ \, , \, , ,}$	9°10°15°
Press $\boxed{\circ \, , \, , ,}$ once more	9.170833333

2 To enter 9 hours 10 minutes:

 9°10°

Press [° , ,,] once more 9.166666667

3 To enter 9 minutes 10 seconds:

 0°9°10°

Press [° , ,,] once more 0.152777778

Now try:

1 Enter 1.25 [=] [· , ,,] 1°15° (this could be 1 hour 15 minutes, or 1 minute 15 seconds)

2 Enter 1.255 [=] [· , ,,] 1°15°18° (this is 1 hour 15 minutes and 18 seconds)

If your calculator does not work exactly like this you might have to experiment with the shift button as well until you know how to use it.

You might need to change decimal parts of an hour to hours, minutes and seconds, without a calculator.

> **Example 19**
> Change 3.75 hours to hours and minutes.
>
> **Answer 19**
> 0.75 hours = 0.75 × 60 minutes = 45 minutes
> 3.75 hours = 3 hours and 45 minutes

12-hour and 24-hour clocks

You should be able to convert between the 12-hour and 24-hour clocks. To change from the 12-hour to 24-hour clock, follow these steps:

- If the time is a.m., add a zero at the beginning if necessary to write as four figures, and drop the 'a.m.'
- If the time is p.m., add 1200 and drop the 'p.m.'

To change from the 24-hour to the 12-hour clock, follow these steps:

- If the time is less than 1200, add 'a.m.' and remove any zero at the beginning.
- If the time is later than 1200, subtract 1200 and add 'p.m.'

> **Example 20**
> **a** Change to the 24-hour clock:
>   **i** 8.15 a.m.   **ii** 2.45 p.m.
> **b** Change to the 12-hour clock:
>   **i** 0800   **ii** 1514
>
> **Answer 20**
> **a** **i** 8.15 a.m.   **ii** 2.45 p.m.
>   = 0815   = 1445
> **b** **i** 0800   **ii** 1514
>   = 8 a.m.   = 3.14 p.m.

You need to be able to work with timetables and international time.

The rotation of the Earth means that the Sun rises at different times in different parts of the world. To allow for this the world is divided into time zones so that close geographical locations can use the same time.

Example 21

a A train leaves Edinburgh at 0845 and arrives in London at 1515.
   How long does the journey take?

b A television programme starts at 6.55 p.m. and runs for 1 hour and 10 minutes.
   At what time does it finish?

c How much time has elapsed between 1845 on Monday and 0830 on Tuesday?

d The time difference between Paris and New York on a day in summer is 6 hours.
   i If it is 1023 in Paris on Friday what time is it in New York?
   ii If it is 11.15 p.m. in New York on Monday what time is it in Paris?

Answer 21

a Counting-on is often the best way to deal with time.

From 0845 to 0900 is	15 minutes
From 0900 to 1500 is	6 hours
From 1500 to 1515 is	15 minutes

   Hence, total time taken is 6 hours and 30 minutes, or $6\frac{1}{2}$ hours.

b 6.55 p.m. plus 10 minutes is 7.05 p.m.
   7.05 p.m. plus 1 hour is 8.05 p.m.
   Hence, the programme finishes at 8.05 p.m.

c Again, counting-on is probably best.

1845 to 1900 is	15 minutes
1900 to midnight is	5 hours
midnight to 0800 is	8 hours
0800 to 0830 is	30 minutes
Total	13 hours and 45 minutes

d The Earth rotates so that the Sun rises in eastern countries before countries further west.
   That means that the time will be 6 hours earlier in New York than in Paris.
   i It will be 0423 on Friday in New York.
   ii It will be 5.15 a.m. on Tuesday in Paris.

4.14 Rate

Rate is a measure of how one quantity changes as another changes.

Speed

Speed is probably the easiest rate to understand. Speed measures how far you go in a given time. The faster the speed the further you go in this given time, so speed is calculated by dividing distance gone by time taken.

If you travel 32 km in 1 hour your speed is 32 km/h (32 kilometres per hour). A speed of 90 km/h means that you travel 90 kilometres in one hour. Light travels at a speed of nearly 3×10^8 m/s (metres per second). This means that light travels 300 000 kilometres in one second. A snail may travel at a speed of 0.5 m/h (or much less!). This is 0.5 metres in 1 hour.

Key term

Rate is a measure of how one quantity changes as another changes.

Exchange Rates

You will also come across the word 'rate' when you see exchange rates, which represent how the currency of one country relates in value to that of another country.

Table 4.3 gives exchange rates taken from a particular time on a particular day.

Currency	
American dollars	1
Indian rupees	44.613 22
British pounds	0.505 37
Singapore dollars	1.540 75
South African rands	7.183 85
Euros	0.750 50

Table 4.3 Exchange rates based on dollars

This table is based on the American dollar, so it shows how many units of each currency you would get for 1 dollar. The table can also be based on the rupee.

According to the table, the ratio of dollars to rupees is 1: 44.613 22.

To change this ratio to make the ratio rupees (Rs) to dollars we need to divide both parts of the ratio by 44.613 22, as shown below:

$$1 \div 44.613\,22 = 0.022\,41$$

So Re 1 is equivalent to $0.022 41.

Copy and complete Table 4.4 showing the exchange rates based on the Indian rupee. Notice that all the rates are given to 5 decimal places. The table shows how many units of each currency you would get for Re 1.

The exchange rates are constantly changing according to what is happening in the world financial markets, and the rates given above might be completely different by the time you come to read this book. Try to find out some current exchange rates by looking in a newspaper, or on the Internet.

The other thing to remember about exchanging currencies is that the bank or bureau that changes the currency for you will charge a commission to cover the costs of their work, so you will never get the total amount you calculate.

NOTE:
Exchange rates are quoted to several decimal places. When you are using your calculator for questions about money you should remember that the final answer should be rounded to only two decimal places. So a calculation that produced an answer of $12.819 37 should be given as $12.82 (12 dollars and 82 cents).

Currency	
Indian rupees	1
American dollars	0.022 41
British pounds	0.011 23
Singapore dollars	
South African rands	
Euros	

Table 4.4 Exchange rates based in rupees

Gradient

Slope, or gradient is another example of rate. The gradient of a hill is measured by finding how much the hill rises (vertical measurement) for each unit in a horizontal direction (horizontal measurement). So you might say that a gradient is 50 metres rise for every kilometre horizontally. The gradient is 50 m/km.

However, in practice, it is usual to use the same units of measurement both horizontally and vertically which makes it unnecessary to state the units.

So 50 metres per kilometre would be 50 metres per 1000 metres or 1 metre per 20 metres, a gradient of 1 in 20.

$$\text{gradient} = \frac{50 \text{ metres}}{1 \text{ kilometre}}$$
$$= \frac{50 \text{ metres}}{1000 \text{ metres}} = \frac{50}{1000} = \frac{1}{20}$$

Gradients are also given as percentages, so 1 in 20 would become $\frac{1}{20} \times 100 = 5\%$.

Average Rates

You may see a sign at the top or bottom of a steep hill warning drivers to take care. As Figure 4.16 shows, a gradient of a hill given as 20% does not necessarily mean that the gradient is the same all the way up the hill. The gradient would be given as an average gradient, calculated by dividing the total height risen vertically by the total distance covered horizontally.

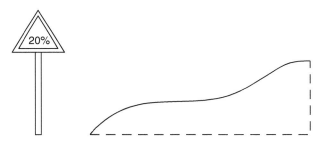

Figure 4.5 The gradient of a hill

The same applies to speed on a journey. You may be asked to calculate the average speed on a journey, which always means total distance travelled divided by total time taken. Parts of the journey might have been faster, and parts slower than the average speed.

4.15 Compound Units

Compound units are units of measurement that are derived from other units. Examples of compound units are km/h or g/cm³. The units themselves tell you how the measurements are calculated. For example, speed measured in kilometres *per* hour means that you find how many kilometres are travelled in one hour, so you have to divide distance gone (in kilometres) by time taken (in hours).

Grams *per* cubic centimetre gives the mass of a body per unit volume, and is calculated by dividing the mass of the body (in grams) by the volume of the body (in cubic centimetres). This is known as the **density** of the body and depends on the material it is made from. Lead has a high density, so quite a small volume has a large mass. Feathers have a low density, so quite a large volume has a low mass.

Key term

Density is the weight per unit volume of a material.

Table 4.5 shows the densities of some metals.

metal	kg/m³
Lead	11 389
Brass	8400
Iron	7850
Copper	8930
Silver	10 490

Table 4.5 Densities of metals

Cents *per* metre of material is the cost of each metre of the material. It would be calculated by dividing the total cost in cents by the total length in metres.

Metres per cents is the number of metres you could buy for each cents and is calculated by dividing the length in metres by the total cost in cents.

Example 22
a Find the average speed in kilometres per hour for a car which travels 100 kilometres in 1.5 hours.
b How far could you go at an average speed of 65 kilometres per hour for 2.5 hours?
c How long would it take to travel 50 kilometres at an average speed of 80 kilometres per hour?
d Change 15 metres per second to kilometres per hour.

Answer 22
a

NOTE:
Remember average speed in km/h is the distance in kilometres travelled in one hour.

100 km in 1.5 hours
$= \frac{100}{1.5}$ km in 1 hour
$= 66.7$ km in 1 hour
Average speed $= 66.7$ kilometres per hour

b 65 km in 1 hour
$= 65 \times 2.5$ km in 2.5 hours
$= 162.5$ km in 2.5 hours
Distance gone $= 162.5$ kilometres

c 80 km in 1 hour
$= 1$ km in $\frac{1}{80}$ hour
$= 50$ km in $50 \times \frac{1}{80}$ hours $= 0.625$ hours
$= 0.625$ hours $= 0.625 \times 60$ minutes $= 37.5$ minutes
Time taken $= 37.5$ minutes

d

Distance gone	Time taken
15 metres in	**1** second
$15 \times 60 \times 60$ metres in	$1 \times 60 \times 60$ seconds
54 000 metres in	1 hour
54 kilometres in	1 hour

So 15 metres per second $= 54$ kilometres per hour

Exercise 4.13

NO CALCULATOR IN THIS EXERCISE

1 Wood costs $4 per cubic metre. Find the cost of a piece of wood 5 m by 20 cm by 50 cm.

2 The world turns through 360° every 24 hours.
a How long does it take to turn through 80°? Give your answer in hours and minutes.
b What angle has the world turned through in 6 hours?

3 Water has a mass of 1000 kg per cubic metre. Calculate the mass of water in a swimming pool measuring 30 m × 20 m × 2 m.

4 A TV film starts at 11.35 p.m. on Wednesday and finishes at 1.20 a.m. on Thursday. How long is the film?

5 A train leaves Delhi at 7.15 a.m. and arrives in Agra at 9.45 a.m. The distance from Delhi to Agra is 206 km. Calculate the speed of the train.

6 A train leaves Kolkata at 2015 and arrives in Patna 10 hours later. At what time does it arrive in Patna?

7 Change 35 grams per cubic centimetre into kilograms per cubic metre.

8 4 cubic metres of a compound has a mass of 5 tonnes. Calculate its density in grams per cubic centimetre. (There are 1000 kg in 1 tonne.)

NOTE:
In question 5 remember that speed is distance gone in one hour.

4.16 Personal and Small Business Finance

Best Buys

It can often happen that manufacturers will offer two different sizes of a commodity at two different prices, and you may wish to work out which one is the best buy. There are two different ways of doing this, either:

- choose the one with the *lowest* cost per unit volume (or mass), or
- choose the one with the *highest* volume (or mass) per unit cost.

An example should make this clear.

Example 23

A shop is offering two sizes of a commodity:

A is a pack with a mass of 100 g costing Rs 75, and **B** is a pack of mass 75 g costing Rs 50. Which is the better buy? You must show all your working.

Answer 23

A
100 g
Rs 75

B
75 g
Rs 50

First method

A: 100 g costs Rs 75   **B:** 75 g costs Rs 50

  1 g costs Rs $\frac{75}{100}$ 1 g costs Rs $\frac{50}{75}$

  1 g costs Rs 0.75   1 g costs Rs 0.67

So **B** is the better buy (1 g costs less).

Alternative method

A: Rs 75 buys 100 g   **B:** Rs 50 buys 75 g

  Re 1 buys $\frac{100}{75}$ g   Re 1 buys $\frac{75}{50}$ g

  Re 1 buys 1.33 g   Re 1 buys 1.5 g

So **B** is the better buy (Re 1 buys more).

Profit and Loss

Profit or loss may be expressed as either an amount of money, or as a percentage *of the original cost price*. Always calculate the actual profit or loss first and then, if required, express as a percentage of the cost price, as shown in the example below.

Example 24

Pierre bought 50 pens for €135, and sold 48 of the pens for €4 each. He kept the remaining two pens to use in his shop. Calculate his percentage profit.

Answer 24

Cost price of pens		= €135.00
Selling price of pens (48 at €4 each)		= €192.00
Actual profit	(selling price − cost price)	= €57.00
Percentage profit	(€57.00 ÷ €135 × 100%)	= 42.2%

Simple and Compound Interest

If you put money into a savings account at a bank you will receive **interest**, which is calculated as a percentage of the **amount** you have in the account. The percentage varies according to the bank and the type of account, and is called the **interest rate**.

There are two ways to calculate this interest, called **simple interest** and **compound interest**.

When simple interest is calculated, the interest earned at the end of each year is not taken into account in the following year. For example, it may be removed from the account for other purposes.

When compound interest is calculated, the interest earned each year is left in the account and the interest for the following year is calculated using this new (larger) sum.

Calculating Simple Interest

Simple interest = amount invested (or borrowed) × interest rate (per annum) × time (in years). So the formula for calculating simple interest is $I = PrT$, where I is the interest, P is the principal (another word for the amount invested or borrowed), r is the interest rate and T is the time.

Calculating Compound Interest

You can use the formula

$$\text{Value of investment} = P\left(1 + \frac{r}{100}\right)^n$$

where P is the amount invested, r is the interest rate and n is the number of years.

Example 25

a Calculate the simple interest earned on an investment of $150 at a rate of 4% per annum for

   i 1 year   **ii** 2 years   **iii** 9 months   **iv** 15 months.

b Using the formula, calculate the annual rate of simple interest as a percentage when an investment of $2000 earns $250 in 2 years.

c Using the formula, calculate the compound interest that will be paid on $1000 invested at 2.01% for 5 years.

Answer 25

a **i** $\text{Interest} = 150 \times \frac{4}{100} \times 1 = \$6.00$ **ii** $\text{Interest} = 150 \times \frac{4}{100} \times 2 = \$12.00$

    iii $\text{Interest} = 150 \times \frac{4}{100} \times \frac{9}{12} = \$4.50$ **iv** $\text{Interest} = 150 \times \frac{4}{100} \times \frac{15}{12} = \$7.50$

b $I = PrT$

    $250 = 2000 \times r \times 2$

    $250 = 4000r$

    $r = \frac{250}{4000} = 0.0625$

    Annual rate of interest $= 6.25\%$

c   Value of investment after 5 years $= 1000\left(1 + \frac{2.01}{100}\right)^5$

                             $= 1104.622125$

                             $= \$1104.62$

    Interest received $= \$1104.62 - \$1000$

                       $= \$104.62$

Interest is also payable on any amount you borrow. It is calculated in exactly the same way.

> **Key term**
>
> **Depreciation** is the loss of value of goods as they age.

Depreciation

The value of many consumer goods decreases as time goes by. For example, a car with a cost when new of, say, $12 000 might have lost 30% of this value by the end of the first year. If it were to carry on depreciating at the same rate the calculation would be the same as that for compound interest, but with the value falling each year instead of increasing. In this case, however, the rate of depreciation is 30% in the first year, but it is likely to be less, say 20% in the succeeding years. The second-hand car trade has tables showing how the values of makes of cars fall each year. The depreciation rate is a factor to take into account when deciding which car to buy.

Discount

You will often see a sale advertised as, for example, '25% off everything'.

In this sale an item normally costing $405 will have 25% of $405 taken off. This is $101.25.

To calculate the amount you will have to pay you can take the discount ($101.25) away from the original price ($405), to give $303.75 to pay.

However, it can be quicker to say that if you have a discount of 25% the percentage you have to pay is 75% of the original price. Then the calculation is: 75% of $405 = $303.75.

Electricity Bills

Electricity and other utility bills (for example, gas, water, and telephone) are usually based on the number of units used as shown on a meter. The units will be a measure used for the particular utility, and we normally refer to them as 'units', without having to worry about what exactly they are. There are then various methods to calculate the total sum to pay, and you will need to read each question carefully and follow the instructions. For example, the cost of the 'first' units used may be different from the remaining units, as you will see in the example given. There could also be a 'standing charge' which you have to pay just for having the service connected, even if you have not used any units.

Example 26

I have just read my electricity meter, one month after the last reading.

Nov 12th	9	9	1	5	3
Dec 12th	9	9	6	7	6

Units cost £0.1276 each for the 'first' 170 units, and £0.0931 each for the remaining units. There is no standing charge, but VAT is added at 5%. Calculate my total bill for this month.

Answer 26

> **NOTE:**
> Remember to take the old reading away from the new reading.

Units used	$99676 - 99153 = 523$ units
First units	170 at £0.1276 = £21.69
Remaining units	$(523 - 170) = 353$ units
	353 at £0.0931 = £32.86
Total before VAT	(£21.69 + £32.86) = £54.55
VAT at 5%	$(5 \times 54.55 \div 100) = £2.73$
Total after VAT	(£54.55 + £2.73) = £57.28
Total bill = £57.28	

Exercise 4.14

1 For each question:
  i   state whether there is a profit or loss,
  ii the actual profit or loss,
  iii the profit or loss as a percentage of the cost price.
  and work out

	Cost price	Selling price
a	$50	$45
b	$50	$55
c	Rs 365	Rs 456.25
d	10 for Rs 786	Rs 85 each
e	150 for £75	£0.55 each

2 a Fred borrows $1000 from the bank. The bank charges 5% simple interest per annum. Calculate the interest payable after

    i 8 months   **ii** 1 year.

  b Calculate how long it would take for an investment of $500 to earn $25 interest at a rate of 2% per annum.

3 On the Island of Equality everyone earns the same amount (€25) per hour and everyone pays annual income tax at the same rate (25%).

There is a personal allowance of €2500 per annum which is tax free.

Calculate the amount each of these people pays in tax per annum.

  a Raj works for 20 hours a week and has three weeks unpaid holiday a year.

  b Tamara works for 175 hours a month and has one month unpaid holiday per year.

  c Anet works for 796 hours per year, and has no extra holiday.

4 An approximation used to convert between kilometres and miles is 8 kilometres ≈ 5 miles.

  a Work out the approximate equivalent of 20 kilometres in miles.

  b Work out the approximate equivalent of 35 miles in kilometres.

5 Change the following to the units stated.

  a 5.5 km/h to m/s

  b 60 miles per hour to kilometres per hour (use the approximate conversion 5 miles ≈ 8 kilometres).

6 Zac is making a paperweight. He will choose between the following:

  a a cuboid 10 cm × 2 cm × 4 cm, made of iron;

  b a cube of side 4 cm, made of copper.

    Use the table of densities, Table 4.5, to work out which will be the heavier paperweight.

7 Assuming the light from a flash of lightning arrives instantaneously, but that the sound travels at 300 m/s, work out how far away a thunderstorm is if you count 10 seconds between seeing the flash and hearing the thunder. Give your answer in kilometres.

8 Supriti buys 10 toy cars for Rs 50 each. She sells 7 for Rs 75 each, and then reduces the remaining three and sells them in her sale at 20% discount on her previous selling price. Calculate her profit as a percentage of the cost price.

9 A large (1 litre) bottle of lemonade costs £1.80, and a small (250 ml) bottle costs £0.44. Which is the better buy?

10 Anita is going to buy a used car. She is making a choice between a Penti hatchback and a Quadri saloon.

The Penti uses 10 litres of fuel to travel 90 kilometres, and the Quadri uses 15 litres to travel 165 kilometres. Which of these two cars would be the most economical to run? You must show all your working.

11 Tomas got 36 marks out of a possible 60 in his mathematics test. He got 52 marks out of 75 in his science test. By calculating his percentage marks for each test find out which was his better test.

12 Niraj bought a new car in 2014 costing $35 000.

The rate of depreciation was 46% in the first year and 19% in the second year. Calculate the value of the car at the end of 2016.

13 A valued customer is offered a 10% discount on an item normally worth $65.70. How much will they have to pay?

14 A video conference is to be arranged between Rome and Tokyo. The time difference is 7 hours. Rome is west of Tokyo. What time would it be in Tokyo if the conference is arranged for 1113 Rome time?

15 Calculate the value of a bond purchased in 2015 at a cost of $5000, with a compound interest rate of 2.35%, when it matures in 2020.

(A bond in this case is a certificate that provides a method of saving, usually for a fixed term or number of years. It 'matures' after the fixed term and can then be converted to cash.)

Exercise 4.15

Mixed exercise

1 A mineral known as 'fool's gold' because it glitters like gold has the chemical formula FeS_2. Fe stands for iron and S stands for sulfur.

This means that 1 molecule of FeS_2 contains 1 atom of iron and 2 atoms of sulfur. How many atoms of (a) iron and (b) sulfur are present in 72 molecules of fool's gold?

2 The air in the classroom contains 0.03% CO_2.

A classroom is 2.5 metres high, 8 metres long and 6 metres wide.

    a Calculate the volume of the room.

    b Work out the volume of CO_2 in the room.

3 A cake requires 275 grams of flour, 250 grams of sugar and 4 eggs.

Amrit wants to make enough cakes to use up all the eggs in his refrigerator.

He finds he has 10 eggs.

    a How much flour and sugar will he need to make the cakes?

    b How many whole cakes can he make?

4 A flight leaves London at 2135 on February 1st and arrives in Bangkok at 1540 London time on February 2nd.

    a How long has the flight taken?

        The distance between London and Bangkok along the plane's route is 8038 miles.

    b Calculate the speed of the plane in miles per hour. 1200 in London is 1800 in Bangkok.

    c What is the time in Bangkok when the plane arrives?

5 Change the following to the stated units.

    a 2 hours and 43 minutes to minutes   **b** 7.15 hours to hours and minutes

    c 3 hours 36 minutes to hours   **d** 27 minutes to hours

6 The mass of Earth is approximately 5.97×10^{24} kg.

The mass of the Moon is approximately $\frac{1}{81}$ of the mass of the Earth.

Calculate the mass of the moon giving your answer to 3 significant figures and in standard form.

7 The distance of the Moon from Earth is 384.4×10^3 km.

    a Write this in standard form.

    b Change to metres, giving your answer in standard form.

Exam-style questions

NO CALCULATOR IN THIS EXERCISE

8 A model of a car has a scale of 1 : 25.
The model is 18 cm long. Calculate, in metres, the actual
length of the car. *(0580 paper 01 Q5 June 2004)*

9 The length of a rectangular rug is given as 0.9 m, correct to the nearest ten centimetres.
The width of the rug is given as 0.6 m, correct to the nearest ten centimetres.
   a Write down the upper bound, in metres, of the length of the rug.
   b Find the lower bound, in metres, of the perimeter
   of the rug. *(4024 paper 12 Q8 June 2012)*

10 Shampoo is sold in two sizes, *A* and *B*.
A contains 800 ml and costs $1.30. *B* contains 1.5 litres and costs $2.30.
Which is the better value for money?
Show your working clearly. *(0580 paper 01 Q14 June 2004)*

11 Carlos buys a box of 50 oranges for $8.
He sells all the oranges in the market for 25 cents each.
   a Calculate the profit he makes.
   b Calculate the percentage profit he makes on the
   cost price. *(0580 paper 01 Q18 June 2004)*

12 a Add 55 minutes to 2.4 hours, giving your answer in hours and minutes.
   b The mass of a bag of sugar is given as 1.5 kg, correct to the nearest tenth of a kilogram.
   Write down the upper bound of this mass, giving your answer in grams.
   (4024 paper 11 Q4 November 2011)

13 The length of a road is 1300 metres, correct to the nearest 100 metres.
Copy and complete this statement.
$$\ldots\ldots\ldots\ldots\ldots\ldots\text{m} \leqslant \text{road length} < \ldots\ldots\ldots\ldots\ldots\ldots\ldots\text{m}.$$
(0580 paper 01 Q8 November 2003)

14 a A bag contains red and blue counters in the ratio 3 : 8.
   There are 24 blue counters.
   How many red counters are there?
   b Amy and Ben share $360 in the ratio 3 : 2.
   How much is Ben's share.
   (4024 paper 12 Q4 June 2012)

15 The diagram shows a pole of length *l* centimetres.

$\longleftarrow$ - - - - - - - - - - - - - - - - - - -   *l* cm   - - - - - - - - - - - - - - - - - - - $\longrightarrow$

   a Hassan says that *l* = 88.2. Round this to the nearest whole number.
   b In fact the pole has a length 86 cm, to the nearest centimetre.
   Copy and complete the statement about *l*.
$$\ldots\ldots\ldots\ldots\ldots\ldots \leqslant l < \ldots\ldots\ldots\ldots\ldots\ldots\ldots$$
(0580 paper 01 Q12 June 2003)

16 Anne took a test in chemistry.
She scored 20 marks out of 50.
Work out her percentage mark.

(0580 paper 01 Q3 June 2005)

17 Write, in its simplest from, the ratio
3.5 kilograms : 800 grams.

(0580 paper 01 Q4 June 2005)

18 Yasmeen is setting up a business.
She borrows $5000 from a loan company.
The loan company charges 6% per year simple interest.
How much interest will Yasmeen pay after 3 years?

(0580 paper 01 Q11 June 2005)

19 $\dfrac{8.95 - 3.05 \times 1.97}{2.92}$

   a **i** Write the above expression with each number rounded to one significant figure.

      ii Use your answer to find an **estimate** for the value of the expression.

(0580 paper 01 Q19a June 2005)

20 Ed goes on a car journey.
The first 60 km of the journey takes 45 minutes.
The remaining 20 km of the journey takes 30 minutes.
Calculate his average speed, in kilometres per hour, for the whole journey.

(4024 paper 11 Q4 June 2010)

21 The scale on a map is 1 : 250000. A road is 4.6 cm long on the map.
Calculate the actual length of the road in kilometres.   (0580 paper 01 Q6 November 2008)

22 a Maryam's height is 1.52 m correct to the nearest centimetre.
State the lower bound of her height.
  b The length of each of Maryam's paces is 0.55 m.
She walks at a constant speed of 2 paces per second.
Calculate the distance, in kilometres, that she walks in one hour.

(4024 paper 01 Q16 June 2004)

23 Matthew invested $500 at 6% simple interest per year.
Calculate how much interest had been earned after 8 months.

(4024 paper 01 Q19b June 2004)

24 a When Peter went to Hong Kong, he changed £50 into $616.
Calculate what one British pound (£) was worth in Hong Kong dollars ($).
  b It takes 8 hours for 5 people to paint a room.
How long would it take 4 people?   (4024 paper 01 Q5 June 2005)

25 A TV programme list shows that a film begins at 2155.
The film lasts for 100 minutes.
At what time will it end?
Express your answer using the 24 hour clock.   (4024 paper 01 Q12a June 2005)

26 The rate of exchange between pounds (£) and dollars ($) was £1 = $2.80. Calculate:
  a the number of dollars received in exchange for £120,
  b the number of pounds received in exchange for $224.   (4024 paper 01 Q3 June 2006)

27 a The time difference between Brunei and London is 7 hours.
So, when it is 1900 in Brunei, it is 1200 in London.
When it is 0330 in Brunei, what time is it in London?
  b An aircraft leaves Brunei at 6.30 p.m. local time.
It arrives in Dubai at 10 p.m. local time.
The flight took $7\frac{1}{2}$ hours.
Calculate the time difference between Dubai and Brunei. (4024 paper 01 Q8 June 2006)

28 a Add together 181 centimetres and 14.85 metres.
Give your answer in metres.

b Express 40 000 square metres in square kilometres. (4024 paper 01 Q5 November 2004)

29 An atom of helium has a mass of 6.8×10^{-27} kilograms.

a Express this mass in grams.
Give your answer in standard form.

b A room contains 9×10^{22} atoms of helium.
Find the mass of helium in the room.
Give your answer in grams as a normal decimal
number. (4024 paper 01 Q12 November 2004)

30 a Calculate 5% of $280 000.

b A single carton of juice costs $4.20.
A special offer pack of 3 cartons costs $9.45.
Ali bought a special offer pack instead of 3 single cartons.
Calculate his percentage saving. (4024 paper 01 Q18 June 2007)

31 By writing each number correct to 1 significant figure, estimate the value of $\frac{8.62 \times 2.04^2}{0.285}$.
(4024 paper 01 Q4 June 2008)

32 It is given that $68.2 \times 0.235 = 16.027$.
Hence evaluate

a 0.0682×2350

b $160.27 \div 0.0235$. (4024 paper 01 Q5 June 2008)

33 a A jar contained 370 g of jam.
Usman ate 30% of the jam.
What mass of jam remained in the jar?

b In 2006 the population of a town was 30 000.
This was 5000 more than the population in 1999.
Calculate the percentage increase in population. (4024 paper 01 Q14 June 2008)

34 The Earth is 1.5×10^8 kilometres from the Sun.

a Mercury is 5.81×10^7 kilometres from the Sun.
How much nearer is the Sun to Mercury than to the Earth?
Give your answer in standard form.

b A terametre is 10^{12} metres.
Find the distance of the Earth from the Sun in terametres. (4024 paper 01 Q18 June 2008)

35 a Convert 0.8 kilometres into millimetres.

b Evaluate $(6.3 \times 10^6) \div (9 \times 10^2)$, giving your answer in standard form.
(4024 paper 01 Q8 June 2009)

36 Five clocks at a hotel reception desk show the local times in five different cities at the
same moment.

LONDON	MOSCOW	SYDNEY	TOKYO	NEW YORK
07 38	10 38	16 38	15 38	02 38

a Rosidah has breakfast at 0800 in Moscow.
What is the local time in Sydney?

b Elias catches a plane in London and flies to New York.
He leaves London at 1130 local time.
The flight time is 8 hours 10 minutes.
What is the local time in New York when he lands? (4024 paper 01 Q10 June 2009)

37 a The rate of exchange between dollars and euros was $0.8 to 1 euro.
  Calculate the number of euros received in exchange for $300.

b Find the simple interest on $450 for 18 months at 4% per year.

(4024 paper 01 Q5 November 2007)

38 a Estimate the value, correct to one significant figure, of $\frac{4.03^2 \times 29.88}{\sqrt{150}}$.

b Sam ran 100 metres in 12 seconds.
  Calculate his average speed in kilometres per hour.

(4024 paper 01 Q19 November 2007)

39 a The local time in Singapore is 7 hours ahead of the local time in London.
  A flight to London leaves Singapore at 0300 local time.
  The flight takes 12 hours and 45 minutes.
  What is the local time in London when it arrives?

b Mai changes £250 into dollars.
  The exchange rate is £1 = $3.10.
  How many dollars does she receive?   (4024 paper 01 Q5 November 2009)

40

Paris to Creil	Paris to Creil
Adult 25 euros	Child 17.50 euros

During a visit to France, a family took a train from Paris to Creil.
The cost of an adult ticket was 25 euros and the cost of a child ticket was 17.50 euros.

i How much did it cost for a family of 2 adults and 3 children?

ii Express the cost of a child ticket as a percentage of the cost of an adult ticket.

(4024 paper 01 Q23a November 2009)

41 The diagram shows a fuel gauge in a car.

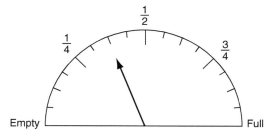

a What fraction does the gauge show?

b The fuel tank holds 48 litres when it is full.
  How many litres must be added to fill the tank?   (4024 paper 01 Q3 November 2005)

42 a The number 3002.05 can be written as $3 \times 10^3 + 2 \times 10^x + 5 \times 10^y$.
  Given that x and y are integers, find the values of x and y.

b A bank exchanged Japanese yen and Singapore dollars ($) at a rate of 66 yen = $1.

  i Calculate, in yen, the amount received for $200.

  ii Calculate, in dollars, the amount received for 33 000 yen.

(4024 paper 01 Q18 November 2005)

43 a An empty tin has a mass of 330 g.
  When filled with powder, the total mass is 2.10 kg.
  Find the mass, in kilograms, of the powder.

b Express 2.45 hours in minutes.   (4024 paper 1 Q2 November 2006)

44 a Find the fraction which is exactly halfway between $\frac{5}{9}$ and $\frac{8}{9}$.

b **Estimate** the value of $\sqrt{5000}$, giving your answer correct to **one** significant figure.

c Evaluate $3^0 \times 4^{\frac{3}{2}}$. (4024 paper 01 Q7 November 2006)

45 It is given that $N = 87 \times 132$.

a Complete these statements.

$88 \times 132 = N + \ldots$

$87 \times 131 = N - \ldots$

b Hence evaluate $88 \times 132 - 87 \times 131$. (4024 paper 01 Q15 June 2005)

46 a A coach left London at 2045 and arrived in Edinburgh the next day at 0505.
How long did the journey take?

b The distance between London and Edinburgh is 660 km.

i A train took 5 hours 30 minutes to complete the journey.
Calculate its average speed.

ii The average speed of another train was 150 km/h.
How long did this train take for the journey?
Give your answer in hours and minutes. (4024 paper 01 Q23 November 2004)

Working with Algebra

Learning Objectives   Syllabus sections 17, 20 and 22

In this chapter you will:
- solve simple equations
- rearrange formulae
- start working with sequences
- solve simple pairs of linear simultaneous equations.

5.1 Introduction

This chapter will provide you with more skills in the use of algebra. You should begin to feel more confident in the language of algebra and the use of letters to replace numbers. Remember to work through each worked example carefully before going on to the exercise that follows it.

The most likely errors you may make usually involve signs, particularly minus signs! Remember the rules for plus and minus signs. Use the number line you made in Chapter 1 when necessary.

5.2 Essential Skills   NO CALCULATOR IN THIS EXERCISE

1 Simplify:

    a $-1-2+4$ **b** -2×5 **c** -1×0 **d** 3×6

    e $(5)^2$ **f** $-2(x-y)$ **g** $-(3+a)$

2 Simplify:

    a $3+0$ **b** 3×0 **c** $0 \div 2$ **d** $2+1$

    e 2×1 **f** $\frac{0}{1}$ **g** $\frac{3}{1}$ **h** $\frac{2}{-3}$

    i $\frac{-2}{-3}$ **j** $3-3$ **k** $\frac{3}{3}$ **l** $4 \div 4$

    m $x \div x$ **n** $0 \times x \times y$ **o** $0-a$ **p** $\sqrt{4}$

    q 3^2 **r** $x-x$

3 Which of the following are expressions and which are equations?

    a $3+x-y$ **b** $6(x-5)=1$ **c** $3+x-y=0$ **d** $6(x-5)$

4 $2x + 3z - 5y - 3x + w$

    a Which is the term in y?

    b Which two terms are like terms?

    c List the variables.

    d What is the coefficient of the first term?

    e Which sign belongs to the term in z?

5 List pairs of these operators that are inverses of (undo) each other.

    square   **divide**   **add**   **subtract**   **multiply**   **square root**

5.3 Solution of Equations

You will remember that we looked at the difference between expressions and equations in Chapter 3. We noted that expressions may be simplified but not solved, but that we can often find solutions to equations. A solution to an equation is a number that can replace the letter (for example, x) and make the equation a true statement.

A simple example of an equation would be $2x + 3 = 11$.

A little thought, or perhaps trial and error, will help you see that if the variable x is replaced by the number 4 the equation becomes $2 \times 4 + 3 = 11$, which is a true statement.

This means that the solution to this equation is $x = 4$.

For simple equations like these it is often easy to just look at the equation and see what the solution must be (you are solving 'by inspection'), but you will rapidly find that the equations become too difficult to solve in this way, so we need to develop a systematic method to find the solution.

It is useful to think of equations as items in a set of balancing scales. Our equation above has two sides, a left side and a right side, and the equals sign in the middle tells us that the two sides are indeed equal to each other. We can use this equation to work out a systematic method for solving equations.

Remembering that x at this moment represents an unknown number, let us imagine that the two sides represent quantities which have mass. If we put the two sides of the equation in the two sides of a set of scales (see Figure 5.1), then the equation tells us that they must balance.

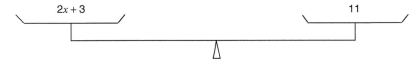

Figure 5.1 Balancing the two sides of an equation

So x represents an unknown number of grams and the scales also carry 3 grams and 11 grams. The left-hand scale pan carries 2 lots of x grams plus 3 grams and the right-hand scale pan carries 11 grams.

They would stay in balance if we removed 3 grams from both pans, so:

$$2x + 3 - 3 = 11 - 3$$
$$2x = 8$$

We can now easily see that if $2x = 8$ then x must be one half of 8.

$$2x = 8$$
$$x = 8 \div 2$$
$$x = 4 \text{ grams}$$

We have arrived at the same solution by this method as we did by inspection.

The basis for our method is: **the equation will stay in balance if we do the same thing to both sides**. You can add, subtract, multiply or divide as long as you do the same to *both sides*.

It is good practice to keep your equals signs in a straight line down the page when you are solving equations, and always write only one statement on each line, as in the worked examples below.

Example 1

Clearly showing your working, solve the following equations.

a $3x + 1 = 7$ **b** $5x - 11 = 4$ **c** $5 + 2x = 8$

d $3x + 6 = 2$ **e** $7 - 2x = 13$

Answer 1

a $3x + 1 = 7$

$\qquad 3x = 7 - 1 \qquad$ (-1 from both sides)

$\qquad 3x = 6$

$\qquad\quad x = 6 \div 3 \qquad$ ($\div 3$)

$\qquad\quad x = 2$

b $5x - 11 = 4$

$\qquad 5x = 4 + 11 \qquad$ ($+11$ to both sides)

$\qquad 5x = 15$

$\qquad\quad x = 15 \div 5 \qquad$ ($\div 5$)

$\qquad\quad x = 3$

c $5 + 2x = 8$

$\qquad 2x = 8 - 5 \qquad$ (-5)

$\qquad 2x = 3$

$\qquad\quad x = 3 \div 2 \qquad$ ($\div 2$)

$\qquad\quad x = \frac{3}{2} \qquad$ (or 1.5)

NOTE:

If there is no sign in front of the first term (in this case 5) it is positive ($+5$), so to remove the 5 take (subtract) 5 from both sides.

d $3x + 6 = 2$

$\qquad 3x = 2 - 6 \qquad$ (-6)

$\qquad 3x = -4$

$\qquad\quad x = -4 \div 3 \qquad$ ($\div 3$)

$\qquad\quad x = -\frac{4}{3}$

e $7 - 2x = 13$

$\qquad -2x = 13 - 7 \qquad$ (-7)

$\qquad -2x = 6$

$\qquad\quad x = \frac{6}{-2} \qquad$ ($\div -2$)

$\qquad\quad x = -3$

NOTE:
$+6 \div -2 = -3$

The steps in these equations are all leading to the line where the x has been isolated by itself on the left-hand side of the equation, leaving the right-hand side to be simplified if necessary. It is as if we are slowly unpicking the equation to get to the unknown or variable x.

Simple equations may also be solved by thinking of number machines. Look at the number machine in Figure 5.2, which represents the equation from Example 1 (d): $3x + 6 = 2$.

The input is x and the output is 2.

Figure 5.2 Number machine for $3x + 6 = 2$

We now solve the equation by running the machine backwards, so that the input is 2 (see Figure 5.3).

Figure 5.3 Running the number machine backwards

The output is $-\frac{4}{3}$, which is the solution to the equation.

This can be a useful technique for rearranging formulae which you will meet later in the chapter, so practise now by writing number machines for the other three equations in the example, and running them in reverse to get the solutions.

Exercise 5.1 **NO CALCULATOR IN THIS EXERCISE**

Solve the following equations either by inspection if they are easy enough or by our systematic method *showing your working* as in the answers to Example 1.

1	$3x + 4 = 10$	**2**	$5x = 20$
3	$x + 3 = 11$	**4**	$6x - 15 = 3$
5	$4x + 3 = 1$	**6**	$7x - 15 = 13$
7	$11x - 10 = 12$	**8**	$7 + 4x = 8$
9	$-2x = -10$	**10**	$-8 - 3x = 10$
11	$-x = 9$	**12**	$-x = -7$
13	$4 - x = 7$	**14**	$-x - 10 = 12$
15	$16 + 2x = 31$	**16**	$2 - 3x = 7$

NOTE:
In question 9 remember that $- \div - = +$

NOTE:
In question 11 $-x$ means $-1x$, so divide both sides by -1.

NOTE:
In questions 15 and 16 you can leave the answer as a fraction, or give it as a decimal if it is an exact decimal.

The next step is to see what happens when the variable appears on both sides of the equation, for example: $3x + 2 = 4 - x$.

The same method will apply, and it may help to gather your terms in x on the left-hand side of the equation, and the number terms on the right-hand side. The x term is subtracted on the right-hand side, so adding x to both sides will remove it from the right-hand side.

$$3x + 2 = 4 - x$$

$$3x + 2 + x = 4 \qquad (+x) \qquad \text{(this takes the } x \text{ to the left-hand side)}$$

$$4x + 2 = 4 \qquad\qquad \text{(this is the line above simplified)}$$

$$4x = 2 \qquad (-2 \text{ from both sides})$$

$$x = \frac{2}{4} \qquad (\div 4)$$

$$x = \frac{1}{2} \qquad\qquad \text{(this is the fraction simplified by dividing top and bottom by 2)}$$

Example 2

Solve the following equations:

a $5x - 3 = 7 + x$ **b** $2 - 4x = 9 + 9x$

c $5x - 7 + 3x = 10x + 6 - 6x - 3$

Answer 2

a $5x - 3 = 7 + x$ **b** $2 - 4x = 9 + 9x$

$5x - 3 - x = 7$ $(-x)$ $2 - 4x - 9x = 9$

$4x = 7 + 3$ $(+3)$ $2 - 13x = 9$

$4x = 10$ $-13x = 9 - 2$

$x = 2.5$ $(\div 4)$ $-13x = 7$

$x = -\dfrac{7}{13}$

c $5x - 7 + 3x = 10x + 6 - 6x - 3$

$8x - 7 = 4x + 3$

$8x - 4x = 3 + 7$

$4x = 10$

$x = 2.5$

> **NOTE:**
> It may be easier to collect like terms on each side of the equation first.

When you are really sure that you know what you are doing you can leave out some of the steps while still showing your working. The first two answers above could be shown as follows:

a $5x - 3 = 7 + x$ **b** $2 - 4x = 9 + 9x$

$5x - x = 7 + 3$ $-4x - 9x = 9 - 2$

$4x = 10$ $-13x = 7$

$x = 2.5$ $x = -\dfrac{7}{13}$

Exercise 5.2

Solve the following equations.

1 $7x + 3 = 2x + 7$ **2** $5x - 1 = 6x + 3$

3 $4 - 8x = 6 - x$ **4** $-10 - x = 7 - 6x$

5 $15 + 2x = 17 - 6x$ **6** $23 - 3x = -7x + 11$

7 $100 + 2x = 50 - 25x$ **8** $-8x + 4 = -16x + 8$

9 $11 - x = 11 + x$ **10** $12a + 6 = 6a - 17$

11 $7x + 3 - 5x + 2 = 6x$ **12** $-8a - 1 + 3a = 7a - 6 + 5a - 3$

13 $-11 - 12y + 10 + 10y = 6y + 7 - 9y$ **14** $10 + 3b - 5 = 12 + b - 3b$

> **NOTE:**
> In question 9 zero divided or multiplied by anything is still zero.

> **NOTE:**
> The variable does not have to be x.

The next type of equation you may have to solve involves brackets, but otherwise is no more difficult. The first thing to do is to multiply out the brackets and then proceed as above.

Example 3

Solve the following equations.

a $7(x - 3) = 3(x + 7)$ **b** $2(x + 3) = -5(2x - 1)$

c $9(3x - 1) - 6(2x - 1) = 5(3 + 5x)$

Answer 3

a $7(x - 3) = 3(x + 7)$ **b** $2(x + 3) = -5(2x - 1)$

$\quad 7x - 21 = 3x + 21$ $\quad 2x + 6 = -10x + 5$

$\quad 7x - 3x = 21 + 21$ $\quad 2x + 10x = 5 - 6$

$\qquad 4x = 42$

$\qquad x = \frac{42}{4} = \frac{21}{2} = 10\frac{1}{2}$ or 10.5 $12x = -1$

$\qquad\qquad x = -\frac{1}{12}$

> **NOTE:**
> Beware of the minus sign!

c $9(3x - 1) - 6(2x - 1) = 5(3 + 5x)$

$\quad 27x - 9 - 12x + 6 = 15 + 25x$

$\quad 27x - 12x - 25x = 15 + 9 - 6$

$\qquad\qquad -10x = 18$

$\qquad\qquad\quad x = -1.8$

Exercise 5.3

NO CALCULATOR IN THIS EXERCISE

Solve the following equations.

1 $5(x + 7) = 4(1 - x)$ **2** $3(x - 1) = 8$

3 $9(3x - 2) = 7x$ **4** $4(5 - x) = 3(2 - 3x)$

5 $-2(7 - 2x) = 7(3 + 2x)$ **6** $-3(-4x + 5) = 2(-x + 6)$

7 $10(3x + 2) - (x - 1) = -7(x + 5)$ **8** $-(3x - 2) = 6(4 + 2x)$

9 $3(x - 2) - 7(x + 1) = -2(2x + 1) - 3(x + 2)$ **10** $a - 8(7 + a) = 16(2a - 1) - 5(a + 3)$

> **NOTE:**
> In question 7 remember that $-(x - 1)$ is the same as $-1(x - 1)$.

Equations are often used to solve problems. The unknown numbers are given a letter or letters and equations are written using the given information. The equations may then be solved algebraically to find the unknown numbers.

Example 4

Alex is 2 years older than Bernard and half Callista's age. Bernard is 42 years younger than Callista. Find the ages of Alex, Bernard and Callista.

Answer 4

Let Alex be x years old.

Then Bernard is $(x - 2)$ years old, and Callista is $2x$ years old.

Since Bernard is 42 years younger than Callista, Bernard is $(2x - 42)$ years old.

We now have two expressions for Bernard's age, and both must, of course, be equal.

$$2x - 42 = x - 2 \qquad (-x + 42)$$
$$2x - x = -2 + 42$$
$$x = 40$$

So, Alex is 40, Bernard is 38 and Callista is 80 years old.

You will find more examples of writing and using equations throughout the book.

Exercise 5.4

NO CALCULATOR IN THIS EXERCISE

Solve the following.

1 $3x = -10$

2 $15 = 5x$

3 $4 = 2x - 3$

4 $11 - 9x = 7x + 23$

5 $7x = 18 - x$

6 $6(a - 5) = 7(a + 2)$

7 $-3(y + 2) = 4(y - 1)$

8 $6(b - 3) + 2(b + 1) = 3(b - 5)$

9 $5x - 3 = 2x$

10 $16x - 10 + 2x = 18x - 12 - 3x$

11 $4(c - 5) - 3(c - 1) = 2(c + 1)$

12 $-(x - 1) + 2(x + 1) = 5$

13 $2(3x - 5) = 5(x - 2)$

14 $-(x + 1) = 2(-x - 1)$

15 $21x - 3 = 4$

16 A triangle has two sides each of length $3x$ centimetres, and one of length $(2x + 5)$ centimetres. The perimeter (sum of all the sides) of the triangle is 33 centimetres.
   a Form an equation in x.
   b Solve your equation.
   c Hence write down the lengths of the sides of the triangle.

17 Tomas has a pencil case containing only red, blue and green pencils. There are twice as many red pencils as blue pencils and two more red pencils than green pencils. There are 23 pencils altogether in the pencil case.
   Let the number of red pencils be x.
   a Write down expressions for the number of blue pencils and the number of green pencils in terms of x.
   b Form an equation in x.
   c Solve the equation.
   d Hence write down the number of each colour of pencil.

18 An examination paper is to have 20 questions altogether. It has to cover algebra, shape and graphs.

   There will be 4 more questions on algebra than on graphs, and twice as many questions on shape as on graphs.
   a Let the number of questions on graphs be x.
         Write down expressions for the numbers of questions on algebra and shape in terms of x.
   b Form an equation in x.
   c Solve the equation to find x.
   d How many questions will there be on algebra?

19 The sum of three consecutive numbers is 114.
   Let the first of the numbers be x.
   Form an equation in x and solve it to find the three numbers.

20 The sum of three consecutive odd numbers is 135.
   Find the three numbers.

5.4 Rearranging or Transforming Formulae

Key terms

The **subject** of a formula is the quantity the formula is designed to find; for example, in $s = ut + \frac{1}{2}at^2$, s is the subject.

Transforming a formula means rearranging it to change the subject of the formula.

We have already met some formulae. The formula below is used to find the speed of an object such as a car (v) when it was initially travelling at a certain speed (u) and then accelerated (a) for a certain time (t). *We will assume that the units for speed, acceleration and time are correct so that we do not have to worry about them.*

The formula is $v = u + at$, which we could read as 'the final speed of the car is equal to its initial speed plus the acceleration multiplied by the time for which the car has been accelerating'.

The formula is arranged so that it is easy to find v. We say that v is the **subject** of the formula.

For example, if $u = 10$, $a = 2$ and $t = 4$,

$$\text{using } v = u + at$$
$$v = 10 + 2 \times 4$$
$$v = 10 + 8$$
$$v = 18$$

But suppose we wanted to find, say, u? The best way is to *rearrange* (or **transform**) the formula so that u is the subject. This means getting u on its own.

It can be helpful to underline the variable that is to become the subject of the formula.

$$v = \underline{u} + at$$

Then the first step could be to write the equation the other way round.

$$\underline{u} + at = v$$

Then, just as in the solution of equations, we do the same thing to both sides of the formula, in this case take away at

$$\underline{u} = v - at \qquad (-at)$$

and this is the answer.

Now we can find u, given $v = 20$, $a = 10$ and $t = 0.5$:

$$u = v - at$$
$$u = 20 - 10 \times 0.5$$
$$u = 20 - 5$$
$$u = 15$$

This was an easy rearrangement, but suppose we were asked to make a the subject of the formula. We will work through the method at the same time as solving a similar equation with numbers instead of letters.

$8 = 2 + 3a$	compare with	$v = u + at$
$3a + 2 = 8$		$u + at = v$ (turning round)
$3a = 8 - 2$ (-2)		$at = v - u$ $(-u)$

At this stage we must divide both sides by t to leave the a on the left-hand side. We must divide the whole of the right-hand side by t, so it is safest to put brackets round the right-hand side. This is equivalent to working out the numbers $(8 - 2)$ in the example.

$3a = 6$	$\underline{a}t = (v - u)$

$$a = \frac{6}{3} \qquad\qquad a = \frac{(v-u)}{t}$$

The formula has been rearranged to make a the subject.

Now we can find a given that $v = 32$, $u = 14$ and $t = 4$:

$$a = \frac{(v-u)}{t}$$
$$a = \frac{32-14}{4}$$
$$a = \frac{18}{4}$$
$$a = 4.5$$

In these examples we have been using mainly whole numbers or simple fractions, but if we have to use numbers that require a calculator, then we should give the answer rounded, probably to 3 significant figures.

> **Example 5**
> Solve the equations and rearrange the corresponding formulae to find a in each case.
>
> **a** **i** $2a + 3 = 17$ **ii** $2a + b = c$
>
> **b** **i** $7 = \frac{a}{5}$ **ii** $x = \frac{a}{b}$
>
> **c** **i** $14 = \frac{28}{a}$ **ii** $p = \frac{q}{a}$
>
> **d** **i** $5(a-1) = 3(a+1)$ **ii** $b(a-c) = d(a+1)$
>
> **Answer 5**
>
> **a** **i** $2a + 3 = 17$ **ii** $2a + b = c$
> $\quad 2a = 17 - 3 \qquad\qquad 2a = c - b$
> $\quad 2a = 14 \qquad\qquad\quad 2a = (c-b)$
> $\quad\;\; a = 7 \qquad\qquad\qquad a = \frac{(c-b)}{2}$
>
> **b** **i** $7 = \frac{a}{5}$ **ii** $x = \frac{a}{b}$
> $\quad \frac{a}{5} = 7 \qquad\qquad\qquad \frac{a}{b} = x$
> $\quad a = 7 \times 5 \qquad\qquad a = x \times b$
> $\quad a = 35 \qquad\qquad\quad a = bx$
>
> **c** **i** $14 = \frac{28}{a}$ **ii** $p = \frac{q}{a}$ (× a both sides)
> $\quad 14 \times a = 28 \qquad\qquad p \times a = q$
> $\quad a = \frac{28}{14} \qquad\qquad\quad a = \frac{q}{p}$
> $\quad a = 2$
>
> **d** **i** $5(a-1) = 3(a+1)$ **ii** $b(a-c) = d(a+1)$
> $\quad 5a - 5 = 3a + 3 \qquad\quad ab - bc = ad + d$
> $\quad 5a - 3a = 3 + 5 \qquad\quad ab - ad = d + bc$ (factorise out a)
> $\quad 2a = 8 \qquad\qquad\qquad a(b-d) = (d+bc)$
> $\quad a = \frac{8}{2} \qquad\qquad\qquad\quad a = \frac{(d+bc)}{(b-d)}$
> $\quad a = 4$

NOTE:
In question **d ii** the variable appears twice, and terms containing it must be collected first.

The next exercise provides some practice in rearranging formulae by comparing with simple equations.

Exercise 5.5

NO CALCULATOR IN THIS EXERCISE

Solve the equations and rearrange the corresponding formulae to make x the subject.

1 a $x + 2 = 5$ **b** $x + b = d$

2 a $\frac{x}{3} = 6$ **b** $\frac{x}{y} = z$

3 a $2x - 5 = 7$ **b** $ax - b = c$

4 a $2x + 4x = 9$ **b** $ax + bx = c$

5 a $4x - 2 = x$ **b** $ax - 2 = bx$

6 a $3 + x = 4x$ **b** $3 + x = ax$

7 a $5 + 9x = x - 7$ **b** $a + bx = xc$

8 a $\frac{1}{3} = \frac{2}{x}$ **b** $\frac{1}{a} = \frac{b}{x}$

9 a $7 = \frac{15}{x}$ **b** $y = \frac{3}{x}$

10 a $\frac{1}{2}x = 10$ **b** $\frac{1}{a}x = b$

NOTE:
Factorise first in question **4 b**

As was mentioned earlier, another way to look at rearranging simple formulae is to use number machines. The following examples show both methods.

Example 6

a Given $S = \frac{1}{2}n(a + l)$, **without using your calculator**,

  i   find S when $n = 10$, $a = 5$ and $l = 15$;

  ii   make a the subject of the formula;

  iii   find a when $S = 100$, $n = 8$ and $l = 23$.

b Given $t = 2\pi\sqrt{\dfrac{l}{g}}$, **using your calculator**,

  i   find t when $l = 15$ and $g = 9.8$, giving your answer correct to 3 significant figures;

  ii   make l the subject;

  iii   find l when $t = 5$ and $g = 9.8$, giving your answer correct to 3 significant figures.

Answer 6

a $S = \frac{1}{2}n(a + l)$

  i $S = \frac{1}{2} \times 10 \times (5 + 15)$

      $S = 100$

  ii $S = \frac{1}{2}n(a + l)$

      $\frac{1}{2}n(a + l) = S$

        $n(a + l) = 2S$

           $a + l = \frac{2S}{n}$

             $a = \frac{2S}{n} - l$

  iii $a = \frac{2 \times 100}{8} - 23$

       $a = 2$

An alternative answer to part (ii):
Rearranging the formula using a number machine (see Figure 5.4). Always start by inputting the letter you want to make the new subject.

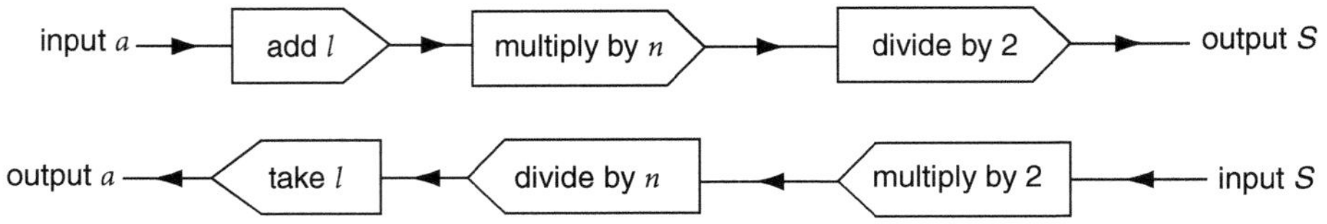

input a → add l → multiply by n → divide by 2 → output S

output a ← take l ← divide by n ← multiply by 2 ← input S

Figure 5.4 Using a number machine

Result: $a = \dfrac{2S}{n} - l$

> **NOTE:**
> The number machine method only works when the new subject appears only once.

> **NOTE:**
> Rearranging this formula in a slightly different order can lead to an answer that at first appears to be different.
> $$n(a + l) = 2S$$
> $$na + nl = 2S$$
> $$na = 2S - nl$$
> $$a = \dfrac{2S - nl}{n}$$
> In fact this is the same as before, but expressed differently.

b $\quad t = 2\pi\sqrt{\dfrac{l}{g}}$

  i $\quad t = 2 \times \pi \times \sqrt{\dfrac{15}{9.8}}$

     $t = 7.77$

  ii $\quad t = 2\pi\sqrt{\dfrac{l}{g}}$

     $2\pi\sqrt{\dfrac{l}{g}} = t$

     $\sqrt{\dfrac{l}{g}} = \dfrac{t}{2\pi}$

     $\dfrac{l}{g} = \left(\dfrac{t}{2\pi}\right)^2$

     $l = \left(\dfrac{t}{2\pi}\right)^2 \times g$

> **NOTE:**
> Remember that squaring is the inverse of (undoes) finding the square root.

  iii $\quad l = \left(\dfrac{5}{2\pi}\right)^2 \times 9.8$

      $l = 6.21$

An alternative answer for part (ii):

Number machine method for rearrangement (see figure 5.5).

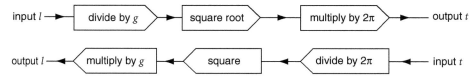

input l → divide by g → square root → multiply by 2π → output t

output l ← multiply by g ← square ← divide by 2π ← input t

Figure 5.5 Using a number machine

Result: $l = \left(\dfrac{t}{2\pi}\right)^2 \times g$

Exercise 5.6

In each of the formulae in questions 1 to 10 make the letters written in **bold** the subject of the formula.

1 $F = \dfrac{Gm\mathbf{M}}{d^2}$

2 $F = \dfrac{G\mathbf{m}M}{d^2}$

3 $u = a + (n-1)\mathbf{d}$

4 $u = a + (\mathbf{n} - 1)d$

5 $c = \dfrac{\mathbf{a}}{h}$

6 $c = \dfrac{a}{\mathbf{h}}$

7 $s = \dfrac{\mathbf{d}}{t}$

8 $s = \dfrac{d}{\mathbf{t}}$

9 $P = \dfrac{F}{\mathbf{A}}$

10 $F = \dfrac{9}{5}\mathbf{C} + 32$

11 $S = ut + \dfrac{1}{2}at^2$ Show that $a = \dfrac{2(s - ut)}{t^2}$.

12 $\dfrac{a}{b} = \dfrac{c}{d}$. Make:

    a a **b** c **c** b **d** d the subject.

13 $2y + 3x = 5$

    a Make y the subject of the formula.   **b** Find y when $x = 6$.

14 $A = \pi r^2$

    a Make r the subject of the formula.

    b **Using your calculator** find r when $A = 20$, giving your answer to 3 significant figures.

15 $I = \dfrac{b}{c}$

    a Find I when $b = 5$ and $c = 3$.

    b Rearrange the formula, and **without using your calculator** find c when $I = 1.5$ and $b = 20$.

16 $A = \dfrac{1}{2}(a + b) \times h$

    a Make h the subject of the formula.

    b **Without using your calculator** find h when $A = 15$, $a = 12$ and $b = 9$.

5.5 Sequences

Key term

A **sequence** is a list of numbers or terms which vary according to some rule. Each term is related to the previous term, or to its place in the sequence.

Sequences are patterns of numbers that follow some rule so that, once the rule is known, any member of the sequence may be calculated.

Each member of the sequence is called a **term**, and has its own place in the sequence.

For example, think of the sequence of square numbers. The rule would be 'square each member of the set of counting numbers' and the terms of the sequence would be

$$1, 4, 9, 16, 25, 36, \ldots$$

As usual, the dots show that the sequence goes on and on.

In this sequence the *first* term is 1, the *second* term is 4, the *third* term is 9 and so on.

Can you see that the *ninth* term would be 81?

It can help to arrange the sequence vertically, as in Table 5.1.

Term number	Term	Calculation
1	1	1^2
2	4	2^2
3	9	3^2
4	16	4^2
5	25	5^2
6	36	6^2
7	49	7^2
8	64	8^2
9	81	9^2

Table 5.1 Sequence of squares

We now think about a general term. We will call it term number n or the nth term (see Table 5.2).

Term number	Term	Calculation
n	n^2	n^2

Table 5.2 nth term of sequence of squares

The formula for this sequence is: **nth term** $= n^2$. Using this formula you can find any term in the sequence.

Questions about sequences will give you the start of a sequence, probably ask you to find the next term or two, and then ask you to find the formula for the nth term.

The questions will often start by giving you a set of diagrams from which you can find the sequence of numbers.

These questions on sequences can be treated like puzzles. You think of a possible formula, test it, and adjust it until you get it right. The sequences themselves provide the clues you need.

Key term

The **nth term** in a sequence provides the rule for working out every term in the sequence, for example if the nth term $= 3n + 1$ then the *second* term is $3 \times 2 + 1 = 7$.

Finding the Clues

One way to find a formula for the nth term is to write down the differences between successive terms (how much you need to add to or subtract from a term to get the next term in the sequence).

Take the sequence: 5, 8, 11, 14, 17, 20, 23, …

Write it in a vertical table, as in Table 5.3.

Term number	Term	Difference
1	5	
		+3
2	8	
		+3
3	11	
		+3
4	14	
		+3

Term number	Term	Difference
5	17	
		+3
6	20	
		+3
7	23	

Table 5.3 Term differences

For this sequence the difference between each term is a constant (+3).

This means that the formula for the nth term is based on the three times table, or $3n$.

This is the basis for the formula, but you now need to test one or two terms because you need to add another number to obtain the correct starting point. (The three times table would normally start with 3.)

Using the formula $3n$:

when $n = 1$ (the first term) the term would be $3 \times 1 = 3$, but it is actually 5.

when $n = 2$ (the second term) the term would be $3 \times 2 = 6$, but it is 8.

We have to add 2 each time to make the correct sequence.

The nth term is $3n + 2$.

Check by calculating the 7th term.

The 7th term $= 3 \times 7 + 2 = 21 + 2 = 23$, which is correct, so we have found the correct formula.

Sometimes you might have to find a second set of differences before they become constant. This changes the form of the formula.

Look at the sequence: 4, 7, 12, 19, 28, 39, 52, ..., and look at the differences shown in Table 5.4.

Term number	Term	First difference	Second difference
1	4		
		+3	
2	7		+2
		+5	
3	12		+2
		+7	
4	19		+2
		+9	
5	28		+2
		+11	
6	39		+2
		+13	
7	52		

Table 5.4 Second differences

The differences have settled down and become constant in the second column.

This means that the formula is based on n^2.

Testing the first two terms:

$$1^2 = 1, \text{ but the term is } 4$$
$$2^2 = 4, \text{ but the term is } 7$$

We need to add 3 each time to generate the correct sequence, so the formula is:

$$n\text{th term} = n^2 + 3$$

Check the 7th term: $7^2 + 3 = 49 + 3 = 52$, so the formula is correct.

As you get used to doing these questions you will probably not have to write the terms in a vertical table, but it can help at first. The examples show the setting out horizontally to save space.

Example 7

a Write down the first three terms and the 100th term when nth term $= 2n^2 - 3$.

b Find the nth term for the following sequences:

   i $-4, 1, 6, 11, 16, 21, 26, \ldots$ **ii** $6, 9, 14, 21, 30, \ldots$

   iii $10, 9, 8, 7, 6, \ldots$

c For each of the sequences in part (b) find the 30th term.

Answer 7

a $2 \times 1^2 - 3 = -1$

      $2 \times 2^2 - 3 = 5$

      $2 \times 3^2 - 3 = 15$

      $2 \times 100^2 - 3 = 19\,997$

b **i**

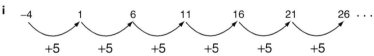

        formula is based on $5n$

        first term: $-4 = 5 \times 1 - 9$

        nth term $= 5n - 9$

   ii

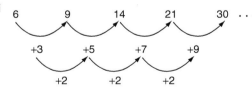

        formula is based on n^2

        first term: $6 = 1^2 + 5$

        nth term $= n^2 + 5$

   iii

        formula is based on $-1n$ (or just $-n$)

        first term: $10 = -1 + 11$

        nth term $= -n + 11$

c **i**   30th term $= 5 \times 30 - 9 = 141$ **ii**   30th term $= 30^2 + 5 = 905$

   iii   30th term $= -30 + 11 = -19$

Exercise 5.7

NO CALCULATOR IN THIS EXERCISE

1 4, 5, 6, 7, …

For the sequence shown above find:

a the 50th term, **b** the nth term.

2 7, 8, 9, 10, …

Find: **a** the 50th term, **b** the nth term.

3 −6, −3, 0, 3, 6, 9, …

Find: **a** the next two terms, **b** the nth term, **c** the 103rd term.

4 16, 25, 36, 49, …

Find: **a** the next two terms, **b** the nth term, **c** the 55th term.

5 3, 6, 11, 18, 27, 38, …

Find: **a** the next two terms, **b** the nth term, **c** the 19th term.

6

shape number	1	2	3	4	5	6
			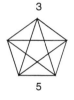			
number of sides	3	4	5	6	7	……..
number of diagonals	0	2	5	9	……..	……..

a Copy the diagram above and fill in the blank spaces.
b How many **sides** would there be in the 50th shape?
c Find the nth term for the sides.

The nth term for the diagonals is given by: nth term $= \dfrac{n^2 + n - 2}{2}$

d Find the number of diagonals in the 50th shape.

5.6 Simultaneous Equations

We have solved equations with one variable (usually x), and now need to study equations with two variables, for example, $y = 2x + 3$.

This equation is called a ***linear equation*** for reasons you will see in a later chapter. There is not just one value of x which will satisfy this equation because the value of y needs to be taken into account as well.

We can usually find pairs of values for x and y which satisfy the equation.

Suppose we make $x = 4$?

Then $y = 2x + 3$
becomes $y = 2 \times 4 + 3$
$y = 8 + 3$
$y = 11$

> **Key term**
>
> A **linear equation** is an equation in two variables which will produce a straight line when it is drawn on a graph (see Chapter 7), for example $y = 2x - 1$.

and we can say that $x = 4$ and $y = 11$ satisfy the equation, or make it true.

These values can be written as a pair of numbers in brackets: (4, 11).

Notice that the x value is always written first.

We can find an infinite number of solutions to the equation, all of them pairs of values for x and y.

Another example, suppose $x = 100$?

$$y = 2x + 3$$
$$y = 2 \times 100 + 3$$
$$y = 203$$

So (100, 203) is also a solution to the equation.

We will pick a few solutions to the equation, and you should check if they are correct.

$$y = 2x + 3$$

Some solutions: (4, 11), (1, 5), (−1, 1), (0, 3), (5, 13), (100, 203).

Looking at another equation:

$$y = 3x − 2$$

and some of its solutions, choosing the same values of x to try:

$$(4, 10), (1, 1), (−1, −5), (0, −2), (5, 13), (100, 298)$$

Comparing the two lists you should see that one solution, (5, 13), appears in both lists.

You will see in a later chapter that for any pair of linear equations there will be only one solution which satisfies them both.

Solving a pair of linear equations to find the solution which belongs to them both is called solving them *simultaneously*. The two equations are called **simultaneous equations**.

Sometimes two equations have no common solution, but all the simultaneous equations you will be given to solve will have a solution that is true for both of them.

We need to find a method for solving simultaneous equations because just trying solutions might take forever before we find the correct pair of values.

The method we will use is called ***elimination*** because we put the two equations together in a way which *eliminates* one of the variables, either x or y, to give an equation with only one variable, which we can solve.

For example, consider the pair of equations

$$y + 2x = 7$$
and
$$y + \ x = 4.$$

If we take the second equation away from the first we will eliminate the y terms.

$$y + 2x = 7$$
$$\underline{y + x = 4}\ \text{subtract}$$
$$0 + x = 3$$
$$x = 3$$

Now we know x we can substitute $x = 3$ into either of the original equations.

Key terms

Simultaneous equations are two equations, each with two variables, which have a solution which satisfies both equations. When drawn on a graph the lines cross at this solution.

Elimination is a method for finding the solution which satisfies both simultaneous equations.

Substituting $x = 3$ in the first equation:

$$y + 2 \times 3 = 7$$
$$y + 6 = 7$$
$$y = 1$$

We would get the same result if we substituted $x = 3$ into the second equation.

Try it yourself to check this.

The solution for these two equations is (3, 1).

You may have to add or subtract the two equations as the example shows.

Example 8
In each case solve the given pairs of equations simultaneously.

a $y - x = 7$ **b** $3y + 2x = 6$
     $2y + x = 5$ $-3y - x = 3$

Answer 8

a $y - x = 7$
     $\underline{2y + x = 5}$ add
     $3y + 0 = 12$
         $y = 12 \div 3$
         $y = 4$

> **NOTE:**
> In this case adding the two equations will eliminate x because $-x + +x = 0$.

Substituting $y = 4$ into the first equation
     $4 - x = 7$ (-4)
       $-x = 3$ $(\times -1)$
         $x = -3$

Solution for these two equations is (−3, 4).

b $3y + 2x = 6$
     $\underline{-3y - x = 3}$ add
     $0 + x = 9$

> **NOTE:**
> Adding the two equations will eliminate the $3y$ terms.

Substituting $x = 9$ into the first equation
     $3y + 18 = 6$ (-18)
        $3y = -12$
         $y = -4$ $(\div 3)$
Solution is (9, −4)

Now do this exercise, but remember that you are trying to eliminate x or y. If, for example, you add the equations when you should have subtracted then you will end up with another equation in both x and y, which will get you nowhere. If this happens try again!

Exercise 5.8   **NO CALCULATOR IN THIS EXERCISE**

Solve these pairs of simultaneous equations.

1 $x + 5y = 6$ **2** $3x + y = 8$
    $x + 3y = 2$ $2x - y = 2$

3 $y + 4x = 1$ **4** $5y + 7x = 8$
    $3y - 4x = 3$ $5y + 4x = 2$

The two equations may not always have a term that can be eliminated straight away, and you may have to multiply one of them by a number first to get two terms that are same.

For example, if we were asked to solve:

$$y + 3x = 11$$
$$2y + x = 2$$

we could multiply the first equation all through by 2 first so that both equations have the term $2y$ in them. We could then subtract to eliminate the $2y$ terms, leaving an equation in x only.

The following method makes your working very clear and easy to follow.

$$y + 3x = 11 \xrightarrow{\times 2} 2y + 6x = 22 \text{ subtract}$$
$$2y + x = 2 \longrightarrow \frac{2y + x = 2}{0 + 5x = 20}$$
$$x = 4$$

Substitute $x = 4$ into the first equation.

$$y + 3 \times 4 = 11$$
$$y = -1$$

Solution is $(4, -1)$.

It is easier to add the two equations than subtract because the chances of making a mistake with the signs are less. If the two terms you are trying to eliminate have the same sign there is something you can do to help prevent sign errors.

For example, look at these two equations:

$$y + 3x = 8$$
$$3y - 2x = 2$$

Set out the working as above, and instead of subtracting, multiply the whole of the second equation by -1 so that you can add. This is easy because all it means is that you change *every* sign in the second equation.

$$y + 3x = 8 \xrightarrow{\times 3} 3y + 9x = 24 \longrightarrow 3y + 9x = 24$$
$$3y - 2x = 2 \longrightarrow 3y - 2x = 2 \xrightarrow{\times -1} \frac{-3y + 2x = -2}{0 + 11x = 22} \text{ add}$$
$$x = 2$$

Substituting in the first equation gives $y = 2$, so the solution is $(2, 2)$.

Points to watch out for:

- Remember that the aim is to eliminate one of the terms from each equation.
- Look for terms in either x or y which have the same coefficients in each equation.
- If you need to multiply one equation by a number to equalise the coefficients then remember to multiply the *whole equation* (including the right-hand side).
- If the signs of the terms that you want to eliminate are the *same*, it is easier to multiply one equation by -1 and *add* the equations.
- If you multiply one equation through by -1, just change *every* sign (including the right-hand side) in that equation.
- If the signs of the two terms you need to eliminate are *different* you just add the two equations.

Example 9

Solve each pair of equations simultaneously.

a $7x - 3y = 11$ b $2y + x = 5$

  $x + y = -3$ $2x + y = 7$

Answer 9

a

$$7x - 3y = 11 \longrightarrow \quad 7x - 3y = 11$$

$$x + y = -3 \xrightarrow{\times 3} \quad \frac{3x + 3y = -9}{10x \quad\; = 2}$$

$$x = \frac{1}{5}$$

Substitute $x = \frac{1}{5}$ in the second equation:

$$\frac{1}{5} + y = -3$$

$$y = -3 - \frac{1}{5}$$

$$y = \frac{-16}{5} \qquad\qquad \text{Answer: } \left(\frac{1}{5}, \frac{-16}{5}\right)$$

b $2y + x = 5$

 $2x + y = 7$

Rearrange the first equation

$$x + 2y = 5 \xrightarrow{\times 2} \quad 2x + 4y = 10 \longrightarrow \quad 2x + 4y = 10$$

$$2x + y = 7 \longrightarrow \qquad 2x + y = 7 \xrightarrow{\times -1} \frac{-2x - y = -7}{3y = \; 3} \text{ add}$$

$$y = \; 1$$

Substitute $y = 1$ in the first equation:

$$x + 2 \times 1 = 5$$

$$x = 3 \qquad\qquad \text{Answer: } (3, 1)$$

Exercise 5.9   **NO CALCULATOR IN THIS EXERCISE**

Solve each pair of equations simultaneously.

1 $-y + x = 15$ **2** $y = 6x - 10$ **3** $16x = 3y - 5$ **4** $5x + 6y = 7$

 $2y + 3x = 5$ $3y = x + 4$ $4x = y - 1$ $x + 2y = 1$

5 $2x + y = 5$ **6** $2p - q = 4$ **7** $3x + y = -10$ **8** $3x + 2y = 10$

 $x + 2y = 4$ $p - 3q = 2$ $x + 2y = -5$ $5x - 4y = 2$

9 $5x - 2y = 17$ **10** $7x - 2y + 5 = 0$

 $3x + 4y = 5$ $3x - 8y + 45 = 0$

Simultaneous equations may be used to solve problems with unknown numbers. A letter is assigned to each number that is unknown. The information available is used to write down equations using these letters. The equations are then solved simultaneously to find these unknown numbers.

NOTE:

There must be at least as many independent equations as there are unknown numbers. In other words, if there are two unknowns, such as x and y, there must be at least two different bits of information linking x and y. If you work through the next example you will see what is meant by independent equations.

Example 10

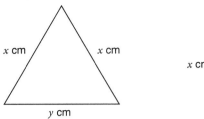
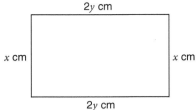

Figure 5.6 Perimeters

Figure 5.6 shows a triangle and a rectangle with sides of unknown lengths.

The perimeter of the triangle is 10 centimetres, and the perimeter of the rectangle is 28 centimetres.

a Write down two independent equations in x and y using the above two separate pieces of information.

b Solve these two equations simultaneously to find x and y.

c Write down the lengths of the sides of the rectangle.

Answer 10

a $2x + y = 10$ (from the triangle)

   $2x + 4y = 28$ (from the rectangle)

> **NOTE:**
> These two equations are derived from different pieces of information, and so are independent. You *could* write the equation for the rectangle as $x + 2y = 14$ (that is, two of the sides added together are equal to half the perimeter), which is a perfectly true statement. It would give the correct answer when used with the equation for the perimeter of the triangle. However, $x + 2y = 14$ and $2x + 4y = 28$ are not independent so you could not obtain any information about x and y by trying to solve these two simultaneously.

b $2x + y = 10$

   $\underline{2x + 4y = 28}$ subtract

   $-3y = -18$ $(\div -3)$

   $y = 6$

   substitute $y = 6$ into the first equation:

   $2x + 6 = 10$ (-6)

   $2x = 10 - 6$

   $2x = 4$ $(\div 2)$

   $x = 2$

   $x = 2$ and $y = 6$

c The rectangle has sides 2 centimetres and 12 centimetres.

Exercise 5.10   NO CALCULATOR IN THIS EXERCISE

Mixed exercise

1 Solve these equations:

   a $3x = x + 2$ **b** $4x - 5 = 2x - 8$ **c** $6 = 5(2x + 3)$

   d $7x + 6 - 2x = 9x - 2$ **e** $3(x - 5) = 2(4 - 3x)$ **f** $5(x - 3) = -15x$

g $2x + 3 = x - 3$ **h** $3x - 2(x + 1) = 2(x - 1)$

i $4a + 3(3 - a) = 2(a + 1) - (2a - 1)$

j $\frac{b}{2} = 4b - 7$

2 Rearrange these formulae to make the letters in **bold** the subject.

a $A = \pi \boldsymbol{r}^2$ **b** $V = \frac{1}{2}b\boldsymbol{h}l$ **c** $V = \frac{d}{\boldsymbol{t}}$ **d** $A = \frac{1}{2}(a + b)\boldsymbol{l}$

e $D = \frac{M}{\boldsymbol{V}}$ **f** $a^2 = \boldsymbol{b}^2 + c^2$ **g** $p = \frac{q + r}{\boldsymbol{s}}$ **h** $A = B(\boldsymbol{x} + c)$

i $\frac{x}{a} - \boldsymbol{b} = c$ **j** $3a^2 + \boldsymbol{x}^2 = b^2$ **k** $V = a\boldsymbol{h}$ **l** $a = \frac{b + c}{\boldsymbol{d}}$

m $A = \frac{1}{2}(\boldsymbol{a} + b)l$

3 **a** Copy the pattern below, and draw the next shape.

shape number

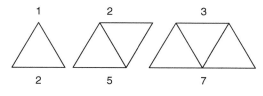 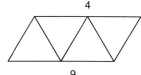

number of lines   2   5   7   9

b Find the nth term for the number of lines.

c Find the number of lines in the 99th shape.

4 Find the nth term for the following sequences.

a   2   6   10   14 ...

b   −3   0   3   6 ...

c   4   2   0   −2 ...

5 Solve the following pairs of simultaneous equations.

a $y = 3x + 5$ **b** $2y + 3x = 6$ **c** $5y + 3x = 19$

    $y = -x + 1$ $y + x = 3$ $y + x = 4$

6 Yasmin thinks of two numbers. She says that the sum of the two numbers is 57, and the difference between the two numbers is 15.

a Let the numbers be x and y.

Form two equations in x and y.

b Solve the two equations simultaneously to find the two numbers that Yasmin thought of.

7

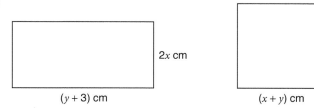

2x cm

$(y + 3)$ cm $(x + y)$ cm

The perimeter of the rectangle is 36 centimetres, and the perimeter of the square is 48 centimetres.

Use the information given to calculate the dimensions of the rectangle.

8 As we have seen in Chapter 4, the formula used to calculate simple interest is $I = PrT$ where I is the simple interest, P is the principal (or amount), r is the rate of interest (as a percentage) and T is the time (in years).

a Rearrange the formula to make P the subject.

b Copy and complete the table by calculating the missing values.

NOTE: It can be easier to make the calculation if you convert the percentage rate into a decimal first.

	I ($)	P ($)	r (%)	T (years)
i		1000	3.25	0.5
ii	75		10	2
iii	1500	2500		10
iv	66.50	100	13.3	

Exam-style questions

9 Make s the subject of the formula $p = st - q$. (0580 paper 01 Q12 June 2005)

10 Solve the equation $5x - 7 = 8$. (0580 paper 01 Q5 November 2005)

11 $b = m(a - c)$
  a Evaluate b when $m = 5$, $a = 8$ and $c = -3$.
  b Rearrange the formula to make c the subject. (4024 paper 11 Q10 June 2013)

12 a The term-to-term rule for a sequence is

  > multiply the previous term by 3 and subtract 1.

  The first three terms in this sequence are 1, 2 and 5.
  Write down the next two terms in this sequence.
  b The nth term of a second sequence is given by the expression $4n - 3$.
  Find the number in this sequence that is closest to 150.
  c The nth term of a different sequence is given by the expression $n^2 + 1$.
    i Write down the first four terms of this sequence.
    ii Hence write down an expression, in terms of n, for the nth term of the following sequence.

    $$0 \quad 3 \quad 8 \quad 15 \quad \ldots$$
    (4024 paper 11 Q18 November 2014)

13 a Solve the equations:
    i $3x - 4 = 14$
    ii $\frac{y+1}{5} = 5$
    iii $3(2z - 7) - 2(z - 3) = -9$.
  b Donna sent p postcards and q letters to her friends.
    i The total number of postcards and letters she sent was 12.
    Write down an equation in p and q.
    ii A stamp for a postcard costs 25 cents and a stamp for a letter costs 40 cents.
    She spent 375 cents on stamps altogether.
    Write down another equation in p and q.
    iii Solve these equations to find the values of p and q. (0580 paper 03 Q4 June 2008)

14 $s = \frac{n}{2}(a + b)$
  a Evaluate s when $n = 200$, $a = 3.6$ and $b = 5.7$.
  b Rearrange the formula to make b the subject. (4024 paper 11 Q12 November 2014)

15 Solve the simultaneous equations
$$3x + y = 95,$$
$$x + y = 29.$$
(4024 paper 01 Q9 June 2005)

16 $C = \frac{5}{9}(F - 32)$

    a Calculate C when $F = -4$.

    b Express F in terms of C.
(4024 paper 01 Q9 June 2005)

17 a Write down the next two terms in the sequence $20, 16\frac{1}{2}, 13, 9\frac{1}{2}, 6, \ldots$

    b Write down an expression, in terms of n, for the nth term of the sequence $1, 4, 7, 10, 13, \ldots$
(4024 paper 01 Q4 November 2004)

18 The nth term of a sequence is $\frac{4}{n^2}$.

    a Write down the first three terms of the sequence, expressing each term in its simplest form.

    b The kth term in the sequence is $\frac{1}{100}$.

       Find the value of k.
(4024 paper 1 Q21a and b June 2009)

19 Solve the simultaneous equations
$$2x - y = 16,$$
$$3x + 2y = 17.$$
(4024 paper 01 Q16 November 2007)

20 The force acting on an object during a collision is given by the formula $F = \frac{mv - mu}{t}$.

    a Given that $m = 4$, $v = 5$, $u = 3$ and $t = 0.01$, find the value of F.

    b Rearrange the formula to make m the subject.
(4024 paper 01 Q9 November 2009)

21 A series of diagrams, using three types of triangle, is shown below. The triangles are grey, white or black.

   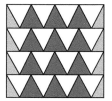

Diagram 1   Diagram 2   Diagram 3   Diagram 4

The table below shows the numbers of each type of triangle used in the diagrams.

Diagram	1	2	3	4		n
Grey triangles	2	4	6			x
White triangles	1	4	9			y
Black triangles	0	2	6			z

    a Complete the column for Diagram 4.

    b By considering the number patterns in the table, find, in terms of n, expressions for x, y and z.
(4024 paper 01 Q24 November 2007)

6 Geometry and Shape I

Learning Objectives · Syllabus sections 28, 29, 30, 31, 32, 33

In this chapter you will:
- practise drawing accurately using a ruler, compasses and a protractor
- learn facts about angles connected with triangles, parallel lines, polygons and circles
- learn about symmetry
- construct triangles accurately

- learn the properties of three-dimensional shapes and their nets
- start learning about similar and congruent shapes
- have an introduction to locus
- make simple scale drawings

6.1 Introduction

For this chapter you will need a protractor, a pair of compasses, a ruler, a pair of scissors and some tracing paper.

There is quite a lot of practical work and accurate drawing in this chapter. This is designed to help you understand the shapes and their properties and thus memorise them. You will find out for yourself many of the facts that you need to know. However, bear in mind that these are not *proofs* of the facts. For this course you do not need to know the proofs, but you do need to be able to recall the facts.

It is an essential part of your course that you have skills in using geometrical instruments. If you feel confident that you can use a protractor and a pair of compasses correctly, and you measure the lines and angles in the essential skills exercise accurately, you can go straight on to Section 6.4, 'Lines and angles'; otherwise, read Section 6.3, 'Geometric instruments'.

6.2 Essential Skills   NO CALCULATOR IN THIS EXERCISE

1   Use a protractor to measure the angles between each of these pairs of lines.

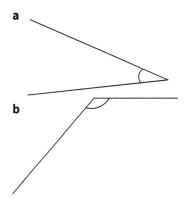

2 Use a ruler to measure these lines.

a ———————————————   **b**

6.3 Geometric Instruments

The easiest protractor to use is the circular type illustrated in Figure 6.1, as simple as possible, with angles up to 360°. With a 360° protractor you can measure angles greater than 180° without having to do a calculation.

When you use the protractor make sure that the zero lies accurately on one of the arms of the angle, and that you count round the scale which starts at zero, round to the other arm, as shown in the illustrations.

The centre of the protractor must coincide with the point of the angle if you are measuring an angle, as shown in Figure 6.1**a**. It must coincide with the end of the line on which you want to draw the angle as shown in Figure 6.1**b**. If you have any doubts about your use of the protractor check the examples carefully and make sure that you can obtain the values given in the answers.

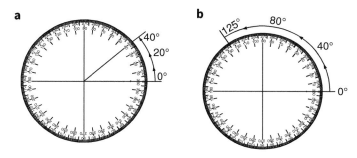

Figure 6.1 a Measuring an angle: the angle measures 40°   **b** Drawing an angle: the angle being drawn is 125°

The best pair of compasses have a small wheel in the centre which you rotate to open the compasses to the required length, and a piece of lead rather than a pencil to draw the curve. These will not slip while you are using them, which frequently happens with other types. Figure 6.2 shows an example of this type of compass, and a 180° protractor.

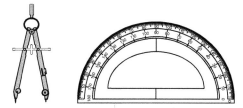

Figure 6.2 A pair of compasses and a 180° protractor

Make sure that your pencil is sharp to minimise experimental error!

Most of the diagrams in this chapter are **not** drawn to scale, so unless you are asked to measure an angle or side you will need to calculate it.

NOTE:
In questions on shape and geometry, you may be asked to *construct*, to *draw* and *measure*, or to *calculate* an answer. If the question says *calculate* you **have not answered it** if you rely on drawing and measuring. So you must answer the question as set, and particularly you must show a calculation if that is required.

6.4 Lines and Angles

Angles are measured in degrees. One degree is a complete turn divided into 360 equal parts, so 360° is a complete turn. If you stand in a room facing the door and turn round until you are facing the door again you have turned through 360°. This might sound a strange number to use when we are used to the metric system in which we might expect a complete turn to be divided into 100 or 1000 equal parts. However, 360 turns out to be a very good choice because the number 360 has so many different factors. This means that more fractions of complete turns may be written as a whole number of degrees. For example, one sixth of a complete turn is 60°, but one sixth of 100 is 16.6666666…

To start with, we must make sure that we are all talking about the same types of angles, which are illustrated in Figures 6.3–6.8.

- An angle between 0° and 90° is called an **acute angle**.
- An angle of 90° is a **right angle**.
- An angle between 90° and 180° is an **obtuse angle**.
- An angle of 180° is a **straight angle**.
- An angle between 180° and 360° is a **reflex angle**.
- An angle of 360° is a **complete turn**.

Also note:

- Angles on a straight line add up to 180°.
- Angles round a point add up to 360°.

Exercise 6.1

Measure the angles **a** to **f** shown below and check with the answers in the back of the book to make sure that you have the correct measurements.

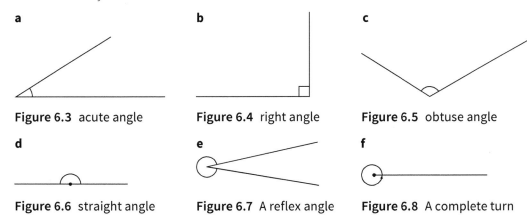

a **b** **c**

Figure 6.3 acute angle   **Figure 6.4** right angle   **Figure 6.5** obtuse angle

d **e** **f**

Figure 6.6 straight angle   **Figure 6.7** A reflex angle   **Figure 6.8** A complete turn

Angles and lines are usually given capital letters to name them in a diagram, as shown in Figure 6.9.

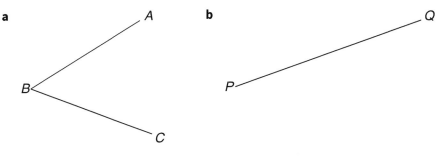

a **b**

Figure 6.9 a Angle *ABC*   **b** Line *PQ*

The angle shown in Figure 6.9a is angle ABC (or CBA). Follow the letters round so that the letter at the point of the angle is in the centre of the three letters. (In this case the centre of A<u>B</u>C is B, and the sides of the angle are the lines A<u>B</u> and <u>B</u>C.)

Notation:

NOTE:
In this chapter either symbol may be used.

- Abbreviations for angle ABC are $\angle ABC$ or $A\hat{B}C$.
- If there is **no** doubt about which angle we are referring to it may be called just $\angle B$ or $\hat{B}$.
- The line is more simply referred to as the line PQ (or QP).

The order of the letters does not matter except that, as stated above, angles must have the letter at the point of the angle in the centre of the group of three letters.

Example 1

In the triangle shown below name the angles marked x, y and z.

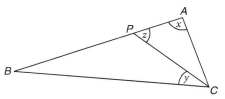

Answer 1

x is either $\angle CAB$ or $\angle CAP$ (or $C\hat{A}B$ or $C\hat{A}P$) or, because there is no doubt about which angle we are referring to, it can be called $\angle A$ (or $\hat{A}$).

y is $\angle PCB$. It cannot be called $\angle C$ because there are three angles at C ($\angle ACP$, $\angle PCB$ and $\angle ACB$).

z is $\angle APC$, (to distinguish it from $\angle BPC$).

Exercise 6.2

1 Name the angles and sides shown by small letters in the diagrams below.

a 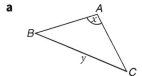 **b**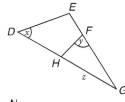

c 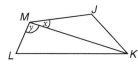 **d**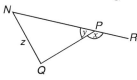

2 Measure the angles and sides named in the diagrams below.

a 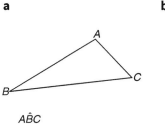 **b**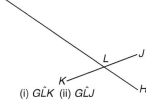

$A\hat{B}C$ (i) $G\hat{L}K$ (ii) $G\hat{L}J$

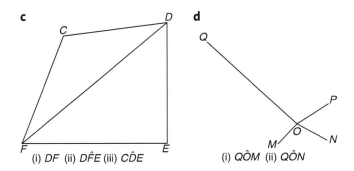

(i) *DF* (ii) *DÊE* (iii) *CD̂E*   (i) *QÔM* (ii) *QÔN*

3 For each of the angles below, state whether it is acute, obtuse, reflex or a right angle.

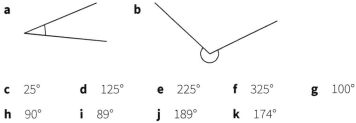

a   **b**

c 25°   **d** 125°   **e** 225°   **f** 325°   **g** 100°

h 90°   **i** 89°   **j** 189°   **k** 174°

4 Using the facts that angles on a straight line add up to 180° and angles around a point add up to 360°, find the value of *x* in each of the following diagrams.

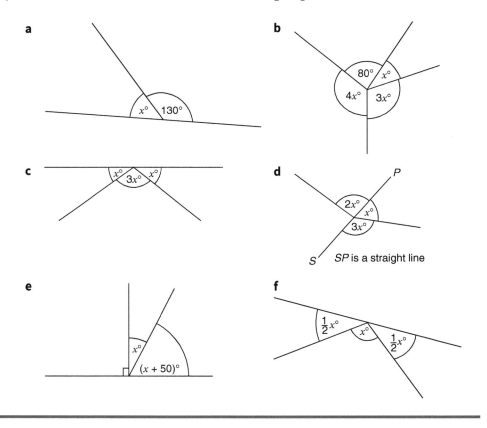

a

b

c

d   *SP* is a straight line

e

f

6.5 Pairs of Lines

A pair of lines drawn on paper can be **parallel** (they never meet), or if they are not parallel they must **intersect** at some point. This point of intersection may not be on the paper, but if the lines were **extended** they would eventually intersect somewhere.

If the lines intersect at right angles they are said to be **perpendicular** to each other.

Figures 6.10–6.13 show: parallel lines and the arrows that we use to signify that the lines are parallel; lines that are not parallel but do not intersect on the page; intersecting lines; perpendicular lines with the little square which indicates a right angle.

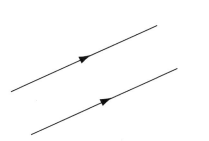

Figure 6.10 Parallel lines

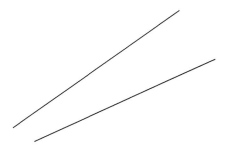

Figure 6.11 Lines that are not parallel

Key terms

Horizontal lines are parallel to the surface of the Earth.

Vertical lines are perpendicular to the surface of the Earth.

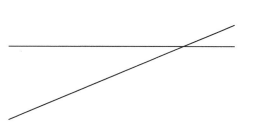

Figure 6.12 Intersecting lines

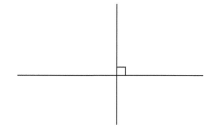

Figure 6.13 Perpendicular lines

Lines may also be **horizontal** (parallel to the surface of the earth, or to the horizon if it is not hilly), or **vertical** (at right angles, or perpendicular, to the ground).

It is usual to draw horizontal lines across the page and vertical lines up and down the page, as in Figure 6.14.

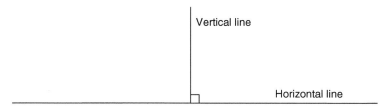

Vertical line

Horizontal line

Figure 6.14 Vertical and horizontal lines

Exercise 6.3

Use the words parallel, intersecting, perpendicular, horizontal or vertical to describe the following:

1 Railway lines.

2 An electricity pole.

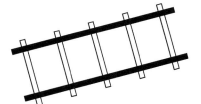

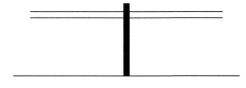

3 The side of a house.

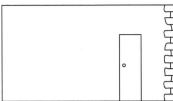

4 The top and side of a door.

5 Two edges of a pyramid.

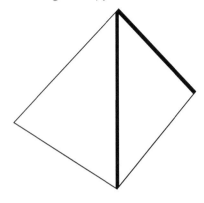

6 The two lines that make up the letter X.

7 A fence post.

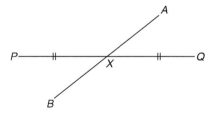

8 The rails of the fence.

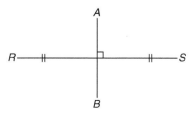

If one line divides another line into two equal parts it is called the **bisector** of the line. In Figure 6.15 the line *AB* bisects the line *PQ* at the point *X*. The two dashes on each side of *X* show that *PX* and *XQ* are equal in length.

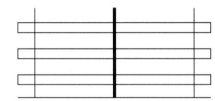

If one line divides another line into two equal parts *and* is at right angles it is called the **perpendicular bisector** of the line. This is shown in Figure 6.16 where *AB* is the perpendicular bisector of *RS*.

Figure 6.15 Bisector

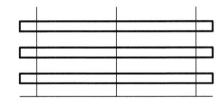

If the lines are both divided into equal parts they are the bisectors of each other, as shown in Figure 6.17 (they could also be the perpendicular bisectors of each other as shown in the second diagram). The single dashes on one of the lines show that both parts are equal in length, but are not equal to the lines with double dashes.

Figure 6.16 Perpendicular bisector

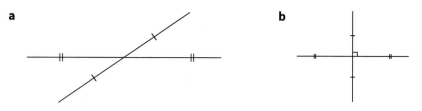

Figure 6.17 **a** Equal bisectors **b** Equal perpendicular bisectors

Investigation

The shortest distance from a point to a line

Measure the lengths of all the lines between the point *A* and the line *XY* in the diagrams in Figure 6.18.

In which diagram is the line the shortest?

What could you say about the two lines (or the angles) in the diagram you have chosen?

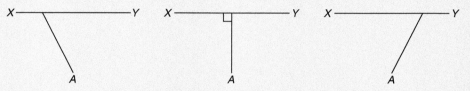

Figure 6.18 Shortest distance from a point to a line

You should find that the shortest distance from a point to a line is the perpendicular from the point to the line.

The shortest distance between two parallel lines

Measure the lengths *AB* shown in Figure 6.19.

What could you say about the line which has the shortest length? If you are to measure the distance between two lines, you have to use the shortest distance.

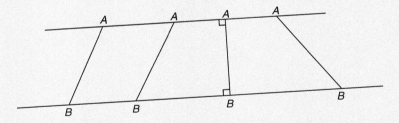

Figure 6.19 Shortest distance between two parallel lines

You should find that the shortest distance between parallel lines is along the line which is perpendicular to both of them.

6.6 Triangles

Triangles may either be:

- **scalene** (with no sides or angles equal to each other)
- **isosceles** (with two sides and two angles equal)
- **equilateral** (with all three sides equal and all three angles equal to 60°).

They may also be:

- **right-angled** (with one angle equal to 90°)
- **acute-angled** (with all three angles less than 90°)
- **obtuse-angled** (with one angle greater than 90° and less than 180°).

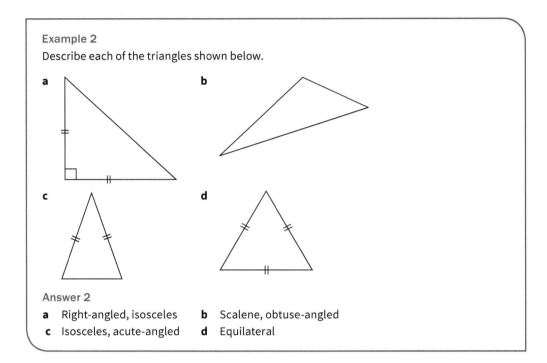

Example 2
Describe each of the triangles shown below.

a

b

c

d

Answer 2

  a Right-angled, isosceles   **b** Scalene, obtuse-angled

  c Isosceles, acute-angled   **d** Equilateral

Practical work

Sum of the angles of a triangle

1 For each of the triangles shown below measure the angles and find the sum of the angles.

a

b

c

d

2 Draw any triangle, and cut it out.

Tear off each angle as shown in Figure 6.20.

Rearrange the torn-off angles to fit on a straight line.

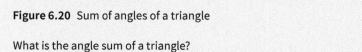

Figure 6.20 Sum of angles of a triangle

What is the angle sum of a triangle?

In each of these cases you should find that the angles add up to about 180°.

In fact, the angle sum of a triangle is 180°.

You will be asked to draw triangles accurately using either a ruler and protractor, or a ruler and compasses, or maybe all three. You will be asked to leave in your 'construction' lines to show how you have drawn the triangle. This shows your working and you will probably lose marks if you rub them out.

6.7 Methods for Constructing Triangles Accurately

Follow the constructions below to make sure that you are able to reproduce the triangles yourself.

1 In triangle ABC, $AB = 7$ cm, $\angle BAC = 30°$, $\angle CBA = 50°$.

> **NOTE:**
> Before drawing any diagram accurately make a rough sketch with the given measurements marked on it, as in Figure 6.21. It does not matter which way up you draw the triangles, but in this case it is convenient to make the given side the base of the triangle.

Rough sketch

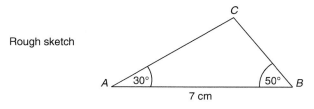

Figure 6.21 Rough sketch of required triangle

The information we have been given to draw this triangle is two angles, one at each end of a side. It is known as *angle, side, angle* and abbreviated to **asa**.

Method

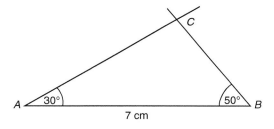

Figure 6.22 Constructing the triangle

Draw the base 7 cm long, followed by the correct angles at each end of the base. Make the arms of the angles long enough so that they cross. Do not rub out the surplus lengths, as this is part of your construction method (see Figure 6.22).

Measure AC and CB in your diagram. They should be about 5.4 cm and 3.6 cm.

2 In triangle DEF, $DE = 5$ cm, $EF = 4$ cm and $DF = 3$ cm.

This information is known as *side, side, side* and is abbreviated to **sss**.

Again, start with a rough sketch (see Figure 6.23).

Rough sketch

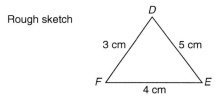

Figure 6.23 Rough sketch

Method

Draw *FE* 4 cm long. Open the compasses to 3 cm and, with the point at *F*, draw an arc above the line as shown. Repeat for the other side, with the point of the compasses at *E*, making sure that the arcs cross. Join the sides (see Figure 6.24). Do not rub out your construction lines.

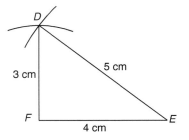

Figure 6.24 Constructed triangle

Measure your angle *DFE*. It should be about 90°.

3 In triangle *GHJ*, *GH* = 8 cm, *HJ* = 9 cm and ∠*GHJ* = 70°.

This information is *side, angle, side* and is abbreviated to **sas**. It is important to note that the angle given is *between* the two given sides (see the rough sketch in Figure 6.25). This is known as the **included angle**.

Rough sketch

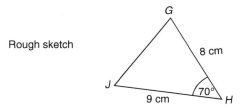

Figure 6.25 Rough sketch

This method is straightforward, and you should draw your own. Check that it is correct by measuring *GJ*. It should be about 9.8 cm.

Example 3
Try to draw each of the following triangles accurately. If it is impossible, explain why.

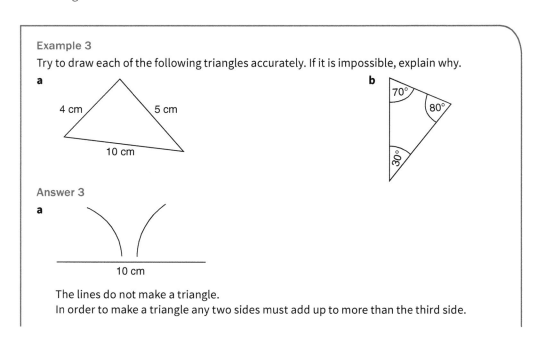

a

b

Answer 3

a

10 cm

The lines do not make a triangle.
In order to make a triangle any two sides must add up to more than the third side.

b We cannot even start on this one because there are no length measurements given, so we do not know how large to make it.

Example 4

Calculate the angles marked with letters in these triangles.

a Calculate the values of x and y and hence write down the sizes of the angles in the triangle *ABC*.

b Calculate the value of x and hence write down the sizes of the angles in triangle *DEF*.

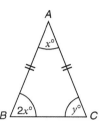

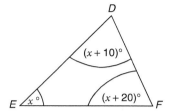

Answer 4

a $y = 2x$ (isosceles triangle)

  $x + 2x + y = 180$ (angle sum of a triangle)

so $x + 2x + 2x = 180$

     $5x = 180$ ($\div 5$)

      $x = 36$

 The angles are 36°, 72° and 72°.

b $x + (x + 10) + (x + 20) = 180$ (angle sum of a triangle)

   $3x + 30 = 180$ (-30)

     $3x = 150$ ($\div 3$)

      $x = 50$

 The angles are 50°, 60° and 70°.

Exercise 6.4

1 Try to draw accurately each of the triangles described or sketched below.

If they are impossible to draw try to describe why, and then see if you can write down some rules about the information you need to draw triangles.

In each case where you have been able to draw the triangle, (i) measure the angles or sides marked with a letter, and (ii) write down the abbreviation for the information given.

> **NOTE:**
> Calculate the third angle first.

a

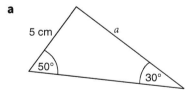

b

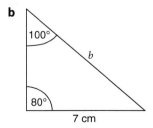

c

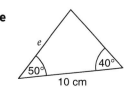

d

e

Before you carry on with this exercise, check your answers to question 1 with the answers at the back of the book.

2 Construct accurately each of these triangles. Measure the remaining sides and angles.

a Use compasses and ruler only for construction.

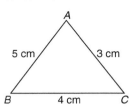

b Use compasses and ruler only for construction.

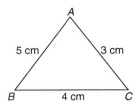

c

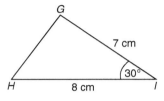

d

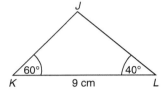

e

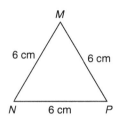

3 Find the values of the letters in the diagrams below.

a

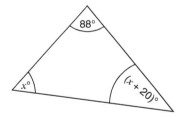

b

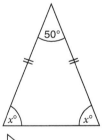

c

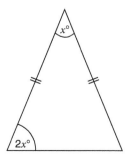

d

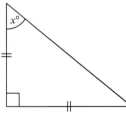

e

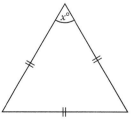

f

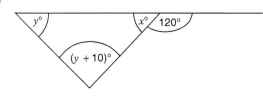

6.8 Angles in Parallel Lines

A line crossing a pair of parallel lines is called a **transversal**. You do not have to remember this name, but it makes explaining diagrams easier. A transversal produces sets of equal angles, as shown in Figure 6.26. The angles marked with a dot are all equal and the angles marked with a cross are also all equal.

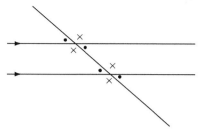

Figure 6.26 Angles made by a transversal

You *do* need to remember the names of pairs of angles in parallel lines.

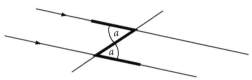

Figure 6.27 Alternate angles

The angles marked with an *a* in Figure 6.27 are called **alternate angles**. You can recognise them because they are in a Z shape, or because they are on *alternate* sides of the transversal.

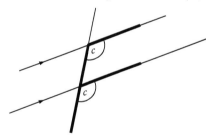

Figure 6.28 Corresponding angles

The angles marked with the letter *c* in Figure 6.28 are **corresponding angles**. They can be recognised by being in an F shape, or that they are in corresponding positions between the transversal and the parallel lines.

Finally, there are angles that are not associated with parallel lines. These are shown in Figure 6.29, marked with a *v*, and are called **vertically opposite angles**. They are recognised as angles in an X shape, or because they are opposite at the vertex of two angles made between intersecting *straight* lines.

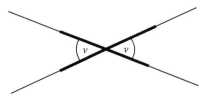

Figure 6.29 Vertically opposite angles

Of course, the two obtuse angles in the intersection are also vertically opposite and equal.

Example 5

Find the sizes, in degrees, of the angles marked with letters in the diagram. Give reasons for your answers.

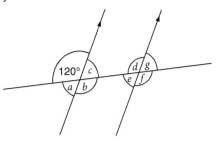

Answer 5

$a = 60°$ (angles on a straight line add up to 180°)
$b = 120°$ (either vertically opposite to the given angle, or angles on a straight line with a)
$c = 60°$ (vertically opposite to a)
$d = 120°$ (b and d are alternate angles, or d is corresponding with the given angle)
$e = 60°$ (c and e are alternate angles, or a and e are corresponding angles)
$f = 120°$ (either vertically opposite to d or corresponding to b)
$g = 60°$ (either vertically opposite to e or corresponding to c)

As you can see, most angles made with parallel lines are the same! There is often more than one way to reach the answer.

Exercise 6.5

Find the sizes, in degrees, of the angles marked with letters.

1

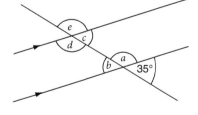

2

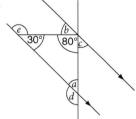

3

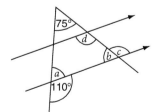

4

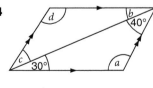

Key terms

A shape has **line symmetry** if it fits exactly on itself when it is folded along its **line of symmetry**.

6.9 Symmetry

Line Symmetry

A shape is said to have **line symmetry** if you can fold it over along a line so that one side fits exactly on top of the other. The line along which you fold the shape is called an **axis** or **line**

of symmetry. In this case either *axis* (plural *axes*) or *line* of symmetry can be used. There may be more than one axis of symmetry. In the shapes shown below the axes of symmetry are marked with dotted lines, and the number of axes of symmetry is given for each shape.

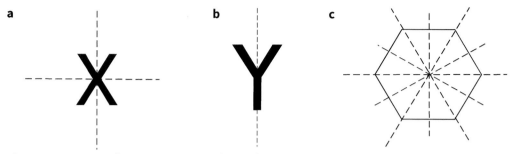

Figure 6.30 Axes of symmetry, **a** Two lines of symmetry **b** One line of symmetry **c** Six lines of symmetry

Example 6
Copy the diagrams and draw the axes (if any) of symmetry. State the number of axes or lines of symmetry in each case.

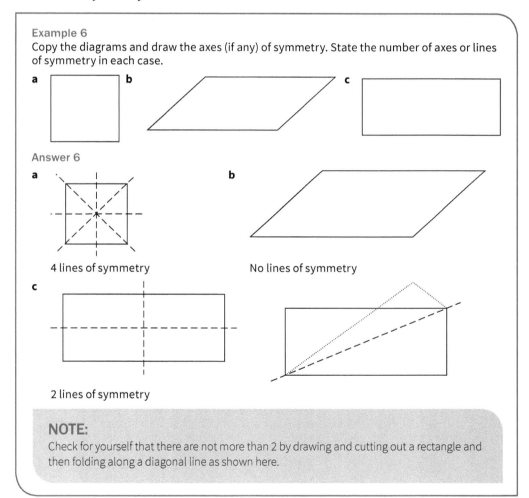

NOTE:
Check for yourself that there are not more than 2 by drawing and cutting out a rectangle and then folding along a diagonal line as shown here.

Key term

A shape has **rotational symmetry** about a point if it fits exactly on itself when rotated about that point through an angle less than 360°.

Rotational Symmetry

A shape is said to have **rotational symmetry** if it can be picked up and rotated (but not turned over) through an angle less than 360° to fit again into its own outline. The number of ways it can be made to fit is called the **order of rotational symmetry**.

Figure 6.31 shows an equilateral triangle with one corner marked with an **x** so that we can more easily see it turn and count the number of times it fits into its own outline.

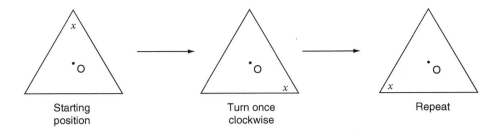

Figure 6.31 Rotational symmetry

One more turn returns the triangle to its starting position. It has taken three turns, so the rotational symmetry is of order 3.

O marks the **centre of rotational symmetry** of the triangle.

Key term

A shape has **rotational symmetry** about a point if it fits exactly on itself when rotated about that point through an angle less than 360°.

The number of times it will fit on itself before a complete rotation is its **order of symmetry**.

Example 7

Find the order of rotational symmetry of each of these shapes.

a

b

Answer 7

a Marking part of the shape with a dot, we see that it can be turned twice.

This shape can fit into its own outline in two different ways, so it has order of symmetry = 2.

b

If necessary mark one of the points of the star with a dot, to help you see that it can be turned five times to reach its original position. It has order of rotational symmetry = 5.
Notice that the letter Z has no lines of symmetry, and the star has five lines of symmetry.

Exercise 6.6

State the number of lines of symmetry (if any) and the order of rotational symmetry for each of the shapes shown below.

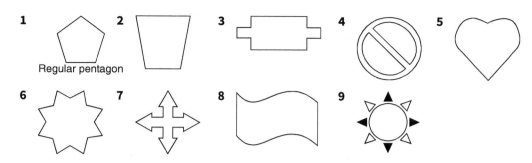

1 Regular pentagon

Using Symmetry

We have seen that a line of symmetry in a shape means that the shape can be folded along that line and one side will fit exactly over the other. This means that pairs of angles on each side are equal and lengths of corresponding sides are equal. In particular, if a line, *AB*, crosses a line of symmetry, *XY*, then the line of symmetry must be the perpendicular bisector of the line *AB*. This is shown in Figure 6.32.

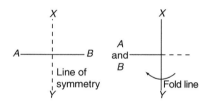

Figure 6.32 Line crossing line of symmetry

Example 8
The following shape has a line of symmetry, marked *XY* on the diagram.
Find the values of *a*, *b*, *c*, *d*, and *e*.

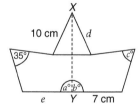

Answer 8
We are told that the line *XY* is a line of symmetry, so we can use symmetry to find the required sides and angles.

$a = b = 90°$ $c = 35°$ $d = 10\,\text{cm}$ $e = 7\,\text{cm}$

6.10 Quadrilaterals

A **quadrilateral** is a shape with four straight line sides. The sum of its four angles is 360°. The lines joining opposite angles are called diagonals. You need to know the names and properties of the special quadrilaterals given in Table 6.1.

This is presented in the form of a table which you should copy and complete, and then check your answers at the back of the book before continuing.

Exercise 6.7

Copy and complete Table 6.1.

Shape						
Name	square	rectangle	parallelogram	rhombus	trapezium	Kite
Sides	all equal; opposite sides parallel	opposite sides equal in length; opposite sides parallel	opposite sides equal in length; opposite sides parallel	all sides equal; opposite sides parallel	one pair of opposite sides parallel	two pairs of equal sides; no parallel sides
Angles	all 90°	(a)	opposite angles equal	(b)	(c)	one pair of opposite angles equal
Diagonals	equal lengths; bisect each other at right angles	(d)	different lengths; bisect each other	(e) (f)	different lengths; do not bisect	different lengths; one bisects the other at right angles
Lines of symmetry	4	(g)	0	(h)	(i)	(j)
Order of rotational symmetry	(k)	2	(l)	(m)	no rotational symmetry	no rotational symmetry

Table 6.1 Quadrilaterals

Example 9

Find the angles marked with letters in the following quadrilaterals. In each case state your reasons.

a Find the value of x in the diagram and hence write down the sizes of the angles. State your reasons.

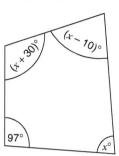

b Find, stating your reasons, the values of a, b, c and d in the diagram.

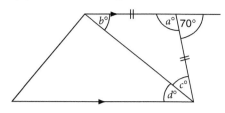

Answer 9

a $97 + x + (x - 10) + (x + 30) = 360$ (the angle sum of a quadrilateral is 360)

$97 + 3x - 10 + 30 = 360$

$117 + 3x = 360$ (-117)

$3x = 243$ $(\div 3)$

$x = 81$

The angles are: 81°, 71° and 111°.

b $a = 180 - 70$ (angles on a straight line)

$a = 110$

$b + c = 180 - 110$ (angle sum of a triangle)

$b + c = 70$

$b = c = 35$ (isosceles triangle)

$c + d = 70$ (alternate angles)

$d = 70 - c = 35$

Example 10

Using the diagram below explain how you know that AD is parallel to BC.

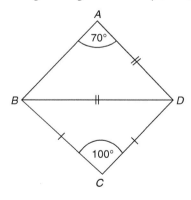

Answer 10

$\angle ABD = 70°$ (isosceles triangle)

$\angle ADB = 180 - 70 - 70 = 40°$ (angle sum of a triangle)

$\angle CBD = \angle DBC = \frac{180 - 100}{2} = 40°$ (angle sum of an isosceles triangle)

So $\angle ADB = \angle DBC = 40°$

and AD and BC are parallel, with $\angle ADB$ and $\angle DBC$ alternate angles.

Exercise 6.8

Find the values of the letters in the following shapes.

1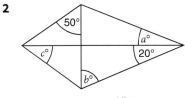

Parallelogram

2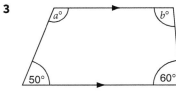

Kite

3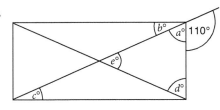

Trapezium

4

Rectangle

5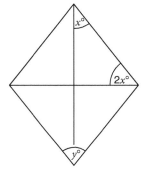

Rhombus

6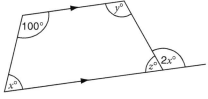

Trapezium

7 Explain how you know that *PQ* is parallel to *RS* in the diagram.

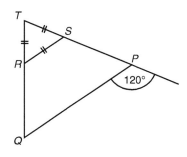

6.11 Polygons

Polygons are many-sided shapes. They include triangles and quadrilaterals. You need to know the names of the **regular polygons** shown in Table 6.2. Regular means that all the sides are of the same length and all the angles are the same. Although we do not usually say it, a regular triangle would be an equilateral triangle (all the sides have the same length and all angles 60°), and a regular quadrilateral would be a square (all the sides have the same length and all angles 90°).

Investigation

1   Copy Table 6.2 for use in parts 2 and 3 of the investigation. You do not need to draw the shapes until you have read through part 2, but leave plenty of space in the last column where you will construct the shapes.

Name	Number of sides	Interior angle	Shape
Square (regular quadrilateral)	4 sides	90°	▢
Regular pentagon	5 sides		⬠
Regular hexagon	6 sides		⬡
Regular heptagon	7 sides		
Regular octagon	8 sides		⯃
Regular nonagon	9 sides		
Regular decagon	10 sides		

Table 6.2 Regular polygons

2   Drawing regular polygons.

   a   Using angles at the centre.

   Regular polygons can be constructed from isosceles triangles as shown in Figure 6.33.

   The angle shown at the centre of the pentagon is obtained by dividing 360° (the complete turn) by 5 (the number of sides in the pentagon), to give 72°.

   The angles are drawn accurately, and the sides of the triangles are drawn all having the same length. An easy way to do this is to use your compasses, opening them to the length that you need to draw the pentagon; 2 centimetres is a convenient size. With the compass point on the centre, mark each line as shown.

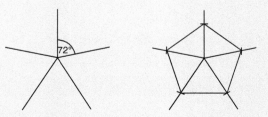

Figure 6.33 Constructing a regular pentagon

b The hexagon is the only polygon that is made up from equilateral triangles. It can be drawn by the above method or by drawing a circle, then stepping round the circumference using the compasses, as shown in Figure 6.34. If you keep your compasses at exactly the same length as the radius of the circle you should be able to fit in six steps round the circumference. Join these to form the hexagon.

 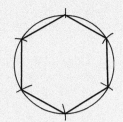

Complete the right-hand column of Table 6.2 by drawing each of the polygons as accurately as possible.

Figure 6.34 Constructing a regular hexagon

3 Calculating the interior and exterior angles in regular polygons.

Figure 6.35 is a diagram of part of a polygon, showing an interior and an exterior angle.

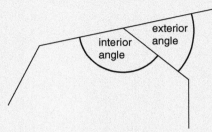

Figure 6.35 Interior and exterior angles

You will see that the interior angle = 180° − exterior angle.

You need to be able to calculate these angles in any polygon. There are several methods for doing this. We will look at two.

a Calculating the exterior angle first.

The pentagon in Figure 6.36 has all the exterior angles shown.

Imagine that you are walking round the outside of the pentagon, each time you come to a corner you turn through the angle shown. You start facing the sun at A and continue round, turning five times until you face the sun again, back at A. You have turned through 360°. Since we are talking about a regular pentagon each turn is one fifth of a complete turn (see Figure 6.37).

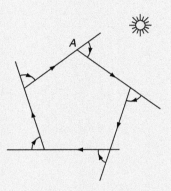

Figure 6.36 Exterior angles of a pentagon

Each exterior angle $= \frac{360}{5} = 72°$.
Each interior angle $= 180 - 72 = 108°$ (angles on a straight line).

b Finding the total interior angle first.

The pentagon in Figure 6.38 has been divided into three triangles, with all of them drawn from one point on the pentagon. Each of these triangles has a total angle sum of 180°, so the total interior angle of the pentagon is $3 \times 180 = 540°$.

Each individual interior angle of the regular pentagon is thus $\frac{540}{5} = 108°$.

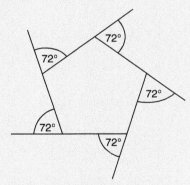

Figure 6.37 Exterior angles of a pentagon are 72°

c Using a formula.

If you prefer to learn formulae you could use the following, where n is the number of sides in the polygon.

Total interior angle of *any* polygon $= 180 \times (n - 2)$

Interior angle of a *regular* polygon $= \frac{180 \times (n-2)}{n}$

There are other methods. Look at your constructions of regular polygons and see if they suggest another method.

Complete the final column of Table 6.2 by calculating the interior angles for each polygon.

What do you notice about the size of the interior angle of a regular polygon as the number of sides increases?

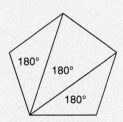

Figure 6.38 Pentagon divided into triangles

Exercise 6.9

1   Calculate the total interior angle for a 15-sided polygon.

2   Calculate the exterior angle in a regular 12-sided polygon.

3   Calculate the angle a in this regular hexagon.

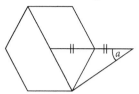

NOTE:

This is a long question. Make it easier by drawing a larger version of the diagram and marking in each angle as you *calculate* it.

4   *ABCDE* is a regular pentagon, with centre *O*, and side *DE* extended to *F*.

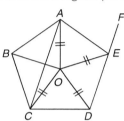

Calculate:

a   *AEF*   **b**   *AED*   **c**   *AEO*   **d**   *OAE*

e   *AOC*   **f**   *CAO*   **g**   *CAE*

Hence explain how you know that *AC* and *DE* are parallel.

5   The diagram shows the exterior angle of part of a regular polygon with n sides. Calculate n.

6   The total interior angles of a regular polygon add up to 2520°. Calculate:

a   the number of sides

b   the interior angle of the polygon.

6.12 Circles

Once again there are words connected with circles that you need to know. Figures 6.39–6.44 show these names, many of which you will probably know already.

Figure 6.39 Circumference

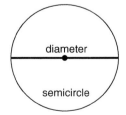

Figure 6.40 Diameter and semicircle
The **diameter** divides the circle into two halves. Each half is a **semicircle**.

Figure 6.41 Radius

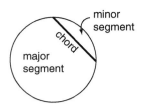

Figure 6.42 Chord

A chord divides a circle into two parts. Each part is a **segment**.

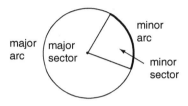

Figure 6.43 Arc and Sector

Two radii (plural of radius) divide a circle into two parts. Each part is a **sector**. Each part of the circumference is an **arc**.

Figure 6.44 Tangent

A tangent is a line outside the circle which *just* touches the circle, making a single point of contact.

Practical work

Try these two constructions, making your drawings as accurate as possible (sharp pencil!).

1   Draw a circle with your compasses, radius 10 cm. Mark the centre accurately.

Draw a tangent at any point, making sure it just touches the circle, as in Figure 6.44.

From the point of contact of the tangent and the circle draw a radius to the centre of the circle.

Measure the angle between the radius and the tangent.

If you have been accurate you should find that the **angle between a tangent and the radius at the point of contact is 90°** (see Figure 6.45).

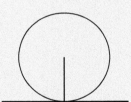

Figure 6.45 Radius and tangent

This also makes sense if you consider the symmetry of the diagram in Figure 6.46.

The diameter is a line of symmetry of the circle. The tangent is a straight line. Folding the diagram along the diameter makes one half of the diagram fit onto the other half, as in Figure 6.46. In particular, the angles between the diameter and the tangent must be the same. They must both be half a straight angle, and so must both be 90°.

2   Draw a circle of radius 10 centimetres and mark the centre.

Draw a diameter accurately through the centre of the circle. Mark the diameter with the letters *A* and *B*.

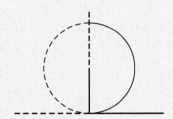

Figure 6.46 Tangent, radius and symmetry

Mark a point, *X*, anywhere on the circumference.

Join this point to the ends of the diameter as shown in Figure 6.47, making a triangle *ABX*.

Measure the angle *AXB*.

Repeat with other positions of *X* on the same circle, and with circles with different radii.

If you have been accurate you should find that the angle *AXB* is always 90°.

This angle is referred to as the angle in a semicircle because the diameter divides the circle into two semicircles.

You have shown that **the angle in a semicircle is a right angle**.

> **NOTE:**
> There is one other point to notice about circles. In many questions about circles you will find isosceles triangles, because all the radii are equal length, and a triangle made with two radii and a chord will be an isosceles triangle. **Look out for isosceles triangles in questions on circles!**

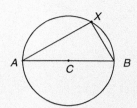

Figure 6.47 Angle in a semicircle

Example 11

The diagram shows a circle with centre O. AOB is a diameter, DBT is a tangent, and $\angle COB = 40°$. Find, giving reasons,

a $\angle ACB$ **b** $\angle ABD$ **c** $\angle OCB$

d $\angle OCA$ **e** $\angle CAO$ **f** $\angle ODB$

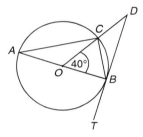

Answer 11

a $\angle ACB = 90°$ (angle in a semicircle)

b $\angle ABD = 90°$ (angle between tangent and radius)

c $\angle OCB = \dfrac{180 - 40}{2} = 70°$ (isosceles triangle)

d $\angle ACO = 90 - 70 = 20°$ (ACB is a right angle)

e $\angle CAO = 20°$ (isosceles triangle)

f $\angle ODB = 180 - 90 - 40 = 50°$ (triangle ODB is right-angled)

Exercise 6.10

Calculate the values of the letters in these diagrams. O is the centre of each circle.

1

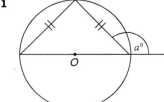

2

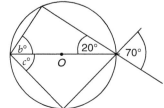

3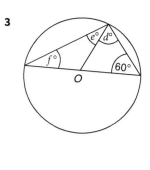

4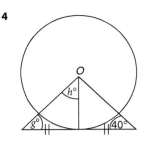

5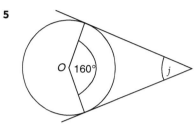

6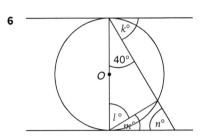

6.13 Solid Shapes

There are a few basic solid shapes that you need to know.

Solid figures are shapes in three dimensions, and are not easy to draw on two-dimensional paper. They have **faces**, **edges** and **vertices** (the plural of **vertex**). These are shown in the diagram of a cube in Figure 6.48.

An edge is the line where two faces meet, and a vertex is the point where more than two faces meet. If you look at Figure 6.48, you should be able to see that it has 6 faces (only three are visible), 12 edges (only 9 are visible) and 8 vertices (only 7 are visible). If you find this difficult to visualise try drawing in the invisible edges with dotted lines, as in Figure 6.49.

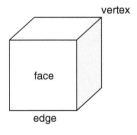

Figure 6.48 Parts of a cube

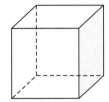

Figure 6.49 The hidden edges of a cube

Key term

A **prism** is a solid which has the same cross-section all the way throughout its length.

Table 6.3 is divided into **prisms** and other solids which we shall call non-prisms. Prisms are solids which have the same **cross-section** all the way through the shape. An example of a prism would be an unsharpened hexagonal pencil, as in Figure 6.50, because you could cut through it at right angles anywhere along its length and the cross-section would always be the same hexagon.

A cylinder is also a prism because you can cut through it at any place along its length and its cross-section will always be the same circle.

Figure 6.50 A hexagonal prism

Exercise 6.11

Copy and complete Table 6.3.

Prisms					
Name	Shape	Example	Number of faces	Number of edges	Number of vertices
Cube		dice	6	12	8
Cuboid		box of matches	6	(a)	(b)
Cylinder			3	2	0
Triangular prism			(c)	(d)	(e)
Non-prisms					
Sphere		rubber ball	1	0	0
Tetrahedron (triangular based pyramid)			(f)	(g)	(h)
Square (or square-based) pyramid		the pyramids of Egypt	(i)	(j)	(k)
Cone			2	(l)	(m)

Table 6.3 Solid shapes

6.14 Nets

As we mentioned earlier, solids are difficult to draw on paper, so it is useful to be able to draw the **net** of a solid. This is a two-dimensional shape that can be cut and folded to make the three-dimensional shape. Two examples are shown in Figure 6.51.

Figure 6.51 Nets. **a** A cube **b** A square pyramid

Some nets are not as obvious as these. Copy the diagrams in Figure 6.52 onto paper or card, cut them out and see if they can be folded into any of the shapes given in the table.

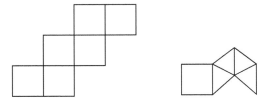

Figure 6.52 Nets

Not all shapes with six squares will make a cube. Try this one in Figure 6.53.

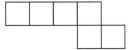

Figure 6.53 A net?

Example 12
Draw accurately a net for a tetrahedron (triangular-based pyramid) with all edges = 2 cm.

Answer 12
In the diagram *AB* was drawn first.

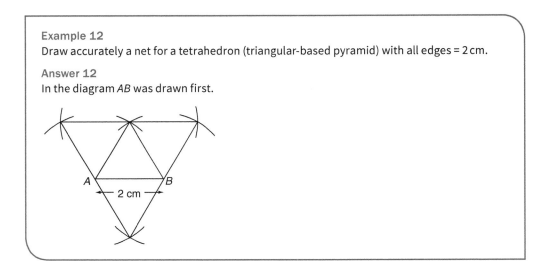

Exercise 6.12

1 Draw accurately a net for the cuboid shown below.

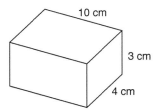

2 What solid would this net make?

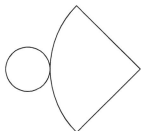

6.15 Similar and Congruent Shapes

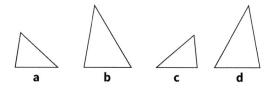

Figure 6.54 Triangles

Look at the triangles in Figure 6.54. They all have the same angles and all look the same shape, but some are different sizes.

Figures that have exactly the same shape *and* exactly the same size are called **congruent**. The pair of triangles **b** and **d** above are a set of congruent triangles. Triangles **a** and **c** are also another pair of congruent triangles, but they are not congruent with the first set of triangles.

Figures which have exactly the same shape but different sizes are called **similar**. For example, triangles **c** and **d** are similar.

Similar triangles are easy to recognise because they have equal angles, but it is not so easy to recognise similar quadrilaterals. For example, look at the rectangles in Figure 6.55.

All the rectangles have angles of 90°, but only **a** and **b** are similar.

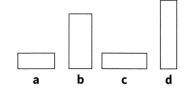

Figure 6.55 Rectangles

For quadrilaterals the sides have also to be in the same ratio. In the rectangles **e** and **f** in Figure 6.56, rectangle *ABCD* has sides of 3 centimetres and 7 centimetres, and rectangle *WXYZ* has sides of 4.5 centimetres and 10.5 centimetres. The ratios of the corresponding sides are 2 : 3, as shown. Therefore, **e** and **f** are similar.

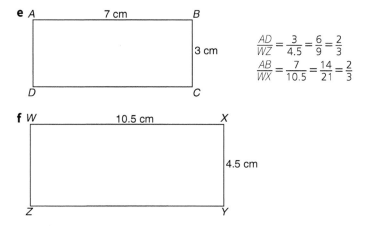

$$\frac{AD}{WZ} = \frac{3}{4.5} = \frac{6}{9} = \frac{2}{3}$$

$$\frac{AB}{WX} = \frac{7}{10.5} = \frac{14}{21} = \frac{2}{3}$$

Figure 6.56 Similar rectangles

Regular polygons with the same number of sides are all either similar or congruent to each other. For example, all equilateral triangles are either similar or congruent and all regular pentagons are either similar or congruent.

You will notice that congruent figures are also similar, but similar figures are not necessarily congruent.

Example 13

Match pairs of:

a   congruent   **b**   similar figures from the shapes below.

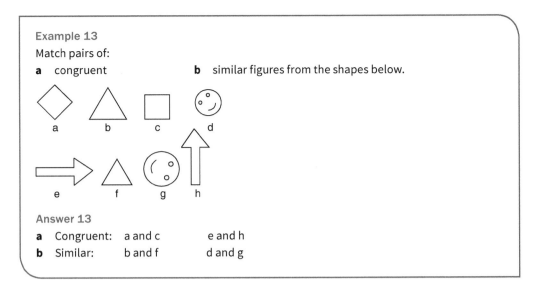

Answer 13

a   Congruent: a and c   e and h
b   Similar: b and f   d and g

Exercise 6.13

1   Match pairs of similar letters from the selection below.

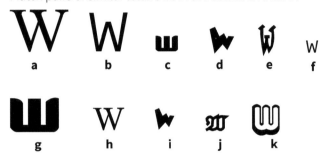

2   Match pairs of congruent figures from the selection below.

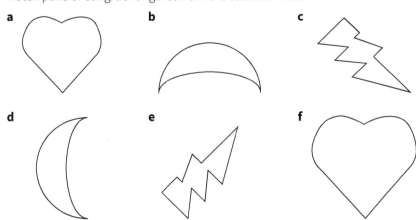

6.16 Scale Drawings

You have already met scales on maps and on diagrams and solid objects. We will now practise constructing some accurate scale drawings.

Example 14

An architect is drawing the plan of a proposed house. She uses a scale of 1 centimetre to represent 1 metre. She starts with a rough sketch on which she can mark the proposed measurements.

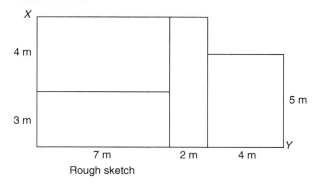

Rough sketch

a Draw an accurate plan of the house.

b Measure the diagonal length from **X** to **Y**.

c What will be the length of this diagonal, in metres, in the finished house?

Answer 14

a

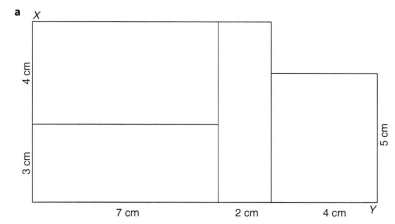

b 14.8 cm

c 14.8 m

Exercise 6.14

1 A ship sails 20 kilometres due east from port *P*. The captain then alters course to avoid a busy shipping lane and sails 22 kilometres due south. The ship then turns due east again and sails for 36 kilometres, to reach a point *Q*.

The sketch shows this information.

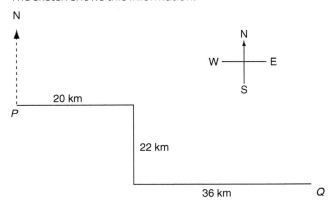

a   Make a scale drawing using a scale of 1 centimetre to 5 kilometres.
b   Join *P* and *Q*, and measure the length of the line in centimetres.
c   How far is the ship from port *P*?

2   The diagram shows the relationship of four towns, *A*, *B*, *C* and *D*.

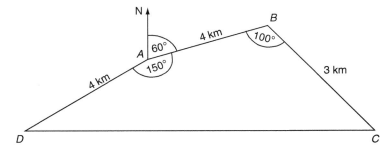

a   Make a scale drawing, using a suitable scale.
b   Use your drawing to find the distance, in kilometres, between *A* and *C*.

NOTE:
Start by drawing the North line at *A*.

Key term

A **locus** (plural loci) of points is the possible positions of those points defined by some rule. The positions may be in one (a line), two (an area) or three (a volume) dimensions.

NOTE:
This locus of points is also called a *region*.

6.17 Locus in Two Dimensions

The Latin word *locus* means 'place'. Think of the words 'location' or 'locality'.

The plural of locus is loci. The loci we will be constructing are based on the shapes we have studied in this chapter.

Methods for Constructing Loci

Construct the following loci to ensure that you know how to do each one. The first locus is a circle.

1 a   Construct the locus of points in two dimensions that are 1.5 cm from a point marked *A*.
   b   Shade the locus of points that are more than 1.5 centimetres from *A*.

Method

If you are not sure about what the locus in any question would be, make a rough sketch showing some of the points that you know would be in the locus. This will help you to see what shape you should be drawing.

The required locus is a circle, radius 1.5 cm, with its centre at *A*, because all the points on a circle are an equal distance from the centre (see Figure 6.57).

NOTE:
It is no good measuring with a ruler and then adding fake 'construction lines' afterwards.

You will be expected to draw loci accurately, and sometimes you will be asked to draw them with a restricted set of instruments such as a pair of compasses and a straight edge only. The 'straight edge' means that you can use your ruler to draw lines, but not to measure anything. You cannot use a protractor or set square.

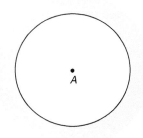

Figure 6.57 Locus of points 1.5 cm from *A* (the line) and more than 1.5 cm from *A* (the shading).

The method you have used is shown by your construction lines, which *must* be left in. This is equivalent to showing your working when asked to do so in other questions. If you do not leave in your construction lines you will probably get *no marks* for that part of the question.

The examples show what is meant by construction lines.

The next two loci are based on the shape of a rhombus.

NOTE:
In all these constructions make your arcs reasonably large. The smaller they are the less accurate your results will be.

Before you start drawing the next locus, follow the method to construct the rhombus shown in Figure 6.58.

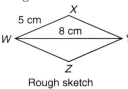

Figure 6.58 Rough sketch of a rhombus

Draw a line *WY* 8 cm long.

Open your compasses to 5 cm and, with the compass point at *W*, draw arcs above and below the line *WY*. Without altering the compasses move the compass point to *Y* and draw arcs above and below to intersect the first set of arcs at *X* and *Z*.

Join *X* and *Z* to *W* and *Y*.

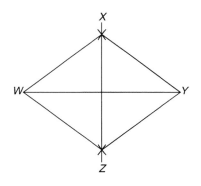

Figure 6.59 Constructed rhombus

Join *X* and *Z* to get the rhombus shown in Figure 6.59.

From our study of the symmetry of the rhombus earlier in the chapter we know that the diagonals of a rhombus bisect each other at right angles, so *XZ* is the perpendicular bisector of *WY*.

Look at the rhombus *PQRS* in Figure 6.60. *Any* point on the diameter *QS* is the same distance from *P* as it is from *R*. Copy the figure, mark a few points on *QS* extended in either direction and measure the distances to check this fact.

The dotted lines in Figure 6.60 show one example. Here, *PT* = *TR*.

This is the fact that is used in the construction of the next locus.

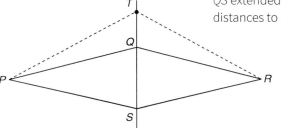

Figure 6.60 Distances from vertices of a rhombus

2 a Construct the locus of points that are equidistant (equal distance) from two points *A* and *B*. Use a straight edge and compasses only.

b Shade the region which is closer to *B* than to *A*.

c Join *AB*. What is the name given to the line of the locus you drew in part (a) in relation to the line *AB*?

Method

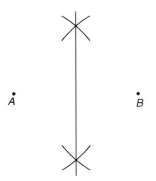

Figure 6.61 Locus of points equidistant from points A and B

If you are not sure what to draw, mark one point that is at the same distance from *A* as it is from *B*. Try to find another, and then another, until you know what is required.

Open your compasses to more than the half the distance between the two points. Put the compass point on *A* and draw a pair of arcs above and below the line between *A* and *B*.

Keep the compasses exactly the same but place their point on *B*. Draw two more arcs above and below which should intersect with the first pair of arcs. Use your ruler as a straight edge to join the two points of intersection. The finished answer should look like Figure 6.61.

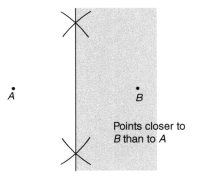

Points closer to B than to A

Figure 6.62 Points closer to B than to A

a We have drawn a rhombus, but without joining two of the sides. As we have seen above, the symmetry of the rhombus means that we have drawn the perpendicular bisector of *AB*.

b Figure 6.62 repeats the diagram for clarity, but you would not be expected to do this. As before, think of points that are closer to *B* than to *A*.

c The locus we have drawn is the perpendicular bisector of *AB*.

The next locus is also based on a rhombus but with a slightly different method of construction. Before you go on to the next locus, draw accurately the rhombus sketched in Figure 6.63.

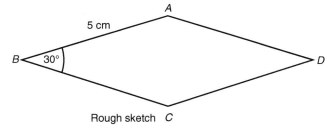

Figure 6.63 Rough sketch of rhombus

Draw a line *BC*, longer than 5 cm, and measure and draw the angle *ABC* = 30°.

Open your compasses to 5 cm and, with the compass point at *B*, draw an arc on both arms of the angle *ABC*. These intersections are *A* and *C*.

Keeping your compasses to the same measurement, put the point at A and then at C, drawing intersecting arcs as in Figure 6.64.

The intersection of these two arcs is D. Join BD.

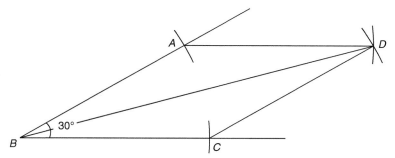

Figure 6.64 Constructed rhombus

Once again we have constructed a rhombus. In this case we are going to use the fact that the symmetry of the rhombus means that BD is the bisector of angle ABC.

In particular, any point on BD is at the same distance from BA or BA extended as it is from BC or BC extended. As before, check a few points on BD to confirm this. Figure 6.65 shows one such point with dotted lines to indicate the shortest distance to BA extended, and to BC extended. Remember that the shortest distance from a point to a line is the perpendicular from the point to the line.

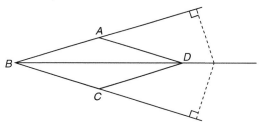

Figure 6.65 Shortest distances to extended sides

3 **a** Using a straight edge and compasses only, draw the locus of points that are equidistant from the lines AB and BC shown in Figure 6.66.

   b Shade the locus of points *within the triangle ABC* which are closer to AB than to BC.

   c What is the name used to describe the line you drew in part (a)?

Method

As before, if you are not sure what the locus would look like always try to find a few points that would be on the locus until you see what has to be drawn.

If you worked through the last example you should be able to see from the diagram how this locus is constructed.

Start with your compass point on B, marking an arc on both arms of the angle.

Move your compasses to the points of intersection between each arc and line in turn and mark a pair of arcs as shown.

Join the point B to the intersection of the arcs.

We have again drawn part of a rhombus, which as we know from earlier work, has a line of symmetry which, in this case, divides ∠*ABC* into two equal parts.

a

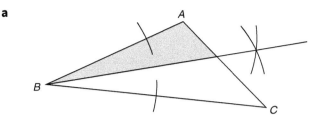

Figure 6.66 Construction of locus of points dividing angle *ABC* into two equal parts

b The shading in part (a) shows the required locus.

c The locus is the bisector of angle *ABC*.

4 Construct the locus of points that are 2 centimetres from the given line segment *AB*.

Method

Imagine that the line is a length of wire that is stretched tightly between two posts. A dog is on a leash that is attached to a ring that is free to run along the line. The locus of points would be represented (in miniature!) by the furthest points the dog could reach.

Open your compasses to 2 centimetres, and at *A* and then at *B* draw semicircles as shown in Figure 6.67.

Join the semicircles to make lines on each side of *AB* that are 2 centimetres from *AB*.

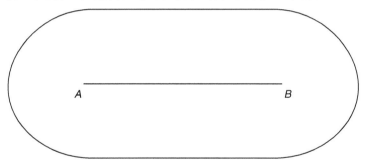

Figure 6.67 Constructed locus

You should now have enough information to answer questions on locus.

Example 15

a Draw a rectangle *ABCD* with *AB* = 8 centimetres and *BC* = 6 centimetres.

b Construct the angle bisector of angle *ABC*.

c Construct the perpendicular bisector of *BC*.

d Shade the region where the points are closer to *BC* than to *AB*, and closer to *AB* than to *DC*.

Answer 15

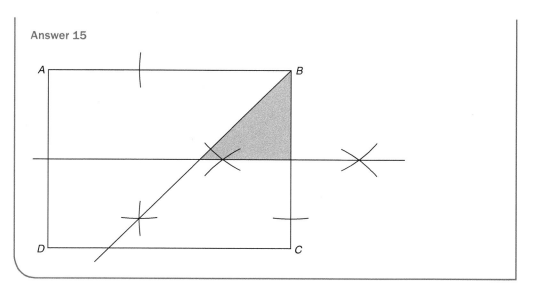

The next example is probably more complex than you need, but it does usefully show how to construct loci.

Example 16
A guard dog is tied to a building on a leash that is 5 metres long. The building is 3 metres by 3 metres, and the dog is tied 1 metre from the end of one of the short sides as shown. Using a scale of 1 centimetre to represent 1 metre, construct a diagram to show the extent of the ground outside the building that the guard dog can patrol.

Answer 16

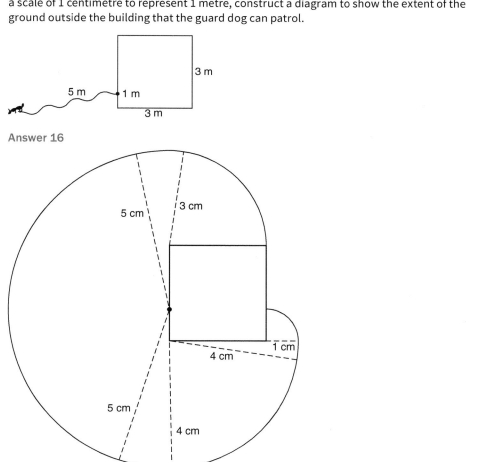

NOTE:
Remember that each time the dog comes to a corner its leash is effectively shortened so the arc drawn needs to have the reduced radius.

Example 17

Do not use a protractor in this construction.
a Construct an equilateral triangle with sides 3 cm.
b Construct the locus of points that are 2 cm outside the triangle.
c Shade the locus of points that are outside the triangle *and* less than 2 cm from the triangle.

Answer 17

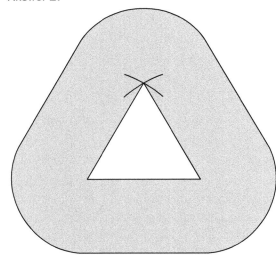

Exercise 6.15

1 Copy the diagram, and construct the bisector of angle *XYZ* using a pair of compasses and a straight edge only.

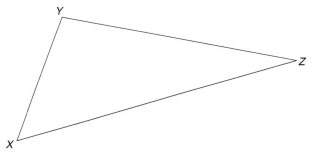

NOTE:
There are two lines of points that are equidistant from these two intersecting lines.

2 Copy the diagram and construct the loci of points that are equidistant from *AB* and *CD*. Use a pair of compasses and a straight edge only.

3 *A*, *B* and *C* are three villages as shown in the diagram.
a Draw an accurate diagram of the location of the three villages using a suitable scale. A radio mast is to be placed in a position that is an equal distance from each of the villages.

b Construct the locus of points that are equidistant from:

    i   *A* and *B*   **ii**   *B* and *C*   **iii**   *A* and *C*.

c Mark the position of the radio mast, labelling it *R*.

d Measure the distance of the mast from the villages, converting your answer to kilometres.

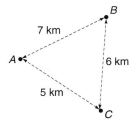

4 Repeat question 3 for the three villages *X*, *Y* and *Z* shown below.

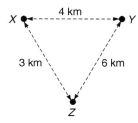

Exercise 6.16

Mixed exercise

1 The diagram shows a triangular park with gates at *A*, *B* and *C*.

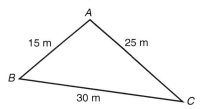

A fountain is to be placed so that it is an equal distance from *BA* and *BC*.

a Using a scale of 1 centimetre to represent 2 metres, draw the triangle accurately.

b Draw the locus of points that are equidistant from *BA* and *BC*, using a straight edge and compasses only.

The fountain is also equidistant from *A* and *B*.

c Draw the locus of points that are equidistant from *A* and *B*, using a straight edge and compasses only.

d Mark the position of the fountain and label it *F*.

The water from the fountain sprays over a circle of radius 2 metres.

e Using the given scale draw the locus of points that are 2 metres from *F*.

f Make appropriate measurements on your drawing to find (in metres):

    i   how close the spray comes to the gate *A*

    ii   the distance of the fountain from gate *C*.

2 Describe the symmetry of each of the diagrams below.

a 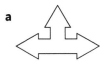 **b** **c**

d **e** x x x x
x x o x
x o x x
x x x x
f

3 Calculate the sizes of the angles and sides marked with letters in the following diagrams. In each case give reasons for your answers and state the units in your answers.

a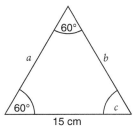

b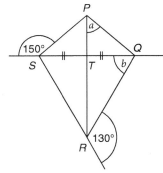

c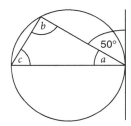

d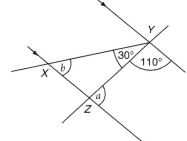

e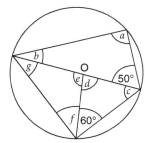

4 Describe the locus of points in three dimensions which lie between 10 cm and 10.5 cm from a fixed point, *A*.

Exam-style questions

Many of these questions are based on diagrams that will have to be copied into your own exercise book. Try using tracing paper.

5 Choose a quadrilateral from the list to complete each statement.

Kite   Parallelogram   Rectangle   Rhombus   Square   Trapezium

a A .... has four equal sides and four angles of 90°.

b A .... has just one pair of parallel sides.

c A .... has just one pair of opposite angles equal and its diagonals bisect at 90°. *(4024 paper 11 Q11 June 2013)*

6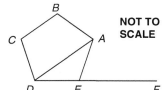

ABCDE is a regular pentagon.

DEF is a straight line.

Calculate:

a angle *AEF*

b angle *DAE*. *(0580 paper 02 Q17 November 2005)*

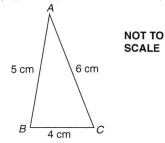

7 a i Using a ruler and compasses only, construct the above triangle accurately.

    ii Using the triangle you have drawn, measure and write down the size of angle *ACB*.

b In the diagram below, two points, *P* and *Q*, are joined by a straight line.

    i Copy the diagram and draw the locus of all the points that are 4 centimetres from the line *PQ*.

    ii On the same diagram, using a straight edge and compasses only, construct the locus of the points that are equidistant from *P* and *Q*. **Show all your construction lines**.

    iii Shade the region which contains the points that are closer to *P* than to *Q* **and** are less than 4 centimetres from the line *PQ*. *(0580 paper 03 Q4 November 2004)*

8 Copy this diagram. (You can use tracing paper.)

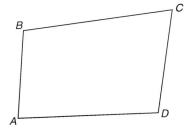

In this question show clearly all your construction arcs.

a Using a straight edge and compasses only, construct on the diagram:

    i the perpendicular bisector of *BD*

    ii the bisector of angle *CDA*.

b Shade the region, inside the quadrilateral, which is nearer to *D* than *B* **and** nearer to *DC* than *DA*. *(0580 paper 02 Q17 June 2004)*

9 Copy this triangle.

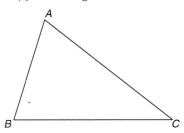

   a In this part of the question use a straight edge and compasses only.
     Leaving in your construction lines,
      i construct the angle bisector of angle *ACB*
      ii construct the perpendicular bisector of *AC*.

           (adapted from 0580 paper 02 Q22 November 2005)

10

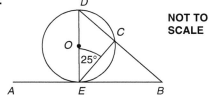

NOT TO SCALE

PQ is a chord of a circle, centre *O*. Angle *OPQ* = 35°.
Calculate angle *POQ*.

           (0580 paper 01 Q11 June 2004)

11

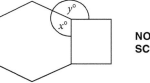

NOT TO SCALE

In the diagram, *DE* is a diameter of the circle, centre *O*.
AEB is the tangent at the point *E*. The line *DCB* cuts the circle at *C*.
Angle *DEC* = 25°.
   a Write down the size of angle *DCE*.
   b Calculate the size of angle *CDE*.
   c Calculate the size of angle *DBE*.   (0580 paper 01 Q23 June 2005)

12 The diagram shows a regular hexagon and a square.

NOT TO SCALE

Calculate the values of *x* and *y*.
        (0580 paper 01 Q15 June 2007)

13 In this question the diagrams are not to scale.

   a   Calculate the value of *s*.   **b**   Calculate the value of *t*.

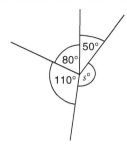 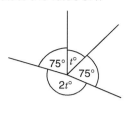

   c **i**   **ii**

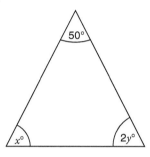 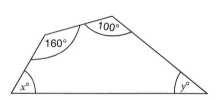

Complete the equation $x + 2y =$ ....   Complete the equation $x + y =$
....

      iii Solve the simultaneous equations given by your answers to parts c(i) and c(ii) to
find the values of *x* and *y*.   (0580 paper 03 Q4 June 2004)

14 The diagram shows three parallel lines.

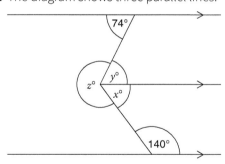

   a   Find *x*.   **b**   Find *y*.   **c**   Find *z*. (4024 paper 11 Q11 November 2010)

15 a   Copy these diagrams and draw all the lines of symmetry on the shapes. (Shape *B* is a
regular polygon.)

 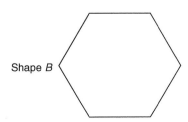

Shape *A*   Shape *B*

   b   Write down the order of rotational symmetry of shape *A*.

                                       (0580 paper 01 Q12 June 2006)

16 a Calculate the size of one exterior angle of a regular heptagon
(seven-sided polygon). Give your answer correct to 1 decimal place.

b

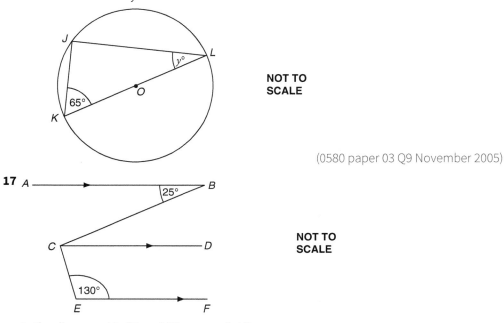

NOT TO SCALE

In the diagram above, *DAE* and *FBCG* are parallel lines.
AC = *BC* and angle *FBA* = 130°.

  i What is the special name given to triangle *ABC*?

  ii Work out the values of *p*, *q*, *r*, *s* and *t*.

c *J*, *K* and *L* lie on a circle with centre *O*.
KOL is a straight line and angle *JKL* = 65°.
Find the value of *y*.

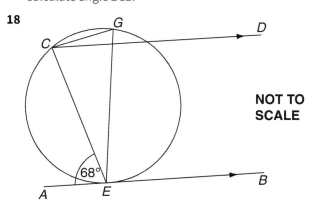

NOT TO SCALE

(0580 paper 03 Q9 November 2005)

17

NOT TO SCALE

In the diagram, *AB*, *CD* and *EF* are parallel lines.
Angle *ABC* = 25° and angle *CEF* = 130°.
Calculate angle *BCE*.

(0580 paper 01 Q10 June 2007)

18

NOT TO SCALE

EG is a diameter of the circle through *E*, *C* and *G*.
The tangent *AEB* is parallel to *CD* and angle *AEC* = 68°.

Calculate the size of the following angles and give a reason for each answer:

a angle *CEG*   **b** angle *ECG*   **c** angle *CGE*   **d** angle *ECD*.

(0580 paper 03 Q4 November 2008)

19 In the diagram, *EAF* is a straight line and *AB* is parallel to *CD*.
AB bisects *FÂC* and *CÂB* = 58°.
Find the value of
a *x*
b *y*.

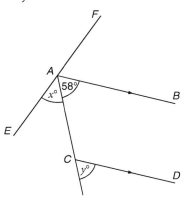

(4024 paper 01 Q5 June 2004)

20 a The interior angle of a regular polygon is 160°.
How many sides does it have?

b *ABCDE…* is part of a regular polygon which has interior angles of 160°.
CDLM is a square.

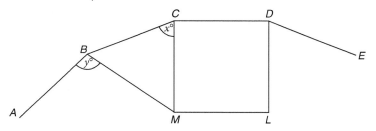

Find
     i the value of *x*   **ii** the value of *y*.   (4024 paper 01 Q20 November 2004)

21 a Three of the angles of a quadrilateral are each 95°.
Find the fourth angle.

b Each interior angle of a regular polygon is 165°.
How many sides has the polygon?   (4024 paper 01 Q10 November 2005)

22 The 7 sided polygon in the diagram has 6 angles of *x*° and one of *y*°.

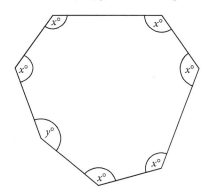

a Draw the line of symmetry on the diagram.

b If *y* = 126, calculate the value of *x*.

(4024 paper 01 Q13 November 2006)

24 In the diagram, the lines *BA*, *DC* and *EF* are parallel.

$A\hat{B}C = 140°$ and $B\hat{C}F = 115°$.

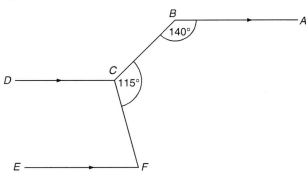

Find

a $D\hat{C}B$

b $D\hat{C}F$

c $E\hat{F}C$. *(4024 paper 01 Q17 June 2007)*

25 The following list gives the names of six shapes.

Square   Rectangle   Equilateral triangle
Kite   Trapezium   Parallelogram

From this list, write down the name of the shape which always has

a rotational symmetry of order 3

b rotational symmetry of order 2 and exactly 2 lines of symmetry

c one line of symmetry only. *(4024 paper 01 Q11 June 2008)*

26 In the diagram, *ABCD* is part of a regular polygon.

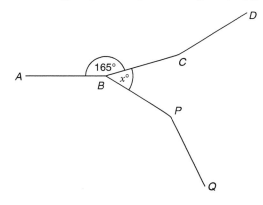

Each interior angle is 165°.

a How many sides does this polygon have?

b *ABPQ* is part of another regular polygon.
This polygon has 12 sides.
Calculate *x*.

(4024 paper 01 Q18 November 2007)

27 Write down the letters of all the shapes which have

a exactly 1 line of symmetry

b rotational symmetry of order 2. *(4024 paper 01 Q2 November 2004)*

Shape *A*   *B*   *C*   *D*   *E*   *F*

Learning Objectives

Syllabus sections 24, 25, 27

In this chapter you will:
- draw straight line graphs by plotting points
- look at some everyday graphs
- learn about gradients of straight line graphs
- use the general equation of a straight line in the form $y = mx + c$

- use graphs to solve simultaneous equations
- draw up tables of coordinates for curves
- plot the curves.

7.1 Introduction

You must have seen graphs in many places in everyday life. A graph is a good visual method for displaying the relationship between two quantities or measures. For example, a newspaper may have a graph to show how the price of oil has increased over a period of time. After working through this chapter you should have a better understanding of both commonly used graphs and those that display algebraic relationships.

7.2 Essential Skills NO CALCULATOR IN THIS EXERCISE

1 Copy and complete these number lines.

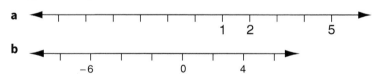

2 Calculate the following:

   a $-2 - 5$　　　b $2 \times (-3)$　　　c $(-3)^2$　　　d -3^2

   e $\frac{10}{-5}$　　　f $1 - (-6)$

3 Simplify the following:

   a $\frac{3}{21}$　　　b $\frac{18}{6}$　　　c $\frac{2}{-10}$　　　d $\frac{-3}{-7}$　　　e $\frac{6}{-1}$

4 List the integer values that satisfy the following inequality:
   $-3 \leqslant x \leqslant 3$

7.3 Axes, Coordinates, Points and Lines

Most graphs you meet will be drawn on a grid with x- and y-axes as in the diagram.

The positive directions of the x- and y-axes are marked with arrows and the letters x and y. The x-axis is always across the page, and the y-axis is up and down the page (see Figure 7.1).

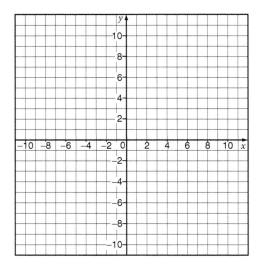

Figure 7.1 x- and y-axes

The axes are marked with scales like the number lines you have already drawn, and the two scales cross at the zero on both lines. This point, where they cross, is called the **origin**, or often just given the letter **O**. It is marked with a zero on the grid. The numbers on the scales mark the grid lines, not the spaces between them.

All the points on the grid can be named by giving their x- **and** y-**coordinates**. The x-coordinate is always given first, and shows how far from the **origin** the point is in the x-direction. Then the y-coordinate shows how far from the origin the point is in the y-direction.

Take, for example, a pair of coordinates (6, 8).

You can plot this point by starting at the origin, going 6 steps in the x-direction (across), and then 8 steps in the y-direction (up).

Figure 7.2 illustrates this.

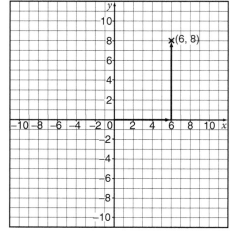

Figure 7.2 Plotting (6, 8)

Example 1

Copy the grid in Figure 7.1 and plot and label the given points.

a   A, (5, 3)   **b**   B, (−2, 4)   **c**   C, (3, −2)   **d**   D, (−3, −5)

Join A, B, C and D to make a four-sided shape.

Answer 1

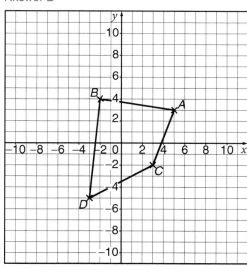

Exercise 7.1

NOTE:

In question **1 b ii** go back (left) 5 and down 3.

1   **a**   Draw a grid with both the axes running from −10 to +10, as in Figure 7.1.

    b   Plot and label the following points:

       i   A, (6, 1)   **ii**   B, (−5, −3)   **iii**   C, (4, −6)   **iv**   D, (−8, 5)

2   **a**   Draw another grid as in question 1.

    b   Plot and label the following points:

       i   A, (3, 2)   **ii**   B, (6, 2)   **iii**   C, (3, 7)

       iv   D, (−6, 2)   **v**   E, (−3, 2)   **vi**   F, (−3, 7)

    c   Join A, B and C to form a triangle.

    d   Join D, E and F to form another triangle.

    e   In what way are the two triangles the same?

    f   In what way are they different?

3   Write down the coordinates of all the points in the diagram below.

NOTE:

To get to B from the origin you go along zero and up 8. Hence the x-coordinate is 0 and the y-coordinate is 8. B is the point (0, 8).

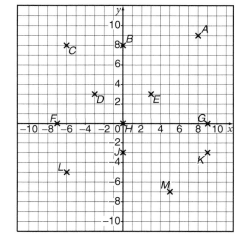

We can now see how points are specified, with their **x**- and **y**-coordinates given in that order, and written in brackets. The points can also be given capital letters to distinguish them.

Next we need to see how to specify lines on the grid.

Example 2

Draw three more grids as above.

a **i** On the first grid plot and join up all the points with x-coordinate 3, that is, points from the set:

$\{(3, -10), (3, -9), (3, -8), ..., (3, 10)\}$

ii What can you say about all the points on the line you have drawn?

b **i** On your second grid plot and join up all the points from the set:

$\{(-5, -10), (-5, -9), (-5, -8), ..., (-5, 10)\}$

ii What do you think this line would be called?

c **i** On your third grid plot and join up all the points which have the x- and y-coordinates equal to each other.

That is, all the points from the set:

$\{(-10, -10), (-9, -9), (-8, -8), ..., (10, 10)\}$

ii What would you call this line?

Answer 2

a **i**

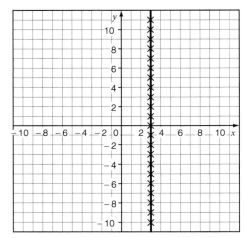

ii All the points have their x-coordinate equal to 3.
The line is called $x = 3$, and its equation is $x = 3$.

b **i**

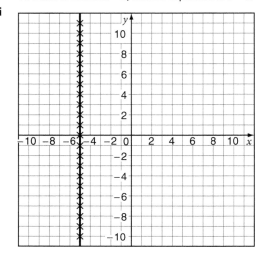

ii This is the line $x = -5$.

---

c i

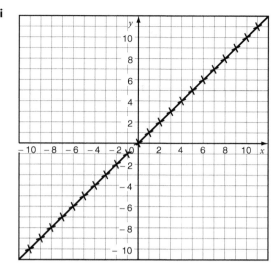

ii   This line connects all the points with equal x- and y-coordinates, so it is the line $y = x$.

Exercise 7.2

1   On a grid draw the lines:

    a $y = 7$ **b** $x = -3$ **c** $y = -x$

2   Write down the names for the lines l and m drawn in the diagram below.

> **NOTE:**
> The last line $(y = -x)$ (in question **1 c**) would join up all the points from the set:
> $\{(-10, 10), (-9, 9), \ldots,$
> $(8, -8), (9, -9), (10, -10)\}$.
> In all the points in this set the x- and y-coordinates have opposite signs.

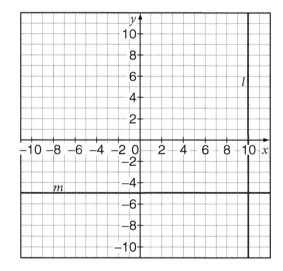

We have been referring to the *names* of lines, but from now on they will be referred to as the *equations* of the lines.

So for example, the line going up and down through $x = -1$ will be called the line with equation $x = -1$, or merely the line $x = -1$.

The lines do not have to go through integer values of x or y. The line $y = 0.75$ would join all the points whose y-coordinates were equal to 0.75.

7.4 Everyday Graphs

You will see graphs in newspapers, on television, in advertisements and so on. We will look at line graphs in this chapter, and in the chapters on statistics you will see examples of other kinds of graphs, for example bar charts and pie charts.

The graph in Figure 7.3 is an example of the change of value of the US dollar compared with the UK pound over five days in one particular week. The points show the values at the close of business each evening.

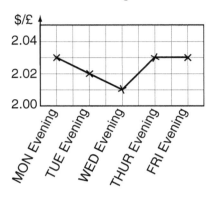

Figure 7.3 Dollar/pound exchange rate

We can see that on Tuesday evening the financial markets closed with $2.02 = £1. This is shown on the vertical axis as 2.02 $/£, in other words for every 1 pound you get 2.02 dollars.

Example 3

The diagram shows a travel graph for a walking trip Abel and Gerry made. They both set out from Abel's home, and an hour later they were at a point *B*, 5 kilometres from Abel's home. They rested for a short time and then continued for one more kilometre to *D* before turning round and going home. The whole trip took 4 hours.

a Find their average speed from:
  i *A* to *B* **ii** *B* to *C* **iii** *C* to *D* **iv** *D* to *E*.

b For how long did they rest?

c What was their average speed from *A* to *D*?

d What was their average speed for the whole trip?

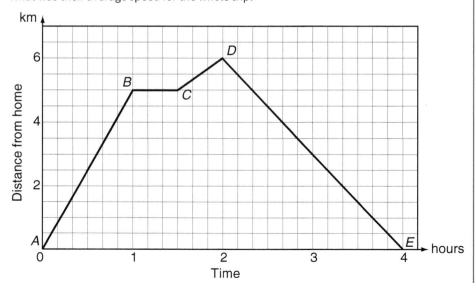

Answer 3

a **i** There are two methods for calculating speed, the first is to use the formula:

$$\text{average speed} = \frac{\text{distance gone}}{\text{time taken}}$$ (see chapter 4)

Average speed = 5 km / 1 hour = 5 km/h

ii Average speed = 0 km/h, since they did not move

iii Average speed = 1 km / $\frac{1}{2}$ hour = 2 km/h

An alternative method which you might prefer is to work out how far they would have gone in one hour.

They travelled 1 kilometre in half an hour, so they would have gone 2 kilometres in 1 hour if they had continued at the same pace. So their average speed is 2 km/h.

iv From D to E they travelled six kilometres in 2 hours, so they would have travelled three kilometres in one hour.

Average speed is 3 km/h.

b From B to C the line is horizontal, the distance from home does not change, but the time changes by half an hour, so they rested for half an hour.

c From A to D is 6 kilometres, and they took 2 hours altogether. That is 3 kilometres in 1 hour, so again the average speed is 3 km/h.

d The total journey, there and back, was 12 kilometres and took 4 hours, so their average speed was 12 ÷ 4 = 3 km/h.

> **NOTE:**
> Remember that average speed for a whole journey is:
>
> $$\frac{\text{total distance gone}}{\text{total time taken}}$$

Example 4

a Draw a conversion graph to convert kilometres per hour into miles per hour for $0 \leqslant$ kilometres per hour $\leqslant 280$, using the fact that 5 miles = 8 kilometres. Use 2 mm graph paper.

b The speed restriction in Britain in built-up areas is 30 mph. Use the graph to convert this to km/h.

c The fastest Formula One average speed recorded in a certain year was 243 km/h correct to 3 significant figures. Change this to miles per hour.

d Cricketers are fast bowlers if they bowl at speeds between 140 and 160 km/h. Find the difference between these two values expressed in miles per hour.

Answer 4

a 5 miles = 8 kilometres, so 50 miles = 80 kilometres.

Travelling 50 miles in one hour is the same as travelling 80 kilometres in one hour, so 50 mph = 80 km/h.

The line is drawn through (0, 0) and through (80, 50), as shown.

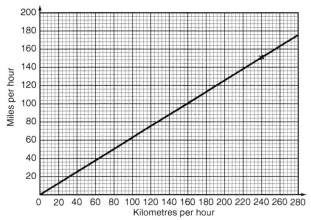

b The line goes through (48, 30), so 30 mph = 48 km/h.

c From the graph, 243 km/h = 152 mph.

d From the graph, 140 km/h = 88 mph and 160 km/h = 100 mph.
The difference between the two speeds is 12 mph.

Example 5

Stopping distances for cars with good tyres, good brakes and on a dry road surface are shown in the table.

speed (kilometres/hour)	0	32	48	64	80	96	112
distance (metres)	0	12	23	36	53	73	96

a Use the table to plot a graph with distance on the vertical axis, and speed on the horizontal axis. Use 2 mm graph paper.

b If the average length of a car is 4 metres, find how many car lengths will be needed to stop if a car is travelling at 90 km/h.

c Find the minimum safe distance you should allow between your car and the one in front if both cars are travelling at 60 km/h.

Answer 5

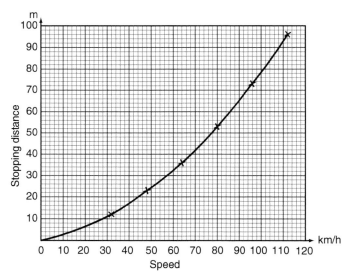

b From the graph, stopping distance at 90 km/h = 64 metres.
One car = 4 metres, so 64 metres = 64 ÷ 4 = 16 car lengths.

c From the graph, stopping distance at 60 km/h = 32 metres, so the minimum safe distance is 32 metres.

Exercise 7.3

1 The graph shows the number of daylight hours for a certain town in the northern hemisphere on the first day of every month.

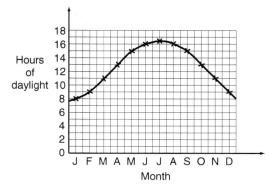

a Which month has the most daylight?

b For how many months are there more than 10 hours of daylight?

2 On a certain day the exchange rate for UK pounds (£) to Indian rupees (Rs.) was 1 pound = 80 rupees.

a Draw a graph to show this information, for $0 \leqslant$ pounds (£) $\leqslant 100$. Use 5 mm squared paper.

b Use the graph to find:

i the value of £75 in rupees (Rs.)

ii the number of pounds you would get in exchange for Rs. 3000.

3 An electrician charges $10 callout fee and $15 per hour worked. The callout fee is charged regardless of how much work is done, if any, and has to be added to every bill.

a Draw horizontal axes with $0 \leqslant$ time in hours $\leqslant 10$ and vertical axes with $0 \leqslant$ cost in dollars $\leqslant 180$.

Use 5 mm squared paper.

b Draw a graph showing charges for up to 10 hours work.

c From the graph how much would be charged for 5.5 hours?

d A bill came to $122.50. How many hours did the electrician work?

4 The graph shows two journeys made by Anton and Bethany from school.

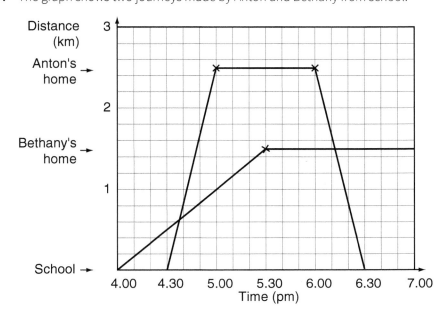

Anton left at 4.30 p.m., had a meal at home and then returned for an evening games match. Bethany left school at 4.00 p.m.

a How long did Anton spend at home?

b How long did it take Bethany to reach home?

c How far is Bethany's home from the school?

d What was Bethany's average speed on her journey home?

e Who travelled the fastest?

We have been studying distance-time graphs in this section. We will go on to study speed-time graphs in Chapter 18.

7.5 Graphs with Algebra

Graphs can also be drawn to illustrate algebraic equations which show the relationship between two variables, commonly x and y.

Look, for example, at the equation $y = 2x + 3$.

There is no single solution to this equation but there is a set of solutions that can be shown on an x–y graph.

We can find a few members of this solution set by trying different values for x and calculating the corresponding values of y.

Trying $\qquad x = 1$,

then $\qquad y = 2 \times 1 + 3$

$\qquad\qquad y = 5$

This shows that $x = 1$, $y = 5$ is one solution to this equation.

This solution can be plotted on the graph as (1, 5).

We could try other values of x, for example, $x = 91.5$:

$$y = 2 \times 91.5 + 3 = 186$$

So the point (91.5, 186) would also represent a solution to the equation and could be plotted on a graph.

Negative values of x also can be tried. For example,

when $\qquad\qquad x = -2, \quad y = 2 \times -2 + 3$,

so $\qquad\qquad y = -1$,

giving the point (−2, −1).

This is clearly a rather haphazard way of finding solutions, and it is more usual to decide a set of values for x and calculate the corresponding values of y, and put this solution set in a table.

Drawing Straight Line Graphs

As an example of the method, using the equation $y = 2x + 3$ we will draw the graph for values of x: $-3 \leqslant x \leqslant 3$.

When $\qquad\qquad x = -3, \quad y = 2 \times -3 + 3$,

so $\qquad\qquad y = -3$.

Table 7.1 shows the values of x and y for $x = -3$ to $x = 3$.

x	-3	-2	-1	0	1	2	3
y	-3	-1	1	3	5	7	9

Table 7.1 $y = 2x + 3$

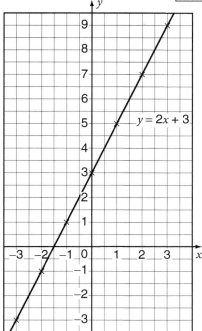

Figure 7.4 $y = 2x + 3$

Check these values for yourself to make sure you know how to find them.

This type of question will often give you some of the values of y, but not all, and you will be asked to find the others.

The table shows that y varies from -3 to 9, so the y-axis must be drawn for values of y: $-3 \leqslant y \leqslant 9$ (see Figure 7.4).

Note the following points:

- Straight lines should always be drawn with a ruler.
- Use the ruled, coordinate lines on the graph paper to find the x and y values.
- The line may be continued to the edge of the grid although in this case we have only been asked to plot points between $x = -3$ and $x = 3$.
- Write the equation for the line beside the line you have drawn on the graph.
- Make sure that whatever scale you choose is evenly spaced on both axes.

For example, do *not* label an axis like in Figure 7.5.

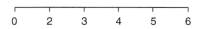

Figure 7.5 Incorrectly labelled axis

Example 6

Draw the graph of $y = -x + 5$ for values of x: $-3 \leqslant x \leqslant 3$.

Answer 6

x	-3	-2	-1	0	1	2	3
y	8	7	6	5	4	3	2

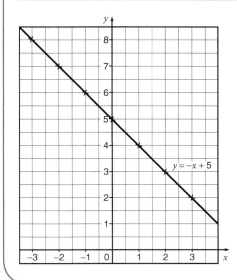

Example 7

a Draw and label each of the following lines on the same graph.

    i $x = 3$ **ii** $x = -2$ **iii** $y = -4$ **iv** $y = 1$

b **i**   Where do all the points whose x-coordinate is 0 lie?

    ii   What is the equation of the y-axis?

c What is another name for the line $y = 0$?

Answer 7

a

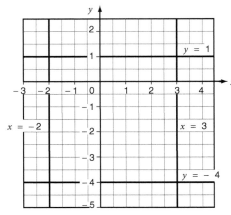

b **i**   The points with x-coordinate equal to zero lie on the y-axis.

    ii   The equation of the y-axis is $x = 0$.

c The line $y = 0$ is the x-axis.

> **NOTE:**
> It is very easy to make the mistake of thinking that the equation of the y-axis is $y = 0$. Make sure that you LEARN that the y-axis goes through all the points where $x = 0$. For example, $(0, -4)$, $(0, -3)$, $(0, 2)$ and so on. Also learn that the x-axis is $y = 0$.

Exercise 7.4

For questions 1 to 7 draw the straight line graphs for the values of x given. Use the same scale on both axes.

Beside each graph write its equation and the value of y where the line cuts the y-axis.

1 $y = x$ $-3 \leqslant x \leqslant 3$ **2** $y = x + 2$ $-3 \leqslant x \leqslant 3$

3 $y = x - 1$ $-3 \leqslant x \leqslant 3$ **4** $y = 2x$ $-3 \leqslant x \leqslant 3$

5 $y = 2x + 2$ $-3 \leqslant x \leqslant 3$ **6** $y = 3x - 3$ $-2 \leqslant x \leqslant 4$

7 $y = 5$ $-2 \leqslant x \leqslant 4$

8 What did you notice about the equation of each line and the value of y where the line cuts the y-axis?

Key term

The **y-intercept** is the point where a line cuts the y-axis.

The value of y where the line cuts the y-axis is called the y-**intercept**, and you should have seen in the exercise above that it is the same as the constant term in each equation. Where there is no constant term the line goes through the origin (the y-intercept is 0).

Understanding Straight Line Graphs

An equation will be a straight line when it is plotted on a graph if it only has terms in x and/or y, and a constant term. If the constant term is zero it will not be shown in the equation, and the line will go through the origin as you have seen.

The equations of straight lines do not have terms in y^2, y^3, x^2, xy or $\frac{1}{x}$, or any other terms like these.

Earlier we looked at the graph of $y = 2x + 3$.

When $x = 0$, $y = 3$. Therefore we know that the y-intercept (where the line cuts, or intercepts, the y-axis) is 3, as we found when we plotted and drew the graph.

The equation could have been written in other ways:

$$y = 2x + 3$$
$$y - 2x = 3$$
$$y - 2x - 3 = 0$$
$$x = \frac{y - 3}{2}$$
or
$$2x - y + 3 = 0$$

These are all the same equation and will give the same straight line graph when plotted.

The first form is the easiest to use, and gives us the most immediate information about the graph, such as that it cuts the y-axis at $y = 3$. It also tells us about the gradient of the graph, as we shall see.

Gradients

For the rest of this section we are going to use equal scales on both axes so that we can count the squares to calculate the gradient.

Remember that gradient is the steepness of a line, and is measured by

$$\text{gradient} = \frac{\text{change in } y}{\text{change in } x}$$

You might find it helps you to remember which way up this fraction should be if you draw a triangle (like a hill) and fit in the words 'up' and 'along'. Hills have gradients and the words fit conveniently, as shown in Figure 7.6.

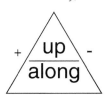

Figure 7.6 Gradients

The gradient of a line that slopes *up* from left to right is positive, while one that slopes *down* from left to right is negative. These signs could be added to the hill as shown in Figure 7.7.

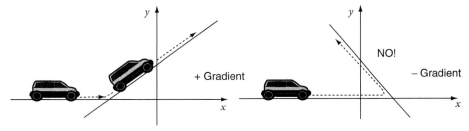

Figure 7.7 Positive and negative gradient

Example 8

Find the gradients of these line segments. Give your answer in its simplest terms. (A line *segment* is just part of a line. In general a line could go on forever!)

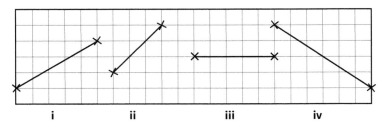

Answer 8

> **NOTE:**
> Draw a right-angled triangle at any convenient point on the line and count the number of squares up and the number along. Remember to make the answer negative if the line slopes backwards.

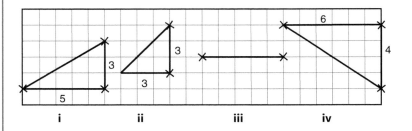

i $\dfrac{\text{up}}{\text{along}} = \dfrac{3}{5}$

   gradient $= \dfrac{3}{5}$

ii   gradient $= \dfrac{3}{3}$

   gradient $= 1$

iii $\dfrac{\text{up}}{\text{along}} = \dfrac{0}{5}$

   gradient $= 0$

iv   Line slopes backwards, so comparing with $\dfrac{\text{up}}{\text{along}}$.

   gradient $= \dfrac{-4}{6}$ or $\dfrac{4}{-6}$, which simplifies to: gradient $= \dfrac{-2}{3}$ or $-\dfrac{2}{3}$

Example 9

Draw line segments with the following gradients:

a   2

b   −1

c $-\dfrac{2}{3}$

d $\dfrac{2}{3}$

e $\dfrac{5}{2}$

Answer 9

> **NOTE:**
> Compare each fraction with $\dfrac{\text{up}}{\text{along}}$, and remember that negative gradients slope backwards.

a $2 = \frac{2}{1}$. Therefore, along 1 and up 2 (or, along 3 and up 6):

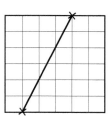

b Either $-1 = \frac{-1}{1}$, therefore, along 1 and *down* 1;

or $-1 = \frac{1}{-1}$, therefore *back* 1 and up 1(or *back* 6 and up 6):

You should see that either way of looking at it gives a line sloping backwards.

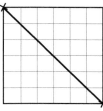

c Either $-\frac{2}{3} = \frac{-2}{3}$, therefore along 3 and *down* 2;

or $-\frac{2}{3} = \frac{2}{-3}$, therefore *back* 3 and up 2.

Again, either way gives a line sloping backwards.

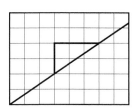

d $\frac{2}{3}$ is 3 along and 2 up:

e $\frac{5}{2}$ is 2 along and 5 up:

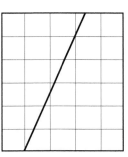

- Looking at these examples, you can see that it makes no difference to the gradient of the line if we count 5 mm squares or 1 cm squares, as long as we use the *same in both directions*.
- Have you noticed that a gradient of 1 slopes at 45° to the horizontal?
- What can you say about a gradient of zero?
- Gradients between 0 and 1 (such as $\frac{2}{3}$ in the example above) slope at *less* than 45°.
- Gradients bigger than 1 (such as $\frac{5}{2}$) are *steeper* than 45°.
- Gradients which are negative make the same angles with the horizontal, but slope backwards.
- Along 1 and up 2 is the same as along 2 and up 4 and so on. Always give your gradient in its simplest form.

NOTE:
Draw the triangle at the points where the line crosses the intersections of the grid lines. The points in **a** have been marked with two crosses to show this.

As you have seen there are three ways that might help you to deal with negative gradients.

The first is to notice that negative gradients slope backwards, and deal with them accordingly.

The second is instead of *along* and *up* to count *along* and *down*. So $-\frac{2}{3}$ is $\frac{-2}{3}$, that is 3 along and 2 down.

The third is instead of *along* and *up* to count *back* and *up*. So $-\frac{2}{3}$ is $\frac{2}{-3}$, that is 3 back and 2 up.

Whatever you do, do not count *back* and *down* or you will end up with a positive gradient again!

Noticing these things will help you ensure that you get the correct answer.

Exercise 7.5

1 Find the gradients of the following line segments. Give each answer in its simplest terms.

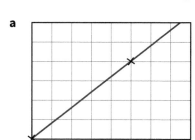 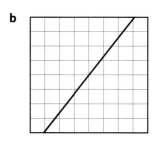 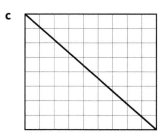 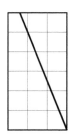

2 Draw line segments with the following gradients:

a $\frac{1}{2}$ **b** 3 **c** $-\frac{1}{4}$ **d** -8

e 0 **f** 1 **g** $\frac{6}{5}$

3 Match these line segments with their possible gradients.

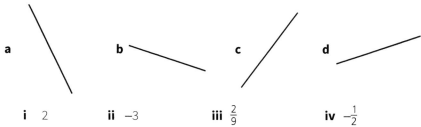

i 2   **ii** -3 **iii** $\frac{2}{9}$ **iv** $-\frac{1}{2}$

4 Copy and complete the table below for the following gradients of lines and the angle each line would make with the *x*-axis.
Two have been done for you.

a gradient $=\frac{1}{2}$ **b** gradient $=\frac{2}{2}$ **c** gradient $=\frac{3}{5}$

d gradient $=5$ **e** gradient $=\frac{1}{5}$ **f** gradient $=\frac{4}{3}$

Angle made with *x*-axis	less than 45°	exactly 45°	between 45° and 90°
Gradient	$\frac{1}{2}, \frac{1}{5},$		

Drawing Straight Line Graphs without Using a Table of Values

We now know enough to be able to recognise and sketch straight line graphs very quickly. For example, looking at $y = 3x + 1$, we know that it crosses the *y*-axis at 1, and has a gradient of 3.

3 is the same as $\frac{3}{1}$, so comparing with $\frac{up}{along}$, we get 1 along and 3 up.

Go to the y-intercept $(0, 1)$, and draw a line with a gradient of 3 by stepping 1 along and 3 up repeatedly, as in Figure 7.8.

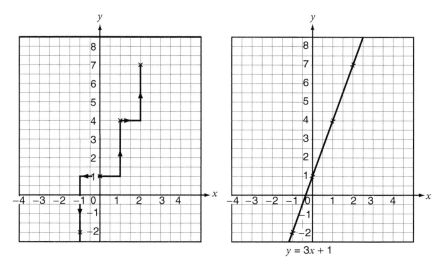

Figure 7.8 Drawing $y = 3x + 1$

Of course, 1 along and 3 up is the same as 1 *back* and 3 *down*, as you can see.

Example 10

a Sketch the graphs of:

   i $y = 2x + 2$ **ii** $y = -x - 2$

b Match the following diagrams with their possible equations.

   i

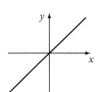

   ii

   iii

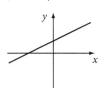

   iv

   A. $y = \frac{1}{2}x + 1$ B. $y = x$ C. $y = -6x + 1$ D. $x = 4$

Answer 10

a   **i**

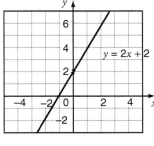
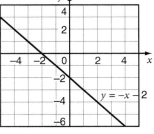

b   **i**   B   **ii**   D   **iii**   A   **iv**   C

Drawing a Straight Line Graph When It is not in the Form $y = mx + c$

Example 11

Draw the graph of $3y + 2x = 6$.

Answer 11

When $x = 0$, $\quad 3y + 0 = 6 \quad\quad 3y = 6 \quad\quad y = 2$
The graph goes through the point $(0, 2)$.
When $y = 0$, $\quad 0 + 2x = 6 \quad\quad 2x = 6 \quad\quad x = 3$
The graph goes through the point $(3, 0)$.
Checking with one more point:
When $x = 2$, $\quad 3y + 2 \times 2 = 6 \quad\quad 3y + 4 = 6 \quad\quad 3y = 2 \quad\quad y = \frac{2}{3}$
The checkpoint is $(2, \frac{2}{3})$.

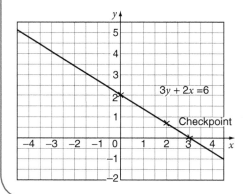

Exercise 7.6

Draw the following straight line graphs by any of the methods we have used.

1 $y = -2x - 3$ **2** $2y - 3x = 12$ **3** $y = \frac{1}{4}x + 2$

4 $5y + 2x = 10$ **5** $6y - 3x + 12 = 0$ **6** $y = x + 5$

The General Form of a Straight Line Equation

We have been working so far with equations in the form of $y =$ a term in x and a constant term, for example:

$$y = 5x + 3$$

When the equation is arranged in this way it can be compared with the **general equation** of a straight line, which is

$$y = mx + c$$

In this general form, m represents the gradient and c represents the y-intercept.

For example, for the equation

$$y = 5x + 3$$
$$m = 5 \text{ and } c = 3$$

It is important to notice that the y term has to be $1y$ for this to be true.

For example, if you have the equation,

$$3y = 5x - 6$$

then you need to rearrange it first into the correct form:

$$3y = 5x - 6 \qquad (\div 3)$$
$$y = \frac{5}{3}x - 2$$

Now $m = \frac{5}{3}$ and $c = -2$.

The line $3y = 5x - 6$ cuts the y-axis at -2 and has a gradient of $\frac{5}{3}$.

The equations may also be given in other forms and have to be rearranged.

Example 12

For each equation find the values of m and c.

a $2y = 5x - 4$ **b** $3y - 3x - 5 = 0$ **c** $5x = 4y + 1$

Answer 12

a $2y = 5x - 4 \qquad (\div 2)$
$\quad y = \frac{5}{2}x - 2$
$\quad m = \frac{5}{2} \qquad c = -2$

b $3y - 3x - 5 = 0 \qquad (+3x+5)$
$\quad 3y = 3x + 5 \qquad (\div 3)$
$\quad y = x + \frac{5}{3}$
$\quad m = 1 \qquad c = \frac{5}{3}$

c $5x = 4y + 1 \qquad$ (turn around)
$\quad 4y + 1 = 5x \qquad (-1)$
$\quad 4y = 5x - 1 \qquad (\div 4)$
$\quad y = \frac{5}{4}x - \frac{1}{4}$
$\quad m = \frac{5}{4} \qquad c = -\frac{1}{4}$

> **NOTE:**
> Be careful! Remember you want $y = \ldots$

> **NOTE:**
> In question 9 is the same as $y = 0x + 6$.

> **NOTE:**
> In question 10 is the same as $y = 1x + 0$.

Exercise 7.7

For each equation find the value of m and the value of c.

1 $y = \frac{1}{2}x - 5$ **2** $2y + x = 3$ **3** $2x = 4 - 5y$

4 $x + y + 1 = 0$ **5** $5x - 4y = 20$ **6** $y = \frac{x+1}{2}$

7 $2x + 3y - 4 = 0$ **8** $y = \frac{x}{2} + 3$ **9** $y = 6$

10 $y = x$ **11** $y = -10$ **12** $y = 2x$

13 $y = -x$ **14** $x + y = 4$

Finding Gradients When the Scales Are Not the Same on Both Axes

---

Example 13

a Find the gradient of the line shown on the grid below.

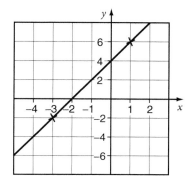

---

b Find the gradient of the line joining the points $(3, -4)$ and $(-2, -1)$.

Answer 13

a

> **NOTE:**
> Choose two points on the graph, for example $(1, 6)$ and $(-3, -2)$ as shown.
> The change in y and the change in x have to be read from the axes. Counting the squares will not work when the scales are different on both axes.

For the change in y, think 'how do you get from -2 to 6?' These are the two y-coordinates.
The answer is you add 8.
So the change in $y = 8$.
For the change in x, think 'how do you get from -3 to 1?' The answer is you add 4.
So the change in $x = 4$.
The gradient of the line is $\frac{\text{change in } y}{\text{change in } x} = \frac{8}{4} = 2$

> **NOTE:**
> In this particular case you could have chosen the points where the line crosses each axis, $(-2, 0)$ and $(0, 4)$, and read 4 units on the y-axis and 2 units on the x-axis, giving a gradient of $\frac{4}{2} = 2$. However, it is important that you understand the first method because the line you are given might not be shown cutting both axes.

b The points are: $(3, -4)$ and $(-2, -1)$.
For the change in y, ask yourself 'how do you get from -4 to -1?'
Change in $y = +3$.
For the change in x, 'how do you get from 3 to -2?'
Change in $x = -5$.
The gradient of the line is $\frac{\text{change in } y}{\text{change in } x} = \frac{3}{-5} = -\frac{3}{5}$

If you prefer you can plot the two points on a grid and find the gradient from the grid, taking account of the scale you have chosen.

Finding the Equation of the Straight Line on a Graph

To find the equation of a straight line, find its gradient (m) and the y-intercept (c) and use $y = mx + c$.

> **Example 14**
> Find the equation of the line shown on the grid in Example 13 above.
> **Answer 14**
> Gradient, $m = 2$, and y-intercept, $c = 4$.
> So $y = mx + c$ becomes $y = 2x + 4$.

Exercise 7.8

Find the equation for each of the lines shown in questions 1 to 4.

1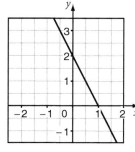

2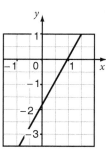

3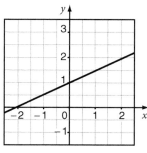

4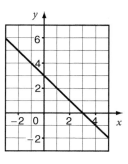

5 Find the gradient of the line joining the point (2, 4) to the point (10, 5).

6 Find the gradient of the line joining the points (1, −3) and (−2, 6).

Parallel Lines

Parallel lines have the same gradient, but will cut the y-axis at different places.

For example, $y = 5x + 6$ and $y = 5x - 2$ both have a gradient of 5, but cut the y-axis at 6 and −2 respectively.

You may be asked to find parallel lines when the equations are not arranged conveniently in the $y = mx + c$ form, so you may have to rearrange the equations into this form first.

Example 15

a Find a pair of parallel lines from these equations.

   i $y - 3x + 5 = 0$ ii $y - 2x + 4 = 0$ iii $2y - 3 = 4x$ iv $5y = 2x$

b Write down the equation of a line which is parallel to $y = -x + 4$.

Answer 15

a i $y - 3x + 5 = 0$ ii $y - 2x + 4 = 0$

       $y = 3x - 5$ $y = 2x - 4$

       $m = 3$ $m = 2$

  iii $2y - 3 = 4x$ iv $5y = 2x$

       $2y = 4x + 3$ $y = x$

       $y = 2x + \frac{3}{2}$ $m = \frac{2}{5}$

       $m = 2$

So the lines $y - 2x + 4 = 0$ and $2y - 3 = 4x$ both have the same gradient and are parallel.

b Any line parallel to the given line will be acceptable.

   For example, $y = -x + 6$.

Exercise 7.9

1 Find the pair of parallel lines.

   a $3y = x - 9$ **b** $2y - 6x = 9$ **c** $15y - 5x + 7 = 0$

2 Write down the equation of a line parallel to $2y = \frac{1}{2}x - 3$.

3 Find the gradients of each of these lines to find a pair that are parallel.

   a 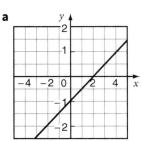   **b** 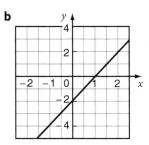   **c**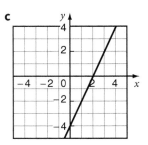

Using Graphs to Solve Simultaneous Equations

We have already solved simultaneous equations using algebra in Chapter 5. We shall now look at a graphical method.

The graphs of straight lines link every single point whose x- and y-coordinates obey the equation for the line. This includes all the rational numbers as well as the integers. No other point on the grid has x- and y-coordinates which obey this equation.

Look at the first diagram in Figure 7.9, which is the graph of $y = 2x + 1$.

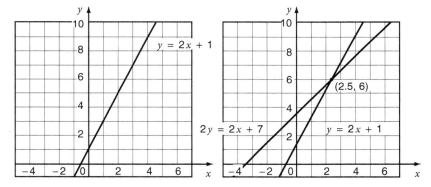

Figure 7.9 Solving simultaneous equations

You can see that when, for example, $x = 2.5$, then $y = 6$.

But this point also lies on the line $2y = 2x + 7$.

(Check: when $x = 2.5$, $2y = 5 + 7$, $2y = 12$, $y = 6$.)

If this equation is plotted on the graph you will see that it crosses the $y = 2x + 1$ at the point $(2.5, 6)$, as in the second diagram in Figure 7.9.

Simultaneous equations are equations which share a point in common, so that the x- and y-coordinates obey *both* equations. If two simultaneous equations are plotted on a graph then the point where they cross is a solution to *both* equations. When you are asked to solve two equations simultaneously, you are looking for the point which satisfies both of the equations.

Two straight lines will always cross unless they are parallel, in which case they never meet.

Example 16

a **i** Find graphically the solution to these two simultaneous equations:

$y = x + 2$ $\qquad$ $3x + 2y = 9$

ii Solve the two equations simultaneously by an algebraic method.

b Show that these two equations cannot be solved simultaneously:

$y = 2x + 1$ $\qquad$ $3y = 6x + 1$

Answer 16

a **i** $y = x + 2$

$m = 1, c = 2$

$3x + 2y = 9$

when $x = 0, y = 4.5$

when $y = 0, x = 3$

Checkpoint: when $x = 2, y = 1.5$

Solution: $x = 1, y = 3$

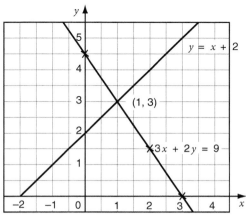

ii $y = x + 2 \quad \longrightarrow \quad y - x = 2 \quad \xrightarrow{\times 2} \quad 2y - 2x = 4$

$3x + 2y = 9 \quad \longrightarrow \quad 2y + 3x = 9 \quad \longrightarrow \quad \begin{array}{l} 2y + 3x = 9 \\ \underline{-5x = -5} \end{array}$ subtract

$x = 1, y = 3$

b $y = 2x + 1, m = 2$

$3y = 6x + 1$ $\qquad$ $(\div 3)$

$y = 2x + \frac{1}{3},$ $\qquad$ $m = 2$

The lines are parallel and will never meet.

NOTE:

A question may ask you to solve two simultaneous equations by using algebra, or by using a graph. It is important to read the question carefully to ensure that you are using the required method to find the solution. If you have been asked to calculate the solution that is what you must do.

Exercise 7.10

1 $y + x = 7$

$y - 2x = 1$

Solve this pair of simultaneous equations:

a by a graphical method $\qquad$ **b** by an algebraic method.

2 Solve these pairs of simultaneous equations by a graphical method.

a $x + y = 2$ $\qquad\qquad$ **b** $y = 3x + 8$

$\quad\ y = x + 4$ $\qquad\qquad\qquad\ 2x + y = 3$

7.6 Drawing Curves

So far we have looked at equations that produce straight line graphs, but other equations produce curves which you need to be able to draw.

Equations of straight lines are easy to plot, and are often drawn on 5 mm squared paper.

However, curves may well be drawn on 2 mm squared graph paper to allow points to be plotted more accurately. The scales on the two axes need not be the same, and they often need to be different to get more of the graph on a reasonable amount of paper.

The approach is still the same. You write down a set of values for x, and calculate the corresponding values of y. Draw up a table, and then plot the curve.

Some examples will make this clear.

Example 17

Draw the graph of the equation $y = x^2$ for values of x: $-3 \leqslant x \leqslant 3$.
Use a scale of 1 centimetre to represent 1 unit on each axis.

Answer 17

$y = x^2$

x	-3	-2	-1	0	1	2	3
y	9	4	1	0	1	4	9

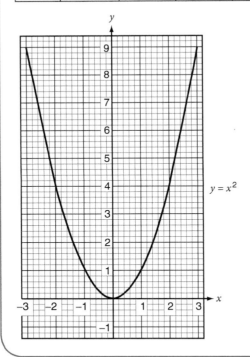

$y = x^2$

NOTE:
The shape this graph makes is called a *parabola*. It may be this way up, or upside down. It may be symmetrical about the y-axis as this is, or about some other line parallel to the y-axis.

Example 18

The table shows values of x and y for x: $-2 \leqslant x \leqslant 2$ for the equation $y = 2x^2 - 3$.

x	-2	-1	0	1	2
y	5	-1	-3	-1	5

a Use the table to draw the graph of $y = 2x^2 - 3$.
Use a scale of 1 centimetre to represent 1 unit on the y-axis and 2 centimetres to represent 1 unit on the x-axis.

b Use your graph to solve the equation $2x^2 - 3 = 0$.
Give your answers correct to 1 decimal place.

Answer 18

a

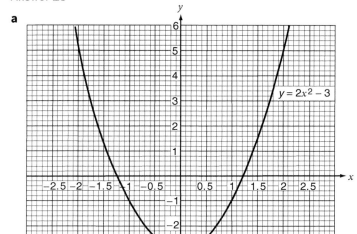

b $2x^2 - 3 = 0$ is found on the graph of $y = 2x^2 - 3$ when $y = 0$. The line $y = 0$ is the x-axis, so the solutions to the equation $2x^2 - 3 = 0$ are the points where the curve cuts the x-axis: $x = -1.2$ or $x = 1.2$.

Example 19

x	-4	-2	-1	$-\frac{1}{2}$	$-\frac{1}{4}$	$\frac{1}{4}$	$\frac{1}{2}$	1	2	4
y	$-\frac{1}{4}$	$-\frac{1}{2}$	-1	-2	-4	4	2	1	$\frac{1}{2}$	$\frac{1}{4}$

Use this table of values of x and y to draw the graph of $y = \frac{1}{x}$ for x: $-4 \leqslant x \leqslant 4$.
Use a scale of 1 centimetre to represent 1 unit on both axes.

Answer 19

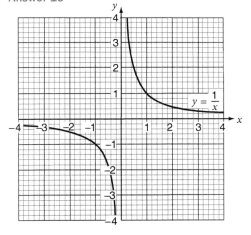

In the answer to the last example, you will see a different kind of graph. This graph never cuts the y-axis. Why is this? To find where a graph cuts the y-axis we must put $x = 0$ into the equation.

When $x = 0$, $y = \frac{1}{x}$ becomes $y = \frac{1}{0}$, or $y = 1 \div 0$.

$1 \div 0$ means 'how many zeros go into 1?' This makes no sense. To try to understand this use your calculator to find the answer to the following division sums:

$$1 \div 0.1 =$$
$$1 \div 0.01 =$$
$$1 \div 0.001 =$$
$$1 \div 0.0001 =$$
$$1 \div 0.00001 =$$
$$1 \div 0.00000001 =$$

NOTE:
Remember that you must never divide by zero.

Divide by a smaller and smaller number, the answer gets larger and larger. You could say that zero is infinitely small so $1 \div 0$ must be infinitely large. In the graph of $y = \frac{1}{x}$ you see the curve getting closer and closer to the y-axis, but we could never draw a graph large enough to find where it might touch the y-axis.

Similarly, see if you can work out an argument to show why y can never be zero when $y = \frac{1}{x}$. Try different values of x to see how close you could get to $y = 0$.

NOTE:
For this question you do not need to copy the graph; laying your ruler across the diagram in the correct place will help you find the answers.

Example 20
The figure shows the graph of $y = x^3 - 4x$ for x: $-2.5 \leqslant x \leqslant 2.5$. Use the graph to find the solutions to $x^3 - 4x = 1$.

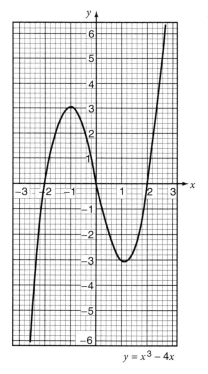

$$y = x^3 - 4x$$

Answer 20
When $y = 1$, $1 = x^3 - 4x$.
Laying a ruler along the line $y = 1$ we see that where this line cuts the curve at $x = -1.9$ or $x = -0.3$ or $x = 2.1$.

Completing a Table of Values for a Curve

Example 21

Find the missing values from the table for the equation
$y = 2x^2 - 3x - 5$ for values of x: $-3 \leqslant x \leqslant 3$.

x	-3	-2	-1	0	1	2	3
y	a	b	c	d	e	f	g

NOTE:

$(-3)^2$ means -3×-3 which means $+9$, and $-3 \times (-3)$ is also $+9$.

Answer 21

a $y = 2x^2 - 3x - 5$
$y = 2 \times (-3)^2 - 3 \times (-3) - 5$
$y = 2 \times 9 + 9 - 5$
$y = 18 + 9 - 5 = 22$
$a = 22$

b $y = 2 \times (-2)^2 - 3 \times (-2) - 5$
$y = 8 + 6 - 5 = 9$
$b = 9$

c $y = 2 \times (-1)^2 - 3 \times (-1) - 5$
$y = 2 + 3 - 5 = 0$
$c = 0$

d $y = 2 \times (0)^2 - 3 \times 0 - 5$
$y = 0 - 0 - 5 = -5$
$d = -5$

e $y = 2 \times 1^2 - 3 \times 1 - 5$
$y = 2 - 3 - 5 = -6$
$e = -6$

f $y = 2 \times 2^2 - 3 \times 2 - 5$
$y = 8 - 6 - 5 = -3$
$f = -3$

g $y = 2 \times (3)^2 - 3 \times (3) - 5$
$y = 18 - 9 - 5 = 4$
$g = 4$

Exercise 7.11

Copy and complete the table for each of the equations given.

x	-3	-2	-1	0	1	2	3
y	a	b	c	d	e	f	g

NOTE:

$-(-3)^2 = -(9) = -9$

1 $y = x^2$

2 $y = x^3$

3 $y = \dfrac{3}{x}$ ($x \neq 0$, so you cannot find d in this case)

NOTE:

$-(-3)^3 = -(-3) \times (-3) \times (-3) = -(-27) = 27$

4 $y = x^2 + x$

5 $y = x^2 - x$

6 $y = x^3 + 2$

7 $y = -x^2$

8 $y = -x^3$

9 $y = x^2 - x - 5$

10 $y = -x^2 - 2x + 1$

When you are satisfied that you have the correct answers to the above exercise then carry on to the next exercise, taking careful note of the following points.

- The scales do not have to be the same on both axes.
- Curves should never be drawn with a ruler.
- Curves should be smooth, without angles.
- If you have to suddenly change direction to include one point you have probably made an error, either in the calculation or in the plotting of the point. Go back and check.
- Write the equation beside the curve and see if you can make connections between the equation and the shape of the graph.

Exercise 7.12

Using the values you found in the above exercise, draw the following curves for $x: -3 \leqslant x \leqslant 3$.

1 $y = x^2$ $0 \leqslant y \leqslant 9$ **2** $y = x^3$ $-27 \leqslant y \leqslant 27$

3 $y = \dfrac{3}{x}$ $(x \neq 0)$ $-3 \leqslant y \leqslant 3$ $(y \neq 0)$ **4** $y = x^2 + x$ $-1 \leqslant y \leqslant 12$

5 $y = x^2 - x$ $-1 \leqslant y \leqslant 12$ **6** $y = x^3 + 2$ $-25 \leqslant y \leqslant 29$

7 $y = -x^2$ $-9 \leqslant y \leqslant 0$ **8** $y = -x^3$ $-27 \leqslant y \leqslant 27$

9 $y = x^2 - x - 5$ $-6 \leqslant y \leqslant 7$ **10** $y = -x^2 - 2x + 1$ $-14 \leqslant y \leqslant 2$

> **NOTE:**
> For question 3 see
> Example 19 on
> page 197.

Exercise 7.13

Mixed exercise

1 The graph shows the flight of a ball thrown from a height of 1 metre above the ground.
   a How far away from the person who threw it does it land on the ground?
   b What is its maximum height?
   c Will the ball clear a wall 1.5 metres high 7.2 metres away?

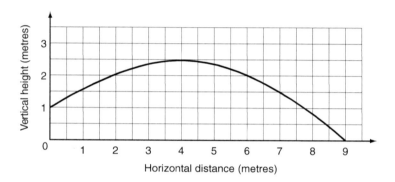

2 What is the equation of the line going through each of the following sets of points?
   a $(1, 1), (0, 0), (3, 3), (-2, -2)$
   b $(1, -1), (0, 0), (3, -3), (-2, 2)$
   c $(5, 0), (5, 1), (5, 3), (5, -4)$
   d $(1, -2), (3, -2), (-1, -2), (0, -2)$

> **NOTE:**
> For each line plot the
> points on squared paper
> first.

3 For values $x: -3 \leqslant x \leqslant 3$ draw each of the following lines:
   a $y = x$ **b** $y = x + 2$ **c** $y = x - 4$
   d $y = 2x$ **e** $y = -2x$

4 For values of $x: -3 \leqslant x \leqslant 3$ draw each of the following curves:
   a $y = x^2$ **b** $y = x^2 + 2$
   c $y = -x^2$ **d** $y = x^2 - 3$

5 An examiner is marking the following answers to questions on curves. All of them lose marks. Can you see why?

     a 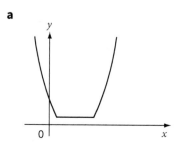   **b**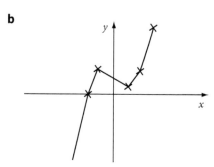

c

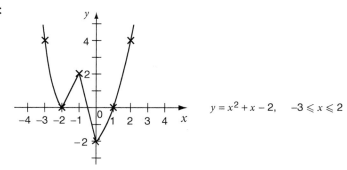

$y = x^2 + x - 2, \quad -3 \leqslant x \leqslant 2$

6 From your knowledge of the graphs in this chapter, try to match each graph to a possible equation.

a

b

c

d

e

f

i $y = x^3$

ii $y = x^2$

iii $y = 1 - x$

iv $y = -x^2 + 1$

v $y = x^2 - 2$

vi $y = \frac{1}{x}$

7 Find the gradients of each of these lines.

a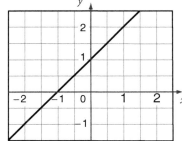

b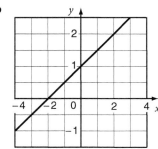

c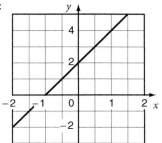

8 a Draw a graph to show the conversion of Singapore dollars to Swiss francs. The exchange rate is:

1 Singapore dollar = 0.8 Swiss francs.

The horizontal axis should show:

$0 \leqslant$ Singapore dollars $\leqslant 100$

b Use your graph to convert 45 Swiss francs to Singapore dollars.

Exam-style questions

9 a Copy the table and the grid. The table shows corresponding values of x and y for the function:

$y = \dfrac{60}{x}$ $(x \neq 0)$.

x	−6	−5	−4	−3	−2	−1		1	2	3	4	5	6
y		−12	−15		−30			60				12	10

  i Fill in the missing values of y in the table above.

  ii Plot the points on the grid below and draw the graph for $-6 \leqslant x \leqslant -1$ and $1 \leqslant x \leqslant 6$.

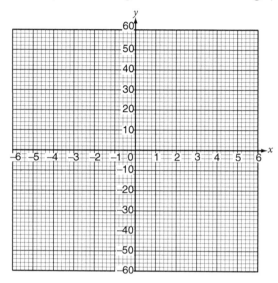

  b Write down the order of rotational symmetry of the graph.

(0580 paper 03 Q4a June 2007)

10

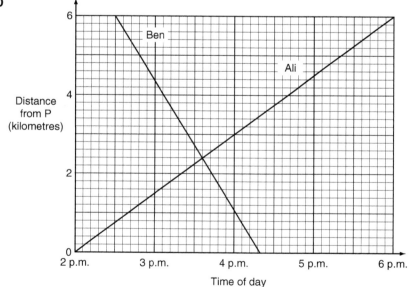

Ali and Ben each made a journey between two towns, P and Q, that are 60 km apart.

These two journeys are shown on the travel graph.
a Calculate Ali's speed.
b Find the number of minutes after 3 p.m. that Ali and Ben passed each other.
c Find how far Ben had travelled when he met Ali.
d Chris left P at 3 p.m. and travelled to Q at a speed of 30 km/h.
On a copy of the diagram, draw the graph that represents Chris's journey.

(4024 paper 11 Q23 November 2011)

11 The graph below shows the amount a plumber charges for up to 6 hours work.

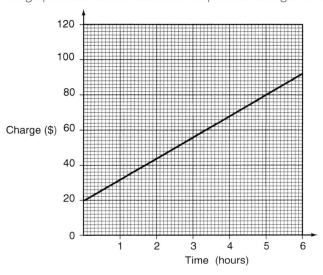

Copy the grid and answer the following questions.

a How much does he charge for $3\frac{1}{2}$ hours work?
b The plumber charged $50.
How many hours did he work?
c Another plumber charges $16 per hour.
  i Draw a line on the grid to show his charges. Start your line at (0, 0).
  ii Write down the number of hours for which the two plumbers charge the same
    amount.

(0580 paper 01 Q21 November 2005)

12 Write down the equation of the straight line through (0, −3) which is parallel
to $y = 2x + 3$.

(0580 paper 01 Q12 June 2007)

13

	Monday	Tuesday	Wednesday	Thursday	Friday	Saturday	Sunday
Minimum temperature °C	4	6	0	−2	−4	2	
Maximum temperature °C	8	10	5	7	2	7	

The table shows the minimum and maximum temperatures on six days of a week. Copy
the table and the grid.
a **i** On Sunday the minimum temperature was 5 °C lower than on Saturday.
    The maximum temperature was 2 °C higher than on Saturday.
    Use this information to complete the table.
  ii Find the difference between the minimum and maximum temperatures on
    Thursday.

b Use the table to complete the graphs below for all seven days.

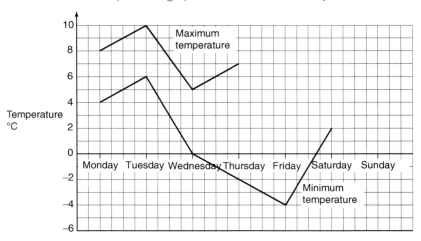

c Use your graphs to find:
 i on how many days the temperature fell below −1 °C,
 ii which day had the largest difference between minimum and maximum temperatures.

d The formula for changing degrees Celsius (C) to degrees Fahrenheit (F) is

$F = \dfrac{9C}{5} + 32.$

Use the formula to change 6 degrees Celsius to degrees Fahrenheit.

Show all your working. (0580 paper 03 Q3 June 2005)

14 A walker leaves his house at 1000 and walks towards a shopping centre at a constant speed of 5 km/h.

A cyclist leaves the same house 10 minutes later.

He travels along the same road at a constant speed of 20 km/h until he reaches the shopping centre which is 6 km from the house.

The cyclist stops at the shopping centre for 14 minutes.

He then returns to the house along the same road at a constant speed of 20 km/h.

a The distance–time graph for the walker is drawn below. On a copy of the axes, draw the distance–time graph for the cyclist.

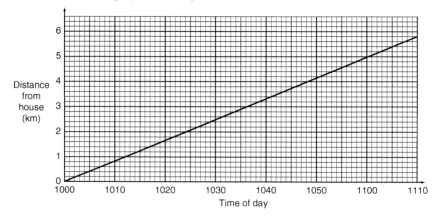

b Using the graphs, find
 i the time when the cyclist, on his return journey, meets the walker,
 ii the distance from the house when this meeting takes place.

(4024 paper 11 Q22 June 2010)

15 a Copy and complete the table of values for the equation $y = x^2 + x - 3$.

x	-4	-3	-2	-1	0	1	2	3
y	9		-1	-3		-1		9

b On a copy of the grid, draw the graph of $y = x^2 + x - 3$.

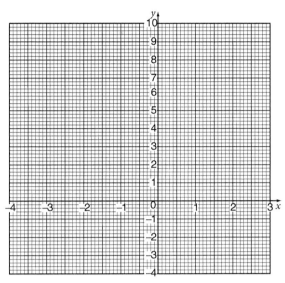

c Write down the coordinates of the lowest point of the curve.
d **i** Draw the line of symmetry of the graph.
  ii Write down the equation of the line of symmetry.

(0580 paper 03 Q7 November 2008)

16 The diagram shows the distance–time graphs of the journeys of Ali and Bala from home to school.

They leave home together and follow the same route.

Ali runs to school and Bala cycles.

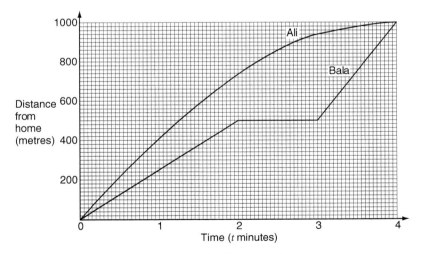

a How long does it take Ali to run the first 700 m?
b Estimate the distance between Ali and Bala when $t = 3$.
c Find Bala's speed when $t = 2.6$.
d Find Bala's speed when $t = 3.5$.

(4024 paper 01 Q21 November 2004)

Length, Area and Volume I

Learning Objectives

Syllabus sections 10, 34, 35

In this chapter we carry on the work started in Chapter 4, and in particular you will:
- learn about units of length, area and volume
- carry out calculations involving lengths and perimeters

- calculate areas of rectangles, triangles, circles and trapezia
- work out total surface area and volumes of three-dimensional objects

8.1 Introduction

The measurement and calculation of lengths, areas and volumes are an essential part of modern life. We may be building a house, making clothes, drawing maps, planning routes from one city to another, calculating the area of a field or the volume of water in a reservoir. You will be able to think of many more examples.

We looked at length, area and volume briefly in Chapter 4. This chapter goes into it in more detail. Avoid using your calculator where possible.

8.2 Essential Skills

1   Copy this table showing conversions for length, area and volume units, and fill in the missing numbers.
    Keep for future reference.

Measurement	Unit	Equivalent	Working
Length	1 cm	...10....mm	
	1 m	..........cm	
Area	1 cm²	..........mm²	10 mm × 10 mm
	1 m²	..........cm²	100 cm × 100 cm
Volume	1 cm³	..........mm³	......mm × ......mm × ......mm
	1 m³	..........cm³	......cm × ....cm × ....cm
Capacity	1 millilitre	1 cm³	
	1 litre	1000 ml	
	1 litre	1000 cm³	
	1 m³	1000 litres	

2 a How do you 'undo' squaring?
  b What is the inverse of cubing?
  c Use your calculator to find the following. If the answers are not exact, give to 3 significant figures.
    i 13^2 **ii** $\sqrt{13}$ **iii** 13^3 **iv** $\sqrt[3]{13}$

8.3 Length

Key terms

Length is a measurement in one dimension.

A length is a measurement in one dimension. It may be the length of a straight line, or of a curved line *measured along the curve*. Adding lengths together makes a longer length, and multiplying by a number greater than one likewise makes a longer length. For example, $3\,cm + 4\,cm = 7\,cm$, and $2\,cm \times 4 = 8\,cm$. However, multiplying by a number between zero and one makes a shorter length. For example, $0.5 \times 2\,cm = 1\,cm$ (or $\frac{1}{2} \times 2\,cm = 1\,cm$).

Lengths do not have direction, so are always positive.

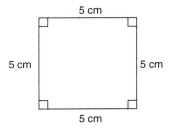

Figure 8.1 Square

Figure 8.1 shows a square with each side of length 5 centimetres. The distance (or length) all the way round the square is called the **perimeter**. The perimeter can either be calculated by adding all the lengths together,

$$5\,cm + 5\,cm + 5\,cm + 5\,cm = 20\,cm$$

or it may be calculated more simply in this case by multiplying one length by 4 since the lengths are all the same:

$$4 \times 5\,cm = 20\,cm$$

You will encounter formulae in this chapter which will help you to calculate lengths, areas and volumes, and it is important that you understand a little about them.

As you can see from the above, if the side of the square was of length a centimetres, then the formula for the perimeter could be either:

$$perimeter = a\,cm + a\,cm + a\,cm + a\,cm$$
or
$$perimeter = 4 \times a\,cm$$

The lengths have either been added together or, since they are all the same, they have been multiplied by 4.

It is not usual to write the units *in* the calculation, but it is done here to make the ideas clearer. However, you must state the units in the answer, and all the measurements in a single calculation must be in the same units. So, for example, you cannot mix centimetres with metres in a single calculation.

Example 1

Find the perimeters of the following shapes.

a

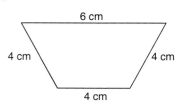

b

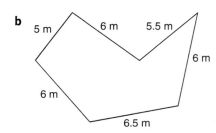

c

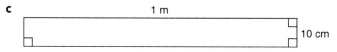

Answer 1

a   Perimeter $= 6 + 3 \times 4 = 6 + 12$
       Perimeter $= 18\,cm$

b   Perimeter $= 5 + 6 + 5.5 + 6 + 6.5 + 6$ (or $5 + 5.5 + 6.5 + 3 \times 6$)
           $= 35\,m$

c   The units of measurement must all be made the same before addition, so either
       Perimeter $= 100 + 10 + 100 + 10$
               $= 220\,cm$
       or
       Perimeter $= 1 + 0.1 + 1 + 0.1$
               $= 2.2\,m$

NOTE:

The perimeter in part a has been calculated by multiplication of a common length by a number *and* by addition of another length.

Practical investigation

As you already know, the perimeter of a circle is called the circumference. For this experiment you need a cylindrical object such as a tin. If possible find one without a lid, or widening, at the end. A piece of drainpipe is ideal, or some other piece of tube. You will also need a strip of tracing paper long enough to wrap round the cylinder.

Rule a pencil mark across the strip of paper, and then wrap it tightly round the cylinder, so that the end overlaps the pencil mark (see Figure 8.2). Trace the pencil mark onto the overlap.

The pencil marks should coincide exactly.

Now take off the paper strip and measure between the pencil marks. This is the circumference of the circle which is the shape of the cross-section of the cylinder.

Also measure the diameter of the cylinder, by taking the largest measurement you can find across the circular end.

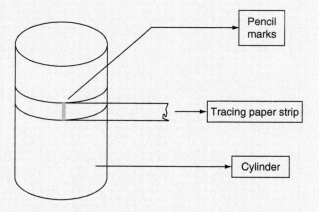

Figure 8.2 Measuring a cylinder

Copy and enter your measurements into Table 8.1. Two sets have already been entered.

circumference	26.3 cm	14.5 cm			
diameter	8.2 cm	4.5 cm			
circumference diameter (to 1 dp)	3.2	3.2			

Table 8.1 Measuring a cylinder

If you can, make the same measurements on one or two other cylinders and include these results.

Possible Experimental Errors

- Not holding the paper strip tightly round the cylinder before tracing the mark.
- Not measuring the diameter correctly (remember that it is the widest part of the circle).
- The cylinder curves out (like the rim of a tin) or in (like the base of a bottle) making it hard to get an accurate measurement.

If you have managed to avoid all these errors you should get a close similarity between the numbers along the bottom row.

The number you have found is an approximation to π (3.141…), a number you met in Chapter 1. Pi (π) is an irrational number. However, it is the ratio of the circumference of a circle to its diameter. How can we say it is an irrational number *and* that it is the ratio of the circumference to the diameter of a circle? The reason is that to be rational a number must be capable of being expressed as the ratio of two *integers*. It is impossible to find a circle which has integer measurements for both diameter and circumference.

We now have the information to write a formula for the circumference of a circle in terms of its diameter.

If the diameter is d, then the circumference $= \pi d$.

You already know that the diameter of a circle is twice the radius, so if the radius

is r, then the circumference $= \pi \times 2r = 2\pi r$.

Example 2
Calculate:

a the circumference of a circle which has a radius of 15 cm

b the diameter of a circle which has a circumference of 34 cm

c the length of one side of a square which has a perimeter of 13 cm

d the perimeter of the shape below, which is a semicircle and a rectangle.

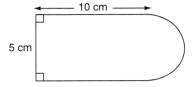

Answer 2

a   Circumference $= 2\pi r$
$$= 2 \times \pi \times 15$$
$$= 94.247\,779\ldots$$
Circumference $= 94.2$ cm

b   Circumference $= \pi \times$ diameter
$$34 = \pi \times \text{diameter} \qquad (\div \pi)$$
$$\text{diameter} = \frac{34}{\pi}$$
$$= 10.822\,536\ldots$$
diameter $= 10.8$ cm

c   The perimeter of a square is the four sides added together, or 4 times the length of one side.
Perimeter $= 4 \times$ side
$$13 = 4 \times \text{side} \qquad (\div 4)$$
$$\text{side} = \frac{13}{4}$$
The length of one side of the square $= 3.35$ cm

d   Draw a dotted line to show the semicircle and the rectangle.

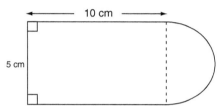

The semicircular end of the shape has a diameter of 5 cm (the same as the other side of the rectangle).
Curved end $= \frac{1}{2} \times \pi \times 5$
$$\text{Perimeter} = 10 + 5 + 10 + \frac{1}{2} \times \pi \times 5$$
$$= 32.853\,98\ldots$$
Perimeter $= 32.9$ cm

Example 3

A triangle has sides of length x, $x + 2$ and $2x - 1$ centimetres. The perimeter of the triangle is 30 cm. Calculate the lengths of the sides of the triangle.

Answer 3

The perimeter $= x + (x + 2) + (2x - 1)$
$$= 4x + 1$$
The perimeter $= 30$ cm
$$4x + 1 = 30$$
$$4x = 29 \qquad (-1)$$
$$x = 29 \div 4 = 7.25 \text{ cm} \qquad (\div 4)$$
The sides of the triangle are 7.25 cm, $(7.25 + 2)$ cm and $(2 \times 7.25 - 1)$ cm.
The sides are 7.25 cm, 9.25 cm and, 13.5 cm.

NOTE:
In all the following examples the dotted lines are only there to help you; they are not part of the perimeter, area or volume of the shape. Arrows on sides indicate parallel lines, and single or double marks on sides indicate equal lengths. Diagrams are not drawn to scale, so you cannot assume that the sides are in proportion to those shown in the diagrams.

NOTE:
In all these examples it is wise to copy the diagram and mark in the lengths of all the sides before you try to calculate the answers. For example, if you are asked to find the perimeter of a shape which has pairs of equal sides, then mark the lengths on all the sides. See example 4.

NOTE:
Can you explain why, in this example, the perimeter is the same as that of a simple rectangle measuring 14 cm by 8 cm? If you were to make this shape with, say, a length of string it would require exactly the same length as for the simple rectangle!

Example 3

A triangle has sides of length x, $x + 2$ and $2x - 1$ centimetres. The perimeter of the triangle is 30 cm. Calculate the lengths of the sides of the triangle.

Answer 3

The perimeter $= x + (x + 2) + (2x - 1)$
$$= 4x + 1$$
The perimeter $= 30$ cm
$$4x + 1 = 30$$
$$4x = 29 \qquad (-1)$$
$$x = 29 \div 4 = 7.25 \text{ cm} \qquad (\div 4)$$
The sides of the triangle are 7.25 cm, $(7.25 + 2)$ cm and $(2 \times 7.25 - 1)$ cm.
The sides are 7.25 cm, 9.25 cm and, 13.5 cm.

Example 4

Calculate the perimeter of the following shape. All the angles are right angles.

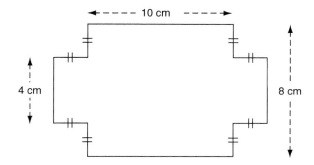

Answer 4

Copying the diagram and enlarging to allow room for the extra numbers:

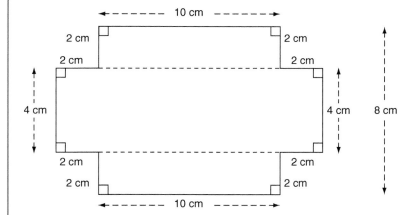

It is now easy to find the perimeter.
Perimeter $= (8 \times 2) + 2 \times 4 + 2 \times 10 = 16 + 8 + 20 = 44$ cm

Exercise 8.1

1 Calculate the perimeters of the following shapes.

a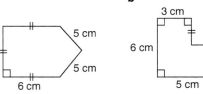

b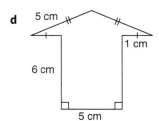

c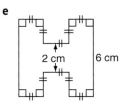

d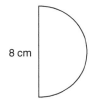

e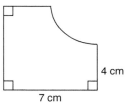

2 Calculate the circumferences of the following circles:

    a radius 5 cm   **b** diameter 5 cm

    c radius 7.15 m   **d** diameter 105 cm

3 Calculate the perimeters of the following shapes:

    a A semicircle, radius 4 cm.   **b** A square, with a quarter of a circle removed from the corner.

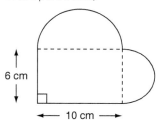

    c A rectangle with a semicircle on two of the sides. (The dotted lines are drawn to help you see the shape; they are not part of the perimeter.)   **d** A rectangle with a semicircle removed from one edge.

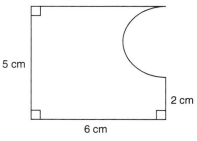

    e Two semicircles joined by two straight lines each 1 cm long.

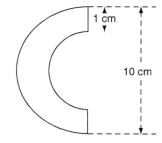

4 Calculate x in each of the following.

a Perimeter = 20 cm

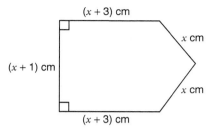

b A circle with circumference = 15 cm and diameter = x cm.

c A circle with radius x m and circumference = 11 m.

d A rectangle with perimeter = 24 cm.

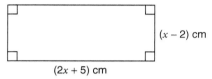

5 Find, by calculation:

a the length of the shortest side

b the length of the longest side in the diagram below.

All the measurements are in centimetres and the perimeter is 37 cm.

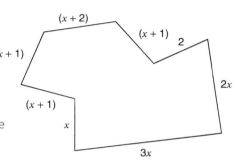

8.4 Area

An area is a measurement in two dimensions. For example, it could be a measurement of the amount of surface on one page of this book. If you think of the amount of surface on a postage stamp compared with the amount of surface on the envelope you will get some idea of area. You could make a reasonable guess at how many stamps would be needed to cover the whole surface of the envelope. Areas of rectangles are reasonably easy to visualise, it is a little harder when the shape is irregular or even has curved edges.

Because the area of a shape is a measurement in two dimensions it needs two length measurements to define it. For example, the area of a rectangle is calculated by multiplying its length by its breadth (Figure 8.3).

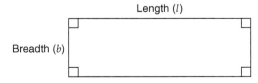

Figure 8.3 Area of a rectangle

Area of rectangle = lb

The units of area are square units. Suppose the length and breadth are measured in centimetres:

area = l cm $\times$ b cm = lb cm $\times$ cm = lb cm^2

This means that the two measurements must be in the same units (that is, both in centimetres, or both in metres, and so on).

The unit of area, $1\,cm^2$, is the amount of surface covered by a square measuring 1 cm by 1 cm, as shown in Figure 8.4.

1 cm
1 cm

Figure 8.4 Unit square

The area of a rectangle is the number of 1 centimetre squares that it covers. For example, looking at the rectangle drawn on the one centimetre squared paper shown in Figure 8.5, you will see that we can actually count the number of squares.

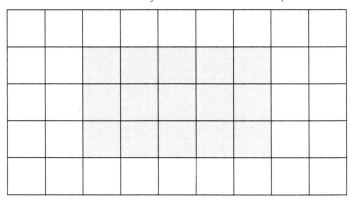

Figure 8.5 Area of a rectangle

The rectangle is 5 centimetres long and 3 centimetres wide, and covers $5 \times 3 = 15$ centimetre squares. The area of the rectangle is $15\,cm^2$.

The length and breadth may not necessarily be whole numbers.

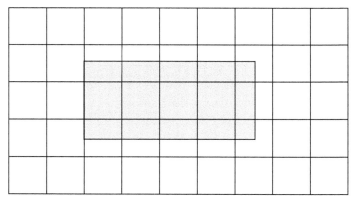

Figure 8.6 Rectangle

The rectangle in Figure 8.6 covers 4 whole squares, 9 half squares and 2 quarter squares.

This is $4 + 9 \times \frac{1}{2} + 2 \times \frac{1}{4} = 4 + 4.5 + 0.5 = 9$ centimetre squares.

The rectangle measures 4.5 cm by 2 centimetres, so its area is $4.5 \times 2 = 9\,cm^2$.

> • **Area of a rectangle = length × breadth**

NOTE:
The lengths of the sides may be called length, breadth, width or height. Whatever they are called they must be measurements at right angles to each other.

Area of a Triangle

Other shapes that you know can be related to the rectangle by various means. For example, the right-angled triangle is half a rectangle, as shown in Figure 8.7.

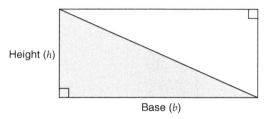

Figure 8.7 Area of a right-angled triangle

The area of the rectangle is base × height, so the area of the triangle is half the base × height.

The formula for the area of this triangle is $\frac{1}{2}bh$.

A rectangle can be drawn round any triangle, as shown in Figure 8.8.

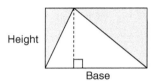

Figure 8.8 Area of any triangle

The area of the rectangle is base × height, and you should be able to see that the area of the triangle is half that of the rectangle, so the area of the triangle is half the base times the height. However, it is essential to see that the height is a line drawn from one vertex of the triangle *perpendicular* to the opposite side. The 'base' and the 'height' of the triangle are *always* perpendicular to each other. The 'base' does not always have to be at the bottom of the triangle as long as the two measurements are at right angles, as you can see from the other examples of triangles in Figure 8.9.

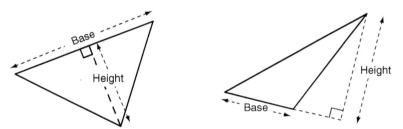

Figure 8.9 Height and base measurements for any triangle

In each case the base and the height are at right angles to each other.

- **The area of a triangle $= \frac{1}{2} \times$ base $\times$ perpendicular height**

Example 5

Calculate the area of this shape.

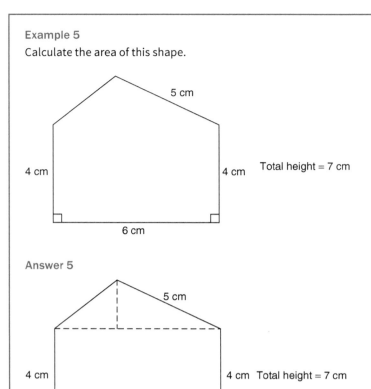

Answer 5

The shape is a rectangle with a triangle on top. The height of the triangle is 7 cm − 4 cm = 3 cm, and the base of the triangle is 6 cm.

Area of rectangle = 4 × 6 = 24 cm²

Area of triangle = $\frac{1}{2}$ × 6 × 3 = 9 cm²

Total area of shape = 24 + 9 = 33 cm²

NOTE:

You do not always have to use all the measurements given, in this case the 5 cm on one side of the triangle is not used.

Example 6

Calculate the area of the shape in Example 4.

Answer 6

Redrawing the shape with all its measurements marked on it:

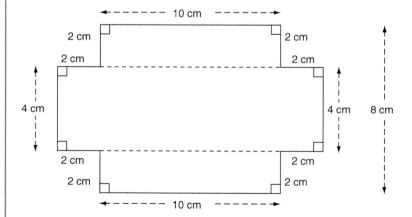

There are different ways to work through this question.

You could divide it into rectangles in different ways. Take, for example, the dotted lines shown above. There are now 2 rectangles measuring 10 cm by 2 cm, and one measuring 14 cm by 4 cm.

Area = $2 \times 10 \times 2 + 14 \times 4 = 40 + 56 = 96$ cm^2.

Or, you could calculate the area of the rectangle measuring 14 cm by 8 cm, and take away 4 squares each measuring 2 cm by 2 cm.

Area = $14 \times 8 - 4 \times 2 \times 2 = 112 - 16 = 96$ cm^2.

In the question about the perimeter of this diagram, we saw that the perimeter was, in fact, the same as that of the 14 cm by 8 cm rectangle. In the case of the area, however, it is not the same.

This shows that two different shapes with the same perimeter will not necessarily have the same area.

Exercise 8.2

All the measurements in this exercise are in centimetres.

1 Calculate the areas of the following shapes by dividing them up into rectangles and triangles when necessary.

Remember:

The double marks on the sides of the diagrams indicate equal lengths.

The dotted lines are there to help you; the areas to be found are enclosed by solid lines.

a

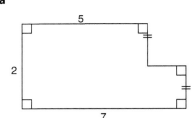

b

c

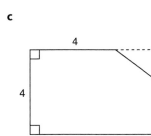

NOTE:
The triangle at the left in shape *f* end could be cut out and fitted in the right-hand end.

d

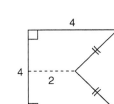

e

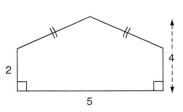

f

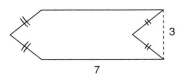

2 Calculate *x* in each of these diagrams.

a Area = 10 cm^2

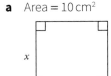

b Area = 30 cm^2

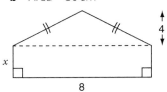

The Area of a Circle

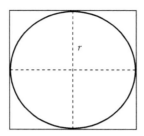 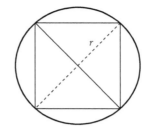

Figure 8.10 Area of a circle

In the first diagram in Figure 8.10, you can see that the area of the circle is less than the total area of the four squares. The area of each square is r^2, where r is the radius of the circle. So the area of the circle is less than $4r^2$.

In the second diagram in Figure 8.10 you can see that the area of the circle is more than the area of the inside square. This square is made up from two triangles; each with a base $2r$ in length, and each with a height of r. The area of one triangle is:

$$\tfrac{1}{2} \times \text{base} \times \text{height} = \tfrac{1}{2} \times 2r \times r = r^2$$

So the area of the circle is more than $2r^2$.

$$2r^2 < \text{area of circle} < 4r^2$$

It seems possible that the area is about 3 times the radius squared, and you can check this by drawing circles on graph paper and counting the squares.

In fact the magic number is once again π.

- **The area of a circle is πr^2.**

We now have two formulae connected with circles:

- **Circumference $= \pi d$ or $2\pi r$**
- **Area $= \pi r^2$**

NOTE:
Remember that an area needs two length measurements multiplied together, in this case the radius $\times$ the radius (r^2).

NOTE:
Remember that the circumference is a length and has one length measurement multiplied only by numbers (π is just a number, approximately 3.14…).

Example 7

Calculate the area of this shape. It is a square with side 4 cm with a semicircle removed from it.

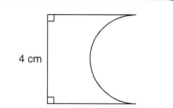

4 cm

Answer 7

The area of the square $= 4 \times 4 = 16 \text{ cm}^2$
The radius of the circle is 2 cm ($\tfrac{1}{2} \times 4$)
The area of the whole circle is $\pi r^2 = \pi \times 2^2 = 4\pi \text{ cm}^2$
The area of the semicircle is $\tfrac{1}{2} \times 4\pi = 2 \times \pi = 6.283\,18… \text{ cm}^2$

The area of the shape = square − semicircle

$$= 16 - 6.283\,18\ldots$$

$$= 9.716\,81\ldots$$

The area of the shape = 9.72 cm²

> **NOTE:**
> Check for yourself whether this seems reasonable.

Exercise 8.3

1 Calculate the areas of the following:
   - **a** a circle with radius 6 cm
   - **b** a circle with radius 3.2 metres
   - **c** a circle with diameter 8 cm
   - **d** a semicircle with radius 6 cm
   - **e** a semicircle with diameter 8.1 cm

2 Calculate the areas of the shapes shown in Exercise 1, question 3.

3 Calculate x in each of the following:
   - **a** a circle, area 17 cm², radius x cm
   - **b** a circle, area 12 cm², diameter x cm
   - **c** a semicircle, area 5 cm², radius x cm
   - **d** a semicircle, area 6 cm², diameter x cm

> **NOTE:**
> *What* In question **3 c** what would be the area of the whole circle if the semicircle is 5 cm²?

4 Calculate the shaded area. The large circle has a diameter = 7.5 cm, and the small circle has diameter = 3 cm.

> **Key terms**
>
> A **trapezium** (plural trapezia) is a quadrilateral with two parallel sides.

The Area of a Trapezium

In Figure 8.11, the solid line shows a trapezium, *WXYZ*. The lengths of the two parallel sides are a cm and b cm. The distance between the parallel sides, or height of the trapezium, is h cm. A dotted line is drawn across a diagonal dividing the trapezium into two triangles, triangle *WXZ* and triangle *XYZ*. The base of triangle *WXZ* is a cm and its height is h cm. The base of triangle *XYZ* is b cm and its height is h cm.

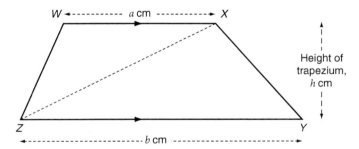

Figure 8.11 Area of a trapezium

The area of triangle XYZ $= \frac{1}{2} \times$ base $\times$ height

$= \frac{1}{2}bh$

And the area of triangle WXZ $= \frac{1}{2}ah$

So the area of the trapezium $= \frac{1}{2}bh + \frac{1}{2}ah$

The area of the trapezium is usually written as:

NOTE:
Remember that it is the *perpendicular* distance between the parallel sides.

- **Area of trapezium** $= \frac{1}{2}(a+b) \times h$

You may prefer to remember in words:

- **Area of trapezium** $= \frac{1}{2} \times$ **the sum of the parallel sides** $\times$ **the distance between them**

Example 8
Calculate the areas of the following shapes.

a $ABCD$ is a parallelogram.

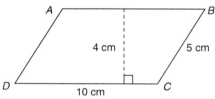

b $PQRS$ is a trapezium.

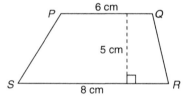

c Calculate the shaded area of the shape shown below. The diameter of the circle is 3 cm.

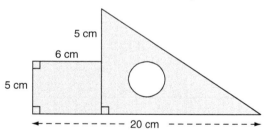

Answer 8

a Draw a line from C perpendicular to AB. The resulting right-angled triangle could be moved so that its hypotenuse BC fits along AD, forming a rectangle.

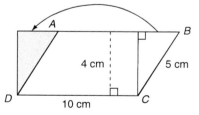

NOTE:
The length of the side BC (5 cm) was not required for the calculation.

The area of the rectangle is $10 \times 4 = 40 \, \text{cm}^2$.
Area of $ABCD = 40 \, \text{cm}^2$

b The area of a trapezium $=\frac{1}{2}\times$ the sum of the parallel sides $\times$ the distance between them

$$=\frac{1}{2}\times(6+8)\times5$$

$$=\frac{1}{2}\times14\times5$$

Area of trapezium $=35\,\text{cm}^2$

c This shape is made up from a rectangle, a right-angled triangle and a circle.
Separating out the shapes:

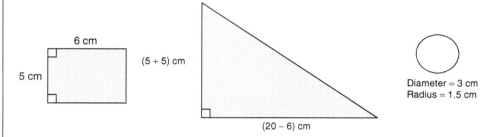

Area of rectangle $=6\times5=30\,\text{cm}^2$

Area of triangle $=\frac{1}{2}\times(20-6)\times(5+5)$

$$=\frac{1}{2}\times14\times10=70\,\text{cm}^2$$

Area of circle $=\pi r^2=\pi\times1.5^2=7.0685\ldots$

Total area of shape $=$ rectangle $+$ triangle $-$ circle

$$=30+70-7.0685\ldots$$

$$=92.931\ldots\text{cm}^2$$

Total area $=92.9\,\text{cm}^2$

In the answer to Example 8 (a), we calculated the area of the parallelogram by transforming it into a rectangle. This will always be possible.

However, if you prefer to learn a formula, then you can use the following:

- **the area of a parallelogram $=$ the length of one of the parallel sides $\times$ the perpendicular distance between them.**

Exercise 8.4

Calculate the shaded areas of these shapes.

1

7 cm

3 cm

3 cm

2

6 cm   6.5 cm

9 cm

3

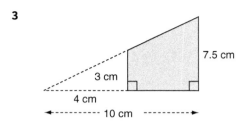

4 Triangle base = height = 5 cm
Square, side = 5 cm
Circle diameter = 5 cm

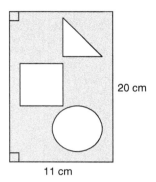

5

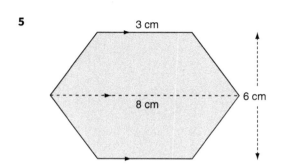

6

5 cm   7 cm

6 cm

Total Surface Area

You may be asked to calculate the total surface area of a three-dimensional or solid shape. This is the areas of all the faces of the solid added together. It can be useful to draw the net of the solid first (see Chapter 6).

Imagine you are going to make the solid out of card. The total surface area is the amount of card you would use.

Remember that a solid cuboid would be made of six rectangles or squares, while a box without a lid would have only five rectangle or square faces, with the sixth side being open.

Example 9
Calculate the total surface area of the following:

a

b

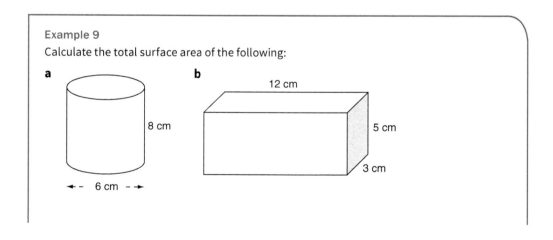

Answer 9

a Draw the net of the cylinder.

The net consists of a rectangle and two circles.
The length of the rectangle is the same as the
circumference of the circular ends.
Length of rectangle $= \pi \times$ diameter $= \pi \times 6$ cm $= 18.849\ldots$ cm
Area of rectangle $= 8 \times 18.849\ldots = 150.796\ldots$ cm^2
Radius of circular ends $= 3$ cm
Area of one circle $= \pi r^2 = \pi \times 3^2 = 28.274\ldots$ cm^2
Total surface area $=$ rectangle $+$ 2 circles
$$= 150.796\ldots + 2 \times 28.274\ldots$$
$$= 207.34\ldots \text{ cm}^2$$
Total surface area $= 207$ cm^2
The surface area of a cylinder can always be calculated by drawing the net, as you can
see in this example.
However, if you prefer to learn a formula you can use the following:

- **The total surface area of a cylinder of height h and radius r is given by:**
  Total surface area $= 2\pi r^2 + 2\pi rh$

NOTE:
If you find this difficult to visualise, think of a tin with a label all round it. Take off the label which will be a rectangle. The two ends of the tin are the circles.

b The cuboid has six rectangular surfaces.
There are 2 rectangles 12×5, 2 rectangles 3×5 and 2 rectangles 12×3.
Total surface area $= 2 \times 12 \times 5 + 2 \times 3 \times 5 + 2 \times 12 \times 3$
$$= 120 + 30 + 72 \text{ cm}^2$$
Total surface area of cuboid $= 222$ cm^2

NOTE:
If you find it difficult to visualise the rectangles, sketch a simple net of the cuboid.

Exercise 8.5

Calculate the total surface area of the following:

1 a box with no lid

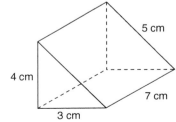
2 cm
2 cm
8 cm

2 a food can with its lid still on

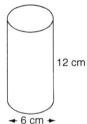
12 cm
6 cm

3

5 cm
4 cm
7 cm
3 cm

4

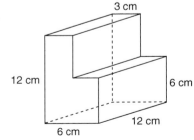
3 cm
12 cm
6 cm
6 cm
12 cm

8.5 Volume

A volume is a measurement in three dimensions. For example, the amount of water that a bottle can hold, or the amount of space a brick takes up. As you will realise by now, three dimensions means that three length measurements are needed to calculate a volume. You can also use an area and a length to calculate a volume because the area is already made up from two length measurements multiplied together.

A volume can either be measured in cubic units, for example, cm³, or in units of *capacity*. **Capacity** is, for example, the amount of a liquid that a container can hold.

Units of capacity are, for example, litres and millilitres. The calculations are the same, it is only the units used which are different. (see the table in Section 8.2 at the beginning of the chapter for conversions.)

The unit of volume in Figure 8.12 is a cube with sides measuring 1 cm, and its volume is $1 \text{ cm} \times 1 \text{ cm} \times 1 \text{ cm} = 1 \text{ cm}^3$.

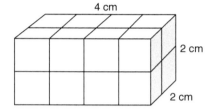

Figure 8.12 Volume of a cuboid

The cuboid measures $4 \text{ cm} \times 2 \text{ cm} \times 2 \text{ cm}$. It is made up from 16 one centimetre cubes, so its volume is $4 \times 2 \times 2 \text{ cm}^3$.

The formula for the volume of a cuboid is:

- **volume of cuboid = length × breadth × height.**

Volume of a Cylinder or Prism

A prism is a shape which has the same cross-section throughout, and for our purposes, it has its ends at right angles to its length.

A cylinder is a prism, as is a cube or a cuboid.

A prism can have a triangular cross-section, or a pentagonal or hexagonal cross-section. Many pencils have hexagonal cross-sections; before it is sharpened such a pencil would be a hexagonal prism. Some containers for sweets are triangular prisms. Beams made from steel for the construction of buildings can have complicated cross-sections, such as **H** shapes, but they are still prisms.

The volume of each of these prisms is calculated by multiplying the area of the cross-section by the length (or height if it is standing up!) of the prism.

- **Volume of a prism = area of cross-section × length.**
- **Volume of a cylinder = area of circular end × height**
$$= \pi r^2 h$$

Example 10

Calculate the following:

a The volume of a triangular prism which has a cross-section which is a triangle with a height of 3 cm and a base of 4 cm. The length of the prism is 15 cm.

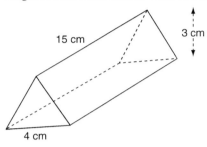

b A pipe has a cross-section which is a circle with diameter 2.5 cm. The length of the pipe is 105 m. How much water can it hold? Give your answer in litres.

Answer 10

a The area of the triangular end (or cross-section) of the prism is:

$\frac{1}{2} \times$ base $\times$ height

Area of end $= \frac{1}{2} \times 4 \times 3 = 6\,cm^2$

Volume $=$ area of end $\times$ length

$\qquad = 6 \times 15 = 90\,cm^3$

Volume of prism $= 90\,cm^3$

b The area of the circular end of the pipe $= \pi r^2$

The radius of the pipe $= \frac{1}{2} \times 2.5 = 1.25\,cm$

The units must be the same for the radius and the length, so we can choose either centimetres or metres.

Working in metres:

the radius of the pipe $= 0.0125\,m$

Area of end $= \pi \times 0.0125^2\,m^2$

Volume of pipe $=$ area of end $\times$ length

$\qquad = \pi \times 0.0125^2 \times 105\,m^3$

$\qquad = 0.051\,541\ldots\,m^3$

Volume $= 51.541$ litres $(1\,m^3 = 1000$ litres$)$

Volume of pipe $= 51.5$ litres

Exercise 8.6

1 Calculate the capacity of the cuboid in Exercise 8.5, Question 1.
(1 millilitre $= 1\,cm^3$)

2 Calculate the capacity of the cylinder in Exercise 8.5, Question 2.

3 Calculate the volume of the prism in Exercise 8.5, Question 3.

4 Calculate the volume of the prism in Exercise 8.5, Question 4.

5 Calculate the volumes of these prisms:

a

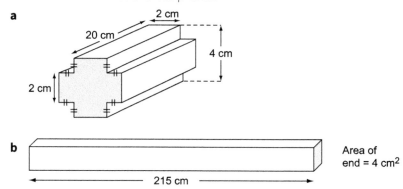

b

Area of
end = 4 cm²

215 cm

6 A cuboid has a volume of 25 cm³. Its length is 5 cm, and its breadth is 2.5 cm. Calculate the height of the cuboid.

7 The length of a triangular prism is 16 cm, and its volume is 36 cm³. Calculate the area of the cross-section of the prism.

8 The volume of a cylinder is 18 cm³, and its height is 4 cm. Calculate the radius of the circular cross-section of the cylinder.

9 A plastic pipe has a cross-section as shown in the diagram. The outer circle has a radius of 20 cm, and the inner circle has a diameter of 10 cm.
  a Calculate the shaded area.
  b The pipe is 1 metre long. Calculate the volume of plastic used to make the pipe.
  c Calculate the capacity of the pipe, giving your answer in millilitres.

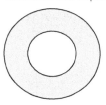

Calculations 'in Terms of π'

In your non-calculator paper you may be asked to give your answer to questions involving circles 'in terms of π'. This avoids having to make calculations with π (= 3.141 59…) when a calculator is not available.

> **Example 11**
> **Without using a calculator** work out the volume of a cylinder of radius 7 cm and height 15 cm. Give your answer in terms of π.
>
> **Answer 11**
> Volume of cylinder = area of cross-section × height
> $$= \pi \times 7^2 \times 15$$
> $$= \pi \times 7 \times 105$$
> $$= \pi \times 735$$
> Volume = 735π cm³

You might also have to give your answer in terms of other letters as well, which can avoid all calculation.

Example 12

A cylinder has a base radius x cm and a volume of 20 cm³.
Work out the height of the cylinder in terms of π and x.

Answer 12

Volume of cylinder = area of base × height

So height $= \dfrac{\text{volume}}{\text{area of base}}$

Area of base $= \pi \times x^2$

height $= \dfrac{20}{\pi x^2}$ cm

Exercise 8.7   **NO CALCULATOR IN THIS EXERCISE**

1 The figure shown below is made from two semicircles, of diameters 10 cm and 4 cm.
Giving your answers in terms of π, calculate
   a the perimeter   **b** the area of the shape.

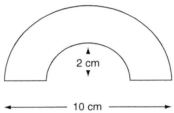

2 cm

10 cm

2 The figure shown in question 1 is the cross-section of a prism with a volume of V cm³.
Giving your answer in terms of V and π, find an expression for the length of the prism.

3

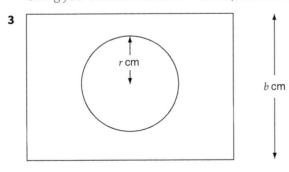

r cm

b cm

l cm

The diagram above shows a rectangle with a circle removed from it. Find, in terms of b, l, r and π expressions for

   a the total perimeter, and   **b** the area of the remaining piece.

Exercise 8.8

Mixed exercise

1 A farmer has three steel drinking troughs.
A has a semicircular cross-section, B has a triangular cross-section, and C is a cuboid. All are open at the top.

a Calculate the area of steel required to manufacture each trough (that is: the total surface area of each trough).

b Calculate the capacity of each trough.

c Find the ratio $\dfrac{\text{volume}}{\text{surface area}}$ for each trough.

d Which is the most economical shape (maximum volume for minimum steel)?

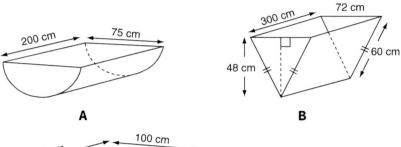

A

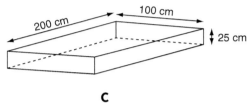

B

C

2 A laboratory measuring cylinder has a capacity of 250 millilitres when filled to the top.
It has a diameter of 5 cm and a height of h cm.
Calculate h.

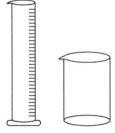

3 Another measuring cylinder is 20 centimetres tall and has a capacity of 100 millilitres when filled to the top with water.

a Calculate the radius of this cylinder.

b The contents of the measuring cylinder are poured into a container which is a cylindrical beaker with a radius of 2.5 cm. How deep is the water in the beaker?

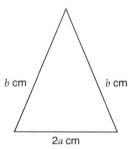

4 The diagram shows a rectangle and a triangle. The perimeter of the rectangle is 20 cm, and the perimeter of the triangle is 16 cm.

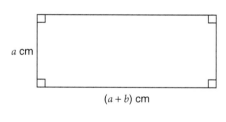

Using the information given:

a Show that, for the rectangle, $4a + 2b = 20$.

b Find the equation connecting the sides of the triangle and its perimeter.

c Solve the two equations simultaneously to find a and b.

d Write down the length and breadth of the rectangle.

5 The diagram shows a parallelogram and a rectangle. The perimeter of the parallelogram is 22 cm, and the perimeter of the rectangle is 14 cm.

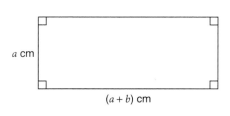
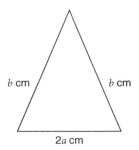

Form two equations in *x* and *y*, and solve them simultaneously to find the dimensions of the parallelogram.

Exam-style questions Part 1

6

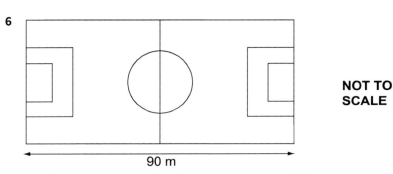

NOT TO SCALE

a The diagram shows the plan for a new soccer field.
The length of the pitch is 90 metres.
The ratio length : width is 5 : 3.
Calculate the width of the pitch.

b The centre circle has a circumference of 57.5 metres.
Calculate the radius.

(0580 paper 01 Q17 June 2006)

7

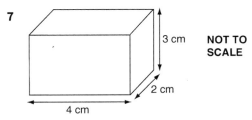

3 cm   **NOT TO SCALE**

2 cm

4 cm

The solid shown is a cuboid with length 4 cm, width 2 cm and height 3 cm.

a Draw an accurate net of the cuboid on 1 centimetre squared paper.

b Using your net, calculate the total surface area of the cuboid.

(0580 paper 01 Q18 June 2006)

8

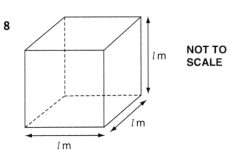

l m   **NOT TO SCALE**

l m

l m

A cube of side *l* metres has a volume of 20 cubic metres.
Calculate the value of *l*.

(0580 paper 01 Q5 June 2006)

9 A 400 metre running track has two straight sections, each of length 120 metres, and two semicircular ends.

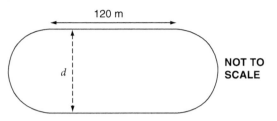

120 m

d

NOT TO SCALE

a Calculate the **total** length of the **curved** sections of the track.

b Calculate *d*, the distance between the parallel straight sections of the track.

(0580 paper 01 Q18 November 2005)

10

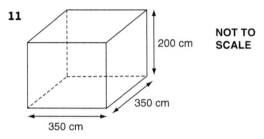

80 cm

30 cm

NOT TO SCALE

The diagram shows a cylindrical tank.

The radius is 30 cm and the height is 80 cm.

a Calculate the area of the base of the tank.

b Calculate the volume of the tank **in litres**.

(0580 paper 01 Q19 June 2004)

11

200 cm

350 cm

350 cm

NOT TO SCALE

A large tank, in the shape of a cuboid, has a square base of side 350 cm and height 200 cm. The tank is filled with water.

Find, in **litres**, the volume of water it holds when full.

(0580 paper 01 Q15 November 2004)

12

A   O   B

NOT TO SCALE

The diagram shows half of a circle, centre *O*.

a What is the special name of the line *AB*?
  i Calculate the perimeter of the shape.
  ii Calculate the area of the shape.

b *AB* = 12 cm.

(0580 paper 01 Q22 November 2004)

13 The diagram shows a swimming pool with cross-section *ABCDE*.
The pool is 6 metres long and 3 metres wide.
AB = 2 m, *ED* = 1 m and *BC* = 3.6 m.

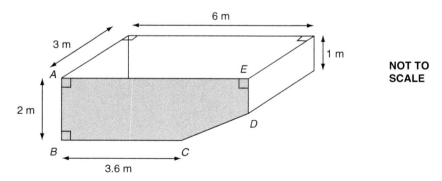

6 m

3 m

A

E

1 m

2 m

B

C

D

3.6 m

NOT TO SCALE

a i Calculate the area of the cross-section *ABCDE*. **Show your working.**
   ii Calculate the volume of the water in the pool when it is full.
      Give your answer in **litres**. [1 cubic metre is 1000 litres.]
   iii One litre of water evaporates every hour for each square metre of the water surface.
      How many litres of water will evaporate in 2 hours?

b Another pool holds 61 500 litres of water.
   Jon uses a hosepipe to fill this pool.
   Water flows through the hosepipe at 1000 litres per hour.
   i Calculate how long it takes to fill the pool.
      Give your answer in hours and minutes.
   ii Change 61 500 litres to gallons.
      [4.55 litres = 1 gallon.]
   iii Every 10 000 **gallons** of water needs 2.5 litres of purifier.
      How many litres of purifier does Jon use for this pool?
   iv The purifier is sold in 1 litre bottles.
      How many **bottles** of purifier must Jon buy for this pool?

(0580 paper 03 Q6 November 2005)

14 The area of a square is 42.25 cm².
Work out the length of one side of the square.   *(0580 paper 01 Q4 November 2008)*

15 a i Calculate the area of a circle with radius 3.7 centimetres.
    ii A can of tomatoes is a cylinder with radius 3.7 centimetres and height h
      centimetres. The volume of the cylinder is 430 cubic centimetres. Calculate h.
  b Twelve cans fix exactly inside a box 3 cans long, 2 cans wide and 2 cans high.

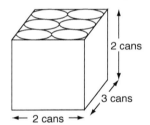

    i Write down the length, width and height of the box.
    ii Calculate the volume of the box.
    iii Calculate the percentage of the volume of the box
       occupied by the cans.

(0580 paper 03 Q5 June 2008)

Exam-style questions Part 2

**NO CALCULATOR
IN THIS EXERCISE**

16 A block of wood is a cuboid, 10 cm by 6 cm by 2 cm.
Find
  a its volume
  b its surface area.

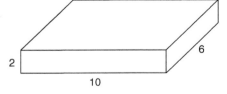

(4024 paper 01 Q7 November 2004)

17 In this shape all the lengths are in centimetres.

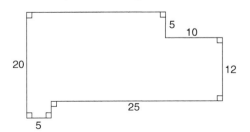

Work out

  a the perimeter,
  b the area.

(4024 paper 11 Q1 June 2013)

18 In the diagram, *ABCD* is a diameter of the circle centre *P*.
AB = *BC* = *CD* = 2*x* centimetres.

a Find an expression, in terms of *x* and π, for the
circumference of this circle.

b The perimeter of the shaded region consists of
two semicircles whose diameters are *AB* and *CD*,
and two semicircles whose diameters are *AC* and *BD*.
Find an expression, in terms of *x* and π, for the area
of the shaded region.

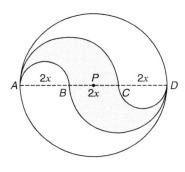

(4024 paper 01 Q14 June 2007)

19 The diagram shows a solid cuboid with base 10 cm by 6 cm.
The height of the cuboid is *x* centimetres.

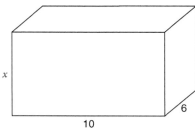

a Find an expression, in terms of *x*, for the total
surface area of the cuboid.

b The total surface area of the cuboid is 376 cm².
Form an equation in *x* and solve it to find the
height of the cuboid.

(4024 paper 01 Q7 June 2008)

20

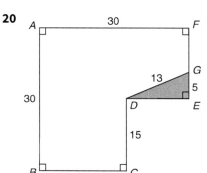

ABCDEF represents an L-shaped piece of glass with
AB = *AF* = 30 cm and *CD* = 15 cm.
The glass is cut to fit the window in a door and the
shaded triangle *DEG* is removed. *DG* = 13 cm and
EG = 5 cm.

a Show that *DE* = 12 cm.

b For the remaining piece of glass *ABCDEF*, find

i its perimeter

ii its area. (4024 paper 01 Q22a and b June 2009)

21 The diagram shows a container consisting of two
cylinders fastened together.
The lower cylinder has radius *r* centimetres and
height 2*h* centimetres.
The upper cylinder has radius 2*r* centimetres and
height *h* centimetres.
Water was poured into the container at a constant rate.
The container was filled in 12 minutes.

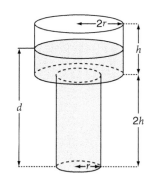

a Calculate the time taken to fill the lower cylinder.

b On the axes below, draw the graph showing how the depth,
d centimetres, of water, changes during the 12 minutes.

(4024 paper 01 Q13 November 2007)

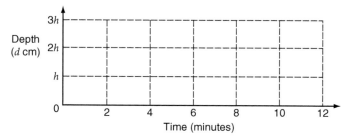

22

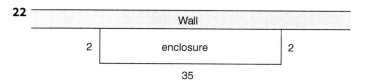

A farmer wishes to build a rectangular enclosure against a straight wall.
He has 39 identical fence panels, each 1 metre long.
One possible arrangement, which encloses an area of 70 m², is shown in the diagram and recorded in the table below.
Find the length of the enclosure which would contain the largest area.
Write down this length and the largest area.
Record all your trials in the table.
Marks will be awarded for clear, appropriate working.

Width (m)	2			
Length (m)	35			
Area (m²)	70			

(4024 paper 01 Q15 November 2007)

23 The diagram shows a solid prism of length 20 cm.
The cross-section, *ABCD*, is a trapezium.
AB = 2 cm, *BC* = 5 cm, *CD* = 6 cm, *DA* = 3 cm
and angle *ADC* = 90°.

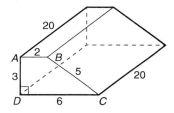

a Calculate the area of trapezium *ABCD*.

b Calculate the **total** surface area of the prism.

(4024 paper 01 Q16 November 2011)

9 Trigonometry I

Learning Objectives Syllabus section 36

In this chapter you will learn about:
- the tangent, sine and cosine ratios in right-angled triangles
- Pythagoras' theorem
- bearings
- angles of elevation and depression

9.1 Introduction

Trigonometry involves the calculations of the angles and the lengths of sides in triangles.

You have seen that triangles need three measurements to define them exactly. In this chapter, one of these measurements will be a right angle. The other two measurements may be two sides or one side and another angle.

You will need graph paper or squared paper, protractor, ruler and a scientific calculator for this chapter.

Please note that if you are asked to **calculate** measurements in triangles you **must** show your calculation and not rely on a scale drawing! This does not mean that you cannot occasionally make a scale drawing to check your own work, or to try to understand a problem better. Do not, however, give it as your final answer!

9.2 Essential Skills

1 Round to 3 significant figures.
     a 56.1935   **b** 7.9514   **c** 6.1445

2 Round to 1 decimal place.
     a 60.199   **b** 72.954   **c** 14.578 01

3 Find x, giving your answers to 3 significant figures if not exact.
     a $x^2 = 4$ **b** $x^2 = 5$ **c** $x^2 = 10.34$

4 Calculate x, giving your answers to 3 significant figures if necessary.
     a $6.9x = 5.1$ **b** $7.3 = \dfrac{x}{4.6}$ **c** $9.2 = \dfrac{7.9}{x}$

5 Make x the subject:
     a $ax = b$ **b** $a = \dfrac{x}{b}$ **c** $a = \dfrac{b}{x}$

6 **a** Find the area of a square of side 3.9 centimetres.

 b Find the length of the sides of a square with area 5.7 cm², giving your answer to 3 significant figures.

NOTE:

In your answers to the questions in this chapter give all angles to 1 decimal place, and the lengths of all sides to 3 significant figures unless otherwise stated or the answers are exact. Always give the units of the lengths as part of your answer.

9.3 The Tangent Ratio

Practical Investigation

To get the most out of this work you need to be as accurate as possible, so have a sharp pencil and work carefully.

Before you start work make sure that your calculator is in *degree mode*.

Try this to check: press ⎡tan⎤ ⎡45⎤ ⎡=⎤. If your calculator has a different logic you might have to press ⎡45⎤ ⎡tan⎤. Either way you should get 1 *exactly*. If you get either 1.6... or 0.85..., your calculator is in the wrong mode and you may have to refer to your instruction book to change it to degrees. Most calculators will show either a D or *deg* on the display if they are in degree mode, but it can be very small and difficult to read.

It is very important that you get to know your own calculator, its logic (the order in which things must be entered) and its settings.

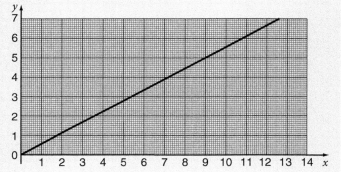

* Take a sheet of 1 mm or 2 mm squared graph paper and draw x- and y-axes with scales of 1 cm to represent 1 unit on each axis.

* Draw an angle with its vertex at the origin and one side along the x-axis as in the top diagram in Figure 9.1. Make it a different angle from the one shown, and make the lines at least 12 cm long.

* At convenient places (where the line crosses the intersection of two grid lines) draw some perpendiculars from the top line down to the base line as in the lower diagram in Figure 9.1, thus making a set of similar triangles.

* Starting with the smallest triangle, copy and complete Table 9.1 for your own drawing. The y-measurement is the height of the triangle, and the x-measurement is the length of the base of the same triangle.

* Calculate $\frac{y}{x}$ to 2 decimal places.

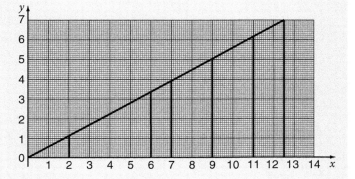

Figure 9.1 The tangent ratio

y-measurement	1.1	3.3	3.9	5	6.1	7
x-measurement	2	6	7	9	11	12.6
$\dfrac{y}{x}$	0.55	0.55	0.56	0.56	0.55	0.56

Table 9.1 The tangent ratio

Table 9.1 has been filled in for the angle shown in Figure 9.1, but yours will not be the same, because you will have drawn a different angle and different perpendiculars.

You should notice that the bottom row of your table has nearly the same value all the way along. The values may not be exactly the same because of experimental error (even the thickness of your pencil line can make the work less accurate), but they should be very similar. If one is very different have another look at it and make sure that you have not made a mistake.

Find the mean of all your values. Calculating the mean involves adding up all the values along the bottom row and dividing by the number of values you have entered in that row.

For Table 9.1:

the mean value of the ratio $\dfrac{y}{x} = \dfrac{0.55 + 0.55 + 0.56 + 0.56 + 0.55 + 0.56}{6} = \dfrac{3.33}{6}$

$$= 0.555 = 0.56 \text{ to 2 decimal places}$$

The next thing to do is to measure your angle as carefully as you can. It is about 29° in Figure 9.1, but the printing processes make it difficult to be as accurate here as you can be in your own diagram.

Using your calculator press ⌜shift⌝⌜tan⌝ (or ⌜2nd⌝⌜tan⌝, depending on your calculator) and enter your mean value. Press ⌜=⌝.

The answer *should* be approximately the size of the angle you have drawn.

For Figure 9.1 the mean is 0.56, and ⌜shift⌝⌜tan⌝⌜0.56⌝ gives the angle 29.2°. The measured angle is 29°, so that is pretty good!

Now press ⌜tan⌝ followed by your angle. You should get approximately the same as your ratio mean value.

Without clearing the calculator display in between, first enter ⌜tan⌝ *your angle*, note the decimal value, then press ⌜shift⌝⌜tan⌝⌜=⌝ and get the angle back. Pressing ⌜tan⌝⌜=⌝ again gives you your decimal value once more.

This shows that ⌜tan⌝ and ⌜shift⌝⌜tan⌝ are *inverses* of each other.

Key term

In a right-angled triangle the side opposite the right angle is the longest side and is called the **hypotenuse.**

What can we learn from this?

In our right-angled triangles we measured the angle at the origin, and then worked out the value of the ratio $\dfrac{y\text{-measurement}}{x\text{-measurement}}$. Does this remind you of the gradient of a line?

Can you see that the *y-measurement* is the length of the side **opposite** the angle, and the *x-measurement* is the length of the *side next to* the angle?

The mathematical name for something which is next to (or next door to) is **adjacent**.

The triangle has one more side, the one opposite the right angle, which is the longest side and is called the **hypotenuse**.

The names of the sides are summarised in Figure 9.2.

If you have trouble seeing which side is adjacent to and which is opposite your angle, draw a straight line arrow from within the angle, as in Figure 9.2. The side it points to is the *opposite* side. The longest side is the hypotenuse, so the one remaining is the adjacent side.

It is important that you are sure you can work out and remember which side is which before you go on.

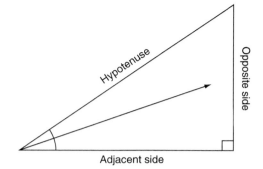

Figure 9.2 Opposite, adjacent and hypotenuse

Also, you need to note that although the hypotenuse is always the longest side, and always opposite the right angle, the other two sides can change places according to which of the other two angles you are using. If you are interested in the other angle, as you can see in Figure 9.3, the opposite and adjacent change places.

Looking back at our investigation work, you may have wondered why we pressed shift tan on the calculator.

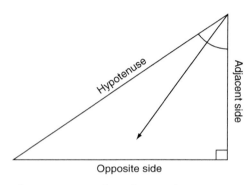

Figure 9.3 For the other angle

The reason is that the ratio $\frac{\text{opposite side}}{\text{adjacent side}}$ for any angle in a right-angled triangle has been given the name **tangent**, and tan is short for tangent. Here, the word 'tangent' does not refer to a line touching a curve, which is also called a tangent.

We say that the tangent of an angle in a right-angled triangle is the ratio $\frac{\text{opposite side}}{\text{adjacent side}}$.

A Note about Calculators

NOTE:
You need plenty of practice with your own calculator. Make sure that it is the same as the one you will be using in your examination!

NOTE:
Sometimes you might see the term *arctan* used to mean inverse tan (or tan⁻¹), but in this book we will use tan⁻¹.
From now on, tan⁻¹ will mean shift tan, or 2nd tan.

If your calculator has a key labelled Ans, you can press it to enter the answer to the previous calculation. If it does not have this key you may be able to use the = key. You can see this in the example below.

Your calculator probably shows the tan key with *tan⁻¹* written above it. This is a very convenient notation for inverse tan, or shift tan. Pressing tan 20 finds the tangent of 20° (0.363970234…), and shift tan (or tan⁻¹) 0.363970234 gives the angle back again.

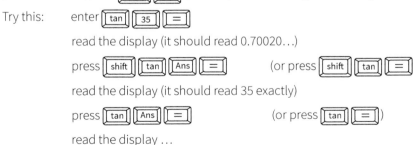

Try this: enter tan 35 =

         read the display (it should read 0.70020…)

         press shift tan Ans =   (or press shift tan =)

         read the display (it should read 35 exactly)

         press tan Ans =   (or press tan =)

         read the display …

This is just to convince you that tan and tan⁻¹ are inverses of each other!

Example 1

a Find the tangents of the following angles. Give your answers to 4 decimal places.

  i 20°   **ii** 38°   **iii** 43.1°   **iv** 77.2°

b Giving your answers correct to 1 decimal place if not exact, find the angles whose tangents are:

  i 0.3249   **ii** 0.8916   **iii** 1   **iv** 6.5184

Answer 1

a **i** $\tan 20° = 0.3640$ **ii** $\tan 38° = 0.7813$

   iii $\tan 43.1° = 0.9358$ **iv** $\tan 77.2° = 4.4015$

b **i** $\tan^{-1} 0.3249 = 18.0°$ **ii** $\tan^{-1} 0.8916 = 41.7°$

   iii $\tan^{-1} 1 = 45°$ **iv** $\tan^{-1} 6.5184 = 81.3°$

NOTE:
Think 'the angle whose tangent is …' when you see $\tan^{-1}$…

Exercise 9.1

1 Find the tangents of the following angles. Give your answers to 4 decimal places.

  a 56°   **c** 27.12°   **e** 60°

  b 75°   **d** 30°   **f** 49.4°

2 Giving your answers correct to 1 decimal place if they are not exact, find the angles whose tangents are:

  a 0.1651   **c** 1.6571   **e** 14.5710

  b 0.8013   **d** 5.9503   **f** 0.5

We now are able to make use of the tangent ratio, and first we will find an angle in a right-angled triangle where two of the sides are known.

Here is a good routine to follow in order to get the best possible answer.

- Remember that the tangent ratio is $\frac{\text{opposite side}}{\text{adjacent side}}$, which is often abbreviated to $\frac{\text{OPP}}{\text{ADJ}}$.
- Check that the triangle has a right angle.
- If necessary sketch the triangle.
- Label the sides in the triangle OPP and ADJ, in relation to the angle you are calculating.
- Calculate the tangent ratio as a decimal.
- Write down the decimal, but *do not clear your calculator*.
- Press ⬚shift⬚ ⬚tan⬚ ⬚Ans⬚ (or ⬚shift⬚ ⬚tan⬚ ⬚=⬚) to get the angle.
- *Without rounding* write down the angle to a few decimal places.
- Give the answer correct to 1 decimal place.

Example 2

In the diagram, triangle *ABC* has angle *BAC* = 90°, *BA* = 5 cm and *CA* = 7 cm. Find angle *BCA*. Give your answer correct to 1 decimal place.

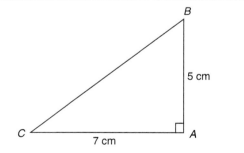

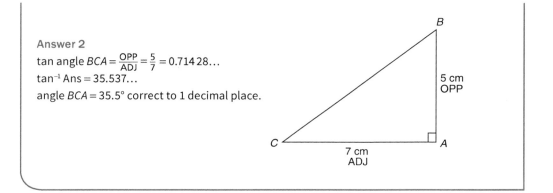

Answer 2

$\tan \text{ angle } BCA = \dfrac{OPP}{ADJ} = \dfrac{5}{7} = 0.714\,28\ldots$

$\tan^{-1} \text{ Ans} = 35.537\ldots$

angle $BCA = 35.5°$ correct to 1 decimal place.

Exercise 9.2

Calculate the angle B in each of these triangles. Measurements are all in centimetres. Give your answers correct to 1 decimal place unless exact.

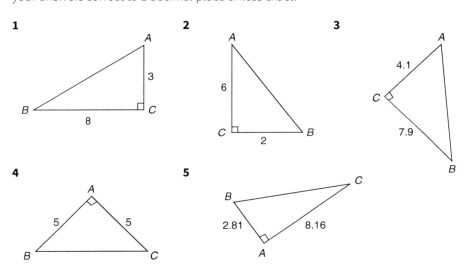

6 In triangle ABC, $\angle BAC = 90°$, $AB = 10$ cm and $AC = 7$ cm. Calculate $\angle ABC$.

7 In triangle ABC, $\angle BCA = 90°$, $AC = 7.96$ cm and $BC = 3.52$ cm. Calculate $\angle ABC$.

Finding a Side

If you are given an angle and the length of the opposite side you can use the tangent ratio to find the length of the adjacent side. Alternatively, if you are given the length of the adjacent side and an angle you can find the length of the opposite side.

Finding the Opposite Side

We will start with finding the length of an opposite side. Using the triangle PQR in Figure 9.4 as an example, we will calculate the length of QR.

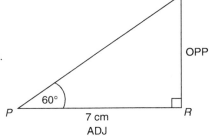

Figure 9.4 Finding the opposite

The routine is as follows.

- Check the right angle.
- Label the sides.
- Write down: $\quad$ tan angle $QPR = \dfrac{\text{OPP}}{\text{ADJ}}$
- Fill in the known measurements: $\quad$ tan $60° = \dfrac{\text{OPP}}{7}$
- Using normal algebra methods rearrange: $\quad$ $7 \times \tan 60° = \text{OPP} \quad (\times 7)$
- Enter into calculator: $\quad$ $7 \times \tan 60° =$
- Write down calculator display: $\quad$ 12.124 35…
- Round to 3 significant figures: $\quad$ 12.1
- Answer: $\quad$ $QR = 12.1$ cm

Finding the Adjacent Side

Using triangle *XYZ* in Figure 9.5 as an example, calculate side *YZ*.

This is a good time to start using a convenient new notation. If the length of a side is unknown it may be referred to by using the lower case letter of the opposite angle, as shown in Figure 9.5. We use x to represent the length of the side opposite *X*.

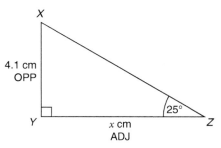

Figure 9.5 Finding the adjacent

- Check the right angle.
- Label the sides.
- Write down: $\quad$ tan angle $YZX = \dfrac{\text{OPP}}{\text{ADJ}}$
- Fill in the known measurements: $\quad$ tan $25° = \dfrac{4.1}{x}$
- Use algebra methods to rearrange: $\quad$ $x \times \tan 25° = 4.1 \quad (\times x)$
  $$x = \dfrac{4.1}{\tan 25°} \quad (\div \tan 25°)$$
- Enter into calculator: $\quad$ $4.1 \div \tan 25° =$
- Write down calculator display: $\quad$ 8.792 47…
- Give answer to 3 significant figures: $\quad$ 8.79
- Answer: $\quad$ $YZ = 8.79$ cm

Example 3

In triangle *DEF*, angle *DEF* is a right angle, angle *FDE* is 56°, and *EF* is 6.3 centimetres. Calculate the length of *DE*.

Answer 3

$\tan = \dfrac{\text{OPP}}{\text{ADJ}}$

$\tan 56° = \dfrac{6.3}{f}$

$f \times \tan 56° = 6.3 \quad (\times f)$

$f = \dfrac{6.3}{\tan 56°} \quad (\div \tan 56°)$

$f = 4.249\,40…$

$f = 4.25$

Answer: $DE = 4.25$ cm

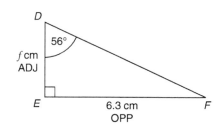

Exercise 9.3

1 Calculate the lengths of each side marked with a letter in the following triangles. The lengths are all in centimetres.

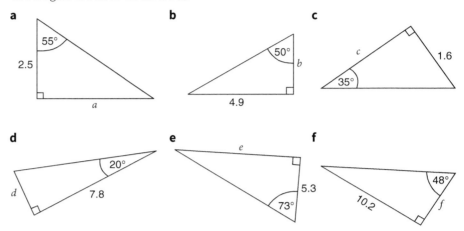

2 Calculate the sizes of the angles or the lengths of the sides marked with letters in the following triangles. All the lengths are in centimetres.

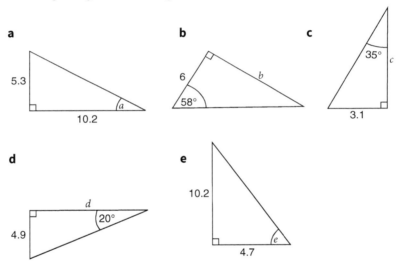

9.4 The Sine and Cosine Ratios

If you were to repeat the practical work at the start of this chapter, but this time measure the length of the hypotenuse in each triangle, you would find that not only is the tangent ratio $\left(\dfrac{y}{x}, \text{ or } \dfrac{OPP}{ADJ}\right)$ constant for each angle, but so are the ratios $\dfrac{OPP}{HYP}\left(\dfrac{y}{HYP}\right)$ and $\dfrac{ADJ}{HYP}\left(\dfrac{x}{HYP}\right)$.

The ratio $\dfrac{OPP}{HYP}$ is called the SINE of the angle, normally abbreviated to SIN.

The ratio $\dfrac{ADJ}{HYP}$ is called the COSINE of the angle, normally abbreviated to COS.

You will need to learn the three ratios.

A made up 'word' is often used to remember these ratios:

SOHCAHTOA

Key terms

The sine of an angle in a right-angled triangle is the ratio of the length of the opposite side to the length of the hypotenuse.

The cosine of an angle in a right-angled triangle is the ratio of the length of the adjacent side to the length of the hypotenuse.

This stands for:

$$\mathbf{S}IN = \mathbf{O}PP / \mathbf{H}YP, \quad \mathbf{C}OS = \mathbf{A}DJ / \mathbf{H}YP, \quad \mathbf{T}AN = \mathbf{O}PP / \mathbf{A}DJ$$

It may be helpful to write:

$$\begin{array}{ccc} \mathbf{O} & \mathbf{A} & \mathbf{O} \\ \mathbf{S} \quad \mathbf{H} & \mathbf{C} \quad \mathbf{H} & \mathbf{T} \quad \mathbf{A} \end{array}$$

to show that, for example, **S**ine equals **O**pposite *over* **H**ypotenuse.

You may want to make up your own way of remembering the ratios, but whatever you do, you need to learn them!

The routines for using sines and cosines are the same as for tangents, but it is now more important to label the sides of the triangle to work out which ratio to use.

We will work through one example to show this step.

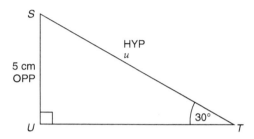

Figure 9.6 Finding the hypotenuse

Find the length of the hypotenuse in triangle *STU* in Figure 9.6.

In this triangle, we are given an angle and the opposite side and are asked to find the hypotenuse.

- Label the sides we are using (in this case OPP and HYP).
- Choose appropriately sine, cosine or tangent. Using SOHCAHTOA we can see that it is SINE, which links OPP and HYP.
- Write down: $\sin = \dfrac{OPP}{HYP}$
- Fill in the measurements. $\sin 30° = \dfrac{5}{u}$
- Use algebra to rearrange: $u \times \sin 30° = 5 \quad (\times u)$

  $u = \dfrac{5}{\sin 30°} \quad (\div \sin 30°)$
- Enter 5 ÷ sin 30° into calculator.
- Write down display: 10
- Answer is exact so $u = 10$
- Answer: $ST = 10\,\text{cm}$

Example 4

Calculate the measurements represented by letters in the following triangles. State the units in your answers.

a

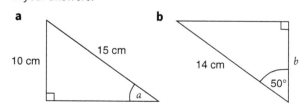

c

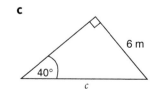

NOTE:

Remember, we are always referring to the ratios of the lengths of sides. The lengths must always be expressed in the same units. (For example, in cm or m or km, but not in mixtures of any two!)

NOTE:

The maximum value of the sine or cosine of any angle is 1. If you enter, for example, $\sin^{-1} 1.21$ into your calculator you will get an error message, and if this is the result of a calculation then you must have made a mistake in the calculation. However, the tangent of an angle can be any number. But, note that the tangent of 90° does not exist!

Answer 4

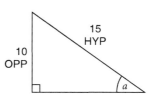

a $\sin = \dfrac{OPP}{HYP}$

$\sin a = \dfrac{10}{15} = 0.666\,66...$

$\sin^{-1} \text{Ans} = 41.813...$

$a = 41.8°$

b $\cos = \dfrac{ADJ}{HYP}$

$\cos 50° = \dfrac{b}{14}$

$14 \times \cos 50° = b \qquad (\times 14)$

$b = 8.999\,020...$

$b = 9.00\,\text{cm}$

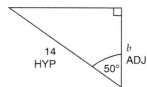

c $\sin = \dfrac{OPP}{HYP}$

$\sin 40° = \dfrac{6}{c}$

$c \times \sin 40° = 6 \qquad (\times c)$

$c = \dfrac{6}{\sin 40°} \qquad (\times \sin 40°)$

$c = 9.3343...$

$c = 9.33\,\text{m}$

Exercise 9.4

Use the sine and cosine ratios to answer the following questions.

1 Calculate $\angle ACB$.

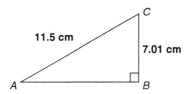

2 Calculate *DF*.

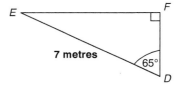

NOTE:

In questions 5 to 10 draw the triangles and label the sides before trying to do the calculations. In each question just sketch a right-angled triangle and make sure that you write the correct letter beside the right angle, otherwise your answer will be wrong!

3 Calculate $\angle IGH$.

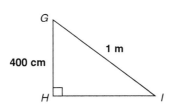

4 Calculate *JK*.

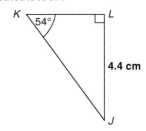

5 In triangle *MNP*, $\angle P = 90°$, $\angle M = 31°$, $NP = 10.6\,\text{cm}$. Calculate the length of *NM*.

6 In triangle *QRS*, $\angle Q = 90°$, $RS = 9.46\,\text{cm}$, $SQ = 5.12\,\text{cm}$. Calculate $\angle S$.

7 In triangle *TVW*, $\angle V = 90°$, $VW = 11.5\,\text{cm}$, $\angle T = 80°$. Calculate the length of *WT*.

8 In triangle *XYZ*, $\angle Y = 90°$, $ZX = 51$ metres, $\angle X = 57°$. Calculate the length of *ZY*.

9 In triangle *ABC*, $\angle C = 90°$, $AB = 12.7\,\text{cm}$, $AC = 11.3\,\text{cm}$. Calculate $\angle B$.

10 In triangle *DEF*, $\angle F = 90°$, $\angle D = 37°$, $DF = 7.23$ metres. Calculate the length of *DE*.

9.5 Pythagoras' Theorem

There is one more useful relationship that you need to know, this time connecting the lengths of all the sides of a right-angled triangle. The theorem actually connects the *areas* of the *squares* drawn on each of the sides, and from these we can work out the lengths of the sides.

Pythagoras was a Greek philosopher who lived 2500 years ago. He found that the 'square on the hypotenuse of a right-angled triangle is equal to the sum of the squares on the other two sides'.

This has been very important ever since and is used every day in, for example, architecture, engineering, surveying, science and so on. It was especially important for the Greeks in their architecture.

Figure 9.7 illustrates Pythagoras' theorem.

You will see that the 'square on the hypotenuse' and the 'squares on the other two sides' have been drawn.

If you trace this diagram and cut the two smaller squares up into smaller pieces you will be able to fit these pieces exactly onto the larger square, showing that the sum of the *areas* of the two smaller squares is indeed equal to the *area* of the largest square.

Figure 9.8 shows an easy method for cutting one of the two smaller squares into pieces which can be rearranged with the smallest square to fit exactly on the largest square. You can use this method for any right-angled triangle if you want to check this theorem.

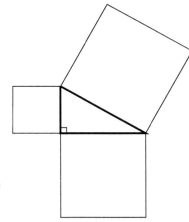

Figure 9.7 Pythagoras' theorem

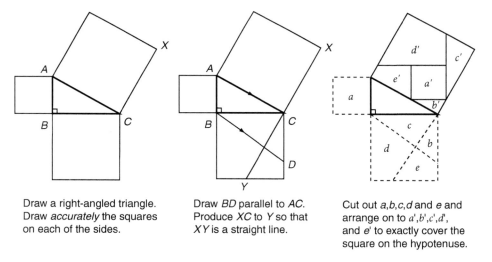

Draw a right-angled triangle. Draw *accurately* the squares on each of the sides.

Draw *BD* parallel to *AC*. Produce *XC* to *Y* so that *XY* is a straight line.

Cut out *a,b,c,d* and *e* and arrange on to *a',b',c',d'*, and *e'* to exactly cover the square on the hypotenuse.

Figure 9.8 Proving Pythagoras' theorem

In practice the use of this theorem means that we can find the lengths of any of the three sides of a right-angled triangle if we know those of the other two sides.

For example, suppose we need to find the third side when the hypotenuse is 10 cm, and one of the other sides is 4 cm. We will call the unknown side *x*. The lengths of the sides are in centimeters (see Figure 9.9).

- Sketch the triangle.
- Draw the squares *as recognisable squares*.
- The areas of the two smaller squares add to make the area of the largest square, so the area of the square we want must be the *difference* between the other two.

$x^2 = 100 - 16$

$x^2 = 84$

- We undo squaring by square rooting.

$x = \sqrt{84}$

$x = 9.165\,15\ldots$

- Answer: $x = 9.17\,\text{cm}$

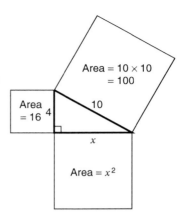

Figure 9.9 Using Pythagoras' theorem

Example 5

In triangle ABC, $AB = 6.5$ centimetres, $BC = 2.3$ centimetres and angle $ABC = 90°$.
 a Sketch the triangle, showing all the given measurements.
 b Calculate the length of AC.

Answer 5

a

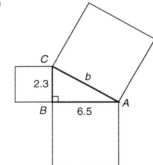

 b The area of the square on the side $CB = 2.3^2$
 The area of the square on the side $AB = 6.5^2$
 The area of the square on the side $AC = b^2$
 From the figure we can see that $b^2 = 2.3^2 + 6.5^2$

$$b^2 = 47.54$$
$$b = \sqrt{47.54}$$
$$b = 6.894\,92\ldots$$

 Answer $AC = 6.89\,\text{cm}$

Work through the following exercise using the same routine, drawing the triangle and the squares on each side.

Exercise 9.5

1 Calculate *BC*.

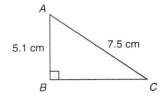

2 Calculate *EF*.

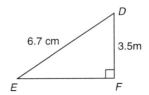

3 In triangle *PQR*, ∠*PRQ* = 90°, *PR* = 6 m, *QR* = 11 m. Calculate *PQ*.

4 In triangle *XYZ*, ∠*ZYX* = 90°, *ZY* = 4.2 cm, *ZX* = 5.7 cm. Calculate *XY*.

Once you are confident that you can see which two squares on which sides add to give the square on the third it is no longer necessary to draw the squares, but remember that the two smaller squares add to give the largest.

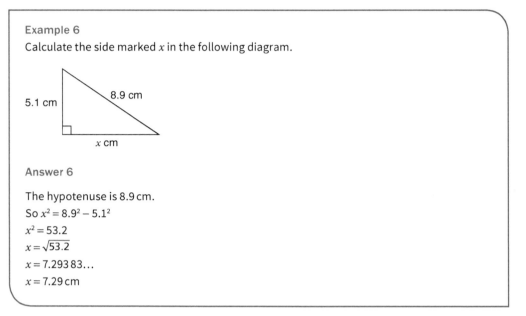

Example 6

Calculate the side marked *x* in the following diagram.

Answer 6

The hypotenuse is 8.9 cm.

So $x^2 = 8.9^2 - 5.1^2$

$x^2 = 53.2$

$x = \sqrt{53.2}$

$x = 7.293\,83\ldots$

$x = 7.29$ cm

> **NOTE:**
> Always finish by checking whether the answer is reasonable. If you find the side ***x*** to be longer than the hypotenuse you have made a mistake! Remember, however, that the diagrams will not be drawn to scale.

Exercise 9.6

Calculate the lengths of the sides marked with letters in the following diagrams. State the units in your answers.

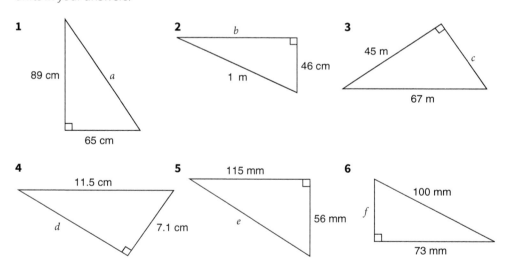

We will now practise choosing Pythagoras' theorem or the sine, cosine and tangent ratios to solve right-angled triangles before going on to use them to solve problems.

* Remember that these only apply to right-angled triangles.
* Draw the diagram and write in the given measurements.
* Write a small letter beside each measurement you are asked to find.
* You now need to look carefully at the diagram to decide how to calculate the information.
* If you are given two sides and asked to find the third you will need to use Pythagoras' theorem.

- If you are given two sides and asked to find an angle, or given an angle and a side, you will need to use the sine, cosine or tangent ratios. In this case label the sides OPP, ADJ and HYP to help you decide which ratio to use.
- Remember SOHCAHTOA.

Exercise 9.7

1 Calculate *BC*.

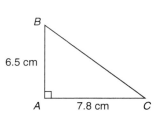

2 Calculate *EF*.

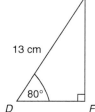

3 Calculate *GI*.

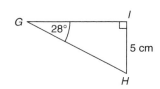

4 Calculate *JK*.   **5** Calculate *NM*.   **6** Calculate *PR*.

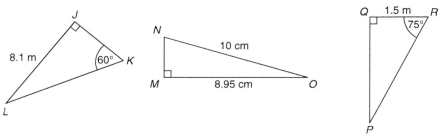

7 In triangle *STU*, ∠*TUS* = 90°, *ST* = 10.5 cm, *SU* = 7 cm. Calculate ∠*STU*.

8 In triangle *VWX*, ∠*XVW* = 90°, *WX* = 8 cm, *XV* = 6.81 cm. Calculate ∠*VXW*.

9 In triangle *XYZ*, ∠*XYZ* = 90°, *XY* = 5.7 cm, *ZY* = 4.3 cm. Calculate ∠*XZY*.

Example 7

The diagram shows the triangle *ABC* and the perpendicular *AD* from *A* to the side *BC*.
Using the information on the diagram, calculate:

a *AD*

b *AB*

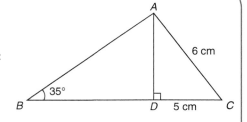

Answer 7

Let *AD* be *x* cm and *AB* be *y* cm as shown in the diagram.

a

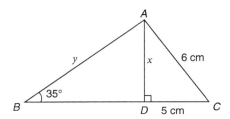

In triangle *ADC*, *AC* is the hypotenuse.

Using Pythagoras' theorem, $x^2 = 6^2 - 5^2$

$x^2 = 11$

$$x = \sqrt{11}$$
$$x = 3.316\,624\ldots$$
$$x = 3.32$$
$$AD = 3.32\,\text{cm}$$

Let AB be y cm as shown in the diagram.

b

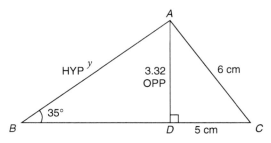

In triangle ABD, angle $ABD = 35°$, AD is the OPP side, and AB is the HYP.

$$\sin = \frac{\text{OPP}}{\text{HYP}}$$
$$\sin 35° = \frac{3.316\,624\ldots}{y}$$
$$y \times \sin 35° = 3.316\,624\ldots \qquad (\times y)$$
$$y = \frac{3.316\,624\ldots}{\sin 35°} \qquad (\div \sin 35°)$$
$$y = 5.782\,357\ldots$$
$$y = 5.78$$
$$AB = 5.78\,\text{cm}$$

There are other shapes which have right-angled triangles, although they are not necessarily immediately obvious.

For example, the line of symmetry of an isosceles triangle, or the diagonal of a rectangle, both divide the diagram into two equal right-angled triangles as shown in Figure 9.10.

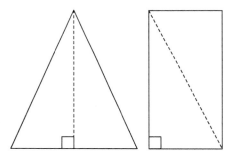

Figure 9.10 Finding right-angled triangles

Example 8
ABC is an equilateral triangle with side 10 centimetres. Calculate the height of the triangle.

Answer 8
Sketch the triangle and draw the perpendicular height, AD.
Let the height be h cm.
D is the midpoint of CB (symmetry of an equilateral triangle).
In triangle ACD, $AC = 10$ cm, $CD = 5$ cm and $\angle ADC = 90°$.
Using Pythagoras' theorem,
$$h^2 = 10^2 - 5^2$$
$$h^2 = 75$$
$$h = \sqrt{75} = 8.660\,25\ldots$$
$$h = 8.66\,\text{cm}$$
The height of the triangle is 8.66 centimetres.

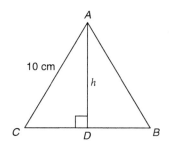

Exercise 9.8

NOTE: When necessary draw sketches before answering the questions.

1 Pythagorean triples are sets of whole numbers which, when used as the lengths of the sides of a triangle, make it a right-angled triangle.
For example, 3, 4 and 5, because $3^2 + 4^2 = 5^2$.

   a Find the missing number from each of these sets of Pythagorean triples.

   i 5, …, 13   **ii** 6, 8, …   **iii** …, 24, 25

   b A set square is a right-angled triangle used for drawing or setting out right angles. Lena was on a building site and needed to lay out a rectangle for the foundation of a building. She had one strip of wood 5 metres long and another 7 metres long, a saw and a tape measure. Describe how she could make a set square.

2 Calculate the length of the diagonal of a square which has sides of 4 cm.

3 Calculate the height of an equilateral triangle which has sides of length 10 cm.

4 The diagram shows the side of a house with a pitched roof. *BC* and *CD* are 4.5 metres each. *AB* and *DE* are 6 metres and *AE* is 8 metres.

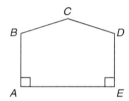

Calculate the total height of the house.

NOTE:
Copy the diagram and draw a perpendicular from *B* down to the side *CD* to make a triangle and a rectangle.

5 *ABCD* is a trapezium. *AB* is 5 centimetres, *AD* is 4 centimetres and *DC* is 8.5 centimetres.

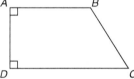

Calculate

   a *BC*   **b** ∠*BCD*   **c** ∠*ABC*.

6 Using the diagram, calculate the length *AE*.

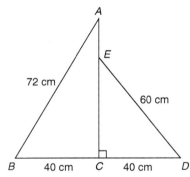

7 In the diagram below, *AB* = 16 centimetres, *AD* = 20 centimetres, *CD* = 15 centimetres.

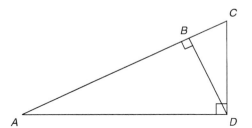

Calculate

   a *BD*   **b** *BC*   **c** ∠*BDC*.

9.6 Bearings

A **bearing** is the direction of one place from another, using due north as the reference direction.

The **mariner's compass**, shown in Figure 9.11, uses the four main directions, **N**orth, **S**outh, **E**ast and **W**est. These can then be divided into four more directions, as shown in the diagram. The order of the letters for each bearing is always given with the main bearing first, with north and south before east and west. For example, we would say north-west, not west-north.

Half way between north and north-east is north-north-east or NNE, and in between north-east and east is east-north-east or ENE.

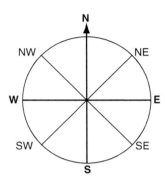

Figure 9.11 The mariner's compass

Example 9

Name, and give the abbreviations for, the following bearings:
a Halfway between south-west and west
b Halfway between south-east and south.

Answer 9

a West-south-west, or WSW.
b South-south-east, or SSE.

With the mariner's compass there is a limit to how accurately you can measure bearings because the naming of the bearings would become very confusing.

The bearings used more often today are three-figure bearings.

For **three-figure bearings**, north is 000°, east is 090°, south is 180°, and west is 270°.

This is shown in Figure 9.12.

As you will see, the angles are measured in a clockwise direction, starting from north, 000°, and going all the way round to 360°, which is north again. This allows many more directions to be specified clearly, for example, 021° which would be difficult to express with the mariner's compass. Angles less than 100° normally have a zero in front to make them three-figure.

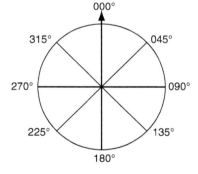

Figure 9.12 Three-figure bearings

Using Three-figure Bearings

Figure 9.13 shows two towns, Alpha and Beta. We need to know the bearing of Alpha *from* Beta.

The way this is written is important, because *from* Beta means that you must imagine yourself standing at Beta and turning to look towards Alpha.

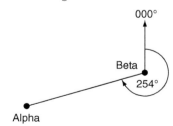

Figure 9.13 Using three-figure bearings

Stand at Beta, face north (000°) and turn to your right (clockwise) until you are facing Alpha. The angle you have turned through is the three-figure bearing of Alpha from Beta.

It is very convenient to have a 360° protractor for measuring bearings. If you do not have a 360° protractor, you need to either measure the obtuse angle in the above diagram and subtract it from 360°, or draw the south (180°) line in the diagram, measure the acute angle and add 180°.

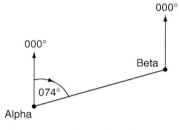

Figure 9.14 Bearing of Beta from Alpha

Check with the diagram above that you can get the correct bearing by measuring. It should be about 254°, allowing for slight errors in the printing process.

The next thing to be aware of is that the bearing of Beta from Alpha is not the same as the bearing of Alpha from Beta. For this you need to draw in another north line at Alpha, making sure that it is parallel to the north line at Beta (Figure 9.14).

Now imagine you are standing at Alpha looking north, and then turn to your right (clockwise) until you are facing Beta. The angle you have turned through will give you the bearing of Beta from Alpha. It is 074° as shown in Figure 9.14.

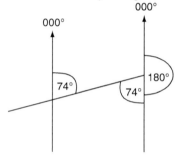

Figure 9.15 Relationship between bearings

You should be aware that angles in parallel lines frequently come into bearings questions because north lines are always parallel. Drawing in the south lines will often help with calculations. Figure 9.15 shows how the south lines help to show the relationship between the bearings of Alpha from Beta (254°) with the bearing of Beta from Alpha (74°) above. In Figure 9.15, 254° is split into 180° and 74°.

If you are not sure about these angles, revise *corresponding*, *alternate* and *vertically opposite* angles.

The next example uses alternate angles to calculate a bearing.

Example 10

The diagram shows the relative locations of a hospital helipad (*H*) and a casualty (*C*).

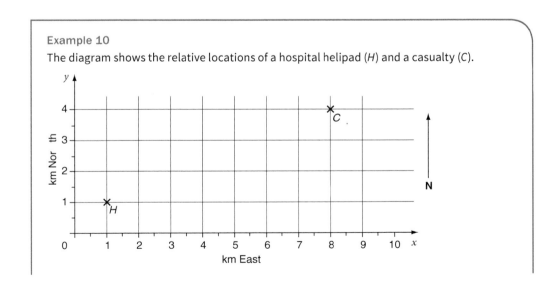

Using trigonometry and Pythagoras' theorem, **calculate**:

a the bearing on which the helicopter must fly in order to reach the casualty

b the distance from the hospital to the casualty

c the bearing on which the helicopter must fly in order to return to the hospital.

Answer 10

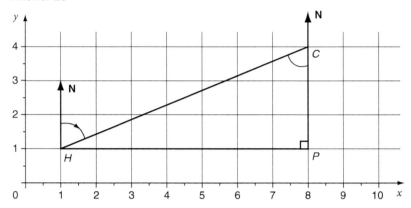

Using the right-angled triangle *HCP* shown on the diagram:

a The bearing of the casualty from the hospital is the same as angle *HCP* (alternate angles).

$$\tan \text{angle } HCP = \frac{\text{OPP}}{\text{ADJ}} = \frac{HP}{CP} = \frac{8-1}{4-1}$$

$$\tan \angle HCP = \frac{7}{3} = 2.33333\ldots$$

$$\tan^{-1} 2.33333\ldots = 66.801\ldots$$

$$\angle HCP = 66.8°$$

The bearing of the casualty from the hospital is 066.8°.

b Using Pythagoras' theorem:

HC is the hypotenuse.

$$HC^2 = 3^2 + 7^2 = 58$$

$$HC = \sqrt{58}$$

$$HC = 7.61577\ldots$$

The distance of the casualty from the hospital is 7.62 km.

c The bearing of the hospital from the casualty is $180° + \angle HCP = 180° + 66.8° = 246.8°$

Example 11

The diagram shows three ships, *A*, *B* and *C*.

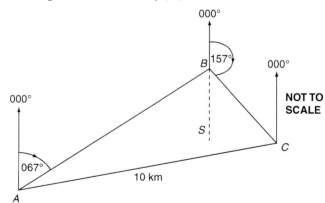

The bearing of *C* from *A* is 083°.

a Using the bearings given show that triangle ABC has a right angle at B. The distance between A and C is 10 kilometres.

b Calculate the distance between A and B.

Answer 11

a BS is the south (180°) line from B.

$\angle ABS = 67°$ (alternate angles)

$\angle CBS = 180 - 157 = 23°$ (angles on a straight line)

So $\angle ABC = 67° + 23° = 90°$

b $\angle BAC = 83 - 67 = 16°$

$\cos = \dfrac{\text{ADJ}}{\text{HYP}}$

$\cos 16° = \dfrac{AB}{10}$

$AB = 10 \times \cos 16°$ ($\times\,10$)

$AB = 9.6126\ldots$

The distance between A and B is 9.61 km.

Exercise 9.9

1 Find the angle marked with a letter in each of the diagrams below.

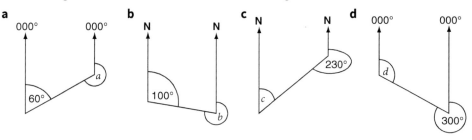

a   000°   000°   60° a

b   N   N   100° b

c   N   N   230° c

d   000°   000° d 300°

2 The bearing of A from B is 060°. Make a sketch showing A and B and their north lines and find the bearing of B from A.

3 Repeat question 2 for C and D where the bearing of C from D is 195°.

4 A, B and C are three villages.

The bearing of B from A is 050°, and the bearing of C from B is 135°.

The distance of B from A is 10 kilometres, and the distance of C from B is 15 kilometres.

Make an accurate scale drawing using a scale of 1 cm represents 1 km, and find:

a the distance of C from A, and

b the bearing of A from C.

5 A ship sails 6 nautical miles due west from port, and then 15 nautical miles due north. (A nautical mile is a unit of distance used at sea.)

Draw a diagram to show this journey and **calculate** the distance of the ship from port, and the bearing on which it will have to sail to return to port.

6 A ship's captain sees a marker buoy on a bearing of 073°, and a port on a bearing of 090°. The captain knows that the marker buoy is 5 kilometres due north of the port. Draw a sketch to show this information and **calculate** the distance, in kilometres, that the ship has to sail to reach port.

7 **a** Change the three-figure bearings (i) 135° (ii) 315° using the mariner's compass.

   b Express (i) E and (ii) SW as three-figure bearings.

9.7 Trigonometry Without a Calculator

In your non-calculator paper you may be asked for some simple trigonometry with sufficient information given to solve the problem without the use of a calculator. You may have to make a suitable choice from this information as the example below shows.

Example 12

Triangle *ABC* is shown below.

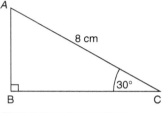

tan 30°	0.577
sin 30°	0.5
cos 30°	0.866

Using the information in the table, and without using your calculator, calculate

a *AB*   **b** *BC*

Answer 12

a $\sin A\hat{C}B = \dfrac{AB}{AC}$

   $\sin 30° = \dfrac{AB}{8}$

   $AB = 8 \times \sin 30° = 8 \times 0.5 = 4$

   $AB = 4\,\text{cm}$

b $\cos A\hat{C}B = \dfrac{BC}{AC}$

   $\cos 30° = \dfrac{BC}{8}$

   $BC = 8 \times \cos 30° = 8 \times 0.866 = 6.928$

   $BC = 6.93\,\text{cm}$

Exercise 9.10   NO CALCULATOR IN THIS EXERCISE

1 In triangle *PQR*, $P\hat{Q}R = 90°$, $PR = 5\,\text{cm}$ and $QR = 3\,\text{cm}$.
    Calculate the length of *PQ*.

2 In triangle *XYZ*, $X\hat{Z}Y = 90°$, $XZ = 9\,\text{cm}$ and $X\hat{Y}Z = 48°$.
    Using the information given in the table, calculate the length of *YZ*.

tan 42°	0.9004
tan 48°	1.1106

3 *ABCD* is a rectangle. The side *AB* = 7 cm, and the diagonal *AC* = 10 cm.

a Using the information given in the table calculate the length of *AD*, giving your answer correct to 3 significant figures.

$\sqrt{149}$	12.2065
$\sqrt{51}$	7.1414

b Calculate

i sin *CÂD* **ii** cos *CÂD* **iii** tan *AĈD*

9.8 Angles of Elevation and Depression

Key terms

An angle of elevation measures the angle between the line of sight of an object *above* an observer and the horizontal.

An angle of depression: measures the angle between the line of sight of an object *below* the observer and the horizontal.

If you are sitting on the ground and looking at the base of a tall vertical pole you will need to lift your eyes to see the top of the pole. The angle through which you raise your eyes is called the **angle of elevation**, and is illustrated in Figure 9.16. For simplicity the diagram ignores the fact that your eyes will not be at ground level.

Pole (vertical)

e

Ground level (horizontal)

Figure 9.16 Angle of elevation

The angle of elevation is labelled *e*.

If the ground is horizontal and the pole is vertical, the angle that the pole makes with the ground is a right angle, so we are able to do calculations using right-angled triangles.

Similarly, if you are on the top of a cliff looking out to sea, the angle through which you have to lower your eyes from the horizontal to look at a ship is called the **angle of depression**, and is illustrated in Figure 9.17.

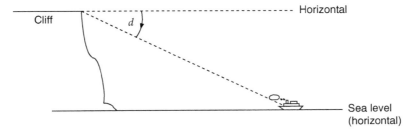

Horizontal

Cliff

d

Sea level (horizontal)

Figure 9.17 Angle of depression

The angle of depression is labelled *d*.

In Figure 9.16 you can see that, because the two horizontal lines must be parallel, the angle of elevation from the ship to the top of the cliff is also *d* (alternate angles).

Example 13

The angle of elevation of the top of a building seen by an observer from a distance of 10 metres away on horizontal ground is 60°. How tall is the building? (Ignore the height of the observer.)

Answer 13

The diagram shows a sketch of the building and the angle of elevation.

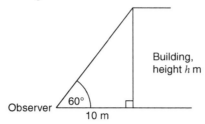

Let h be the height of the building.

$\text{Tan } 60° = \dfrac{h}{10}$

$10 \times \tan 60° = h$

$h = 17.320\ldots$

The height of the building is 17.3 metres, to 3 significant figures.

Exercise 9.11

1 Ramiro is surveying a building. He is using a theodolite, which is an instrument for measuring angles. The theodolite is on a pole 170 centimetres above ground level. The building is 25 metres away on horizontal ground. Ramiro measures the angle of elevation of the top of the building. It is 50°.
  How tall is the building?

2 The given diagram shows the position of a theodolite on the top of a hill. It is being used to measure the height of a tower 70 metres away in a horizontal direction. The angle of depression of the bottom of the tower is 25°, and the angle of elevation of the top of the tower is 30°.
  Calculate
  a the height of the hill   b the height of the tower.

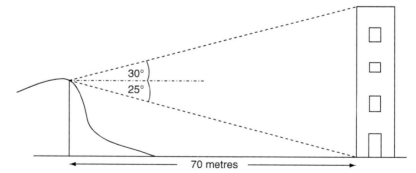

Exercise 9.12

Mixed exercise

1 Calculate the angles or lengths of sides marked with letters in these diagrams. In each case state the units in your answers.

a
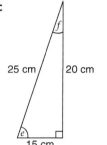

b 3.72 cm
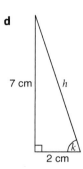

c

d

2 The diagram shows a ladder leaning against a house. The safe angle between a ladder and the ground (to minimise the risk of sliding or toppling) is 75°. The ladder is 3 metres long. How high up the wall will it reach when it is leaning at the safe angle?

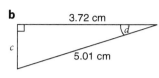

3 Calculate the height of the isosceles triangle shown below.

NOTE:
Remember that when the question says 'calculate' you have not answered the question if you rely on a scale drawing.

4 Two ships are carrying divers who are going to investigate an ancient wreck. The ship *Explorer* (*E*) is on a bearing of 030° from the wreck (*W*), and the ship *Discovery* (*D*) is on a bearing of 300° from the wreck.
The bearing of *Explorer* from *Discovery* is 070°, and the distance between the ships is 10 kilometres.

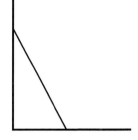

NOT TO SCALE

a Copy the diagram, and show that ∠*DWE* is 90°.
b Find the values of the letters marked on the diagram.
c Calculate the distance of *Discovery* from the wreck.
d Calculate the distance of *Explorer* from the wreck.

5

The gradient of a hill is $\frac{1}{5}$. Calculate the angle (*a*°) it makes with the horizontal.

Exam-style questions Part 1

6 a

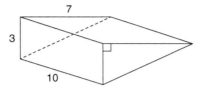

The diagram shows a solid triangular prism. The dimensions are in metres.
i Calculate the volume of the prism.
ii Calculate the total surface area of the prism (Unit for answer: m^3).

b

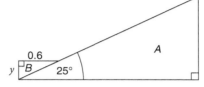 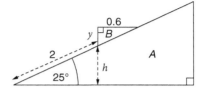

The diagrams show the cross-sections of a ramp A and a triangular prism B.
The triangular prism B can move up and down the ramp A.
The ramp is inclined at 25° to the horizontal.
i When the prism has moved 2 m up the ramp, it has risen h metres vertically.
Calculate h.
ii As it moves, the uppermost face of the prism B remains horizontal.
The length of the horizontal edge of the face is 0.6 m.
The length of the vertical edge of the prism is y metres.
Calculate y.   (4024 paper 22 Q4 November 2014)

7

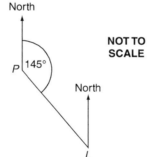

The bearing of a lighthouse, L, from a port, P, is 145°.
Find the bearing of P from L.

(0580 paper 01 Q7 June 2007)

NOT TO SCALE

8

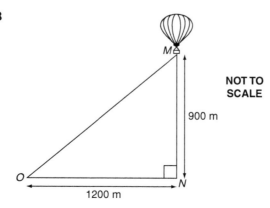

NOT TO SCALE

A hot air balloon, M, is 900 metres vertically above a point N on the ground.

A boy stands at a point, O, 1200 metres horizontally from N.
a Calculate the distance, OM, of the boy from the balloon.
b Calculate angle MON.

(0580 paper 01 Q18 June 2007)

9 Write as a 3-figure bearing the direction:
   a West
   b North-East.   (0580 paper 01 Q6 November 2004)

10

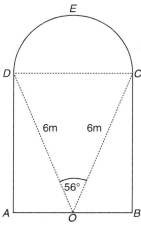

NOT TO
SCALE

ABCED is the cross-section of a tunnel.
ABCD is a rectangle and *DEC* is a semicircle. *O* is the midpoint of *AB*.
OD = *OC* = 6 m and angle *DOC* = 56°.

  a **i**   Show that angle *COB* = 62°.
     ii   Calculate the length of *OB*.
     iii Write down the width of the tunnel, *AB*.
     iv Calculate the length of *BC*.

  b Calculate the area of:
     i   the rectangle *ABCD*
     ii the semicircle *DEC*
     iii the cross-section of the tunnel.

  c The tunnel is 500 metres long.
     i   Calculate the volume of the tunnel.
     ii A car travels through the tunnel at a constant speed
        of 60 kilometres per hour.
        How many seconds does it take to go through
        the tunnel?   (0580 paper 03 Q6 June 2007)

11

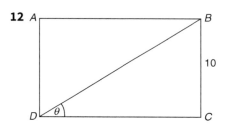

NOT TO
SCALE

6 cm

4 cm

NOT TO
SCALE

8 cm

The diagram above shows a cuboid and its net.

a Calculate the total surface area of the cuboid.

b Calculate the volume of the cuboid.

c An ant walks directly from *A* to *C* on the surface of the cuboid.

  i Draw a straight line on the net to show this route.

  ii **Calculate** the length of the ant's journey.

  iii **Calculate** the size of angle *CAB* on the net. (0580 paper 03 Q8 June 2005)

Exam-style questions Part 2

DO NOT USE A CALCULATOR IN THE REST OF THIS EXERCISE

12

$\sin \theta$	$\frac{5}{13}$
$\cos \theta$	$\frac{12}{13}$
$\tan \theta$	$\frac{5}{12}$

A   *B*

10

D θ *C*

ABCD is a rectangle with *BC* = 10 cm.
Using as much information from the table as is necessary, calculate *BD*. (4024 paper 01 Q6 June 2008)

13 *A* is due north of *O*.

a A ship sailed from *O* to *B*, where $A\hat{O}B = 12°$.
Write down the bearing of *B* from *O*.

b At *B*, the ship turned and sailed to *C*, where $O\hat{B}C = 50°$.
Calculate the bearing of *C* from *B*.

(4024 paper 01 Q4 June 2005)

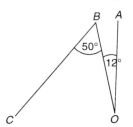

14

North

D •   • A

S

C •   • B

The bearing of a lighthouse from a ship, S, is 220°.
The position of S is marked on the diagram.

a Which of the four points A, B, C or D is a possible position of the lighthouse?

b Write down the bearing of S from the lighthouse.

(4024 paper 11 Q5 June 2010)

15 A man who is 1.8 m tall stands on horizontal ground 50 m from a vertical tree.
The angle of elevation of the top of the tree from his eyes is 30°.
Use as much of the information below as is necessary to calculate an estimate of the height of the tree.
Give the answer to a reasonable degree of accuracy.
[sin 30° = 0.5, cos 30° = 0.866, tan 30° = 0.577]   (4024 paper 01 Q24 June 2004)

16

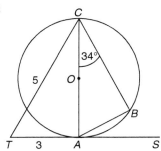

In the diagram, the circle, centre O, passes through A, B and C.
AC is a diameter of the circle and the line TAS is the tangent at A.
$\angle ACB = 34°$, $TA = 3$ cm and $TC = 5$ cm.

a Find $\angle BAC$.

b Calculate the radius of the circle.

(4024 paper 01 Q4 November 2007)

Learning Objectives

Syllabus sections 37 and 39

In this chapter you will study:
- reflection, translation, rotation and enlargement
- vectors and how to use them

10.1 Introduction

Transformations are movements and changes of a shape on a plane (flat surface) according to various rules.

For this chapter you require squared paper, a ruler, pencil, eraser and tracing paper. A small mirror would be helpful. It is advisable to draw your transformations in pencil so that any mistakes can be corrected. Neatness and reasonable accuracy in your drawings will help you avoid mistakes.

10.2 Essential Skills

1 Match the equation of each line to a graph
   a $y = x$ **b** $x = 1$ **c** $y = -3$ **d** $x = -3$ **e** $y = -x$ **f** $y = x + 2$

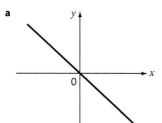
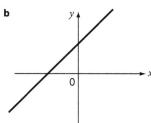
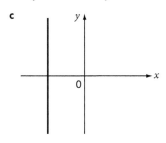
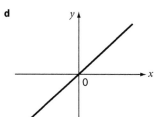
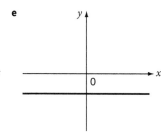
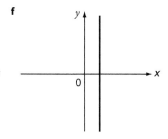

NOTE:
In question 3 what number does it pass through on the *x*-axis?

NOTE:
Learn the four proper names, and their spellings.

Key term

Transformation is the collective name for a group of movements or changes of shape or size of a two-dimensional object on a plane according to certain rules.

Reflection is the image of an object in a mirror.

2   Write down the equation of the vertical line which passes through 2 on the *x*-axis.

3   Write down the equation of the *y*-axis.

10.3 Transformations

For this course we need to study each of a set of four transformations:

reflection, translation, rotation and **enlargement**.

Try not to confuse the words transformation and translation.

We will study these transformations further in Chapter 22.

10.4 Reflection

A reflection is the image you see when you look in a mirror.

Look at the two diagrams in Figure 10.1.

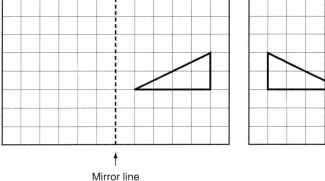

Mirror line   Mirror line

Figure 10.1 Reflection

If you hold a small mirror upright so that its lower edge is on the mirror line in the first diagram, with its mirror surface pointing towards the triangle, you should see an image that looks like the second diagram.

The triangles are the same, but they face in opposite directions. In fact, they are **mirror images** of each other. If you put the mirror on the mirror line in the second diagram, facing either way, you will see the same picture.

A *reflection* is the first of the transformations we will study.

In Figure 10.2 you will see two different reflections of triangle *A* drawn. In each case triangle *A* is called the **object** and the result of the transformation (*B* or *C*) is called the **image**.

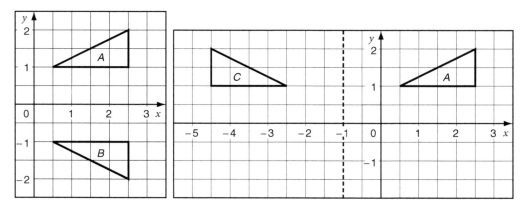

A maps to *B* under reflection in the *x*-axis.   *A* maps to *C* under reflection in the line $x = -1$.

Figure 10.2 Reflection in a line

Underneath each diagram in Figure 10.2 is the correct description of the transformation. As you will have seen, we say '*A* maps to *B*' rather than '*A* is transformed to *B*'.

Note that if you are asked for the description of a **single** transformation, you have not answered the question if you describe one transformation after another. We will discuss this again later.

Looking at Figure 10.2 you should see that the shape and size of the object and image are exactly the same, but the object has been turned over to create the image.

Check this by tracing the triangles on tracing paper and then folding your drawing along the mirror line. In each case they should fit exactly on top of each other.

This also means that the object and image are the same distance from the mirror line, but on opposite sides.

NOTE:
When you are asked to *describe* a transformation you are expected to use the correct words, and not just describe it in your own words!

How to recognise a reflection
A reflection is a transformation in which:

- the **object** and **image** are exactly the same shape and size
- the object and image face in opposite directions
- the **image** is as far behind the **mirror line** as the **object** is in front of it.

How to describe a reflection
To describe a reflection you must:

- name the transformation (reflection)
- name the mirror line or give its equation.

How to draw a reflection
- Take one point on the object at a time, and measure or count the number of squares from the point to the mirror line.
- The distance must be measured in the direction perpendicular to the mirror line.
- Measure or count the squares the same distance beyond the mirror line and mark the point.
- Repeat with all the other points, and join your new points together to draw the image.

To make this clear, Figure 10.3 shows the steps in the reflection of a different shape in the line LM.

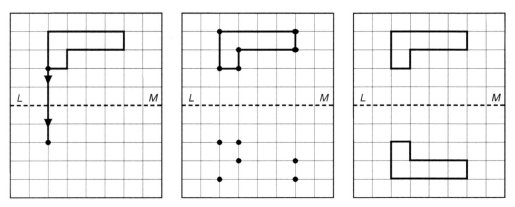

Count 2 squares to the mirror line and 2 squares beyond
Repeat for all corners
Draw the image

Figure 10.3 Drawing a reflection

For a diagonal mirror line you need to count the diagonals instead of the squares, as shown in Figure 10.4.

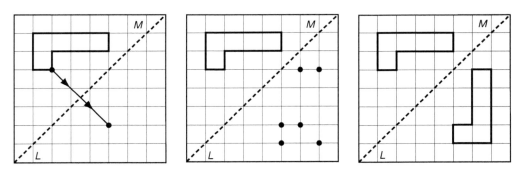

Figure 10.4 Reflection in a diagonal line

If the mirror line goes through the object the reflection produces what at first seems like a completely different picture, as in Figure 10.5.

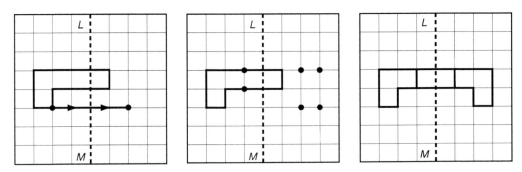

Figure 10.5 Line of reflection through the object

Example 1

Copy these diagrams and draw the images of the shapes in the dotted mirror lines.

a

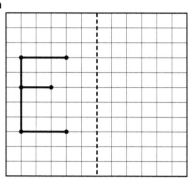

b

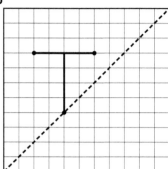

c

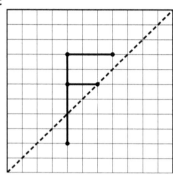

NOTE:
In (b) and (c) remember to count the diagonals instead of the sides of the squares.

Answer 1

a

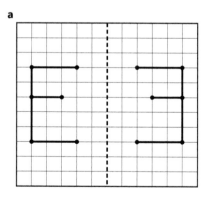

b

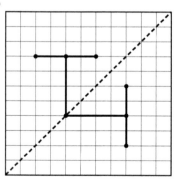

c

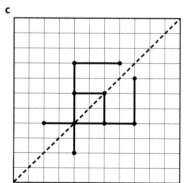

NOTE:
You will see that any point which is on the mirror line maps onto itself under the reflection. We say that such a point is 'invariant' under the transformation because it does not change.

NOTE:
It pays to be NEAT in your diagrams. Preferably use a ruler unless you can draw *very good* straight lines for the smaller diagrams!

Exercise 10.1

1 Copy the following diagrams and draw the images of the shapes in the dotted mirror lines.

a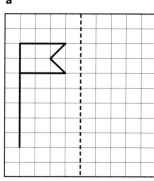

b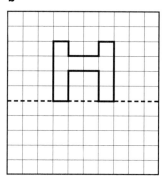

c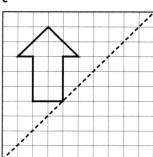

d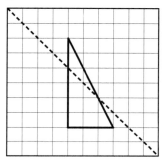

2 Draw x- and y- axes from −5 to +5, with 1 cm representing each unit on each axis.

a Plot the following points:

(1, 1), (3, 1), (3, 2)

Join up the points to form a triangle and label the triangle A.

b Reflect A in:

i the y-axis, labelling the image B

ii the line $y = -1$, labelling the image C

iii the line $y = x$, labelling the image D

iv the line $y = -x$, labelling the image E.

NOTE:
It can be confusing reflecting in the axes because the scales on the axes tend to get in the way. Remember that you are reflecting in the *line*, not in the line and numbers. The diagrams in Figure 10.6 show this. The first diagram is wrong, the second one is correct.

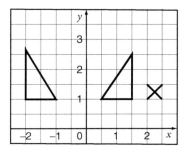 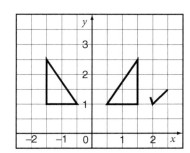

Figure 10.6 Reflection in the y-axis

Example 2

Describe the following transformations.

a

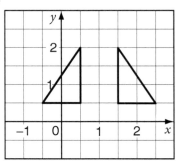

b

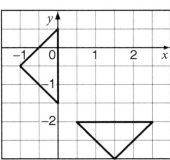

c

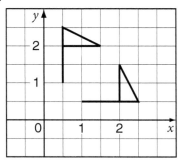

d

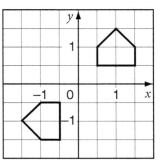

NOTE:
Use tracing paper to check. If you fold your tracing along the mirror line the object and image should coincide exactly.

Answer 2

a   Reflection in the line $x = 1$.

b   Reflection in the line $y = x - 2$.

c   Reflection in the line $y = x$.

d   Reflection in the line $y = -x$.

Exercise 10.2

Describe the following transformations.

1

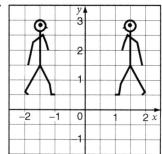

2

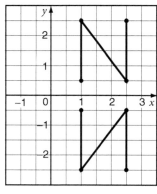

3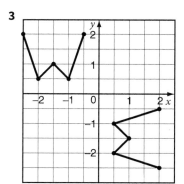

4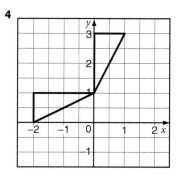

5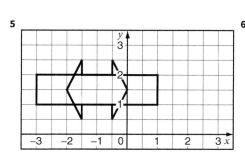

6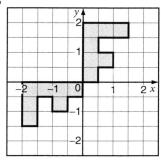

10.5 Translations and Vectors

A **translation** is a movement in which only the position of the object changes.

The image remains facing the same way as the object, and stays the same size and shape.

For example, in Figure 10.7 the object A has been moved two squares to the right (**+x** direction) and 4 squares down (**−y** direction) to give the image B.

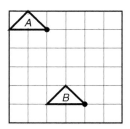

Figure 10.7 Translation

This translation is described by breaking it down into the two movements, each parallel to one of the two axes.

These movements are written in the form of a **vector**, also called a **column vector**, so in this diagram the vector would be written in tall brackets with the **x**-direction at the top: $\begin{pmatrix} 2 \\ -4 \end{pmatrix}$.

You can think of a vector as a method of clearly showing direction of movement.

When written, the *column vector* is always in tall brackets, and always with the **x**-direction on top.

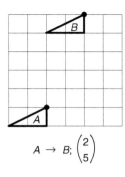

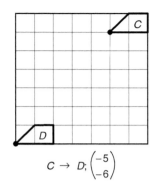

$$A \rightarrow B; \begin{pmatrix} 2 \\ 5 \end{pmatrix}$$

$$C \rightarrow D; \begin{pmatrix} -5 \\ -6 \end{pmatrix}$$

Figure 10.8 Translations and vectors

NOTE:
Follow the dot!

The two examples in Figure 10.8 should help you understand the concept.

In the first diagram, to get from A to B you move two squares in the **+x** direction and five squares in the **+y** direction. This vector would be written as $\begin{pmatrix} 2 \\ 5 \end{pmatrix}$.

In the second diagram, to get from C to D you would move five squares *back* in the **x**-direction, and six squares *down* in the **y**-direction. This column vector is $\begin{pmatrix} -5 \\ -6 \end{pmatrix}$.

How to Label a Vector

There are two ways to label a vector.

In Figure 10.9, the vector to get from A to B can be labelled $\overrightarrow{AB}$ or with a lower case letter printed in bold, for example **a**. Notice also the arrow in the diagram.

The arrow over the $\overrightarrow{AB}$ shows that the direction is from A to B.

In handwriting the bold **a** is written with an underline, $\underline{a}$, because it is not easy to write a recognisable bold letter by hand.

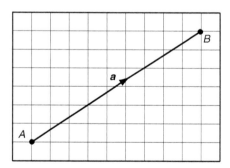

Figure 10.9 Vector $\overrightarrow{AB}$

Important Points to Notice When Working with Vectors

- The vector **a** does not have to have just one *position*, but can be applied anywhere in the diagram, always in the same direction.
- The vector written as $\overrightarrow{AB}$ shows that this particular vector is the one joining A to B in the direction A to B.
- The vector is not a fraction, and should *not* be written with a fraction line.
- The vector should always be written with the **x**-direction above the **y**-direction.

- When you draw a vector in a diagram remember to add the arrow to show its direction.
- Sometimes, in some textbooks, you may see row vectors, for example (2 −4), but it will be much safer and clearer if you use column vectors in this course. Row vectors will not be used, and could be confused with coordinate points. You are strongly advised *not* to use them.

Figure 10.10 shows three examples of the same vector: $\mathbf{v} = \begin{pmatrix} 4 \\ -3 \end{pmatrix}$, and also an example of the opposite vector: $-\mathbf{v}$ which is $\begin{pmatrix} -4 \\ 3 \end{pmatrix}$.

As you might expect, opposite vectors are negatives of each other. (That is, they have opposite signs.) The first vector can also be written as $\overrightarrow{PQ}$ because it goes from the point P to the point Q.

So $\mathbf{v} = \overrightarrow{PQ}$ and $-\mathbf{v} = \overrightarrow{QP}$.

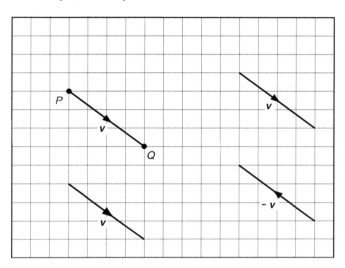

Figure 10.10 Vector **v**

How to recognise a translation

A translation is a transformation in which:

- the object and image have exactly the same shape and size
- the *orientation* (direction in which the object and image face) remains the same.

How to describe a translation

A translation is described by:
- the name of the transformation (translation)
- a column vector.

How to use a column vector
- The vector shows the direction of movement broken down into a movement parallel to the x-axis and another movement parallel to the y-axis.
- Mark a point on the object and the corresponding point on the image and count the number of units moved in the x-direction and the number moved in the y-direction.
- The column vector is written in tall brackets with the x-direction on top of the y-direction.
- A column vector is not a fraction and has no fraction line.

How to draw a translation
- Mark one corner of the image with a dot.
- Count along (or back if the number is negative) the number of units shown on top in the column vector.
- Then count up (or down if negative) the number of units shown at the bottom of the column vector.
- Mark a dot.
- Repeat for all the corners.
- Join the dots to show the image.

Figure 10.11 should help you see how to draw a translation, in this case $\begin{pmatrix} 4 \\ -6 \end{pmatrix}$.

a

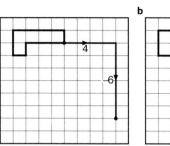

b

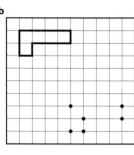

c

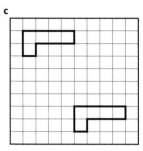

Figure 10.11 Drawing a translation

Example 3

Draw a grid on 5 mm squared paper with both the x- and y-axes from −5 to 5, using one centimetre (2 squares) per unit.

a i A: {(−4, 3), (−4, 5), (−3, 3)} B: {(3, 1), (4, 1), (3, 3)}

Mark these two sets of points and join them to form two triangles, A and B.

ii Describe fully the single transformation which maps A onto B.

iii Describe fully the single transformation which maps B onto A.

b i Draw the image of A under the translation $\begin{pmatrix} 2 \\ -3 \end{pmatrix}$.

Label the image C.

ii Draw the image of B under the translation $\begin{pmatrix} -1 \\ -2.5 \end{pmatrix}$.

Label the image D.

c Plot and label the points E (−4, −1) and F (−2, −4).

i Write $\overrightarrow{EF}$ as a column vector.

ii Write $\overrightarrow{FE}$ as a column vector.

d Describe fully the single transformation which maps A onto D.

Answer 3

a i

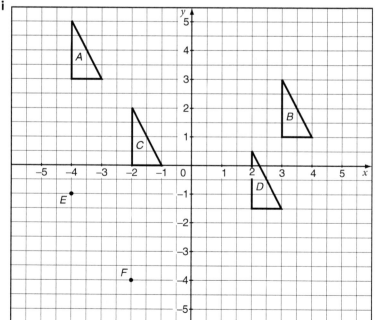

NOTE:

Here the units to be counted are centimetres, not small squares. Always check the scale!

a **ii** Translation $\begin{pmatrix} 7 \\ -2 \end{pmatrix}$ **iii** Translation $\begin{pmatrix} -7 \\ 2 \end{pmatrix}$

c **i** $\overrightarrow{EF} = \begin{pmatrix} 2 \\ -3 \end{pmatrix}$ **ii** $\overrightarrow{FE} = \begin{pmatrix} -2 \\ 3 \end{pmatrix}$

d Translation $\begin{pmatrix} 6 \\ -4.5 \end{pmatrix}$

Example 4

On 1 centimetre squared paper draw:

a 3 examples of the vector $\begin{pmatrix} 3 \\ -1 \end{pmatrix}$ **b** 3 examples of the vector $\begin{pmatrix} 1 \\ -3 \end{pmatrix}$.

Answer 4

a

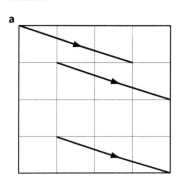

b

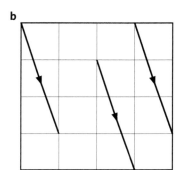

Exercise 10.3

1 Copy the diagrams and in each case draw the image of each shape under the translation given.

a

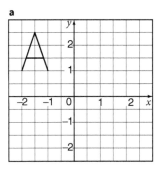

$\begin{pmatrix} 3 \\ -3 \end{pmatrix}$

b

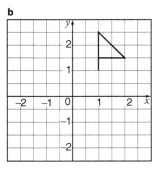

$\begin{pmatrix} -2 \\ -3 \end{pmatrix}$

c

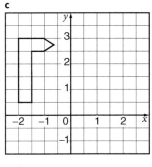

$\begin{pmatrix} 3 \\ 0 \end{pmatrix}$

2 Copy the diagram and draw two examples of the vector **c** = $\overrightarrow{AB}$, and one example of −**c**.

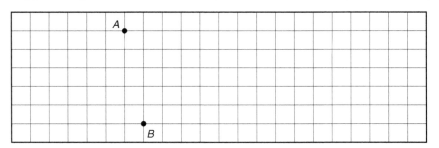

3 Draw *x*- and *y*-axes from −5 cm to +5 cm.
Plot the following points and join to form a triangle. Label the triangle *A*.
(−1, 0)   (−1, −2)   (−2, −2)

   a Draw *B*, the image of *A* under the translation $\begin{pmatrix} -1 \\ 4 \end{pmatrix}$.

   b Draw *C*, the image of *A* under the translation $\begin{pmatrix} 3 \\ 1 \end{pmatrix}$.

   c Describe **fully** the **single** transformation which maps *B* onto *C*.

4 Describe fully the following single transformations.
   a **i** *A* maps to *B*   **ii** *A* maps to *C*   **iii** *B* maps to *C*

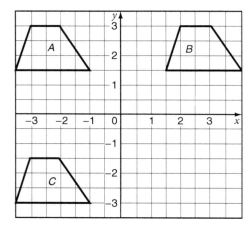

   b **i** *A* maps to *B*   **ii** *C* maps to *B*   **iii** *B* maps to *C*

10.6 Rotation

A rotation is a turning about some central point. Think of a bicycle wheel. Each spoke turns or *rotates* about one of its ends: the one which is attached to the centre of the wheel. The valve on the rim also rotates about the centre of the wheel even though it is not directly attached to it.

A rotation of an object can be about a point on the object (as the spoke of the wheel rotates about one end) or about some other point (as the valve rotates about a point further away).

In a rotation the object and image are exactly the same size and shape, but they face different ways.

A rotation needs four pieces of information to describe it fully.

As well as the correct word (rotation) it needs the centre of rotation, the angle of rotation and the *sense* or direction of rotation. It is best to use 'clockwise' or 'anticlockwise' to describe the sense of the rotation.

Key term

Rotation is the turning of an object about a given point through a given angle.

The exception to this is a rotation of 180° because it does not matter whether the object is turned clockwise or anticlockwise, it still arrives in the same place.

Figure 10.12 shows two examples of rotations and their correct descriptions.

The rotations are in the plane of the paper.

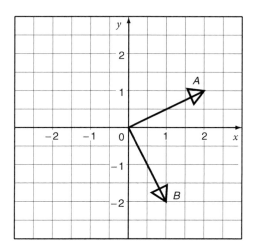 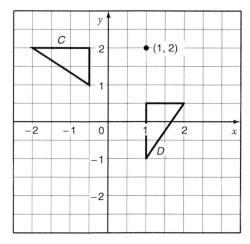

A maps to B under a rotation of 90° clockwise about the origin.

C maps to D under a rotation of 90° anticlockwise about (1, 2).

Figure 10.12 Rotations

You can find the centre of rotation by trial and error using a piece of tracing paper. There is a geometrical method which we will look at in Chapter 22.

Trace the object and the axes, and mark the axes **x** and **y** (see Figure 10.13).

Keeping the two pieces of paper together put your pencil point down firmly at different points on the tracing paper and carefully rotate the tracing paper until you find the point where the tracing of the object fits exactly over the image.

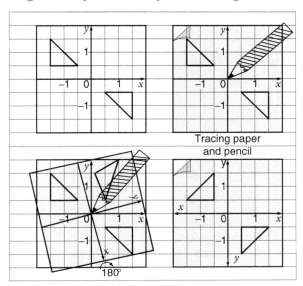

It can take a bit of time to find the centre, but try the obvious places first. The centre will usually be at a grid point.

Now compare the positions of the **x**-axis before and after the rotation to see the angle and sense through which direction the object has been rotated.

Figure 10.13 Finding the centre of rotation

NOTE:
A rotation of 90° clockwise is equivalent to a rotation of 270° anticlockwise.

How to recognise a rotation

A rotation is a transformation in which:

- the object and the image are exactly the same size and shape
- the object and image are facing different ways, (but have not been turned over as in a reflection)
- all the points on the object and image remain the same distance from the centre of rotation
- To be sure, check with a piece of tracing paper that you can find the centre, angle and sense of the rotation.

How to fully describe a rotation

A rotation is a transformation described by:

- the name of the transformation (rotation)
- the centre of rotation
- the angle and sense of the rotation.

How to draw a rotation, using tracing paper

- Trace the object and at least one of the axes onto your tracing paper.
- Put the point of your pencil firmly down on the centre of rotation.
- Turn the paper through the given angle and sense. The axis that you have traced will help here.
- Copy the image from the tracing onto the original diagram.

How to draw a rotation without tracing paper

- Draw vectors in the *x* and *y* directions from the centre of rotation to the various points on the object.
- Rotate the vectors to find the new positions of these points.
- The vectors must all turn through the same angle, and remain of the same length.

NOTE:

It is much easier to use tracing paper. Remember that the points on the object are usually on grid lines, and so the points of the image will also be on grid lines. This should help you to draw accurate images. You will be allowed tracing paper in your examination.

Example 5

Copy the diagrams.

a Rotate *A* 180° about the origin (0, 0), draw the image and label it *P*.

b Rotate *B* 90° anticlockwise about the point marked with a cross. Draw the image and label it *Q*.

c Describe fully the single transformation that will map *C* onto *D*.

a

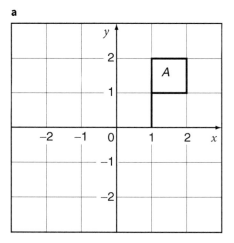

b

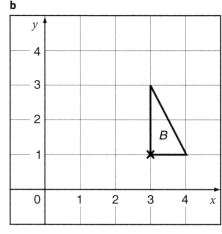

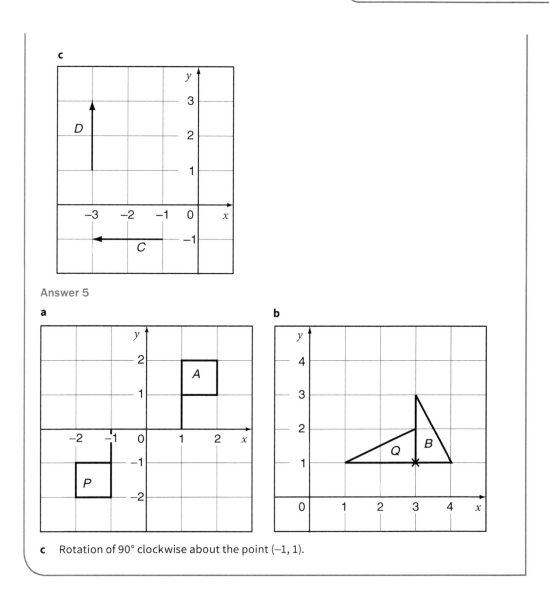

Answer 5

c Rotation of 90° clockwise about the point (−1, 1).

Exercise 10.4

1 Copy the diagrams.
Rotate the triangles about the centres marked with a cross and through the angles stated.

a

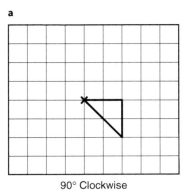

90° Clockwise

b

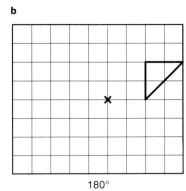

180°

c

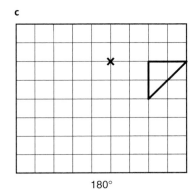

180°

d

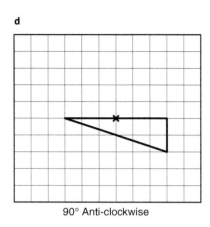

90° Anti-clockwise

e

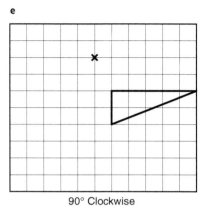

90° Clockwise

2 Describe fully the following single transformations.

a

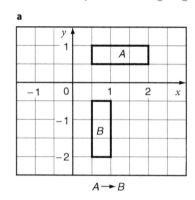

$A \longrightarrow B$

b

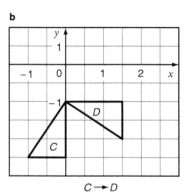

$C \longrightarrow D$

c

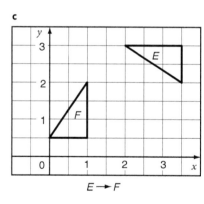

$E \longrightarrow F$

d

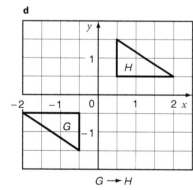

$G \longrightarrow H$

e

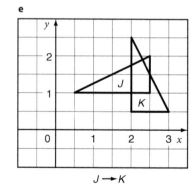

$J \longrightarrow K$

f

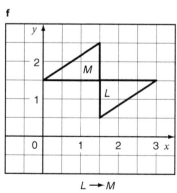

$L \longrightarrow M$

g

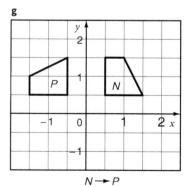

$N \longrightarrow P$

10.7 Enlargement

An enlargement can, as its name suggests, make the image larger than the object. Confusingly it is also called an enlargement if it makes the image smaller than the object!

The difference is in the **scale factor** of the enlargement. A scale factor greater than 1 will make the image larger than the object, but a scale factor less than 1 will make it smaller.

You can demonstrate an enlargement by shining a torch onto a shape, such as your hand, and looking at the shadow of your hand on a wall. Your hand should be parallel to the wall.

The size of the shadow changes according to how close your torch is to your hand, and the position of the shadow changes according to the position of the torch.

The torch is called the **centre** of the enlargement, and you can see that it is important that the centre is defined when you are describing an enlargement.

How to recognise an enlargement

An enlargement is a transformation in which:
- the image is larger or smaller than the object
- the image is exactly the same *shape* as the object so all angles remain the same and the sides of the image are all multiplied by the same scale factor
- the image remains facing the same way as the object
- the position of the image depends on the position of the centre of enlargement.

How to describe an enlargement

An enlargement is described by giving:
- the name of the transformation (enlargement)
- the scale factor
- the centre of the enlargement.

How to draw an enlargement

An enlargement may be drawn by drawing 'rays' from the centre to each of the corners of the object and beyond, but this is less accurate than the following method.
- From the centre of the enlargement count the number of squares (or centimetres) along (or back) and up (or down) to get to one corner of the object.
- Multiply these distances by the scale factor.
- *Go back to the centre* and count along and up the new distances.
- Repeat for the other corners of the object, until you are certain how to complete the image, bearing in mind that all the angles remain the same and all the sides are multiplied by the same scale factor.

As usual, a set of diagrams will make this clearer.

Figure 10.14 shows the centre of the enlargement marked with a cross. The scale factor is 2.

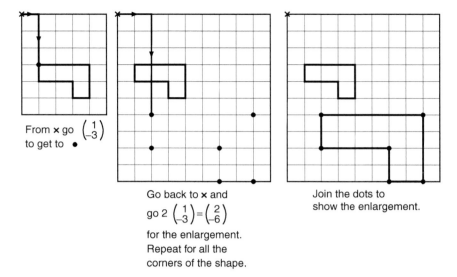

From × go $\begin{pmatrix} 1 \\ -3 \end{pmatrix}$
to get to •

Go back to × and
go 2 $\begin{pmatrix} 1 \\ -3 \end{pmatrix} = \begin{pmatrix} 2 \\ -6 \end{pmatrix}$
for the enlargement.
Repeat for all the
corners of the shape.

Join the dots to
show the enlargement.

Figure 10.14 Enlargement

Figure 10.15 shows how important the centre of enlargement is, and how moving the centre of enlargement completely changes the position of the image. In each case the small square is enlarged to the big square with a scale factor 3.

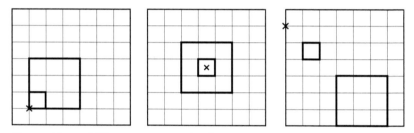

Figure 10.15 Different centres of enlargement

Example 6

Copy the diagrams.

a Draw an enlargement of A, centre the origin and scale factor 2. Label the image B.

b Draw an enlargement of C, centre the point (1, −1) and scale factor $\frac{1}{2}$. Label the image D.

c Describe the single transformation which maps E onto F.

a

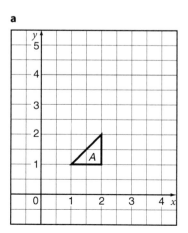

b

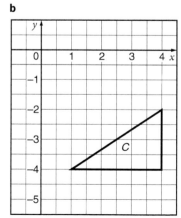

c

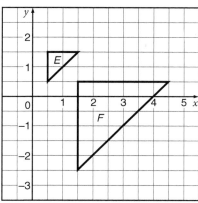

Answer 6

a

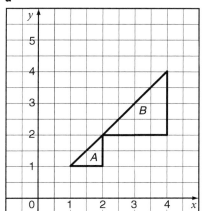

b

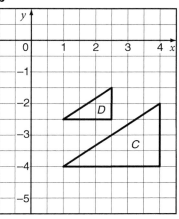

NOTE:
To find the centre of the enlargement join corresponding points on object and image with straight lines. The lines meet at the centre of the enlargement.

c

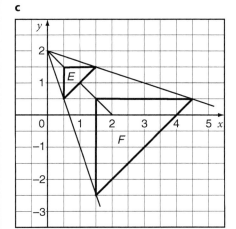

E maps to *F* under enlargement, centre (0, 2), scale factor 3.

Exercise 10.5

1 Copy the diagrams.
   Draw the enlargements with the given scale factors and the centres marked with a cross.

a

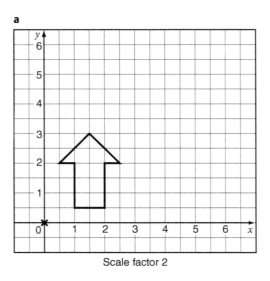

Scale factor 2

b

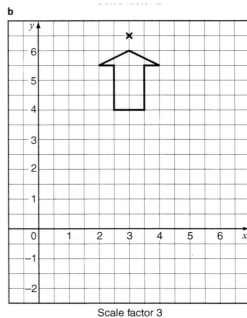

Scale factor 3

2 For each of the diagrams below describe fully the single transformations which map A onto B.

a

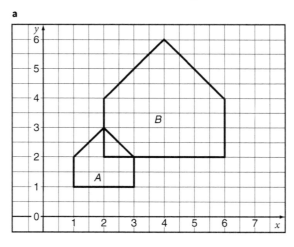

b

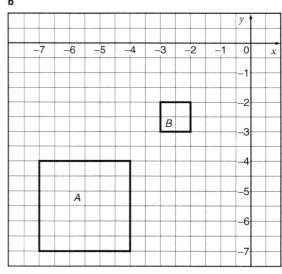

10.8 More About Vectors

Negative Vectors

As we have seen, if the vector $\mathbf{a} = \begin{pmatrix} 2 \\ -3 \end{pmatrix}$, then the same vector, pointing in the opposite direction is $-\mathbf{a}$ or $\begin{pmatrix} -2 \\ 3 \end{pmatrix}$ (see Figure 10.16). Notice that both components of the vector have had their signs changed.

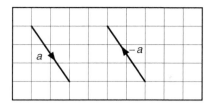

Figure 10.16 Vectors *a* and negative *a*

Adding Vectors

Vectors may be added to produce a new vector which has the same effect as the original two applied one after another. The *x* components are added, and the *y* components are added, producing the new vector, taking account of the signs of the components.

$$\begin{pmatrix} -1 \\ 2 \end{pmatrix} + \begin{pmatrix} 3 \\ 5 \end{pmatrix} = \begin{pmatrix} -1+3 \\ 2+5 \end{pmatrix} = \begin{pmatrix} 2 \\ 7 \end{pmatrix}$$

Figure 10.17 shows this effect.

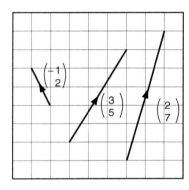
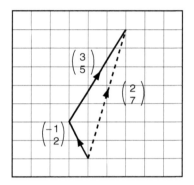

Figure 10.17 Adding vectors

You will see in the second diagram that if we move the two vectors which are to be added until they are joined 'head to tail' (you can follow the arrows round) the result of the addition joins the 'tail' of the first to the 'head of the second'.

Vectors may also be subtracted by subtracting the *x* components and the *y* components. For example,

$$\begin{pmatrix} -2 \\ 6 \end{pmatrix} - \begin{pmatrix} 1 \\ 3 \end{pmatrix} = \begin{pmatrix} -2-1 \\ 6-3 \end{pmatrix} = \begin{pmatrix} -3 \\ 3 \end{pmatrix}$$

Multiplying a Vector by a Number

A vector may be multiplied by a number to change its length. Both components are multiplied by the same number.

Figure 10.18 shows the vectors $\begin{pmatrix} 4 \\ 1 \end{pmatrix}$, $2\begin{pmatrix} 4 \\ 1 \end{pmatrix}$ and $\frac{1}{2}\begin{pmatrix} 4 \\ 1 \end{pmatrix}$. The last two vectors may be simplified to $\begin{pmatrix} 8 \\ 2 \end{pmatrix}$ and $\begin{pmatrix} 2 \\ 0.5 \end{pmatrix}$. You will see that the vectors are all parallel to each other, but are of different lengths.

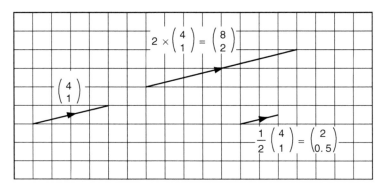

Figure 10.18 Multiplying a vector by a number

Example 7

Simplify the following:

a $3\binom{5}{-2}$

b $2\binom{1}{5}-\binom{0}{3}$

c $\frac{1}{2}\binom{5}{6}+3\binom{-1}{-2}$

d $2\binom{5}{1}-\frac{1}{2}\binom{-6}{4}$

Answer 7

a $\binom{15}{-6}$

b $\binom{2-0}{10-3}=\binom{2}{7}$

c $\binom{2.5+(-3)}{3+(-6)}=\binom{-0.5}{-3}$

d $\binom{10-(-3)}{2-2}=\binom{13}{0}$

Example 8

a   From this list of vectors pick two that are parallel to **a**.

$\mathbf{a}=\binom{1}{2}$ $\mathbf{b}=\binom{-1}{2}$ $\mathbf{c}=\binom{-2}{-4}$ $\mathbf{d}=\binom{3}{6}$ $\mathbf{e}=\binom{2}{1}$

b   Comment on the vectors you have chosen.

Answer 8

a   First take out any common factors in the vectors.

$\mathbf{c}=-2\binom{1}{2}$ $\mathbf{d}=3\binom{1}{2}$

So $\mathbf{c}=-2\mathbf{a}$ and $\mathbf{d}=3\mathbf{a}$.

c and **d** are parallel to **a**.

b   **c** is twice as long as **a** and points in the opposite direction.
   d is three times as long as **a** and points in the same direction.

Vectors can form equations which can be solved algebraically to find unknown values. Remember that if two vectors are equal then the x-directions must be equal and the y-directions must be equal. The next example shows this.

Example 9

a $2\begin{pmatrix} a \\ 5 \end{pmatrix} + 3\begin{pmatrix} a \\ b \end{pmatrix} = \begin{pmatrix} 10 \\ -8 \end{pmatrix}$

Using the above vector equation write down an equation in a and an equation in b and solve them to find a and b.

b $\begin{pmatrix} k \\ 2k \end{pmatrix} + \begin{pmatrix} 2m \\ m \end{pmatrix} = \begin{pmatrix} 4 \\ 5 \end{pmatrix}$

Form two equations in k and m and solve simultaneously to find k and m.

Answer 9

a

$2a + 3a = 10$ $\qquad\qquad\qquad\qquad 2 \times 5 + 3 \times b = -8$

$\quad\; 5a = 10$ $\qquad\qquad\qquad\qquad\qquad\; 10 + 3b = -8$

$\qquad a = 2$ $\qquad\qquad\qquad\qquad\qquad\qquad 3b = -18$

$\qquad\qquad\qquad\qquad\qquad\qquad\qquad\qquad\qquad b = -6$

b $k + 2m = 4 \xrightarrow{\times 2} 2k + 4m = 8$

$2k + m = 5 \rightarrow \underline{2k + m = 5}$ subtract

$\qquad\qquad\qquad\qquad 3m = 3$

$\qquad\qquad\qquad\qquad\; m = 1$

Substituting in the first equation: $\quad k + 2 \times 1 = 4, \qquad k = 2$

Exercise 10.6

1 Simplify the following:

a $3\begin{pmatrix} \frac{1}{2} \\ \frac{1}{3} \end{pmatrix}$
 b $-2\begin{pmatrix} 5 \\ 0 \end{pmatrix}$
 c $\frac{1}{2}\begin{pmatrix} -6 \\ 12 \end{pmatrix} + \begin{pmatrix} 5 \\ 3 \end{pmatrix}$
 d $6\begin{pmatrix} 5 \\ 4 \end{pmatrix} + \frac{1}{2}\begin{pmatrix} 60 \\ 8 \end{pmatrix}$

2 $\begin{pmatrix} a \\ 10 \end{pmatrix} + \begin{pmatrix} a \\ -5 \end{pmatrix} = \begin{pmatrix} 8 \\ 5 \end{pmatrix}$

Find a.

3 $\begin{pmatrix} 2x \\ 15 \end{pmatrix} - \begin{pmatrix} 8 \\ y \end{pmatrix} = \begin{pmatrix} -4 \\ 12 \end{pmatrix}$

Find x and y.

4 Draw these vectors on squared paper and list those that are parallel to each other:

$\mathbf{a} = \begin{pmatrix} -1 \\ 2 \end{pmatrix}, \qquad \mathbf{b} = \begin{pmatrix} -2 \\ 4 \end{pmatrix}, \qquad \mathbf{c} = \begin{pmatrix} 2 \\ -1 \end{pmatrix}, \qquad \mathbf{d} = \begin{pmatrix} 1 \\ -2 \end{pmatrix}, \qquad \mathbf{e} = \begin{pmatrix} -2 \\ -4 \end{pmatrix} \qquad \mathbf{f} = \begin{pmatrix} 3 \\ -6 \end{pmatrix}.$

5 How can you tell that the vectors $\begin{pmatrix} 1 \\ 4 \end{pmatrix}$ and $\begin{pmatrix} 3 \\ 12 \end{pmatrix}$ are parallel and that one is three times longer than the other?

6 What can you say about the vectors $\begin{pmatrix} -1 \\ 3 \end{pmatrix}$ and $\begin{pmatrix} -2 \\ 6 \end{pmatrix}$?

10.9 Recognising Transformations

Example 10

a Describe **fully** the **single** transformations shown in each of the diagrams. *A* maps onto *B* in each case.

i
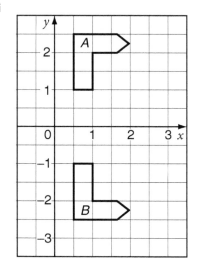

ii
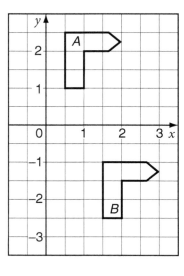

iii
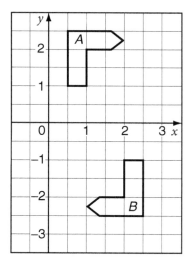

iv
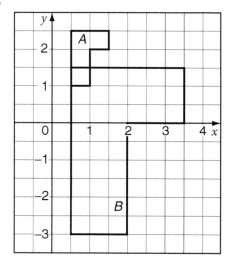

b Name each of the following transformations of the outline of a left hand.

i

ii
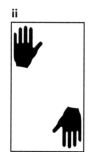

iii

iv
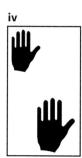

Answer 10

a **i** Reflection in the line $y = 0$ (or the x-axis).

ii Translation $\begin{pmatrix} 1 \\ -3.5 \end{pmatrix}$

iii Rotation 180° about $(1.5, 0)$.

iv Enlargement, centre $(0.5, 3)$, scale factor 3.

b **i** Translation **ii** Rotation **iii** Reflection **iv** Enlargement

Exercise 10.7

Mixed exercise

1 Copy the diagrams.

a

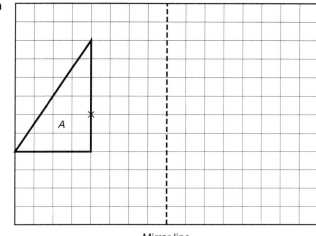

Mirror line

i Rotate A 180° about X.

ii Reflect A in the dotted mirror line.

b

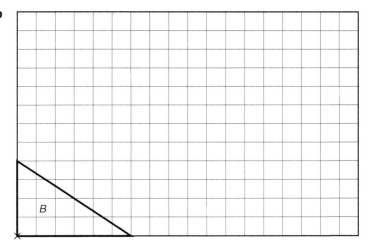

i Enlarge B, centre X, scale factor 3.

ii Translate B using the vector $\begin{pmatrix} 4 \\ 3 \end{pmatrix}$.

2 Copy the diagram.

   a Describe fully the single transformation which maps

      i *A* onto *B*   **ii** *B* onto *C*.

   b **i** Enlarge *D*, scale factor 2, centre the origin. Label the image *E*.

      ii Rotate *B*, 90° anticlockwise, centre the origin. Label the image *F*.

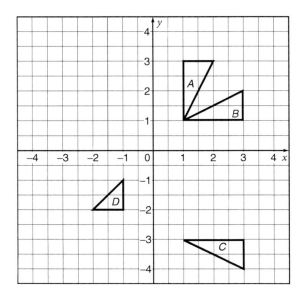

Exam-style questions

NOTE:
In the actual examinations the answers are to be written on the question paper, so in an examination situation you would not normally have to draw the diagrams yourself.
Here, to avoid drawing on this book, you will need to copy the diagrams first.
The questions have been slightly edited to remind you to copy the diagrams.

3 The diagram shows two triangles, *A* and *B*.

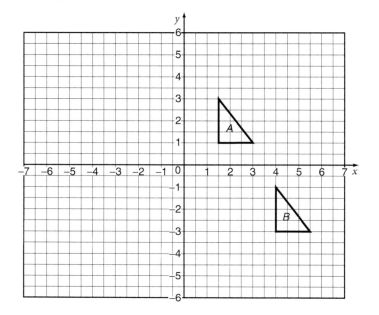

a Write down the vector that represents the translation that maps triangle *A* onto triangle *B*.

b Triangle *C* is an enlargement of triangle *A* with centre (5, 3) and scale factor 3.
On a copy of the diagram, draw and label triangle *C*.

(4024 paper 12 Q13 June 2012)

4

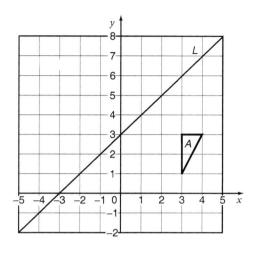

The grid shows triangle *A* and line *L*. Copy the grid.

i Triangle *A* is mapped onto triangle *B* by a reflection in line *L*.
Draw and label triangle *B*.

ii Triangle *A* is mapped onto triangle *C* by a clockwise rotation of 90°, centre (0, 3).
Draw and label triangle *C*.

iii Triangle *C* is mapped onto triangle *D* by a reflection in the line *L*.
Describe the single transformation that maps triangle *B* onto triangle *D*.

(4024 paper 21 Q11b November 2012)

5 $\overrightarrow{AB} = \begin{pmatrix} -1 \\ 4 \end{pmatrix}$ and $\overrightarrow{CD} = 3\overrightarrow{AB}$.

a Write $\overrightarrow{CD}$ as a column vector.

b Make two statements about the relationship between the lines *AB* and *CD*.

(0580 paper 01 Q15 June 2006)

6 The points *A* and *B* are marked on the diagram.

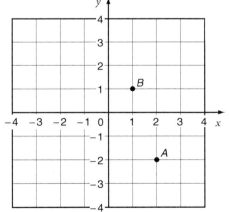

a Write $\overrightarrow{AB}$ as a column vector.

b $\overrightarrow{BC} = \begin{pmatrix} -3 \\ -2 \end{pmatrix}$.

Write down the coordinates of *C*.

(0580 paper 01 Q8 June 2007)

7

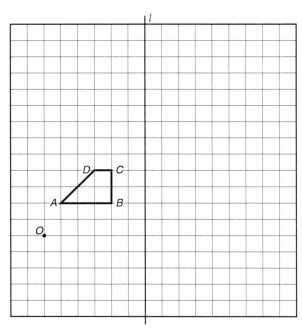

A quadrilateral *ABCD*, a line *l* and a point *O* are shown on the grid given on the previous page.

a Write down the mathematical name for the quadrilateral *ABCD*.

b Copy the grid above, and draw the images of the quadrilateral *ABCD* under the following transformations.

  i Translation by the vector $\begin{pmatrix} 9 \\ -3 \end{pmatrix}$. Label this image *P*.

  ii Reflection in the line *l*. Label this image *Q*.

  iii Rotation, centre *A*, through 90° anticlockwise. Label this image *R*.

  iv Enlargement, centre *O* and scale factor 3. Label this image *S*.

(0580 paper 03 Q7 June 2007)

8

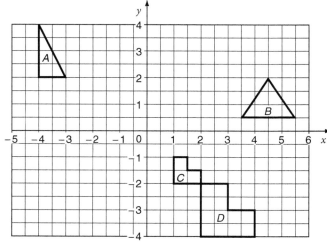

a A translation is given by $\begin{pmatrix} 6 \\ 3 \end{pmatrix} + \begin{pmatrix} -3 \\ -4 \end{pmatrix}$.

  i Write this translation as a single column vector.

  ii On a copy of the grid, draw the translation of triangle *A* using this vector.

b Another translation is given by $-2\begin{pmatrix} 1 \\ -1 \end{pmatrix}$.

   i Write this translation as a single column vector.

   ii On your copy of the grid, draw the translation of triangle B using this vector.

c Describe fully the single transformation that maps shape C onto shape D.

d

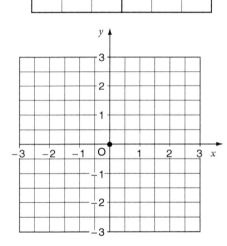

The triangle in the diagram left is isosceles.

   i How many lines of symmetry does this triangle have?

   ii Write down the order of rotational symmetry of this triangle.

   iii On a copy of the grid above, draw the rotation of this triangle about O through 180°.

   iv Describe fully another single transformation that maps this triangle onto your answer for part (d) (iii).

(0580 paper 03 Q7 June 2007)

9

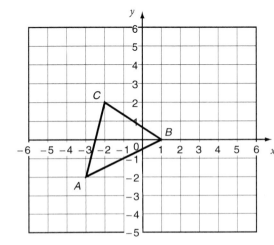

$\mathbf{p} = \begin{pmatrix} 2 \\ -3 \end{pmatrix}$ and $\mathbf{q} = \begin{pmatrix} 3 \\ 1 \end{pmatrix}$.

a Write $\mathbf{p} + \mathbf{q}$ as a column vector.

b The point O is marked on the grid below. Draw the vector $\overrightarrow{OP}$ where $\overrightarrow{OP} = \mathbf{p}$.

(0580 paper 01 Q11 November 2005)

10

Triangle ABC is drawn on the grid.

a **i** Write down the coordinates of A.

   ii Write $\overrightarrow{AB}$ and $\overrightarrow{BC}$ as column vectors.

b Translate triangle ABC by the vector $\begin{pmatrix} 4 \\ -3 \end{pmatrix}$. Label the image T.

c $\overrightarrow{AP} = 2\overrightarrow{AB}$ and $\overrightarrow{AQ} = 2\overrightarrow{AC}$.

   i Plot the points P and Q on the grid.

   ii Describe fully the single transformation which maps triangle ABC onto triangle APQ.

d Rotate triangle ABC through 180° about the midpoint of the side AB. Label the image R.

(0580 paper 03 Q8 November 2008)

11 $\overrightarrow{AB} = \begin{pmatrix} 8 \\ -4 \end{pmatrix}$, $\overrightarrow{BC} = \begin{pmatrix} 6 \\ 4 \end{pmatrix}$.

    a Express $\overrightarrow{AC}$ as a column vector.

    b It is given that $\overrightarrow{CD} = \begin{pmatrix} -11 \\ h \end{pmatrix}$.

       Find the two possible values of **h** which will make *ABCD* a trapezium.
       You may use squared paper to help you with your investigation.

(4024 paper 01 Q13 November 2004)

12

On the grid below, $\overrightarrow{OP} = \mathbf{p}$ and $\overrightarrow{OQ} = \mathbf{q}$.

a Given that $\overrightarrow{OR} = \mathbf{p} - \mathbf{q}$, mark the point *R* clearly on the grid.

b The point *S* is shown on the grid. Given that $\overrightarrow{OS} = \mathbf{q} + h\mathbf{p}$, find *h*.

(4024 paper 01 Q8 June 2007)

13

The diagram shows triangles *A* and *B*.

a The translation $\begin{pmatrix} -3 \\ 2 \end{pmatrix}$ maps $\triangle A$ onto $\triangle C$. On a copy of the diagram, draw and label $\triangle C$.

b The rotation 90° clockwise, centre (2, 0), maps $\triangle A$ onto $\triangle D$. On your copy of the diagram, draw and label $\triangle D$.

c Describe **fully** the **single** transformation which maps $\triangle A$ onto $\triangle B$.

(4024 paper 01 Q20 June 2009)

14 a

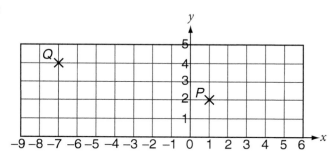

The grid above shows the points *P*(1, 2) and *Q*(−7, 4).

  i *P* can be mapped onto *Q* by a translation. Write down its column vector.

  ii *P* can also be mapped onto *Q* by an enlargement, centre (5, 1). Write down its scale factor.

b

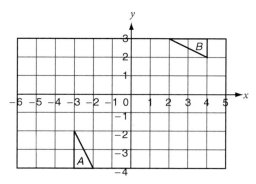

The diagram shows triangles A and B.

i Describe **fully** the **single** transformation that maps triangle A onto triangle B.

ii Triangle A can also be mapped onto triangle B by a reflection in the line $x = -1$ followed by a rotation.

Write down the centre of this rotation.

(4024 paper 01 Q20 June 2009)

11 Statistics I

Learning objectives   (Syllabus sections 41 and 42)

In this chapter we will look at:
- how statistical data is collected and organised
- bar charts and simple histograms
- scatter diagrams and correlation
- frequency polygons
- pie charts
- mean, median, mode and range
- frequency distributions
- statistics in the media

11.1 Introduction

Statistics are all around us in the modern world, so it is necessary to have some knowledge of how statistics are used and the strengths and failings of statistics. This chapter introduces quite a lot of new words which you need to become familiar with. You will need a ruler, protractor and compasses for this chapter.

11.2 Essential Skills

Spend a little time (with your calculator where necessary) working on these questions. It will help you answer some of the questions in this chapter. Check each answer with your calculator as you go along.

1 $\frac{360}{18} = 20$ $\frac{18}{360} = 0.05$

   Using the above information copy and fill in the blanks:

   a $20 \times 18 = \ldots\ldots$
   b $360 \times 0.05 = \ldots\ldots$
   c $360 \div \ldots\ldots = 18$
   d $18 \div \ldots\ldots = 360$
   e $20 \times \ldots\ldots = 1$

2 Copy and fill in the blanks:

   a $360 \times \ldots\ldots = 30$
   b $360 \div \ldots\ldots = 30$
   c $360 \times \ldots\ldots = 12$
   d $360 \div \ldots\ldots = 12$
   e $10 \times \ldots\ldots = 360$
   f $360 \times \ldots\ldots = 10$
   g $360 \div \ldots\ldots = 10$
   h $360 \times \ldots\ldots = 720$
   i $360 \div \ldots\ldots = 540$
   j $1440 \times \ldots\ldots = 360$

3 Copy and fill in the blanks:

   a $100 \times \ldots\ldots = 360$
   b $72 \times \ldots\ldots = 54$
   c $690 \div \ldots\ldots = 23$
   d $690 \times \ldots\ldots = 23$
   e $72 \div \ldots\ldots = 24$
   f $42 \div \ldots\ldots = 28$
   g $55 \times \ldots\ldots = 99$
   h $81 \div \ldots\ldots = 36$
   i $81 \times \ldots\ldots = 36$
   j $90 \times \ldots\ldots = 72$
   k $90 \div \ldots\ldots = 72$

11.3 Why do we need Statistics?

Statistics are used by governments to determine such diverse things as how many schools and hospitals need to be built in the next decade, how the proportion of elderly people in the population will change, and consequently how much support for the elderly will be needed. Doctors need to find out whether the undesirable side effects of a particular drug outweigh its benefits. Businesses may need to predict their stock requirements for the coming years, based on population statistics and current trends. Universities will need to predict the proportion of students who will want to study mathematics next year. You may need to know the likelihood of rain tomorrow. Insurance companies need to know things such as life expectancy of individuals of different ages.

All these things will use statistics. Proper use of statistics involves many steps such as:

- defining the problem that needs to be answered
- collecting data and organising it in a way that can be used
- illustrating the results with pictures, graphs or charts in a way that can be easily understood
- interpreting the data so that useful conclusions can be drawn
- and finally, testing the conclusions to see how valid they may be.

Statistics is different from the rest of the mathematics you are studying because it can only assess the probability of certain conclusions from given data. However, it is an enormously important branch of mathematics for today's world.

It is very important that you should understand that interpreting the statistics can sometimes lead to wrong conclusions. People may want to prove a favourite theory and in some way distort the statistics to support their theory. This does not necessarily mean fraud, but it can mean that other people are misinformed. In particular the public can be misinformed by the distortion of statistical diagrams, as you will see later in the chapter.

Good statistical arguments depend on the collection of sufficient data in an unbiased manner.

For example, you could not predict the number of people in the general population who would be interested in going to the Olympic Games by only asking the members of a sports club. Also, you could not make a sensible prediction based on asking only a small number of people.

Key terms

Data is the set of pieces of information, usually numbers, which will be examined statistically.

A **survey** is a collection of information.

A **sample** is taken when the entire set of data is too large to be conveniently used.

The **population** is the entire set of data from which the sample is taken.

11.4 Collecting and Organising Data

A **data** set consists of individual pieces of information that you may collect in order to solve a problem.

A typical collection of data would be made by a **survey**.

A survey is an organised collection of sufficient and relevant data that can be used to help solve a problem. It is collected from a **sample** of the whole possible set of data (which is the **population**). It can then be used to make predictions for the whole population.

11.5 Examples of Surveys

SURVEY 1 Traffic Congestion

The volume of traffic passing through a very small village is endangering the lives of pedestrians, particularly young children attending the village school, so the authorities are considering building a new road to bypass the village.

The first step towards deciding whether to spend the money necessary to build the bypass is to find the number of cars passing a particular point (point A) in the village at different times of the day.

The authorities commission a survey. The cars are counted throughout the day, over many days to collect enough data. The method used is to count every car that passes point A during each hour during the day. The term 'car' in this survey includes all motorised vehicles, even lorries, motorbikes and tractors.

An easy way to count cars in this situation is to use a **tally chart**. Using a tally chart could be as simple as making a mark on paper every time a car passes. In order to make it easier to add up the marks it is usual to put a strike through the previous four marks to represent the fifth mark for each set of five marks. Table 11.1 shows how such a chart might look.

You will notice that the 'Time of day' column shows entries such as '0700 to before 0800'. This means that a car passing at exactly 0800 goes into the next row labelled '0800 to before 0900'.

A more technical method would be to have some sort of hand-held data logging device which could be clicked every time a car passes and would record all the data and the time of day automatically.

A survey would normally have much more data than this, but this will be sufficient for our purposes.

DATE		
PLACE		
Time of day	**Tally**	**Total**
0700 to before 0800	ЖΤ ЖΤ ЖΤ ЖΤ ЖΤ	25
0800 to before 0900	ЖΤ ЖΤ ЖΤ ЖΤ ЖΤ ЖΤ ЖΤ ЖΤ ЖΤ		46
0900 to before 1000	ЖΤ ЖΤ ЖΤ ЖΤ ЖΤ ЖΤ ЖΤ ЖΤ ЖΤ ЖΤ ЖΤ ЖΤ ||	63
1000 to before 1100 and so on	ЖΤ ЖΤ ЖΤ ЖΤ ЖΤ ЖΤ ЖΤ ЖΤ		41

Table 11.1 Cars passing point A at different times of the day

Table 11.1 is an example of a **frequency distribution**. The frequency of an event is another way of expressing how often it occurs. The column labelled 'Total' is the same as the frequency, so a **frequency table** of the data above might look like Table 11.2.

Time of day	Frequency
0700 to before 0800	25
0800 to before 0900	46
0900 to before 1000	63
1000 to before 1100	41
and so on	

Table 11.2 Cars passing point *A* at different times of the day

This is actually a **grouped frequency table** because the individual times at which the cars passed are not given, but they have been grouped into hourly intervals or classes.

SURVEY 2 Wild Flower Meadow

A botanist wants to estimate the number of wild flowers in a particular meadow. To save having to survey the whole meadow, **sample** squares are taken at different places across the meadow. Each section is 1 metre square. For this survey a tally chart is not necessary as the flowers can just be counted. In the survey the sections were labelled *A, B, C, D* and *E* and the results were as shown in Table 11.3.

Section of meadow	Frequency
A	15
B	14
C	21
D	8
E	20

Table 11.3 Wild flowers per square metre

Again, a proper survey would need much more data, but this will be sufficient for our work. Further statistical work could make a prediction of the number of flowers in the whole meadow.

SURVEY 3 Reduction of Pollution

Our third survey has been commissioned by a city council because they are trying to find ways of cutting down on pollution in a city. They would like people taking children to school in the mornings to try to share transport.

They commission a survey to find how many passengers there are in each car, in the morning rush hour, entering the city past a certain point on one of the main roads into the city.

The results are shown in Table 11.4.

Number of passengers	0	1	2	3	4	5
Number of cars	64	38	41	27	10	2

Table 11.4 Numbers of passengers per car

The first thing you may notice about this frequency table is that, unlike the previous two surveys, it is presented horizontally instead of vertically. You must be able to recognise which row is the frequency, and which is the data you are counting. In this case the number of cars is the frequency; the data you are counting is the number of passengers per car.

11.6 Types of Data

In the first survey we are counting the numbers of cars which pass a particular point at different times of the day. You have seen that we have had to make a decision about where a car passing at 0800 belongs. The time of day is **continuous data**. Continuous data is measured data. Examples would include heights of buildings, volumes of liquids and so on.

In the second survey we are counting the numbers of flowers in different sections of a meadow. There is no doubt about to which section any particular flower belongs. The sections are separate, or **categorical**. **Categorical data** could include colours of sweets, countries of the world and so on.

In the third survey we are counting the numbers of cars which carry passengers. Again there is no doubt as to where each car belongs. It must carry either 0, 1, 2, 3, 4 or 5 passengers. This is **discrete data**. Discrete data can be counted. Examples could be scores at a games match, examination marks and so on.

11.7 Illustrating the Data

One possible method to illustrate the data would be a **pictogram**.

A pictogram uses a small picture or symbol to represent a given number of the pieces of data. For example, using the frequency distribution from Survey 1 (Traffic congestion), we might use a small car to represent a frequency of, say, ten cars (see Figure 11.1). Less than ten cars would have to be represented by a part of a car, so this is not a very accurate method, but it does present the data in a pictorial way, which gives everyone an immediate idea of the scale of the problem.

0700 to before 0800

0800 to before 0900

0900 to before 1000

1000 to before 1100

represents 10 cars

Figure 11.1 Cars passing point *A* at different times of the day

Points to note about pictograms:
- The pictogram needs a key to show how many objects are represented by each whole symbol.
- Parts of a symbol are used to represent smaller numbers, but these are not very accurate.
- The pictogram needs a title.

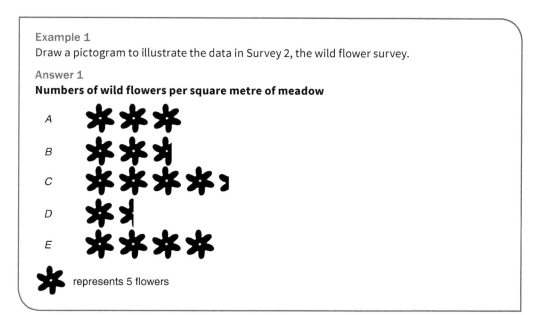

Example 1
Draw a pictogram to illustrate the data in Survey 2, the wild flower survey.

Answer 1
Numbers of wild flowers per square metre of meadow

✳ represents 5 flowers

Pictograms are not very accurate representations of the data. Precise illustrations are provided by **bar graphs** (or **bar charts**) or **simple histograms**.

Bar charts illustrate data which can be divided into completely *separate* categories.

The wild flower survey can be illustrated by a bar chart because the data is divided into separate sections *A*, *B*, *C*, *D* and *E* of the meadow (see Figure 11.2).

In a bar chart the vertical axis represents frequency, and the horizontal axis distinguishes each bar with a label. The bars can be separated because there is no actual connection between them.

Key terms

A **bar chart** is a graph in which *separated* bars are drawn to illustrate the frequency of categorical or discrete data.

A **simple histogram** is similar to a bar chart, but is used to represent continuous data that has been grouped into classes of equal size. The bars are not separate but must be of equal width.

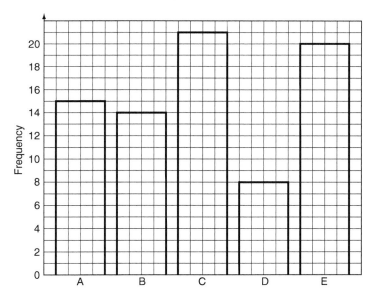

Figure 11.2 Numbers of wild flowers per square metre of meadow

You will also see bar graphs with the bars drawn horizontally and the frequency on the horizontal axis.

Points to note about bar graphs:
- The bars can be separated by blank areas.
- The bars are labelled, not the grid lines.
- The height of each bar represents the frequency.
- The bars are all the same width.
- The bar chart needs a title.

The traffic congestion survey (Survey 1) could be illustrated by a simple histogram (Figure 11.3). This is very similar to a bar chart, but is used to represent data that is **continuous**. As we have seen, continuous data is not divided into separate parts but can take any value.

The data is still represented by bars, but the bars cannot be separated by blank spaces because there is no gap in the possible measurements.

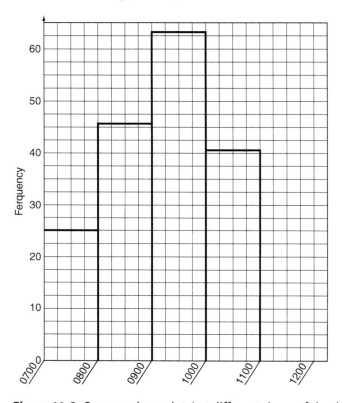

Figure 11.3 Cars passing point *A* at different times of the day

It is important to note that a *simple* histogram can only be used if the data is divided into groups of *equal width* (as in the above example where the groups are each of one hour). Histograms for groups of varying widths are slightly more complicated. We will study these in Chapter 23.

Points to notice about simple histograms:
- The bars touch each other and are not separated by blank spaces.
- The grid lines are labelled, not the bars.
- **The widths of the bars are all the same.**
- The height of each bar represents the frequency.
- The histogram needs a title.

Example 2

Draw a bar chart to illustrate the data in Survey 3, the reduction of pollution survey.

Answer 2

Number of passengers per car

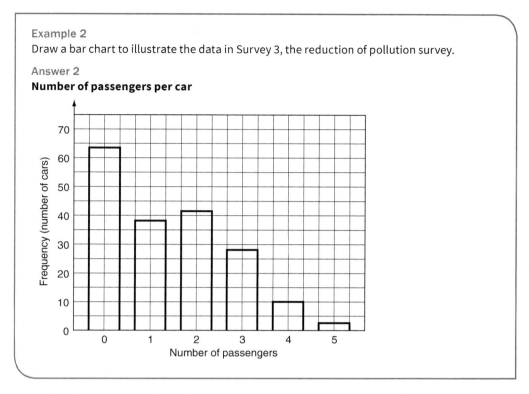

Some data has so many values that it is better to group it into **classes** before drawing any conclusion, as the next survey shows.

SURVEY 4 Waiting Times in a Surgery

The data set in Table 11.5 records the time patients had to wait in a surgery before they were able to see a doctor. The times are given to the nearest minute. The data is an example of **raw data** which has not yet been sorted in any way.

10	3	15	7	8	4	21	33	11	31	27	25
7	5	9	11	27	17	28	16	14	8	23	35
19	10	28	21	16	15	19	19	19	27	6	9
26	7	2	18	23	14	10	10	9	32	29	3

Table 11.5 Waiting times for patients in a doctor's surgery

This data is shown in the frequency table in Table 11.6 with the waiting times grouped into classes.

NOTE:

Take your time when working with statistics. It is easy to leave out or repeat values when you are counting data values. Hold a ruler under the line you are working on, or run a finger along the data.

Time (to the nearest minute)	Tally	Frequency
1–5	卌	5
6–10	卌 卌 |||	13
11–15	卌		6
16–20	卌 |||	8
21–25	卌	5
26–30	卌 ||	7
31–35	||||	4
	Total frequency	48

Table 11.6 Frequencies of surgery waiting times

Table 11.6 has presented us with a problem. To illustrate the data, do we use a bar chart or histogram?

Time is continuous, but these classes appear to be for discrete data because the times have been rounded to the nearest minute. However, this means that a time of 5.4 minutes would be rounded to 5 minutes, and a time of 5.5 minutes would be rounded to 6 minutes. Just as measurements are rounded according to our known rules, so the classes into which continuous items of data will be entered have **upper** and **lower class boundaries**, and the data is effectively rounded into these boundaries. The class boundaries in the histogram are calculated as $\frac{5+6}{2}$, $\frac{10+11}{2}$, $\frac{15+16}{2}$ and so on.

If the data had not previously been rounded it could have been entered into a table like Table 11.7, with the classes shown. The result is still the same, but the table now makes it clear that we should draw a histogram.

Time (t minutes)	Frequency
$0.5 \leqslant t < 5.5$	5
$5.5 \leqslant t < 10.5$	13
$10.5 \leqslant t < 15.5$	6
$15.5 \leqslant t < 20.5$	8
$20.5 \leqslant t < 25.5$	5
$25.5 \leqslant t < 30.5$	7
$30.5 \leqslant t < 35.5$	4
Total frequency	48

Table 11.7 Surgery waiting times

The waiting times are illustrated in the histogram in Figure 11.4, and as you can see *the class boundaries must be shown on the horizontal axis.*

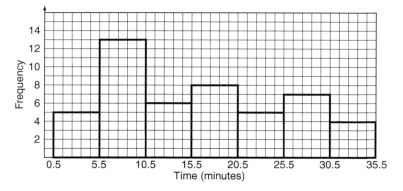

Figure 11.4 Waiting time for patients in a doctor's surgery

When do we draw a bar chart and when do we draw a simple histogram?
- **Bar charts** are drawn to illustrate **discrete** or **categorical** data which are separate or *counted* data.
- Examples could be numbers of students, colours, votes for political parties, types of farm animals.
- The data can still be grouped into classes.
- The bars can be separate.
- **Histograms** are drawn to illustrate **continuous** data which is *measured* data.
- Examples could be journey times, long jump records, weights of bags of flour.
- The data can be grouped into classes, but decisions must be made as to where values fit in the boundaries between classes.
- There is no space between the bars (unless one class has a frequency of zero).

Exercise 11.1

1 **a** Construct a frequency table for the following scores on the spinning of a spinner numbered from 1 to 6.

2	5	6	3	3	3	4	1	5	1	5
5	5	6	3	4	4	2	2	3	4	5
1	6	1	3	2	3	3	2	5	2	5
2	6	4	1	3	5	5	2	1	4	3

   b Draw a bar chart to illustrate the frequency of each score.

2 **a** Draw up a grouped frequency table for the following *discrete* data.
   Use the classes 1–10, 11–20, 21–30, 31–40, 41–50.

1	45	50	37	3	3	36	5	48	38	17
19	21	12	36	46	49	29	29	29	20	40
34	31	42	45	40	50	32	5	11	28	35
2	8	41	9	10	17	18	49	37	33	30
21	41	5	8	10	11	13	5	8	23	9

   b Use your frequency table to draw a bar chart.

3 a Draw up a grouped frequency table for the following data. Use the classes 0 to less than 10, 10 to less than 20, 20 to less than 30 and so on.

1.6	63.1	57.3	3.1	6.7	54.6	55.5	52.7	13.6	41.7	8.1
56.9	42.8	46.9	9.5	53.2	12.7	56	3.9	8	5.7	1.1
44.1	17.6	9	17.8	27.4	57.3	52	33.8	34	52.9	7.5
49.3	59.9	0	0.5	17.8	27	53.1	37.3	0.7	51.1	1.1

b Draw a simple histogram to show this data.

4 The heights of 25 students were measured, and the results are shown below.

SURVEY 5 Heights of Students

160	155.5	128.5	161	152	152.5	153	154.7	141	163.4	129.2
164.2	151.9	150	150.3	145	138	136.6	129	149	148.2	135.1
132.8	143	141.5								

NOTE:
This means that 129.9 would go in the first class and 130 would go in the second class and so on.

a Draw up a frequency table with the data grouped into the following classes: 120 to <130, 130 to <140, 140 to <150, 150 to <160 and 160 to <170.

b Draw a simple histogram with the horizontal axis labelled from 120 to 170.

5 The bar chart shown below shows the numbers of a group of students taking examinations in maths, physics, chemistry, English and economics in one week in an examination period. 26 students are taking the chemistry examination, and 15 are taking the economics examination.

a Copy the bar chart and complete the frequency scale on the vertical axis. (The scale runs from zero.)

b Draw in the missing bar for economics.

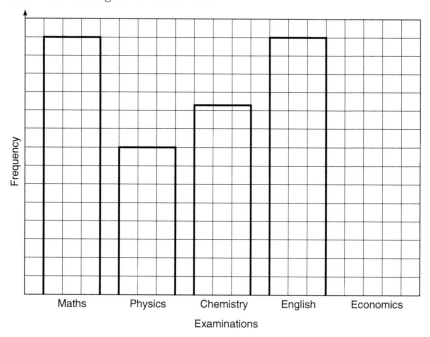

c How many examinations will be taken all together?

6 Liam counts the numbers of different colours in a bag of sweets.
He finds 12 red sweets, 9 green sweets, 4 yellow sweets and 7 purple sweets.
Draw a bar chart to illustrate the numbers of sweets of each colour.

7 A hotel manager leaves a questionnaire in each room for visitors to rate their stay. Feedback from the questionnaire should give the hotel managers valuable insight into how they can improve their customer satisfaction.

The questionnaire asks the visitors to tick boxes which best describe their satisfaction with different aspects of the hotel.

The boxes are numbered 0: very dissatisfied
1: fairly dissatisfied
2: neither satisfied nor dissatisfied
3: fairly satisfied
4: very satisfied
5: don't know.

After a week the questionnaires were studied.

The answers to the question: 'How satisfied were you with the hotel breakfast?' are shown below.

5	4	1	0	1	1	0	4	4	3	2
5	2	5	2	3	4	1	0	0	1	2
2	3	3	4	3	2	5	1	0	3	3
4	0	1	3	3	4	2	2	3	3	4

a Use the data above to draw up a frequency table.
b Illustrate the data by means of a bar chart.

11.8 Scatter Diagrams

A **scatter diagram** shows the relationship, if any, between *two* variables. It is drawn on a grid, with each axis representing one of the variables.

For example, you could investigate the possible relationship between minimum temperatures per month over 12 months in Sydney and in Delhi, for one particular year.

The data, in degrees Celsius, is shown in Table 11.8.

Month	Jan	Feb	Mar	Apr	May	Jun	July	Aug	Sept	Oct	Nov	Dec
Sydney	19	19	18	15	12	9	8	9	1 I	14	16	18
Delhi	7	10	15	21	26	28	27	26	24	19	13	8

Table 11.8 Minimum temperatures

We know that Sydney is in the southern hemisphere and Delhi is in the northern hemisphere, so we would expect that when the temperature is *high* in one city it would be *low* in the other. This is called negative correlation. To see if this is the case, and to investigate how strongly the data conforms to this expectation we draw a scatter diagram in Figure 11.5. Each dot on the diagram represents one month.

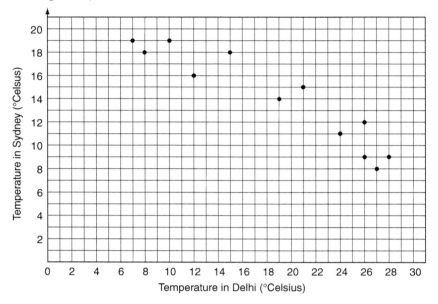

Figure 11.5 Minimum temperatures in Delhi and Sydney

Figure 11.5 shows that there is indeed a **negative correlation**, and it is a strong correlation because the results cluster close to a line. For our purposes we could say that they are close to a straight line, although in this case it looks as though it could possibly be a curve and would need further investigation to establish whether this is so. We are not concerned with that amount of detail here.

The diagrams in Figure 11.6 show the types of scatter diagrams you might see, and how the correlation would be described in each case.

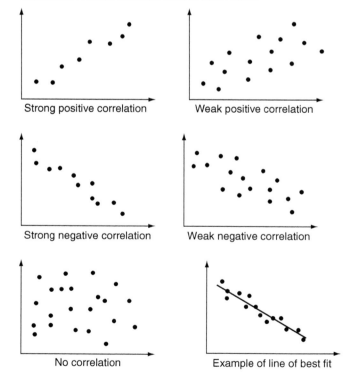

Figure 11.6 Correlation and line of best fit

Sometimes you might be asked to draw a line of best fit through the points. This is a straight line through, or close to, as many of the points as possible, and with approximately the same number on each side. This is always an approximation so no two people will necessarily have exactly the same answers. Sometimes the mean, or average, of the points will be found and the line drawn through that point.

Example 3

Two judges are judging a diving competition independently. Their marks should be close together, but because marking this sort of competition is not exact but depends to a certain extent on each judge's personal opinion, the marks will not necessarily be identical. The marks are out of 10. The organisers of the competition want to make sure that the judges are reasonably consistent.

The table shows the results.

Competitor number	1	2	3	4	5	6	7	8	9	10
Judge A	5	4	3	7	9	9	10	3	1	4
Judge B	6	4	5	6	8	9	9	2	2	4

a Draw a scatter diagram to show these results.
b Comment on the diagram.
c In your opinion should the organisers of the competition appoint these two judges next time they hold a diving competition?

Answer 3

a

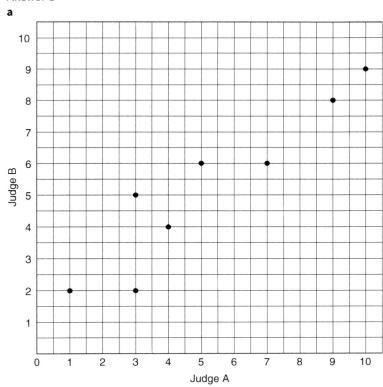

b The diagram shows a reasonably strong consistency between the two judges.

c The organisers could safely ask the judges back next time.

Exercise 11.2

1 The table shows the average maximum and minimum temperatures in degrees Celsius for each month in a city in the northern hemisphere.

Anita assumes that there will be a **positive correlation** between the maximum and minimum temperatures.

	Jan	Feb	Mar	Apr	May	Jun	July	Aug	Sept	Oct	Nov	Dec
Av Max	21	22	29	37	39	37	34	33	34	33	28	23
Av Min	7	9	15	22	26	28	27	26	25	19	13	8

Draw a scatter diagram and comment on the result.

Key term

Positive correlation is seen if as one set of data increases in value the other also increases. For example, as the population of a city increases more schools are needed.

2 As part of her chemistry project Zaida is investigating the properties of the noble gases. She suspects that there is an association between the melting point in K and the atomic number. (K is temperature measurement with respect to absolute zero, so it is the normal degrees Celsius + 273°. It saves having to use large negative numbers.)

She finds the following values in a table of the chemical elements, and uses them to plot a scatter graph.

Element	Abbreviation	Atomic number	Melting point (K)
Argon	Ar	18	83.8
Helium	He	2	0.95
Krypton	Kr	36	116.6
Neon	Ne	10	24.5
Radon	Rn	86	202
Xenon	Xe	54	161.3

a Draw a scatter diagram showing this data.

b Comment on the result.

3 Joel is interested in code-breaking.

a He decides to see what the relationship is between the numbers of vowels and the numbers of consonants in words of different lengths. He writes down the number of each in the first one-letter word, then the first two-letter word and the first three-letter word he comes to in a book he is reading. He manages to find words of length up to 14 letters, and one of 18 letters.

His results are shown in the table.

Word length	1	2	3	4	5	6	7	8	9	10	11	12	13	14	15	16	17	18
Vowels	1	1	1	1	2	2	4	3	3	5	4	4	7	6				8
Consonants	0	1	2	3	3	4	3	5	6	5	7	8	6	8				10

i Draw a scatter diagram to show these results.

ii Comment on the diagram.

b Joel decides that this is not going to help very much.

He thinks that the most commonly used letters in the English language could be a, e, d, r, s, t.

Joel makes a tally chart by looking at the number of times these letters occur in the first paragraph of his book.

From the tally chart he draws up the following frequency table.

Letter	*a*	*e*	*d*	*r*	*s*	*t*
Frequency	35	59	10	30	36	36

Draw a bar chart to show this data.

c How do you think he could improve his investigation?

4 Pierre and Mignon have to be in school by 0900.

Their father drives them to school but the rush hour traffic causes delays.

They keep a note of the time they leave the house each day and the length of time it takes to get to school (to the nearest minute) for 12 days.

The results are shown in the table.

Time of day	0800	0712	0805	0815	0825	0845	0724	0746	0738	0700	0835	0750
Time taken	18	10	22	25	23	27	13	25	20	9	22	22

a Draw a scatter diagram to show these times.
b Draw the line of best fit.
c Use your line of best fit to estimate how long the journey will take if they leave home at 0730.
d Estimate how many minutes late will they might be if they leave home at 0840.

Practical investigations

1 Investigate the possible relationship between people's hand span and the length of their feet. The hand span is the furthest distance between the outstretched thumb and little finger that a person can spread their fingers.
2 Investigate whether people find it easier to estimate lengths than areas.
3 Investigate a possible relationship between the length of a person's middle finger and their musical ability.
4 Investigate a possible relationship between a person's ability in mathematics and their ability in music.

11.9 Frequency Polygons

Key term

A **frequency polygon** is formed when the midpoints of the tops of the bars of a simple histogram are joined by straight lines.

Joining the midpoints of the tops of the bars of a simple histogram produces a **frequency polygon**.

The steps needed to produce a frequency polygon are shown in the two diagrams in Figure 11.7.

Step 1: Join the midpoints of the tops of the bars with straight lines.

Step 2: Complete the polygon by joining the midpoint of the first bar to the horizontal axis at the point corresponding to the position of a previous bar with a frequency of zero. In the same way, join the midpoint of the last bar to the horizontal axis at the point corresponding with the midpoint of the next zero frequency bar.

The second diagram in Figure 11.7 shows the completed frequency polygon.

Points to notice about the frequency polygon:

- The area under the frequency polygon is the same as the total area of the bars of the histogram because the amount cut off each bar is the same as the amount gained above each bar, as you can see in the second diagram in Figure 11.7.
- It is not necessary to draw a histogram before drawing a frequency polygon; the polygon may be plotted using the midpoint of each class and the corresponding frequency.
- The main use of frequency polygons is to compare data. Showing two or more histograms on one graph is often confusing, but two or more frequency polygons produce a good visual comparison. The best comparisons are obtained by using the same number of data items (total frequency) and the same classes.
- The class with the most items of data (modal class: see Section 11.12) is the class with the highest point on the frequency polygon.
- The frequency polygon also gives some idea of the spread of the data (see Section 11.11).

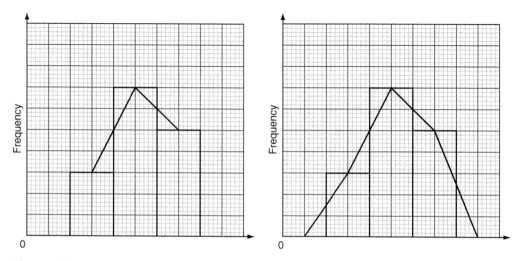

Figure 11.7 Frequency polygon

Example 3

a A teacher gave his class a surprise spelling test one Friday. The results are shown in the table below. The marks are percentages.

mark (m)	$20 \leqslant m < 40$	$40 \leqslant m < 60$	$60 \leqslant m < 80$	$80 \leqslant m < 100$
frequency	7	12	6	5

Draw a frequency polygon to illustrate these marks.

b The teacher warned his class that they would have to repeat the spelling test next Friday. The results of the second test are shown in the next table.

mark (m)	$20 \leqslant m < 40$	$40 \leqslant m < 60$	$60 \leqslant m < 80$	$80 \leqslant m < 100$
frequency	0	10	14	6

On the same axes as you used in part (a) draw a frequency polygon to represent these new results.

c Compare the results of the two spelling tests.

Answer 3

a

mark (m)	$20 \leqslant m < 40$	$40 \leqslant m < 60$	$60 \leqslant m < 80$	$80 \leqslant m < 100$
frequency	7	12	6	5
class midpoint	30	50	70	90

b

mark (m)	$20 \leqslant m < 40$	$40 \leqslant m < 60$	$60 \leqslant m < 80$	$80 \leqslant m < 100$
frequency	0	10	14	6
class midpoint	30	50	70	90

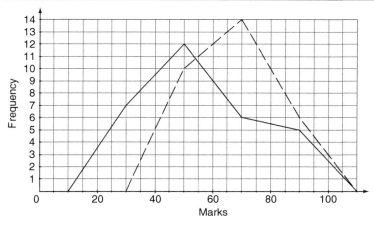

c The students have improved. For the first test results, the class with the most students is $40 \leqslant m < 60$, while for the second test it is $60 \leqslant m < 80$. We can see immediately that more students gained high marks when they were prepared for the test.

The spread of the second set of results is less than that of the first set.

Exercise 11.3

1 The table shows the times between buses on one particular day on a certain bus route. The times are in minutes, rounded to the nearest minute.

Class	$10 \leqslant t < 15$	$15 \leqslant t < 20$	$20 \leqslant t < 25$	$25 \leqslant t < 30$	$30 \leqslant t < 35$
Frequency	5	7	8	10	2

  a Draw a simple histogram.
  b On your simple histogram draw a frequency polygon.
  c Identify the modal class (the class with the highest frequency).

2 The following set of raw data shows the heights of seedlings measured to the nearest centimetre on a certain day.

4	3	7	5	4	8	6	5	5	3	4
2	3	8	7	5	9	10	6	11	6	7
3	4	5	9	8	2	3	10	5	7	6

  a Draw a grouped frequency table with the data grouped into classes:
    $2 \leqslant h < 4, 4 \leqslant h < 6, 6 \leqslant h < 8, 8 \leqslant h < 10, 10 \leqslant h < 12$
  b Draw a frequency polygon.
  c Identify the modal class.

Key term

A **pie chart** is a circle divided into sectors to represent categories with angles at the centre proportional to the frequency of each category.

11.10 Pie Charts

A pie chart is so called because it looks like a pie divided into slices. Who gets the biggest slice? It is used to represent how the whole of a group is divided up into categories. The sizes of the 'slices' are proportional to the numbers in each category. The sizes are dependent on the angle at the centre of each, so, for example, if the total number in the group is 36 and the number in one of the categories is 5, then the angle at the centre of the slice is a fraction $\left(\frac{5}{36}\right)$ of the complete turn.

For example, suppose you want to illustrate the composition of a local orchestra which has the following members:

    32   string players

    8   woodwind players

    5   brass players

    3   others (percussionist, conductor and pianist).

The first step is to make a table, like Table 11.9.

Players	Number	Calculation	Angle
Strings	32		
Woodwind	8		
Brass	5		
Percussionist, conductor and pianist	3		
Total	48	$\frac{360}{48} = 7.5$	360°

Table 11.9 Orchestra composition

The total number of players is 48, which is represented by the whole circle (360°).

This is a question on proportion, so find the multiplier to get from 48 to 360.

This is $\frac{360}{48} = 7.5$, so $48 \times 7.5 = 360°$. Now we can calculate the angles: $32 \times 7.5 = 240°$, and so on.

The table becomes Table 11.10.

Players	Number	Calculation	Angle
Strings	32	$32 \times 7.5 =$	240°
Woodwind	8	$8 \times 7.5 =$	60°
Brass	5	$5 \times 7.5 =$	37.5°
Percussionist, conductor and pianist	3	$3 \times 7.5 =$	22.5°
Total	48	$48 \times 7.5 =$	360°

Table 11.10 Orchestral composition

The pie chart can now be drawn (Figure 11.8).

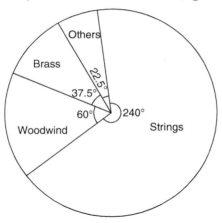

Figure 11.8 Pie chart showing composition of an orchestra

Points to remember when drawing a pie chart:
- Be as accurate as possible.
- Mark the centre as soon as you have drawn the circle (it is easy to lose the centre when you remove your compass point!).
- It does not matter where you start, but the first thing to do is to draw in one radius and start measuring angles from there.
- Draw each slice as soon as you have measured it. (Do not try to measure all the angles at once unless you have a 360° protractor, and even then it is easy to make a mistake.)
- A pie chart measurer is not necessarily the best thing to use as it will probably be marked in percentages instead of angles.
- Each slice must be labelled.
- The pie chart needs a title.
- If you end up with some pie left over you have miscalculated. Check your original calculation and that you have found the correct multiplier or divisor.

Example 4
The pie chart shows the proportion of pencils of various colours in Ethan's pencil case. Ethan has five red pencils.
Colours of pencils in pencil case

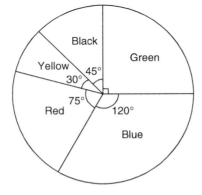

The angles are shown in the diagram.

a Draw up a table to show the information given.

b Calculate the numbers of pencils of each colour and complete the table.

NOTE:
We are not given the total number of pencils, but we are told that 75° represents five pencils.

NOTE:
We are not given the total number of pencils, but we are told that 75° represents five pencils.

NOTE:
Check that dividing by 15 gives a reasonable answer: $90 \div 15 = 6$, which is reasonable, but $90 \times 15 = 1350$, which is *not* reasonable!

NOTE:
Check your answers by adding the number of pencils (24) and by calculating $360 \div 15 (= 24)$.

Answer 4

a

Colour	Angle	Numbers of pencils
Green	90°	
Blue	120°	
Red	75°	5
Yellow	30°	
Black	45°	
Total	360°	

b

First we must find the multiplier or divisor to get from 75 to 5.

$\frac{75}{5} = 15$, so $\frac{75}{15} = 5$, and *dividing* by 15 will convert each angle to the number of pencils it represents.

Colour	Angle	Calculation	Numbers of pencils
Green	90°	90 ÷ 15	6
Blue	120°	120 ÷ 15	8
Red	75°	75 ÷ 15	5
Yellow	30°	30 ÷ 15	2
Black	45°	45 ÷ 15	3
TOTAL	360°	360 ÷ 15	24

Exercise 11.4

1   The owners of a village store need to decide how much floor space to devote to different classes of goods.

These are fresh produce, groceries, household products, magazines and stationery, and frozen goods.

As an initial study the contents of the shopping baskets of customers are analysed over a week and the results entered into a computer spreadsheet.

The total numbers of items in each category are printed out and the results are shown below.

Fresh produce	Groceries	Household products	Magazines and stationery	Frozen goods	Total
351	183	66	315	165	

   a Copy and complete the table.
   b Draw a pie chart to show this information.
   c If the store has 100 square metres of floor space available, calculate the area which should be dedicated to each category, showing your results in a table. Give your answers to 1 decimal place.

2   The electricity consumption on a farm is recorded in units of energy/day for four consecutive quarters of a year.

The results, in the order they were recorded, are: 23   11   21   65

a Draw up a table to show these results and calculate the angles required to show them on a pie chart. The pie chart will show how the electricity consumption for one year is used in the different seasons.

b Draw and label the pie chart.

3 A newsagent stocks the following groups of items:

Newspapers   35% of total stock
Magazines   50% of total stock
Snacks   15% of total stock

  a Copy and complete the table.

	Percentage of total stock	Angle on pie chart
Newspapers		
Magazines		
Snacks		
Total		

  b Draw and label a pie chart to show this information.

4 **a** Copy and complete this table showing the angles on a pie chart which is being drawn up to represent the numbers of students taking psychology, sociology, economics and history out of a group of students.

	Number of students	Angle on pie chart
Psychology	14	
Sociology	20	
Economics		110
History		80
Total	72	

  b Draw the pie chart.

11.11 Mean, Median, Mode and Range

The mean, median and mode are used to find the average of a set of data. They represent the *central tendency* of the data. For example, you might want to find the average of your set of examination results to compare with those of your friend (or rival!).

Suppose this is your set of results (all in percentages):

$$35 \quad 56 \quad 81 \quad 19 \quad 73 \quad 49 \quad 5 \quad 76 \quad 56 \quad 82 \quad 90 \quad 50$$

The three averages will usually give different results, and are used in different circumstances.

We will start with the **mean**.

The mean is calculated by adding up each value in the set of data (examination results), and dividing by the number of values.

So to calculate the mean of your results calculate

$$\frac{35+56+81+19+73+49+5+76+56+82+90+50}{12} = \frac{672}{12} = 56$$

The mean of your examination results is 56%.

Key term

The **median** is the middle value when all the values are arranged in order of size.

Now the **median**.

The median is found by putting the values in order of size, and then finding the middle value. The median should divide the ordered set of data into two equal groups.

If there is an even number of values in the set, say 10, then the mean of the middle two values (5th and 6th values) is the median. If there is an odd number, say 59, take one out to represent the middle value and divide the remainder (58) into two equal groups (29 in each), then the median is the 30th value.

Rearranging the results:

5 19 35 49 50 56 56 73 76 81 82 90

There are 12 values, so there is no particular middle value. The values divide equally into two sets of six. The median in this case is found by taking the sixth and seventh values and finding their mean (or the value half way between them).

5 19 35 49 50 56 … 56 73 76 81 82 90

Key term

The **mode** is the most frequent value.

In this case the required numbers are the same (56 and 56), so their mean is 56.

The median value is 56%.

Lastly the **mode**.

The mode is the value which appears the most frequently. It is easiest to see in the ordered values used for the median. Once again it is 56.

The mode is 56%.

It was only by chance that these examination results had the same mean, median and mode.

We will now look at your friend's results:

37 45 32 76 65 48 79 24 79 35 76 85

It would be difficult to compare them with yours without finding an average.

The mean $= \dfrac{37 + 45 + 32 + 76 + 65 + 48 + 79 + 24 + 79 + 35 + 76 + 85}{12}$

$= \dfrac{681}{12} = 56.75\%$

The median:

24 32 35 37 45 48 65 76 76 79 79 85

Again there are 12 values so we need to find the mean of the sixth and seventh values.

24 32 35 37 45 48 … 65 76 76 79 79 85

$$\frac{48+65}{2} = \frac{113}{2} = 56.5\%$$

Key term

The **range** is the difference between the highest and lowest values. It is a measure of the spread of the data.

This time there are two modes (76 and 79)! This is not unusual.

There is one more useful statistic which can be quoted, and that is the **range**.

The range gives an idea of the *spread* of the values, and is simply the difference between the largest and the smallest values.

The range of your marks is $90 - 5 = 85$.

The range of your friend's marks is $85 - 37 = 48$.

Let us look again at your marks. There is one very low mark of only 5%. Perhaps you were feeling rather ill when you took that examination, or perhaps you really do not like that particular subject. How would it change your averages if we left it out?

First the mean $= \dfrac{35+56+81+19+73+49+76+56+82+90+50}{11}$

$= \dfrac{667}{11} = 60.6\%$

This is looking much better!

The median:

$$19 \quad 35 \quad 49 \quad 50 \quad 56 \quad 56 \quad 73 \quad 76 \quad 81 \quad 82 \quad 90$$

Now that there are 11 values we can pick out a middle value and divide the remaining 10 into two groups of 5, making the median the 6th value:

$$19 \quad 35 \quad 49 \quad 50 \quad 56 \quad \ldots \quad 56 \quad \ldots \quad 73 \quad 76 \quad 81 \quad 82 \quad 90$$

The median is again 56%, so that has made no difference.

Also the mode is still 56%, so no difference there either.

Your new averages:

Mean	60.6%
Median	56%
Mode	56%

Your new range is $90 - 19 = 71$.

This shows that the mean can be so affected by unusual or extreme values (at either end of the set of values) that it is not always the best average to use. The median and the mode are not so affected, sometimes not at all as you can see.

Another student has the following set of results:

$$23 \quad 45 \quad 78 \quad 56 \quad 23 \quad 79 \quad 34 \quad 98 \quad 80 \quad 82 \quad 57 \quad 89$$

The mean is 62%.

The median:

$$23 \quad 23 \quad 34 \quad 45 \quad 56 \quad 57 \quad \ldots \quad 78 \quad 79 \quad 80 \quad 82 \quad 89 \quad 98$$

$$\frac{57+78}{2} = 67.5\%$$

But the mode is 23%! Perhaps this student had two bad days!

The mode is clearly not a suitable average in this case, as it says nothing about the overall ability of the student.

Now consider the following.

A shopkeeper keeps a record of the sizes of shoes sold in one day. They were:

$$5\ 6\ 3\ 8\ 5\ 4\ 5\ 5\ 5\ 8\ 4\ 5\ 5\ 6\ 5\ 4\ 5\ 7\ 8\ 5\ 5$$

Which is the most popular size?

The mode is clearly 5, and this would be the size that this shopkeeper would need to keep in stock in larger numbers than the other sizes. In this case the mode is the most suitable average to consider.

> **To summarise:**
> - The **mean** is found by adding up all the values and dividing by the number of values.
> - The **median** is found by arranging the values in size order and finding the middle value if there are an odd number of values, or the mean of the two middle values if there are an even number of values.

- The **mode** is the most frequently occurring value.
- The mean is probably the most used average.
- The median can be a better average if there are non-typical values at either end of the set of values, which could distort the mean.
- The mode is best for deciding which of a set of values is most popular.
- The mean may not be a whole number even if, for example, it represents people. (One old example of this is the strange report that the average family in Britain has 2.4 children.) The mean can be rounded, but not necessarily to a whole number. The usual rounding rule should be applied.
- The mean can be used to make further predictions about the data, as you will see later.
- The **range** is the difference between the largest and smallest values, and shows the spread of the data.

You should appreciate by now that the popular phrase 'on average' is imprecise, and may be misleading.

NOTE:
If you have difficulty remembering which average is which, try the following:
- the <u>med</u>ian is the <u>mid</u>dle value (when arranged in order)
- the <u>mo</u>de is the <u>mo</u>st popular
- which leaves the mean, which is the other one!

Example 5

Find:

a the mean   **b** the median

c the mode   **d** the range

of the following data:

7	1	9	6	2	8	1	4	5	1	6
9	4	6	2	7	6					

Answer 11.5

a The mean $= \frac{84}{17} = 4.94$

b

1	1	1	2	2	4	4	5	6	6	6
6	7	7	8	9	9					

There are 17 values so the values divide into 2 groups of 8 values with one value in the middle, like this:

    first group of 8   1   last group of 8

The median is the 9th value, which is 6.

Median $= 6$

c Mode $= 6$

d Range $= 9 - 1 = 8$

NOTE:
In part **b** check that you have not left any values out when you rearrange them by counting the total in the rearranged list.

Sometimes it is necessary to combine mean values. To do this we have to calculate the original totals and then recalculate the new mean, as in the following example.

> **Example 6**
> The mean of a list of four numbers is 20. Six more numbers, with a mean of 32, are added to the list. What is the new mean?
>
> **Answer 6**
> Sum of numbers in the list of $4 = 4 \times 20 = 80$. Sum of extra 6 numbers $= 6 \times 32 = 192$
> $$\text{Mean of new list} = \frac{80 + 192}{4 + 6} = \frac{272}{10} = 27.2$$

Exercise 11.5

1 Find:
   i the mean   **ii** the median   **iii** the mode   **iv** the range for each of these sets of data.

a	5	6	9	4	10	3	1	9
b	1	1	1	2	3	3	5	
	7	7	7	7	8	8	9	
c	2.5	2.6	2.6	3.1	4.2	4.8	5.1	5.3	5.6

NOTE:
In question 2 remember that the mean height will be the total height of the enlarged group divided by the new total number of students.

2 The mean height of a group of five students is 160 cm.
   a What is their total height?
      Two new students join them. Their mean height is 156 cm.
   b What is the new mean height of the group?

3 The total number of students in a school is 856.
   a There are 30 classrooms available. Calculate the mean number of students per classroom, giving your answer to 3 significant figures.
   b It has been decided that 25 should be the maximum number of students per classroom. Calculate how many new classrooms should be built.
   c What is the new mean number of students per classroom?

4 The mean number of potatoes in each of 25 bags of potatoes is 60.
   a How many potatoes are there altogether?
   b The potatoes are going to be put into smaller bags, and the new mean is 15. Calculate the number of bags used.

11.12 The Mean, Median and Mode from a Frequency Table

How can these averages be calculated from data which is already drawn up into a frequency table?
We will start by examining the following set of data.

2	7	5	3	9	1	7	2	5	5	3	4
7	1	9	1	5	8	2	6	3	8	6	1
2	4	6	8	2	0	1	7	8	7	7	0

To calculate the **mean** we need to add up all the numbers and divide by 36:
$$\frac{2+7+5+3+9+1+7+2+5+5+\ldots}{36}$$

This is going to take some time and probably be prone to errors.

It would be quicker to look along the rows of data and find the numbers of each item; for example, there are 5 ones, 5 twos, 3 threes and so on.

$$\frac{5 \times 1 + 5 \times 2 + 3 \times 3 + 2 \times 4 + 4 \times 5 + 3 \times 6 + 6 \times 7 + 4 \times 8 + 2 \times 9}{36}$$

$$= \frac{5 + 10 + 9 + 8 + 20 + 18 + 42 + 32 + 18}{36}$$

$$= \frac{162}{36}$$

$$= 4.5$$

But the frequency table sets it up for us, and all we have to do is add another column where the number can be multiplied by the number of times it appears (the frequency); see Table 11.11.

Number	Frequency	Number × Frequency
0	2	0
1	5	5
2	5	10
3	3	9
4	2	8
5	4	20
6	3	18
7	6	42
8	4	32
9	2	18
Totals	36	162

Table 11.11 Extended frequency table

Now all that has to be done is to divide the sum of all the values by the total frequency:

$$\text{mean} = \frac{162}{36} = 4.5$$

The **median** is also easy from the frequency table, because the table has automatically ordered the data for us.

There are 36 items of data, which will divide into two groups without a middle value:

first group has 18 items ...... second group has 18 items

The median is the mean of the 18th and 19th items.

Using the frequency column we can count down to the 18th and 19th entries, by making a running total.

There are two zeroes, 5 ones, 5 twos, 3 threes, and 2 fours, which accounts for the first 17 items ($2 + 5 + 5 + 3 + 2 = 17$), so the first 17 data items are made up of the numbers 0 to 4.

The 18th and 19th items are both 5, so the median is 5.

The **mode** is simply the most frequent, that is the number with the highest frequency.

Looking down the frequency column we see that the highest frequency is 6, and it corresponds to the data item 7 (there are 6 sevens).

The mode is 7.

NOTE:
Remember that the mode is the item from the data set which has the highest frequency, and it is not the frequency itself. The highest frequency is 6, but this corresponds with the data item which is 7, so the mode is 7.

Mean, Median and Mode from a Grouped Frequency Distribution

So far we have looked at the mean, median and mode in an ungrouped frequency table. Once the data has been grouped into classes we lose the individual data items and cannot find the averages so easily. We will look at ways in which we can estimate the mean and the median from grouped frequency distributions in Chapter 23.

As we have seen in Example 3 earlier in this chapter we can identify the **modal class** as being the class with the highest frequency, although we cannot find the actual mode. In a grouped frequency table, a simple histogram or a frequency polygon it is simple to identify the modal class. We will use a different technique in Chapter 23 when the data items are grouped into classes of unequal widths.

Key term

The **modal class** is the class with the highest frequency in a grouped frequency distribution.

Exercise 11.6

Copy each of these frequency tables, and use them to:

a calculate the mean
b work out the median
c find the mode

for each data set.

1

Data value	Frequency
100	7
110	10
120	15
130	2
140	6
150	3
160	7

2

Data value	25	26	27	28	29	30	31
Frequency	51	70	69	32	15	43	15

3

Data value	Frequency
12.4	3
12.5	5
12.6	2
12.7	1
12.8	0
12.9	5
13.0	0
13.1	2

11.13 Statistics in the Media

Statistics should be treated with caution, and you should try to think behind those statistics that are published in the newspapers and other media, and which can cause alarm or panic in the general population. The following headlines are imaginary, but you may have read similar examples.

People with a BMI of greater than 30 are officially obese!

What does this mean?

BMI stands for Body Mass Index and is calculated by dividing your mass in kilograms by the square of your height in metres.

This actually makes some rugby players or other athletes obese!

Examinations are getting easier! The number of students getting A grades is the highest for 3 years!

What could be the possible reasons for this result?

1 Examinations are getting easier.
2 Teaching is improving.
3 Students are working harder.
4 Discipline in schools is improving.
5 Homework is being checked more rigorously.
6 The results are within the normal statistical variation.

Can you think of any other possible reasons?

Numbers of unemployed have fallen under the Hot Air Party!

(This would be just before the next election is due.)

1 How do these figures get counted?
2 Has the school leaving age been raised so that fewer young people are looking for jobs?
3 Has the government made more university places available?
4 Have some other group of people been excluded from these figures, for example, the over 60s?

Can you think of any other reasons?

Look at the two pie charts in Figure 11.9, both showing the same information. What do you think about the way the second one is presented?

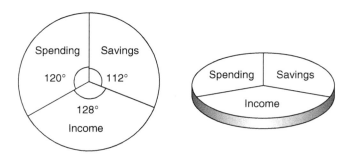

Figure 11.9 Pie graph presentation

What about the two line graphs in Figure 11.10?

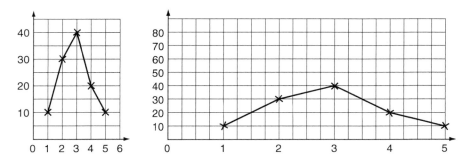

Figure 11.10 Line graph presentation

And the two bar charts in Figure 11.11.

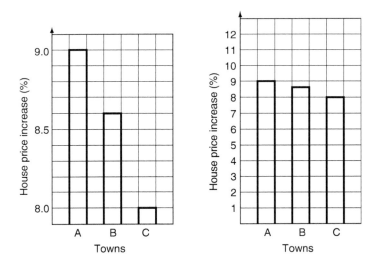

Figure 11.11 Bar chart presentation

All this shows that one needs to be a bit sceptical, particularly when the statistics seem to prove something sensational. However, we still need to use statistics in every walk of life, so it is an essential subject and a powerful tool if used correctly.

Exercise 11.7

Mixed exercise

1 The numbers of days each of a group of people were absent from work due to sickness in one year are shown below.

6	8	21	3	24	4	10	11	8	3	15
12	18	0	2	25	3	10	14	8	9	4
7	0	1	11	5	8	9	15	2	13	5

a Find the mode and range of these values.

b Copy and complete the grouped frequency table shown below.

Days absent	Frequency
0 to 4	10
5 to 9	
10 to 14	
15 to 19	
20 to 24	
25 to 30	
Total frequency	

c Draw a bar chart for the data using the classes above.

2 A survey was made of 100 students from a school, and among the topics on the survey were some questions about pets. The students were asked how many pets they each owned.
The mean number of pets per student was 0.8.
In the whole school there were a total of 1050 students.
a What is the likely number of pets owned by all the students in the school?
The median number of pets in the survey was 2, and the mode was 1.
b Do these averages give any information about the pets in the whole school?

3 You are given the following information about a set of data.
There are 5 items in the set. They are: 2 a b c c,
arranged in order of increasing size.
The mean = 5
The mode = 7
The median = 6
The range = 5
Use the information given to work out the values of a, b and c.

4 The time (to the nearest minute) some students took to complete a test was recorded, and the results are shown in the table below.

Time to the nearest minute	Number of students
1–10	2
11–20	10
21–30	6
31–40	2
Total	

Using class boundaries (0.5 to less than 10.5, and so on), draw a simple histogram to show these results.

5 Calculate the mean and median from the frequency table you drew up in Exercise 11.1, question 1. What can you say about the mode?

6 5   4   7   8   3   1   7   4   4   6

Calculate the mean and find the median and mode of the data given above.

7 Calculate the mean number of passengers per car in Survey 3 in Section 11.5.

8 The table shows the distance travelled per litre of fuel for the Gofaster car at different speeds. We will call this the 'fuel economy'.

Speed (kilometres per hour)	Fuel economy (kilometres per litre)
80	12
96	11
112	10
128	9
135	8
144	7
160	6

a Draw a scatter diagram to show this information.
b Calculate
   i the mean speed   **ii** the mean fuel economy.
c Plot the point showing the mean speed and mean fuel economy on your scatter diagram, and draw a line of best fit through this point.
d Comment on the correlation shown between fuel economy and speed.
e Use your line of best fit to estimate the fuel economy when the car is travelling at 115 kilometres per hour.
f Estimate the possible speed when the fuel economy is 7.5 kilometres per litre.

Exam-style questions | NO CALCULATOR IN THIS EXERCISE

9 Ahmed selected a sample of 10 students from his school and measured their hand spans and heights. The results are shown in the table below.

Hand span (cm)	15	18.5	22.5	26	19	23	17.5	25	20.5	22
Height (cm)	154	156	164	178	162	170	154	168	168	160

He calculated the mean hand span to be 20.9 cm and the range of hand spans to be 11 cm.

   a Calculate:
      i the mean height
      ii the range of heights.

b In order to compare the two measures, he used a scatter diagram.
The first three points are plotted on the grid.

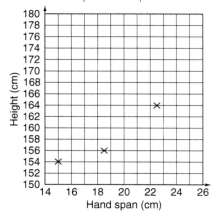

i Copy and complete the scatter diagram by plotting the remaining seven points.
ii Draw the line of best fit on the grid.
iii Use the line of best fit to estimate the height of a student with hand span 21 cm.
iv Which of the following words describes the correlation?
    Positive   Negative   Zero
v What does this indicate about the relationship between hand span and height?

(0580 paper 03 Q6 June 2006)

10 Which word describes the correlation in the scatter graph below?
    positive   negative   none

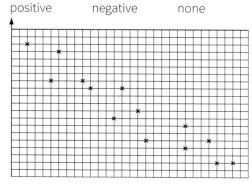

(0580 paper 01 Q3 November 2006)

11 Daniel plots a scatter diagram of speed against time taken.
As the time increases, speed decreases.
Which one of the following types of correlation will his scatter graph show?
    Positive   Negative   Zero   (0580 paper 01 Q5 June 2007)

12 A country has three political parties, the Reds, the Blues and the Greens.
The pie chart shows the proportion of the total vote that each party received in an election.

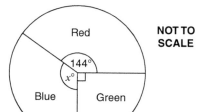

NOT TO SCALE

a Find the value of x.
b What percentage of the votes did the Red party receive? (0580 paper 01 Q4 November 2003)

13 In a school, the number of students taking part in various sports is shown in the table below.

Sport	Number of students
Basketball	40
Soccer	55
Tennis	35
Volleyball	70

Draw a bar chart below to show this data.
Show your scale on the vertical axis and label the bars. (0580 paper 01 Q17 June 2004)

14 Grades were awarded for an examination.
The table below shows the number of students in the whole school getting each grade.

Grade	Number of students	Angle on a pie chart
A	5	
B	15	
C	40	
D	20	
E	10	
Totals	90	

a Complete the table above by calculating the angles required to draw a pie chart.
b Draw an accurate pie chart to show the data in the table.
Label the sectors A, B, C, D and E. (0580 paper 03 Q1b June 2004)

15 The table gives the average surface temperature (°C) on the following planets.

Planet	Earth	Mercury	Neptune	Pluto	Saturn	Uranus
Average temperature	15	350	−220	−240	−180	−200

a Calculate the range of these temperatures.
b Which planet has a temperature 20 °C lower than that of Uranus?
(0580 paper 02 Q3 June 2006)

16 15 students estimated the area of the rectangle shown below:

Their estimates, in square centimetres, were:

45	44	50	50	48
24	50	46	43	50
48	20	45	49	47

a Work out:
  i the mode **ii** the mean **iii** the median.
b Explain why the mean is not a suitable average to represent this data.
(0580 paper 01 Q20 June 2007)

17 Yousef asked 24 students to choose their favourite sport.

He recorded the information in the table below so that he could draw a pie chart.

a Complete the table.

Sport	Volleyball	Football	Hockey	Cricket
Number of students	6	9	7	2
Angle on pie chart	90°	135°		

b Complete the pie chart accurately to show this data.

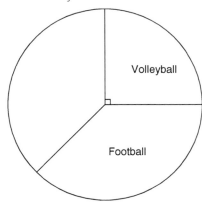

c Which is the modal sport?   (0580 paper 01 Q16 June 2006)

18 The table summarises the times, in minutes, taken by a group of people to complete a puzzle.

Time (*t* minutes)	$0 < t \leqslant 4$	$4 < t \leqslant 8$	$8 < t \leqslant 12$	$12 < t \leqslant 16$	$16 < t \leqslant 20$
Frequency	4	8	7	4	2

a On a copy of the grid, draw a frequency polygon to represent this information.

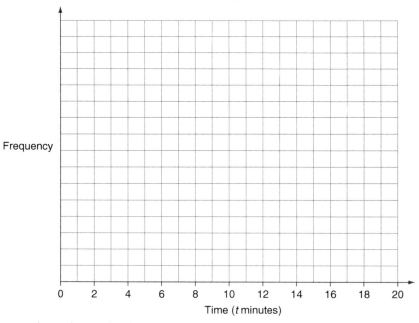

b Write down the modal class.

c How many people took more than 8 minutes to complete the puzzle?

d Imran says:

'The longest time to complete the puzzle was 20 minutes.'

Explain why he may not be correct. (4024 paper 12 Q23 June 2012)

19 A dentist recorded the number of fillings that each of a group of 30 children had in their teeth. The results were:

2	4	0	5	1	1	3	2	6	0
2	2	3	2	1	4	3	0	1	6
1	4	1	6	5	1	0	3	4	2

a Copy and complete this frequency table.

Number of fillings	Frequency
0	
1	
2	
3	
4	
5	
6	

b What is the modal number of fillings?

c Find the median number of fillings.

d Work out the mean number of fillings.

e These 30 children had been chosen from a larger group of 300 children. Estimate how many in the larger group have no fillings in their teeth. (0580 paper 03 Q4(part) November 2003)

20 Marie counts the number of people in each of 60 cars one morning.

a She records the first 40 results as shown below.

Number of people in a car	Tally	Number of cars
1	卌	
2	卌 卌	
3	卌 I	
4	卌 I	
5	卌 II	
6	卌 I	

The remaining 20 results are:

2, 2, 5, 2, 2,   4, 2, 6, 5, 3,   4, 5, 4, 6, 2,   5, 3, 2, 1, 6.

i Use these results to complete the frequency table above.

ii On the grid below, draw a bar chart to show the information for the 60 cars.

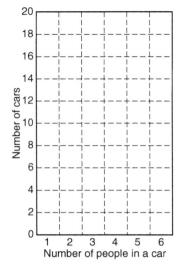

iii Write down the mode.   **iv** Find the median.   **v** Work out the mean.

b Manuel uses Marie's results to draw a pie chart.
   Work out the sector angle for the number of cars with 5 people.

(0580 paper 03 Q3 June 2008)

21 The colours of the cars which passed a house were noted.
The results are shown in the pie chart below.

There were 12 blue cars.
How many cars

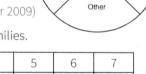

a passed the house?

b were red?   *(4024 paper 01 Q8 November 2009)*

22 The table below shows the number of pets owned by 20 families.

Number of pets	0	1	2	3	4	5	6	7
Number of families	2	5	3	2	4	1	1	2

Find

a the modal number of pets

b the mean number of pets.   *(4024 paper 01 Q11 November 2009)*

23 The times taken for a bus to travel between five stops *A*, *B*, *C*, *D* and *E* are shown below.

A _____   *B* _____   *C* _____   *D* _____   *E* _____

   4 minutes $1\frac{1}{2}$ minutes   75 seconds   2 minutes   35 seconds

Expressing each answer in minutes and seconds, find

a the total time for the journey for *A* to *E*

b the mean time taken between the stops

c the range of times taken between the stops.   *(4024 paper 01 Q15 June 2009)*

24 Some children were asked how many television programmes they had watched on the previous day. The table shows the results.

Number of programmes watched	0	1	2	3
Number of children	7	3	1	*y*

a If the median is 2, find the value of *y*.

b If the median is 1, find the greatest possible value of *y*.   *(4024 paper 01 Q9 June 2004)*

25 a A TV programme list shows that a film begins at 2155. The film lasts for 100 minutes.
At what time will it end?
Express your answer using the 24 hour clock.

b The times taken by an athlete to run three races were 3 minutes 59.1 seconds,
4 minutes 3.8 seconds and 4 minutes 1.6 seconds.
Calculate the mean time. (4024 paper 01 Q12 June 2005)

26 The diagram shows a gauge for measuring the water level in a reservoir.

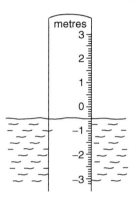

Readings, in metres, taken over a certain period were as follows:

$-2.3, -1.6, -0.4, 0.1, -0.5, 0.3, -1.2$.

For these readings,

a find the difference, in metres, between the highest and lowest levels
b find the median
c calculate the mean. (4024 paper 01 Q20 June 2006)

27 Fifty students were asked how long they each took to travel to school. The results are
summarised in the table below.

Time of travel (t minutes)	$4 \leqslant t < 6$	$6 \leqslant t < 8$	$8 \leqslant t < 10$	$10 \leqslant t < 12$
Frequency	21	11	13	5

Draw a frequency polygon on a copy of the grid below to illustrate this data.

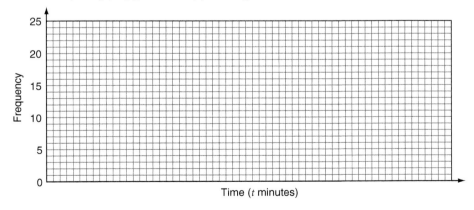

(4024 paper 01 Q24b June 2008)

12 An Introduction to Probability

Learning Objectives   Syllabus section 40

This chapter provides an introduction to:
- the calculation of probability

- the use of relative frequency as a measure of probability.

12.1 Introduction

At the end of this chapter you will know the words commonly used in the study of probability and will be able to work out simple probabilities, both calculated and by experiment.

> *How likely is it to rain tomorrow?*
>
> *Which side might bat first in the next Test Match?*
>
> *What are the chances of my reaching my 60th birthday?*
>
> *What is the most likely score if I throw two dice?*
>
> *How sure is the airline that their plane will arrive on time?*

We often hear questions like these in everyday life.

Mathematicians attempt to find numerical answers to these and many other questions by studying probability. It is a complex but very useful subject.

We will look at the basics so that you can get an idea of what it is about.

12.2 Essential Skills   NO CALCULATOR IN THIS EXERCISE

Take a little time to check that you can do the following questions correctly before you start to study Chapter 12.

1   Work out:

　　a $\frac{2}{3}+\frac{1}{6}$　　　　**b** $\frac{5}{8}-\frac{2}{5}$　　　　**c** $\frac{3}{10}+\frac{4}{5}-\frac{3}{20}$　　　　**d** $1-\frac{3}{5}$　　　　**e** $1-\frac{17}{40}$

2   Simplify:

　　a $\frac{4}{6}$　　　　**b** $\frac{9}{27}$　　　　**c** $\frac{44}{110}$

3 Change to decimals:

    a $\frac{3}{5}$ **b** $\frac{3}{4}$ **c** $\frac{17}{100}$ **d** $\frac{5}{8}$ **e** $\frac{6}{25}$

4 Change to percentages:

    a $\frac{1}{5}$ **b** $\frac{3}{8}$ **c** 0.39   **d** 0.165

5 Work out:

    a $\frac{1}{2} \times \frac{2}{3}$ **b** $\frac{1}{5} \times \frac{3}{2}$ **c** $\frac{3}{1} \times \frac{5}{6}$ **d** $\frac{4}{7} \times \frac{3}{5}$ **e** $\frac{2}{3} \times \frac{4}{5} \times \frac{6}{7}$

12.3 Some Terms used in the Study of Probability

Events and Outcomes

An **outcome** is the result of an experiment or other situation involving uncertainty. An **event** is any collection of outcomes of an experiment.

To understand these terms consider the following experiment.

Experiment 1

Put 3 blue pencils, 2 red pencils and 5 green pencils in a pencil case. Now take out one pencil without looking in the case. You may find that you have chosen a blue pencil. Taking out a blue pencil is an example of an event.

Because there are 3 blue pencils there are three possible choices of pencil which will result in this event (taking out a blue pencil) occurring. Each of these choices is an outcome. So the event 'taking out a blue pencil' is the collection of these outcomes.

Another event would be 'getting a pencil which is not red'. In this case there are 8 possible outcomes, which are the 3 choices of a blue pencil and the 5 choices of a green pencil.

Probability Scale

We measure **probability** on a scale of zero to one. A probability of zero is for an impossible outcome, while a probability of one is for a certain outcome. The probabilities of other outcomes lie somewhere in between. The numbers in between can be fractions or decimals, but are *never* given as a ratio.

Probability is sometimes measured as a percentage. Then the scale is zero to one hundred.

We could safely say that:

a The probability that you will fly to the moon tomorrow is zero (no chance).

b The probability that the world will still be turning tomorrow is one (certain).

c The probability that the next baby born in the world will be a boy is just over 0.5 (there are slightly more boys born than girls).

Key terms

An **outcome** is the result of an experiment or other situation involving uncertainty.

An **event** is any collection of outcomes of an experiment.

Key terms

The **probability scale** is a fraction lying between 0 (impossible) and 1 (certain to happen).

Probability measures how likely it is that something will happen.

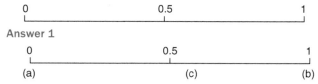

Example 1

Place the above events (a, b and c) on the probability scale shown below.

0   0.5   1

Answer 1

0   0.5   1

(a)   (c)   (b)

Try to think of some more examples, and show them on the probability scale.

Bias

Bias describes how fair an event is. For example if you toss a coin, an **unbiased** coin is equally likely to land heads up or tails up. But if there is something in the coin which makes it more or less likely to land heads up it is a **biased** coin.

If we toss an unbiased coin we expect either heads or tails to be equally likely. The probability of it landing heads up is $\frac{1}{2}$ (or 0.5 or 50%).

You might hear someone say 'There is a fifty–fifty chance of the coin landing heads up'. By that they mean that there is a fifty percent chance of the coin landing heads up. You should note however, that fifty-fifty, although commonly used, is not a correct mathematical expression.

The toss of a coin is often used to choose between two options. For example, the side to bat first in a cricket match is decided by tossing a coin.

Random

Random means completely without order. If you make a list of random numbers then every number is equally likely to be anywhere in the list. One way of getting a list of random numbers is to use a specially written calculator or computer program. These programs are called *random number generators*. Find out if your calculator can produce random numbers.

You cannot make a proper list of random numbers just by writing down the next number to come into your head. Why do you think this is?

If you choose a card from a pack of cards that has been shuffled and laid face down on the table, and if there is absolutely nothing to make you choose one more than any other, you will be making a random choice.

Probability may be calculated or found by experiment.

12.4 Theoretical (or Calculated) Probability

We use the following definition:

Theoretical probability of an event $= \dfrac{\text{number of outcomes favourable to the event}}{\text{total number of possible outcomes}}$

When you toss a coin, what is the *theoretical* probability of getting a head? How many heads might you expect to get in 20 tosses?

When we calculate a theoretical probability it is important that we know that each outcome is equally likely. Look at Example 2, noting that probability can be referred to using a 'P'.

Example 2

Tariq has a pencil case like the one in Experiment 1, with 3 blue pencils, 2 red pencils and 5 green pencils. Tariq chooses one pencil without looking in the case.

The pencils are identical apart from colour so he is making a random choice, and each choice is equally likely.

Work out the probability that he chooses a blue pencil.

Answer 2

There are 3 blue pencils and 10 pencils altogether, so P(blue pencil) $= \frac{3}{10}$.

As you can see from this answer it is useful to refer to the probability of choosing a blue pencil as P(blue pencil) or even just P(blue).

Try to work through the next example before you look at the answers given below.

Example 3

a In Example 2 above how many green pencils are there in Tariq's pencil case?
b What is the probability of Tariq choosing a green pencil?
c What is the probability of Tariq choosing a yellow pencil?
d Find P(red pencil).
e Calculate P(blue pencil) + P(green pencil) + P(red pencil).
f Find P(*not* a red pencil).
g Tariq needs either a blue pencil or a green pencil, it does not matter which.
Find P(blue *or* green).

> **NOTE:**
> How many pencils are not red?

Answer 3

a There are 5 green pencils in the pencil case
b P(green pencil) $= \frac{5}{10}$
c P(yellow pencil) $= 0$ (there are no yellow pencils in the pencil case)
d P(red pencil) $= \frac{2}{10}$
e P(blue) + P(green) + P(red) $= \frac{3}{10} + \frac{5}{10} + \frac{2}{10} = 1$
f There are 8 pencils which are not red, so
P(*not* red) $= \frac{8}{10}$
g There are 3 blue and 5 green pencils so P(blue *or* green) $= (3+5) \div 10 = \frac{8}{10}$

You can see from part (e) in the example above that if all the possible outcomes have been accounted for then the probabilities must add up to 1. This is an important result.

Also, in part (f) we calculated the probability of *not* red to be 8/10.

So because the pencils can either be red or not red and there is no other possibility, then:

$$P(\textit{not } red) + P(red)$$
$$= \frac{8}{10} + \frac{2}{10}$$
$$= 1$$

Of course, if we are working in percentages,

$$P(\textit{not } \text{red}) + P(\text{red})$$
$$= 80\% + 20\%$$
$$= 100\%$$

You can see that:

> **probability of an event happening = 1 − probability of the event *not* happening**

We can also see in part (g) that we can find the probability of blue *or* green either by counting the pencils, or use the fact that P(blue *or* green) = P(blue) + P(green).

This is because picking a green pencil and picking a blue pencil are *mutually exclusive* events. They cannot happen together because the pencils are *either* blue *or* green but not both.

> **Two mutually exclusive events cannot happen at the same time.**
> If A and B are **mutually exclusive** events then P(A or B) = P(A) + P(B).

Key term

Two results are **mutually exclusive** if they cannot possibly happen at the same time.

Example 4

A game consists of a circular board divided into six **equal** sectors, with each sector numbered 1, 2 or 3, as shown on the diagram. A dart is thrown and lands on the board in one of the sectors. The score is the number written in that sector.

Write down the probabilities of scoring 1, 2 or 3, assuming that the dart always lands in a random position.

Answer 4

The probability of the dart landing on any particular number depends on the total area for that number, in this case, how many sectors there are for that number.

$$P(1) = \frac{2}{6} \qquad\qquad P(2) = \frac{1}{6} \qquad\qquad P(3) = \frac{3}{6}$$

Exercise 12.1   NO CALCULATOR IN THIS EXERCISE

1

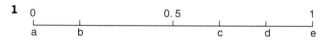

From this list of words choose those that could be used on the above number line in the positions a, b, c, d and e.

  i   unlikely   **ii**   certain   **iii**   impossible
  iv   quite likely   **v**   very likely

2 Choose suitable words from the list below to complete the sentences.
    mutually exclusive   outcome   random   biased   bias
  a When Iravan threw a 6 ten times in twenty throws of a die he decided that the die was probably ....
  b Scoring 6 and scoring 3 with a single roll of a die are .... events.

c Choosing a tall girl and choosing a girl with glasses to partner you in a game of tennis doubles are not .... events.

d A .... choice is one in which every .... is equally likely.

3 Which of the following pairs of events are always mutually exclusive?
  a Throwing a five and throwing a six with a six-sided die.
  b There are some clouds in the sky and the sun is shining.
  c Paula won the high jump competition and Paul broke the record for the high jump in the same competition.
  d Tomorrow is Wednesday and tomorrow is Thursday.
  e Tomorrow is Wednesday and yesterday was Monday.

4 The weather forecasters have said that there is a 40% chance of rain tomorrow.
  What is the probability that it will *not* rain tomorrow?

5 A bag contains 12 coloured discs. There are 3 yellow, 5 red and the rest are blue. Paris takes one disc out without looking.
  a Write down the probability that it is a red disc.
  b Find P(blue disc).
  c What is the probability of a green disc?
  d Find P(not blue).

6 A 'lucky dip' has two sorts of prizes hidden in a tub. One sort is a model car and the other a model aeroplane. They are in identical boxes so it is not possible to feel which is which. The probability of picking an aeroplane is 3/5.
  What is the probability of picking a car?

7 'Drawing the short straw' is a way of picking a person to do an unpopular job.
  To decide who does the washing up Theresa holds 5 straws concealed in her hand with only the ends showing. One of the straws is shorter than the others. I pick a straw.
  What is the probability that I will be doing the washing up?

8 The letters of the word STATISTICS are written on cards which are then shuffled and laid face down on a table. One card is chosen.
  a Write down the probability of choosing an S.
  b Find P(S or T).
  c Find P(a vowel).
  d What is the probability of choosing a B?

NOTE:
The sections on the spinner are numbered 1 to 6.

9 A six-sided spinner is spun once.

Write down the probability of this spinner landing on 3.

10 A word game consists of small tiles, each with a letter of the alphabet on it. The tiles are put in a bag. The bag contains three letter 'A', five letter 'B' and ten letter 'C'. There are no other tiles in the bag.
  Erin chooses one letter at random without looking in the bag.
  What is the probability that Erin chooses a 'B'?

11 Another game consists of throwing a counter to land on the rectangle shown below.

4	3
2	1

The score is the number shown on the area on which the counter lands.
Give a reason why the probability of scoring 3 is not $\frac{1}{4}$.

12 The pie chart shows the distribution of the colours of the cars already sold and awaiting collection in a manufacturer's car park. The cars are either red, blue or black. There are no other colours.

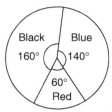

a Why is the probability that the next car collected will be blue not $\frac{1}{3}$?
b What is the probability that the next car collected will be red?
c What is the probability that the next car collected will be white?
d What is the probability that the next car collected will not be black?

12.5 Experimental Probability or Relative Frequency

I have just done an experiment. I had 10 counters in a bag, coloured red, blue or green. I did not know how many of each. I picked out a counter at random, noted its colour on a tally chart, and replaced it. I repeated the experiment many times, with the results shown in Table 12.1.

Number of trials	Red	Blue	Green
30	13	15	2
100	48	43	9
200	83	97	20

Table 12.1 Results of experiment

Key term

Relative frequency
is a measure of how often a particular result occurs in a repeated experiment.

The **relative frequency** of an event is the number of times it happens divided by the total number of trials.

$$\text{Relative frequency of an event} = \frac{\text{number of times that event occurs}}{\text{the number of trials}}$$

So the relative frequency of red $= \dfrac{\text{number of times red was chosen}}{\text{the number of trials}}$.

Table 12.2 shows the results of calculating the relative frequencies (to 2 decimal places) in the experiment above.

For example, the relative frequency of red after 30 trials $= \frac{13}{30} = 0.43$.

Number of trials	Red	Blue	Green
30	0.43	0.50	0.07
100	0.48	0.43	0.09
200	0.42	0.49	0.10

Table 12.2 Relative frequencies

If the number of trials were increased the relative frequencies would start to settle down. If we were able to do the experiment enough times and if we were *sure* that we were picking the counters at random (so that each event is equally likely) we would find that the relative frequencies would eventually come out very close to the calculated or theoretical probabilities.

So finding the relative frequencies of events is a way of *approximating* to the probabilities of those events.

After 200 trials I looked in the bag and discovered that I had 4 red counters, 5 blue counters and 1 green counter. I calculated the theoretical probabilities and compared them with the relative frequencies from the experiment (Table 12.3).

	Theoretical probability	Relative frequency after 200 trials
Red	$\frac{4}{10} = 0.40$	0.42
Blue	$\frac{5}{10} = 0.50$	0.49
Green	$\frac{1}{10} = 0.10$	0.10

Table 12.3 Comparing relative frequency and theoretical probability

Calculating the probabilities as decimals makes it easier to compare the values.

Experiment 2

Take a coin and decide which side is 'heads' and which is 'tails'. Now toss the coin 20 times, and each time record whether it lands 'heads' or 'tails' on top. Calculate the relative frequency of, say, 'heads'.

Repeat your experiment, noting your results after 50, 100 and 200 trials. How close do your relative frequencies get to the theoretical probability of 'heads'?

Experiment 3

Use a bag with 20 coloured counters in it to repeat my experiment. Ask someone else to put in the counters so that you do not know what the colours are, or how many there are of each colour.

Take out one counter at a time, note its colour and then replace it. Repeat 100 times, and see if you can work out how many counters of each colour there are in the bag.

You should see that:

**the expected number of any coloured counter = relative frequency of that colour ×
the total number of counters in the bag.**

Example 5

Akash and Namita are tossing an unbiased coin. They have repeated the experiment 30
times and the results are 11 heads and 19 tails. Akash says that the next coin will be more
likely to land heads up. Namita says she is wrong. Who is correct and why?

Answer 5

Namita is correct because each toss of the coin is *independent* of the one before and so each
time the coin is tossed it has exactly the same probability of landing heads up.

Key term

Two results are
independent if one
does not affect the other.

This is another important aspect of probability. If the trials are **independent** of each other
the probability of a certain event remains the same for each trial. The *trend* is for the relative
frequency to come close to the expected probability if enough trials are carried out.

Independent events are not affected by other events.

12.6 Combined Events

Amarus tosses an unbiased coin and rolls a fair five-sided spinner. The spinner is equally likely
to stop on any of the numbers from 1 to 5.

To find P(heads *and* 4) he can list all the possible outcomes:

H,1   H,2   H,3   H,4   H,5   T,1   T,2   T,3   T,4   T,5

There are ten possible outcomes and only one which is heads and 4, so P(heads *and* 4) $= \frac{1}{10}$.

This was a relatively easy list to write down, but some can be much longer.

Key term

A **possibility** or
probability space
diagram illustrates all
the possible outcomes
of combined events.

A **possibility diagram**, also known as a **probability space diagram**, is an aid to drawing up
the list so that no outcomes are forgotten.

For this example, where the events are independent of each other, a suitable diagram would
be as shown in Table 12.4.

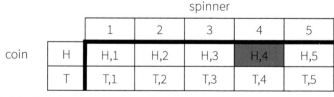

		spinner				
		1	2	3	4	5
coin	H	H,1	H,2	H,3	H,4	H,5
	T	T,1	T,2	T,3	T,4	T,5

Table 12.4 Outcomes for spinner and coin

It is easy to see that there are ten possible outcomes in the table. This is the number of
outcomes from the coin times the number of outcomes from the spinner.

We are interested in one particular event, that is heads *and* 4, which occurs for one outcome
only, so P(H,4) $= \frac{1}{10}$.

What is P(H) × P(4)?

Can you see that this is $\frac{1}{2} \times \frac{1}{5} = \frac{1}{10}$?

Work out P(T) × P(odd number). Does this agree with P(T, odd number) from the table?

We will find out more about this later in the chapter.

An alternative method is to mark the outcomes on a grid like a graph. Each outcome is represented by a grid point or coordinates, as in Figure 12.1.

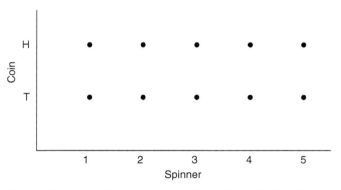

Figure 12.1 Graphical representation of possibility diagram

If the spinner had eight sides, with the numbers 1 to 8 on it, and the coin was tossed again, how many dots would there be on the grid?

Example 6

Suppose two spinners are used instead of a spinner and a coin.

One spinner (A) goes from 1 to 4, and the other (B) from 1 to 5.

a   How many dots would be on the grid now?

b   How many possible outcomes would there be?

c   What would be the probability of scoring a double two (2 *and* 2) with these spinners?

d   Check that P(2 on spinner A) × P(2 on spinner B) = P(2, 2).

Answer 6

a   20 dots (4 × 5). Draw the grid if you are not sure.

b   20

c $\frac{1}{20}$

d $\frac{1}{4} \times \frac{1}{5} = \frac{1}{20}$

Example 7

In an experiment, two six-sided dice are thrown, one red and the other blue.

The scores on the two dice are then added together, and the resulting totals are noted.

The possible outcomes are shown below:

		Red die					
	+	1	2	3	4	5	6
Blue die	1	2	3	4	5	6	7
	2	3	4	5	6	7	8
	3	4	5	6	7	8	9
	4	5	6	7	8	9	10
	5	6	7	8	9	10	11
	6	7	8	9	10	11	12

a How many possible outcomes are there?

b Find P(a total of 6).

c Find P(a double).

d Find P(a total of *less* than 5).

e Find P(both dice showing even numbers).

f What is the most likely total?

g Find P(total of 1).

h Find P(total less than 12).

Answer 7

> **NOTE:**
> It is acceptable to leave your answers to probability questions as unsimplified fractions unless otherwise specified in the question.

a 36 possible outcomes.

b There are 5 totals of six, and 36 possible outcomes, so $p(six) = \frac{5}{36}$.

c There are six doubles (for example 1,1 and so on), so $P(a\ double) = \frac{6}{36}$.

d There are six ways of getting a total of less than 5 (they are 2, 3, 3, 4, 4, 4). So $P(total\ less\ than\ 5) = \frac{6}{36}$.

e There are 9 ways in which both dice could show even numbers (for example, 2, 4). So $P(both\ showing\ even\ numbers) = \frac{9}{36}$.

f $P(a\ total\ of\ seven) = \frac{6}{36}$. All the others are less than this, so the most likely total is seven.

g $P(total\ of\ 1) = 0$.

h $P(total\ less\ than\ 12) = 1 - P(total\ of\ 12) = 1 - \frac{1}{36} = \frac{35}{36}$.

Example 8

Bakari tosses a coin twice and notes both outcomes.

He gets tails both times.

He says the probability of this happening is $\frac{1}{3}$, because there are three possible outcomes: two heads, a head and a tail, and two tails.

Seema says he is wrong, and that the probability should be $\frac{1}{4}$.

Who is right?

Answer 8

Seema is right.

There are 4 possible outcomes: H,H T,T H,T T,H

(If this does not seem right, think of tossing two different coins, say a pound and a dollar. Then the outcomes would be: $H, £H $T, £T $H, £T $T, £H.)

Exercise 12.2

1 The possible outcomes of an experiment in which the scores of two five-sided spinners are added together are shown on the grid below. Each outcome is represented by a point on the grid.

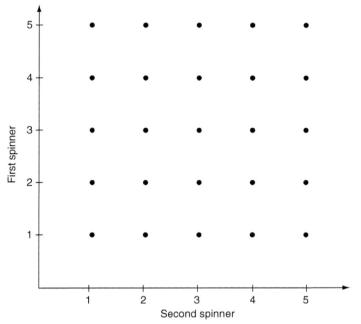

a How many possible outcomes are there?

b Find P(total score of 4).

c Find P(total score greater than 6).

d Find P(a double).

e How many outcomes are there where the score on the first spinner is greater than the score on the second?

f What is the most likely total score?

2 Patony is doing an experiment with two bags containing coloured counters.
In one bag there are four counters, one each of red, blue, green and yellow.
In the other bag there are five counters, one each of red, blue, green, purple and white.
He picks one counter from each bag without looking in the bags.

a Draw a possibility space diagram to show all the possible outcomes of picking a counter from each bag.

b What is the probability of drawing two counters of the same colour?

3 There are two boxes of counters, box A and box B.

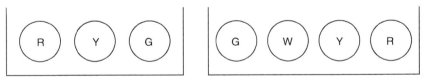

Box A contains 1 red, 1 yellow and 1 green counter.
Box B contains 1 green, 1 white, 1 yellow and 1 red counter.
Meer chooses one counter at random from each box.
Copy and complete the following possibility space diagram.

Box A

	R	Y	G
R	R,R		
Y			
G			
W			

Box B

What is the probability that he chooses
a two counters of the same colour?
b one green counter and one red counter?
c one yellow and one white counter?
d two white counters?

Exercise 12.3

Mixed exercise   **NO CALCULATOR IN THIS EXERCISE**

1 The manufacturers of a certain type of computer part know from experience that the relative frequency of faults in the component is 0.05.
  a What is the probability that the next component picked will not be faulty?
  b **i** How many of these components would you expect to be faulty in a consignment of 1000?
     ii Would you expect there to be *exactly* this number faulty?

2 On average 51% of babies born are boys. What is the probability of the next baby to be born being a girl?

3 An examination paper is made up of 25 multiple-choice questions.
Each question has five different possible answers given for it, only one of which is correct.
Ryan guesses the answer to each question at random.
  a What is the probability that he gets question 1 correct?
  b How many questions could you expect him to get correct on the whole paper?
  c What would his mark be as a percentage?

4 A manufacturing company runs a check on one of its components by taking 100 of them from the assembly line at random, and then checking each of these to see how many are faulty.
The company finds that the relative frequency of faulty components is $\frac{3}{100}$ or 3%.
How many perfect components would the company expect to get in a production run of 4000 components?

5 Nesip picks a sweet at random from a jar containing 15 red sweets, 20 orange sweets and 12 yellow sweets.
  a What is the probability that he picks his favourite orange sweets?
  b What is the probability that he picks a red or an orange sweet?

6 Anaya rolls a seven-sided spinner, with each of the numbers 1 to 7 on it.
  a What is the probability that she gets an even number?
  b What is the probability that she does not get a seven?

7 The average number of wet days in Mumbai in June is 14.
What is the probability that June 13th next year will be wet?

Exam-style questions

8 Aminata has a bag containing 35 beads. The beads are either blue, yellow or red. One bead is chosen at random.
The probability of choosing a blue bead is $\frac{2}{7}$ and the probability of choosing a yellow bead is $\frac{3}{5}$.
Calculate:
  a the number of blue beads in the bag
  b the probability of choosing a red bead.   (0580 paper 01 Q20 November 2004)

9 Grades were awarded for an examination.
The table below shows the number of students in the whole school getting each grade.

Grade	Number of students	Angle on pie chart
A	5	
B	15	
C	40	
D	20	
E	10	
Total	90	

  a Copy and complete the table above by calculating the angles required to draw a pie chart.
  b Draw an accurate pie chart to show the data in the table.
    Label the sectors A, B, C, D and E.
  c What is the probability that a student chosen at random from the group taking the examination was awarded
    i grade C?   **ii** grade D or E?   (0580 paper 03 Q1b June 2004)

10 A dentist recorded the number of fillings that each of a group of 30 children had in their teeth. The results were:

2   4   0   5   1   1   3   2   6   0

2   2   3   2   1   4   3   0   1   6

1   4   1   6   5   1   0   3   4   2

  a One of these children is chosen at random.
    Find the probability that this child has:
    i exactly one filling   **ii** more than three fillings.
  b These 30 children had been chosen from a larger group of 300 children. Estimate how many in the larger group have no fillings in their teeth.
        (0580 paper 03 Q4e and f November 2003)

11 a 85% of the seeds in a packet will produce red flowers.
    One seed is chosen at random. What is the probability that it will **not** produce a red flower?
  b A box of 15 pencils contains 5 red, 4 yellow and 6 blue pencils. One pencil is chosen at random from the box. Find the probability that it is
    i yellow   **ii** yellow or blue   **iii** green.
        (0580 paper 01 Q20 November 2008)

12 A bag contains 24 discs.

10 discs are red, 9 discs are green and 5 discs are yellow.

a A disc is chosen at random.

Find, **as a fraction**, the probability of each of the following events.

   i Event A: the disc is red.

   ii Event B: the disc is red or yellow.

   iii Event C: the disc is **not** yellow.

b

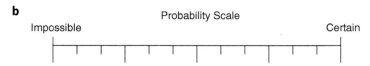

The diagram shows a horizontal probability scale. Copy the diagram and show on the diagram the probability of

   i an impossible event   **ii** a certain event.

c Mark the positions of A, B and C, your answers to part (a), on your probability scale.

(0580 paper 03 Q5b, c and d June 2007)

13 a There are 11 boys and 12 girls in a choir.

The teacher chooses one choir member at random.

What is the probability that it is a girl? Write your answer as a fraction.

b The probability that Carla arrives at school before 0800 is $\frac{9}{20}$.

What is the probability that Carla does not arrive before 0800?

Write your answer as a fraction. *(0580 paper 01 Q12 June 2008)*

14 The diagram shows a six-sided spinner.

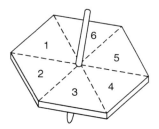

a Amy spins a biased spinner and the probability she gets a two is $\frac{5}{36}$.

Find the probability she

   i does not get a two   **ii** gets a seven

   iii gets a number on the spinner less than 7.

b Joel spins his blue spinner 99 times and gets a two 17 times.

Write down the relative frequency of getting a two with Joel's spinner.

c The relative frequency of getting a two with Piero's spinner is $\frac{21}{102}$.

Which of the three spinners, Amy's, Joel's or Piero's, is most likely to give a two?

(0580 paper 01 Q23 November 2006)

15 A fair five-sided spinner is numbered using the prime numbers 2, 3, 5, 7 and 11.

    a   In a game, players spin it twice and add the two numbers obtained.

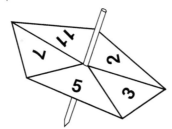

+	2	3	5	7	11
2	4	5			
3					
5			10	12	
7			12		
11					

    i   Complete the possibility diagram.

    ii Find the probability that the total of the two numbers is

       a   a prime number   **b**   a perfect square.   (4024 paper 01 Q21a June 2006)

13 Real Numbers

Learning Objectives Syllabus sections 2, 5

In this chapter you will learn
- more about sets, including the notation used with sets
- about Venn diagrams and how to use them
- some more about square roots, irrational numbers, fractions, decimals and percentages.

13.1 Introduction

The set of real numbers includes all the numbers we need in everyday life. Your course for Cambridge O Level Mathematics is based entirely on the set of real numbers. You may wonder what other numbers there could possibly be. If you study mathematics further you will eventually meet the set of imaginary numbers, which are the square roots of negative numbers. As you know, it is not possible to multiply a number by itself to make a negative number, so the square root of a negative number does not exist. However, mathematicians need to work with the square roots of negative numbers, so they are called imaginary numbers. Imaginary numbers form the basis of a very interesting branch of mathematics and you might like to find out more about them.

13.2 Essential Skills NO CALCULATOR IN THIS EXERCISE

1. 100 π 22.5 1 9 18 5 24 6 0 $\sqrt{2}$ $\sqrt{25}$ $2\frac{2}{7}$ 49
   From the list above select
   a the natural numbers
   b the integers
   c the rational numbers
   d the irrational numbers
   e the prime numbers
   f the factors of 45
   g the multiples of 6
   h the cube root of 8
   i the square of 7
   j the square root of 81

2. a List the set of factors of 144.
   b List the set of prime factors of 144.
   c Write 144 as a product of its prime factors.

3. Insert a correct symbol between each of the following pairs of numbers:
   $\sqrt{64}$, 2^3 $\sqrt{64}$, 3^2 19, 18

4. List the set of prime numbers between 20 and 40.

5. Without using a calculator, calculate the following:
   a $2\frac{2}{7} - \frac{4}{7}$ b $2\frac{2}{7} \times \frac{4}{7}$ c $2\frac{2}{7} \div \frac{4}{7}$

6 Find 16% of 54.

7 Find 28 as a percentage of 63.

8 Find a fraction that lies between $\frac{4}{7}$ and $\frac{5}{7}$.

13.3 More about Sets

We have already studied some sets of numbers. These were the sets of natural numbers, integers, rational numbers, real numbers and prime numbers.

A set is a collection of objects, ideas or numbers that can be clearly defined.

Clearly defined means that we can tell with certainty whether or not something belongs to the set.

For example:

a The set of colours of the rainbow is {red, orange, yellow, green, blue, indigo, violet}. Brown is a colour, but it does not belong to this set.

b The set of domestic pets may be quite large, but it would not include a brontosaurus! However, a brontosaurus would be included in the set of dinosaurs.

c The set of factors of 10 would include 1, 2, 5 and 10, but not 4.

In each of these cases, the sets are well defined because it is possible to tell whether or not something belongs to the set.

13.4 Defining a Set

There are various ways of defining a **set**.

Key term

A **set** is a collection of objects, ideas or numbers that can be clearly defined.

- We can **list** the members of the set in curly brackets. The set of factors of 10 = {1, 2, 5, 10}.
- If there is no end to the set, we use dots to represent 'and so on'. The set of natural numbers = {1, 2, 3, 4, 5, 6, 7, …}.

- If there is an end to the set, but it is too long to list all the numbers, we can still use dots, but include one or more of the last numbers in the set.

  The set of even numbers between 1 and 99 = {2, 4, 6, 8, 10, …, 96, 98}.

- Sets can also be defined by a description.

  For example, {planets in our solar system} or {capital cities of the world}.

- Sets are often labelled by using capital letters. The letters $\mathbb{N}$, $\mathbb{Z}$, $\mathbb{Q}$ and $\mathbb{R}$ are reserved for the sets we have already met, namely natural numbers, integers, rational numbers and real numbers.

- If we use a capital letter to represent another set we must define it clearly.
  For example,
  $$P = \{\text{the prime numbers between 1 and 20}\}$$
  or
  $$B = \{\text{boys in your class}\}$$

Example 1

a Write down a description of each of the following sets (there could be more than one suitable description).

i {1, 3, 5, 7} **ii** {5, 10, 15, 20, 25, ...} **iii** {1, 2, 3, 4, 6, 12}

b List the following sets:
   i The set of square numbers less than 30.
   ii The set of vowels in the English alphabet.
   iii The set of natural numbers less than 80.
   iv The set of cube numbers.

Answer 1

a **i** The set of odd numbers between 0 and 8, or simply {odd numbers between 0 and 8}.
   ii The set of multiples of 5.
   iii The set of factors of 12.
b **i** {1, 4, 9, 16, 25}
   ii {a, e, i, o, u}
   iii {1, 2, 3, 4, 5, 6, 7, ..., 76, 77, 78, 79}
   iv {1, 8, 27, 64, 125, ...}

13.5 Notation and Symbols Used with Sets

Key term

The members of a set are also called the **elements** of the set.

The members of a set are also called **elements** of the set.

If we define a set C = {primary colours}, then the elements of the set C are red, blue and green. The number of elements or members in the set is referred to as $n(C)$.

In this case, $n(C) = 3$. Of course, $n(Z)$ (the number of elements in the set of integers) is undefined, or infinitely large, because the integers go on forever.

The symbol $\in$, derived from the Greek letter $\mathscr{E}$, is used to mean 'is a member of' or 'is an element of'.

So Monday $\in$ {days of the week}, should be read as 'Monday is an element of the set of days of the week'. If this letter has a cross through it, $\notin$, it reads 'is not an element of'. Hence, April $\notin$ {days of the week}.

We also need the 'empty' set: the **empty set** has no members.

Key term

The **empty set** has no members.

For example, {even prime numbers *greater* than 2} is an empty set because 2 is the *only* even prime number. The symbol used for the empty set is $\varnothing$.

In some textbooks, you may see the empty set written as {}, which is an alternative for $\varnothing$.

Notice that we cannot use {0} as the empty set, because it has a member, which is zero. So far the symbols we have met are:

Number of elements in set A	$n(A)$
'is an element of'	$\in$
'is not an element of'	$\notin$
The empty set	$\varnothing$

Exercise 13.1

1 List the elements of these sets:
   a {square numbers between 10 and 40}   **b** {months of the year beginning with M}
   c {natural numbers $\leqslant 10$}

2 Describe these sets:
   a {1, 3, 5, 7, 9}
   b {Monday, Tuesday, Wednesday, Thursday, Friday, Saturday, Sunday}
   c {a, b, c, d, e, …, x, y, z}

3 Which of the following are empty sets?
   a {people over 5 metres tall}   **b** {birds that swim}
   c {0}   **d** {integers between 1.1 and 1.9}

4 Insert the correct symbol in the following statements.
   a 1 … {prime numbers}   **b** 1000 … {even numbers}

5 $A = \{$letters used in the word 'mathematics'$\}$.
   a List set A.   **b** Find $n(A)$.

13.6 More Notation and Symbols

Key terms

The universal set in a particular context contains all the elements from which the other sets are drawn.

The **intersection** of two or more sets contains all the elements that are present in both or all of the sets.

NOTE:
This symbol, $\cap$, could be likened to a bridge between the two sets.

You will find that when we talk about sets we need to limit the possibilities in some way. For example, if you were to make up a school team to play football, it would be no good including students from another school. The team would be chosen from the set of all the students in *your* school. This is called the **universal set**. The symbol used to denote the universal set is $\mathscr{E}$.

So we could have: $\mathscr{E} = \{$students in your school$\}$

$F = \{$students in your school's football team$\}$

$M = \{$students in your maths class$\}$

Both F and M belong to the universal set $\mathscr{E}$.

Another situation we need to be able to describe is that some students may be in your maths class *and* in the school football team. This is called an **intersection** of sets, and has the symbol $\cap$.

We write {students *both* in the school football team *and* in your maths class} $= F \cap M$.

If there is no one in your maths class who is also in the football team, then $F \cap M = \varnothing$. In this case, the intersection of F and M has no members, so it is the empty set. It is perhaps easier to see this using sets with numbers.

We will use the following sets:

$$A = \{1, 2, 3, 4, 5, 6, 7, 8, 9\}$$
$$B = \{10, 11, 12, 13, 14, 15\}$$
$$C = \{2, 4, 6, 8, 10, 12\}$$
$$D = \{1, 3, 5, 7\}$$

From these sets it will be seen that:

$A \cap C = \{2, 4, 6, 8\}$ because 2, 4, 6 and 8 are in both A and C

and $A \cap B = \varnothing$

What about $A \cap D$?

$$A \cap D = \{1, 3, 5, 7\} = D$$

The whole of set D is in set A.

We say that D is a **proper subset** of A, and we use the symbol $\subset$, so $D \subset A$. You will usually hear a proper subset being referred to as just a subset. Strictly speaking a **subset** is different from a proper subset, which can be shown using the following example.

$$V = \{\text{vowels in the English language}\}$$
$$E = \{\text{letters of the English language}\}$$
$$L = \{a, e, i, o, u\}$$
$$F = \{a, b, c\}$$

V is a proper subset of E because there are elements in E that are *not* in V. However, V could be thought of *either* as equal to L, *or* as a subset of L, so V is not a *proper* subset of L.

Therefore, V is a proper subset of E: $\qquad V \subset E$

V is a subset of L (and V is equal to L): $\qquad V \subseteq L$

The same symbol with a line through it, $\not\subset$, means 'is not a proper subset of'.

V is not a proper subset of L: $\qquad V \not\subset L$

We can also say: $\qquad F \subset E$

$$F \not\subset L$$

and $\qquad F \not\subseteq L$

Suppose we wanted to use the whole of A and B. This would be called the **union** of A and B, and we would use the symbol $\cup$.

$$A \cup B = \{1, 2, 3, 4, 5, 6, 7, 8, 9, 10, 11, 12, 13, 14, 15\}$$
$$A \cup C = \{1, 2, 3, 4, 5, 6, 7, 8, 9, 10, 12\}$$

Notice that the elements that appear in both sets are not listed twice. We can now add to our list of symbols.

Universal set	$\mathscr{E}$	Subset	$\subseteq$
Intersection	$\cap$	Not a subset	$\not\subset$
Proper subset	$\subset$	Union	$\cup$

Example 2

$F = \{10, 20, 30, 40\}$ $\qquad G = \{11, 13, 17, 19\}$

$H = \{10, 11, 12, 13\}$ $\qquad J = \{11, 13\}$

Use these sets to answer the questions.

a List:

  i $G \cap H$ $\qquad\qquad$ **ii** $F \cup H$

b J is a subset of two of the sets. Which are those two sets?

c Suggest a suitable universal set for F, G, H and J.

d What can you say about $F \cap J$?

Answer 2

a i $G \cap H = \{11, 13\}$ (notice that this is also equal to J)

  ii $F \cup H = \{10, 11, 12, 13, 20, 30, 40\}$

b $J \subset G$ and $J \subset H$

c A universal set could be N (the set of natural numbers), or we could restrict it more, say
$\mathscr{E} = \{10, 11, 12, 13, 14, 15, \ldots, 38, 39, 40\}$
or $\mathscr{E} = \{$natural numbers between 10 and 40 inclusive$\}$

d $F \cap J = \varnothing$

There is one more symbol left to add to the list. Look at these sets:

$$\mathscr{E} = \{1, 2, 3, 4, 5\}$$
$$A = \{1, 4\}$$
$$B = \{2, 4, 5\}$$

The new symbol is the letter for the set followed by a dash, for example, A'.

This means everything in the universal set but not in set A. It is called the **complement** of A.

Key term

The complement of a set is all the elements that are not in the set, but that *are* in the universal set.

So $\qquad A' = \{2, 3, 5\}$ and $B' = \{1, 3\}$.

Since $\qquad A \cap B = \{4\}$

then $\qquad (A \cap B)' = \{1, 2, 3, 5\}$

In the same way, can you show that $(A \cup B)' = \{3\}$?

Exercise 13.2

$\mathscr{E} = \{3, 4, 5, 6, 7, 8, 9\}$
$A = \{4, 5, 6\}$
$B = \{$odd numbers between 2 and 8$\}$
$C = \{$square numbers $\leqslant 10\}$
Using the above sets,

1 List:

  a B **b** $A \cap B$ **c** $A \cup B$ **d** A'
  e the complement of B **f** $A \cap B$ **g** $(A \cup B)'$

2 List the intersection of B and C.   **3** List the union of A and C.

4 Write down n(C).   **5** Find n($A \cup C$).

6 Find n(B').

13.7 Venn Diagrams

Key term

A **Venn diagram** shows the relationship between the sets in the universal set.

A **Venn diagram** is a very useful method of visualising the relationship between sets. A rectangular box is drawn to show the universal set, and within this, other shapes, usually ovals or circles, represent sets within the universal set. If there is an intersection between sets, it will be shown by an overlap of the ovals or circles.

The following example should help you to understand the concept of a Venn diagram.

Example 3

$\mathcal{E}$ = {1, 2, 3, 4, 5, 6, 7, 8, 9, 10}

A = {even numbers}

B = {1, 2, 3, 4, 5}

C = {6, 7, 8}

a Draw a Venn diagram to represent the above sets. Show the elements in each set.

b List the following sets:

    i $A \cap B$ **ii** $A \cup B$ **iii** $A \cup C$ **iv** $(A \cup C)'$

    v $A \cup B \cup C$ **vi** $(A \cup B \cup C)'$ **vii** $B \cap C$

Answer 3

a

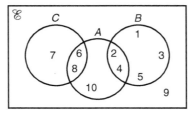

NOTE:

The symbol ($\mathcal{E}$) for the universal set may be placed either inside or outside the rectangle. Either is correct. You may find different symbols used for the universal set in other books, but it should always be clear what is intended.

b   **i** $A \cap B$ = {2, 4}   **ii** $A \cup B$ = {1, 2, 3, 4, 5, 6, 8, 10}

    iii $A \cup C$ = {2, 4, 6, 7, 8, 10}   **iv** $(A \cup C)'$ = {1, 3, 5, 9}

    v $A \cup B \cup C$ = {1, 2, 3, 4, 5, 6, 7, 8, 10}   **vi** $(A \cup B \cup C)'$ = {9}

    vii $B \cap C$ = $\varnothing$

NOTE:

You may find that shading or hatching can help to make the distinction between union and intersection between sets in the Venn diagram more clear.

If you look at the three Venn diagrams in Figure 13.1, you will see that in the first, one set has been hatched in a different direction from the other.

In the second Venn diagram, the two sets show an intersection, where the hatching appears in both directions (cross hatching).

In the third Venn diagram, the union is shown by all the shaded areas, in either direction, taken together.

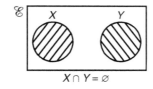

$X \cap Y = \varnothing$

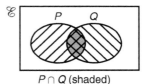

$P \cap Q$ (shaded)

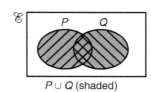

$P \cup Q$ (shaded)

Figure 13.1 Union and intersection in Venn diagrams

Example 4

a Draw three identical Venn diagrams to illustrate the following sets.

    $\mathcal{E}$ = {students in your school}

    C = {students in your class}

    B = {students who come to school by bus}

b **i**   In the first diagram shade and clearly label $B \cap C$.
   ii In the next diagram shade and clearly label $B \cap C$.
   iii In the last diagram shade and clearly label $C \cap B'$.
c How would you describe $B \cap C$ and $C \cap B'$ in words?

Answer 4

a and **b**

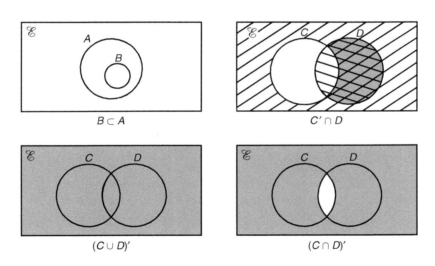

i $B \cap C$ **ii** $B \cup C$ **iii** $C \cap B'$

c $B \cap C$ = {students in the class who come to school by bus}
   $C \cap B'$ = {students in the class who do not come to school by bus}

You should be able to see what a powerful tool Venn diagrams can be in the study of sets. We will use them again later in the course.

Study the four diagrams in Figure 13.2 carefully to see how hatching and shading can clarify the required areas of Venn diagrams.

$B \subset A$

$C' \cap D$

$(C \cup D)'$

$(C \cap D)'$

Figure 13.2 Shading different areas of Venn diagrams

NOTE:
The hatching used above is to help you understand which area of the Venn diagram is required. When you are answering a question you should only shade the area specified in the question.

Venn diagrams can also show the number of elements in each set, as the next example shows.

Example 5

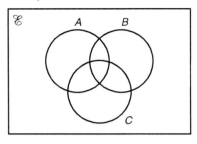

You are given the following information.

$n(\mathscr{E}) = 30$, $n(A) = 11$, $n(B) = 12$, $n(C) = 10$,

$n(A \cap B \cap C) = 3$, $n(A \cap B) = 5$, $n(A \cap C) = 4$, $n(B \cap C) = 6$

a Copy and complete the Venn diagram.

b Find **i** $n(A \cup B \cup C)$ **ii** $n(A \cup B)$.

Answer 5

a Using the information given, it is possible to fill in the Venn diagram in steps.

STEP 1: $n(A \cap B \cap C) = 3$, so 3 goes right in the centre of the diagram.

STEP 2: $n(A \cap B) = 5$, so take away the 3 that is already there, which leaves 2 to go in the rest of the intersection.

$n(A \cap C) = 4$ and $n(B \cap C) = 6$ means we can fill in the other two intersections in the same way. (See the diagram below for steps 1 and 2.)

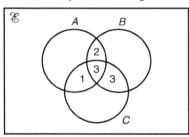

STEP 3: $n(A) = 11$ so take away the 1, 2 and 3 which are already in A, leaving 5 to be written in the remaining part of A.

Use $n(B) = 12$ and $n(C) = 10$ in the same way.

STEP 4: Find $n(A \cup B \cup C)$ by adding all the numbers in your diagram.

$n(A \cup B \cup C) = 5 + 1 + 3 + 2 + 4 + 3 + 3 = 21$

It was given that $n(\mathscr{E}) = 30$, so $n(A \cup B \cup C)' = 30 - 21 = 9$

Write in the 9 to complete the Venn diagram. (See the following diagram for step 4.)

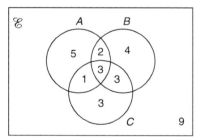

b **i** $n(A \cup B \cup C)' = 9$

  ii $n(A \cup B) = 5 + 1 + 2 + 3 + 4 + 3 = 18$

The answers to these and many other similar questions can now be easily obtained from the diagram.

Exercise 13.3

1 Draw Venn diagrams to illustrate the following:

   a $\mathscr{E} = \mathbb{N}$, $P = \{\text{prime numbers less than 10}\}$, $E = \{2, 4, 6\}$.
(Mark and label each element in its correct place.)

   b $\mathscr{E} = \mathbb{Z}$, $S = \{\text{square numbers}\}$, $E = \{\text{even numbers}\}$.
(The individual elements cannot be labelled because there are an infinite number of elements.)

2 Copy these Venn diagrams and in each case, shade the required areas.

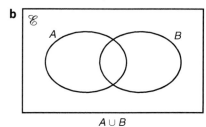

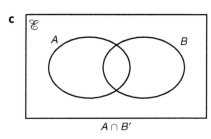

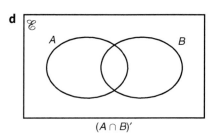

3 Draw Venn diagrams to illustrate each of the following:

   a $A \cap B = \varnothing$ **b** $A \subset B$

4 Draw a Venn diagram to illustrate the following:
$\mathscr{E} = \{\text{natural numbers from 1 to 10}\}$
$P = \{1, 2, 3, 4, 5, 6, 7, 8\}$
$R = \{2, 4, 6, 8\}$
$S = \{1, 2, 3, 4\}$
Mark and label the correct position for each element in the diagram.

5 **a** Draw a Venn diagram to show two sets, A and B, where $B \subset A$.

   b Given that $n(\mathscr{E}) = 48$, $n(A) = 25$ and $n(B) = 10$, find

      i $n(A \cap B')$ **ii** $n(A')$

   c Complete the Venn diagram showing the numbers in each area. Check that all your numbers add up to 48.

6 **a** Draw a Venn diagram showing two sets, P and S, with an intersection.

   b Given that $n(\mathscr{E}) = 20$, $n(P) = 7$, $n(S) = 16$ and $n(P \cup S)' = 0$, find $n(P \cap S)$.

   c Complete the diagram.

NOTE:

Since $n(P \cup S)' = 0$, all 20 of the elements must lie in P and S, but adding 7 and 16 makes too many, so how many must be in the intersection?

13.8 More about Square Roots and Irrational Numbers

In this section of this chapter we will see how we can find the square root of any perfect square, or express irrational square roots in their simplest form, without using a calculator. There are two possible methods.

a In the first, we express the number, as a product of its prime factors (by using a factor tree if necessary).

For example, $900 = 2 \times 2 \times 3 \times 3 \times 5 \times 5$

so $\sqrt{900} = \sqrt{2 \times 2 \times 3 \times 3 \times 5 \times 5}$

This is the same as $\sqrt{2} \times \sqrt{2} \times \sqrt{3} \times \sqrt{3} \times \sqrt{5} \times \sqrt{5}$

We know $\sqrt{2} \times \sqrt{2} = \sqrt{4} = 2,\ \sqrt{3} \times \sqrt{3} = 3$ and $\sqrt{5} \times \sqrt{5} = 5$

This means $\sqrt{900} = \sqrt{2 \times 2 \times 3 \times 3 \times 5 \times 5} = 2 \times 3 \times 5 = 30$

so $\sqrt{900} = 30$

This is also the best method for finding cube roots.

$$\sqrt[3]{216} = \sqrt[3]{2 \times 2 \times 2 \times 3 \times 3 \times 3} = \sqrt[3]{2 \times 2 \times 2} \times \sqrt[3]{3 \times 3 \times 3} = 2 \times 3 = 6$$

b In the second method, we look for factors of the number that are perfect squares themselves, such as 4, 9, 16, 25 and so on.

So $\sqrt{900} = \sqrt{4 \times 9 \times 25} = 2 \times 3 \times 5 = 30$

Either method will also work for numbers whose square roots are irrational. For example, by the first method,

$$\sqrt{450} = \sqrt{2 \times 3 \times 3 \times 5 \times 5} = \sqrt{2} \times \sqrt{3 \times 3} \times \sqrt{5 \times 5} = \sqrt{2} \times 3 \times 5 = 15 \times \sqrt{2}$$

and $15 \times \sqrt{2}$ is usually written $15\sqrt{2}$.

By the second method,

$$\sqrt{450} = \sqrt{9 \times 25 \times 2} = 3 \times 5\sqrt{2} = 15\sqrt{2}.$$

This is as far as you can go easily without using a calculator.

Square roots that are irrational are also called **surds**. The number $15\sqrt{2}$ is a surd because $\sqrt{2}$ is irrational.

Key term

If the square root of a natural number is irrational it is called a **surd**.

Example 6

a Find $\sqrt{255}$ without using a calculator.

b Simplify $\sqrt{432}$ by writing it as a surd, in terms of $\sqrt{2}$ or $\sqrt{3}$ or $\sqrt{5}$.

Answer 6

a $\sqrt{225} = \sqrt{3 \times 3 \times 5 \times 5} = \sqrt{9 \times 25} = 3 \times 5 = 15$

b $\sqrt{432} = \sqrt{2 \times 2 \times 2 \times 2 \times 3 \times 3 \times 3} = \sqrt{16 \times 9 \times 3}$

$4 \times 3 \times \sqrt{3} = 12\sqrt{3}$

Exercise 13.4   NO CALCULATOR IN THIS EXERCISE

1 Without using a calculator (and showing all your working) find the following:

    a $\sqrt{784}$ **b** $\sqrt{1600}$ **c** $\sqrt{625}$

2 Express the following square roots as surds in terms of $\sqrt{2}$, $\sqrt{3}$ or $\sqrt{5}$:

    a $\sqrt{180}$ **b** $\sqrt{98}$ **c** $\sqrt{192}$

3 In each case, show that the following square roots are either rational or irrational:

    a $\sqrt{50}$ **b** $\sqrt{144}$ **c** $\sqrt{45}$

13.9 Fractions, Decimals and Percentages

The basic work on fractions, decimals and percentages was covered in Chapter 2. We will now look at slightly more difficult questions.

Exercise 13.5   NO CALCULATOR IN THIS EXERCISE

1 Write 2.23 as
    a a mixed number   **b** an improper fraction.

2 Arrange in order of size, starting with the smallest:
    0.21% $\frac{21}{500}$ 2×10^{-3} $-\frac{1}{250}$

3 **a** Calculate 65 as a percentage of 50.
    b Calculate 38.2 as a percentage of 40.
    c Calculate 6 as a percentage of 1200.

4 Arrange the following in order of size, starting with the smallest.
    $\frac{1}{6}, \frac{9}{16}, \frac{9}{20}, \frac{19}{40}$ and $\frac{77}{160}$

5 Find a fraction halfway between
    a $\frac{17}{20}$ and $\frac{9}{10}$ **b** $\frac{4}{5}$ and $\frac{5}{6}$

Exercise 13.6

Mixed exercise

1 $\mathscr{E} = \{a, b, c, d, e, f, g, h\}$ $L = \{a, c, e\}$ $M = \{b, c, d, e, f\}$
    a Draw a Venn diagram showing these sets. Shade L in one direction and M in another.
    b List:
        i $L \cap M$ **ii** $L \cup M$ **iii** L'
        iv M' **v** $(L \cap M)'$
    c Draw another Venn diagram, Shade L in one direction and M' in another.
    d List   **i** $L \cap M'$ **ii** $L \cup M'$

2 List the integers from −2 to 2 inclusive. (Inclusive means including −2 and 2.)

3 Describe the following:
    a $\{1, 8, 27, 64\}$ **b** $\{1, 4, 9, 16, 25\}$

4 Without using a calculator, simplify as far as possible:
    a $\sqrt{4096}$ **b** $\sqrt{2450}$

5 Which of the following are irrational numbers?
    a $\sqrt{500}$ **b** $\sqrt{121}$

6 You are given the following information.
    $\mathscr{E} = \{$integers from -10 and 10 inclusive$\}$
    $F = \{2, 4, 6\}$
    $G = \{-2, -1, 0, 1, 2\}$
    $H = \{1, 2, 3, 4, 5, 6, 7, 8\}$

    By first drawing a Venn diagram, find
    a $n(F \cap G)$ **b** $n(F \cup G)$ **c** $n(F \cap G \cap H)$
    d $n(F \cup G \cup H)$ **e** $n(F \cup G \cup H)'$

Exam-style questions

7 From the list of numbers $\frac{22}{7}$, π, $\sqrt{14}$, $\sqrt{16}$, 27.4, $\frac{65}{13}$, write down

    a one integer   **b** one irrational number.

                                                               (0580 paper 02 Q3 November 2004)

8   **a** $\mathscr{E} = \{x : x \text{ is a integer}, 2 \leqslant x \leqslant 14\}$

        $A = \{x : x \text{ is a prime number}\}$

        $B = \{x : x \text{ is a multiple of 3}\}$

        i   List the members of $(A \cup B)'$.

        ii   Find $n(A \cap B)$.

        iii   Given that $C \subset A$, $n(C) = 3$ and $B \cap C = \varnothing$, list the members of a possible set C.

   b   On a copy of the Venn diagram below, shade the set $(P \cup R) \cap Q'$.

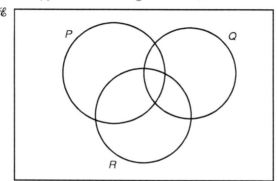

   c   A group of 80 people attended a recreation centre on one day.

      Of these people,   48 used the gym

                            31 used the swimming pool

                            17 used neither the gym nor the swimming pool.

      By drawing a Venn diagram, or otherwise, find the number of people who used both
the gym and the swimming pool.   (4024 paper 22 Q6 June 2012)

9 $\mathscr{E} = \left\{ -2\frac{1}{2}, -1, \sqrt{2}, 3.5, \sqrt{30}, \sqrt{36} \right\}$

   $X = \{\text{integers}\}$

   $Y = \{\text{irrational numbers}\}$

   List the members of

   a X **b** Y.   (0580 paper 02 Q5 November 2003)

10   **a**   Use set notation to describe the shaded subset in the Venn diagram.

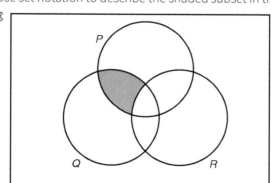

b In a group of students
30 play cricket, 38 play football and 9 play neither cricket nor football.
Find the lowest possible number of students in the group.

(4024 paper 11 Q10 November 2014)

11 In a group of language students, 24 studied Spanish, 23 studied French and 15 studied German. 12 studied Spanish and French, 10 studied German and French, 6 studied Spanish and German and 4 studied all three languages. By drawing a Venn diagram or otherwise, calculate the number of students who studied

a both Spanish and French, but not German

b only one language.

(4024 paper 01 Q18a June 2003)

12 Rearrange the quantities in order with the smallest first.

$\frac{1}{8}\%$, $\frac{3}{2500}$, 0.00126

(0580 paper 02 Q4 November 2003)

13 0.0008 8×10^{-5} 0.8% $\frac{1}{125000}$

Write the above numbers in order, smallest first.

(0580 paper 02 Q6 November 2006)

14 Write down the next prime number after 89.

(0580 paper 02 Q2 June 2006)

15 $\mathscr{E} = \{x : x \text{ is an integer and } x > 5\}$

$P = \{x : x \text{ is a prime number}\}$

$F = \{x : x \text{ is a multiple of 4}\}$

$S = \{x : x \text{ is a multiple of 6}\}$

The Venn diagram shows the universal set and the set F.

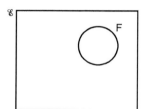

a Copy the Venn diagram and draw and label the two sets P and S to complete it.

b Write down a possible element y such that y is an even number and $y \in (F \cup S)'$.

(4024 paper 11 Q15 November 2011)

16 On the Venn diagrams shade the regions

a $A' \cap C'$

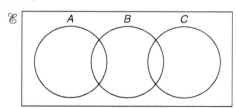

b $(A \cup C) \cap B$

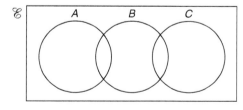

(0580 paper 02 Q8 June 2007)

17 a $\mathscr{E} = \{x : x \text{ is an integer and } 5 \le x \le 15\}$

$A = \{x : x \text{ is a multiple of 3}\}$

$B = \{x : x \text{ is a factor of 60}\}$

$C = \{x : x \text{ is a prime number}\}$

    i   Find n($A \cap B \cap C$).   **ii**   Find ($A \cup B$)'.

    iii   A number, r, is chosen at random from $\mathscr{E}$.

        Find the probability that $r \in A \cap B$.

    iv   Given that $D \subset B$ and $D \subset C$, find D.

b   An activity camp offers 3 sports: tennis, cricket and volleyball.

   One day, 50 children took part in these sports.

   19 children played tennis, 34 children played cricket and 23 children played volleyball.

   2 children played all 3 sports.

   5 children played tennis and cricket.

   10 children played tennis and volleyball.

   By drawing a Venn diagram, or otherwise, find the number of children who played

    i   tennis and cricket but not volleyball,

    ii   cricket and volleyball but not tennis,

    iii   cricket only.   (4024 paper 21 Q2 June 2014)

18 A and B are sets.

Write the following sets in their simplest form.

    a $A \cap A'$ **b** $A \cup A'$ **c** $(A \cap B) \cup (A \cap B')$.

                                                     (0580 paper 02 Q12 November 2007)

19 Work out the value of $1 + \dfrac{2}{3 + \frac{4}{5 + 6}}$.

                                            (0580 paper 21 Q3 November 2008)

20 In a group of 100 students, 80 study Spanish and 35 study French.

x students study Spanish and French.

y students study neither Spanish nor French.

The Venn diagram illustrates this information.

a   Expressed in set notation, the value of x is $n(S \cap F)$. Express the value of y in set notation.

b   Find, in its simplest form, an expression for y in terms of x.

c   Find

    i   the least possible value of x

    ii   the greatest possible value of y.   (4024 paper 02 Q5 June 2004)

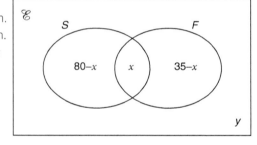

21 The results of a survey of 31 students are shown in the Venn diagram.

$\mathscr{E}$ = {students questioned in the survey}

M = {students who study Mathematics}

P = {students who study Physics}

S = {students who study Spanish}

    i   Write down the value of

        a x **b** $n(M \cap P)$

        c $n(M \cup S)$ **d** $n(P')$.

    ii   Write down a description, in words, of the set that has 16 members.

                                              (4024 paper 02 Q6a June 2006)

22 a The sets A and B are shown on the Venn diagram. The element y is such that $y \in A$ and $y \notin B$. On a copy of the diagram, write y in the correct region.

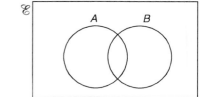

b $\mathscr{E} = \{x : x \text{ is an integer and } 1 \leqslant x \leqslant 8\}$

$P = \{x : x > 5\}$

$Q = \{x : x \leqslant 3\}$

i Find the value of $n(P \cup Q)$.

ii List the elements of $P' \cap Q'$.

(4024 paper 01 Q9 June 2007)

23 a Express, in set notation, as simply as possible, the subset shaded in the Venn diagram.

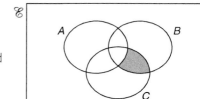

b It is given that $n(\mathscr{E}) = 40$, $n(P) = 18$, $n(Q) = 20$ and $n(P \cap Q) = 7$. Find

i $n(P \cup Q)$,

ii $n(P' \cap Q')$. (4024/01 Oct/Nov 2007 q9)

24 a On a copy of the Venn diagram, shade the set $P \cup Q'$.

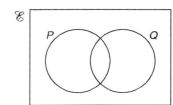

b There are 27 children in a class. Of these children, 19 own a bicycle, 15 own a scooter and 3 own neither a bicycle nor a scooter. Using a Venn diagram, or otherwise, find the number of children who own a bicycle but not a scooter.

(4024 paper 01 Q9 November 2008)

25 a $\mathscr{E} = \{1, 2, 3, 4, 5\}$

$A = \{1, 2, 3\}$

$B = \{5\}$

$C = \{3, 4\}$

List the elements of

i $A \cup C$

ii $B' \cap C$.

b A group of 60 children attend an after school club. Of these, 35 children play football and 29 play hockey. 3 children do not play either football or hockey. By drawing a Venn diagram, or otherwise, find the number of children who play only hockey. (4024 paper 01 Q18 June 2009)

14 Algebra I

Learning Objectives   Syllabus sections 17, 18 and 19

In this chapter you will:
- expand products of algebraic fractions
- factorise quadratic expressions
- factorise differences of squares
- factorise by pairing

- learn more about indices
- work with algebraic fractions

14.1 Introduction

Algebra is a vital tool in mathematics. It is essential that you understand the language of algebra, both the significant words such as 'equation' and 'evaluate', and the shorthand notation that mathematicians use to communicate their ideas.

14.2 Essential Skills   NO CALCULATOR IN THIS EXERCISE

1   $y = 2x + 3$ $\qquad$ $2x + 5y - x - 1$ $\qquad$ $a^2 = b^2 + c^2$
From the selection above, choose
    a   a formula
    b   an equation
    c   an expression.

2   From the expression $2x - x^2 + 3xy - 6 - 4xy$, choose
    a   a term in x
    b   a constant term
    c   the coefficient of the term in x^2
    d   two like terms.

3   Simplify
    a $a^2 \times a^3$
    b $x^3 \times x^5 \times x$
    c $b^5 \div b^2$
    d $(c^2)^5$
    e $(ab^2)^3$

4   Simplify where possible
    a $(-x)^2 + (-x)^3$
    b $-6x \div -2y$
    c $xy + x^2y^2$
    d $-2a \times -3b \div 6a$

5   Simplify
    a $x^4 \times y^5 \times y^2 \times x^3$
    b $2x^3 \div 3x^2 \times 9x^5$
    c $x^{11} \div x^7 \times x^8$
    d $(x^2y^5)^6$

6   Simplify the following expressions:
    a $2x - 3y - 5x + y$
    b $a + b + c - -a + -b - -c$
    c $pqr - qpr$
    d $ab + 3a - 4b - 2ab + 4b + a$

7 Calculate the following:

   a 3^{-1} **b** $2^{-1} \times 2^{-3}$ **c** $\left(\frac{1}{2}\right)^{-2}$ **d** $\left(2\frac{1}{2}\right)^{-2}$

8 In each of the following, find a replacement for n which makes the statement true.

   a $1 = 100^n$ **b** $\frac{3}{4} = \left(\frac{4}{3}\right)^n$ **c** $\left(\frac{2}{3}\right)^n = \frac{9}{4}$ **d** $10 = 10^n$

9 Multiply out the brackets and simplify:

   a $2(x - y) - 2(x + y)$ **b** $pqr - pq(r + 1)$

   c $a^2(a + b^2) + b^2(a^2 + b)$ **d** $x^2 y^2 - (x^2 y^2 - 1) + x^2(y^2 - 1) - y^2(x^2 + 1)$

10 Factorise completely:

   a $5xyz + 10x^2y$ **b** $14x^2y - 21xy^2$ **c** $3a^2 - 6a^3$ **d** $2x^2 - x$

14.3 Expanding Products of Algebraic Factors

You have met examples of multiplying a bracketed expression by a number and letters. An example of a bracketed expression is $(2x + 5y)$.

We now have to look at multiplying two bracketed expressions together, and for simplicity we shall from now on say 'brackets' rather than 'bracketed expression'. Take a simple example:

$$(2 + x) \times (3 + y)$$

This could be separated into:

$$2 \times (3 + y) + x \times (3 + y)$$
$$= 6 + 2y + 3x + xy$$

Note how every term in the first pair of brackets multiplies every term in the second pair of brackets.

It is normal to write the brackets without the multiplication sign using algebraic shorthand:

$$(2 + x)(3 + y) = 6 + 2y + 3x + xy$$

You will get used to doing this multiplication quickly if you are systematic.

Start with the 2 from the first pair of brackets and multiply it first by the 3 and then by the $+y$ from the second pair of brackets, writing down both results. Now move on to the $+x$ and multiply it by first the 3 and then the $+y$, again writing down both results.

Once again we have to take careful notice of any minus signs, as being careless with these is one of the commonest ways to get a wrong answer and lose marks.

Usually you will find that there is a second line of working after you have multiplied out the brackets where you can simplify by collecting like terms, as you will see in the next example. Multiplying out the brackets is sometimes called expanding the brackets.

NOTE:
If you really find this difficult you can draw a table like this:

×	3	+y
2		
+x		

and fill it in. However, this is fine to start with but is too complicated and lengthy for permanent use, so it is much better to practise working in the systematic way described here until it becomes easy for you.

Example 1

Multiply out the brackets and simplify where possible.

a $(x+2)^2$

NOTE:
Be careful! It is the brackets that are squared, not just the x and the $+2$.

b $(x+2)(x-3)$
c $(3a-4)(2a+5)$
d $(x+1)(x-1)$
e $(a+b)(a-b)$
f $(2-s)(5+s)$
g $(x^2+1)(x+2)$
h $(a+b)(a+b+1)$

NOTE:
In part **h**, just be systematic.

NOTE:
In part **h** remember that ba is the same as ab.

Answer 1

a $(x+2)^2 = (x+2)(x+2)$
$= x^2 + 2x + 2x + 4 = x^2 + 4x + 4$

b $(x+2)(x-3) = x^2 - 3x + 2x - 6$
$= x^2 - x - 6$

c $(3a-4)(2a+5) = 6a^2 + 15a - 8a - 20$
$= 6a^2 + 7a - 20$

d $(x+1)(x-1) = x^2 - x + x - 1$
$= x^2 - 1$

e $(a+b)(a-b) = a^2 - ab + ab - b^2$
$= a^2 - b^2$

f $(2-s)(5+s) = 10 + 2s - 5s - s^2$
$= 10 - 3s - s^2$

g $(x^2+1)(x+2) = x^3 + 2x^2 + x + 2$

h $(a+b)(a+b+1) = a^2 + ab + a + ba + b^2 + b$
$= a^2 + 2ab + a + b^2 + b$

Exercise 14.1

Multiply out the brackets and simplify where possible.

1 $(a+1)(a+1)$ **2** $(x+4)(x+5)$ **3** $(x+4)(x-5)$ **4** $(x-4)(x+5)$

5 $(x-4)(x-5)$ **6** $(2b+1)(b+1)$ **7** $(5c-2)(c-2)$ **8** $(6x+5)(2x+3)$

9 $(x+y)(x+y)$ **10** $(x-y)(x-y)$ **11** $(x-y)(x+y)$ **12** $(2d+3e)(2d-3e)$

13 $(7z+1)(2z-1)$ **14** $(2+x)(4+x)$ **15** $(2+x)(2-x)$ **16** $(a^2+b)(a+b)$

17 $(x^2-1)(x+1)$ **18** $(b+c)(2b+2c+1)$ **19** $(x-1)(x^2+x+1)$ **20** $(x^2+1)(x^2-1)$

21 $(2x+3)^2$ **22** $(2x+3)(2x-3)$ **23** $(2x-3)^2$ **24** $(3x-4)(3x+4)$

25 $(2b-1)(2b+1)$ **26** $(2a+3b)(c+d)$

Key term

A **quadratic expression** is a sum of terms usually involving a single variable in which the highest power of that variable is 2. There may also be a term with the variable to the power 1, and a constant term.

14.4 Factorising Quadratic Expressions

A **quadratic expression** in x contains a term in x^2, and can contain a term in x and a constant term, but no other terms. For example, $x^2 + 2x + 1$ is a quadratic expression.

Now that we know how to multiply out two pairs of brackets and simplify the result we need to answer the question 'how do we get back to our original two pairs of brackets?' This needs to be treated like a puzzle which can be solved by trial and error. Try a possible solution, and then multiply out again to see if you get back the original expression.

You will often find that you will not get the correct answer straight away, but this does not mean that you are doing anything particularly wrong, so just try again, with a different combination of letters and numbers. After a while you will begin to see the patterns and will find that you get the correct answer with fewer attempts. It is worth practising these until it becomes easier.

We will start with easy examples, and work on towards the more difficult. First we will look at an example which has been multiplied out, so we can see where the terms come from.

$$(x + 2)(x + 5)$$
$$= x^2 + 5x + 2x + 10$$
$$= x^2 + 7x + 10$$

If you are asked to factorise this expression you can start by drawing two empty pairs of brackets:

$$x^2 + 7x + 10$$
$$= (\quad)(\quad)$$

The term at the beginning of each pair of brackets comes from factorising x^2, so this is easy:

$$x^2 + 7x + 10$$
$$= (x\quad)(x\quad)$$

The term at the end of each pair of brackets comes from factorising the constant term, +10. Beside your working it is a good idea to write down all the factors of +10, as usual being systematic about it.

The factors of 10 are {1, 2, 5, 10}.

Start with the smallest and write it down multiplied by the other factor which gives the product 10. (In this case 1 × 10.) Then move on to the next factor. (In this case 2 × 5.) This is as far as you can go with 10 because you will start repeating pairs of factors. By working in this way you will not be in danger of leaving out any factors when the examples become more difficult.

$$x^2 + 7x + 10 \qquad\qquad 1 \times 10$$
$$= (x\quad)(x\quad) \qquad\qquad 2 \times 5$$

The first part of the puzzle is to decide which of these two pairs of factors you need to choose. If you look back to the multiplying out you will see that the two factors have to add up to +7, so in this example there is not a lot of choice, and we pick 2 and 5, both being positive.

$$= x^2 + 7x + 10 \qquad\qquad 2 + 5$$
$$= (x + 2)(x + 5) \qquad\qquad = 7$$

Things start to get more complicated when the constant term has more pairs of factors, or when there are negative signs as well. We will come to these later.

As usual, you should work through the examples, and then work through the whole exercise.

NOTE:

It is worth repeating that you should always check your answer by multiplying out the brackets again.

Example 2

Factorise the following quadratic expressions:

a $x^2 + 11x + 10$ **b** $x^2 + 10x + 24$ **c** $x^2 + 11x + 24$

Answer 2

a $x^2 + 11x + 10$ 1×10 $1 + 10 = 11$
$= (x \quad)(x \quad)$ 2×5
$= (x + 1)(x + 10)$

b $x^2 + 10x + 24$ 1×24
$= (x \quad)(x \quad)$ 2×12
$= (x + 4)(x + 6)$ 3×8
     4×6 $4 + 6 = 10$

c Using the factors we have already set out in part (b) you should see that $3 + 8 = 11$, so:
$x^2 + 11x + 24$
$= (x + 3)(x + 8)$

NOTE:
Remember to be systematic, as you can see in part (b) of the answer, and work through all the factors in order.

Exercise 14.2

Factorise:

1 $x^2 + 4x + 3$ **2** $x^2 + 6x + 5$ **3** $x^2 + 13x + 12$ **4** $x^2 + 8x + 12$ **5** $x^2 + 7x + 12$

6 $x^2 + 8x + 16$ **7** $x^2 + 17x + 16$ **8** $x^2 + 10x + 16$ **9** $x^2 + 18x + 17$ **10** $x^2 + 2x + 1$

We will now look at quadratic expressions containing minus signs.

Example 3

Factorise

a $x^2 - 5x - 6$ **b** $x^2 + 5x - 6$ **c** $x^2 - 5x + 6$ **d** $x^2 - 7x + 6$

Answer 3

In each one of these we have to factorise 6: 1×6
     2×3

a $x^2 - 5x - 6$ $+1 - 6 = -5,$ **b** $x^2 + 5x - 6$ $-1 + 6 = +5,$
     and $+1 \times -6 = -6$ and $-1 \times +6 = -6$
$= (x + 1)(x - 6)$ $= (x - 1)(x + 6)$

c $x^2 - 5x + 6$ $-2 - 3 = -5,$ **d** $x^2 - 7x + 6$ $-1 - 6 = -7,$
     and $-2 \times -3 = +6$ and $-1 \times -6 = +6$
$= (x - 2)(x - 3)$ $= (x - 1)(x - 6)$

Exercise 14.3

Factorise:

1 $x^2 + 6x + 5$ **2** $x^2 + 4x - 5$ **3** $x^2 - 4x - 5$ **4** $x^2 - 6x + 5$

5 $x^2 - 7x - 8$ **6** $x^2 - 6x + 8$ **7** $x^2 + 2x - 8$ **8** $x^2 + 35x - 36$

9 $x^2 - 16x - 36$ **10** $x^2 - 13x + 36$

Example 4

Factorise:

a $2x^2 + 3x + 1$ **b** $2x^2 + x - 3$ **c** $2x^2 - 5x + 3$ **d** $6x^2 + 17x + 5$

e $6x^2 + 13x + 6$ **f** $6x^2 + 5x - 6$ **g** $6x^2 + 5xy - 6y^2$

Answer 4

a $2x^2 + 3x + 1$
$= (2x + 1)(x + 1)$

> **NOTE:**
> In this case, 1 can only be factorised to 1×1 so there is no choice of combination and the answer is simple.
> $2 = 1 \times 2, 1 = 1 \times 1$

b $2x^2 + 5x + 3$
$= (2x + 3)(x + 1)$

> **NOTE:**
> There is now an element of choice because the 2 and the 3 will both factorise.
> $2 = 1 \times 2$ and $3 = 1 \times 3$
> Try both combinations to find the right one.
> $(2x + 1)(x + 3) = 2x^2 + 7x + 3$
> or $(2x + 3)(x + 1) = 2x^2 + 5x + 3$
> The second combination is the one we want.

c $2x^2 - 5x + 3$
$= (2x - 3)(x - 1)$

> **NOTE:**
> This is like (b), but with minus signs in both pairs of brackets.

d $6x^2 + 17x + 5$
$= (2x + 5)(3x + 1)$

> **NOTE:**
> The 6 will factorise in two different ways, making more choices.
> $6 = 1 \times 6$ $5 = 1 \times 5$
> or $6 = 2 \times 3$
> Again, try each in turn with the factors of 5 until you find the correct combination.
> $(x + 1)(6x + 5) = 6x^2 + 11x + 5$
> or $(x + 5)(6x + 1) = 6x^2 + 31x + 5$
> or $(2x + 1)(3x + 5) = 6x^2 + 13x + 5$
> or $(2x + 5)(3x + 1) = 6x^2 + 17x + 5$
> We see that the last combination gives the correct value (17) for the coefficient of the x term, so this is the solution we want.

e $6x^2 + 13x + 6$
$= (2x + 3)(3x + 2)$

> **NOTE:**
> This is more difficult because there are two sixes, both of which will factorise in two different ways.
> $6 = 1 \times 6$ $6 = 1 \times 6$
> or $6 = 2 \times 3$ $6 = 2 \times 3$
> Systematic trials with all the possible combinations will get you the right answer.

f $6x^2 + 5x - 6$
$(2x + 3)(3x - 2)$

NOTE:
This is probably the most difficult one you would have to tackle, because it is like (e), but also with a minus sign.

g $6x^2 + 5xy - 6y^2$
$= (2x + 3y)(3x - 2y)$

NOTE:
This is the same as (f), but with a term in y at the end of each pair of brackets.

As you can see, you must be prepared for some trial and error when factorising the more difficult quadratics. Practise as much as you can and you will begin to see the solutions without having to write down every possible combination. It does get easier. Always remember to multiply out again to check that you do have the correct solution.

Exercise 14.4

Factorise:

1 $3x^2 + 4x + 1$ **2** $6x^2 + 5x + 1$ **3** $3x^2 + 5x + 2$ **4** $3x^2 + 7x + 2$

5 $3x^2 - 2x - 1$ **6** $3x^2 + 2x - 1$ **7** $3x^2 - 4x + 1$ **8** $6x^2 + 7x + 1$

9 $4x^2 - 7x - 2$ **10** $4x^2 + 8x + 3$ **11** $4x^2 + 13x + 3$ **12** $4x^2 - 4x - 3$

13 $4x^2 + 4x - 3$ **14** $4x^2 - 8x + 3$ **15** $8x^2 + 14x + 3$ **16** $8x^2 + 10x - 3$

NOTE:
Look again at question 24. It is the same as question 21, but in $(xy)^2$ and xy instead of x^2 and x.

17 $8x^2 + 10x + 3$ **18** $8x^2 + 2x - 3$ **19** $8x^2 + 26x + 15$ **20** $9x^2 + 30x + 25$

21 $6x^2 - 25x + 25$ **22** $8x^2 + 26xy + 15y^2$ **23** $9x^2 + 30xy + 25y^2$ **24** $6x^2y^2 - 25xy + 25$

14.5 Factorising a Difference of Squares

Do you remember what happened in some of the questions on multiplying out the brackets in Exercise 14.1, for example $(x + y)(x - y)$?

To take another example:

$$(c + 4d)(c - 4d)$$
$$= c^2 - 4cd + 4cd - 16d^2$$
$$= c^2 - 16d^2$$

Key term
A **difference of squares** is an expression with two terms, both perfect squares, in which one term is subtracted from the other.

This result is called a **difference of squares**. The minus sign means to find the *difference* between c^2 and $16d^2$, and c^2 and $16d^2$ are both terms that are perfect *squares*.

There is no easy way of working out how to factorise a difference of squares, so it is very important that you learn the following result:

$$x^2 - y^2 = (x + y)(x - y)$$

This *only works for a difference of squares*, so do not try to find something similar for a sum of squares, which will not factorise in this way.

One example to look out for is:

$$x^2 - 1 = (x - 1)(x + 1)$$

This is not obvious until you remember that 1 is the same as 1^2.

Example 5
Factorise where possible:

a $1 - 25x^2$ **b** $9y^2 - 16x^2$ **c** $y^2 + x^2$

Answer 1

a $1 - 25x^2$
$= (1 - 5x)(1 + 5x)$

b $9y^2 - 16x^2$
$= (3y - 4x)(3y + 4x)$

c $y^2 + x^2$
Nothing can be done with this because it is a sum of squares, not a difference.

Exercise 14.5

Factorise:

1 $x^2 - y^2$ **2** $a^2 - 1$ **3** $x^2 - 9$ **4** $4y^2 - 9$

5 $25 - a^2$ **6** $36a^2 - 49b^2$ **7** $a^2b^2 - x^2y^2$ **8** $1 - 4c^2$

14.6 Factorising by Pairing

Looking back at Exercise 14.1 question 26:

$$(2a + 3b)(c + d)$$
$$= 2ac + 2ad + 3bc + 3bd$$

We see that it is not always possible to finish off by simplifying two of the terms. These expressions can often be factorised by first putting them into two pairs.

For example,

$$ab + xy + ay + bx$$

This can be grouped into two pairs in which each of the pairs has a common factor. We rewrite

$$ab + xy + ay + bx$$
$$= ab + ay + xy + bx$$
$$= a(b + y) + x(y + b)$$

Remembering that $b + y$ is the same as $y + b$, we can take $(b + y)$ out as a common factor.

$$= a(b + y) + x(b + y)$$
$$= (b + y)(a + x)$$

Check that this is correct by multiplying out again.

The same result would have been obtained if the terms had been grouped the other possible way:

$$ab + bx + xy + ay$$
$$= b(a + x) + y(x + a)$$

and so on.

14.7 Factorising Systematically

When you are asked to factorise an expression it is worth looking at the question systematically.

Always look for any common factors first, and take them outside a pair of brackets. Then think about difference of squares, then a quadratic and then pairing.

Factorizing systematically

1   *Are there any common factors?*

    If so, factorise them out first.

2   *Is there a difference of squares?*

    If so, factorise.

3   *Is the expression quadratic?*

    If so, factorise.

4   *Lastly, think about pairing.*

Example 6
Factorise completely:

a $2x^2 - 8$ **b** $x^2y^2 - 4z^2$

c $8ab + 4ay + 4bx + 2xy$ **d** $2a^2 + 6ab + 4b^2$

Answer 6

a $2x^2 - 8$

> **NOTE:**
> You would not be able to carry on if you did not spot the common factor first.

$= 2(x^2 - 4)$
$= 2(x - 2)(x + 2)$

b $x^2y^2 - 4z^2$
$= (xy - 2z)(xy + 2z)$

c $8ab + 4ay + 4bx + 2xy = 2(4ab + 2ay + 2bx + xy)$
$= 2[2a(2b + y) + x(2b + y)]$
$= 2(2b + y)(2a + x)$

d $2a^2 + 6ab + 4b^2$
$= 2(a^2 + 3ab + 2b^2)$
$= 2(a + 2b)(a + b)$

> **NOTE:**
> If you had factorised this without first looking for common factors you might have ended up with $(2a + 4b)(a + b)$, or $(a + 2b)(2a + 2b)$, which is fine, but not completely factorised, and as it stands is only worth part of the marks in an examination. In each case, if you go on to factorise out the common factor of 2 you would have completed the factorisation. A similar problem would have arisen if the common factor in (c) had not been taken out first.

Exercise 14.6

Factorise completely

1 $9a + 15b$ **2** $1 - x^2$ **3** $18 - 2x^2$

4 $2x^2 - x - 1$ **5** $6x^2 - 18x$ **6** $2x^2 - 12x + 18$

7 $20x^3 - 5x$ **8** $3x^2 + 3x - 6$ **9** $2y^3 - 4y^2 + 2y$

10 $16xy^2 - 4x^2y$ **11** $16xy^3 - 4x^3y$ **12** $12ab + 6ay + 3xy + 6bx$

14.8 More about Indices

In Chapter 3 we looked at indices that were taken from the set of integers (positive and negative whole numbers and zero). Now we must look at fractional indices. You should remember that finding a square root is the inverse of squaring, and so squaring a number's square root gives back the number itself. Look at the following statements:

$$\sqrt{2} \times \sqrt{2} = 2$$
$$2^{\frac{1}{2}} \times 2^{\frac{1}{2}} = 2^{\frac{1}{2}+\frac{1}{2}} = 2^1 = 2$$

It makes sense to say that $\sqrt{2}$ is the same as $2^{\frac{1}{2}}$.

In the same way,

$$\sqrt[3]{2} \times \sqrt[3]{2} \times \sqrt[3]{2} = 2^{\frac{1}{3}} \times 2^{\frac{1}{3}} \times 2^{\frac{1}{3}} = 2^{\frac{1}{3}+\frac{1}{3}+\frac{1}{3}} = 2^1 = 2$$

You can see that the root is denoted by the denominator in a fractional index. Thus a cube root is written as a power of $\frac{1}{3}$, a fourth root is written as a power of $\frac{1}{4}$ and so on.

> **NOTE:**
> In part **b** the power of one fifth means means the fifth root of 32. In other words, which number raised to the power 5 would equal 32?
> When you are trying to find the root of a number, start investigating small numbers first. You will not be given anything too difficult, the most likely roots are 2, 3, 4 or 5.

Example 7

Calculate:

a $25^{\frac{1}{2}}$

b $32^{\frac{1}{5}}$

Answer 7

a $25^{\frac{1}{2}}$ means the square root of 25, which is 5

$25^{\frac{1}{2}} = 5$

b $32^{\frac{1}{5}}$ trying 2 first, $2 \times 2 \times 2 \times 2 \times 2 = 32$

$32^{\frac{1}{5}} = 2$

The normal rules for working with indices apply to fractional indices as well. In particular it is useful to understand the following:

$$32^{\frac{3}{5}} = (32^3)^{\frac{1}{5}} = (32^{\frac{1}{5}})^3 = 2^3 = 8$$
$$32^{\frac{3}{5}} = (32^3)^{\frac{1}{5}} = 32768^{\frac{1}{5}} = 8$$

Hence, you can multiply the indices in any order but it is much simpler to take the root first so that you are dealing with smaller numbers.

NOTE:
In answer **b ii**
$-\frac{1}{2}+\frac{5}{2}=\frac{4}{2}=2$

NOTE:
In answer **b iii**
$-\frac{3}{2}\times-4=+6$

NOTE:
In answer **c i** which power of 5 would make 25?

5 squared equals 25, so the square root of 25 = 5

NOTE:
In answer **c ii** check your answer! Remember that while $27^{\frac{1}{3}}=3$
$27^3\neq3$, so the answer is $x=\frac{1}{3}$, not $x=3$!

NOTE:
In answer **C iii** 4 to the power 4 equals 256, so the fourth root of 256 = 4

Example 8

a Without using a calculator work out

  i $(100)^{\frac{3}{2}}$ **ii** $(27)^{\frac{-2}{3}}$

b Simplify

  i $(x^{\frac{1}{2}}\times y^{\frac{3}{2}})^2$ **ii** $x^{-\frac{1}{2}}\times x^{\frac{5}{2}}$ **iii** $(x^{-\frac{3}{2}})^{-4}$

c Find replacements for x which will make the following statements true:

  i $25x=5$ **ii** $27x=3$ **iii** $256x=4$

Answer 8

a i $(100)^{\frac{3}{2}}=(100^{\frac{1}{2}})^3=10^3=1000$

  ii $(27)^{-\frac{2}{3}}=\frac{1}{27^{\frac{2}{3}}}=\frac{1}{\left(27^{\frac{1}{3}}\right)^2}=\frac{1}{3^2}=\frac{1}{9}$

b i $(x^{\frac{1}{2}}\times y^{\frac{3}{2}})^2=x^{(2\times\frac{1}{2})}\times y^{(2\times\frac{3}{2})}=x\times y^3=xy^3$

  ii $x^{-\frac{1}{2}}\times x^{\frac{5}{2}}=x^{\left(-\frac{1}{2}+\frac{5}{2}\right)}=x^2$

  iii $(x^{-\frac{3}{2}})^{-4}=x^{\left(-\frac{3}{2}\times-4\right)}=x^6$

c i $25^x=5$

     $5^2=25$, so $25^{\frac{1}{2}}=5$

     $x=\frac{1}{2}$

  ii $27^x=3$

     $3^3=27$, so $27^{\frac{1}{3}}=3$

     $x=\frac{1}{3}$

  iii $256^x=4$

     $4^4=256$, so $256^{\frac{1}{4}}=4$

     $x=\frac{1}{4}$

NOTE:
Ask yourself the questions in part **c** the other way round.

Exercise 14.7

Without using a calculator, work out:

1 $8^{\frac{1}{4}}$ **2** $81^{-\frac{1}{4}}$ **3** $81^{-\frac{3}{4}}$

Simplify, giving your answer in a form with positive powers.

4 $2x^{\frac{2}{5}}+5x^{\frac{2}{5}}$ **5** $2x^{\frac{2}{5}}\times5x^{\frac{2}{5}}$ **6** $2x^{\frac{2}{5}}\div5x^{\frac{2}{5}}$ **7** $2x^{\frac{2}{5}}\times5x^{-\frac{2}{5}}$

8 $2x^{-\frac{2}{5}}\times5x^{-\frac{2}{5}}$ **9** $2x^{\frac{2}{5}}\div5x^{-\frac{2}{5}}$ **10** $2y^{\frac{3}{4}}\times y^{\frac{1}{2}}$ **11** $2y^{\frac{3}{4}}\div y$

12 $(x^{\frac{1}{2}}+1)(x^{\frac{1}{2}}-1)$ **13** $(xy^2)^{\frac{1}{2}}$ **14** $2x^{-\frac{1}{2}}(x^{\frac{1}{2}}+x)$ **15** $(2x)^{\frac{2}{5}}\times(16x)^{\frac{2}{5}}$

16 $(x^{\frac{1}{2}}-1)^2$ **17** $(x^{\frac{1}{2}}-x^{-\frac{1}{2}})^2$

18 Find replacements for x which would make each of the following statements true.

  a $32^x=2$ **b** $81^x=3$ **c** $125^x=5$

14.9 Algebraic Fractions

In this section we are going to see how we can simplify algebraic fractions, and also how to add, subtract, multiply and divide algebraic fractions. The same rules apply as for arithmetic, with a few changes to allow for the variables (letters).

Simplifying Algebraic Fractions

Look at the expressions below.

$$\frac{x}{2}, \quad \frac{y^2}{y+1}, \quad \frac{3}{a}, \quad \frac{\frac{1}{a}+\frac{1}{b}}{\frac{a}{b}}$$

These are all examples of algebraic fractions.

Now we must see how to simplify some typical examples following the familiar rules of arithmetic.

The fraction $\frac{10}{15}$ can be simplified by dividing the denominator and numerator by the highest common factor. In this case it is 5.

$$\frac{10}{15} = \frac{5 \times 2}{5 \times 3} = \frac{2}{3}$$

In a similar way, $\frac{abc^2}{a^2c}$ can be simplified by dividing the numerator and denominator by the HCF of abc^2 and a^2c, which is ac.

$$\frac{abc^2}{a^2c} = \frac{ac \times bc}{ac \times a} = \frac{bc}{a}$$

Remember

- You *must* check that whatever you are dividing by can in fact divide the *whole* of the numerator and the *whole* of the denominator.
- It **really** is best to factorise first to avoid one of the most common mistakes in algebra. Two further examples should demonstrate this:

$$\frac{xy + zy}{y^2} = \frac{y(x + z)}{y \times y} = \frac{x + z}{y}$$

but

$$\frac{xy + yz}{2y + z} = \frac{y(x + z)}{2y + z}$$

The y cannot divide the whole of the denominator, so no further simplifying can be done.

Complicated fractions can often be simplified by *multiplying* the denominator and numerator by the same number or letter, as in this example:

$$\frac{\frac{1}{2} + \frac{2}{3}}{\frac{2}{3}}$$

The lowest common multiple of the denominators 2 and 3 is 6, so if the top and bottom of this fraction are multiplied by 6 these denominators can be cancelled out.

It is a good idea to multiply by $\frac{6}{1}$ to avoid mistakes.

Remember that $\frac{1}{2} \times \frac{6}{1} = 3$ and $\frac{2}{3} \times \frac{6}{1} = 4$.

$$\frac{\frac{1}{2} + \frac{2}{3}}{\frac{2}{3}} = \frac{\left(\frac{1}{2} + \frac{2}{3}\right) \times \frac{6}{1}}{\frac{2}{3} \times \frac{6}{1}} = \frac{(3 + 4)}{4} = \frac{7}{4} = 1\frac{3}{4}$$

Work through this carefully to make sure you understand what is happening.

To avoid some of the common errors in working with complex algebraic fractions it is best, if the numerator or denominator (or both) contain sums or differences of terms, to draw pairs of brackets round them before you start any work.

For example,

$$\frac{x+y}{x-y}$$

should be written as $\frac{(x+y)}{(x-y)}$ before any work is done.

Remember:

*   Before starting work with algebraic fractions draw pairs of brackets round the numerator and denominator if necessary.

> **NOTE:**
> In example **a** multiply top and bottom by 12

> **NOTE:**
> In example **b i** multiply top and bottom by ab.

> **NOTE:**
> In example **b ii** factorise the denominator.

> **NOTE:**
> In example **b iii** factorise Factorise the numerator (a difference of squares).

> **NOTE:**
> In example **b vi** factorise both the numerator and the denominator.

Example 9

a   Calculate $\dfrac{1+\frac{2}{3}}{\frac{1}{12}+\frac{3}{4}}$

b   Simplify

i $\dfrac{\frac{1}{a}+\frac{1}{b}}{\frac{1}{ab}}$

ii $\dfrac{x+y}{3x+3y}$

iii $\dfrac{x^2-y^2}{x+y}$

iv $\dfrac{x-1}{x^2+x-2}$

v $\dfrac{x-2y}{x^2-xy-2y^2}$

vi $\dfrac{a^2+3a+2}{a^2+a-2}$

Answer 9

a $\dfrac{1+\frac{2}{3}}{\frac{1}{12}+\frac{3}{4}} = \dfrac{\left(1+\frac{2}{3}\right)}{\left(\frac{1}{12}+\frac{3}{4}\right)} = \dfrac{\left(1+\frac{2}{3}\right)\times12}{\left(\frac{1}{12}+\frac{3}{4}\right)\times12} = \dfrac{12+8}{1+9} = \dfrac{20}{10} = 2$

b   Simplify

i $\dfrac{\frac{1}{a}+\frac{1}{b}}{\frac{1}{ab}} = \dfrac{\left(\frac{1}{a}+\frac{1}{b}\right)\times\frac{ab}{1}}{\frac{1}{ab}\times\frac{ab}{1}} = \dfrac{b+a}{1} = b+a$

ii $\dfrac{x+y}{3x+3y} = \dfrac{(x+y)}{(3x+3y)} = \dfrac{(x+y)}{3(x+y)} = \dfrac{1}{3}$

iii $\dfrac{x^2-y^2}{x+y} = \dfrac{(x+y)(x-y)}{(x+y)} = x-y$

iv $\dfrac{x-1}{x^2+x-2} = \dfrac{(x-1)}{(x+2)(x-1)} = \dfrac{1}{x+2}$

v $\dfrac{x-2y}{x^2-xy-2y^2} = \dfrac{(x-2y)}{(x-2y)(x+y)} = \dfrac{1}{(x+y)}$

vi $\dfrac{a^2+3a+2}{a^2+a-2} = \dfrac{(a+2)(a+1)}{(a+2)(a-1)} = \dfrac{a+1}{a-1}$

Exercise 14.8

Without using a calculator, simplify:

1 $\dfrac{\frac{1}{2}-\frac{1}{3}}{1+\frac{1}{6}}$

2 $\dfrac{2-\frac{2}{5}}{\frac{2}{25}+\frac{4}{5}}$

3 $\dfrac{\frac{2}{3}+\frac{3}{4}}{\frac{1}{6}+\frac{5}{2}}$

4 $\dfrac{4x-8}{2}$

5 $\dfrac{3}{6x+9}$

6 $\dfrac{xy+xz}{x}$

7 $\dfrac{xy+xz}{2y+2z}$

8 $\dfrac{3x}{9xy+15xz}$

9 $\dfrac{6x^2+4x}{10x^2-8x}$

10 $\dfrac{3xyz}{xy-4xz}$

11 $\dfrac{x+y}{x^2-y^2}$

12 $\dfrac{4x^2-9}{2x-3}$

13 $\dfrac{y+2}{y^2+3y+2}$

14 $\dfrac{x^2-1}{x^2-2x+1}$

15 $\dfrac{x^2-1}{x^2+2x+1}$

16 $\dfrac{\frac{1}{x}\times\frac{1}{y}}{\frac{3}{x}\times\frac{3}{y}}$

17 $\dfrac{\frac{1}{x}+\frac{x}{y}}{\frac{1}{y}+\frac{y}{x}}$

18 $\dfrac{\frac{a}{b}+\frac{b}{a}}{\frac{1}{ab}}$

Multiplying and Dividing Algebraic Fractions

Let us revise how to multiply and divide fractions involving numbers only:

$$\frac{2}{5}\times\frac{3}{7}=\frac{2\times3}{5\times7}=\frac{6}{35}\qquad\text{and}\qquad\frac{2}{5}\div\frac{3}{7}=\frac{2}{5}\times\frac{7}{3}=\frac{14}{15}$$

You can save work by cancelling before multiplying where possible. For example,

$$\frac{5}{12}\div\frac{15}{4}=\frac{5}{12}\times\frac{4}{15}=\frac{1\times4}{12\times3}=\frac{1\times1}{3\times3}=\frac{1}{9}$$

The numerator and denominator were first divided by 5 and then by 4, but these two divisions can be done at the same time.

The alternative is:

$$\frac{5}{12}\div\frac{15}{4}=\frac{5}{12}\times\frac{4}{15}=\frac{20}{180}$$

which then has to be simplified.

The same applies to multiplying and dividing algebraic fractions.

> **NOTE:**
> In all work with algebraic fractions, if the denominator of the simplified answer is factorised it is better to leave it that way.
> For example, $\dfrac{x}{(x+1)(x+2)}$
> is preferable to $\dfrac{x}{x^2+3x+2}$.

Example 10

a Calculate

  i $\dfrac{3}{8}\times\dfrac{4}{9}$

  ii $\dfrac{3}{8}\div\dfrac{1}{6}$

b Simplify

  i $\dfrac{x}{y+1}\times\dfrac{y}{x+1}$

  ii $\dfrac{x}{y+1}\div\dfrac{x^2}{(y+1)^2}$

  iii $\dfrac{x^2+2x-3}{x}\div\dfrac{x+3}{x-1}$

Answer 10

  a **i** $\dfrac{3}{8}\times\dfrac{4}{9}=\dfrac{3\times4}{8\times9}=\dfrac{1\times1}{2\times3}=\dfrac{1}{6}$ **ii** $\dfrac{3}{8}\div\dfrac{1}{6}=\dfrac{3}{8}\times\dfrac{6}{1}=\dfrac{3\times6}{8\times1}=\dfrac{3\times3}{4}=\dfrac{9}{4}$

  b **i** $\dfrac{x}{y+1}\times\dfrac{y}{x+1}$

       $=\dfrac{x}{(y+1)}\times\dfrac{y}{(x+1)}$

       $=\dfrac{xy}{(y+1)(x+1)}$

> **NOTE:**
> In this case no further simplification is possible.

NOTE:
Divide top and bottom by $(y+1)$ and x.

ii $\dfrac{x}{y+1} \div \dfrac{x^2}{(y+1)^2} = \dfrac{x}{(y+1)} \div \dfrac{x^2}{(y+1)^2}$

$= \dfrac{x}{(y+1)} \times \dfrac{(y+1)^2}{x^2}$

$= \dfrac{y+1}{x}$

NOTE:
Divide top and bottom by $(x+3)$.

iii $\dfrac{x^2+2x-3}{x} \div \dfrac{x+3}{x-1} = \dfrac{(x^2+2x-3)}{x} \div \dfrac{(x+3)}{(x-1)}$

$= \dfrac{(x+3)(x-1)}{x} \times \dfrac{(x-1)}{(x+3)}$

$= \dfrac{(x-1)^2}{x}$

Exercise 14.9

Without using a calculator, work out:

1 $\dfrac{4}{9} \times \dfrac{2}{3}$ **2** $\dfrac{4}{9} \div \dfrac{2}{3}$

Simplify

3 $\dfrac{1}{xy} \times \dfrac{x^2y^2}{x^2+y^2}$ **4** $\dfrac{x}{x-1} \times \dfrac{x-1}{xy}$ **5** $\dfrac{x}{x-1} \div \dfrac{x+1}{xy}$

6 $\dfrac{x-y}{x^2+y^2} \times \dfrac{x-y}{x^2-y^2}$ **7** $\dfrac{xyz}{x^2+y^2} \times \dfrac{x-y}{x^2-y^2}$ **8** $\dfrac{x^2+2x+1}{x} \times \dfrac{1}{(x+1)^2}$

Adding and Subtracting Algebraic Fractions

As with numerical fractions, the common denominator has to be found first. Also, finding the lowest common denominator saves time, as it avoids extra cancelling at the end.

$$\dfrac{2}{3} + \dfrac{3}{4} = \dfrac{2 \times 4}{3 \times 4} + \dfrac{3 \times 3}{4 \times 3} = \dfrac{8}{12} + \dfrac{9}{12} = \dfrac{17}{12}$$

Remember:

• You *cannot* cancel across the addition sign.

If, as in the last case, the lowest common denominator is merely the product of the two denominators, you might find that a mental picture helps you to work more quickly, as in Figure 14.1.

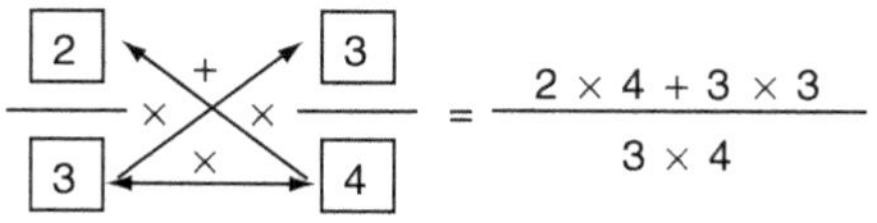

Figure 14.1 Adding and subtracting fractions

Example 11

a Calculate $\frac{2}{5} + \frac{3}{8}$

> **NOTE:**
> The common denominator is 40, so multiply the first fraction top and bottom by 8 and the second one by 5.

b Write as a single fraction in its simplest form

i $\frac{3}{x} - \frac{x}{y}$

> **NOTE:**
> The common denominator is xy.

ii $\frac{3}{x-1} - \frac{4}{2x+1}$

> **NOTE:**
> The common denominator is $(x-1)(2x+1)$. Start by putting brackets round both denominators, then multiply the first fraction top and bottom by $(2x+1)$ and the second by $(x-1)$. Beware of the minus sign.

iii $\frac{2x-1}{x-1} + \frac{x+1}{2x+1}$

iv $\frac{3}{xy} - \frac{x}{y}$

> **NOTE:**
> The common denominator is xy, so you only have to multiply the second fraction top and bottom by x.

v $\frac{1}{x(x-1)} - \frac{1}{(x-1)(x-2)}$

> **NOTE:**
> The common denominator is $x(x-1)(x-2)$, so multiply the first fraction top and bottom by $(x-2)$ and the second by x.

vi $\frac{1}{x-1} - \frac{1}{x^2-1}$

> **NOTE:**
> Factorise the second denominator first to find the lowest common denominator.

Answer 11

a $\frac{2}{5} + \frac{3}{8} = \frac{2 \times 8}{5 \times 8} + \frac{3 \times 5}{8 \times 5} = \frac{16}{40} + \frac{15}{40} = \frac{31}{40}$

b **i** $\frac{3}{x} - \frac{x}{y} = \frac{3y}{xy} - \frac{x^2}{xy}$

$= \frac{3y - x^2}{xy}$

NOTE:
Here you can see the importance of the brackets, because in this case the last term in the numerator is the product of two negative numbers.

ii $\frac{3}{x-1} - \frac{4}{2x+1} = \frac{3}{(x-1)} - \frac{4}{(2x+1)}$

$= \frac{3(2x+1)}{(x-1)(2x+1)} - \frac{4(x-1)}{(2x+1)(x-1)}$

$= \frac{3(2x+1) - 4(x-1)}{(x-1)(2x+1)}$

$= \frac{6x + 3 - 4x + 4}{(x-1)(2x+1)}$

$= \frac{2x + 7}{(x-1)(2x+1)}$

iii $\frac{2x-1}{x-1} + \frac{x+1}{2x+1} = \frac{(2x-1)}{x-1} + \frac{(x+1)}{(2x+1)}$

$= \frac{(2x-1)(2x+1)}{(x-1)(2x+1)} + \frac{(x-1)(x+1)}{(x-1)(2x+1)} = \frac{(4x^2 - 1) + (x^2 - 1)}{(x-1)(2x+1)}$

$= \frac{5x^2 - 2}{(x-1)(2x+1)}$

NOTE:
It is usual to leave the denominator in factorised form unless the question says otherwise.

iv $\frac{3}{xy} - \frac{x}{y} = \frac{3}{xy} - \frac{x^2}{xy} = \frac{3 - x^2}{xy}$

v $\frac{1}{x(x-1)} - \frac{1}{(x-1)(x-2)} = \frac{(x-2)}{x(x-1)(x-2)} - \frac{x}{x(x-1)(x-2)}$

$= \frac{x - 2 - x}{x(x-1)(x-2)} = -\frac{2}{x(x-1)(x-2)}$

vi $\frac{1}{x-1} - \frac{1}{x^2-1} = \frac{1}{(x-1)} - \frac{1}{(x-1)(x+1)}$

$= \frac{(x+1)}{(x-1)(x+1)} - \frac{1}{(x-1)(x+1)}$

$= \frac{x + 1 - 1}{(x-1)(x+1)}$

$= \frac{x}{(x-1)(x+1)}$

Exercise 14.10

Write in the simplest form

1 $\frac{2}{3} + \frac{3}{5}$

2 $1 + \frac{1}{x}$

3 $\frac{x}{3} + \frac{x}{4}$

4 $\frac{x}{y} - \frac{y}{x}$

5 $\frac{1}{a-b} + \frac{1}{a+b}$

6 $\frac{1}{a-b} - \frac{1}{a+b}$

7 $\frac{3}{x-1} + \frac{3}{x}$

8 $\frac{3}{x-1} - \frac{3}{x}$

9 $\frac{2x-3}{3} + \frac{2-3x}{4}$

10 $\frac{2x-3}{3} - \frac{2-3x}{4}$

11 $\frac{4}{x+y} + \frac{3}{x+2y}$

12 $\frac{x}{x-y} - \frac{y}{x+y}$

13 $\frac{x}{x-y} + \frac{y}{x+y}$

14 $\frac{a+b}{a-b} + \frac{a-b}{a+b}$

15 $\frac{a+b}{a-b} - \frac{a-b}{a+b}$

16 $\frac{x}{2x-y} - \frac{2x-y}{x+y}$

17 $\frac{2x-1}{xy} + \frac{x-2}{y}$

18 $\frac{1}{x(x-1)} + \frac{1}{x^2-1}$

Exercise 14.11

Mixed exercise

1 Without using a calculator, simplify:

a $\frac{15}{27} \times \frac{9}{15}$

b $\dfrac{\frac{1}{2} + \frac{1}{6}}{\frac{3}{4} - \frac{5}{12}}$

c $(27)^{-\frac{4}{3}}$

d $\left(36^{-2}\right)^{\frac{1}{4}}$ **e** $8^2 + 8^0$ **f** $\dfrac{1}{64^{-\frac{2}{3}}}$

g $\left(\dfrac{6}{7}\right)^{-1}$ **h** $\dfrac{6^{-1}}{7}$ **i** $\dfrac{6}{7^{-1}}$

2 Simplify:

a $\left(x^0 y^3\right)^{-\frac{2}{3}}$ **b** $y^{\frac{1}{2}} \div y^{\frac{5}{6}}$ **c** $\dfrac{(2x^2)^2}{(x^{\frac{1}{2}})^2}$

d $3a^{\frac{3}{2}} \times 4b^{\frac{1}{3}} \times (4b)^{\frac{1}{2}} \times (ab)^2$ **f** $\left(\dfrac{x^2}{y^{-3}}\right)^{-1} \times \dfrac{x^{\frac{5}{2}}}{y^{-1}}$

3 Expand the brackets and simplify:
  a $(3x + 7)(2x - 7)$ **b** $(x - 1)^2$ **c** $(x^2 - y^2)^2$
  d $(xy + 1)(xy - 1)$ **e** $(x + a)(y + b)$ **f** $(3a - 5b)(2c + 3d)$

4 Factorise completely:
  a $3x^2 + x - 2$ **b** $x^2 - 5x - 50$ **c** $2x^2 - 21x + 49$
  d $50x^2 - 18$ **e** $x^3y - xy$ **f** $6x^2 - 15x - 36$
  g $2ac + ad + 2bc + bd$ **h** $2ac - 2bc + bd - ad$ **i** $8a^3b - 18ab^3$

5 Simplify:

a $\dfrac{ax}{a^2x^2 - ax}$ **b** $\dfrac{x^2 - 1}{x^2 + 5x - 6}$ **c** $\dfrac{20x}{10x^2}$

d $\dfrac{4xy + 2x^2y}{4xy - 2x^2y}$ **e** $\dfrac{2x^2y}{5x} \times \dfrac{15xy^2}{4y^3}$ **f** $\dfrac{\frac{1}{x} + \frac{x}{y}}{1 + \frac{x}{y}}$

6 Simplify:

a $\dfrac{a}{a+b} + \dfrac{a}{a-b}$ **b** $\dfrac{x+1}{x-1} - \dfrac{x-1}{x+1}$ **c** $\dfrac{x+1}{x-1} \div \dfrac{x-1}{x+1}$ **d** $\dfrac{x+1}{x-1} \times \dfrac{x-1}{x+1}$

7 Write as a single fraction in its lowest terms:

a $\dfrac{c}{c-d} - \dfrac{1}{c^2 - d^2}$ **b** $\dfrac{c}{c-d} + \dfrac{1}{c^2 - d^2}$

Exam-style questions Part 1

8 Work out the value of $\dfrac{-\frac{1}{2} - \frac{3}{8}}{-\frac{1}{2} + \frac{3}{8}}$. (0580 paper 02 Q7 June 2004)

9 a $3^x = \dfrac{1}{3}$. Write down the value of x.
  b $5^y = k$. Find 5^{y+1} in terms of k. (0580 paper 02 Q8 November 2003)

10 a Factorise fully $10x^2y + 15xy^2$.
  b Factorise $25a^2 - b^2$.
  c Simplify $\dfrac{3}{(x+1)^2} - \dfrac{2}{x+1}$.

  d Simplify $\dfrac{3a^2}{10bc} \div \dfrac{9a}{5b^2c}$. (4024 paper 11 Q25 June 2013)

11 Work out as a single fraction
  $\dfrac{2}{x-3} - \dfrac{1}{x+4}$. (0580 paper 02 Q10 June 2003)

12 a Factorise $(a - 2b) - 3c(a - 2b)$
  b Simplify $5t(t + 3) - 3(5t - 2)$ (4024 paper 01 Q22a and b November 2004)

13 Express as a single fraction in its simplest form: $\dfrac{2}{x-3} - \dfrac{1}{x+2}$. (4024 paper 01 Q8 June 2004)

14 Find a, b and c when

   a $3^a \div 3^5 = 27$ **b** $125^b = 5$ **c** $10^c = 0.001$.

                             (4024 paper 01 Q12 November 2003)

15 a It is given that $5^{-2} \times 5^k = 1$.   **b** It is given that $\sqrt[3]{7} = 7^m$.

      Write down the value of k.   Write down the value of m.

                               (4024 paper 01 Q7 June 2003)

16 a Expand and simplify $(x-1)(x^2+x+1)$.

   b Factorise $ax - bx - 3ay + 3by$.   (4024 paper 01 Q20 June 2003)

17 Simplify

   $\dfrac{x+2}{x} - \dfrac{x}{x+2}$.

   Write your answer as a fraction in its simplest form.   (0580 paper 02 Q16 June 2005)

18 Simplify

   a $\left(\dfrac{x^{27}}{27}\right)^{\frac{2}{3}}$,   **b** $\left(\dfrac{x^{-2}}{4}\right)^{-\frac{1}{2}}$ (0580 paper 02 Q18 November 2005)

19 Factorise

   a $4x^2 - 9$ **b** $4x^2 - 9x$ **c** $4x^2 - 9x + 2$. (0580 paper 02 Q19 June 2006)

20 Factorise

   a $2x^2 - 7x - 15$ **b** $2yt - 8ys - zt + 4zs$.   (4024 paper 01 Q21 June 2007)

21 a Simplify

     i $x(3x+2) - (2x+4)$ **ii** $\dfrac{ax^2 - x^2}{ax - x}$

   b Factorise completely $7x^2 - 63$.   (4024 paper 01 Q23 June 2006)

22 Write as a fraction in its simplest form $\dfrac{x-3}{4} + \dfrac{4}{x-3}$.   (0580 paper 02 Q10 June 2007)

23 a $\sqrt{32} = 2^P$. Find the value of p.

   b $\sqrt[3]{\dfrac{1}{8}} = 2^q$. Find the value of q.   (0580 paper 02 Q17 June 2007)

24 Simplify $\dfrac{x}{3} + \dfrac{5x}{9} - \dfrac{5x}{18}$.   (0580 paper 21 Q2 June 2008)

25 Simplify $(27x^3)^{\frac{2}{3}}$.   (0580 paper 21 Q8 June 2008)

26 Write as a single fraction in its simplest form

   $\dfrac{4}{2x+3} - \dfrac{2}{x-3}$ (0580 paper 21 Q11 November 2008)

27 Find the value of n in each of the following statements:

   a $32^n = 1$ **b** $32^n = 2$ **c** $32^n = 8$ (0580 paper 02 Q7 November 2006)

28 a Simplify $(27x^6)^{\frac{1}{3}}$.   **b** $(512)^{-\frac{2}{3}} = 2^p$. Find p.   (0580 paper 02 Q21 November 2007)

29 Write as a single fraction in its simplest form.

   $\dfrac{1}{c} + \dfrac{1}{d} - \dfrac{c-d}{cd}$

                           (0580 paper 21 Q10 June 2009)

30 a Remove the brackets and simplify

     i $4(3 - 2p) - 3(1 - p)$

     ii $(3q - r)(q + 2r)$.

   b Factorise completely $18t^2 - 2$.

c Given that $y = 18 + 3x^2$,

  i find the value of y when $x = -2$

  ii find the values of x when $y = 93$

  iii express x in terms of y. (4024 paper 02 Q1 June 2005)

31 a i Factorise completely $5x^2 - 20$.

  ii Simplify $\dfrac{5x^2 - 20}{10x^2 + 10x - 20}$.

  b Express as a single fraction in its simplest form

  $\dfrac{4}{y-3} - \dfrac{3}{y+5}$. (4024 paper 02 Q1a and b November 2006)

32 Factorise completely

  a $15a^2 + 12a^3$ **b** $1 - 16b^2$ **c** $6cx - 3cy - 2dx + dy$.

  (4024 paper 01 Q20 November 2007)

33 Express as a single fraction in its simplest form

  $\dfrac{3}{2t-1} - \dfrac{2}{t+2}$. (4024 paper 01 Q15 June 2008)

34 a Factorise completely

  i $15x^2 + 10x$ **ii** $t^2 - 2t - 15$.

  b Solve $4(x - 0.3) = 3(x - 0.2)$. (4024 paper 01 Q19 June 2008)

Exam-style questions Part 2

DO NOT USE A CALCULATOR IN THE REST OF THIS EXERCISE

35 Evaluate

  a 17^0 **b** $4^{\frac{5}{2}}$ **c** $(0.2)^{-2}$. (4024 paper 01 Q12 June 2007)

36 Evaluate

  a 9^0 **b** 9^{-2} **c** $9^{\frac{3}{2}}$. (4024 paper 01 and Q8 June 2008)

37 a Evaluate $5^2 + 5^0$.

  b Simplify

  i $\left(\dfrac{1}{x}\right)^{-2}$

  ii $(x^6)^{\frac{1}{2}}$ (4024 paper 01 Q13 June 2006)

15 Working with Numbers II

Learning Objectives   Syllabus sections 10, 12

In this chapter you will:
- use upper and lower bounds in calculations
- use reverse percentages.

15.1 Introduction

This is a short chapter, but together with Chapter 4 it covers much of the mathematics you need in everyday life. The mixed exercise at the end of the chapter will give you a good idea of the variety of questions you might meet in your examination.

15.2 Essential Skills   Part 1

1   Calculate (a) the area, and (b) the perimeter of a rectangle measuring 15 metres by 7 centimetres, stating the units in your answer.

2   Round the following to the degree of accuracy stated.
   a   4.6749 to 2 decimal places
   b   500.612 to 3 significant figures
   c   0.0093 to 2 decimal places
   d   0.010 56 to 3 significant figures
   e   516.2 centimetres to the nearest centimetre
   f   99.8 kilograms to the nearest kilogram
   g   9197 to the nearest 10
   h   999 to the nearest hundred.

3   Copy and complete the following to show the limits of accuracy in each case.
   a $\ldots \leqslant 439 < \ldots$ given that 439 is correct to the nearest whole number.
   b $\ldots \leqslant 5670 < \ldots$ given that 5670 is correct to three significant figures.

4   Calculate the volume of a cuboid measuring 100 centimetres by 2 metres by 10 metres, giving your answers in standard form
   a   in mm^3
   b   in cm^3
   c   in m^3.

5   Change
   a $50\,mm^2$ to cm^2
   b   500 ml to litres
   c   12 kilograms to grams.

6   By writing each number correct to 1 significant figure estimate the answers to each of these calculations, giving your answers to 1 significant figure. Do not use a calculator.
   a 659×0.712
   b $\frac{76}{81} \div \frac{218}{389}$
   c $\frac{1112.5}{501.9} + \frac{359}{31.6}$.

7   Calculate, giving your answers in standard form:
   a $(7.5 \times 10^{-5}) \times (1.9 \times 10^2)$
   b $(9.35 \times 10^3) \div (3.76 \times 10^{-9})$
   c $(1.23 \times 10^3) - (1.23 \times 10^2)$
   d $(5.49 \times 10^{-5}) + (5.12 \times 10^{-6})$.

8 Calculate, giving your answers correct to 3 significant figures:

a $\dfrac{5.76 + 7.93}{4.1 + 2.98}$

b $\dfrac{5.76}{4.1} + \dfrac{7.93}{2.98}$

c $\dfrac{5.76 + 7.93}{4.1} + 2.98$

d $\sqrt{\dfrac{5.76}{4.1}} + \sqrt{\dfrac{7.93}{2.98}}$

e $\sqrt{\dfrac{5.76}{4.1} + \dfrac{7.93}{2.98}}$

Part 2   DO NOT USE A CALCULATOR IN THE REST OF THIS EXERCISE

9 Simplify the following ratios.

a $50 : 625$

b 7 centimetres : 28 metres

c $\dfrac{2}{3} : \dfrac{1}{6}$

d $1\dfrac{3}{5} : 2\dfrac{5}{6}$

e $70 : 35 : 350$

f $1.85 : 25$.

10 Write the ratio 900 litres : 180 millilitres in the form

a $1 : n$

b $n : 1$.

15.3 Upper and Lower Bounds in Calculations

You have seen how to find the upper and lower limits or bounds of measurements that have been approximated to a given significant figure, decimal place or other unit. You also need to be able to use these values in calculations, and find the upper and lower bounds of the results of the calculations.

Let us assume that x and y are two measurements that have been given to a stated approximation.

The *largest* possible value of $x + y$ would obviously be obtained by adding the *upper* bounds of the two measurements together. Conversely, the smallest value would come from the two lower bounds.

The *largest* possible value of $x - y$ would come from subtracting the *lower* bound of y from the *upper* bound of x to give the greatest possible difference.

But how would you get the largest possible value of $x \times y$?

Also how would you get the largest possible value of $\dfrac{x}{y}$?

In the following example we are using just numbers, without putting them in any context in order to make the idea clear.

Example 1

Given that $x = 35$ correct to the nearest whole number and that $y = 25$ correct to the nearest whole number, copy and complete the following table.

		Value	Lower bound	Upper bound
a	x	35	34.5	35.5
b	y	25		
c	$x + y$	60		
d	$x - y$	10		
e	$x \times y$	875		
f	$x \div y$	1.4		
g	$2x + 3y$			
h	x^2			

Answer 1

		Value	Lower bound	Upper bound
a	x	35	34.5	35.5
b	y	25	24.5	25.5
c	$x+y$	60	$34.5+24.5=59$	$35.5+25.5=61$
d	$x-y$	10	$34.5-25.5=9.0$	$35.5-24.5=11$
e	$x\times y$	875	$34.5\times24.5=845.2$	$35.5\times25.5=905.25$
f	$x\div y$	1.4	$34.5\div25.5=1.35$ (3 s.f.)	$35.5\div24.5=1.45$ (3 s.f.)
g	$2x+3y$	120	$2\times34.5+3\times24.5=142.5$	$2\times35.5+3\times25.5=147.5$
h	x^2	1225	1190.25	1260.25

Exercise 15.1

1 Given that $x=14$ and $y=12$, both to the nearest whole number, work out (i) the lower bound, and (ii) the upper bound of the following:

    a $x-y$ **b** x^2y^2 **c** xy **d** $\frac{x}{y}$.

2 Given that $a=16.9\,\text{cm}$, $b=7.3\,\text{cm}$ and $c=5.8\,\text{cm}$, all to 1 decimal place, work out (i) the lower bound, and (ii) the upper bound of the following:

    a abc **b** $\frac{ab}{c}$ **c** $\frac{(a+b)}{2}\times c$.

Give your answers correct to 4 significant figures if not exact.

15.4 Reverse Percentages

Calculating a reverse percentage is a method for finding an original value if you have only been given the value *after* a percentage change has been made.

To understand how reverse percentages work we will first look at some simple percentage examples.

A shop offers a 20% reduction in a sale.

An item costing Rs 60 will be reduced by 20% of 60.

Reduction $=\text{Rs}\,(\frac{20}{100}\times60)$ $=\text{Rs }12$

Sale price $=\text{Rs }(60-12)$ $=\text{Rs }48$

There is another, quicker method for calculating the sale price.

The original price is 100%, so taking off 20% leaves 80% to pay in the sale.

Sale price $=80\%$ of Rs 60

$$=\text{Rs}\,(\frac{80}{100}\times60)\qquad=\text{Rs }48$$

So if you want to calculate the *reduction* you use 20%, but if you want to calculate the *new price* you calculate 80%. Either way, the original price is 100%.

Setting this out another way:

original price	−	reduction	=	new price
100%	−	20%	=	80%
$\times 0.6$		$\times 0.6$		$\times 0.6$ $(60\div100=0.6)$
Rs 60	−	Rs 12	=	Rs 48

The same method is used for an increase in price. If a price is increased by 20% then the new amount is $(100 + 20)\% = 120\%$.

$$\text{Rs } 60 \text{ increased by } 20\% = \text{Rs } \left(\tfrac{120}{100} \times 60\right) = \text{Rs } 72$$

As before, if you want to calculate the *increase* use 20%, but if you want to calculate the *new price* use 120%.

Setting this out the other way:

original price   +   increase   =   new price
100%   +   20%   =   120%
$\Big) \times 0.6$ $\Big) \times 0.6$ $\Big) \times 0.6$
Rs 60   +   Rs 12   =   Rs 72

This leads us easily into calculating reverse percentages.

An example should show you how this is done.

Example 2

a An item in a sale costs \$36, after a 10% reduction. Calculate the original price.

b A shop buys its goods at **wholesale** prices, it then adds a 40% **mark-up** (this is the extra they charge in order to make a profit). The **retail price** is the price the shop charges its customers. An item in the shop is marked at \$70. (This is the retail price.) Calculate the price the shop paid for the item. (This is the wholesale price.)

Answer 2

a Original price   −   reduction   =   sale price
100%   −   **10%**   =   90%
$\Big) \times 0.4$ $\Big) \times 0.4$ $\Big) \times 0.4$ $(36 \div 90 = 0.4)$
?   −   \$4   =   **\$36**
Original price $= 100 \times 0.4 = \$40$

b Wholesale price   +   mark up   =   retail price
100%   +   **40%**   =   140%
$\Big) \times 0.5$ $\Big) \times 0.5$ $\Big) \times 0.5$ $(70 \div 140 = 0.5)$
?   +   \$20   =   **\$70**
The wholesale price was $100 \times 0.5 = \$50$.

Exercise 15.2

1 A toy was reduced by 20% in a sale. The sale price was \$72. Calculate the price before the reduction.

2 Niko is given an increase of 6% on his hourly rate. He now earns \$13.25 per hour. Calculate his previous hourly rate.

3 In 2010 a new car costs \$10 063. This is an increase of 16% on its new price in 2009. Calculate the increase in dollars.

4 An item in a sale is reduced by 15%. The actual reduction is Rs 72. Calculate
    a the original price   **b** the sale price.

Exercise 15.3

Mixed exercise

1 A rectangle measures 6.5 cm by 3.5 cm, each measurement correct to 1 decimal place. Calculate the lower bound of
    a the perimeter   **b** the area of the rectangle.
    Give your exact answer.

2   Yash is cutting short pieces of wood from a longer piece. The shorter pieces of wood are 10 cm long, correct to the nearest centimetre, and the whole piece is 1 metre, correct to the nearest centimetre.

   a Show that it may not be possible for him to cut 10 shorter pieces of wood.

   b What is the maximum amount that might be left over?

3   **a** The length (l metres) of a piece of wood is given as 3.50 metres correct to the nearest centimetre.

      Copy and complete the statement below.

      .... $\leqslant l$ metres $<$ ....

   b Using the above statement work out the maximum possible error if instead the length is given as 3.5 metres, correct to the nearest 10 cm.

NOTE:
Depreciation is defined on page 93.

4   In 2015 a car is valued at $8607 when it is 1 year old. The rate of depreciation in the first year is 58%.

   a What did the car cost in 2014 when it was new?

   b Calculate its value in 2017 if the depreciation rate is 20% per annum for these two years. Give your answers to the nearest dollar.

5   **a** A shop has a mark-up of 46% on an item selling at €49.64. Calculate the wholesale price.

   b The shop has a sale. An item is marked at €160 after a reduction of 20%. Calculate the amount saved if the item is purchased at the sale price rather than the normal price.

Exam-style questions

6   The population of Newtown is 45 000.

   The population of Villeneuve is 39 000.

   a Calculate the ratio of these populations in its simplest form.

   b In Newtown, 28% of the population are below the age of twenty.

      Calculate how many people in Newtown are below the age of twenty.

   c In Villeneuve, 16 000 people are below the age of twenty.

      Calculate the percentage of people in Villeneuve below the age of twenty.

   d The population of Newtown is 125% greater than it was fifty years ago.

      Calculate the population of Newtown fifty years ago.

   e The two towns are combined and made into one city called Monocity.

      In Monocity the ratio of men : women : children is 12 : 13 : 5.

      Calculate the number of children in Monocity.   *(0580 paper 04 Q1 November 2004)*

7   A square has sides of length d metres.

   This length is 120 metres, correct to the nearest 10 metres.

   a Copy and complete this statement.

      .... $\leqslant d <$ ....

   b Calculate the difference between the largest and the smallest possible areas of the square.   *(0580 paper 02 Q13 November 2004)*

8 A train left Sydney at 2320 on December 18th and arrived in Brisbane at 0204 on December 19th.
How long, in hours and minutes, was the journey? (0580 paper 02 Q1 June 2004)

9 A rectangle has sides of length 6.1 cm and 8.1 cm correct to 1 decimal place.
Calculate the upper bound for the area of the rectangle as accurately
as possible. (0580 paper 21 Q7 November 2008)

10

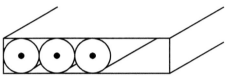

Pencils are packed in a box.
Each pencil has a diameter of 7 mm, correct to the nearest millimetre.
a Write down the lower bound of the diameter of a pencil.
b Find the smallest width of a box that can **always** hold 8 pencils side by side.
Give your answer in centimetres. (4024 paper 11 Q9 June 2010)

11 The ratios of teachers : male students : female students in a school are 2 : 17 : 18.
The total number of **students** is 665. Find the number
of **teachers**. (0580 paper 02 Q5 June 2003)

12 A holiday in Europe was advertised at a cost of €245.
The exchange rate was $1 = €1.06.
Calculate the cost of the holiday in dollars, giving your answer correct
to the nearest cent. (0580 paper 21 Q5 June 2008)

13 Write the number 1045.2781 correct to
a 2 decimal places
b 2 significant figures. (0580 paper 21 Q7 June 2008)

14 Marcus receives $800 from his grandmother.
a He decides to spend $150 and to divide the remaining $650 in the
ratio savings : holiday = 9 : 4.
Calculate the amount of his savings.
b **i** He uses 80% of the $150 to buy some clothes.
Calculate the cost of the clothes.
ii The money remaining from the $150 is $37\frac{1}{2}$% of the cost of a day trip to Cairo.
Calculate the cost of the trip. (0580 paper 04 Q1a and b June 2009)

15 A student played a computer game 500 times and won 370 of these games.
He then won the next x games and lost none.
He has now won 75% of the games he has played.
Find the value of x. (0580 paper 21 Q17 June 2008)

16 In January Sunanda changed £25 000 into dollars when the exchange rate was $1.96 = £1.
In June she changed the dollars back into pounds when the exchange rate was $1.75 = £1.
Calculate the profit she made, giving your
answer in pounds (£). (0580 paper 21 Q11 June 2009)

17 In 2005, there were 9 million bicycles in Beijing, correct to the nearest million.
The average distance travelled by each bicycle in one day was 6.5 km correct to 1 decimal
place.
Work out the upper bound for the **total** distance travelled by
all the bicycles in one day. (0580 paper 21 Q6 June 2009)

18 A rectangle has sides of length 6.1 cm and 8.1 cm correct to 1 decimal place.
Calculate the upper bound for the area of the rectangle as
accurately as possible.   (0580 paper 21 Q7 November 2008)

19 Beatrice has an income of $40 000 in one year.

  a She pays
    no tax on the first $10 000 of her income;
    10% tax on the next $10 000 of her income;
    25% tax on the rest of her income.
    Calculate
    i the total amount of tax Beatrice pays,
    ii the total amount of tax as a percentage of the $40 000.
  b Beatrice pays a yearly rent of $10 800.
    After she has paid her tax, rent and bills, she has $12 000.
    Calculate how much Beatrice spends on bills.
  c Beatrice divides the $12 000 between shopping and saving in the ratio shopping :
    saving = 5 : 3.
    i Calculate how much Beatrice spends on shopping in one year.
    ii What fraction of the original $40 000 does Beatrice **save**?
    Give your answer in its lowest terms.
  d The rent of $10 800 is an increase of 25% on her previous rent.
    Calculate her previous rent.   (0580 paper 04 Q1 November 2008)

20 At 0506 Mr Ho bought 850 fish at a fish market for $2.62 each.
95 minutes later he sold them all to a supermarket for $2.86 each.

  a What was the time when he sold the fish?
  b Calculate his total profit.   (0580 paper 21 Q3 June 2009)

21 Vreni took part in a charity walk.
She walked a distance of 20 kilometres.

  a She raised money at a rate of $12.50 for each kilometre.
    i How much money did she raise by walking the 20 kilometre?
    ii The money she raised in part (a) (i) was $\frac{5}{52}$ of the total money raised. Work out the
    total money raised.
    iii In the previous year the total money raised was $2450.
    Calculate the percentage increase on the previous year's total.
  b Part of the 20 kilometres was on a road and the rest was on a footpath.
    The ratio road distance : footpath distance was 3 : 2.
    i Work out the road distance.
    ii Vreni walked along the road at 3 km/h and along the footpath at 2.5 km/h. How
    long, in hours and minutes, did Vreni take to walk the 20 kilometres?
    iii Work out Vreni's average speed.
    iv Vreni started at 0855. At what time did she finish?
  c On a map, the distance of 20 kilometres was represented by a length of 80 centimetres.
    The scale of the map was 1 : n.
    Calculate the value of n.   (0580 paper 04 Q1 June 2008)

22 Angharad sleeps for 8 hours each night, correct to the nearest 10 minutes.
The total time she sleeps in the month of November (30 nights) is T hours.
Between what limits does T lie?   (0580 paper 02 Q4 November 2006)

23 $p = \dfrac{0.002751 \times 3400}{(9.8923 + 24.7777)^2}$

    a Write each number in this calculation correct to 1 significant figure.

    b Use your answer to part (a) to **estimate** the value of p.

(0580 paper 02 Q6 November 2007)

24 **a** In October the cost of a car in euros was €20 000.
      The cost of this car in pounds was £14 020.
      Calculate the **exact** value of the exchange rate in October, writing your answer in the form €1 = £….

    b In November the car still cost €20 000 and the exchange rate was €1 = £0.6915.
      Calculate the difference, in pounds, between the cost in October and November.

(0580 paper 02 Q8 November 2007)

25 Carmen spends 5 minutes, correct to the nearest minute, preparing one meal.
    She spends a total time of T minutes preparing 30 meals. Between what limits does T lie?

(0580 paper 02 Q6 June 2007)

26 The cost of a chair $\$x$, is $70 correct to the nearest $10.
    The cost of a desk, $\$y$, is $900 correct to the nearest $50.

    a Complete the table.

    b Find the lower bound of the total cost of a desk and 4 chairs.

	Lower bound	Upper bound
x		
y		

(4024 paper 01 Q14 November 2004)

27 **a** The population of a city is given as 280 000, correct to the nearest ten thousand.
      State the greatest possible error in the given value.

    b The dimensions of a rectangular card are 7 cm by 4 cm, correct to the nearest centimetre.
      Calculate the smallest possible perimeter of the card.   (4024 paper 01 Q6 June 2005)

28 **a** Two varieties of tea, 'High Blend' and 'Normal Blend', are made by mixing Grade A leaves and Grade B leaves.

      i In High Blend, the ratio of the masses of Grade A leaves to Grade B leaves is 3 : 2.
         Find the mass of Grade A leaves used in making 250 g of High Blend.

      ii 1 kg of Normal Blend is made by using 450 g of Grade A leaves.
         Find, **in its simplest form**, the ratio of the masses of Grade A to Grade B leaves in Normal Blend.
         Give your answer in the form $m : n$, where m and n are integers.

      iii 250 g of High Blend is mixed with 1 kg of Normal Blend.
         Calculate the percentage of the mass of this mixture that consists of Grade A leaves.

    b During a sale, a shop sold packets of tea for 20% less than the price shown on their labels. Elizabeth and Peter each bought a packet of tea in the sale.

      i Elizabeth's packet had a label price of $4.50.
         How much did she pay?

      ii Peter paid $6.20 for his packet.
         Calculate the price shown on its label.   (4024 paper 02 Q2 June 2005)

29 a A rectangular table top is 100 cm long and 75 cm wide.
Both lengths are correct to the nearest 5 cm.
Find the least possible perimeter of the table.

b The area of a rectangular room is 22 m², correct to the nearest square metre.
The width is 3 m, correct to the nearest metre.
Find the greatest possible length of the room. (4024 paper 01 Q17 November 2005)

30 James and Dan are partners in a small company.
From each year's profit, James is paid a bonus of $15 000 and the remainder is shared
between James and Dan in the ratio 2 : 3.

a In 1996 the profit was $20 000.
Show that Dan's share was $3000.

b In 1997 the profit was $21 800.
Calculate
i the percentage increase in the profit in 1997 compared to 1996,
ii the total amount, including his bonus, that James received in 1997.

c In 1998 Dan received $7500.
Calculate the profit in 1998.

d In 1999, the profit was $$x$, where $x > 15 000$.
i Write down an expression, in terms of x, for the amount Dan received.
ii Given that Dan received half the profit, write down an equation in x and hence find
the amount that Dan received. (4024 paper 02 Q7 June 2006)

31 Do not use a calculator in this question.

a Write the following numbers in order of size, starting with the **smallest**.

$$0.7, \quad 0.7^2, \quad \frac{7}{11}, \quad \frac{7}{9}$$

b In a school election, John received 220 votes.
This was 55% of the total number of votes.
Find the total number of votes. (4024 paper 01 Q5 November 2006)

32 a One day the rate of exchange between pounds (£) and United States dollars ($) was
£1 = $1.65.
On the same day, the rate of exchange between pounds (£) and euros was £1 = 1.44
euros.
i Alan changed £500 into dollars.
Calculate how many dollars he received.
ii Brenda changed 900 euros into pounds.
Calculate how many pounds she received.
iii Clare changed $792 into euros.
Calculate how many euros she received.

b The cost of manufacturing a television was $15 000.
i It was sold to a wholesaler at a profit of 8% of the cost.
Calculate the price the wholesaler paid for the television.
ii The wholesaler sold the television to a shop at a profit of 8% of the price he paid for
it. The shop then sold the television to John at a profit of 8% of the price it paid.
Calculate how much the television cost John.
iii Calculate the percentage increase in the cost of the television from its manufacture
till John owns it.

c The shop sold a home entertainment system to Leslie for $46 480. The shop made a
profit of 12% on the price it paid for the system.
Calculate how much the shop paid for the system. (4024 paper 02 Q5 November 2006)

33 Do not use a calculator in this question.

The mass of a marble is given as 5.4 grams, correct to the nearest tenth of a gram.

The mass of a box is given as 85 grams, correct to the nearest 5 grams.

a Complete the table.

b Find the lower bound for the total mass of the box and 20 identical marbles.

	Lower bound	**Upper bound**
Mass of 1 marble	_____ g	_____ g
Mass of the box	_____ g	_____ g

(4024 paper 01 Q11 June 2007)

34 a Anne's digital camera stores its images on a memory card.

The memory card has 128 units of storage space.

When 50 images were stored, there were 40 units of **unused** storage space on the memory card.

  i Calculate the percentage of unused storage space on the memory card.

  ii Calculate the average amount of storage space used by each image.

b Shop A charged 60 cents for each photograph.

Shop B charged 63 cents for each photograph and gave a discount of $1 on all purchases more than $10.

  i Anne bought 24 photographs from Shop A and paid with a $20 note.

  Calculate the change she received.

  ii Find how much cheaper it was to buy 24 photographs from Shop B than from Shop A.

  iii Find the smallest number of photographs for which it was cheaper to use Shop B. (4024 paper 02 Q2 June 2008)

35 a During a 20 week period in 2007, a bank made a profit of $378 million.

  i Calculate the average profit it made each second.

  ii During the same 20 week period in 2008, the profit was $945 million.

  For this 20 week period, calculate the percentage increase in the profit from 2007 to 2008.

  iii Find the ratio of $378 million to $945 million.

  Give your answer in the form $m : n$, where m and n are the smallest possible integers.

b Mary changed 480 euros into dollars.

The exchange rate was $1 = 0.6 euros.

The bank took, as commission, 2% of the amount that had been changed.

Calculate the number of **dollars** the bank took as commission. (4024 paper 02 Q2 June 2009)

36 a 100 g of spaghetti contains 3.6 g of fibre.

Express mass of fibre : mass of spaghetti as the ratio of two integers in its simplest form.

b A tin contains 210 g of beans.

  i 100 g of beans contains 4.5 g of protein.

  Calculate the mass of protein in the tin.

  ii 100 g of beans contains 0.3 g of fat.

   a What percentage of the beans is fat?

   b The recommended daily amount of fat is 70 g.

  Calculate what percentage of the recommended daily amount is in the tin.

    iii The mass of salt in 100 g of beans is 1.0 g, correct to 1 decimal place.

       Calculate an upper bound for the mass of salt contained in the tin.

c A tin of soup contains 166 calories.

  This is 8.3% of the recommended daily number of calories.

  Calculate the recommended daily number of calories.

(4024 paper 02 Q6 November 2009)

Learning Objectives

In this chapter you will:
- solve quadratic equations by factorising, using a formula and completing the square
- work with more sequences

- solve more simultaneous equations
- simplify inequalities
- learn about variation
- rearrange more complex formulae.

16.1 Introduction

In this chapter we start to develop algebra as a tool for solving problems. We will work more with techniques you have already learned and introduce some new ones.

16.2 Essential Skills

1 Rearrange the formulae to make x the subject.

a $s = \dfrac{x}{h}$

b $A = lx$

c $V = xy + c$

d $v^2 = u^2 - 2ax$

e $A = \frac{1}{2}(a+b)x$

f $c = \dfrac{b}{x}$

2 Find the nth term in the following sequences.

a $2, 7, 12, 17, \ldots$

b $-10, -5, 0, 5, \ldots$

c $2, 5, 10, 17, 26, \ldots$

d $10, 8, 6, 4, 2, \ldots$

e $1, 4, 9, 16, 25, \ldots$

3 Use each of the following formulae to find (i) the first term, and (ii) the 100th term in the sequence.

a $n\text{th term} = \dfrac{(n+2)^2}{2}$

b $n\text{th term} = n^2 - 10n$

c $n\text{th term} = -8n - 1$

4 Solve these pairs of simultaneous equations:

a $x + y = 7$
$x + 2y = 3$

b $2x - y = 1$
$y + x = 5$

c $3x + y = 2$
$x + 2y = 4$

d $2x - y = 6$
$2y - x = 3$

16.3 More Equations

You will be expected to solve more difficult equations, putting into practice the techniques you have already learned in Chapter 5 and in Chapter 14.

Example 1
Solve the following equations.

a $\dfrac{x+2}{3} - \dfrac{x-1}{4} = \dfrac{3}{2}$

b $1.3x + 2.5 = 4x$

Answer 1

a $\dfrac{x+2}{3} - \dfrac{x-1}{4} = \dfrac{3}{2}$

$12 \times \left(\dfrac{x+2}{3} - \dfrac{x-1}{4} = \dfrac{3}{2} \right)$

$4(x-2) - 3(x-1) = 6 \times 3$

$4x + 8 - 3x + 3 = 18$

$x = 18 - 11$

$x = 7$

In the first fraction $12 \div 3 = 4$, and so on.

Be careful with the minus sign in front of the second bracket!!

b $1.3x + 2.5 = 4x$

$13x + 25 = 40x$

$13x - 40x = -25$

$-27x = -25$

$x = \dfrac{-25}{-27}$

$x = \dfrac{25}{27}$

> **NOTE:**
> Remember that you can do the same thing to both sides of an equation, so to get rid of the fractions multiply the whole equation by the lowest common multiple of 3, 4 and 2. This is called the *lowest common denominator*.
> Now multiply each term by 12, and 3, 4 and 2 will all divide into the twelve, removing the denominators of each fraction.

> **NOTE:**
> This time the equation would look more friendly multiplied by 10.

Exercise 16.1

Solve the following equations

1 $2.5x - 1.5 = 6$

2 $\dfrac{x}{2} + \dfrac{x}{3} = 5$

3 $\dfrac{x}{2} - \dfrac{x}{3} = \dfrac{7}{3}$

4 $\dfrac{x+1}{5} - \dfrac{x-1}{2} = \dfrac{1}{10}$

5 $\dfrac{1}{4}(x-1) - \dfrac{3}{8}(x+1) = 2$

6 $\dfrac{1}{x} - \dfrac{3}{8x} = 1$

7 $\dfrac{x}{x+1} + 1 = 10$

8 $x(x+2) + 2 = x^2$

> **NOTE:**
> In question **6** multiply all through by $8x$.

> **NOTE:**
> In question **7** multiply all through by $(x+1)$.

> **NOTE:**
> In question **8** multiply out the brackets then subtract x^2 from both sides.

16.4 Quadratic Equations

Quadratic equations have an x squared term, and also possibly an x term and a number term. For example, $y = x^2 + 2x - 3$ is a quadratic equation. It has two variables, x and y. There are an infinite number of solutions to this equation.

Two possible solutions are $x = 0$, $y = -3$ or $x = 2.6$, $y = 8.96$, because both these sets of values 'satisfy' the equation. 'Satisfy' in this case means 'make the equation true'.

Later in the course you will plot equations like this on an $x - y$ graph, and by joining up the points you plot will be able to see where all the solutions lie, and the shape of curves produced by quadratic equations.

For the moment we will be finding solutions algebraically.

Of particular interest are those quadratic equations where $y = 0$.

For example, $x^2 + 2x - 3 = 0$.

This is an equation in a single variable, x, and we may be able to find values of x which satisfy it.

What happens when we replace x by 1?

$$x^2 + 2x - 3$$
$$= 1^2 + 2 \times 1 - 3$$
$$= 0$$

so $x = 1$ is a solution to this equation.

There is another solution ($x = -3$) and we could try different values for x until we find it, but this could take some time, and would be impossible in many cases, so we must learn the algebraic methods.

Solving Quadratic Equations by Factorising

Look at the equation $2x^2 + 5x + 2 = 0$.

The left-hand side of the equation can be factorised to give:

$$(2x + 1)(x + 2) = 0$$

The left-hand side of the equation is now written as two brackets multiplied together. If the x in this equation is replaced by a number, for example 3, the equation would become:

$$(2 \times 3 + 1)(3 + 2) = 0$$
$$7 \times 5 = 0$$
$$35 = 0$$

This is clearly nonsense since 35 is not equal to zero!

The only way that two different numbers or terms can be multiplied to give zero is if one of them is already zero. So either $(2x + 1) = 0$ or $(x + 2) = 0$, which gives us two possible answers to the quadratic equation.

Setting out the answer to a question asking you to solve a quadratic equation:

$$2x^2 + 5x + 2 = 0$$
$$(2x + 1)(x + 2) = 0$$

either

$$2x + 1 = 0 \quad \text{or} \quad x + 2 = 0$$
$$x = -\frac{1}{2} \qquad \qquad x = -2$$

The two solutions are $x = \frac{1}{2}$ or $x = -2$.

Finally, to test that this has worked correctly we can substitute each solution into the original equation:

when
$$x = -\frac{1}{2}$$
$$2x^2 + 5x + 2$$
$$= 2 \times \left(-\frac{1}{2}\right)^2 + 5 \times \left(-\frac{1}{2}\right) + 2$$
$$= \frac{1}{2} - \frac{5}{2} + 2$$
$$= 0$$

So $x = -\frac{1}{2}$ is a solution to the quadratic equation $2x^2 + 5x + 2 = 0$.

You should check for yourself that the other solution is also correct.

Warning! This method *only* works for two terms multiplied together to give *zero*.

It cannot be used unless one side is zero because the method depends on the special fact that the only way two (or more) different numbers can be multiplied together to give zero is if one of them is zero. This of course does not apply to two numbers multiplied together to give, for example, 2.

Example 2
Solve the quadratic equations

a $x^2 + 2x - 3 = 0$ **b** $3x^2 - 11x + 8 = 0$

Answer 2

a $x^2 + 2x - 3 = 0$

$(x + 3)(x - 1) = 0$

either $x + 3 = 0$ or $x - 1 = 0$

$\qquad\qquad x = -3 \qquad\qquad x = 1$

b $3x^2 - 11x + 8 = 0$

$(3x - 8)(x - 1) = 0$

either $3x - 8 = 0$ or $x - 1 = 0$

$\qquad\qquad 3x = 8 \qquad\qquad x = 1$

$\qquad\qquad x = \frac{8}{3}$ or $\qquad x = 1$

Exercise 16.2

Solve the following equations

1 $x^2 + 5x + 6 = 0$ **2** $x^2 + x - 2 = 0$ **3** $x^2 - 6x + 5 = 0$

4 $2x^2 - x - 1 = 0$ **5** $x^2 - 1 = 0$ **6** $2x^2 - 7x + 5 = 0$

7 $3x^2 - x - 4 = 0$ **8** $4x^2 - 8x + 3 = 0$ **9** $4x^2 - 9 = 0$

10 $x^2 - 8x + 15 = 0$ **11** $4x^2 - 16 = 0$ **12** $x^2 + 2x + 1 = 0$

13 $3x^2 - 6x + 3 = 0$ **14** $6x^2 - 22x + 16 = 0$

NOTE:

Question 5: Remember how to factorise a difference of squares?

Question 11: Divide the equation by 4 first, remembering that $\frac{0}{4} = 0$.

Question 12: The two solutions to this equation are the same.

Question 13: Remember to check for common factors first!

Using the Quadratic Formula to Solve Quadratic Equations

Some quadratic equations may not factorise easily, because their solutions are not whole numbers or simple fractions.

For these we may use a formula, often called the **quadratic formula**. We will derive a simplified form of it in the next section, but for the moment we will get used to using it. The formula refers to the general equation:

$$ax^2 + bx + c = 0$$

and states that:

$$x = \frac{-b \pm \sqrt{b^2 - 4ac}}{2a}$$

To see how it works we will use it to solve the equation $x^2 + 2x - 3 = 0$, which we have already solved by factorising in Example 2(a).

Comparing

$$x^2 + 2x - 3 = 0$$

with

$$ax^2 + bx - c = 0,$$

we see that $a = 1$, $b = 2$ and $c = -3$.

Using the quadratic formula:

$$x = \frac{-b \pm \sqrt{b^2 - 4ac}}{2a}$$

$$x = \frac{-2 \pm \sqrt{2^2 - 4 \times 1 \times (-3)}}{2 \times 1}$$

$$x = \frac{-2 \pm \sqrt{4 + 12}}{2}$$

$$x = \frac{-2 \pm \sqrt{16}}{2}$$

$$x = \frac{-2 \pm 4}{2}$$

NOTE:
Notice that the whole numerator is divided by $2a$. It is a very common mistake to only divide the square root by $2a$, and this will give you the wrong answer.

The $\pm$ sign means 'plus or minus', and gives us the two solutions:

either

$$x = \frac{-2 - 4}{2} \quad \text{or} \quad x = \frac{-2 + 4}{2}$$
$$x = -3 \quad \text{or} \quad x = 1$$

This is more time-consuming than the method used in Example 2(a), so you should use the method of factorising if it is possible. However, questions often ask you to solve the given quadratic equation giving the answers correct to two decimal places, or correct to three significant figures. This is a big hint that it is not going to factorise and you should then use the formula without spending time attempting a factorisation.

Example 3
Solve the following equations, giving your answers to 3 significant figures if not exact.
a $5x^2 + 2x - 1 = 0$ **b** $2x^2 - x - 1 = 0$

Answer 3
a $5x^2 + 2x - 1 = 0$
Comparing with $ax^2 + bx + c = 0$
then $a = 5$, $b = 2$ and $c = -1$
Using $x = \frac{-b \pm \sqrt{b^2 - 4ac}}{2a}$

$$x = \frac{-2 \pm \sqrt{2^2 - 4 \times 5 \times -1}}{2 \times 5} \quad x = \frac{-2 \pm \sqrt{4 + 20}}{10}$$

$$x = \frac{-2 + \sqrt{24}}{10} \quad \text{or} \quad x = \frac{-2 - \sqrt{24}}{10}$$

$$x = 0.290 \quad \text{or} \quad x = -0.690 \text{ to 3 significant figures}$$

b $2x^2 - x - 1 = 0$

In this equation $a = 2$, $b = -1$ and $c = -1$

$$x = \frac{-b \pm \sqrt{b^2 - 4ac}}{2a}$$

$$x = \frac{1 \pm \sqrt{(-1)^2 - 4 \times 2 \times (-1)}}{2 \times 2}$$

$$x = \frac{1 \pm \sqrt{1 + 8}}{4}$$

$$x = \frac{1 + 3}{4} \quad \text{or} \quad x = \frac{1 - 3}{4}$$

$$x = 1 \qquad\qquad x = -\frac{1}{2}$$

These answers are exact, so do not need to be given to 3 significant figures. In fact the equation could have easily been solved by factorising.

You must take great care with the plus and minus signs in this formula.

For example, in the answer to part 1(b) you will see that:

$$-b = -(-1) = +1,$$

$$b^2 = (-1)^2 = +1 \text{ and}$$

$$-4ac = -4 \times 2 \times (-1) = +8$$

Exercise 16.3

Solve the following, giving your answers to 3 significant figures.

1 $x^2 + 5x - 7 = 0$
        2 $x^2 - 5x - 7 = 0$
        3 $3x^2 + 10x + 2 = 0$

4 $x^2 - x - 1 = 0$
        5 $-x^2 + x + 4 = 0$
        6 $2x^2 - 7x + 2 = 0$

Completing the Square to Solve Quadratic Equations

Key term

Completing the square is a method used to solve quadratic equations. The quadratic formula is derived using this method.

You may sometimes be asked to rearrange a quadratic expression or solve a quadratic equation by **completing the square**. This method sometimes seems a bit daunting at first, but is relatively easy if you follow a routine. The easiest way to show you this routine is by one or two examples.

$$x^2 + 2x - 3 = 0$$

To solve the above equation by completing the square the equation first needs to be written in another form. We begin by rewriting the first two terms of the equation:

- Take the first two terms:

$$x^2 + 2x$$

- Open a bracket, insert x, $+$, and *half* the coefficient of the x term, close the bracket and square it:

$$(x + 1)^2$$

- Squaring this bracket gives:

$$(x + 1)(x + 1)$$

$$= x^2 + 2x + 1$$

- Comparing this with the first two terms of our original equation we can see that we have acquired an extra +1, so this must now be subtracted, and the rest of the original equation put in place:

$$(x + 1)^2 - 1 - 3 = 0$$

- Collecting the last two terms finishes the rearrangement and completes the square:

$$(x + 1)^2 - 4 = 0$$

You should multiply out the brackets again to check that this equation is still the same as the original equation.

Before going on to use this new form to solve the equation it would be beneficial to practise some rearrangements.

NOTE:

Part c: Divide the expression by 2 to get the x^2 term with a coefficient of 1, keeping the 2 outside the brackets as a factor.

Using square brackets helps to show that the 2 has divided the whole expression, and avoids confusion with the other set of brackets.

The factor 2 outside the square brackets now multiplies the terms inside these brackets to finish the working.

Example 4

a $x^2 - 4x + 3$ **b** $x^2 + 5x - 4$ **c** $2x^2 + 4x - 1$

Write these expressions in the form $(x + b)^2 + c$ or $a(x + b)^2 + c$.

Answer 4

a $x^2 - 4x + 3$

$\quad (x - 2)^2 = x^2 - 4x + 4$ so subtract 4

$\quad\quad\quad\quad = (x - 2)^2 - 4 + 3$ and replace the $+3$

$\quad\quad\quad\quad = (x - 2)^2 - 1$

b $x^2 + 5x - 4$

$\quad \left(x + \frac{5}{2}\right)^2 = x^2 + 5x + \frac{25}{4}$ so subtract $\frac{25}{4}$

$\quad = \left(x + \frac{5}{2}\right)^2 - \frac{25}{4} - 4$ and replace the -4

$\quad = \left(x + \frac{5}{2}\right)^2 - \frac{41}{4}$

c $2x^2 + 4x - 1$

$\quad = 2\left[x^2 + 2x - \frac{1}{2}\right]$

$\quad = 2\left[(x + 1)^2 - 1 - \frac{1}{2}\right]$

$\quad = 2\left[(x + 1)^2 - \frac{3}{2}\right]$

$\quad = 2(x + 1)^2 - 3$

Exercise 16.4

Write these expressions in the form $(x + b)^2 + c$ or $a(x + b)^2 + c$.

1 $x^2 - 6x + 1$ **2** $x^2 + 5x + 2$ **3** $x^2 - 3x - 3$

4 $2x^2 + 4x - 5$ **5** $3x^2 - 6x - 4$ **6** $2x^2 - 3x + 2$

7 $2x^2 + 5x - 5$

Solving the Equation after Completing the Square

This is now quite straightforward.

Looking again at our original quadratic equation:

$$x^2 + 2x - 3 = 0$$

- Rewrite in the completed square form:

$$(x + 1)^2 - 4 = 0$$

- Add 4 to both sides:

$$(x + 1)^2 = 4$$

- Square root both sides:

$$x + 1 = \pm \sqrt{4}$$
$$x + 1 = \pm 2$$

- Subtract 1 from both sides:

$$x = +2 - 1 \quad \text{or} \quad x = -2 - 1$$
$$x = 1 \qquad\qquad x = -3$$

We have now solved our original equation in three different ways. The choice of method depends on the type of equation, or on the question you have been set. There is a fourth method, which you will see when you work on Chapter 18.

Example 5

Solve these quadratic equations by completing the square. Leave your answers in surd form where appropriate. (A *surd* is the square root of a number which itself is not a perfect square. So leaving in *surd* form means leaving in square root form.)

a $x^2 + 3x - 5 = 0$ **b** $2x^2 + x - 3 = 0$ **c** $x^2 + bx + c = 0$

Answer 5

a $x^2 + 3x - 5 = 0$

$$\left(x + \frac{3}{2}\right)^2 - \frac{9}{4} - 5 = 0$$

$$\left(x + \frac{3}{2}\right)^2 - \frac{29}{4} = 0$$

$$\left(x + \frac{3}{2}\right)^2 = \frac{29}{4}$$

$$x + \frac{3}{2} = \pm \sqrt{\frac{29}{4}}$$

$$x = -\frac{3}{2} \pm \frac{\sqrt{29}}{2} \qquad\qquad \left(\text{or } \frac{-3 \pm \sqrt{29}}{2}\right)$$

b $2x^2 + x - 3 = 0$ We can now divide the equation all through by 2.

$$x^2 + \frac{x}{2} - \frac{3}{2} = 0 \qquad\qquad \text{Remember that } 0 \div 2 = 0!$$

$$\left(x + \frac{1}{4}\right)^2 - \frac{1}{16} - \frac{3}{2} = 0 \quad \left(x + \frac{1}{4}\right)^2 - \frac{25}{16} = 0$$

$$x + \frac{1}{4} = \pm \sqrt{\frac{25}{16}}$$

$$x = -\frac{1}{4} + \frac{5}{4}$$

either $x = -\frac{3}{2}$ or $x = 1$

c $x^2 + bx + c = 0$

$$\left(x + \frac{b}{2}\right)^2 - \frac{b^2}{4} + c = 0$$

$$\left(x + \frac{b}{2}\right)^2 = \frac{b^2}{4} - c$$

$$\left(x + \frac{b}{2}\right)^2 = \frac{b^2 - 4c}{4}$$

$$x + \frac{b}{2} = \pm\sqrt{\frac{b^2 - 4c}{4}}$$

$$x = -\frac{b}{2} \pm \frac{\sqrt{b^2 - 4c}}{2}$$

$$x = \frac{-b \pm \sqrt{b^2 - 4c}}{2}$$

This is the proof of the simplified version of the quadratic formula, with $a = 1$.

Exercise 16.5

Solve these equations by completing the square and leaving in surd form (square root form) if the answers are not exact.

1 $x^2 + x - 1 = 0$ **2** $x^2 - \frac{1}{2}x - 2 = 0$ **3** $x^2 - 4x - 5 = 0$

4 $4x^2 + 8x - 1 = 0$ **5** $x^2 - 7x + 2 = 0$ **6** $2x^2 - 3x + 1 = 0$

Exercise 16.6

Solve the following equations by any appropriate method, giving your answers to 3 significant figures if they are not exact.

1 $x^2 - x - 1 = 0$ **2** $x^2 + 8x + 1 = 0$ **3** $x^2 - 2x + 1 = 0$ **4** $2x^2 + x - 6 = 0$

5 $5x^2 - 5x - 2 = 0$ **6** $x^2 - 3x + 1 = 0$ **7** $x^2 - 3x - 1 = 0$ **8** $3x^2 + 4x + 1 = 0$

9 $3x^2 - 4x - 1 = 0$ **10** $-x^2 + 2x - 1 = 0$ **11** $8x^2 + 342x + 35 = 0$ **12** $6x^2 - 13x - 15 = 0$

Quadratic equations may appear in disguise, so you may need to do a little algebraic work before they are ready to solve.

The next example should make this clear.

Example 6

Solve for x:

a $-\frac{1}{x} = 3x - 4$

b $\frac{3x - 1}{x} + \frac{x + 1}{x - 1} = \frac{1}{x(x - 1)}$

$x \neq 0$ and $x \neq 1$ (because we cannot divide by zero)

Answer 6

a $-\frac{1}{x} = 3x - 4$

Multiply both sides by x:

$-1 = x(3x - 4)$

$-1 = 3x^2 - 4x$

$0 = 3x^2 - 4x + 1$

$0 = (3x - 1)(x - 1)$

either $(3x - 1) = 0$ or $(x - 1) = 0$

$\qquad\qquad x = \frac{1}{3} \qquad\qquad x = 1$

b $\dfrac{3x-1}{x}+\dfrac{x+1}{x-1}=\dfrac{1}{x(x-1)}$

$$\frac{(3x-1)}{\cancel{x}}\times\frac{\cancel{x}(x-1)}{1}+\frac{(x+1)}{\cancel{(x-1)}}\times\frac{x\cancel{(x-1)}}{1}=\frac{1}{\cancel{x}\cancel{(x-1)}}\times\frac{\cancel{x}\cancel{(x-1)}}{1}$$

(Cancel out common factors in numerator and denominator of each fraction)

$$(3x-1)(x-1)+x(x+1)=1$$
$$3x^2-4x+1+x^2+x-1=0$$
$$4x^2-3x=0$$
$$x(4x-3)=0$$
either $x=0$ or $(4x-3)=0$
$$x=\frac{3}{4}$$

Alternative Method for (b):

Multiplying all through by the lowest common denominator can look very cumbersome when the denominators are algebraic as in the above example.

An alternative method is to multiply each fraction top and bottom by the factor or factors that are needed to make all the denominators the same.

In the above example, the first fraction $\dfrac{3x-1}{x}$ needs to be multiplied top and bottom by $(x-1)$ and the second needs to be multiplied top and bottom by x. The right-hand side already has the common denominator.

Thinking of this in the simplest way: you decide what the lowest common denominator is, and then, taking each fraction in turn, look for what is 'missing' in its denominator, and correct it. Your first line of working would become:

$$\frac{(3x-1)(x-1)}{x(x-1)}+\frac{x(x+1)}{x(x-1)}=\frac{1}{x(x-1)}$$

Now the denominators are all the same we can see that multiplying the whole equation by $x(x-1)$ would cancel the denominators, so the next line of working will be:

$$(3x-1)(x-1)+x(x+1)=1$$

Then proceed as before.

Example 7
Solve the following equation

$$\frac{1}{x}-\frac{1}{x+2}=\frac{2}{2x+1}$$

Answer 7

$$\frac{1}{x}-\frac{1}{x+2}=\frac{2}{2x+1}$$

The lowest common denominator is $x(x+2)(2x+1)$, so multiply the first fraction top and bottom by the 'missing' factors $(x+2)$ and $(2x+1)$, multiply the second top and bottom by x and $(2x+1)$ and so on.

$$\frac{(x+2)(2x+1)}{x(x+2)(2x+1)}-\frac{x(2x+1)}{x(x+2)(2x+1)}=\frac{2x(x+2)}{x(x+2)(2x+1)}$$

Now the whole equation has a common denominator, so multiplying through by that common denominator will cancel it out of every term, leaving:

$$(x+2)(2x+1) - x(2x+1) = 2x(x+2)$$

This can now be multiplied out and simplified (taking care with the minus sign):

$$(2x^2 + 5x + 2) - (2x^2 + x) = (2x^2 + 4x)$$
$$2x^2 + 5x + 2 - 2x^2 - x - 2x^2 - 4x = 0$$
$$-2x^2 + 2 = 0$$

Dividing through by -2:

$$x^2 - 1 = 0$$
$$x = 1 \quad \text{or} \quad x = -1$$

Exercise 16.7

Solve the following:

1 $\quad x + 3 + \dfrac{2}{x} = 0$

2 $\quad 2 - \dfrac{5}{x} + \dfrac{2}{x^2} = 0$

3 $\quad \dfrac{6x}{x-1} + (x-2) = 0$

4 $\quad x^3 - x(x^2 - x) = 6 - x$

5 $\quad \dfrac{1}{x(x+1)} = \dfrac{1}{2}$

6 $\quad \dfrac{x-4}{x+1} + \dfrac{1}{x(x+1)} = -1$

7 $\quad \dfrac{x^2}{(5+x)(6-x)} + \dfrac{1}{5+x} = \dfrac{1}{6-x}$

8 $\quad \dfrac{1}{x} + \dfrac{1}{x+1} = \dfrac{3}{3x-1}$

9 $\quad \dfrac{1}{x-1} - \dfrac{1}{x} = \dfrac{2}{x+2}$

NOTE:
Factorise $2x^2 + 5x$ before proceeding as normal.

10 $\quad \dfrac{x}{2x+5} - \dfrac{1}{x} = \dfrac{3x-9}{2x^2+5x}$

11

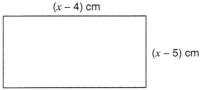

(x − 4) cm

(x − 5) cm

NOTE:
Remember that the area of a rectangle is obtained by multiplying the length by the width.

The area of the rectangle is 12 square centimetres.
   a Form an equation in x.
   b Solve your equation for x.
   c Write down the dimensions of the rectangle.

NOTE:
In question 12, let the two numbers be x and $x + 1$.

12 The sum of the squares of two consecutive numbers is 145. Calculate the numbers.

13 The product of two consecutive **even** numbers is 168. Calculate the numbers.

14 The length of a rectangle is 3 cm more than its breadth. The area of the rectangle is 40 cm². Let the breadth of the rectangle be x cm.
   a Show that this information leads to the equation $x^2 + 3x - 40 = 0$.
   b Solve this equation.
   c Write down the dimensions of the rectangle.

16.5 More Sequences

You will be expected to be able to answer slightly more difficult questions on sequences.

Example 8

a   Find the nth term of the following sequence

$$\frac{1}{3} \quad \frac{3}{5} \quad \frac{5}{7} \quad \frac{7}{9} \;\ldots$$

b   The nth term of a sequence is given by $n^2 + n + 1$.
   i   Calculate the 50th term.   **ii**   Find n when the nth term $= 111$.

c   Find the nth term of the following sequences
   i   16   25   36   49 …   **ii**   2   6   12   20   30 …

Answer 8

a   The numerators and denominators form separate sequences.
   The numerators are   1   3   5   7 …
   The nth term is $2n - 1$
   The denominators are   3   5   7   9 …
   The nth term is $2n + 1$
   So the nth term for the sequence is $= \dfrac{2n-1}{2n+1}$

b   i nth term $= n^2 + n + 1$
   50th term $= 50^2 + 50 + 1$
        $= 2551$

   ii nth term $= 111$
   $n^2 + n + 1 = 111$
   $n^2 + n - 110 = 0$
   $(n + 11)(n - 10) = 0$
   $n = -11$ or $n = 10$
   So the 10th term $= 111$

c   i   16   25   36   49 …
   This sequence is clearly based on the sequence of square numbers, but the first term is 16 (4^2), not 1^2, and the second term is 25 (5^2) not 2^2.
   So the nth term is not n^2, but $(n + 3)^2$.
   nth term $= (n + 3)^2$

   ii   2   6   12   20   30 …
   The *first* set of differences is
   $+4$ $+6$ $+8$ $+10$ …
   and the *second* set is
   $+2$ $+2$ $+2$ …
   so the sequence is based on n^2.
   For the first term $1^2 + 1 = 2$, for the second term $2^2 + 2 = 6$, and for the third term $3^2 + 3 = 12$.
   So the formula for the nth term is $n^2 + n$.
   nth term $= n^2 + n$

You may have to find patterns across different sequences as the next example shows.

Example 9

a   Find the nth term for the following sequence:
   3, 6, 11, 18, 27, …

b   Using your answer to part (a) find the nth term for this sequence
   4, 8, 14, 22, 32, …

c Using your answer to part (a) find the nth term for
$6, 11, 18, 27, 38, \ldots$

Answer 9

a $3, 6, 11, 18, 27, \ldots$
The first set of differences is
$3, 5, 7, 9, \ldots$
The second set of differences is
$2, 2, 2, \ldots$
So the sequence is based on n^2, with 2 added to each term.
nth term $= n^2 + 2$

b $4, 8, 14, 22, 32, \ldots$
The new sequence is
$3 + 1, 6 + 2, 11 + 3, 18 + 4, 27 + 5, \ldots$
This is the old sequence with n added to each term.
nth term $= n^2 + 2 + n$

c $6, 11, 18, 27, 38, \ldots$
Comparing with $3, 6, 11, 18, 27, \ldots$, we can see that:
the 1st term of the new sequence is the 2nd term of the old,
the 2nd term of the new sequence is the 3rd term of the old,
the 3rd term of the new sequence is the 4th term of the old.
So the nth term of the new sequence is the $(n + 1)$th term of the old.
nth term $= (n + 1)^2 + 2$

Example 10

A sequence of diagrams is shown below.

1	2	3	4

a Complete the following table showing the number of dots in each successive diagram in the sequence, including the next diagram (diagram number 5).

Diagram number (D_n)	1	2	3	4	5
Number of dots (n)					

b These numbers are called triangular numbers because of the way the dots can be arranged.
The formula for the nth term is:
$$n\text{th term} = D_n = \tfrac{1}{2}n(n + 1)$$
Calculate the 99th triangular number, D_{99}.

c What is the difference between
  i the 4th and 5th,
  ii the 5th and 6th,
  iii the 99th and 100th triangular numbers?

d **i** Complete the following:
    $D_1 + D_2 = 1 + 3 = 4$
    $D_2 + D_3 = 3 + 6 =$
    $D_3 + D_4 =$
  ii What special numbers are produced by adding successive terms in the sequence of triangular numbers?

Answer 10

a

Diagram number (D_n)	1	2	3	4	5
Number of dots (n)	1	3	6	10	15

b $D_{99} = \frac{1}{2} \times 99 \times (99 + 1) = 4950$

c **i** $D_5 - D_4 = 15 - 10 = 5$ **ii** $D_6 - D_5 = 21 - 15 = 6$ **iii** $D_{100} - D_{99} = 100$

d **i** $D_1 + D_2 = 1 + 3 = 4$

     $D_2 + D_3 = 3 + 6 = 9$

     $D_3 + D_4 = 6 + 10 = 16$

   ii Square numbers

Exercise 16.8

1 Find the first four terms of the following sequences:

   a nth term $= n^2$ **b** nth term $= n^2 - 2$ **c** nth term $= n^2 - 2n$

   d nth term $= n^2 - 2n - 2$ **e** nth term $= \frac{n}{n+1}$ **f** nth term $= \frac{n}{n^2+1}$

   g nth term $= (n-1)^2$ **h** nth term $= n^3$ **i** nth term $= n^3 + 2$

   j nth term $= n^3 - n$ **k** nth term $= 3n$

2 Find the nth term of the following sequences:

   a 1×2 2×3 3×4 4×5 $\ldots$

   b 0 2 6 12 20 30 $\ldots$

   c 4 9 16 25 $\ldots$

   d 2 8 18 32 50 $\ldots$

   e $\frac{1}{2}$ $\frac{4}{3}$ $\frac{9}{4}$ $\frac{16}{5}$ $\ldots$

   f $\frac{3}{4}$ $\frac{6}{5}$ $\frac{9}{6}$ $\frac{12}{7}$ $\frac{15}{8}$ $\ldots$

3 The nth term of a sequence is given by $2n^2 + 1$.

   a   Find the 3rd, 7th and 10th terms.

   b   Find n when the nth term is

     i   33   **ii**   243.

4 The nth term of a sequence is given by $n^2 + 2n$.

   a   Find the 4th, 7th and 100th terms.

   b   Find n when the nth term is

     i   3   **ii**   99   **iii**   120   **iv**   288

16.6 More Simultaneous Equations

You will be expected to solve simultaneous equations which might require rearranging or simplifying first or where *both* equations need to be multiplied by constants in order to equalise coefficients.

The method is called **elimination** because one of the variables is eliminated to give an equation in the other.

Key term

Elimination is a method used to solve simultaneous equations.

For example, solve this pair of simultaneous equations:

$$-2x + 3y = 4$$
$$5x = 8 + 6y$$

It is convenient to number the two equations so that you can explain your method.

$$-2x + 3y = 4 \qquad \ldots(i)$$
$$5x = 8 + 6y \qquad \ldots(ii)$$

Rearrange (ii):

$$5x - 6y = 8 \qquad \ldots(iii)$$

Multiply (i) by 5 and (iii) by 2:

$$-10x + 15y = 20$$
$$10x - 12y = 16$$

Add these two equations to eliminate the x terms.

$$0 + 3y = 36$$
$$y = 12$$

Substitute for y in (ii)

$$5x = 8 + 6 \times 12$$
$$5x = 8 + 72$$
$$5x = 80$$
$$x = \frac{80}{5}$$
$$x = 16$$

So $x = 16$ and $y = 12$.

This example shows the method when both equations are multiplied by constants, and the x terms have been eliminated. But in this particular case it would have been simpler to multiply (i) by 2, and then solve simultaneously with (iii), eliminating the y terms first. Try this to check the answer.

Shown below is a convenient and clear method for showing your working.

Example 11

Solve these two equations by the method of elimination

$$3x - 2y = 4$$
$$5x - 3y = 7$$

Answer 11

$$\text{(i)} \quad \ldots 3x - 2y = 4 \xrightarrow{\times 5} 15x - 10y = 20 \xrightarrow{} 15x - 10y = 20$$
$$\text{(ii)} \quad \ldots 5x - 3y = 7 \xrightarrow{\times 3} 15x - 9y = 21 \xrightarrow{\times -1} -15x + 9y = -21 \quad \text{add}$$
$$\overline{-y = -1}$$
$$y = 1$$

> **NOTE:**
> Substitute $y = 1$ in equation (ii) to check the working.

Substitute $y = 1$ in (i)
$$3x - 2 \times 1 = 4$$
$$3x = 6$$
$$x = 2$$

$x = 2$ and $y = 1$.

In the example above we have equalised the x coefficients to eliminate the x terms. Try the same question yourself, equalising the y coefficients by multiplying equation (i) by 3 and equation (ii) by 2, to eliminate the y terms.

Key term

Substitution is another method used to solve simultaneous equations.

Exercise 16.9

Solve these simultaneous equations by the method of elimination.

1 $3x + 4y = 5$
$3y + 2x = 4$

2 $7y = 5 - 3x$
$4y = 3 - 2x$

3 $3x + 3y = 2$
$2x - 8y = 3$

4 $6x - 5y = 2$
$5x + 3y = 16$

In some cases an alternative method, called solving by **substitution**, may be simpler. For example, look at this pair of simultaneous equations:

$$3x + 5y = 15$$

$$y = 2x - 1$$

In this case putting the right-hand side of the second equation in brackets gives:

$$y = (2x - 1)$$

which can be substituted for y in the first equation:

$$3x + 5(2x - 1) = 15$$

We now have a linear equation in x only, so we can solve it in the normal way.

$$3x + 10x - 5 = 15$$
$$13x = 20$$
$$x = \frac{20}{13}$$

Now substitute for x in one of the equations (the second one is simpler).

$$y = \left(2 \times \frac{20}{13} - 1\right)$$
$$y = \frac{40}{13} - 1$$
$$y = \frac{40 - 13}{13}$$
$$y = \frac{27}{13}$$

Your questions will probably have simpler calculations than this, but there is no reason why fractions cannot be involved.

Example 12

Solve the following pair of equations:

$$\frac{1}{2}y + \frac{1}{5}x = 2$$
$$y - x = 5$$

Answer 12

Number the two equations so that you can explain your method:

$$\frac{1}{2}y + \frac{1}{5}x = 2 \quad \text{...(i)}$$
$$y - x = 5 \quad \text{...(ii)}$$

Multiply equation (i) by 10 to simplify.

$$5y + 2x = 20 \quad \text{...(iii)}$$

Rearrange equation (ii):

$$y = 5 + x \quad \text{...(iv)}$$

Substitute $(5 + x)$ for y in (iii)

$$5(5 + x) + 2x = 20$$
$$25 + 5x + 2x = 20$$
$$7x = 20 - 25$$
$$7x = -5$$
$$x = -\frac{5}{7}$$

Substitute for x in (iv):

$$y = 5 + \left(-\frac{5}{7}\right)$$
$$y = \frac{35 - 5}{7}$$
$$y = \frac{3}{7}$$
$$\text{so } x = -\frac{5}{7} \text{ and } y = \frac{30}{7}$$

As you should see, equations (ii) and (iii) can also be solved by elimination, either by multiplying (ii) by 5 to eliminate y, or by multiplying (ii) by 2 to eliminate x. You could try these for practice.

Exercise 16.10

Solve these pairs of equations by the method of substitution.

1 $y + 2x = 5$
$3y - 5x = 4$

2 $y = 5x + 4$
$3y - 2x + 1 = 0$

3 $x - 3 = 4y$
$7y + 2x = 31$

4 $3x + y = 4$
$2(y - 5) = -5x$

5 $x + 3y = 3$
$5x = 6 - 5y$

6 $\frac{3}{2}x - y = \frac{1}{4}$
$x + \frac{1}{2}y = 1$

The method you choose to use to solve your simultaneous equations is your choice, but by practising both methods you will have a choice and be able to choose the simplest for each particular pair of equations.

Exercise 16.11

Solve the following pairs of simultaneous equations:

1 $3y + 2x = 12$
$y + x = 4$

2 $5y = x - 15$
$x + y = 9$

3 $2x + 3y = 15$
$3x + 2y = 15$

4 $4y = x - 10$
$3y - 2x = 5$

5 $0.1x - 0.2y = 2$
$x + y = 17$

6 $1.4x + 3.9y = 6.4$
$0.2x - 1.3y = 1.2$

7 $x = 7 - 2y$
$y = 5 + 2x$

8 $\frac{1}{2}x - \frac{3}{4}y = 5$
$x + y = 5$

9 $-x + 3y = 10$
$2x + 5y = 2$

10 $\frac{2}{3}x + \frac{1}{4}y = 1$
$5x + y = 1$

16.7 Inequalities

You have already seen the inequality signs: $> \geqslant < \leqslant$.

Key term

An **inequality** is like an equation, but its solution is a range of values rather than discrete values

It is useful to be able to represent inequalities on a number line, using a circle and an arrow. If the **inequality** is strict (< or >) use an open circle, otherwise (⩽ or ⩾) use a filled circle to show that the inequality includes the end number. If the inequality has no end, use an arrow to show it continuing in that direction.

This is best made clear by some examples, as in Figures 16.1–16.3.

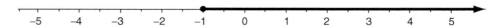

Figure 16.1 $x \geqslant -1$

Figure 16.2 $-2 < x \leqslant 4$

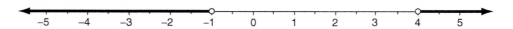

Figure 16.3 $x < -1$ or $x > 4$

Inequalities are similar to equations, but the solutions are generally a range of values rather than individual values. The methods used to solve inequalities are the same as those for equations with one very important exception which you must remember.

For example, consider the following:

$$x - 4 < 3x + 6$$
$$x - 3x < 6 + 4 \qquad \text{(taking } 3x \text{ from both sides}$$
$$-2x < 10 \qquad \text{and adding 4 to both sides)}$$

The next step is to divide both sides by −2, which we will do, but *at the same time* the inequality sign must be changed from 'less than' to 'greater than'.

$$x > \frac{10}{-2}$$
$$x > -5$$

The rule is: **When you multiply or divide an inequality by a negative number you must change the direction of the inequality sign.**

There are several ways to explain why it is necessary to turn the sign around.

Look at the number line in Figure 16.4, and remember that numbers on the right are larger than numbers on the left.

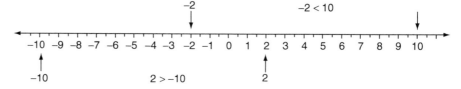

Figure 16.4 Positions on the number line

We can see from the number line that $-2 < 10$; however, if we multiply both sides of this inequality by −1 is it still true that $2 < -10$? From the number line you can see that it is not, and in fact $2 > -10$.

When you are working with inequalities try to picture (or sketch) a number line and think of its symmetry around zero to help you remember to alter the sign.

Another approach is to avoid multiplying or dividing by negative numbers.

Going back to the inequality above, when we reached the stage where we were about to divide by −2, we could do the following instead:

$$-2x < 10$$

Now add $-2x$ to both sides and take 10 from both sides:

$$-10 < 2x$$

Divide both sides by 2:

$$-5 < x$$

Now, since −5 is less than x it follows that x is greater than −5, and the answer may be given as:

$$x > -5$$

Note, however, that without this last step your solution is incomplete.

NOTE:
Remember that it is only when multiplying or dividing by a negative number that the sign has to be changed, not when adding or subtracting.

Example 13

a Solve the following inequalities
   i $5x - 3 \geqslant 2x - 1$ **ii** $2 \leqslant 3x - 5 < 7$

b List the integers which satisfy the following inequality
    $3.5 < -x < 10.5$

Answer 13

a **i** $5x - 3 \geqslant 2x - 1$
        $5x - 2x \geqslant -1 + 3$ (taking $2x$ from both sides and adding 3 to both sides)
        $3x \geqslant +2$
        $x \geqslant \frac{2}{3}$

   ii $2 \leqslant 3x - 5 < 7$ (add 5 to each part of the inequality)
         $2 + 5 \leqslant 3x < 7 + 5$
         $7 \leqslant 3x < 12$ (divide all through by 3)
         $\frac{7}{3} \leqslant x < 4$

         or $2\frac{1}{3} \leqslant x < 4$

         so x is greater than or equal to $2\frac{1}{3}$ and less than 4, which could be shown on the number line as:

b $3.5 < -x < 10.5$ (multiply all through by −1, and remember to change the inequality signs)
           $-3.5 > x > -10.5$ or $-10.5 < x < -3.5$
    This is shown on the number line below:

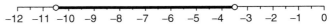

    so the solution is {−10, −9, −8, −7, −6, −5, −4}.

(Drawing the number line makes it easier to see which integers are included. You will note that −10 is included, but −3 is outside the range of the inequality.)

Two inequalities might have to be solved simultaneously. It is convenient to show both on a number line, as shown in the next example.

Example 14

$3x \geqslant x + 4$

$3x - 15 < 0$

a Show the solution to these inequalities on a number line.

b List the integers which satisfy both inequalities.

c Write the solution as an inequality.

Answer 14

a $3x \geqslant x + 4$ $\qquad\qquad$ $3x - 15 < 0$

$\quad$ $2x \geqslant 4$ $\qquad\qquad\qquad$ $3x < 15$

$\quad$ $x \geqslant 2$ $\qquad\qquad\qquad\quad$ $x < 5$

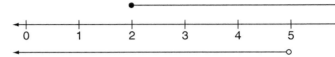

b $\{2, 3, 4\}$ $\qquad\qquad\qquad\qquad$ **c** $2 \leqslant x < 5$

Exercise 16.12

1 Solve the following inequalities, showing the solutions on a number line:

a $-2x < 1$ $\qquad\qquad$ **b** $6x > 7 - x$ $\qquad\qquad$ **c** $3(x + 1) \leqslant x - 2$

d $2(3x - 2) \leqslant 7(x - 1)$ $\qquad$ **e** $\frac{1}{2}x - 3 < x + \frac{1}{5}$ $\qquad$ **f** $-7 < 2x < 4$

g $1 \leqslant x - 1 < 6$ $\qquad\qquad$ **h** $3 < -x < 5$

2 List the integers which satisfy the following inequalities:

a $7x < -14$ $\qquad$ **b** $-3x \geqslant 6$ $\qquad$ **c** $2x - 1 < 2$ $\qquad$ **d** $-5 < 2x + 1 < 2$

e $-2 \geqslant x - 1 < 3$ $\qquad$ **f** $1 \leqslant -x \leqslant 4$ $\qquad$ **g** $-1 < -x < 3$

3 $-x \leqslant 6$

$3x - 5 < -11$

a List the integers which satisfy both inequalities.

b Write the solution as an inequality.

16.8 Variation

We have already looked at the ideas of direct and inverse proportion, and now we must think about them algebraically, or in more general terms.

An example of *direct* proportion would be the number of similar items you buy (*N*) and the total cost (*T*) of those items, because as the number *increases* the total cost will *increase* in proportion.

An example of *inverse* proportion would be the number of items you could buy (*N*) for a given amount of money and the individual cost (*c*) of those items, because as the cost of each item *increases* the number you could buy *decreases*.

Key term

Variation relates two or more variables which are in direct or inverse proportion in an algebraic way.

We will now look at how you are able to express these variations algebraically.

To demonstrate direct proportion or **variation** we can think of the first example above. If N = number of items and T = the total cost then we can say that T is directly proportional to N and write:

$$T \propto N$$

where $\propto$ is the sign meaning 'is proportional to'. We read this as 'T is proportional to N', or 'T varies as (or with) N'.

For inverse proportion, as in the second example, if N is the number of items you can buy for the amount of money you have and c is the cost of each item, then we can say that N is inversely proportional to c, and write:

$$N \propto \frac{1}{c}$$

This is read 'N is inversely proportional to c' or 'N varies inversely as (or with) c'. Having written down the statement showing the variation we then replace the $\propto$ sign by '$= k \times$', where k is a constant, known as the constant of variation:

$$T \propto N \quad \text{and} \quad N \propto \frac{1}{c}$$

$$T = k \times N \qquad N = k \times \frac{1}{c}$$

Before we can make use of these equations it is necessary in each case to find the value of the constant k. Questions on variation will give you a pair of values so that you can find k. Work through the example to see how this is done.

The constant of variation may of course be any letter, but k is often used to represent a constant.

For example, we may be told that when the total cost, T, is Rs 980 and the number of items, N, is 20.

Substituting in the equation:

$$T = k \times N$$
$$980 = k \times 20$$
$$k = 49$$

We now have a formula:

$$T = 49N$$

This formula can now be used to find other values of T or N.

A quantity may be directly or inversely proportional to a simple function of another quantity, such as the cube, or the square root as shown in the example below.

Example 15

a Given that N varies inversely as c, and that $N = 550$ when $c = 0.20$, find a formula connecting N and c.

b Given that x is inversely proportional to y^3, and that $x = 1$ when $y = 2$, find a formula connecting x and y.

c Given that h is proportional to the square root of A, and that $h = 3$ when $A = 81$,

   i find a formula connecting h and A,

   ii use your formula to find h when $A = 16$.

d You are given that $y \propto x^2$. What happens to y if the value of x is doubled (multiplied by 2)?

Answer 15

a $N \propto \dfrac{1}{c}$

$N = k \times \dfrac{1}{c}$

Given $N = 550$ when $c = 0.20$

$550 = k \times \dfrac{1}{0.20}$

$550 \times 0.20 = k$

$k = 110$

So thte formula is $N = \dfrac{110}{c}$

b $x \propto \dfrac{1}{y^3}$

$x = \dfrac{k}{y^3}$

given that $x = 1$ when $y = 2$

$1 = \dfrac{k}{2^3}$

$k = 8$

The formula is $x = \dfrac{8}{y^3}$

c i $h \propto \sqrt{A}$

$h = k\sqrt{A}$

Given that $h = 3$ when $A = 81$

$3 = k \times \sqrt{81}$

$3 = k \times 9$

$k = \dfrac{1}{3}$

The formula is $h = \dfrac{1}{3}\sqrt{A}$

ii When $A = 16$

$h = \dfrac{1}{3}\sqrt{16}$

$h = \dfrac{4}{3}$

d $y \propto (2x)^2$

$y \propto 4x^2$

so y is quadrupled (multiplied by 4).

Exercise 16.13

NO CALCULATOR IN THIS EXERCISE

1 The total cost (T) of a number of similar items (N) is directly proportional to the number of items.
   a Given that the total cost for 30 items is Rs 990, find an equation connecting T and N.
   b What does the constant of variation represent in this example?

2 Given that y is proportional to x^2, and that $y = 4$ when $x = 3$, find an equation in x and y.

3 **a** W is proportional to V and the constant of variation is d.
      Given that when $W = 10\,$kg, $V = 7\,$m³ find the numerical value of d.
   b D is inversely proportional to V.
      When $D = 6\,$mg/m³, $V = 3.5\,$m³.
      Find a formula connecting D and V.

4 Given that a varies inversely as the square root of b, and that when $b = 9$, $a = 4$, find
   a the formula connecting a and b,
   b the value of a when $b = 16$,
   c the value of b when $a = 2.5$, giving your answer to 3 significant figures.

5 Gordon is making a set of cubic glass paperweights of various sizes.
   The mass, $m\,$g, of each paperweight varies as the cube of the length of one of its sides, $l\,$cm.
   A paperweight of side 5 cm has a mass of 375 g.
   a Find a formula to calculate the mass of each paperweight, given the length of one side.
   b Calculate the mass of a paperweight that measures 6 cm on each side.

6 The force of attraction (F) between two planets is inversely proportional to the square of the distance (d) between the planets.

The units to measure force are Newtons.

When $F = 10^{20}$ newtons, $d = 10^9$ metres.

a Find a formula connecting F and d.

b Find the force between the two planets when they are 10^{15} metres apart.

16.9 Rearranging Formulae

We will now look at rearranging (or transforming) more complicated formulae. Remember that you are, in a sense, working backwards to rearrange the formulae, undoing each operation, so inverses need to be used, and BoDMAS may have to be used backwards. As before, it is helpful to underline the variable we want to make the subject of the formula. For example, a formula connecting speed (u), distance (d), time (t) and acceleration (a) is:

$$s = ut + \frac{1}{2} at^2$$

The formula is written in a way that makes it easy to find s, the distance. Rearrange this formula to make a the subject.

- Turn the formula round so that a is on the left-hand side, and underline a.

$$ut + \frac{1}{2} \underline{a}t^2 = s$$

- Subtract ut from both sides.

$$\frac{1}{2} \underline{a}t^2 = s - ut$$

- Multiply both sides by 2.

$$\underline{a}t^2 = 2(s - ut)$$

- Divide both sides by t^2.

$$\underline{a} = \frac{2(s - ut)}{t^2}$$

The formula is now written in a way that makes it easy to find a, the acceleration, and you may have noticed that, contrary to BoDMAS, subtraction came before multiplication and division.

Example 16

a $A = P\left(1 + \dfrac{r}{100}\right)^2$

Rearrange the formula to make r the subject.

b $ax - by = cx - d$

Rearrange the formula to make x the subject.

Answer 16

a $A = P\left(1 + \dfrac{r}{100}\right)^2$

$$P\left(1 + \frac{r}{100}\right)^2 = A$$

$$\left(1 + \frac{r}{100}\right)^2 = \frac{A}{P}$$

$$1 + \frac{r}{100} = \sqrt{\frac{A}{P}}$$

$$\frac{r}{100} = \sqrt{\frac{A}{P}} - 1$$

$$r = 100\left(\sqrt{\frac{A}{P}} - 1\right)$$

b $ax - by = cx - d$

$$ax - cx = -d + by$$

$$x(a - c) = by - d$$

$$x = \frac{by - d}{a - c}$$

NOTE:

x appears on both sides of the formula so the first step is to collect the x terms on one side.

There are two methods available to help you if you are not able to rearrange a formula. One is to compare it with a numerical version, so in part (a) of the example above we could write $20 = 5\left(1 + \frac{r}{100}\right)^2$, calculate r, and note the steps which had to be taken to find r. The numbers used are not too important as they are only there to help you understand the method.

The alternative is to use a number machine.

Always input the letter you need to make the new subject, and then work backwards. See Figure 16.5 for this particular example.

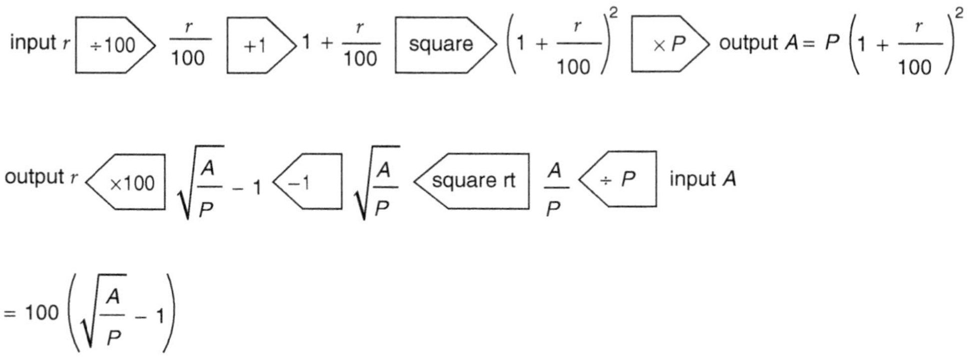

$$r = 100\left(\sqrt{\frac{A}{P}} - 1\right)$$

Figure 16.5 Using a number machine to rearrange the formula in Example 16 a

Exercise 16.14

1   $V = \frac{1}{12}(b - a)^2$ make b the subject   2 $S = \frac{a}{1-r}$ make r the subject

3   $C = \frac{x^2 + y^2 - z^2}{2xy}$ make z the subject   4 $y = 4ax$ make a the subject

5   $S = \frac{m}{2}[2a + (n-1)d]$ make a the subject   6 $E = \frac{1}{2}m(v^2 - u^2)$ make v the subject

7   $e = \frac{W}{W + w}$

    a   make w the subject,
    b   make W the subject.

                                                  8   $v^2 - u^2 = 2as$ make u the subject

9   $t = 2\pi\sqrt{\frac{l}{g}}$ make l the subject   10 $a^2 = b^2 + c^2 - 2bA$ make A the subject

11   $ax + by = ac$ make a the subject

12   $2x - 3y = ax + by$

    a   make x the subject,   **b**   make y the subject,   **c**   make b the subject.

Using Algebra to Solve Real Life Problems

Example 17

Tom is going to have 10 hectares of his grass cut to make hay (a hectare is $10\,000\,\text{m}^2$). The grass will be cut, left to dry in the sun and then made into large bales of hay. The hay will then be carted into his barn.

    a   Ben quotes for this work using the following charges:

        Cutting $30 per hectare

Baling $6 per bale

Carting and stacking $2 per bale.

Write down and simplify an equation for the cost in dollars (y) of making x bales if Ben does this work.

b Amos quotes for the same work as follows:

Daily rate for use of machinery $500

Surcharge per bale $2

He estimates that the work will take three days.

Write down and simplify an equation for the cost in dollars (z) of making x bales if Amos does the work.

c Amos' quotation comes to $516 more than Ben's.

Calculate the number of bales that Tom is expecting to be made.

Answer 17

a $y = 30 \times 10 + 6x + 2x$ **b** $z = 3 \times 500 + 2x$

     $y = 300 + 8x$ $z = 1500 + 2x$

c $z - y = 516$

     $1500 + 2x - (300 + 8x) = 516$

     $1200 - 6x = 516$

     $1200 - 516 = 6x$

     $114 = x$

Tom expects to have 114 bales made.

Exercise 16.15

Mixed exercise   **DO NOT USE A CALCULATOR IN QUESTIONS 1 TO 9**

1 Solve the following equations:

   a $\dfrac{4x+1}{2} = \dfrac{x+5}{5}$ **b** $\dfrac{5x-1}{x+1} = 6$

2 Solve the following equations, giving your answers correct to 3 significant figures if they are not exact.

   a $9x^2 - 25 = 0$ **b** $2x^2 + 3x - 27 = 0$ **c** $3x^2 + 8x - 4 = 0$

3 Write $x^2 - x - 5$ in the form $(x + a)^2 + b$.

4 Find the nth term of the following sequences:

   a $\dfrac{1}{3} \quad \dfrac{3}{6} \quad \dfrac{5}{9} \quad \dfrac{7}{12} \cdots$

   b $0 \quad \dfrac{1}{4} \quad \dfrac{4}{9} \quad \dfrac{9}{16} \cdots$

> **NOTE:**
>
> $\dfrac{0}{1} = 0$

5 Given that y is inversely proportional to $\sqrt{x}$, and that $y = 10$ when $x = 9$, find

   a   a formula connecting x and y

   b **i** y when $x = 40$ **ii** x when $y = 20$.

6 Rearrange the following formulae:

   a $\dfrac{A-b}{c} = D$ make B the subject

   b $\dfrac{A}{a} = \dfrac{B}{b}$ make B the subject

7 Solve the following inequality.

   $3x - 5 < 5x \leqslant 3x + 2$

8 Solve the following pairs of simultaneous equations

a $2y + 3x = 10$
$3y - 2x = -11$

b $7y - x = 17$
$5x + y = -73$

9 The nth term of a sequence is $\dfrac{(n-2)^2}{(n+2)^2}$. Write down the first 5 terms.

Exam-style questions

DO NOT USE A CALCULATOR IN QUESTIONS 10 TO 31

10 a

The set $A = \{x : 1 \leqslant x < 3\}$ is shown on the number line above.

i Set B is shown on the number line below.

Complete the description given below.

$B = \{x : \ldots\ldots\ldots\ x \ldots\ldots\ldots\}$

ii The set $C = \{x : x \leqslant -3\}$.

Illustrate the set C' using the number line given below.

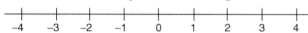

b $X = \{1, 3, 5\}$, $Y = \{3, 5\}$, $Z = \{(x, y) : x \in X, y \in Y, x \neq y\}$.

List the members of Z.

satisfy both

$2x + 7 < 3$ and $x \geqslant -4$. (4024 paper 01 Q20 June 2005)

11 It is given that $p = \dfrac{12}{\sqrt{q}}$.

a Describe the relationship between p and q in words.

b Calculate q when $p = 4$. (4024 paper 01 Q6 June 2006)

12 a Factorise fully $5x^2 - 10x$.

b Solve $3y + 6 = 7y - 10$.

c Solve $3p(p + 2) = 0$. (4024 paper 01 Q11 November 2005)

13 a The first five terms of a sequence are 1, 3, 6, 10, 15.

The nth term of this sequence is $\frac{1}{2}n(n + 1)$.

Find the 19th term.

b Write down an expression, in terms of n, for the nth term of the sequence

3, 6, 10, 15, 21, … (4024 paper 01 Q6 November 2005)

14 Solve the simultaneous equations

$3x = 7y$

$12y = 5x - 1$. (4024 paper 01 Q 11 June 2006)

15 a Given that $x = 6$ is a solution of $\frac{x^3}{3} + k = 0$ find the value of k.

   b Solve $2y^2 - 3y - 2 = 0$.   *(4024 paper 01 Q17 June 2006)*

16 a Solve $-7 \leqslant 3x - 4 < 2$.

   b Write down all the integers which satisfy $-7 \leqslant 3x - 4 < 2$. *(4024 paper 01 Q9 June 2006)*

17 a When an object is falling, the air resistance varies as the square of the speed.
       At a certain speed, the resistance is 30 newtons.
       What is the resistance at twice this speed?

   b y is inversely proportional to x.
       Given that $y = 6$ when $x = 4$, find the value of y when $x = 3$.

                                              (4024 paper 01 Q12 November 2007)

18 Solve the equations

   a $\frac{24}{x-4} = 1$,   **b** $12 - 2(5 - y) = 5y$.   *(4024 paper 01 Q14 November 2007)*

19 a Solve $8 - 3t > 14 + t$.

   b Evaluate $x^2 - 6xy + 2y^2$ when $x = 2$ and $y = -3$.   *(4024 paper 01 Q21 June 2008)*

20 a The nth term of a sequence is $7 - 2n$.
       Write down the 23rd term in this sequence.

   b i The first five terms of another sequence are

                   4   7   10   13   16.

          Write down an expression, in terms of n, for the nth term of this sequence.

     ii The first five terms of another sequence are

$$\frac{4}{1} \quad \frac{7}{4} \quad \frac{10}{9} \quad \frac{13}{16} \quad \frac{16}{25}.$$

        a Write down the next term in this sequence.

        b Write down an expression, in terms of n, for the nth term of this sequence.

                                      (4024 paper 01 Q 22 June 2008)

21 It is given that y is directly proportional to the square of x and that $y = 1$ when $x = \frac{1}{2}$.
   Find

   a the formula for y in terms of x,

   b the values of x when $y = 9$.   *(4024 paper 01 Q10 June 2008)*

22 T is inversely proportional to the square of L.
   Given that $T = 9$ when $L = 2$, find

   a the formula for T in terms of L,

   b the values of L when $T = 25$.   *(4024 paper 01 Q10 November 2008)*

23 a Solve the inequality $3 - 2x < 5$.

   b Solve the equation $3(y + 2) = 2(2y - 7) + y$.   *(4024 paper 01 Q16 November 2008)*

24 y is directly proportional to the square root of x.
   Given that $y = 12$ when $x = 36$,
   find

   a the formula for y in terms of x,

   b the value of x when $y = 10$.   *(4024 paper 01 Q12 June 2009)*

25 a Express $\frac{2m}{5} + \frac{m}{4}$ as a single fraction in its simplest terms.

   b Solve the inequality $5(x + 4) < 7x$.   *(4024 paper 01 Q13 November 2009)*

26 y is inversely proportional to x.
Given that $y = 250$ when $x = 4$, find y when $x = 80$. (4024 paper 01 Q6 November 2009)

27 a Solve
i $9 - k < 7$ **ii** $\frac{5}{2t} = \frac{1}{12}$

b Solve the simultaneous equations $x + y = 29$,
$4x = 95 - 2y$. (4024 paper 01 Q22 June 2007)

28 Solve the simultaneous equations $\frac{1}{2}x + 2y = 16$,
$2x + \frac{1}{2}y = 19$. (0580 paper 02 Q8 June 2005)

29 $c = \frac{b(a - b)}{a}$
a Find c when $a = 4$ and $b = -2$.
b Rearrange the formula to make a the subject. (4024 paper 12 Q11 June 2012)

YOU MAY USE A CALCULATOR FOR THE REST OF THIS EXERCISE

30 a i The cost of a book is $\$x$.
Write down an expression in terms of x for the number of these books which are bought for $40.
ii The cost of each book is increased by $2.
The number of books which are bought for $40 is now one less than before.
Write down an equation in x and show that it simplifies to $x^2 + 2x - 80 = 0$.
iii Solve the equation $x^2 + 2x - 80 = 0$.
iv Find the original cost of one book.

b Magazines cost $\$m$ each and newspapers cost $\$n$ each. One magazine costs $2.55 more than one newspaper. The cost of two magazines is the same as the cost of five newspapers.
i Write down two equations in m and n to show this information.
ii Find the values of m and n. (0580 paper 04 Q8 November 2005)

31

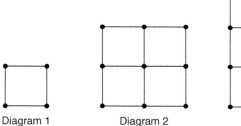 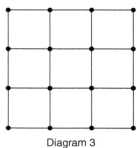

Diagram 1   Diagram 2   Diagram 3

The first three diagrams in a sequence are shown above.
The diagrams are made up of dots and lines. Each line is one centimetre long.
a Make a sketch of the next diagram in the sequence.
b The table below shows some information about the diagrams.

Diagram	1	2	3	4	....	n
Area	1	4	9	16	....	x
Number of dots	4	9	16	p	....	y
Number of one centimetre lines	4	12	24	q	....	z

    i Write down the values of p and q.

   ii Write down each of x, y and z in terms of n.

c The **total** number of one centimetre lines in the first n diagrams is given by the expression

$\frac{2}{3}n^3 + fn^2 + gn$

    i Use $n = 1$ in this expression to show that $f + g = \frac{10}{3}$.

   ii Use $n = 2$ in this expression to show that $4f + 2g = \frac{32}{3}$.

  iii Find the values of f and g.

  iv Find the total number of one centimetre lines in the first 10 diagrams.

(0580 paper 04 Q9 June 2007)

32 Solve the inequality $4 - 5x < 2(x + 4)$.   (0580 paper 02 Q16 November 2005)

33 The length, y, of a solid is inversely proportional to the square of its height, x.

  a Write down a general equation for x and y.

       Show that when $x = 5$ and $y = 4.8$ the equation becomes $x^2 y = 120$.

  b Find y when $x = 2$.

  c Find x when $y = 10$.

  d Find x when $y = x$.

  e Describe exactly what happens to y when x is doubled.

  f Describe exactly what happens to x when y is decreased by 36%.

  g Make x the subject of the formula $x^2 y = 120$.   (0580 paper 04 Q5 June 2006)

34 Make c the subject of the formula

    $\sqrt{3c - 5} = b$.   (0580 paper 04 Q5 June 2006)

35 Make d the subject of the formula

    $c = \frac{d^2}{2} + 5$.   (0580 paper 02 Q12 November 2005)

36 Use the formula $P = \frac{V^2}{R}$ to calculate the value of P when $V = 6 \times 10^6$ and $R = 7.2 \times 10^8$.

(0580 paper 02 Q2 November 2007)

37 Solve the equations

  a $\frac{2x}{3} - 9 = 0$ **b** $x^2 - 3x - 4 = 0$

(0580 paper 02 Q14 November 2007)

38 Solve the inequality

    $\frac{2x - 5}{8} > \frac{x - 4}{3}$

(0580 paper 21 Q13 June 2008)

39 a There are 10^9 nanoseconds in 1 second.
Find the number of nanoseconds in 5 minutes, giving your answer in standard form.

b Solve the equation
$5(x + 3 \times 10^6) = 4 \times 10^7$

(0580 paper 21 Q14 June 2009)

40 a i Factorise $x^2 - x - 20$.

ii Solve the equation $x^2 - x - 20 = 0$.

b Solve the equation: $3x^2 - 2x - 2 = 0$.
Show all your working and give your answers correct to 2 decimal places.

c $y = m^2 - 4n^2$.

i Factorise $m^2 - 4n^2$.

ii Find the value of y when $m = 4.4$ and $n = 2.8$.

iii $m = 2x + 3$ and $n = x - 1$.
Find y in terms of x in its simplest form.

iv Make n the subject of the formula $y = m^2 - 4n^2$.

d i $m^4 - 16n^4$ can be written as $(m^2 - kn^2)(m^2 + kn^2)$.
Write down the value of k.

ii Factorise completely $m^4 n - 16n^5$.

(0580 paper 04 Q2 June 2008)

41 The length of time, T seconds, that the pendulum in a clock takes to swing is given by the formula

$$T = \frac{6}{\sqrt{(1 + g^2)}}$$

Rearrange the formula to make g the subject.

(0580 paper 02 Q17 November 2007)

42 a Factorise $ax^2 + bx^2$.

b Make x the subject of the formula $ax^2 + bx^2 - d^2 = p^2$.

(0580 paper 21 Q8 November 2008)

43 The quantity p varies inversely as the square of $(q + 2)$.
$p = 5$ when $q = 3$.
Find p when $q = 8$.

(0580 paper 21 Q13 November 2008)

44 Rearrange the formula to make y the subject.

$$x + \frac{\sqrt{y}}{9} = 1.$$

(0580 paper 21 Q9 June 2006)

45 Solve the simultaneous equations $2x + \frac{1}{2}y = 1$,

$6x - \frac{3}{2}y = 21$.

(0580 paper 02 Q7 November 2007)

46 a Solve the equation $\frac{m-3}{4} + \frac{m+4}{3} = -7$.

b i $y \frac{3}{x-1} - \frac{2}{x-3}$
Find the value of y when $x = 5$.

ii Write $\frac{3}{x-1} - \frac{2}{x+3}$ as a single fraction.

iii Solve the equation $\frac{3}{x-1} - \frac{2}{x+3} = \frac{1}{x}$.

c $p = \frac{t}{q-1}$
Find q in terms of p and t.

(0580 paper 04 Q3 November 2009)

47 It is given that $y = \frac{3x^2 - 12}{5}$.

   a Find y when $x = -3$.

   b Find the values of x when $y = 0$.

   c For values of x in the range $-3 \leqslant x \leqslant 2$, write down

      i the largest value of y **ii** the smallest value of y.

   d Express x in terms of y.

   e It is also given that $y = \frac{t-3}{2}$ when $x = t$.

      i Show that t satisfies the equation $6t^2 - 5t - 9 = 0$.

      ii Solve the equation $6t^2 - 5t - 9 = 0$, giving each answer
correct to **two significant figures**.   (4024 paper 02 Q10 June 2007)

48 a Solve the equation $7a^2 + 12a - 11 = 0$, giving your answers correct to two decimal places.

   b Ann drove for 4 hours at an average speed of x km/h and then for 6 hours at an average speed of y km/h.
She drove a total distance of 816 km.

      i Write down an equation in terms of x and y, and show that it simplifies to $2x + 3y = 408$.

      ii Ken drove for 3 hours at an average speed of x km/h and then for 5 hours at an average speed of y km/h.
He drove a total distance of 654 km.
Write down an equation, in terms of x and y, to represent this information.

      iii Solve these two equations to find the value of x and the value of y.

                                       (4024 paper 02 Q6 November 2006)

49 a Solve the equation $3x^2 - 4x - 5 = 0$, giving your answers correct to two decimal places.

   b Remove the brackets and simplify $(3a - 4b)^2$.

   c Factorise completely $12 + 8t - 3y - 2ty$.   (4024 paper 02 Q1 June 2006)

50 A road tanker holds 24 tonnes of oil.

   a In cold weather it can pump out x tonnes of oil per minute.
Write down an expression, in terms of x, for the number of minutes it takes to empty the tanker in cold weather.

   b In hot weather it can pump out $(x + 0.5)$ tonnes of oil per minute.
Write down an expression, in terms of x, for the number of minutes it takes to empty the tanker in hot weather.

   c It takes 2 minutes longer to empty the tanker in cold weather than in hot weather.
Write down an equation in x, and show that it simplifies to $2x^2 + x - 12 = 0$.

   d Solve the equation $2x^2 + x - 12 = 0$, giving the solutions **correct to 3 decimal places**.

   e Find the time taken, in minutes and seconds, correct to the nearest second, to empty the tanker in cold weather.   (4024 paper 02 Q6 November 2005)

51 a Solve the equation $\frac{3t+1}{2} = 4$.

   b Solve the simultaneous equations
$2x + y = 12$
$3y - 2x = 56$

   c Simplify $\frac{3y^2 + 8y + 4}{y^2 - 4}$.

   d Given that $3h + 2x = 2f - gx$, express x in terms of f, g and h.

                                       (4024 paper 02 Q2 November 2005)

52 Solve the equations

a $2^y = 8$

b $3p + 4 = 8 - 2(p - 3)$

c $\dfrac{18}{q} - \dfrac{16}{q+2} = 1$

d $5x^2 + x - 7 = 0$, giving each solution correct to 2 decimal places.

(4024 paper 02 Q1 November 2009)

53 a Each diagram in the sequence below consists of a number of dots.

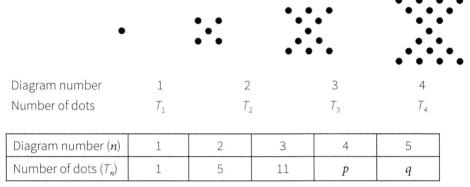

Diagram number	1	2	3	4
Number of dots	T_1	T_2	T_3	T_4

Diagram number (n)	1	2	3	4	5
Number of dots (T_n)	1	5	11	p	q

i Write down the value of p.

ii Find the value of q.

b Another sequence of patterns of dots is shown below.

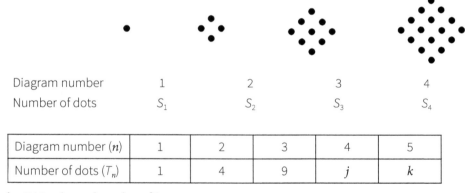

Diagram number	1	2	3	4
Number of dots	S_1	S_2	S_3	S_4

Diagram number (n)	1	2	3	4	5
Number of dots (T_n)	1	4	9	j	k

i Write down the value of j.

ii Find the value of k.

iii Express S_n in terms of n.

c Another sequence is formed whose nth term U_n is $T_n - S_n$.

$U_1 = T_1 = S_1 = 1 - 1 = 0,$ $U_2 = T_2 - S_2 = 5 - 4 = 1,$ $U_3 = T_3 - S_3 = 11 - 9 = 2.$

i Evaluate U_4 and U_5.

ii Express U_n in terms of n.

iii Hence, using your expression for S_n found in (b)(iii), express T_n in terms of n.

(4024 paper 02 Q6 November 2008)

54 A light aircraft flew from Maseru to Nata and returned to Maseru.

a The distance from Maseru to Nata is 1080 km.

i On the outward flight, the average speed of the aircraft was x kilometres per hour.
Write down an expression, in terms of x, for the time taken in hours.

ii On the return flight, the average speed was 30 km/h greater than the average speed on the outward flight.
Write down an expression, in terms of x, for the time taken, in hours, on the return flight.

b The time taken on the return flight was half an hour less than the time taken on the outward flight.

Form an equation in x and show that it reduces to $x^2 + 30x - 64\,800 = 0$.

c Solve the equation $x^2 + 30x - 64\,800 = 0$.

d Calculate

i the time taken, in hours, on the outward flight

ii the average speed for the whole flight from Maseru to Nata and back to Maseru.

(4024 paper 02 Q7 November 2008)

55 a Solve the equation $\frac{2p+1}{3} = 1 + \frac{p-3}{2}$.

b Simplify $\frac{2v-6}{v^2-2v-3}$.

c The tens digit of a number is x and the units digit is y.

Hence the value of the number is $10x + y$.

For example, if $x = 5$ and $y = 6$, the number would be $10 \times 5 + 6 = 56$.

i When the digits x and y are reversed, the value of the number is increased by 63.

Show that $y - x = 7$.

ii The sum of the original number and the number with reversed digits is 99.

a Show that $x + y = 9$.

b Hence find the value of x and the value of y. *(4024 paper 02 Q3 November 2008)*

56 a It is given that $x = a + \sqrt{a^2 + b^2}$.

i Calculate x when $a = 0.73$ and $b = 1.84$.

Give your answer correct to 2 decimal places.

ii Express b in terms of x and a.

b A shopkeeper sells pens and pencils.

Each pen costs \$5 and each pencil costs \$3.

One day he sold x pens.

On the same day he sold 9 more pens than pencils.

i Write down an expression, in terms of x, for his total income from the sale of these pens and pencils.

ii This total income was less than \$300. Form an inequality in x and solve it.

iii Hence write down the maximum number of pens that he sold.

(4024 paper 02 Q2 November 2007)

Learning Objectives
Syllabus sections 28, 31 and 32

In this chapter we
- look at symmetry in three-dimensional shapes
- investigate more circle facts
- work with irregular polygons.

17.1 Introduction

This chapter develops the ideas that began in Chapter 6. It is essential that you fully understand that work.

You will need a ruler, compasses, protractor and possibly tracing paper.

17.2 Essential Skills

1 Construct accurately a triangle with sides 6 cm, 4 cm and 5 cm. Measure the angles of the triangle.

2 Calculate the interior angle of a regular nonagon.

3 Calculate the total interior angle of a 13-sided polygon.

4 Name the quadrilaterals with the following properties:
   a The diagonals bisect each other but not at right angles.
   b One diagonal is the perpendicular bisector of the other.
   c One pair of opposite sides is parallel.
   d Each diagonal is the perpendicular bisector of the other. The diagonals are different lengths.

5 Describe the symmetry of each figure shown below

   a **H**   b **%**   c   d ⊠

6 The figure below is the net for which solid shape?

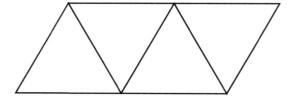

7

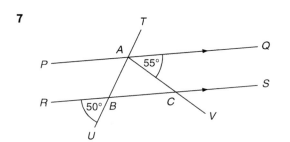

a Name a pair of corresponding angles.
b Name a pair of alternate angles.
c Name a pair of vertically opposite angles.
d Calculate the size of angle *BAC*, giving reasons for your answer.

17.3 Symmetry in Three-Dimensional Shapes

We have seen that two-dimensional shapes can have lines of symmetry, with one side of the line of symmetry perfectly matching the other when the shape is folded along the line. The line of symmetry is a mirror line, and one side of the line of symmetry is the mirror image of the other. In a similar way, three-dimensional shapes can have **planes of symmetry**. One side of the plane of symmetry perfectly matches the other, and is in fact the mirror image of the other side.

A simple example is a cuboid as is shown in Figure 17.1. The cuboid has three planes of symmetry: one in a horizontal direction, as shown in the first diagram, and two in vertical directions, shown in the second and third diagrams.

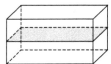 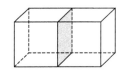 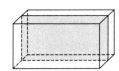

Figure 17.1 Planes of symmetry of a cuboid

Example 1

a Draw a plane of symmetry in these shapes:
   i a square-based pyramid
   ii a regular tetrahedron (triangular-based pyramid)
   iii a cylinder.

b How many planes of symmetry are there in
   i the square-based pyramid?
   ii the regular tetrahedron?
   iii the cylinder?

Answer 1

a **i** 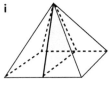   **ii**   **iii**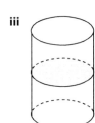

b i 4

ii 6

iii 1 horizontal plane of symmetry as shown
in part (a), but an infinite number of vertical planes of symmetry.

NOTE:
Remember the diagonals.

We have also seen that a two-dimensional shape may have rotational symmetry about a point, or centre of symmetry. The order of rotational symmetry is given by the number of different ways that the shape can be rotated and fitted into its own outline until it returns to the first position.

A three-dimensional shape may also have rotational symmetry, but it will be about an axis, rather than a centre. An example is shown in the diagrams of a square-based pyramid in Figure 17.2; this has a vertical axis of rotational symmetry, and the symmetry is of order 4 because the pyramid will fit its own outline in four different ways. One vertex of the base of the pyramid is marked with a cross to show the four different positions.

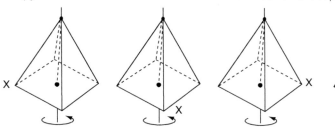

Figure 17.2 Rotational symmetry

Example 2
The cuboid shown below has two square faces and four rectangular faces.

a Describe the symmetry of the cuboid about the axis of symmetry *XY*.
b How many other axes of symmetry does the cuboid have?
c Copy the diagram, draw in the other axes of symmetry, and beside each axis write down the order of symmetry about that axis.

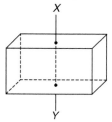

Answer 2
a The cuboid has rotational symmetry of order 2 about the axis of symmetry *XY*.
b The cuboid has two more axes of symmetry.
c

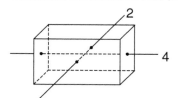

Example 3

a Sketch a cone.

b Draw an axis of symmetry of the cone.

c What is the order of rotational symmetry of the cone about this axis?

Answer 3

a, b

c The order of rotational symmetry is infinite.

Exercise 17.1

1 a Sketch an equilateral triangular prism.

  b How many axes of symmetry does the prism have?

  c Draw two of the axes of symmetry on your sketch, and beside each one write down the order of rotational symmetry about that axis.

  d How many planes of symmetry does the prism have?

2 a Sketch a regular tetrahedron.

  b Draw one of its axes of symmetry.

  c Write down the order of rotational symmetry beside this axis.

3 Describe the symmetry of the shapes shown below.

a
circular
base

b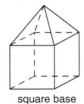
square base

c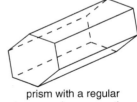
prism with a regular
hexagonal cross-section

17.4 Further Circle Facts

We have seen how the two-dimensional symmetry of the circle means that the tangent at a point is at right angles to the radius at that point. We now look at three more properties of the circle which are due to its symmetry. In Figures 17.3–17.5, a line of symmetry is drawn as a dotted line. In each case folding the circle along that line will result in one side fitting exactly over the other.

- **Equal chords are equidistant from the centre of the circle:**
  $AB = CD$
  OP is perpendicular to AB
  OQ is perpendicular to CD
  $OP = OQ$

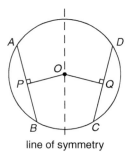

line of symmetry

Figure 17.3 Equal chords

- **The perpendicular bisector of a chord passes through the centre of the circle:**

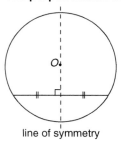

line of symmetry

Figure 17.4 Perpendicular bisector of a chord

- **Tangents from a point outside the circle are equal in length:**

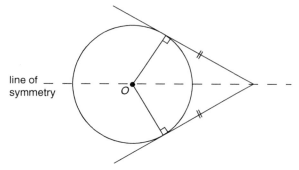

Figure 17.5 Tangents from an external point

You need to be able to recall these facts and use them in solving circle problems.

Example 4

1

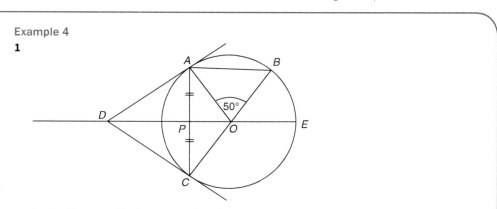

In the diagram, O is the centre of circle, angle $AOB = 50°$, and DA and DC are tangents to the circle. BOC is a straight line. $AP = PC$.

a   Show that AB is parallel to DE.

b   Find angle ADC.

Answer 4

a $\angle BAC = 90°$ (angle in a semicircle)

     $\angle APD = 90°$ (perpendicular bisector of a chord

                               passes through the centre of the circle)

     So AB is parallel to DE (alternate angles)

b $\angle AOC = 180 - 50 = 130°$ (angles on a straight line)

     $\angle DAO = \angle DCO = 90°$ (angle between a tangent and a radius)

     $\angle ADC = 360 - 130 - 2 \times 90$ (angle sum of a quadrilateral)

     $\angle ADC = 50°$

NOTE:

This is just one way to arrive at the answer. There are other ways also.

Exercise 17.2

1

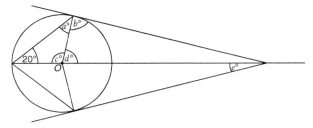

In the diagram, O is the centre of the circle. Find a, b, c, d and e.

2

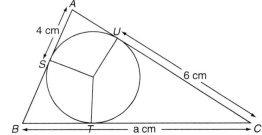

The perimeter of the triangle is 29 cm. Find a, giving reasons.

3

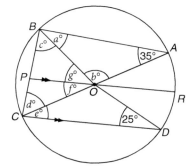

In the diagram, O is the centre of the circle and PR is parallel to CD. AOC is a straight line.
Find a, b, c, d, e, f and g, giving reasons.

Investigations

In each of these investigations draw the diagrams and measure the angles accurately. Record the measured angles for comparison.

1   Draw a circle, centre *O* and radius 6 centimetres. Mark the centre with a dot as soon as you remove your compass point so that you can find it accurately.

Choose any three points on the circumference, and label them *A*, *B* and *C* as in Figure 17.6.

Join *AB*, *AO*, *BC* and *OC* as shown.

Measure angles *ABC* and *AOC*.

Repeat with circles of different radii and different positions on the circumference. You should find that:

- **The angle at the centre of the circle is twice the angle at the circumference.**

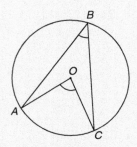

Figure 17.6 Angles at centre and circumference

2   Draw another circle, centre *O* and radius 6 centimetres.

Mark four points on the circumference and label them *A*, *B*, *C* and *D* as shown in Figure 17.7.

Join *AB*, *BD*, *AC*, *CD* and *AD* as shown.
Measure angles *ABD* and *ACD*.

Repeat with other circles and points on the circumference.

Draw some with *C* above the chord *AD* and some with *C* below the chord *AD* as shown in Figure 17.8.

Remember that the chord *AD* divides the circle into two segments. When *B* and *C* are both above the chord they are in the same segment; when one is below the chord they are in opposite segments.

You should have found that:

- **Angles in the same segment standing on the same chord are equal.**
- **Angles in opposite segments standing on the same chord add up to 180°.**
The term for pairs of angles which add up to 180° is **supplementary**, so we can reword the second of the above facts:

- **Angles in opposite segments are supplementary.**

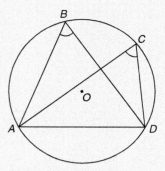

Figure 17.7 Angles subtended by chord

3   Draw one final circle and mark any four points on the circumference. Join the points to form a quadrilateral, as shown in Figure 17.9. Measure all the angles.
You should find that the opposite angles of the quadrilateral add up to 180°.

This also follows from the fact that we have just found, namely that angles in opposite segments of the circle are supplementary, because the diagonals of the quadrilateral form chords which divide the circle into segments.

A quadrilateral that has its vertices on a circle is called a **cyclic quadrilateral**, so we have a new fact:

- **Opposite angles of a cyclic quadrilateral are supplementary.**
A cyclic quadrilateral can have a circle drawn through all its vertices, but this does not apply to all quadrilaterals. We can use the fact that if opposite angles of a quadrilateral are supplementary then the quadrilateral is a cyclic quadrilateral.

- **If the opposite angles of a quadrilateral are supplementary then the quadrilateral is cyclic.**
It follows that all squares and rectangles are always cyclic quadrilaterals. Why? Which of the other special quadrilaterals *can* be cyclic, and what conditions would apply?

To test your answers to the above try to draw each type of quadrilateral in a circle, and see if you are right.

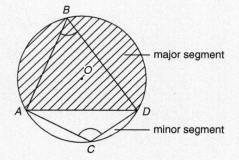

Figure 17.8 Major and minor segments

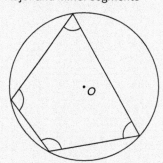

Figure 17.9 Cyclic quadrilateral

17.5 Finding the Centre of a Circle

We can use the fact that the perpendicular bisector of a chord passes through the centre of the circle to find the centre of any circle.

Try the following:

- Draw carefully round any circular object, such as a tin lid or a cylinder.
- Draw a chord, and construct the perpendicular bisector of the chord.
- Draw another chord, and construct the perpendicular bisector of the second chord. The two perpendicular bisectors will intersect at the centre of the circle.

Example 5

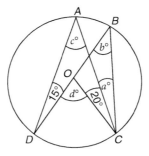

Find a, b, c and d, giving reasons.

Answer 5

$\angle ACB = \angle ADB = 15°$	(angles in the same segment standing on the same chord or arc, AB)
$a = 15°$	
$\angle OBC = \angle OCB = 20 + 15 = 35°$	(isosceles triangle)
$b = 35°$	
$\angle DAC = \angle DBC = 35°$	(angles in the same segment standing on the same chord or arc, DC)
$c = 35°$	
$d = 70°$	(angle at the centre is twice the angle at the circumference)

NOTE:
The chords AB and DC are not drawn in the diagram, so we could say 'standing on the same arc AB' instead. It makes no difference.

Example 6

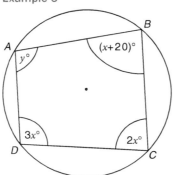

Calculate x and y.

Answer 6

$3x + (x + 20) = 180$ (opposite angles of a cyclic quadrilateral)

$4x + 20 = 180$

$4x = 160$

$x = 40$

$y + 2x = 180$ (opposite angles of a cyclic quadrilateral)

$y + 2 \times 40 = 180$

$y = 100$

Exercise 17.3

1   Find the angles marked x in the diagrams below. Give reasons for your answers.

a

b

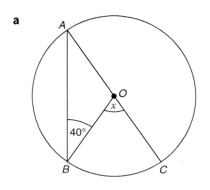

AB and CB are tangents to the circle, centre O.

In questions 2, 3 and 4, use the information in the diagrams to find the angles marked with letters. Give reasons.

2

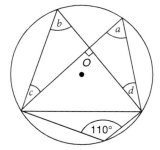

3

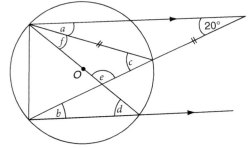

4

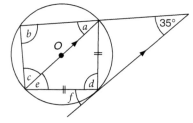

5

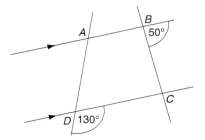

Show that $ABCD$ is a cyclic quadrilateral.

17.6 Irregular Polygons

Regular polygons have all angles and all sides equal, but this does not apply to irregular polygons. However, the angle sum of irregular polygons can be calculated in the same way as before. Figure 17.10 shows an irregular hexagon divided into four triangles. The angle sum is $4 \times 180° = 720°$.

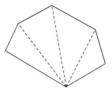

Figure 17.10 Irregular polygon

The exterior angles of each irregular polygon add up to 360° as before.

Example 7

Calculate x in the following polygons.

a
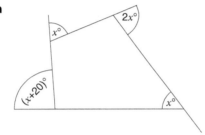

b
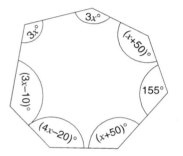

Answer 7

a Using the fact that the exterior angles add up to 360°.

$$x + 2x + (180 - x) + (x + 20) = 360$$
$$3x + 200 = 360$$
$$3x = 160$$
$$x = 53\frac{1}{3}$$

b The angle sum of the interior angles $= (7 - 2) \times 180 = 900°$

$$3x + 3x + (x + 50) + 155 + (x + 50) + (4x - 20) + (3x - 10) = 900$$
$$15x + 225 = 900$$
$$15x = 675$$
$$x = 45$$

Exercise 17.4

1 An irregular polygon has an angle sum of 1980°. How many sides does the polygon have?

2 An irregular nonagon (9 sides) has interior angles $2x°$, $(2x + 1)°$, $(x - 1)°$, $x°$, $3x°$, $(2x - 1)°$, $3x°$, $(x + 1)°$ and $2(x + 1)°$. Calculate x.

3 An irregular pentagon has angles $3a°$, $(a + b)°$, $2b°$, $3b°$ and 40°. A triangle has angles $a°$, $b°$, and $(a + b)°$.
Form two equations in a and b and solve them simultaneously to find a and b.

Exercise 17.5

Mixed exercise

1

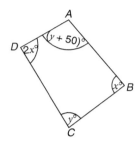

ABCD is a cyclic quadrilateral.
Calculate *x* and *y*.

2

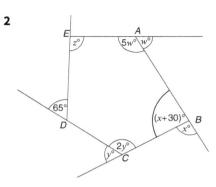

ABCDE is an irregular pentagon. Calculate
w, *x*, *y* and *z*.

3

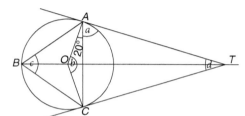

a Find the angles marked *a*, *b*, *c* and *d*.
b Show that *AOCT* is a cyclic quadrilateral.
c Describe where the centre of the circle
AOCT would be located.

4 Describe the symmetry of a pyramid whose base is a regular hexagon.

5 What can you say about (a) *AE* and *BD*, (b) *AF*, *FE*, *BC* and *CD* in this diagram?
Give reasons for your answers.

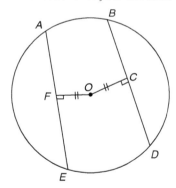

NOT TO SCALE

6

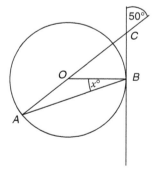

Find *x*, giving reasons for your answer.

7

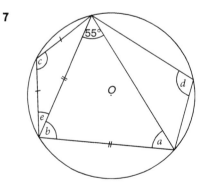

Find the angles marked *a*, *b*, *c*, *d* and *e*,
giving reasons for your answers.

Exam-style questions

8

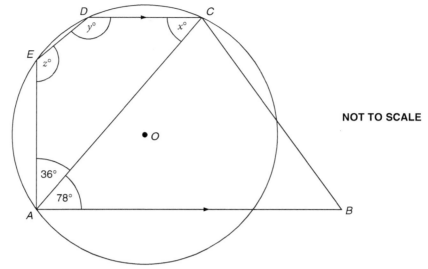

NOT TO SCALE

ABCDE is a pentagon.

A circle, centre *O*, passes through the points *A*, *C*, *D* and *E*.

Angle *EAC* = 36°, angle *CAB* = 78° and *AB* is parallel to *DC*.

a Find the values of *x*, *y* and *z*, giving a reason for each.

b Explain why *ED* is **not** parallel to *AC*.

c Find the value of angle *EOC*.

d *AB = AC*.

Find the value of angle *ABC*. (0580 paper 04 Q8 November 2008)

9

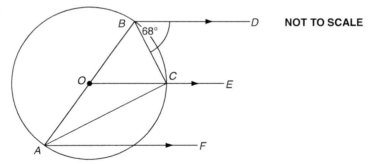

NOT TO SCALE

Points *A*, *B* and *C* lie on a circle, centre *O*, with diameter *AB*.

BD, *OCE* and *AF* are parallel lines.

Angle *CBD* = 68°.

Calculate

a angle *BOC*　　　　　　**b** angle *ACE*. (0580 paper 21 Q19 November 2009)

10 In the diagram, *AB* touches the circle, centre *O*, at *T*.
OB intersects the circle at *C*.

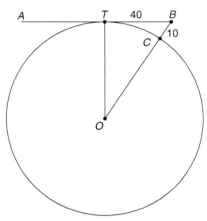

a State, with a reason, the value of *BT̂O*.

b Given that *TB* = 40 cm, *CB* = 10 cm, and the radius of the circle is *x* centimetres, form an equation in *x*, and hence find the radius of the circle.

(4024 paper 11 Q26 November 2011)

11 *A*, *B*, *C* and *D* lie on a circle with centre *O*. *AC* is a diameter of the circle. *AD*, *BE* and *CF* are parallel lines. Angle *ABE* = 48° and angle *ACF* = 126°.

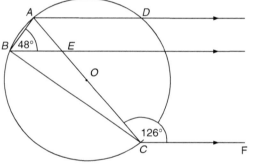

NOT TO SCALE

Find

a angle *DAE*   **b** angle *EBC*   **c** angle *BAE*.

(0580 paper 02 Q15 November 2005)

12 a In the diagram, *ABCD* is a parallelogram.
ADE and *BFE* are straight lines.
AF = *BF*.
AB̂F = 54° and *CB̂F* = 57°.
Find the value of

    i *t*   **ii** *u*

    iii *x*   **iv** *y*.

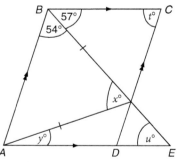

b This hexagon has rotational symmetry of order 3. Calculate the value of *z*.

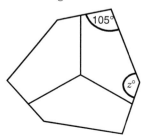

(4024 paper 02 Q3a, b June 2005)

13

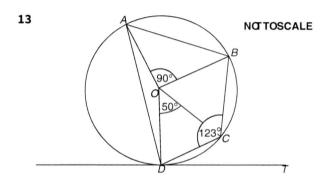

NOT TO SCALE

The points A, B, C and D lie on a circle centre O.
Angle *AOB* = 90°, angle *COD* = 50° and angle *BCD* = 123°.
The line *DT* is a tangent to the circle at *D*.
Find

a angle *OCD*   **b** angle *TDC*
c angle *ABC*   **d** reflex angle *AOC*.   (0580 paper 02 Q20 November 2007)

14

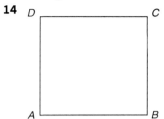

ABCD is a square.
It is rotated through 90° clockwise about *B*.
Copy the square and draw accurately the locus of the point *D*.
(0580 paper 21 Q5 November 2008)

15

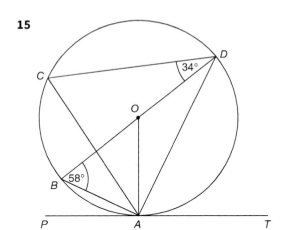

16

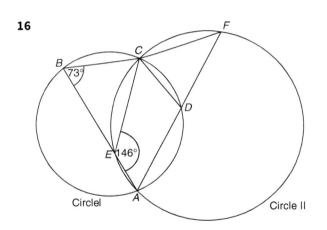

In the diagram, the points A, B, C and D lie on circle I.
The points A, E, C and F lie on circle II.
AEB and ADF are straight lines.
$E\hat{B}C = 73°$ and $A\hat{E}C = 146°$.

a Calculate
  i $A\hat{D}C$
  ii $C\hat{F}A$.

b Explain why the centre of circle I lies on circle II. *(4024 paper 01 Q22 June 2004)*

17 a

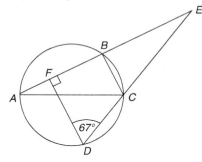

A, B, C and D are points on the circumference of the circle and AC is a diameter.
AFBE and DCE are straight lines.
DF is perpendicular to AE and $C\hat{D}F = 67°$.

  i Find $A\hat{E}D$.
  ii Find $C\hat{B}E$, giving a reason for your answer.
  iii Explain why DF is parallel to CB.

b

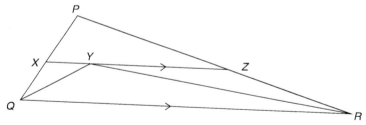

In the triangle PQR, the bisectors of $P\hat{Q}R$ and $P\hat{R}Q$ intersect at Y.
The straight line XYZ is parallel to QR.
Prove that the perimeter of triangle $PXZ = PQ + PR$. *(4024 paper 22 Q2 November 2014)*

18

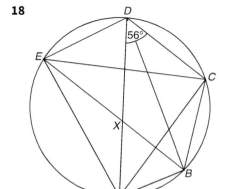

The points A, B, C, D and E lie on a circle.
AD is a diameter of the circle.

DB bisects angle *ADC*.
Angle *ADC* = 56°.

a Giving your reasons, write down
    i angle *DCA*   **ii** angle *DAC*   **iii** angle *CBA*   **iv** angle *AEB*.

b It is given that *EB* is parallel to *DC* and that *EB* cuts *AD* at *X*.
    [You **must not** assume that *X* is the centre of the circle.]
    Show that triangle *BDX* is isosceles.

c Find angle *EBA*.

d Hence or otherwise show that *X* is the centre of the circle.

(4024 paper 02 Q3 November 2005)

19

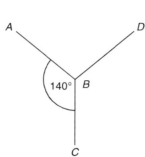

AB and *BC* are adjacent sides of a regular polygon.
$A\hat{B}C = 140°$.

a Calculate the number of sides of the polygon.

b *CB* and *BD* are adjacent sides of a congruent
    regular polygon.
    Calculate $A\hat{B}D$.   (4024 paper 01 Q12 June 2006)

20

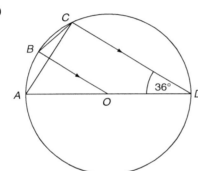

The diagram shows a circle, centre *O*, passing
through *A*, *B*, *C* and *D*.
AOD is a straight line, *BO* is parallel to *CD* and
$C\hat{D}A = 36°$.
Find

a $B\hat{O}A$

b $B\hat{C}A$

c $D\hat{C}B$

d $O\hat{B}C$.   (4024 paper 01 Q14 June 2009)

21

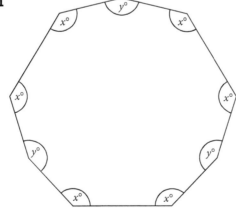

In the diagram, the 9-sided polygon has 6 angles of $x°$ and 3 angles of $y°$.

i For this polygon, state
    a the number of lines of symmetry
    b the order of rotational symmetry.

ii **a** Show that the sum of the interior angles of a 9-sided polygon is 1260°.
    b Find an expression for y in terms of x.
    c Given also that $y = 12 + x$, find x.   (4024 paper 02 Q4a June 2009)

22

The quadrilateral *ABCD* has its vertices on the circumference of a circle.
AE is a tangent to the circle and $A\hat{E}D = 20°$.
The centre of the circle, *O*, lies on the straight line *DE*.

a Find $A\hat{D}O$.

b Given that *DE* is the perpendicular bisector of *AB* and $D\hat{B}A = 55°$,
  i write down $B\hat{A}D$
  ii find $B\hat{C}D$.

(4024 paper 01 Q20 June 2009)

Algebra and Graphs II

Learning Objectives   Syllabus sections 24, 26 and 27

In this chapter you will
- work with distance–time and speed–time graphs
- plot and sketch graphs of curves

- calculate gradient, length, and midpoint of a straight line segment
- work with parallel and perpendicular lines.

18.1 Introduction

This chapter continues the work in Chapter 7. Travel graphs, straight line graphs, and curves are studied in more depth.

18.2 Essential Skills

1   Write down the gradients and y-intercepts of the graphs of the following lines:
    a $y = x + 1$ b $y = -x - 3$ c $y = \frac{1}{2}x$
    d $y = 5$ e $y = -2x + 1$

2   By writing in the form $y = mx + c$ find the y-intercept and the gradient of the line $2x = -5y + 3$.

3   a   Draw a graph for converting degrees Centigrade (°C) to degrees Fahrenheit (°F), given that $0°C = 32°F$ and that $100°C = 212°F$. (The graph should be a straight line connecting these two points.)

    b   Use your graph to convert (i) 25°C to °F and (ii) 125°F to °C.

4   a   Complete the table of values for $y = x^2 - x - 2$.

x	−3	−2	−1	0	1	2	3	4
y	10	4	0	−2	−2	0	4	10

    b   What is the equation of the line of symmetry of this graph?

18.3 Distance-time Graphs

We will now look in more detail at travel graphs.

In Chapter 7 you studied distance-time graphs, and saw that the gradient of the line gave the speed of movement because speed $= \dfrac{\text{distance gone}}{\text{time taken}}$, which is the gradient of the line (gradient $= \dfrac{\text{up}}{\text{along}}$) when the distance travelled is on the vertical (y) axis and the time taken is on the horizontal (x) axis.

You may, for example, need to use a distance-time graph to work out when and where one object overtakes another. The graph in Figure 18.1 shows the journeys of two cyclists, Brendan and Amit, leaving school and travelling along the same route. Brendan leaves school later than Amit, but travels faster. Brendan overtakes Amit at the precise moment when they are both in the same place at the same time; that is, at point P on the graph.

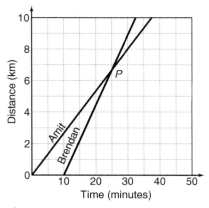

Figure 18.1 Distance–time graph

If the graph shows straight lines, as in the above case, it means that the gradient is the same at any point on each line, so the speed is the same at any point on the journey. The cyclists are travelling at a constant speed.

However, if we think more about a typical journey we realise that the object starts from rest and gradually increases speed until it is travelling at a constant speed. It may then gradually reduce speed until it stops. Such a journey could be shown by the graph in Figure 18.2, showing the short journey of a car.

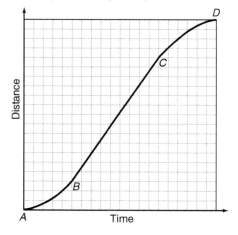

Figure 18.2 Car journey

From *A* to *B* on the graph the car is accelerating (getting faster), from *B* to *C* it is at constant speed, and from *C* to *D* it is decelerating or retarding (getting slower). How could we work out its speed at any precise moment on a curved section, for example when it is accelerating?

Imagine that you could zoom in to look very closely, in great detail, at a curved section. You could imagine it broken into a series of short line segments as in the first diagram in Figure 18.3. The gradient at any point on the curve would be the gradient of the line segment at that point.

  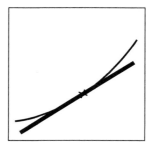

Figure 18.3 Gradient of a curve

We could work out the gradient of the line at that point by extending it as in the second diagram, and then finding $\dfrac{\text{the change in } y}{\text{the change in } x}$ by constructing a right-angled triangle at convenient points.

Now imagine that we can zoom out so that the series of line segments become a smooth curve again, as in the third diagram. The line we have drawn to work out the gradient is now the *tangent* to the curve.

We have shown that the gradient at any point on a curve is the same as the gradient of the tangent at that point. You have met tangents to circles in Chapter 6 and you should know that a tangent is a line that just touches a curve at *one* point. Drawing a tangent to a curve is not something that can be done exactly, but at least it gives an estimate of the speed at any particular time. You will see more about tangents later in this section.

To draw the tangent as accurately as possible it is best to approach the point slowly by sliding your ruler along the paper. If you do this from the inside of the curve, you can make sure that you are cutting off equal arcs on each side of the point until you reach the point where the ruler nearly leaves the curve altogether. Then draw the tangent.

The diagrams in Figure 18.4 show this.

Figure 18.4 Drawing a tangent

The gradient found by drawing a tangent will only give an *estimate* of the speed because it would be impossible to be sure of drawing the tangent at precisely the right place.

18.4 Speed-time Graphs

Finding the Acceleration

Another type of travel graph is a speed-time graph. With **speed** on the vertical (y) axis and time on the horizontal (x) axis the gradient gives $\frac{\text{change in speed}}{\text{time taken}}$ which is, as we know, the acceleration of the object. Constant **acceleration** will give a straight line graph because the gradient (acceleration) stays the same. An example of a speed-time graph is shown in Figure 18.5.

At A the object is stationary. From A to B the object is accelerating with a constant acceleration. From B to C it is travelling at constant speed so the gradient is zero, as is the acceleration. From C to D it is decelerating, until at D it is once again stationary.

The acceleration of the object from A to B in Figure 18.5 is $\frac{45}{20} = 2.25 \text{ m/s}^2$.

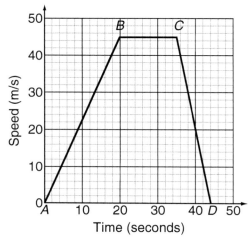

Figure 18.5 Speed-time graph

The deceleration from C to D is $\frac{45}{9} = 5 \text{ m/s}^2$.

You will notice that the gradient while the object is decelerating is negative. We can either say that the acceleration is -5 m/s^2 or that the deceleration (retardation) is 5 m/s^2.

In other words, the word 'deceleration' takes account of the negative gradient.

Finding the Distance Travelled

The area under the graph from the time at A to the time at D in the above diagram gives the distance travelled in that time.

In Figure 18.5 the distance travelled over the whole journey may be calculated by using the formula for the area of a trapezium, or it can be split into triangles and a rectangle.

Using the trapezium formula: Area $= \frac{1}{2}(AD + BC) \times$ distance between them

$$= \frac{1}{2}(44 + 15) \times 45 = 1327.5 \text{ metres}$$

So distance gone during the journey $= 1.33 \text{ km}$.

REMEMBER:

Travel graphs

- On travel graphs the time is shown on the horizontal axis.

Distance-time graphs

- On a distance-time graph the gradient of the line gives the speed.
- A straight line indicates constant speed.
- A curve indicates varying speed, and an estimate of the speed at any time can be found from the gradient of the tangent.
- A horizontal line indicates that the object is stationary.
- A negative gradient indicates that the object has turned round and is heading back to the start. (This means that the distance from the starting point is getting less, not that the object is going back to the origin on the graph.) The gradient still indicates speed, but the sign of the gradient indicates that the object is going in the opposite direction.

Speed-time graphs

- On a speed-time graph the gradient of the line gives the acceleration.
- A straight sloping line indicates constant acceleration.
- A straight horizontal line indicates constant speed.
- A negative gradient indicates that the object is decelerating, but, unlike on a distance-time graph, it does not necessarily mean that the object has turned around.
- The area under the line gives the distance travelled.

Example 1

A car starts from rest at a set of traffic lights at A, shown on the distance-time graph below. It gradually increases speed until it is travelling at a constant speed, shown from B to C on the graph. It then slows to stop at the next set of lights at E.

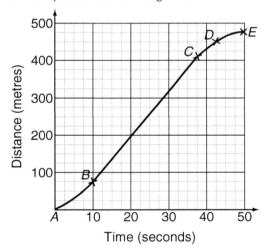

a Calculate the constant speed of the car from B to C.

b Calculate the average speed for the whole time between the traffic lights.
Copy the graph.

c By drawing a tangent, estimate the speed at D.

Answer 1

a The speed of the car from B to C is:

$$\frac{\text{distance gone}}{\text{time taken}} = \frac{410 - 75}{37.5 - 10} = \frac{335}{27.5} = 12.18$$

$$= 12.2 \, \text{m/s to 3 significant figures}$$

b The average speed of the car over the total distance is:

$$\frac{\text{total distance gone}}{\text{total time taken}} = \frac{475}{50} = 9.5\,\text{m/s}$$

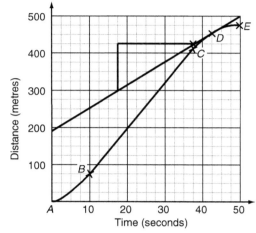

c From the triangle drawn the gradient of the tangent is:

$$\frac{\text{up}}{\text{along}} = \frac{425 - 300}{37.5 - 17.5} = \frac{125}{20}$$

Speed at $D = 6.25\,\text{m/s}$

Example 2

A train leaves station A and steadily increases speed for 60 seconds.

It then travels at a constant speed of 30 metres per second for 2 minutes, finally steadily reducing speed until it comes to rest at station B 5 minutes after leaving station A.

a Draw a speed/time graph to show this journey.

b Calculate the total distance between stations A and B.

c Calculate the acceleration from station A to the maximum speed.

Answer 2

a

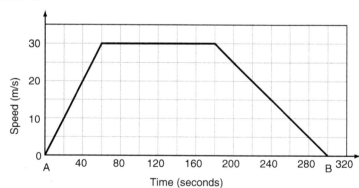

b Total distance = area under graph.

Area of a trapezium $= \frac{1}{2} \times$ sum of the parallel sides $\times$ distance between them

$$= \frac{1}{2}(120 + 300) \times 30 = 6300\,\text{m}$$

Total distance = 6.3 km

c Acceleration = gradient of line $= \frac{30}{60} = 0.5\,\text{m/s}^2$

Exercise 18.1

1 Calculate the areas under the following:

a 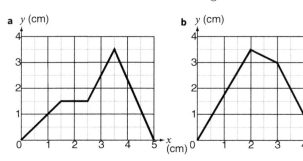 **b**

2 Sister and brother, Svetlana and Igor, go to the same school 2 kilometres from home. Svetlana walks to school, and Igor cycles.
Igor stops on the way at the shops, but Svetlana goes straight to school.
The graph shows their journeys.

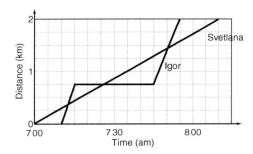

Give your answers to parts **b**, **c** and **e** in kilometres per hour.

a How long does it take Igor to get to school?
b What is his average speed?
c Calculate his speed before and after his visit to the shops.
d At what time does Svetlana overtake Igor?
e Calculate Svetlana's speed.
f When does Igor overtake Svetlana?

3 A small plane leaves an airfield at 1200, and takes 20 minutes to accelerate to its steady cruising speed of 350 km/h. At 1435 it starts to descend for landing. The graph shows this information. (The zig-zag line indicates a break in the scale.)

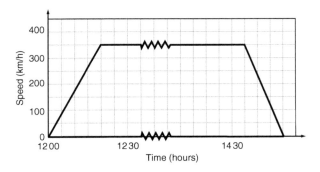

a Calculate the acceleration of the plane during take-off.
b Calculate the total distance the plane travelled.

18.5 More Graphs of Curves

Plotting Graphs of Curves

You need to be able to plot and recognise more curves.

If you do all the questions in the following exercise, you will build up a reference of some of the more frequently used curves together with their equations and special features. You will then be able to recognise curves more easily.

Example 3

Draw the graphs of the following equations for $-3 \leqslant x \leqslant 3$.

a $y = 2^x$ **b** $y = 3 \times 2^x + x^2$

Answer 3

a

x	-3	-2	-1	0	1	2	3
y	0.13	0.25	0.5	1	2	4	8

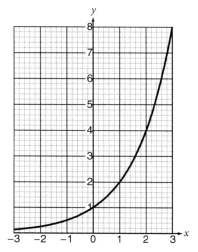

b

x	-3	-2	-1	0	1	2	3
y	9.4	4.8	2.5	3	7	16	33

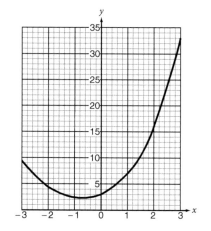

Exercise 18.2

For each of the equations shown below,

   i copy and complete the table, giving your answers correct to 1 decimal place,

   ii draw and label the graph.

1

Question	Equation	x	−3	−2	−1	0	1	2	3
a	$y = x^2$	y	9		1	0			9
b	$y = -x^2$	y			−1	0	−1		−9
c	$y = (x+1)^2$	y	4	1	0	1	4		
d	$y = x^2 - 4$	y		0	−3			0	
e	$y = x^2 - 2^x - 8$	y	7	0		−8	−9		

2

Question	Equation	x	−3	−2	−1	0	1	2	3
a	$y = x^3$	y	−27		−1	0	1		
b	$y = -x^3$	y			1	0			−27
c	$y = (x+1)^3$	y			−1	0		8	
d	$y = x^3 - 4$	y	−31		−5	−4		4	23

3 a

x	−4.5	−4	−3	−2.5	−2	−1.5	−1	−0.5	0	0.5	1
$y = x^3 + 4x^2 + 1$	−9.1	1	10		9		4		1	2.1	6

b

x	−2.5	−2	−1.5	−1	−0.5	0	0.5	1	2
$y = x^3 + x^2 - 2x$	−4.4		1.9	2		0		0	8

c

x	−2.5	−2	−1.5	−1	−0.5	0	0.5	1
$y = x^2(x+2)$	−3.1	0		1	0.4	0		3

d

x	−2.5	−2	−1.5	−1	−0.5	0	0.5	1
$y = -x^2(x+2)$		0		−1	−0.4	0		−3

4

Question	Equation	x	−3	−2.5	−2	−1.5	−1	−0.5	0.5	1	1.5	2	2.5	3
a	$y = \dfrac{3}{x}$	y	−1	−1.2		−2		−6	6	3	2			1
b	$y = \dfrac{9}{x^2}$	y	1		2.3	4	9		36		4		1.4	1
c	$y = x^2 + \dfrac{3}{x}$	y	8		2.5	0.3	−2		6.3	4		5.5		10

5

Equation	x	−0.5	−0.25	0	0.25	0.5	0.75	1
$y = 10^x$	y	0.3		1			5.6	10

Using Graphs of Curves

Having drawn your curve you these are some problems which can be solved using graphs

---

Example 4

The diagram shows the graphs of the curve $y = x^2 + 2x - 1$ and the straight line $y = x + 5$.

   a Use the graph to find the solutions to the equation $x^2 + 2x - 1 = 0$. Give your answers correct to 1 decimal place.

   b Use the curve and the straight line to find the solutions to the equation $-x^2 + x - 6 = 0$.

   c What is the minimum value of $y = x^2 + 2x - 1$?

   d Give the coordinates of the point where the gradient of the curve $= 0$.

   e Find an estimate of the gradient of the curve at the point $(-2, -1)$.

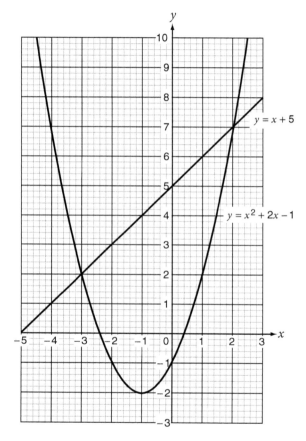

Answer 4

   a The solutions to $x^2 + 2x - 1 = 0$ are the points where $y = 0$ (that is, on the x-axis). So from the graph, the solutions are $x = -2.4$ or $x = 0.4$.

   b The curve and the line meet when the x and y values of the two equations are the same, that is, when they are solved simultaneously.

$$y = x^2 + 2x - 1$$
$$y = x + 5$$

Substituting $y = x + 5$ in the first equation:

$$x + 5 = x^2 + 2x - 1$$
$$x^2 + x - 6 = 0 \qquad\qquad (-x - 5)$$

This is the equation you were asked to solve, so its solutions can be found where the graphs intersect: $x = -3$ and $x = 2$.

> **NOTE:**
> The equation you are asked to solve is in x only, so do not give the y values of the points of intersection!

c The minimum value of $y = x^2 + 2x - 1$ is the minimum value of y as you see it on the graph. The minimum value is $y = -2$.

d The gradient of the curve is zero where the curve is horizontal, so the coordinates are $(-1, -2)$.

> **NOTE:**
> Although you do not need to know this for your course, it might interest you to know that this point is called the turning point, because it is the point at which the curve turns around and the gradient changes from negative to positive.

e The gradient at the point $(-2, -1)$ is estimated by drawing the tangent at that point. This is shown in the next diagram.

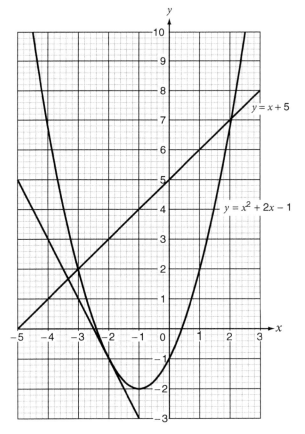

The gradient is $\dfrac{\text{change in } y}{\text{change in } x}$.

From the tangent drawn on the graph an estimate of the gradient is given by

$\dfrac{5 - -3}{-5 - -1}$. Gradient $= \dfrac{8}{-4} = -2$.

Sketching Graphs of Curves

You should have noticed features in the graphs you plotted in Exercise 18.2. For example, the constant term gives the y-intercept just as it does in the equation of a straight line.

The sign in front of the x^2 term in the graph of a parabola also tells us about the parabola. If the sign is negative the graph is 'n' shaped. If the sign is positive the graph is 'u' shaped. If in doubt about the orientation of any curve try putting in a high positive value for x, such as 10 or 100, and see whether the corresponding y value is positive or negative. When you are asked to 'sketch' a curve you do not have to plot points, but just draw a sketch showing key features such as where the curve crosses the axes and its general shape. For a parabola the line of symmetry will always be a vertical line through the midpoint of the two points where the curve crosses the x-axis, as shown in the example below.

Example 5

a For the curve $y = x^2 + x - 2$,
   i factorise the right-hand side.
   ii Hence find the two values of x which make $y = 0$.
   iii Write down the y-intercept.
   iv Sketch the curve.
   v Write down the equation of the line of symmetry.

b Repeat parts (i) to (v) for the curve $y = x^2 - 2x + 1$.

Answer 5

a **i** $y = (x + 2)(x - 1)$
   ii $y = 0$ when $x = -2$ or $x = 1$.
   iii The y-intercept is $y = -2$.
   iv

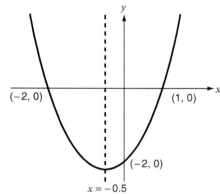

   v The line of symmetry is $x = -0.5$.

b **i** $y = (x - 1)(x - 1)$
   ii $y = 0$ when $x = 1$.

iii The y-intercept is $y = +1$.

iv

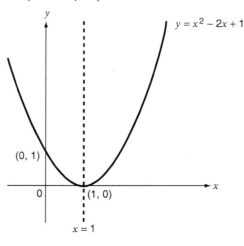

v The line of symmetry is $x = 1$.

Using Function Notation

You will be working with function notation in Chapter 20. Meanwhile, you may meet it briefly in questions about graphs. The following example should show you that you do not have to worry about it at this stage. The $f(x)$ or $g(x)$ just replace y in the equation, as you will see in the example.

Example 6

$$f(x) = \frac{x^2}{x^2 + 1}$$

a Copy and complete the table of values for $0 \leqslant x \leqslant 5$.

x	0	1	2	3	4	5
$f(x)$	0	0.5				0.96

b Using 2 cm to 1 unit on the x-axis, and 10 cm to one unit on the y-axis, draw the graph of $y = f(x)$.

c Why can $f(x) = \frac{x^2}{x^2 + 1}$ never be $\geqslant 1$?

d Why can $f(x) = \frac{x^2}{x^2 + 1}$ never be < 0?

$$g(x) = \frac{5 - x}{5}$$

e On the same axes draw the graph of $y = g(x)$.

f Use your graphs to solve the equation $\frac{x^2}{x^2 + 1} = \frac{5 - x}{5}$, giving your answer to 1 decimal place.

Answer 6

a

x	0	1	2	3	4	5
$f(x)$	0	0.5	0.8	0.9	0.94	0.96

b

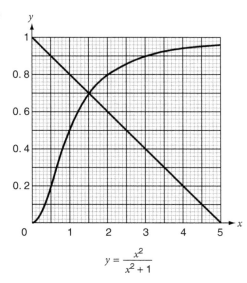

$$y = \frac{x^2}{x^2 + 1}$$

c $f(x)$ can never be greater than or equal to 1 because $x^2 + 1$ is always 1 more than x^2, so that the numerator is always less than the denominator.

d $f(x)$ can never be negative because both the numerator and the denominator will always be positive or zero as x is squared in both, and then 1 is added in the denominator.

e This is a straight line graph.

Using $y = \frac{5-x}{5}$, when $x = 0$, $y = 1$ and when $y = 0$, $x = 5$ so the line goes through $(0, 1)$ and $(5, 0)$ as shown on the graph.

f $x = 1.5$ to 1 decimal place.

Exercise 18.3

1 Draw sketch graphs of the following curves.

On each parabola show the line of symmetry together with its equation. Show the coordinates of the points where the curves cut the axes.

  a $y = 2x^2 + 3x - 5$ **b** $y = x(x - 2)^2$

  c $y = -x^2 + 3x - 2$ **d** $y = (x - 1)(x + 2)(x - 3)$

2 Match the following graphs to their possible equations.

  a   **b**   **c**

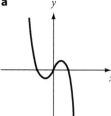   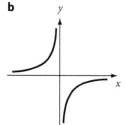   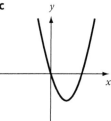

  i $y = \dfrac{1}{x}$ **ii** $y = x^3 - x$

  iii $y = x - x^3$ **iv** $y = 2x - x^2$

  v $y = -\dfrac{1}{x}$ **vi** $y = x^2 - 2x$

3 $y = \dfrac{10x}{(x+1)^2}$

a Copy and complete the following table, giving the values of y to 1 decimal place.

x	0	1	2	3	3.5	4
y	0		2.2			

b Plot these points, using a scale of 2 cm represents 1 unit on each axis.

c By drawing a tangent estimate the gradient when $x = 0.5$.

18.6 Straight Line Segments

Line segments are sections, or segments, of lines.

Two points on a coordinate grid may be joined by a line segment; for example, the line segment AB joining the points (1, 2) and (9, 8) in Figure 18.6.

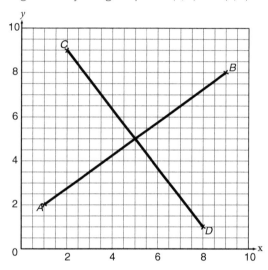

Figure 18.6 Straight line segments

Finding the Gradient of a Line Segment

Since the gradient of a line is $\dfrac{\text{chang in } y}{\text{chang in } x}$, we can easily see from Figure 18.6 that the gradient of the line AB is $\dfrac{6}{8} = \dfrac{3}{4}$.

If you do not have a diagram there are two choices.

Either you can use a formula, or you can write the answer down almost 'by inspection'.

The formula is: **gradient** $= \dfrac{y_2 - y_1}{x_2 - x_1}$

where the line segment joins the points (x_1, y_1) and (x_2, y_2).

In Figure 18.6 the gradient would be calculated using

$$(x_1, y_1) = (1, 2) \qquad \text{and} \qquad (x_2, y_2) = (9.8).$$

$$\text{gradient} = \frac{8-2}{9-1} = \frac{6}{3} = \frac{3}{4}$$

> **NOTE:**
> $\dfrac{y_2 - y_1}{x_2 - x_1} = \dfrac{y_1 - y_2}{x_1 - x_2}$ since both the numerator and the denominator have been multiplied by -1.
> You may choose which points to call (x_1, y_1) and (x_2, y_2), but do not change in mid calculation!

The alternative is to say to yourself 'how do I get from 2 to 8?', and write down +6, followed by 'how do I get from 1 to 9?', and write the +8 under the +6: $\dfrac{+6}{+8} = \dfrac{3}{4}$.

The method you use depends on whether you like learning formulae or not! Either way is acceptable.

The danger with the formula method lies in the misuse of minus signs.

Both methods will be shown in the example.

Finding the Gradient of a Line Perpendicular to a Given Line

Look at the line *CD* in Figure 18.6. *CD* has been drawn perpendicular to *AB*. If you calculate the gradient of *CD* you should see that it is $-\frac{4}{3}$.

This illustrates a new rule:

If m_1 and m_2 are the gradients of two perpendicular lines then $m_1 \times m_2 = -1$.

From our example: $\frac{3}{4} \times \frac{-4}{3} = -1$.

Conversely, to prove that two lines are perpendicular, show that the product of their gradients is -1.

To find a gradient perpendicular to a given gradient you might say to yourself 'turn it upside down and change the sign'. So:

$\frac{-b}{a}$ is perpendicular to $\frac{a}{b}$

$\frac{3}{2}$ is perpendicular to $\frac{-2}{3}$

-1 is perpendicular to 1

-3 is perpendicular to $\frac{1}{3}$.

NOTE:
Remember that 3 is the same as $\frac{3}{1}$.

To summarise:
- Parallel lines have the same gradient.
- Two perpendicular lines have gradients that multiply to give -1.

Finding the Length of a Line Segment

The length of a segment is easily found using Pythagoras' theorem. This important theorem is introduced in Chapter 9. The theorem states that 'the square on the hypotenuse of a right-angled triangle is equal to the sum of the squares on the other two sides.' The hypotenuse is the longest side of a right-angled triangle and is opposite the right angle.

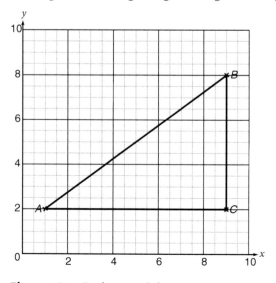

Figure 18.7 Pythagoras' theorem

Figure 18.7 shows a right-angled triangle ABC drawn on the line segment AB. The length of the line AC is $9 - 1 = 8$, and the length of the side BC is $8 - 2 = 6$. By Pythagoras' theorem, $AB^2 = AC^2 + BC^2$, so

$$AB = \sqrt{8^2 + 6^2} = 10 \text{ units.}$$

The formula would be $AB = \sqrt{(x_1 - x_2)^2 + (y_1 - y_2)^2}$.

Notice that it does not matter which way round the subtraction is performed (either $x_1 - x_2$ or $x_2 - x_1$), because the result will be squared, thus losing any minus sign. The alternative would be to think 'how do I get from …?' as before, and straight away write down:

$$AB = \sqrt{8^2 + 6^2} = 10 \text{ units.}$$

Again, the choice is yours, as either method is acceptable.

Finding the Midpoint of a Line Segment

Finding the midpoint could hardly be easier as it is found by taking the *mean* of the x values and the *mean* of the y values. (The mean is dealt with in more detail in Chapter 23 but it is obtained by adding the two values together and then dividing by 2.) In the example above, the midpoint is given by:

$$\left[\frac{1+9}{2}, \frac{2+8}{2}\right] = (5, 5)$$

Check Figure 18.7 and you will see this is correct.

For formula fans, the midpoint is given by $\left[\dfrac{x_1 + x_2}{2}, \dfrac{y_1 + y_2}{2}\right]$.

Example 7

Find
a   the length,
b   the gradient,
c   the midpoint of the line joining A (5, –2) and B (–7, –8).
d   Find the gradient of a line perpendicular to AB.

Answer 7

For this example we will draw a diagram so that you can see that the methods are correct, but normally it is not necessary. However, it does no harm to draw a diagram if that gives you more confidence.

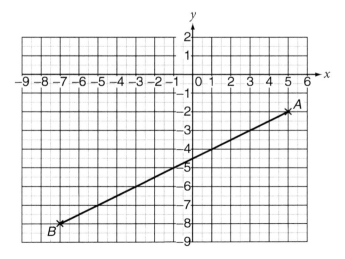

---

a Let $A(5, -2)$ be (x_1, y_1), and $B(-7, -8)$ be (x_2, y_2).

Then AB is given by

$$\sqrt{(5 - -7)^2 + (-2 - -8)^2}$$
$$= \sqrt{12^2 + 6^2}$$
$$= \sqrt{180}$$
$$= 6\sqrt{5}$$

NOTE:
Watch those minus signs!

NOTE:
Leaving the answer as a surd leaves it in its most accurate form. Give to 3 significant figures if requested.

b The gradient of AB is $\dfrac{\text{change in } y}{\text{change in } x}$,

$$= \frac{-8 - -2}{-7 - 5}$$
$$= \frac{-6}{-12} = \frac{1}{2}$$

Or

To get from A to B:

-2 to -8 is subtract 6

5 to -7 is subtract 12,

so gradient $= \dfrac{-6}{-12} = \dfrac{1}{2}$

NOTE:
Remember to go in the same direction (from A to B) each time.

c Midpoint of AB is the mean of the two points.

$$x = \frac{5 + -7}{2} = \frac{-2}{2} = -1$$

$$y = \frac{-2 + -8}{2} = \frac{-10}{2} = -5$$

Midpoint is $(-1, -5)$.

NOTE:
Notice that the two values are added and then divided by 2 to get the mean.

d The gradient of the perpendicular line is $\dfrac{-2}{1} = -2$.

NOTE:
If you are asked to find the equation of the line joining two points, work out the gradient (m) and find the y-intercept (c). Then substitute into $y = mx + c$.

Example 8

a Write down **i** the gradient and **ii** the y-intercept of the line $y = \frac{1}{2}x - 1$.

b Write down the equation of the line parallel to $y = \frac{1}{2}x - 1$ and passing through $(0, 3)$.

c Write down the equation of the line perpendicular to $y = \frac{1}{2}x - 1$ and passing through $(0, 3)$.

d Find the equation of the line passing through A $(2, -5)$ and B $(6, 3)$.

Answer 8

a **i** gradient $= \frac{1}{2}$ **ii** $y = -1$

b $y = \frac{1}{2}x + 3$ **c** $y = -2x + 3$

d gradient $= \frac{8}{4} = 2$

Substituting $m = 2$, $x = 2$ and $y = -5$ (either A or B can be used) into $y = mx + c$:

$-5 = 2 \times 2 + c$

$c = -9$

equation is $y = 2x - 9$.

Exercise 18.4

For each of the line segments joining the following pairs of points find
a its length (giving your answer to 3 significant figures if necessary)
b its gradient (as simplified fractions if not whole numbers)
c its midpoint
d the gradient of a perpendicular line.

   1 $A = (0, 2)$ $B = (1, 6)$
   2 $A = (-1, -1)$ $B = (-2, -2)$
   3 $A = (5, 10)$ $B = (-5, -10)$
   4 $A = (-3, -4)$ $B = (13, 14)$
   5 $A = (4, -7)$ $B = (-3, 1)$
   6 $A = (-1, 3)$ $B = (3, -1)$
   7 $A = (-3, 5)$ $B = (-1, -4)$
   8 $A = (5, 3)$ $B = (1, -2)$

Exercise 18.5

Mixed exercise

1   A ball is thrown vertically up into the air from ground level.

Its height varies with the time of flight according to the following equation:
$h = 15t - 5t^2$

a   Copy and complete the table, giving the values for h correct to 1 decimal place.

t (seconds)	0	0.25	0.5	0.75	1	1.25	1.5	1.75	2	2.25	2.5	2.75	3
h (metres)	0	3.4			10				10				

b   Using scales of 1 cm to represent 1 metre on the vertical axis and 4 cm to represent 1 second on the horizontal axis, draw the distance (height) / time graph for the ball.
c   What is the maximum height of the ball?
d   Draw a tangent to estimate the speed of the ball after 1.25 seconds.
e   What happens to the speed of the ball at its maximum height?
f   With approximately what speed does the ball return to the ground?

2   The speed of the same ball as in the previous question varies with the time according to the following equation:
$speed = 15 - 10t$.

a   Copy and complete the table showing how the speed varies for the first part of the ball's flight.

t (seconds)	0	0.25	0.5	0.75	1	1.25	1.5
speed (m/s)			10	5			

b   Using scales of 1 cm represents 2 metres per second on the vertical axis, and 1 cm represents 0.25 seconds on the horizontal axis, draw the speed-time graph for the first part of the flight of the ball.
c   **i**   What would happen to the graph if you were to carry on and plot the whole of the flight?
     ii   Why is this?
d   Using the graph calculate the height after 1 second.
e   Using the graph calculate the acceleration of the ball.

3   The line $3y + 2x - 12 = 0$ cuts the y-axis at A and the x-axis at B. Find the length of AB.

4 $y = x^2 + \dfrac{1}{x}$

   a Copy and complete the table of values for x and y. Give values of y correct to 1 decimal place.

x	0.1	0.2	0.4	0.6	0.8	1	1.5	2	2.5	3
y	10		2.7				2.9			9.3

   b Using a scale of 1 cm to 1 unit on the y-axis, and 1 cm to 0.2 units on the x-axis, plot the points in the table and draw a smooth curve.

   c On your graph draw the line $y = x$.

   d By drawing a tangent parallel to the line $y = x$, estimate the coordinates of the point where the gradient of the curve = 1. Give the coordinates to the nearest whole number.

   e Write down the equation of the tangent at this point in the form $y = mx + c$, giving c to the nearest whole number.

NOTE:
Be careful! the scales are not the same on each axis!

5 $y = x^2 - x - 6$
$y = -x^2 - x + 6$

   Using a graphical method, solve these two equations simultaneously.
Use integer values of x: $-3 \leqslant x \leqslant 4$.

6 AB is a segment of the line $2y = 3x - 8$.

   a Write down   **i** its gradient, and   **ii** the y-intercept.

   b Find the equation of the line parallel to AB and passing through $(0, 1)$.

   c Find the equation of the line perpendicular to AB and passing through $(0, 1)$.

7 By first finding the gradient of each of the lines below,

   a find two lines which are parallel, and

   b prove that two of the lines are perpendicular.

     AB: $3y - x = 5$

     CD $4y + 2x - 7 = 0$

     EF $y = 3x - 8$

     GH $2y = 5 - x$

     JK $y + 3x = 8$

Exam-style questions

8 The straight line graph of $y = 3x - 6$ cuts the x-axis at A and the y-axis at B.

   a Find the coordinates of A and the coordinates of B.

   b Calculate the length of AB.

   c M is the midpoint of AB.
     Find the coordinates of M.   (0580 paper 12 Q11 June 2012)

9 a P is the point $(-3, 3)$ and Q is the point $(13, -2)$.

Find the coordinates of the midpoint of PQ.

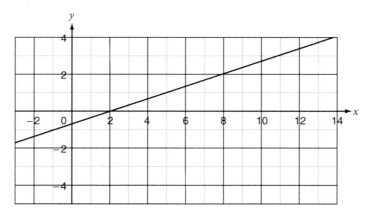

b The line $x - 3y = 2$ is shown on the diagram.
The line $x - 3y = k$ cuts the y-axis at the point $(0, -4)$.
i Copy the diagram and draw the line $x - 3y = k$ on your diagram.
ii Calculate the value of k. *(4024 paper 01 Q13 June 2005)*

10

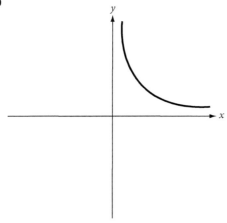

a The diagram is a sketch of the graph of $y = \frac{3}{x}$ for $x > 0$.
Copy the diagram and complete the sketch for $x < 0$.
b Sketch the graph of $y = x$ on the same diagram.
c The graphs of $y = \frac{3}{x}$ and $y = x$ meet at $x = k$.
Find the values of k. *(4024 paper 01 Q22 June 2005)*

11 The table below gives some values of x and the corresponding values of y, correct to one decimal place, where

$$y = \frac{x^2}{8} + \frac{18}{x} - 5$$

x	1	1.5	2	2.5	3	4	5	6	7	8
y	13.2	7.3	4.5	3.0	2.1	1.5	1.7	p	3.7	5.3

a Find the value of p.
b Using a sheet of graph paper and a scale of 2 cm to 1 unit, draw a horizontal x-axis for $0 \leqslant x \leqslant 8$.
Using a scale of 1 cm to 1 unit, draw a vertical y-axis for $0 \leqslant y \leqslant 14$.
On your axes plot the points given in the table, and join them with a smooth curve.

c Use your graph to find
  i the value of x when $y = 8$,
  ii the least value of $\frac{x^2}{8} + \frac{18}{x}$ for values of x in the range $0 \leqslant x \leqslant 8$.
d By drawing a tangent, find the gradient of the curve at the point where $x = 2.5$.
e On the axes used in part (b) draw the graph of $y = 12 - x$.
f The x-coordinates of the points where the two graphs intersect are solutions of the equation
$x^3 + Ax^2 + Bx + 144 = 0$.
Find the value of A and the value of B.   *(4024 paper 02 Q8 June 2006)*

12 a $f(x) = \dfrac{12}{x + 1}$

x	0	1	2	3	4	5	6	7	8	9	10	11
$f(x)$	p	6	4	3	2.4	2	1.71	q	1.33	r	1.09	1

  i Calculate the values of p, q and r.
  ii On a sheet of graph paper draw the graph of $y = f(x)$ for $0 \leqslant x \leqslant 11$.
     Use a scale of 1 cm to 1 unit on each axis.
  iii By drawing a suitable line, find an estimate of the gradient of the graph at the
     point $(3, 3)$.
b On the same grid draw the graph of $y = 8 - x$ for $0 \leqslant x \leqslant 8$.
c i Show that the equation $f(x) = 8 - x$ simplifies to $x^2 - 7x + 4 = 0$.
  ii **Use your graph** to solve this equation, giving your answers correct to 1 decimal
     place.   *(0580 paper 04 Q2 November 2004)*

13 A sketch of the graph of the quadratic function $y = px^2 + qx + r$ is shown in the diagram.

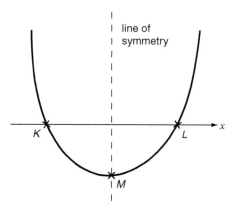

The graph cuts the x-axis at K and L.
The point M lies on the graph and on the lines of symmetry.
a When $p = 1$, $q = 2$, $r = -3$, find
  i the y-coordinate of the point where $x = 4$
  ii the coordinates of K and L
  iii the coordinates of M.
b Describe how the above sketch of the graph would change in each of the following
cases:
  i p is negative   **ii** $p = 1$, $q = r = 0$.
c Another quadratic function is $y = ax^2 + bx + c$.
  i Its graph passes through the origin. Write down the value of c.
  ii The graph also passes through the points $(3, 0)$ and $(4, 8)$. Find the values of a
     and b.   *(0580 paper 04 Q7 November 2004)*

14 The points $A\left(0, \frac{1}{2}\right)$ and $B\left(2, 4\frac{1}{2}\right)$ lie on the curve as shown in the diagram.

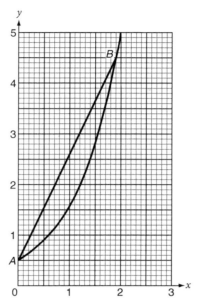

i Calculate the gradient of the straight line *AB*.

ii Using the diagram, estimate the value of *x* at which the gradient of the curve is equal to the gradient of the straight line *AB*.   (4024 paper 01 Q13b June 2007)

15

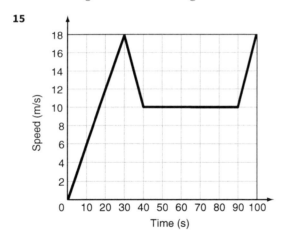

The diagram shows part of a journey by a truck.

a The truck accelerates from rest to 18 m/s in 30 seconds. Calculate the acceleration of the truck.

b The truck then slows down in 10 seconds for some road works and travels through the road works at 12 m/s.
At the end of the road works it accelerates back to a speed of 18 m/s in 10 seconds.
Find the total distance travelled by the truck in the 100 seconds.

(0580 paper 02 Q21 June 2007)

16

Adam stood on a slope, 15 m from the bottom.

He rolled a heavy ball directly up the slope.

After t seconds the ball was y metres from the bottom of the slope.

The table below gives some values of t and the corresponding values of y.

t	0	1	2	2.5	3	3.5	4	4.5	5	5.5
y	15	22	25	25	24	22	19	15	10	4

a Using a scale of 2 cm to represent 1 unit, draw a horizontal t-axis for $0 \leqslant t \leqslant 6$.
Using a scale of 2 cm to represent 5 units, draw a vertical y-axis for $0 \leqslant y \leqslant 30$.
On your axes, plot the points given in the table and join them with a smooth curve.

b Extend the curve to find the value of t when the ball reached the bottom of the slope.

c i By drawing a tangent, find the gradient of the curve when $t = 3.5$.
  ii State briefly what this gradient represents.

d Immediately after he rolled the ball, Adam ran down the slope at a constant speed of 1.5 m/s.
  i Write down the distance of Adam from the bottom of the slope when
    a $t = 0$ **b** $t = 4$.
  ii On the same axes, draw the graph that represents the distance of Adam from the bottom of the slope for $0 \leqslant t \leqslant 6$.
  iii Hence find the distance of Adam from the bottom of the slope when the ball passed him.
                                                                    (4024 paper 02 Q08 June 2007)

17 a Find the values of k, m and n in each of the following equations, where $a > 0$.
  i $a^0 = k$ **ii** $a^m = \dfrac{1}{a}$ **iii** $a^n = \sqrt{a^3}$

b The table shows some values of the function $f(x) = 2^x$.

x	-2	-1	-0.5	0	0.5	1	1.5	2	3
$f(x)$	r	0.5	0.71	s	1.41	2	2.83	4	t

  i Write down the values of r, s and t.
  ii Using a scale of 2 cm to represent 1 unit on each axis, draw an x-axis from -2 to 3 and a y-axis from 0 to 10.
  iii On your grid, draw the graph of $y = f(x)$ for $-2 \leqslant x \leqslant 3$.

c The function g is given by $g(x) = 6 - 2x$.
  i On the same grid as part (b), draw the graph of $y = g(x)$ for $-2 \leqslant x \leqslant 3$.
  ii Use your graphs to solve the equation $2^x = 6 - 2x$.
  iii Write down the value of x for which $2^x < 6 - 2x$ for $x \in$ {positive integers}.
                                                                    (0580 paper 04 Q3 June 2006)

18 $f(x) = 1 - \dfrac{1}{x^2}, x \neq 0$.

a

x	-3	-2	-1	-0.5	-0.4	-0.3	0.3	0.4	0.5	1	2	3
$f(x)$	p	0.75	0	-3	-5.25	q	q	-5.25	-3	0	0.75	p

Find the values of p and q.

b i Draw an x-axis for $-3 \leqslant x \leqslant 3$ using 2 cm to represent 1 unit and a y-axis for $-11 \leqslant y \leqslant 2$ using 1 cm to represent 1 unit.
  ii Draw the graph of $y = f(x)$ for $-3 \leqslant x \leqslant -0.3$ and for $0.3 \leqslant x \leqslant 3$.

c Write down an integer k such that $f(x) = k$ has no solutions.

d On the same grid, draw the graph of $y = 2x - 5$, for $-3 \leqslant x \leqslant 3$.

e i Use your graphs to find solutions of the equation $1 - \frac{1}{x^2} = 2x - 5$.

ii Rearrange $1 - \frac{1}{x^2} = 2x - 5$ into the form $ax^3 + bx^2 + c = 0$, where a, b and c are integers.

f i Draw a tangent to the graph of $y = f(x)$ which is parallel to the line $y = 2x - 5$.

ii Write down the equation of this tangent. (0580 paper 04 Q5 November 2005)

19 During one day, at a point P in a small harbour, the height of the surface of the sea above the seabed was noted.
The results are shown in the table.

Time (t hours) after 8 a.m.	0	1	2	3	4	5	6	7	8	9
Height (y metres) above the seabed	3.8	3.3	2.5	1.8	1.2	1.0	1.2	1.8	2.5	3.3

a Using a scale of 1 cm to represent 1 hour, draw a horizontal t-axis for $0 \leqslant t \leqslant 9$. Using a scale of 2 cm to represent 1 metre, draw a vertical y-axis for $0 \leqslant y \leqslant 4$. On your axes, plot the points given in the table and join them with a smooth curve.

b i By drawing a tangent, find the gradient of the curve at the point where $t = 4$.

ii Explain the meaning of this gradient.

c On the same day, a straight pole was driven vertically into the seabed at the point P.
Work started at 8 a.m.
The pole was driven in at a constant rate.
The height, y metres, of the top of the pole above the seabed, t hours after 8 a.m., is given by the equation $y = 4 - \frac{1}{2}t$.

i Write down the length of the pole.

ii On the same axes as the curve, draw the graph of $y = 4 - \frac{1}{2}t$.

iii How many centimetres was the top of the pole above the surface of the sea at noon?

iv Find the value of t when the top of the pole was level with the surface of the sea. (4024 paper 02 Q8 June 2005)

20 The diagram shows the points $A(1, 2)$, $B(4, 6)$ and $D(-5, 2)$.

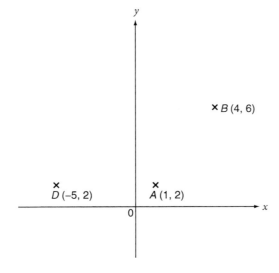

a Find the coordinates of the midpoint of AB.

b Calculate the length of AB.

c Calculate the gradient of the line AB.

d Find the equation of the line AB.

e The triangle ABC has line of symmetry $x = 4$.
Find the coordinates of C.

(4024 paper 01 Q25a–e June 2006)

21

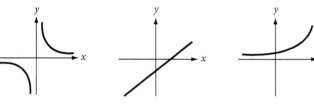

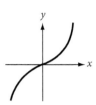

Figure 1   Figure 2   Figure 3

Figure 4   Figure 5   Figure 6

Which of the graphs shown above could be the graph of

a $y = x^3$?   **b** $y = \dfrac{1}{x^2}$?   **c** $y = x - 1$?

(4024 paper 01 Q9 November 2005)

22 A straight line passes through two points with coordinates (6, 8) and (0, 5). Work out the equation of the line.   (0580 paper 21 Q9 June 2008)

23 Find the coordinates of the midpoint of the line joining the points $A(2, -5)$ and $B(6, 9)$.

(0580 paper 21 Q7 June 2009)

24 a The table shows some values for the equation
   $y = \dfrac{x}{2} - \dfrac{2}{x}$ for $-4 \leqslant x \leqslant -0.5$ and $0.5 \leqslant x \leqslant 4$.

x	-4	-3	-2	-1.5	-1	-0.5	0.5	1	1.5	2	3	4
y	-1.5	-0.83	0	0.58			-3.75		-0.58	0	0.83	1.5

   i   Copy the table and write the missing values of y in the empty spaces.
   ii On a sheet of 2 mm graph paper draw the graph of
      $y = \dfrac{x}{2} - \dfrac{2}{x}$ for $-4 \leqslant x \leqslant -0.5$ and $0.5 \leqslant x \leqslant 4$, using a scale of 2 cm to
      represent 1 unit on each axis.
   b Use your graph to solve the equation $\dfrac{x}{2} - \dfrac{2}{x} = 1$.
   c i   By drawing a tangent, work out the gradient of the graph where $x = 2$.
   ii Write down the gradient of the graph where $x = -2$.
   d i   On the grid, draw the line $y = -x$ for $-4 \leqslant x \leqslant 4$.
   ii Use your graphs to solve the equation $\dfrac{x}{2} - \dfrac{2}{x} = -x$.
   e Write down the equation of a straight line which passes through the origin and does
      not intersect the graph of $y = \dfrac{x}{2} - \dfrac{2}{x}$.   (0580 paper 04 Q5 June 2009)

25 The diagram shows the graph of $y = x^2 + x - 12$.
   a The graph cuts the y-axis at K $(0, k)$.
      Write down the value of k.

b The graph cuts the *x*-axis at *L* (*l*, 0) and *M* (*m*, 0).
Find the value of
  i *l*   **ii** *m*.

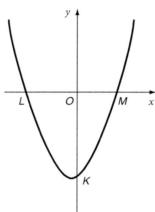

(4024 paper 01 Q11 November 2004)

26 The points *A*, *B* and *C* are (9, 8), (12, 4) and (4, –2) respectively.
  a Find
    i the gradient of the line through *A* and *B*
    ii the equation of the line through *C* which is parallel to *AB*.
  b Calculate the length of the line segment
    i *AB*   **ii** *BC*.
  c Show that *AB* is perpendicular to *BC*.
  d Calculate the area of triangle *ABC*.   (4024 paper 02 Q2 November 2004)

27

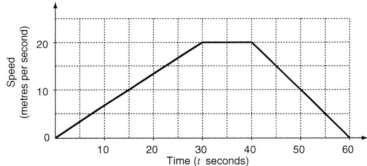

The diagram shows the speed–time graph of a car's journey.
  a Find the speed when *t* = 20.
  b Find the acceleration when *t* = 20.
  c Find the distance travelled in
    i the first 40 seconds   **ii** the first 60 seconds.
  d Part of the distance–time graph for the same journey is shown below. Complete this graph.

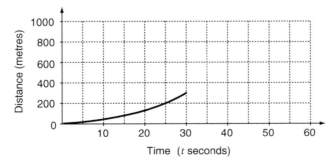

(4024/01 Oct/Nov 2005 q20)

28

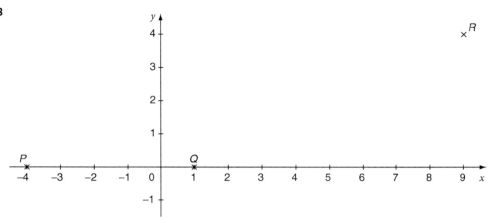

PQRS is a parallelogram.
P is (–4, 0), *Q* is (1, 0) and *R* is (9, 4).
a Find the coordinates of *S*.
b Find the coordinates of the midpoint of *PR*.
c Find the equation of the line *RS*.
d Find the equation of the line *QR*.
e Calculate the area of the parallelogram *PQRS*.   (4024 paper 01 Q21 November 2005)

29 The points *A* and *B* are (5, 3) and (13, 9) respectively.
a Find
    i the midpoint of *AB*
    ii the gradient of the line through *A* and *B*
    iii the length of the line *AB*.
b *C* is the point (–8, 5).
The point *D* is such that $\overrightarrow{DC} = \begin{pmatrix} 4 \\ 3 \end{pmatrix}$.
    i Find the coordinates of *D*.
    ii What type of quadrilateral is *ABCD*?   (4024 paper 02 Q2 November 2006)

30

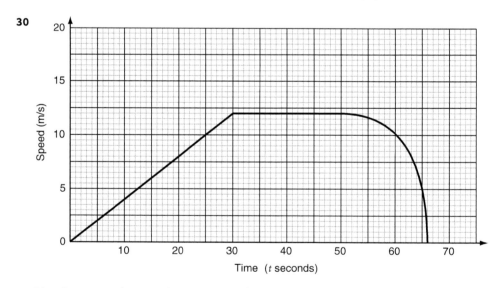

The diagram is the speed–time graph of a cyclist's journey.
a Calculate the time taken to travel the first 300 metres.
b By drawing a tangent, find the retardation of the cyclist when *t* = 55.

(4024 paper 01 Q22 November 2007)

31 The diagram is the speed–time graph of the first 20 seconds of a motorcyclist's journey.

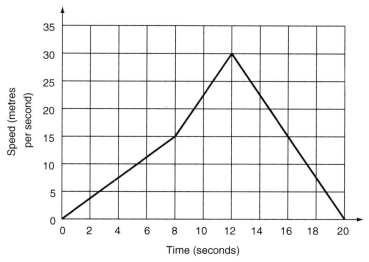

    a Calculate the motorcyclist's retardation during the final 8 seconds.

    b Calculate the distance travelled in the 20 seconds.   (4024 paper 01 Q13 June 2008)

32 A straight line passes through the points P (1, 2) and Q (5, –14).

Find

    a the coordinates of the midpoint of PQ

    b the gradient of PQ

    c the equation of PQ.   (4024 paper 01 Q17 June 2008)

33 The curve $y = x^3 - 5$ is shown on the axes below.

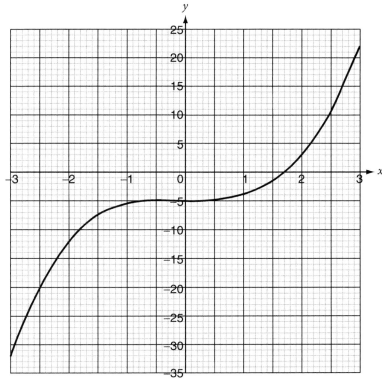

    a Use the graph to find an approximate value of $\sqrt[3]{5}$.

    b **i** On the axes above, draw the graph of $y = 15 - 5x$.

ii Write down the coordinates of the point where the graphs cross.

iii The x coordinate of the point where the graphs cross is a solution of the equation $x^3 = a + bx$.

Find the value of a and the value of b. (4024 paper 01 Q17 November 2008)

34

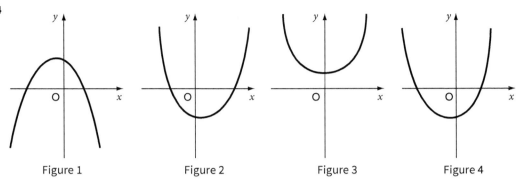

Figure 1   Figure 2   Figure 3   Figure 4

Which of the figures shown above could be the graph of

a $y = x^2 + 2$?

b $y = (x - 2)(x + 1)$?

c $y = 2 - x - x^2$? (4024 paper 01 Q13 June 2009)

35 a

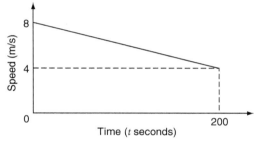

Ali was on a training run.

The diagram is the speed–time graph of part of his run.

At $t = 0$, his speed was 8 m/s.

His speed decreased at a constant rate until it was 4 m/s at $t = 200$.

i Calculate

  a his retardation during the 200 s,

  b the distance he ran during the 200 s,

  c his speed at $t = 150$.

ii Ben ran at a constant speed in the same direction as Ali.

At $t = 0$, Ali and Ben were level.

They ran the same distance in the next 150 seconds.

Calculate Ben's speed.

b Chris ran 200 m, correct to the nearest 10 metres.

He took 25 s, correct to the nearest second.

Find lower bounds for

  i the distance run,

  ii his average speed. (4024 paper 02 Q5 June 2009)

In this chapter we will
- calculate arc lengths and areas of sectors of a circle
- calculate more volumes and surface areas of solid shapes

- use the ratios of lengths, areas and volumes of similar shapes
- work with similar and congruent triangles.

19.1 Introduction

This chapter continues the work from Chapter 8. The essential skills exercise in Section 19.2 will remind you of the work already covered.

19.2 Essential Skills

1 Convert
  a 250 mm to metres
  c 15 m² to square centimetres

  b 20 cm³ to cubic metres
  d 1.7 litres to millilitres.

2 Calculate
  a the circumference,
of a circle with diameter 18 cm.

  b the area

3 Calculate
  a the perimeter,
of each of the following shapes:

  b the area

i

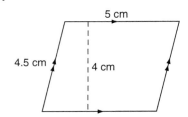

ii

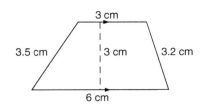

4 Calculate
  a the total surface area,
of a cuboid measuring 12 cm by 5 cm by 10 cm.

  b the volume

5 Calculate
  a the total surface area,   **b** the volume

of a solid cylinder with a radius of 5 cm and a height of 10 cm.

6 Calculate the capacity in millilitres of a cylinder measuring 6 cm in diameter and 25 cm in height.

19.3 Arc Lengths in Circles

As you saw in Chapter 6, an arc is a section of the circumference of a circle.

The diagram in Figure 19.1 is of a circle, centre O and a radius shown as an arrow. If the arrow is rotated clockwise, to the position shown as a dotted line, through an angle of 60° at the centre, it traces out an *arc* shown as the heavy curved line on the circle.

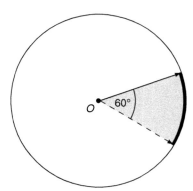

The length of the arc depends on the angle at the centre of the circle. The larger the angle, the longer the arc. The angle at the centre is called the angle *subtended* at the centre by the arc. The angle can be expressed as a fraction of the complete turn (360°).

Figure 19.1 Arc of a circle

In Figure 19.1, the arc length will be $\frac{60}{360} = \frac{1}{6}$ of the whole circumference.

> ## Key term
>
> The angle at the centre of a circle standing on an arc of that circle is called the angle **subtended** at the centre by the arc.

Example 1

Calculate the length of an arc **subtended** by the angle 60° at the centre of a circle, radius 4 cm.

Answer 1

Circumference $= 2\pi r = 2 \times \pi \times 4$ cm

Arc length $= \frac{60}{360} \times 2 \times \pi \times 4 = 4.18879\ldots$

Arc length $= 4.19$ cm

19.4 Sector Areas in Circles

In Figure 19.1, the region between the two arrows (shaded) is a *sector* of the circle. The area of the sector is a fraction of the area of the whole circle, in this case $\frac{60}{360}$ of the total area of the circle.

Example 2

Calculate the area of the sector subtended by the angle 100° at the centre of the circle with radius 4 cm.

Answer 2

Area of the whole circle $= \pi r^2 = \pi \times 4^2$ cm²

Area of the sector $= \frac{100}{360} \times \pi \times 4^2 = 13.96263\ldots$

Area of sector $= 14.0$ cm²

Exercise 19.1

Calculate the quantities represented by letters in the following table.

Angle at the centre	Radius	Length of arc	Area of sector
30°	10 cm	a	b
140°	8 cm	c	d
200°	5 cm	e	f
g	3 cm	10 cm	h
60°	i	12 cm	j
k	15 cm	l	30 cm²
20°	m	n	40 cm²
p	9 cm	q	25 cm²
100°	r	s	60 cm²

19.5 More Volumes and Surface Areas of Solids

NOTE:
In the examination, you will given the necessary formulae

The following worked examples illustrate the types of calculations you might be asked to carry out.

For the total surface area of a solid it can be useful to sketch the net as shown in Example 3.

Example 3

Calculate the total surface area of a square-based pyramid as shown in the diagram below.

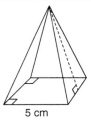

5 cm

The base is a square with side = 5 cm. The four isosceles triangles have a height of 6 cm, shown by the dotted line.

Answer 3

The diagram below shows the net of the pyramid.
The total area of the net = area of square + 4 × area of triangle

$$= 5^2 + 4 \times \frac{1}{2} \times 5 \times 6$$
$$= 85 \text{ cm}^2$$

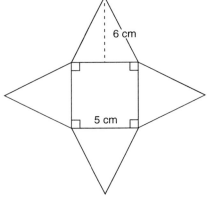

6 cm

5 cm

Cylinders, cones and spheres all have **curved surfaces**.

- For the *total* surface area of a cone you will need to add the area of the circular base as shown in Example 4."
- The net (Chapter 6) of a cylinder is a rectangle and two circles. The rectangle makes the *curved* surface of the cylinder. The length of the rectangle is the circumference of the circular ends. The *total* surface area includes the two circles. You will be expected to be able to calculate the surface area of the cylinder without being given a formula.

Example 4

Calculate the total surface area of a cone with a base radius = 10 cm and a slant height = 30 cm.

(The curved surface area of a cone = $\pi r l$, where l is the slant height.)

Answer 4

The slant height of a cone is the height measured along the surface, as in the diagram.

Curved surface area = $\pi \times 10 \times 30 = 300\pi$ cm^2

Circular base = $\pi \times 10^2 = 100\pi$ cm^2

Total surface area = $100\pi + 300\pi = 1256.637...$ cm^2

Total surface area = 1260 cm^2 to 3 significant figures.

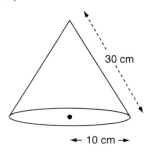

30 cm

10 cm

You might be asked to calculate the volume or surface area of a composite solid such as that shown in Example 5.

Example 5

Calculate the volume of a child's toy which is in the shape of a cone on a hemisphere.

The total height of the toy is 12 cm, and the radius is 4 cm.

(The volume of a cone = $\frac{1}{3}\pi r^3 h$, where h is the perpendicular height, and the volume of a sphere = $\frac{4}{3}\pi r^3$.)

Answer 5

The height of the cone = $12 - 4 = 8$ cm

Volume of cone = $\frac{1}{3}\pi r^2 h = \frac{1}{3} \times \pi \times 4^2 \times 8$ cm^3

Volume of hemisphere = $\frac{1}{2} \times \frac{4}{3}\pi r^3 = \frac{1}{2} \times \frac{4}{3} \times \pi \times 4^3$ cm^3

Total volume = $(\frac{1}{3} \times \pi \times 4^2 \times 8) + (\frac{1}{2} \times \frac{4}{3} \times \pi \times 4^3) = 268.08257...$ cm^3

Total volume of toy = 268 cm^3 to 3 significant figures.

12 cm

4 cm

NOTE:
The height of the cone = total height − radius of hemisphere.

The first diagram in Figure 19.2 shows a cone sliced horizontally into two sections. The top section is a smaller cone and the lower section is called a **frustum**. The second diagram shows the frustum on its own. The volume and surface area of the frustum can be calculated by subtracting the volume or surface area of the smaller cone from that of the larger cone, as the next example shows.

Key term

A **frustum** is the part of a cone left when the pointed part (vertex) of the cone is removed.

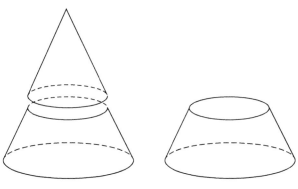

Figure 19.2 Frustum

Example 6

The frustum shown in Figure 19.2 is made by removing a cone with slant height 6 cm from a cone of slant height 12 cm. The radius of the top of the frustum is 2 cm and the radius of the base of the frustum is 4 cm.

Calculate, giving your answers in terms of π:

a the curved surface area of the larger cone

b the curved surface area of the smaller cone

c the **total** surface area of the frustum, given that the frustum is solid.

You are given that the curved surface area of a cone $= \pi r l$.

Answer 6

a The curved surface area of the larger cone $= \pi \times 4 \times 12 = 48\pi \, \text{cm}^2$

b The curved surface area of the smaller cone $= \pi \times 2 \times 6 = 12\pi \, \text{cm}^2$

c The curved surface area of the frustum $= 48\pi - 12\pi = 36\pi \, \text{cm}^2$

The **total** surface area of the frustum $= 36\pi + \pi \times 2^2 + \pi \times 4^2 = 56\pi \, \text{cm}^2$.

Exercise 19.2

You can use the following formulae in this exercise:

Surface area of a sphere $= 4\pi r^2$

Volume of a sphere $= \frac{4}{3}\pi r^3$

Curved surface area of a cone $= \pi r l$, where l is the slant height of the cone

Volume of a cone $= \frac{1}{3}\pi r^2 h$, where h is the perpendicular height of the cone.

1 Calculate the quantities represented by letters in the following table.

	Sphere		Hemisphere	
radius	surface area	volume	total surface area	volume
3 cm	a	b	c	d
7 cm	e	f	g	h
i	20 cm²	j	k	l
m	n	30 cm³	p	q
r	s	t	u	50 cm³

2 Calculate the quantities represented by letters in the following table.

Cone				
radius	slant height	perpendicular height	curved surface area	volume
3 cm	5 cm		a	
6 cm		7 cm		b
c	10 cm	8 cm	60 cm²	d
e	13 cm	10 cm	f	15 cm³

3 Calculate
   a the curved surface area,
   b the total surface area,
   c the volume
   of a cylinder with radius 4.5 cm and height 12 cm.

4 A cylinder has a height of 10 cm and a volume of 283 cm³. Calculate
   a the radius of the cylinder
   b its total surface area.

19.6 Similar Shapes

You have already met similar shapes in Chapter 6, but this is a reminder. Similar shapes have the same shape but are different sizes. This means that they have corresponding angles equal and corresponding sides in proportion. For example, all squares are similar because they all have four angles $= 90°$, and four equal sides.

All cubes are similar because they all have six equal faces at right angles to each other. The diagrams in Figure 19.3 show two lines (A and B) with lengths in the ratio 1 : 2, and two squares (C and D) drawn from sides with these lengths, followed by two cubes (E and F).

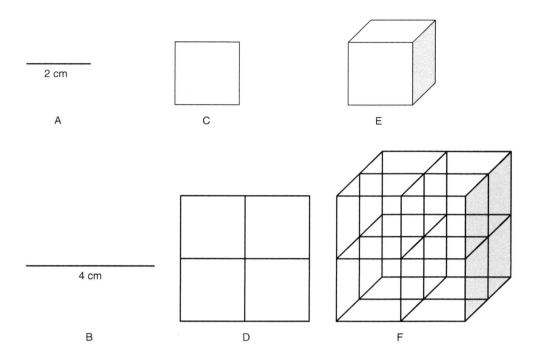

Figure 19.3 The relationship of length, area and volume ratios of similar shapes

The areas of the two squares are $2 \times 2 = 4\,cm^2$ and $4 \times 4 = 16\,cm^2$, so the ratios of the areas of the squares are $4 : 16 = 1 : 4$. The area of D is four times the area of C. The volumes of the two cubes are $2 \times 2 \times 2 = 8\,cm^3$ and $4 \times 4 \times 4 = 64\,cm^3$, so the ratios of the volumes are $8 : 64 = 1 : 8$. The volume of F is eight times the volume of E.

This is an important fact to understand.

If the sides or lengths of two *similar* shapes are in the ratio $1 : 2$, then the areas are in the ratio $1 : 4$ ($1^2 : 2^2$), and the volumes are in the ratio $1 : 8$ ($1^3 : 2^3$). In general, for similar shapes:

- if lengths are in the ratio $a : b$
- then areas are in the ratio $a^2 : b^2$
- and volumes are in the ratio $a^3 : b^3$.

Notice the importance of the word 'similar'. These ratios only apply to similar shapes.

NOTE:

Always check that your answer is sensible. In this case, the surface area is larger for the larger cylinder. Also, if the area of the smaller cylinder had been 32 cm², then the ratio 16 : 25 would have made the larger cylinder 50 cm², so the answer does seem reasonable.

Example 7

The heights of two similar cylinders are 4 cm and 5 cm respectively.
The total surface area of the smaller cylinder is 30 cm².
Calculate the total surface area of the larger cylinder.

Answer 7

Length ratio $= 4 : 5$
Area ratio $= 16 : 25$
Total surface area of small cylinder $= 30\,cm^2$
Total surface area of large cylinder $= 30 \times \frac{25}{16} = 46.875\,cm^2$.

Example 8

The surface areas of two spheres are in the ratio $4 : 9$. The volume of the smaller sphere is 20 cm³. Calculate the volume of the larger sphere.

Answer 8

Area ratio = 4 : 9

Length ratio = $\sqrt{4}:\sqrt{9}$ = 2 : 3

Volume ratio = $2^3 : 3^3$ = 8 : 27

Volume of the smaller sphere = 20 cm³

Volume of the larger sphere = $20 \times \frac{27}{8}$ = 67.5 cm³.

Example 9

The heights of two similar bottles are in the ratio 3 : 5.

The capacity of the larger bottle is 1.5 litres.

Calculate the capacity of the smaller bottle in millilitres.

Answer 9

Capacity is the same as volume.

Length ratio = 3 : 5

Volume ratio = 27 : 125

Capacity of larger bottle = 1.5 litres

Capacity of smaller bottle = $1.5 \times \frac{27}{125}$ = 0.324 litres

Capacity of smaller bottle = 324 millilitres.

NOTE:

This seems reasonable because it is smaller. Also 27 is approximately $\frac{1}{5}$ of 125, and $\frac{1}{5}$ of 1.5 litres is 300 millilitres.

The ratios of lengths, areas and volumes of similar shapes can also be used to find the surface area or volume of a frustum as the next example shows. Slicing a cone parallel to its base gives a small cone which is similar in shape to the original cone.

Example 10

The first diagram below shows a cone of height 20 cm and base radius 5 cm. A small cone is removed from the top of the larger cone to leave a frustum of height 8 cm as shown in the second diagram.

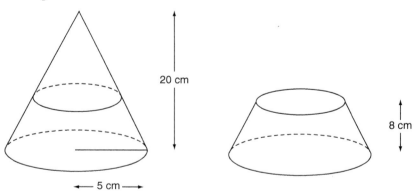

a For the two cones, write down
  i the length ratio
  ii the area ratio
  iii the volume ratio.

b Calculate the volume of the larger cone.

c Using the ratio of the volumes, calculate the volume of the smaller cone and hence the volume of the frustum.

Answer 10

a **i** The height of the small cone = 20 − 8 = 12 cm

The height of the large cone = 20 cm

So length ratio (small cone : large cone) = 12 : 20 = 3 : 5

ii Area ratio (small cone : large cone) = 9 : 25

iii Volume ratio (small cone : large cone) = 27 : 125

b Volume of large cone $= \frac{1}{3}\pi r^2 h$

$$= \frac{1}{3}\pi \times 5^2 \times 20 = 523.598\ldots$$

$$= 525 \text{ cm}^3 \text{ to } 3 \text{ s.f.}$$

c Volume of small cone $= \frac{27}{125} \times 523.598\ldots = 113.097\ldots$

Volume of frustum = 523.598... − 113.097...

$$= 410.500\ldots$$

$$= 411 \text{ cm}^3 \text{ to } 3 \text{ s.f.}$$

Exercise 19.3

1 The volumes of two similar cuboids are in the ratio 1 : 125.

  a Find the ratio of

    i the surface areas   **ii** the lengths

  b Copy and complete the following table for these two cuboids.

	length	height	total surface area	volume
smaller cuboid	20 cm	(i)	(ii)	80 cm³
larger cuboid	(iii)	2 cm	10 600 cm²	(iv)

2 The areas of the two similar 'smiley faces' are in the ratio 10 : 1.

NOT TO SCALE

The height of the larger face is 4 cm. Calculate the height of the smaller face.

3 The volumes of two similar cones are in the ratio 8 : 27.

  a Find the ratio of the heights of the two cones.

  b Find the ratio of the areas of the bases of the two cones.

  c The curved surface area of the smaller cone is 20 cm². Calculate the curved surface area of the larger cone.

4 A soft drink is sold in two different sizes of bottles. The bottles are similar in shape. The height of the smaller bottle is 25 cm and the height of the larger bottle is 35 cm.

  a Calculate the ratio of the volumes.

  b The volume of the smaller bottle is 730 ml.

Calculate the volume of the larger bottle. Give your answer correct to 3 significant figures.

5 A map is in the scale 1 : 25 000.

A lake on the map has an area of 5 cm².

Calculate the area of the actual lake. Give your answer in square metres in standard form.

6 A frustum is cut from a cone with a height of 15 cm, by removing the top section which is a cone of height 10 cm. The volume of the cone which is removed is 40 cm³. Calculate the volume of the frustum.

19.7 Similar Triangles

Similar triangles have the same shape, which means they have equal angles.

The **corresponding sides** of similar triangles are in the same ratio. Corresponding sides are the sides opposite equal angles, as shown in Figure 19.4.

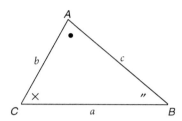 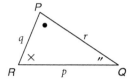

Figure 19.4 Similar triangles

We will use the notation of a single capital letter for each angle where the angle is unambiguous, and the lower case letter for the length of the opposite side.

It is convenient to mark the angles that are equal with the same symbols, as you will see in Figure 19.4.

The corresponding sides are as follows:

a corresponds to p, b corresponds to q and c corresponds to r.

So we can write:

$$\frac{a}{p} = \frac{b}{q} = \frac{c}{r}$$

In order to keep everything in the correct order, as you will see later in the less obvious examples, it is wise to put the triangles in as well.

$$\frac{\text{large triangle}}{\text{small triangle}} : \frac{a}{p} = \frac{b}{q} = \frac{c}{r}$$

However, you must remember that this refers to the lengths of the sides, not to the areas of the triangles!

Conditions for Similarity in Triangles

We have seen that similar triangles have the same shape, which means that they have equal angles. Consider the triangles shown in Figure 19.5.

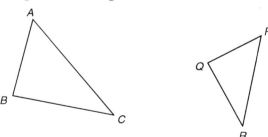

Figure 19.5 Conditions for similarity

To prove that triangles are similar you may prove any of the following conditions:

- Their angles are equal. For example, in Figure 19.5, if
  $\angle A = \angle P$ and $\angle B = \angle Q$ and $\angle C = \angle R$, the triangles are similar.
- Their sides are in the same ratio. For example, if
  $\frac{AB}{PQ} = \frac{BC}{QR} = \frac{AC}{PR}$, the triangles are similar.
- The triangles have one equal angle and the sides making up that angle are in the same ratio. For example, if
  $\angle A = \angle P$ and $\frac{AB}{PQ} = \frac{AC}{PR}$, the triangles are similar.

Example 11

In the diagram, PT is parallel to QS. Find the lengths of QS and PR.

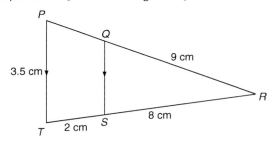

Answer 11

First of all we have to be sure the triangles PRT and QRS are similar.

$\angle P = \angle SQR$ (corresponding angles in parallel lines)

$\angle T = \angle QSR$ (corresponding angles in parallel lines)

$\angle R$ is common to both triangles.

So the angles are equiangular, and therefore the triangles are similar.

Copying the diagram and marking in the equal angles:

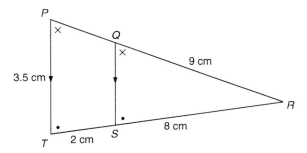

$\dfrac{\text{large triangle}}{\text{small triangle}} : \dfrac{TR}{SR} = \dfrac{PR}{QR} = \dfrac{PT}{QS}$

$\dfrac{2+8}{8} = \dfrac{PR}{9} = \dfrac{3.5}{QS} \qquad \dfrac{10}{8} = \dfrac{PR}{9}$

$PR = 9 \times \dfrac{10}{8} = 11.25\,\text{cm}$

Also, $\dfrac{10}{8} = \dfrac{3.5}{QS}$

$QS \times 10 = 3.5 \times 8$ ($\times QS$ and $\times 8$)

$QS = 3.5 \times \dfrac{8}{10}$ ($\div 10$)

$QS = 2.8\,\text{cm} \quad PR = 11.25 \quad QS = 2.8\,\text{cm}.$

NOTE:

A quick check shows that these are reasonable because PR is in the large triangle, and is larger than QR, and QS is in the small triangle and is smaller than PT.

Example 12

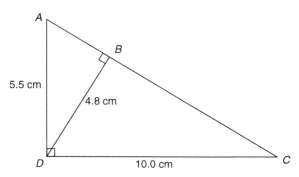

Using the diagram above,

a prove that triangles *ACD* and *ADB* are similar.

b Use similar triangles to calculate the lengths of *AB* and *AC*. All the measurements are correct to 1 decimal place.

Answer 12

a In triangles *ACD* and *ADB*, $\angle ADC = \angle DBA = 90°$ (given in the diagram).

∠*A* is common to both, so $\angle DCA = \angle BDA$ (angle sum of a triangle).

Triangles *ACD* and *ADB* are equiangular so they are similar.

b It is a good idea to split the diagram into the two triangles unless you can easily see which sides are corresponding. Mark the equal angles.

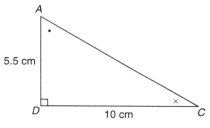 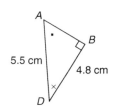

$$\frac{\text{large triangle}}{\text{small triangle}}:\frac{AC}{AD}=\frac{DC}{BD}=\frac{AD}{AB}$$

$$\frac{\text{large triangle}}{\text{small triangle}}:\frac{AC}{5.5}=\frac{DC}{4.8}=\frac{5.5}{AB}$$

$$AC = 5.5 \times \frac{10}{4.8} = 11.5\,\text{cm}$$

$$AB = 5.5 \times \frac{4.8}{10} = 2.6\,\text{cm}$$

All correct to 1 decimal place.

Remember to check that these are reasonable.

Example 13

a Prove that triangle *ABC* is similar to triangle *DEF*.

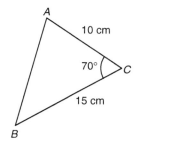 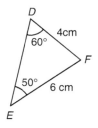

NOTE:

Remember that corresponding sides are opposite the angles marked as equal by using the same signs (× and · and so on).

b Prove that triangle *PQR* is not similar to triangle *STU*.

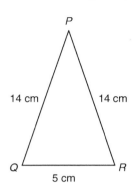

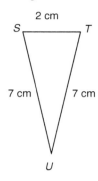

Answer 13

a In triangle *DEF*, $\angle F = 180° - 60° - 50° = 70°$

So $\angle C = \angle F = 70°$

$\frac{AC}{DF} = \frac{10}{4} = 2.5$ and $\frac{BC}{EF} = \frac{15}{6} = 2.5$

so triangle *ABC* and *DEF* are similar (two sides in the same ratio and the included angles equal).

b $\frac{PQ}{SU} = \frac{PR}{TU} = 2$ and $\frac{QR}{ST} = \frac{5}{2} = 2.5$

So the sides are not all in the same ratio and the two triangles are therefore *not* similar.

Exercise 19.4

1 Triangles *ABC* and *PQR* are shown below. *AD* is the height of triangle *ABC* and *PS* is the height of *PQR*. *AD = DC*, and *PS = SR*.

   a Show that triangles *ABC* and *PQR* are similar.

   b Use similar triangles to

     i calculate the length of *SR*

     ii calculate the area of triangle *PQR*, given that the area of triangle ABC is 14 cm².

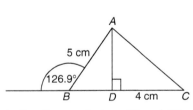

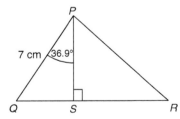

2 In the diagram below, *AB* and *DE* are parallel.

   a Show that triangles *ABC* and *CDE* are similar.

   b Calculate the length of *AB*.

   c The area of triangle *ABC* = 6 cm². Calculate the area of triangle *CDE*.

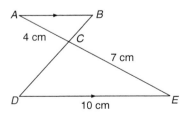

3　**a**　Using your knowledge of cyclic quadrilaterals (Chapter 17), show that triangles *PRT* and *QRS* are similar.

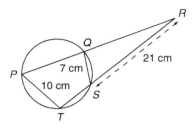

　b　Calculate the length of *PR*.

19.8 Congruent Triangles

Congruent triangles are triangles with exactly the same shape *and* size. This means that, like similar triangles, they have equal corresponding angles, but unlike similar triangles their corresponding sides are also equal in length.

To prove that triangles are congruent you must prove one of the following.
- Each of the sides of one triangle is the same length as a corresponding side of the other triangle. (This can be abbreviated to SSS.)
- Two sides and the included angle in one triangle are equal to two sides and the included angle in the other triangle. (This is abbreviated to SAS.)
- Two angles and one side in one triangle are equal to two angles and the *corresponding* side in the other triangle. (Abbreviated to ASA.)
  NOTE: Remember that corresponding sides are the sides that are opposite equal angles.
- The two triangles are right-angled with equal hypotenuses and one other pair of sides equal. (Abbreviated to RHS.)

Example 14

In the triangles shown below, $AC = QP = YZ$, $A\hat{C}P = P\hat{Q}R = X\hat{Y}Z$ and $B\hat{A}C = P\hat{R}Q = X\hat{R}Y$.

State, giving reasons for your choice, which two of the triangles are congruent.

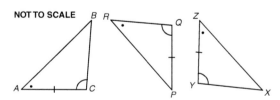

NOT TO SCALE

Answer 14

In triangles *ABC* and *XYZ*,

$B\hat{A}C = X\hat{Z}Y$	(given)
$A\hat{C}B = X\hat{Y}Z$	(given)
$A\hat{B}C = X\hat{Y}Z$	(angle sum of a triangle)
$AC = YZ$	(given)

AC and YZ are corresponding sides because they are opposite to the equal angles $A\hat{B}C$ and $Y\hat{X}Z$.

So triangles ABC and XYZ are congruent (AAS).

Example 15

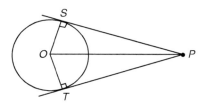

In the diagram O is the centre of a circle, P is a point outside the circle, and PS and PT are tangents drawn from the point to the circle.

a Using the fact that the tangent and the radius drawn to the point of contact of the tangent are at right angles, prove that the tangents are equal in length.

b What other facts can be deduced from this proof?

Answer 15

a In triangles OSP and OTP,

$\angle OSP = \angle OTP = 90°$

OP is common to both triangles

$OS = OT$ (radii of the circle)

So triangles OSP and OTP are congruent (RHS).

In particular, $SP = TP$.

So the two tangents drawn from a point outside the triangle to a circle are equal in length.

b The line OP bisects $\angle SOT$ and $\angle SPT$ and is a line of symmetry of the diagram.

Exercise 19.5

1

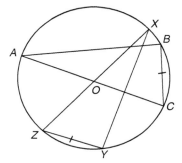

NOT TO SCALE

In the diagram O is the centre of a circle, diameter **d** cm. $BC = YZ = x$ cm.

Prove that triangles ABC and XYZ are congruent.

2   NOT TO SCALE

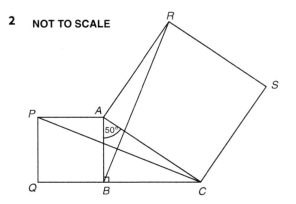

In the diagram, angle *ABC* is a right angle, and angle *BAC* = 50°.
ABQP and *ACSR* are squares.
Prove that triangles *ABR* and *ACP* are congruent.

3

NOT TO SCALE

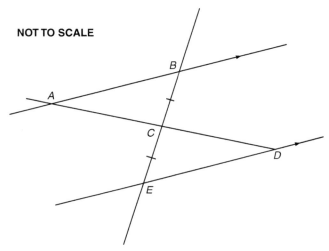

In the diagram *C* is the midpoint of *BE*.
Prove that triangles *ABC* and *CDE* are congruent.

Exercise 19.6

Mixed Exercise

1   A cone is to be made from a thin card. The cone will have a base radius of 4 cm, and a
slant height of 10 cm.
Raj draws a circle of radius 10 cm, and is going to cut out from that a sector to make the
cone. Calculate the angle *x*.

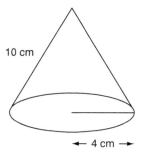

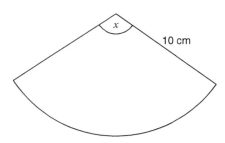

2 A map has a scale of 1 : 2500.
On the map a reservoir has an area of 2 cm².
What is the area of the reservoir? Give your answer in m².

3

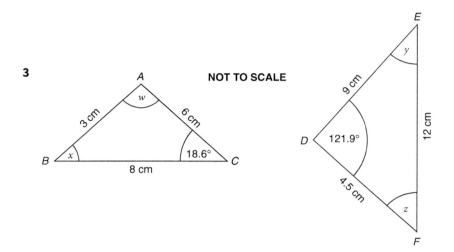

NOT TO SCALE

a By showing that pairs of sides are in the same ratio prove that triangles *ABC* and *DEF* are similar.

b Find the angles marked with letters in the two triangles.

c Calculate the ratio of the areas of the two triangles.

4 A rectangle with length $(x + 6)$ and breadth $(x + 1)$ has the same area as a square with sides $= 2x$. (Measurements in centimetres.)
Calculate the dimensions of the square and rectangle.

5 Two bowls are made from two identical wooden cylinders.
One bowl is made by drilling out a hemisphere with the same radius as the cylinder.
The other is made by drilling out a cone with the same radius as the cylinder, and perpendicular height equal to the height of the cylinder.
The cylinders have height x cm, and radius x cm.

a Calculate the volume of the wood which makes up the hemispherical bowl in terms of x.

b Calculate the volume of the wood which makes up the conical bowl.

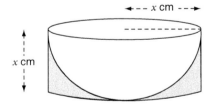

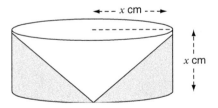

c Comment on your answers to (a) and (b).

Exam-style questions

6 a [The volume of a sphere is $\frac{4}{3}\pi r^3$.]

[The surface area of a sphere is $4\pi r^2$.]

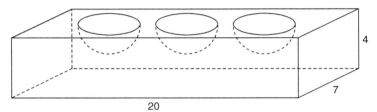

A wooden cuboid has length 20 cm, width 7 cm and height 4 cm.

Three **hemispheres**, each of radius 2.5 cm, are hollowed out of the top of the cuboid, to leave the block as shown in the diagram.

i Calculate the volume of wood in the block.

ii The four vertical sides are painted blue.

Calculate the total area that is painted blue.

iii The inside of each hemispherical hollow is painted white.

The flat part of the top of the block is painted red.

Calculate the total area that is painted

    a white   **b** red.

b The volume of water in a container is directly proportional to the cube of its depth.

When the depth is 12 cm, the volume is 576 cm³.

Calculate

i the volume when the depth is 6 cm

ii the depth when the volume is 1300 cm³.   (4024 paper 02 Q7 June 2007)

7

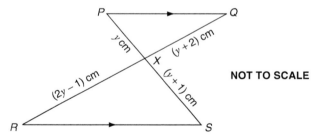

NOT TO SCALE

In the diagram, *PQ* is parallel to *RS*. *PS* and *QR* intersect at *X*.

$PX = y$ cm, $QX = (y + 2)$ cm, $RX = (2y - 1)$ cm and $SX = (y + 1)$ cm.

i Show that $y^2 - 4y - 2 = 0$.

ii Solve the equation $y^2 - 4y - 2 = 0$.

Show all your working and give your answers correct to two decimal places.

iii Write down the length of *RX*.   (0580 paper 04 Q3b June 2007)

8

NOT TO SCALE

0.8 m

0.3 m

1.2 m

The diagram shows water in a channel.
This channel has a rectangular cross-section, 1.2 metres by 0.8 metres.

a When the depth of water is 0.3 metres, the water flows along the channel at 3 metres/**minute**.
Calculate the number of cubic metres which flows along the channel in one hour.

b When the depth of water in the channel increases to 0.8 metres, the water flows at 15 metres/minute.
Calculate the percentage increase in the number of cubic metres of water which flows along the channel in one hour.

c The water comes from a cylindrical tank.
When 2 cubic metres of water leave the tank, the level of water in the tank goes down by 1.3 **millimetres**.
Calculate the radius of the tank, in **metres**, correct to one decimal place.

d When the channel is empty, its **interior** surface is repaired.
This costs $0.12 per square metre. The total cost is $50.40.
Calculate the length, in metres, of the channel. (0580 paper 04 Q7 June 2007)

9 These two cylinders are similar.
The ratio of their volumes is 8 : 27.
The height of cylinder *A* is 12 cm.
Find the height of cylinder *B*.

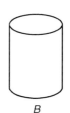

A   *B*

(4024 paper 12 Q10 June 2011)

10

NOT TO SCALE

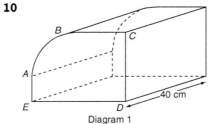

Diagram 1

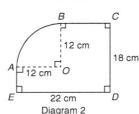

Diagram 2

Diagram 1 shows a closed box. The box is a prism of length 40 cm.
The cross-section of the box is shown in Diagram 2, with all the right angles marked.
AB is an arc of a circle, centre *O*, radius 12 cm. *ED* = 22 cm and *DC* = 18 cm.
Calculate

a the perimeter of the cross-section

b the area of the cross-section

c the volume of the box

d the **total** surface area of the box. (0580 paper 04 Q2 June 2006)

11

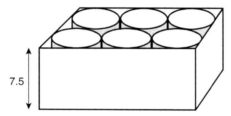

2x + 4

x + 2

x

x² − 40

NOT TO SCALE

The diagram shows a trapezium.
Two of its angles are 90°.
The lengths of the sides are given in terms of x.
The perimeter is 62 units.

   i   Write down a quadratic equation in x to show this information. Simplify your equation.

   ii Solve your quadratic equation.

   iii Write down the only possible value of x.

   iv Calculate the area of the trapezium.   (0580 paper 04 Q8a June 2006)

12 a A candle is in the shape of a cylinder of radius 1.6 cm and height 7.5 cm.
   i   Calculate the volume of the candle. (Unit for answer: cm³).
   ii Six of these candles are packed into a box of height 7.5 cm as shown.

7.5

       a   Find the length and width of the box. (Unit for answer: cm).
       b   Calculate the volume of empty space in the box. (Unit for answer: cm³).

  b The length of a rectangular photo is 17.8 cm, correct to the nearest millimetre.
    The width of the photo is 12.7 cm, correct to the nearest millimetre.
   i   Calculate the lower bound of the area of the photo. (Unit for answer: cm²).
   ii Kate has a rectangular frame with length 18 cm and width 13 cm, both measured correct to the nearest centimetre.
     Will the photo definitely fit into the frame?
     Explain your answer.   (4024 paper 21 Q6 June 2014)

13 A cylindrical glass has a radius of 3 centimetres and a height of 7 centimetres.
A large cylindrical jar full of water is a similar shape to the glass.
The glass can be filled with water from the jar exactly 216 times.
Work out the radius and height of the jar.   (0580 paper 21 Q10 June 2008)

14 A spacecraft made 58 376 orbits of the Earth and travelled a distance of 2.656×10^9 kilometres.
  a Calculate the distance travelled in 1 orbit correct to the nearest kilometre.
  b The orbit of the spacecraft is a circle. Calculate the radius of the orbit.   (0580 paper 21 Q14 November 2008)

15 Two similar vases have heights which are in the ratio 3 : 2.
    a The volume of the larger vase is 1080 cm³.
       Calculate the volume of the smaller vase.
    b The surface area of the smaller vase is 252 cm².
       Calculate the surface area of the larger vase.   (0580 paper 21 Q18 June 2009)

16 A statue two metres high has a volume of five cubic metres.
   A similar model of the statue has a height of four centimetres.
    a Calculate the volume of the model statue in cubic centimetres.
    b Write your answer to part (a) in cubic metres.   (0580 paper 02 Q13 November 2006)

17 The surface area, A, of a cylinder, radius r and height h, is given by the
   formula $A = 2\pi rh + 2\pi r^2$.
    a Calculate the surface area of a cylinder of radius 5 cm and height 9 cm.
    b Make h the subject of the formula.
    c A cylinder has a radius of 6 cm and a surface area of 377 cm².

   Calculate the height of this cylinder.

    d A cylinder has a surface area of 1200 cm² and its radius and height are equal. Calculate
       the radius.   (0580 paper 04 Q8(part) November 2006)

18 a The scale of a map is 1 : 20 000 000.
      On the map the distance between Cairo and Addis Ababa is 12 cm.
      i Calculate the distance, in kilometres, between Cairo and Addis Ababa.
      ii On the map the area of a desert region is 13 square centimetres.
      Calculate the actual area of this desert region, in square kilometres.
    b **i** The actual distance between Cairo and Khartoum is 1580 km.
      On a different map this distance is represented by 31.6 cm.
      Calculate, in the form 1 : n, the scale of this map.
      ii A plane flies the 1580 km from Cairo to Khartoum.
      It departs from Cairo at 1155 and arrives in Khartoum at 1403.
      Calculate the average speed of the plane, in kilometres per hour.
         (0580 paper 04 Q5 June 2007)

19 A rectangle has sides of length 6.1 cm and 8.1 cm correct to 1 decimal place.
   Copy and complete the statement about the perimeter of the rectangle.
   ....cm ⇌ perimeter <...........cm   (0580 paper 02 Q13 November 2007)

20

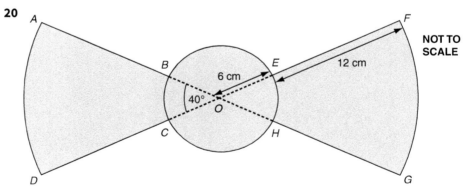

The diagram shows part of a fan.
OFG and *OAD* are sectors, centre *O*, with radius 18 cm and sector angle 40°.
B, *C*, *H* and *E* lie on a circle, centre *O* and radius 6 cm.
Calculate the shaded area.   (0580 paper 04 Q19 June 2009)

21

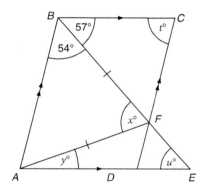

In the diagram, *ABCD* is a square.
Points *P*, *Q*, *R* and *S* lie on *AB*, *BC*, *CD* and *DA* so that *AP* = *BQ* = *CR* = *DS*.

a Giving all your reasons, show that
  i *PB* = *QC*
  ii triangle *BPQ* is congruent to triangle *CQR*
  iii *PQR* is a right angle.

b Write down two reasons to show that *PQRS* is a square.

(4024 paper 02 Q4 November 2004)

22 a In the diagram, *ABCD* is a parallelogram.
  ADE and *BFE* are straight lines.
  AF = *BF*.
  $A\hat{B}F = 54°$ and $C\hat{B}F = 57°$.

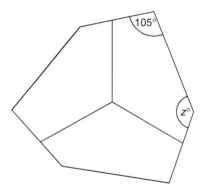

Find the value of
i *t*
ii *u*
iii *x*
iv *y*.

b This hexagon has rotational symmetry of order 3. Calculate the value of *z*.

c In the diagram, triangle *PQR* is similar to triangle *PSQ*.
  $P\hat{Q}R = P\hat{S}Q$.
  PQ = 18 cm, *QR* = 14 cm and *QS* = 21 cm.

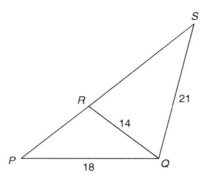

Calculate the length of
i PR
ii RS.

(4024 paper 02 Q3 June 2005)

23 The diagram shows a circle, centre O, with the sector POQ shaded.

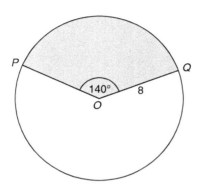

Given that $P\hat{O}Q = 140°$ and the radius of the circle is 8 cm, calculate
   i   the area of the shaded region
   ii the **total** perimeter of the **unshaded** region.   (4024 paper 02 Q3b June 2006)

24

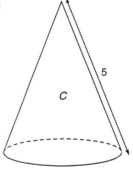
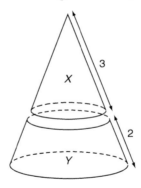

A solid cone, C, is cut into two parts, X and Y, by a plane parallel to the base.
The lengths of the sloping edges of the two parts are 3 cm and 2 cm.
Find the ratio of
a the diameters of the bases of X and C
b the areas of the bases of X and C
c the volumes of X and Y.   (4024 paper 01 Q20 November 2006)

25 [Surface area of a sphere $= 4\pi r^2$]
[Volume of a sphere $= \frac{4}{3}\pi r^3$]

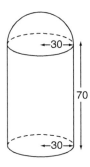

A hot water tank is made by joining a hemisphere of radius 30 cm to an open cylinder of radius 30 cm and height 70 cm.

a Calculate the total surface area, including the base, of the outside of the tank.

b The tank is full of water.

   i Calculate the number of litres of water in the tank.

   ii The water drains from the tank at a rate of 3 litres per second.
      Calculate the time, in minutes and seconds, to empty the tank.

   iii

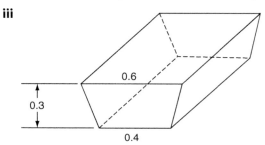

      All of the water from the tank runs into a bath, which it just completely fills.
      The bath is a prism whose cross-section is a trapezium.
      The lengths of the parallel sides of the trapezium are 0.4 m and 0.6 m.
      The depth of the bath is 0.3 m.
      Calculate the length of the bath.   (4024 paper 02 Q7 November 2006)

26 a Compost for growing plants consists of 3 parts of soil to 2 parts of sand to 1 part of peat.

   i Calculate the number of litres of sand in a 75 litre bag of compost.

   ii Compost is sold in 5 litre, 25 litre and 75 litre bags costing $2, $8.75 and $27 respectively.

   Showing your working clearly, state which bag represents the best value for money.

b [The volume of a cone $= \frac{1}{3} \times$ base area $\times$ height.]

The diagram shows a plant pot.
The open end of the plant pot is a circle of radius 10 cm.
The closed end is a circle of radius 5 cm.
The height of the plant pot is 12 cm.
The plant pot is part of a right circular cone of height 24 cm.

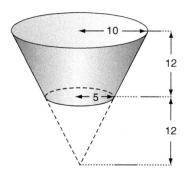

i Calculate the volume of the plant pot. Give your answer in litres.

ii How many of these plant pots can be completely filled from a 75 litre bag of compost?

iii A smaller plant pot is geometrically similar to the original plant pot. The open end of this plant pot is a circle of radius 5 cm.

How many of these plant pots can be completely filled from a 75 litre bag of compost?

(4024 paper 02 Q7 November 2007)

27 a A fuel tank is a cylinder of diameter 1.8 m.

i The tank holds 25 000 litres when full.

Given that 1 m³ = 1000 litres, calculate the length of the cylinder.

Give your answer in metres.

ii

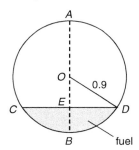

The diagram shows the cross-section of the cylinder, centre *O*, containing some fuel. *CD* is horizontal and is the level of the fuel in the cylinder.

AB is a vertical diameter and intersects *CD* at *E*.

Given that *E* is the midpoint of *OB*,

a show that $E\hat{O}D = 60°$

b calculate the area of the segment *BCD*

c calculate the number of litres of fuel in the cylinder.

b [Volume of a sphere $= \frac{4}{3}\pi r^3$]

A different fuel tank consists of a cylinder of diameter 1.5 m and a hemisphere of diameter 1.5 m at one end.

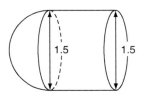

The volume of the cylinder is 10 times the volume of the hemisphere.

Calculate the length of the cylinder.

(4024 paper 02 Q7 November 2009)

Learning Objectives
Syllabus sections 21, 26 and 38

In this chapter you will:
- learn about matrices

- find out more about functions
- use graphs of inequalities.

20.1 Introduction

This chapter completes the algebra part of your course.

You will learn about matrices and functions, and how to find solution sets for inequalities in two variables. The inequalities section leads to some simple programming work. You will see how matrices can be used in Chapter 22, in work on transformations.

20.2 Essential Skills

1 Solve the following simultaneous equations:

a $x + 3y = 5$
$2x + y = 25$

b $y - 6x = -8$
$x - 3y = 7$

2 Substitute:
a $x = 2$ **b** $x = 20$ **c** $x = -6$ into $\dfrac{x+5}{x-10}$

3 Substitute:
a $x = 1$ **b** $x = -7$ **c** $y = -4$ into $y - 2 > x + 4$

20.3 Beginning Matrices

A **matrix** (plural **matrices**) is a rectangular arrangement of numbers.

For example, information about the numbers of boys and girls in years 10 and 11 at a school could be shown in a table, like Table 20.1.

	Year 10	Year 11
Boys	60	56
Girls	58	61

Table 20.1 Boys and girls in Years 10 and 11

If this is presented as a matrix it becomes:

$$\begin{pmatrix} 60 & 56 \\ 58 & 61 \end{pmatrix}$$

The **order** of the matrix is given by the numbers of rows and columns. Rows are always given first. The example above is a square matrix with 2 rows and 2 columns, so it is a **2 × 2 matrix**. This is referred to as a 'two by two matrix' and written '2 × 2'. The sign does not imply multiplication.

Example 1

Write down the order of these matrices:

a $\begin{pmatrix} a & b \\ c & d \end{pmatrix}$ **b** $\begin{pmatrix} 1 & 2 & 3 \\ 4 & 5 & 6 \end{pmatrix}$ **c** $\begin{pmatrix} 10 & 11 \\ 12 & 13 \\ 14 & 15 \end{pmatrix}$ **d** $\begin{pmatrix} x \\ y \\ z \end{pmatrix}$

Answer 1

a 2 × 2   **b** 2 × 3   **c** 3 × 2   **d** 3 × 1

20.4 Operations on Matrices

Matrices of the same order can be added or subtracted by adding or subtracting the corresponding elements in each matrix.

For example, if the school shown above combines with another school we would have the situation shown in Table 20.2.

School A	Year 10	Year 11
Boys	60	56
Girls	58	61

School B	Year 10	Year 11
Boys	43	52
Girls	39	60

Table 20.2 Years 10 and 11 from schools A and B

This can be shown in matrix form as:

$$\begin{pmatrix} 60 & 56 \\ 58 & 61 \end{pmatrix} + \begin{pmatrix} 43 & 52 \\ 39 & 60 \end{pmatrix} = \begin{pmatrix} 103 & 108 \\ 97 & 121 \end{pmatrix}$$

Example 2

Calculate

a $\begin{pmatrix} 5 & 6 \\ 7 & 3 \end{pmatrix} - \begin{pmatrix} 2 & 4 \\ 8 & 1 \end{pmatrix}$ **b** $\begin{pmatrix} 1 & 5 & 9 \\ 2 & 1 & 0 \end{pmatrix} + \begin{pmatrix} 0 & -4 & 8 \\ 3 & 6 & -2 \end{pmatrix}$

Answer 2

a $\begin{pmatrix} 5 & 6 \\ 7 & 3 \end{pmatrix} - \begin{pmatrix} 2 & 4 \\ 8 & 1 \end{pmatrix} = \begin{pmatrix} 3 & 2 \\ -1 & 2 \end{pmatrix}$ **b** $\begin{pmatrix} 0 & -4 & 8 \\ 2 & 1 & 0 \end{pmatrix} + \begin{pmatrix} 0 & -4 & 8 \\ 3 & 6 & -2 \end{pmatrix} = \begin{pmatrix} 1 & 1 & 17 \\ 5 & 7 & -2 \end{pmatrix}$

Key term

A matrix is **transposed** by turning the columns into rows and the rows into columns.

A matrix may be **transposed** by turning the columns into rows and the rows into columns. School A could be shown as in Table 20.3.

	Boys	**Girls**
Year 10	60	58
Year 11	56	61

Table 20.3 School A transposed

In matrix form this is written as:

$$\mathbf{A} = \begin{pmatrix} 60 & 56 \\ 58 & 61 \end{pmatrix}; \text{ A transpose} = \mathbf{A}' = \begin{pmatrix} 60 & 58 \\ 56 & 61 \end{pmatrix}$$

Matrices are normally denoted by capital letters.

Example 3

$C = \begin{pmatrix} 2 & 7 & 0 \\ 5 & 3 & 4 \end{pmatrix}$. Find C'.

Answer 3

$C' = \begin{pmatrix} 2 & 5 \\ 7 & 3 \\ 0 & 4 \end{pmatrix}$

A matrix may be multiplied by a number. For example,

$$3 \begin{pmatrix} 1 & 6 \\ 0 & -1 \end{pmatrix} = \begin{pmatrix} 3 & 18 \\ 0 & -3 \end{pmatrix}$$

You will see that each element is multiplied by the number.

Example 4

Calculate $-\dfrac{1}{2} \begin{pmatrix} 5 & -1 \\ 8 & 0 \end{pmatrix}$

Answer 4

$-\dfrac{1}{2} \begin{pmatrix} 5 & -1 \\ 8 & 0 \end{pmatrix} = \begin{pmatrix} \frac{-5}{2} & \frac{1}{2} \\ -4 & 0 \end{pmatrix}$

Exercise 20.1

1   Write the following information in a table and then in matrix form.
   a   A manufacturer of computers makes laptops and desktops, both in either black or white cases. There are 10 black laptops, 20 white laptops, 4 black desktops, and 15 white desktops.
   b   Four teams, the Reds, the Blues, the Greens, and the Yellows are in a friendly league. The Reds have 2 wins, 2 draws and lose 2 games. The Blues have 3 wins, 2 draws and lose 1 game. The Greens have 1 win, 5 draws and do not lose any games. The Yellows have 1 win, 1 draw and lose 4 games.

2 Work out the following matrix calculations:

a $\begin{pmatrix} 5 & 4 \\ 10 & 3 \end{pmatrix} + \begin{pmatrix} -2 & 6 \\ -18 & 0 \end{pmatrix}$

b $\begin{pmatrix} -5 & 0 \\ 1 & -3 \end{pmatrix} - \begin{pmatrix} -4 & -1 \\ 0 & 4 \end{pmatrix}$

c $\begin{pmatrix} 1 & 0 \\ 3 & -8 \end{pmatrix}$

d $-1\begin{pmatrix} -2 & 5 \\ 0 & 1 \end{pmatrix}$

3 $A = \begin{pmatrix} 5 & 1 & -3 \\ 4 & 5 & 2 \end{pmatrix}$

$B = \begin{pmatrix} 3 & 9 \\ 7 & 1 \end{pmatrix}$

$C = \begin{pmatrix} 1 & 2 & 5 \\ 4 & 9 & 3 \end{pmatrix}$

$D = \begin{pmatrix} 7 & 0 \\ 3 & 1 \end{pmatrix}$

$E = \begin{pmatrix} 5 & 1 \\ 4 & 6 \\ 9 & 3 \end{pmatrix}$

$F = (-1 \quad 2 \quad 6)$

a Write down the order of each matrix.
b Write down the transpose of each matrix.
c Write down the order of
  i D′   **ii** E′   **iii** F′
d Calculate
  i A + C   **ii** D − B   **iii** 4 × F

20.5 Multiplication of Matrices

We have seen that matrices can only be added or subtracted if they are of the same order, because corresponding elements from each matrix have to be added or subtracted.

A similar restriction applies for multiplication of matrices, and we say that matrices have to be **conformable** for multiplication.

Key term

Two matrices are **conformable** for multiplication if the number of columns in the first is the same as the number of rows in the second.

Take four matrices, for example:

$$A = \begin{pmatrix} 2 & 5 & 6 \\ 7 & 1 & 3 \end{pmatrix} \quad B = \begin{pmatrix} 1 & 2 \\ 3 & 4 \end{pmatrix}, \quad C = \begin{pmatrix} 5 & 4 & 1 \\ 9 & 8 & 2 \end{pmatrix}, \quad D = \begin{pmatrix} 1 & 2 \\ 5 & 6 \\ 9 & 1 \end{pmatrix}.$$

The orders of these matrices are:

$$A = 2 \times 3, \qquad B = 2 \times 2, \qquad C = 2 \times 3, \qquad D = 3 \times 2.$$

Matrices are only conformable for multiplication if the number of columns in the first matrix is the same as the number of rows in the second. This means that, unlike in normal arithmetic when 5×10 is the same as 10×5, in matrix multiplication the order of multiplying does matter.

Looking at the matrices **A**, **B**, **C** and **D**, we see that **B** × **A** is possible because **B** has 2 columns and **A** has 2 rows:

$$\begin{array}{ccc} \textbf{B} & & \textbf{A} \\ \text{rows} \quad \text{columns} & & \text{rows} \quad \text{columns} \\ 2 \times 2 & & 2 \times 3 \end{array}$$

these two are equal

However, **A** × **B** is not possible:

$$\begin{array}{ccc} \textbf{A} & & \textbf{B} \\ \text{rows} \quad \text{columns} & & \text{rows} \quad \text{columns} \\ 2 \times 3 & & 2 \times 2 \end{array}$$

these two are not equal

When the two matrices are conformable for multiplication, the order of the resulting matrix is the rows from the first matrix and the columns from the second. Figure 20.1 should make this clearer.

matrix:	$B \times A$		result: **BA**
order:	$2 \times ②$	$② \times 3$	2×3
	conformable		

Figure 20.1 Conformable matrices

Example 5

Using the matrices **A**, **B**, **C** and **D** above, state whether these matrices are conformable *in the order given*, and if they are, the order of the product.

a AC   **b** CA   **c** DA

d DB   **e** BD

Answer 5

a	**A**	**C**		
	$2 \times ③$	$② \times 3$	not conformable	
b	**C**	**A**		
	$2 \times ③$	$② \times 3$	not conformable	
c	**D**	**A**		**DA**
	$3 \times ②$	$② \times 3$	conformable	3×3
d	**D**	**B**		**DB**
	$3 \times ②$	$② \times 2$	conformable	3×2
e	**B**	**D**		
	$2 \times ②$	$③ \times 2$	not conformable	

Exercise 20.2

F, **G**, **H**, **K**, **L** are five matrices. Their orders are

$F = 2 \times 2$, $G = 3 \times 3$, $H = 2 \times 4$, $K = 4 \times 2$, $L = 3 \times 2$.

For each of the following matrix products state whether they are conformable for multiplication, and if so what the order of the product will be.

1 FG	**2** GH	**3** HK	**4** KH
5 LG	**6** GL	**7** LF	**8** FL

We now need to find how to multiply two conformable matrices. The data in question **1b** of Exercise 20.1 produces Table 20.4 and the matrix **A**.

	Win	**Draw**	**Lose**
Reds	2	2	2
Blues	3	2	1
Greens	1	5	0
Yellows	1	1	4

Table 20.4 League results

$$A = \begin{pmatrix} 2 & 2 & 2 \\ 3 & 2 & 1 \\ 1 & 5 & 0 \\ 1 & 1 & 4 \end{pmatrix}$$

In order to decide which team wins the league it is decided to award 5 points for a win, 2 points for a draw, and no points for losing a game. This is shown in Table 20.5 and in matrix form in **B**.

	Points
Win	5
Draw	2
Lose	0

Table 20.5 League scoring

$$\mathbf{B} = \begin{pmatrix} 5 \\ 2 \\ 0 \end{pmatrix}$$

Now we can multiply the two matrices to find the overall winner:

$$\mathbf{AB} = \begin{pmatrix} 2 & 2 & 2 \\ 3 & 2 & 1 \\ 1 & 5 & 0 \\ 1 & 1 & 4 \end{pmatrix} \times \begin{pmatrix} 5 \\ 2 \\ 0 \end{pmatrix}$$

The total points for the Reds are $2 \times 5 + 2 \times 2 + 2 \times 0 = 14$.

Check that you agree with this, and then find the points for the other three teams.

Check that the matrices are conformable for multiplication and find the order of the product.

$$\underset{4 \times 3}{\mathbf{A}} \qquad \underset{3 \times 1}{\mathbf{B}} \qquad\qquad \underset{4 \times 1}{\mathbf{AB}}$$

$$\mathbf{AB} = \begin{pmatrix} 2 & 2 & 2 \\ 3 & 2 & 1 \\ 1 & 5 & 0 \\ 1 & 1 & 4 \end{pmatrix}\begin{pmatrix} 5 \\ 2 \\ 0 \end{pmatrix} = \begin{pmatrix} 2\times5+2\times2+2\times0 \\ 3\times5+2\times2+1\times0 \\ 1\times5+5\times2+0\times0 \\ 1\times5+1\times2+4\times0 \end{pmatrix} = \begin{pmatrix} 14 \\ 19 \\ 15 \\ 7 \end{pmatrix}$$

Which team won the league?

Which team came second?

What would the result have been if 4 points were awarded for a win and 3 for a draw?

What about 3 for a win and 1 for a draw?

Example 6

Using the information above,

a   write down **A**′ and **B**′

b   write down the orders of **A**′ and **B**′

c   multiply **A**′ and **B**′ together in the order in which they are conformable.

Answer 6

a $\mathbf{A'} = \begin{pmatrix} 2 & 3 & 1 & 1 \\ 2 & 2 & 5 & 1 \\ 2 & 1 & 0 & 4 \end{pmatrix}$ $\mathbf{B'} = (5 \quad 2 \quad 0)$

b $\mathbf{A'} = 3 \times 4$ $\qquad\qquad$ $\mathbf{B'} = 1 \times 3$ $\qquad$ c $\mathbf{B'A'} = (14 \quad 19 \quad 15 \quad 7) \times \begin{pmatrix} 2 & 3 & 1 & 1 \\ 2 & 2 & 5 & 1 \\ 2 & 1 & 0 & 4 \end{pmatrix}$

NOTE:
In answer 6 part **c** B′ A′ is a 1×4 matrix, so the multiplication is conformable in that order = (14 19 15 7)

We now need to find a general method for multiplying matrices.

You need to be particularly careful and systematic when multiplying matrices. It is strongly advised that you work out the order of the product and draw a matrix with dots in the positions where each element of the answer will go. We will now go step by step through the process.

For example, we will multiply these two matrices:

$$\mathbf{P} = \begin{pmatrix} 1 & 2 \\ 3 & 4 \\ 5 & 6 \end{pmatrix} \quad \mathbf{Q} = \begin{pmatrix} 7 & 8 \\ 9 & 10 \end{pmatrix} \quad \mathbf{PQ} = \begin{pmatrix} \bullet & \bullet \\ \bullet & \bullet \\ \bullet & \bullet \end{pmatrix}$$

$$\underset{3 \times 2}{\mathbf{P}} \qquad \underset{2 \times 2}{\mathbf{Q}} \qquad \underset{3 \times 2}{\mathbf{PQ}}$$

PQ is conformable, but not **QP**. Check that you agree.

The rule is that you multiply the rows of the first matrix on to the columns of the second matrix, and add the results.

$$\text{row 1} \to \begin{pmatrix} \textcircled{1\ 2} \\ 3 & 4 \\ 5 & 6 \end{pmatrix} \begin{pmatrix} 7 & 8 \\ 9 & 10 \end{pmatrix} = \begin{pmatrix} 1 \times 7 + 2 \times 9 & \bullet \\ \bullet & \bullet \\ \bullet & \bullet \end{pmatrix} = \quad \text{row 1} \to \begin{pmatrix} 25 & \bullet \\ \bullet & \bullet \\ \bullet & \bullet \end{pmatrix}$$

Then repeat for the remaining rows and columns.

$$\text{row 1} \to \begin{pmatrix} \textcircled{1\ 2} \\ 3 & 4 \\ 5 & 6 \end{pmatrix} \begin{pmatrix} 7 & 8 \\ 9 & 10 \end{pmatrix} = \begin{pmatrix} 25 & 1 \times 8 + 2 \times 10 \\ \bullet & \bullet \\ \bullet & \bullet \end{pmatrix} = \quad \text{row 1} \to \begin{pmatrix} 25 & 28 \\ \bullet & \bullet \\ \bullet & \bullet \end{pmatrix}$$

$$\text{row 2} \to \begin{pmatrix} 1 & 2 \\ \textcircled{3\ 4} \\ 5 & 6 \end{pmatrix} \begin{pmatrix} 7 & 8 \\ 9 & 10 \end{pmatrix} = \begin{pmatrix} 25 & 3 \times 7 + 4 \times 9 \\ 28 & \bullet \\ \bullet & \bullet \end{pmatrix} = \text{row 2} \to \begin{pmatrix} 25 & 28 \\ 57 & \bullet \\ \bullet & \bullet \end{pmatrix}$$

Check that you can follow this and complete the multiplication.

$$\begin{pmatrix} 1 & 2 \\ 3 & 4 \\ 5 & 6 \end{pmatrix} \begin{pmatrix} 7 & 8 \\ 9 & 10 \end{pmatrix} = \begin{pmatrix} 25 & 28 \\ 57 & 3 \times 8 + 4 \times 10 \\ 5 \times 7 + 6 \times 9 & 5 \times 8 + 6 \times 10 \end{pmatrix} = \begin{pmatrix} 25 & 28 \\ 57 & 64 \\ 89 & 100 \end{pmatrix}$$

For multiplying matrices:
- Check that the two matrices are conformable.
- Write down the order of the product.
- Open brackets of a suitable size.
- Multiply rows on to columns and add.

Example 7

$$\mathbf{X} = \begin{pmatrix} 2 & 1 & 3 \\ 0 & 5 & 1 \end{pmatrix} \quad \mathbf{Y} = \begin{pmatrix} -1 & 0 \\ 2 & 2 \\ 1 & 4 \end{pmatrix}$$

Calculate

a XY   **b** YX

Answer 7

a

X	Y	XY
2×3	3×2	2×2

$$\begin{pmatrix} 2 & 1 & 3 \\ 0 & 5 & 1 \end{pmatrix}\begin{pmatrix} -1 & 0 \\ 2 & 2 \\ 1 & 4 \end{pmatrix} = \begin{pmatrix} 2\times-1+1\times2+3\times1 & 2\times0+1\times2+3\times4 \\ 0\times-1+5\times2+1\times1 & 0\times0+5\times2+1\times4 \end{pmatrix} = \begin{pmatrix} 3 & 14 \\ 11 & 14 \end{pmatrix}$$

$$\mathbf{XY} = \begin{pmatrix} 3 & 14 \\ 11 & 14 \end{pmatrix}$$

b

Y	X	YX
3×2	2×3	3×3

$$\begin{pmatrix} -1 & 0 \\ 2 & 2 \\ 1 & 4 \end{pmatrix}\begin{pmatrix} 2 & 1 & 3 \\ 0 & 5 & 1 \end{pmatrix} = \begin{pmatrix} -1\times2+0\times0 & -1\times1+0\times5 & -1\times3+0\times1 \\ 2\times2+2\times0 & 2\times1+2\times5 & 2\times3+2\times1 \\ 1\times2+4\times0 & 1\times1+4\times5 & 1\times3+4\times1 \end{pmatrix} = \begin{pmatrix} -2 & -1 & -3 \\ 4 & 12 & 8 \\ 2 & 21 & 7 \end{pmatrix}$$

$$\mathbf{XY} = \begin{pmatrix} -2 & -1 & -3 \\ 4 & 12 & 8 \\ 2 & 21 & 7 \end{pmatrix}$$

NOTE:
This example clearly shows that the order in which two matrices are multiplied matters. In this case **XY** is not equal to **YX**.

Exercise 20.3

1 $\begin{pmatrix} 2 & 5 \\ 0 & 1 \end{pmatrix}\begin{pmatrix} 6 & 7 \\ 3 & 4 \end{pmatrix} = \begin{pmatrix} 27 & a \\ 3 & 4 \end{pmatrix}$

Find a.

2 $\begin{pmatrix} -1 & 6 \\ 4 & 0 \end{pmatrix}\begin{pmatrix} 5 & 2 \\ 3 & -1 \end{pmatrix} = \begin{pmatrix} 13 & b \\ 20 & c \end{pmatrix}$

Find b and c.

3 $\mathbf{A} = \begin{pmatrix} 5 & 1 & -1 \\ 0 & 1 & 3 \end{pmatrix} \mathbf{B} = \begin{pmatrix} 1 & 2 \\ 3 & 4 \end{pmatrix} \mathbf{C} = \begin{pmatrix} 3 & -1 & 2 \end{pmatrix} \mathbf{D} = \begin{pmatrix} 6 & 7 \\ 4 & 2 \\ -1 & 3 \end{pmatrix}$

Where possible calculate

a AB   **b** BA   **c** CD   **d** DA

4 $\begin{pmatrix} 2 & 3 \\ 1 & -1 \end{pmatrix}\begin{pmatrix} 1 & 1 & x \\ -1 & y & 4 \end{pmatrix} = \begin{pmatrix} -1 & 2 & 16 \\ z & 1 & -2 \end{pmatrix}$

Find x, y and z.

5 $E = \begin{pmatrix} -1 & 3 \\ 0 & -2 \end{pmatrix}$

Calculate

a $3E$

b $-E$

c E^2

d $3E + E^2$

e $E + E'$

NOTE:
Part b: $-1 \times E$

NOTE:
Part c: $\mathbf{E} \times \mathbf{E}$

Key term

All the elements of a **zero matrix** are zero.

20.6 The Zero Matrix

Since $a - a = 0$ and $b \times 0 = 0$, can similar results be obtained with matrices?

If $\quad \mathbf{A} = \begin{pmatrix} a & b \\ c & d \end{pmatrix}$ and $\mathbf{X} = \begin{pmatrix} w & x \\ y & z \end{pmatrix}$,

then $\quad \mathbf{A} - \mathbf{A} = \begin{pmatrix} a & b \\ c & d \end{pmatrix} - \begin{pmatrix} a & b \\ c & d \end{pmatrix} = \begin{pmatrix} a-a & b-b \\ c-c & d-d \end{pmatrix} = \begin{pmatrix} 0 & 0 \\ 0 & 0 \end{pmatrix}$

and $\quad \mathbf{X} \times \begin{pmatrix} 0 & 0 \\ 0 & 0 \end{pmatrix} = \begin{pmatrix} w & x \\ y & z \end{pmatrix} \begin{pmatrix} 0 & 0 \\ 0 & 0 \end{pmatrix} = \begin{pmatrix} 0 & 0 \\ 0 & 0 \end{pmatrix}$.

so $\begin{pmatrix} 0 & 0 \\ 0 & 0 \end{pmatrix}$ is the zero 2×2 matrix.

From now on we will be dealing mainly with 2×2 matrices.

Example 8

$\begin{pmatrix} 2 & -3 \\ -c & 10 \end{pmatrix} - \begin{pmatrix} a & -b \\ 5 & -d \end{pmatrix} = \begin{pmatrix} 0 & 0 \\ 0 & 0 \end{pmatrix}$

Find a, b, c and d.

Answer 8

$2 - a = 0 \qquad a = 2$

$-3 - -b = 0 \qquad b = 3$

$-c - 5 = 0 \qquad c = -5$

$10 - -d = 0 \qquad d = -10$

Key term

A 2×2 matrix multiplied by the 2×2 **identity matrix** is unchanged.

20.7 The Identity Matrix and Inverse Matrices

Remembering that $a \times 1 = a$, is there a matrix that has the same property?

We might think that $\begin{pmatrix} 1 & 1 \\ 1 & 1 \end{pmatrix}$ would multiply another matrix and leave it unchanged.

Investigating this we find

$$\begin{pmatrix} a & b \\ c & d \end{pmatrix} \times \begin{pmatrix} 1 & 1 \\ 1 & 1 \end{pmatrix} = \begin{pmatrix} a+b & a+b \\ c+d & c+d \end{pmatrix},$$

so that does not work.

The matrix we are looking for is the **identity matrix**, $I = \begin{pmatrix} 1 & 0 \\ 0 & 1 \end{pmatrix}$.

Testing this:

$$\begin{pmatrix} 1 & 0 \\ 0 & 1 \end{pmatrix}\begin{pmatrix} a & b \\ c & d \end{pmatrix} = \begin{pmatrix} a+0\times c & b+0\times d \\ 0+a\times c & 0+b\times d \end{pmatrix} = \begin{pmatrix} a & b \\ c & d \end{pmatrix}$$

This is an important result because it helps us to find a method for finding inverse matrices. Suppose you need to work out $a \div b$? This can be written $\frac{a}{b}$ or $a \times \frac{1}{b}$. $\frac{1}{b}$ is the multiplicative inverse of b, so $\frac{1}{b} \times b = b \times \frac{1}{b} = 1$.

You do not need to remember the term 'multiplicative inverse', but it is used here to illustrate the use of inverses. $\frac{1}{b}$ is also known as the *reciprocal* of b.

The **inverse of a matrix A** is written as $\mathbf{A}^{-1}$, so $\mathbf{A} \times \mathbf{A}^{-1} = \mathbf{A}^{-1} \times \mathbf{A} = \mathbf{I}$; that is, the matrix **A** multiplied by its inverse should give the identity matrix.

Key term

A 2×2 matrix multiplied by its **inverse matrix** gives the identity matrix.

For example, let $\mathbf{A} = \begin{pmatrix} 2 & 3 \\ 4 & 5 \end{pmatrix}$ and $\mathbf{A}^{-1} = \begin{pmatrix} a & b \\ c & d \end{pmatrix}$.

If $\mathbf{A}^{-1}$ is the inverse of **A** then $\mathbf{AA}^{-1} = \mathbf{I}$.

$$\begin{pmatrix} 2 & 3 \\ 4 & 5 \end{pmatrix} \times \begin{pmatrix} a & b \\ c & d \end{pmatrix} = \begin{pmatrix} 1 & 0 \\ 0 & 1 \end{pmatrix}$$

$$\begin{pmatrix} 2a+3c & 2b+3d \\ 4a+5c & 4b+5d \end{pmatrix} = \begin{pmatrix} 1 & 0 \\ 0 & 1 \end{pmatrix}$$

Comparing each element of the two matrices:

$$2a + 3c = 1 \qquad 2b + 3d = 0$$
$$4a + 5c = 0 \qquad 4b + 5d = 1$$

Solve each pair of equations simultaneously and you will see that $a = \frac{-5}{2}$, $b = \frac{3}{2}$, $c = 2$ and $d = -1$:

$$\mathbf{A}^{-1} = \begin{pmatrix} \frac{-5}{2} & \frac{3}{2} \\ 2 & -1 \end{pmatrix}$$

This can also be written as:

$$\mathbf{A}^{-1} = \frac{1}{2}\begin{pmatrix} -5 & 3 \\ 4 & 2 \end{pmatrix} = -\frac{1}{2}\begin{pmatrix} 5 & -3 \\ -4 & 2 \end{pmatrix}$$

Compare with $A = \begin{pmatrix} 2 & 3 \\ 4 & 5 \end{pmatrix}$

We have shown one particular numerical form of the general rule for finding inverse matrices.

Key term

The **determinant** of a 2×2 matrix $\begin{pmatrix} a & b \\ c & d \end{pmatrix}$ is the number obtained from the difference of the products of the diagonals: $ad - bc$.

If $\quad \mathbf{A} = \begin{pmatrix} a & b \\ c & d \end{pmatrix}, \quad$ then $\quad \mathbf{A}^{-1} = \frac{1}{ad-bc}\begin{pmatrix} d & -b \\ -c & a \end{pmatrix}.$

$ad - bc$ is called the **determinant** of **A** and can be written as det **A** or $|\mathbf{A}|$. Determinants can only be evaluated for square matrices, and here only 2×2 determinants will be considered.

Apart from the determinant, we can see that the elements a and d have changed places, and the elements b and c have remained in the same place but have had their signs changed.

Example 9

Find the determinant of each of these matrices:

a $X = \begin{pmatrix} 1 & 3 \\ 5 & 2 \end{pmatrix}$

b $Y = \begin{pmatrix} -1 & 0 \\ 2 & 4 \end{pmatrix}$

c $Z = \begin{pmatrix} 10 & 3 \\ -7 & -2 \end{pmatrix}$

Answer 9

a $\det X = 1 \times 2 - 5 \times 3 = 13$

b $\det Y = 1 \times 4 - 2 \times 0 = 4$

c $\det Z = 10 \times -2 - -7 \times 3 = -20 + 21 = 1$

If the determinant comes to zero, then the matrix has no inverse because $\frac{1}{0}$ does not exist.

Exercise 20.4

Find the determinant of each of these matrices.

1 $P = \begin{pmatrix} 1 & 5 \\ 3 & 20 \end{pmatrix}$

2 $Q = \begin{pmatrix} 2 & 3 \\ -1 & -2 \end{pmatrix}$

3 $R = \begin{pmatrix} 9 & 1 \\ 0 & 3 \end{pmatrix}$

4 $S = \begin{pmatrix} -3 & 1 \\ 4 & 5 \end{pmatrix}$

Having found the determinants we can find the inverse matrices.

Example 10

$X = \begin{pmatrix} 7 & 1 \\ 3 & 4 \end{pmatrix}$ $Y = \begin{pmatrix} -5 & 6 \\ 2 & -8 \end{pmatrix}$ $Z = \begin{pmatrix} 2 & 4 \\ 3 & 6 \end{pmatrix}$

Find   **a** X^{-1} **b** Y^{-1} **c** Z^{-1}

Answer 10

a $\det X = 7 \times 4 - 3 \times 1 = 28 - 3 = 25$

   $X^{-1} = \frac{1}{25}\begin{pmatrix} 4 & -1 \\ -3 & 7 \end{pmatrix}$

NOTE:
It is acceptable to leave the inverse in this form.

b $\det Y = -5 \times -8 - 2 \times 6 = +40 - 12 = 28$

   $Y^{-1} = \frac{1}{28}\begin{pmatrix} -8 & -6 \\ -2 & -5 \end{pmatrix}$

   $Y^{-1} = \frac{-1}{28}\begin{pmatrix} 8 & 6 \\ 2 & 5 \end{pmatrix}$

NOTE:
In this case the entries could be simplified by factorising out the −1.

c $\det Z = 2 \times 6 - 3 \times 4 = 12 - 12 = 0$

   Z^{-1} does not exist.

NOTE:

D is not the identity matrix **I**, so make sure you can see the difference in the positions of the ones and zeroes.

Exercise 20.5

$A = \begin{pmatrix} 7 & 8 \\ 9 & 10 \end{pmatrix}$ $B = \begin{pmatrix} 2 & -1 \\ -1 & -2 \end{pmatrix}$ $C = \begin{pmatrix} -1 & -6 \\ 3 & 10 \end{pmatrix}$ $D = \begin{pmatrix} 0 & 1 \\ 1 & 0 \end{pmatrix}$

Find: **1** A^{-1} **2** B^{-1} **3** C^{-1} **4** D^{-1} **5** $I = \begin{pmatrix} 1 & 0 \\ 0 & 1 \end{pmatrix}$ Find I^{-1}.

Example 11

a $\mathbf{A} = \begin{pmatrix} 3 & 4 \\ 1 & 2 \end{pmatrix}$

Find $\mathbf{A}^{-1}$.

b Given that $\mathbf{A}\begin{pmatrix} x \\ y \end{pmatrix} = \begin{pmatrix} 10 \\ 6 \end{pmatrix}$,

solve $\mathbf{A}^{-1}\mathbf{A}\begin{pmatrix} x \\ y \end{pmatrix} = \mathbf{A}^{-1}\begin{pmatrix} 10 \\ 6 \end{pmatrix}$.

c Write down the values of x and y

Answer 11

a $\det \mathbf{A} = 3 \times 2 - 1 \times 4 = 2$

$\mathbf{A}^{-1} = \frac{1}{2}\begin{pmatrix} 2 & -4 \\ -1 & 3 \end{pmatrix}$

b $\mathbf{A}\begin{pmatrix} x \\ y \end{pmatrix} = \begin{pmatrix} 10 \\ 6 \end{pmatrix}$

$\mathbf{A}^{-1}\mathbf{A}\begin{pmatrix} x \\ y \end{pmatrix} = \frac{1}{2}\begin{pmatrix} 2 & -4 \\ -1 & 3 \end{pmatrix}\begin{pmatrix} 10 \\ 6 \end{pmatrix}$

$\mathbf{I}\begin{pmatrix} x \\ y \end{pmatrix} = \frac{1}{2}\begin{pmatrix} 2 \times 10 - 4 \times 6 \\ -1 \times 10 + 3 \times 6 \end{pmatrix} = \frac{1}{2}\begin{pmatrix} -4 \\ 8 \end{pmatrix} = \begin{pmatrix} -2 \\ 4 \end{pmatrix}$

since $\mathbf{I}\begin{pmatrix} x \\ y \end{pmatrix} = \begin{pmatrix} x \\ y \end{pmatrix}$,

then $\begin{pmatrix} x \\ y \end{pmatrix} = \begin{pmatrix} -2 \\ 4 \end{pmatrix}$.

> **NOTE:**
> Remember that $\mathbf{A}^{-1}\mathbf{A} = \mathbf{I}$.

c $x = -2, y = 4$

This example illustrates another use for matrices, which is for solving simultaneous equations.

To understand how this works, go back to part (b) of the example.

$$\mathbf{A}\begin{pmatrix} x \\ y \end{pmatrix} = \begin{pmatrix} 10 \\ 6 \end{pmatrix}$$

$$\begin{pmatrix} 3 & 4 \\ 1 & 2 \end{pmatrix}\begin{pmatrix} x \\ y \end{pmatrix} = \begin{pmatrix} 10 \\ 6 \end{pmatrix}$$

Simplifying the left-hand side of this equation we have:

$$\begin{pmatrix} 3x + 4y \\ x + 2y \end{pmatrix} = \begin{pmatrix} 10 \\ 6 \end{pmatrix}$$

These two matrices are equal, so the corresponding elements are equal:

$3x + 4y = 10$

$x + 2y = 6$

Solving these two equations simultaneously gives:

$x = -2$ and $y = 4$.

Using matrices may not be the quickest way to solve a pair of simultaneous equations, but it leads on to solving multiple simultaneous equations in multiple variables. The methods for these are complicated and not required for your course.

Exercise 20.6

$$E = \begin{pmatrix} -1 & 0 \\ 0 & 2 \end{pmatrix} \quad F = \begin{pmatrix} 7 & 1 & 6 \\ 3 & 5 & 2 \end{pmatrix} \quad G = \begin{pmatrix} 0 & 2 \\ 2 & 0 \end{pmatrix}$$

$$H = \begin{pmatrix} 1 \\ 2 \end{pmatrix} \quad J = (4 \quad 6) \quad K = \begin{pmatrix} 1 & -1 \\ 2 & 3 \\ -1 & 0 \end{pmatrix}$$

1 Write down the order of each matrix.

2 Write down the orders of these products:
   a FK **b** KF **c** HJ **d** JH **e** KH

3 Write down **F**' (**F** transpose), and the order of **F**'.

4 Calculate:
   a EF **b** GF **c** HJ **d** JH

5 Write down the identity matrix, **I**.

6 Find
   a E^{-1} (the inverse of **E**)   **b** G^{-1} **c** EE^{-1} **d** IE   **e** GI

7 **a** Simplify

$$\begin{pmatrix} a \\ b \end{pmatrix} = \begin{pmatrix} -1 & 0 \\ 0 & -1 \end{pmatrix} \begin{pmatrix} -5 \\ 7 \end{pmatrix}$$

   b Write down the values of a and b.

8 **a** Simplify

$$\begin{pmatrix} p & q \\ r & s \end{pmatrix} = \begin{pmatrix} 0 & -1 \\ 1 & 0 \end{pmatrix} \begin{pmatrix} -2 & 4 \\ 3 & -4 \end{pmatrix}$$

   b Write down the values of p, q, r and s.

9 Simplify the following:

   a
$$2\begin{pmatrix} 7 \\ 8 \\ 9 \end{pmatrix} - 3\begin{pmatrix} -1 \\ 2 \\ 0 \end{pmatrix}$$

   b
$$x\begin{pmatrix} 1 \\ 2 \\ 3 \end{pmatrix} + 2\begin{pmatrix} 0 \\ 4x \\ x \end{pmatrix}$$

10 Find the values of the letters in these statements:

   a
$$\begin{pmatrix} 3 & 2 \\ -5 & 4 \end{pmatrix} = 2\begin{pmatrix} a & b \\ c & d \end{pmatrix}$$

   b
$$\begin{pmatrix} 4 & 16 \\ 24 & -8 \end{pmatrix} = x\begin{pmatrix} 1 & 4 \\ b & -2 \end{pmatrix}$$

   c
$$\begin{pmatrix} 1 & -2 \\ 3 & -4 \end{pmatrix} = y\begin{pmatrix} 3 & -6 \\ 9 & -12 \end{pmatrix}$$

   d
$$\begin{pmatrix} \frac{1}{2} & \frac{3}{4} \\ r & \frac{-1}{2} \end{pmatrix} = p\begin{pmatrix} 2 & q \\ 28 & -2 \end{pmatrix}$$

11 A car sales person sells two types of cars, called Reliable and Gofaster. She sells 10 blue, 5 red and 2 black Reliables, and 5 blue, 16 red and 3 black Gofasters.

   Reliables retail at $5000 and Gofasters at $6000.

   a Copy and complete the two tables below.

	Reliables	Gofasters
Retail value	$5000	......

	Blue	Red	Black
Reliables	10	......	......
Gofasters	......	16	3

b Copy and complete the two matrices

$$\mathbf{R} = \begin{pmatrix} 5000 & ... \end{pmatrix} \qquad \mathbf{N} = \begin{pmatrix} 10 & ... & ... \\ ... & 16 & 3 \end{pmatrix},$$

where **R** is the matrix of the retail values and **N** is the matrix of the number of cars sold.

c Evaluate **RN**.

d Evaluate $\mathbf{RN} \begin{pmatrix} 1 \\ 1 \\ 1 \end{pmatrix}$.

e What does $\mathbf{RN} \begin{pmatrix} 1 \\ 1 \\ 1 \end{pmatrix}$ represent?

12 Why is it not possible to find the product of

$$\mathbf{A} = \begin{pmatrix} 3 & 5 & 0 \\ -1 & 6 & 7 \end{pmatrix} \qquad \text{and} \qquad \mathbf{B} = \begin{pmatrix} 1 & 2 & 3 & 4 \end{pmatrix}$$

13 Why is it not possible to find the inverse of $\mathbf{C} = \begin{pmatrix} 2 & 6 \\ 3 & 9 \end{pmatrix}$?

20.8 Functions

What is a Function?

A **function** is a **mapping** of one set of numbers on to another according to some rule. For example, the rule might be '**square and add 2**'. If the first set of numbers is {0, 1, 2, 3} the second set would be {2, 3, 6, 11}.

In algebraic notation, this is written as:

$$f: x \rightarrow x^2 + 2$$

which reads 'the function f maps x on to $x^2 + 2$'.

The first set of numbers is called the **domain** (think of 'home'), and the second set is called the **range** (think of going out on to the range).

This can also be shown in a diagram, as in Figure 20.2.

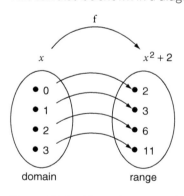

Figure 20.2 A function maps from its domain to its range according to its rule

For this mapping diagram the domain is part of the set of integers, $\{x : 0 \leqslant x \leqslant 3, x \in \mathbb{Z}\}$, and there are only four pairs of values. However, if the domain is part of the set of real numbers, $\{x : 0 \leqslant x \leqslant 3, x \in \mathbb{R}\}$, there are an infinite number of pairs of values in the domain and the function is shown by a line, or in this case a curve, on a graph, as Figure 20.3 shows.

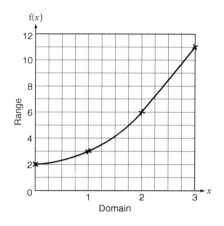

Figure 20.3 Function from a real domain

The graph illustrates the range of the function with the given domain.

As you can see from Figure 20.3, the range is from 2 to 11, which is written $\{f(x) : 2 \leqslant f(x) \leqslant 11, f(x) \in \mathbb{R}\}$, and read as 'the set of values of $f(x)$ such that $f(x)$ is greater than or equal to 2 and less than or equal to 11, $f(x)$ is a member of the set of real numbers'.

There is another, very convenient notation for f. We can write $f(x) = x^2 + 2$, which is read 'f of x equals x squared plus two'. It is convenient because we can then write $f(0) = 0^2 + 2 = 2$, $f(1) = 3$ and so on, as you will see in the next example.

Example 12

Using the domain $\{-2, -1, 0, 1, 2\}$, list the values of $f(x)$ in the range for
a $f(x) = x^2 - 2$ **b** $f(x) = (x + 1)^2$ **c** $f(x) = (3x - 4)$

Answer 12
Using a mapping diagram:

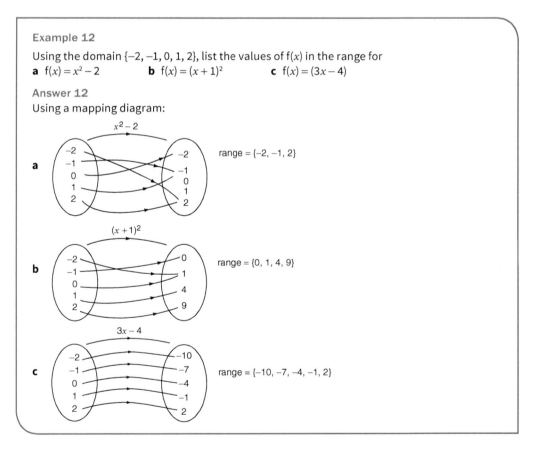

Part (c) of the above example shows what is known as a 'one-to-one' mapping. Every member or element of the domain maps to exactly one member of the range.

Parts (a) and (b) show a 'many-to-one' mapping because two members of the domain sometimes map to one member of the range.

To be a function, every member of the domain must map to one and only one member of the range.

Looking at Figure 20.4, we can see two reasons why this does not represent a function.

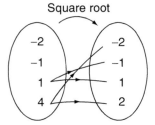

Figure 20.4 Mapping diagram for square root

First of all there are two members of the domain that cannot be mapped to the range, and also there are two members of the domain that map to more than one element of the range.

It is easy to see the different types of mappings in the sketches of graphs in Figures 20.5–20.7.

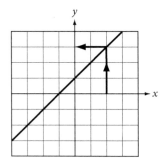

Figure 20.5 A one-to-one mapping; this is a function of x

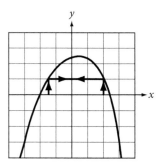

Figure 20.6 A many-to-one (in this case two-to-one) mapping; this is a function of x

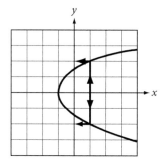

Figure 20.7 A one-to-many mapping; this is **not** a function of x

This should have given you an idea of what makes a function. Now we will go on to use them and you shall see how convenient they are. Functions are usually represented by small letters such as f, g and h.

Example 13

If $f(x) = x^3 + x$ and $g(x) = +\sqrt{x^2 + 1}$, find
a f(1), f(4) and f(−5)
b g(1), g(0) and g(7).

Answer 13
a $f(1) = 1^3 + 1 = 2$
   $f(4) = 4^3 + 4 = 68$
   $f(-5) = -125 - 5 = -130$
b $g(1) = +\sqrt{1^2 + 1} = +\sqrt{2}$
   $g(0) = +\sqrt{1} = 1$
   $g(7) = +\sqrt{7^2 + 1} = +\sqrt{49 + 1} = +\sqrt{50} = +\sqrt{25 \times 2} = +\sqrt{25} \times \sqrt{2} = +5\sqrt{2}$

Example 14

If $f(x) = x^2 + 3x$, find x when $f(x) = 10$.

Answer 14
$x^2 + 3x = 10$
$x^2 + 3x - 10 = 0$
$(x + 5)(x - 2) = 0$
either $x = -5$ or $x = 2$

From now on the domains will all be from the set of real numbers unless otherwise stated. However, you might come across an extra restriction in the description of the domain. Take, for example,

$$f(x) = \frac{1}{x-2}, x \in \mathbb{R}, x \neq 2.$$

The value $x = 2$ has been specifically excluded from the domain because $f(2) = \frac{1}{2-2} = \frac{1}{0}$. As you know, you cannot divide by zero, so f(2) does not exist and $x = 2$ must be excluded from the domain if f(x) is a function. An alternative restriction might be to make $x > 2$, so that you eliminate 2 and all values less than 2.

Exercise 20.7

1 $f(x) = \dfrac{x}{x^2 + 2}$
   Find: **a** f(1)   **b** f(−1)   **c** $f\left(\dfrac{1}{2}\right)$ **d** f(0)

2 $f(x) = 2x^2 + x - 1$
   $g(x) = x^2 - 5x - 6$
   Solve f(x) = g(x).

3 $h(x) = \dfrac{x}{6-x}, x \neq 6$
   Find **a** h(1)   **b** h(1.2)   **c** $h\left(2\dfrac{3}{4}\right)$

4 $g(x) = x^3 + 5$

Find x when $g(x) = -22$.

5

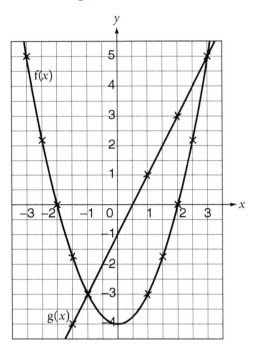

Using the graph evaluate the following:

a $f(2)$　　　　　　　　**b** $f(-2)$　　　　　　　　**c** $g(x) = 0$

d $g(x) = f(x)$　　　　　**e** $f(0)$　　　　　　　　**f** $g(0)$

20.9 Inverse Functions

As usual we have to be able to work backwards to undo anything we have just done.

For example, the mapping of $f(x) = 2x + 1$ on the domain $\{2, 3, 4\}$ can be shown as in Figure 20.8.

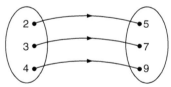

Figure 20.8　$f(x) = 2x + 1$ on the domain $\{2, 3, 4\}$

But how do we get back from 5 to 2, from 7 to 3, and from 9 to 4? The method is quite simple.

- Write $y = 2x + 1$.
- Rearrange to make x the subject.
- Change x to $f^{-1}(x)$, and y to x.

The **inverse** of the function f(x) is written as f^{-1}(x). Going through the steps:

$$f(x) = 2x + 1$$

- $y = 2x + 1$

  $$\frac{y-1}{2} = x$$

- $x = \dfrac{y-1}{2}$

- $f^{-1}(x) = \dfrac{x-1}{2}$

Example 15

Find the inverse of

a $f(x) = \dfrac{1}{x-2},\ x > 2$ **b** $g(x) = \dfrac{x+5}{x},\ x > 0$

Answer 15

a $y = \dfrac{1}{x-2}$

$y(x+2) = 1$

$yx - 2y = 1$

$yx = 1 + 2y$

$x = \dfrac{1+2y}{y}$

$f^{-1}(x) = \dfrac{1+2x}{x}$

b $y = \dfrac{x+5}{x}$

$yx = x + 5$

$yx - x = 5$

$x(y-1) = 5$

$x = \dfrac{5}{y-1}$

$g^{-1}(x) = \dfrac{5}{x-1}$

Exercise 20.8

Find the inverses of the following functions

1 $f(x) = 3x + 1$ **2** $f(x) = 2 - 5x$ **3** $f(x) = \frac{1}{2}x + 1$

4 $f(x) = \frac{3}{4}(x+2)$ **5** $f(x) = \dfrac{5-x}{2}$ **6** $g(x) = \sqrt{x-3},\ x \cdot 3$

7 $g(x) = x^3 - 1$ **8** $g(x) = \dfrac{1}{x+1},\ x \neq -1$ **9** $g(x) = \dfrac{x}{x+1},\ x \neq -1$

10 $g(x) = 3\left(x - \frac{1}{2}\right)$

Example 16

$f(x) = \dfrac{x+1}{x-4},\ x \neq 4$

Find:

a f(2)   **b** f(−3)   **c** f^{-1}(x)

d f^{-1}(3)   **e** x when f(x) = 2

Answer 16

a $f(2) = \dfrac{2+1}{2-4}$

$f(2) = \dfrac{3}{-2}$

$f(2) = \dfrac{-3}{2}$

b $f(-3) = \dfrac{-3+1}{-3-4}$

$f(-3) = \dfrac{-2}{-7}$

$f(-3) = \dfrac{2}{7}$

c $f(x) = \frac{x+1}{x-4}$

$y = \frac{x+1}{x-4}$

$yx - 4y = x + 1$

$yx - x = 1 + 4y$

$x(y - 1) = 1 + 4y$

$x = \frac{1+4y}{y-1}$

$f^{-1}(x) = \frac{1+4x}{x-1}$

d $f^{-1}(3) = \frac{1+4\times3}{3-4}$

$f^{-1}(3) = \frac{13}{2}$

NOTE:
An alternative method to solving for $f(x) = 3$

e $f(x) = 2$

$\frac{x+1}{x-1} = 2$

$x + 1 = 2x - 8$

$0 = x - 9$

$x = 9$

Exercise 20.9

1 If $f(x) = 2x^2 + 3x - 1$, find:

   a $f(0)$ **b** $f(-1)$ **c** x when f$(x) = -2$.

2 $f(x) = x^2 + 1$ $g(x) = \frac{1}{x+1}$, $x^1 \neq -1$ $h(x) = 2x^2 - 3$

Find, simplifying where necessary:

   a $f(1)$ **b** $g(1)$ **c** $g\left(\frac{1}{2}\right)$ **d** $g^{-1}(x)$

   e the values of x when $f(x) = h(x)$.

3 $h(x) = \frac{x+2}{x+3}$, $x \neq -3$; find:–

   a $h\left(\frac{1}{2}\right)$ **b** $h\left(\frac{3}{5}\right)$ **c** $h^{-1}(x)$ **d** x when $h(x) = 0$

   e $h^{-1}(-2)$ **f** $h^{-1}(0)$ **g** x when $h(x) = -2$.

20.10 Graphs of Inequalities

We have already found solutions to linear inequalities in one variable, and shown the results on a number line or one-dimensional graph. We have also illustrated linear equations in two variables as straight lines on graphs.

We now need to illustrate linear inequalities in two variables on graphs. You will see that they have to be shown as areas on graphs.

Taking a simple example, $y \geqslant x + 1$, we can find pairs of values for x and y from the set of real numbers which satisfy this inequality. We will pick a few at random.

	$4 > 1 + 1$	so	$x = 1, y = 4$	satisfies the inequality
and	$2.5 > 0 + 1$		$x = 0, y = 2.5$	
	$-1 > -3 + 1$		$x = -3, y = -1$	
	$-1.5 > -3 + 1$		$x = -3, y = -1.5$	
	$1 > -2 + 1$		$x = -2, y = 1$	
	$3.5 > -1 + 1$		$x = -1, y = 3.5$	all also satisfy the inequality.

If we draw the line $y = x + 1$ on a graph and then plot these points we will see in which region of the graph the points lie (Figure 20.9).

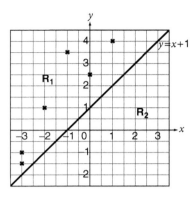

Figure 20.9 Points satisfying $y \geq x + 1$

The line $y = x + 1$ joins all the points with x and y coordinates which satisfy the equation. So the y-coordinate of every point is equal to its x-coordinate plus one. The line also divides the graph into two regions, marked $\mathbf{R_1}$ and $\mathbf{R_2}$. In the region $\mathbf{R_1}$, all the y-coordinates are greater than $x + 1$, and in the region $\mathbf{R_2}$ all the y-coordinates are less than $x + 1$.

The graph is redrawn in Figure 20.10 to make this clear.

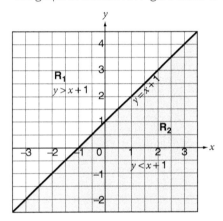

Figure 20.10 $y = x + 1$ splits the plane into two regions

The inequality we are illustrating is $y > x + 1$, so the line $y = x + 1$ is included. The region $\mathbf{R_2}$ is not included, and is shaded to show that it is unwanted.

For a strict inequality, for example $y < -x + 1$, we first draw the line $y = -x + 1$, but because the line is not included ($<$ rather than $\leq$) we draw a broken line as shown in Figure 20.11.

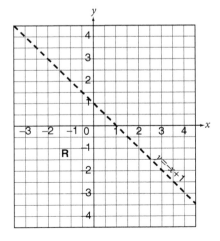

Figure 20.11 The line $y = -x + 1$

We now have to decide which side of the line is the region we want, so we test a point which is not on the line. The origin (0, 0) is convenient.

$$y < x + 1$$
$$0 < 0 + 1$$

This is true: zero *is* less than zero plus one, so the origin lies in the region we want and we can mark **R** on that side of the line.

The region **R** will usually be shown by shading the other side of the line, the unwanted region. You should read the question carefully to decide which side of the line to shade.

Example 17

By shading the unwanted side of the line, show the regions defined by these inequalities:

a $y \leqslant 2x + 1$ **b** $x < 2$ **c** $y \geqslant 0$

Answer 17

a

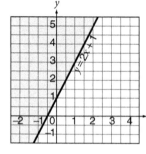

b

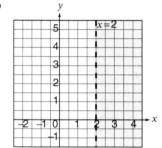

c

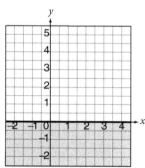

If all three inequalities in the example above are now drawn on one graph with the excluded regions shaded, the remaining unshaded region is the solution of the three inequalities taken simultaneously, as shown in Figure 20.12. All the points in the unshaded region satisfy $y \leqslant 2x + 1$, $x < 2$ and $y \geqslant 0$ at the same time.

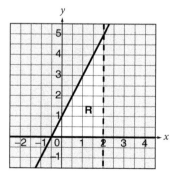

Figure 20.12 Region **R** defined by three inequalities

R represents the region defined by the inequalities.

Example 18

a Show the region defined by the inequalities $x + y < 5$, $x \geqslant 0$, $y \geqslant 1$ on a diagram. Shade the unwanted region.

b Mark with a cross on the diagram all the points which have integer values of x and y, and are in the required region. That is, $\{(x, y): x, y \in \mathbb{Z}\}$.

c List these points.

Answer 18

a, b

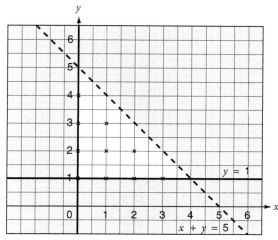

NOTE:
Points such as (1, 4) are not included in the region because they are on the broken line representing the strict inequality $x + y < 5$.

c (0, 1), (0, 2), (0, 3), (0, 4), (1, 1), (1, 2), (1, 3), (2, 2), (2, 1), (3, 1).

Example 19

Show on a diagram the region which satisfies the inequalities
$-3 \leqslant x < 2,$ $2 < y \leqslant 5.$
Shade the unwanted region.

Answer 19

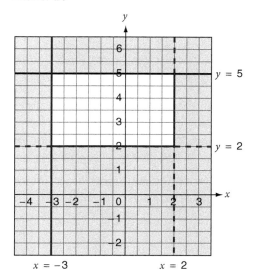

Example 20

Define the region **R** using simultaneous inequalities.

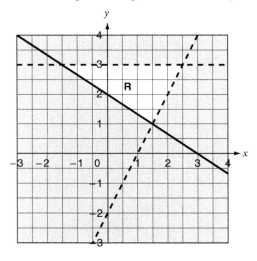

Answer 20

The lines surrounding **R** on the graph are $y = 3$, $y = \frac{-2}{3}x + 2$ and $y = 2x - 2$. It is clear that the required side of the line $y = 3$ is $y < 3$.

Testing $(0, 0)$ for the line $y = \frac{-2}{3}x + 2$, $0 < 0 + 2$.

We want the side which does not contain the origin, so the required inequality is $y \geq -\frac{2}{3}x + 2$.

For the line $y = 2x - 2$, testing the origin, $0 > 0 - 2$. For this line we want the side which does contain the origin so the required inequality is $y > 2x - 2$. Remember that the broken line represents a strict inequality.

The region R is defined by:

$$y < 3 \qquad y \geq \frac{-2}{3}x + 2 \qquad y > 2x - 2.$$

Strictly speaking, the definition should also give the universal set of numbers. If $(x, y) \in \mathbb{Z}$, we are only interested in integer values of x and y. If $(x, y) \in \mathbb{R}$, we are interested in the entire area, as in this case.

Example 21

1 A firm has to manufacture two types of tractors: the Mini and the Maxi.
They already have orders for 4 Maxi tractors and 1 Mini tractor. They can only manufacture 10 tractors in a month, and they want to make more Maxis than Minis.
Let the number of Mini tractors be x and the number of Maxi tractors be y.

a Write down four inequalities to show the above constraints.
b Draw a graph and shade the unwanted regions.
c Mark with crosses all the points with integer values of x and y which lie in the required region.
d List the coordinates of all the points you have marked with crosses.
e The profit on the Mini tractors is \$1500 and on the Maxi tractors is \$2000.

Determine the most profitable combination of tractors the firm should manufacture in the month and write down the total profit.

Answer 21

1 **a** $x + y \leqslant 10, x \geqslant 1, y \geqslant 4, y > x$

b, c

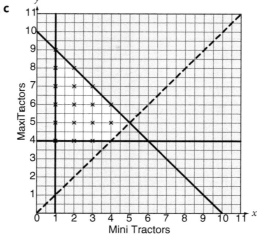

d (1, 4), (1, 5), (1, 6), (1, 7), (1, 8), (1, 9), (2, 4), (2, 5), (2, 6), (2, 7), (2, 8), (3, 4), (3, 5), (3, 6), (3, 7), (4, 5), (4, 6)

e Testing the points marked with crosses shows that (1, 9), which means 1 Mini tractor and 9 Maxi tractors, gives the maximum profit because the total profit becomes
Total Profit = $1 \times \$1500 + 9 \times \$2000 = \$19\,500$

Exercise 20.10

1

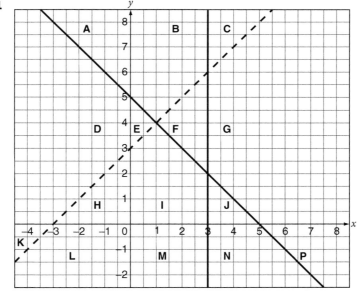

The lines $x = 0$, $x = 3$, $y = 0$, $y = x + 3$ and $x + y = 5$ divide the graph into 15 separate regions.
Use inequalities to define the following regions:

a E **b** J **c** I
d N **e** G and P together **f** A, B and C together
g D and K together.

2 Show the solutions of these sets of inequalities on a graph, shading the unwanted regions and labelling the required region with an **R**.

  a $y \geqslant 0$, $x + y \geqslant 4$, $x \geqslant 0$

  b $4x + 3y < 12$, $y \leqslant 2x$, $y \leqslant 0$

3 **a** Show the solution set of these inequalities on a graph by shading the unwanted regions.

      $y < 3x + 6$, $0 < y < 4$, $x \leqslant 0$.

  b Mark with a cross all the integer solutions.

  c List the points which are integer solutions.

4 A dealer sells Reliable and Gofaster cars. There is room at the showrooms for no more than 10 cars. The dealer knows that more Reliables will be sold than Gofasters so she needs to have more Reliables than Gofasters in stock. The dealer needs to decide how many of each car to keep in stock.

The profit on the Reliables is \$1500 and the profit on the Gofasters is \$1800.

The dealer writes down two matrices. **C** represents the possible combination of numbers of Reliables and Gofasters he could stock. The first column shows the numbers of Reliables and the second column shows the corresponding numbers of Gofasters. **P** represents the profit on the two types of car.

$$\mathbf{C} = \begin{pmatrix} 6 & 4 \\ 7 & 3 \\ 8 & 2 \\ 9 & 1 \end{pmatrix} \quad \mathbf{P} = \begin{pmatrix} 1500 \\ 1800 \end{pmatrix}$$

  a Find the product, **CP**, of the two matrices.

  b What does **CP** represent?

  c How many of each car should the dealer stock and in this case what would her total profit be if she sold all the cars?

Exercise 20.11

Mixed exercise

1 $\mathbf{A} = \begin{pmatrix} 1 & 0 \\ 0 & 1 \end{pmatrix}$ $\mathbf{B} = \begin{pmatrix} 2 & 1 \\ 3 & -1 \end{pmatrix}$ $\mathbf{C} = \begin{pmatrix} 1 & 3 & -5 \\ 2 & 0 & 4 \end{pmatrix}$

     $\mathbf{D} = \begin{pmatrix} 3 & -4 \end{pmatrix}$ $\mathbf{E} = \begin{pmatrix} 1 & 2 \\ 3 & 4 \\ 5 & 6 \end{pmatrix}$ $\mathbf{F} = \begin{pmatrix} 1 \\ 2 \end{pmatrix}$

  a Write down the order of each matrix.

  b Write down the orders of the products:

     i CE   **ii** EC   **iii** DF   **iv** FD

  c Write down **C** transpose (**C**′).

  d Find:

     i det **A**   **ii** AB   **iii** BA

     iv A⁻¹   **v** B⁻¹

2 $f(x) = \dfrac{1}{x^2}$, $f(x) = \dfrac{1}{x}$, $h(x) = x^2 + 1$

  a Find:

     i $f(-1)$ **ii** $h(0)$ **iii** x when $g(x) = 0.25$

     iv $g^{-1}(x)$ **v** $g^{-1}\left(\dfrac{1}{4}\right)$

b Find x when

    i $f(x) = 4$ **ii** $h(x) = 1$ **iii** $g(x) = -2f(x) + 1$

3 **a** $f(x) = \dfrac{1}{2x+3}$. Find $f^{-1}(x)$.   **b** $g(x) = \dfrac{x}{2x+3}$. Find $g^{-1}(x)$.

4 **a** Show, by shading the unwanted regions, the solution set of these inequalities on a graph:

$$-1 \leqslant x < 4$$
$$x + y < 5$$
$$0 \leqslant y < 3$$

    b List all the points which are integer solutions to the set of inequalities.

Exam-style questions

5 **a** The determinant of the matrix $\begin{pmatrix} k & 5 \\ -1 & 2 \end{pmatrix}$ is 14. Find k.

    b Find the inverse of the matrix $\begin{pmatrix} 3 & -1 \\ -4 & 2 \end{pmatrix}$.   *(4024 paper 01 Q15 November 2004)*

6 $\mathbf{A} = \begin{pmatrix} 3 & -1 \\ -2 & 4 \end{pmatrix}$ $\mathbf{B} = \begin{pmatrix} 5 & 3 \\ 0 & -2 \end{pmatrix}$

    a Find $3\mathbf{A} - \mathbf{B}$.

    b Find $\mathbf{A}^2$.

    c Find the 2×2 matrix $\mathbf{X}$, where $\mathbf{AX} = \begin{pmatrix} 1 & 0 \\ 0 & 1 \end{pmatrix}$.   *(4024 paper 11 Q25 June 2014)*

7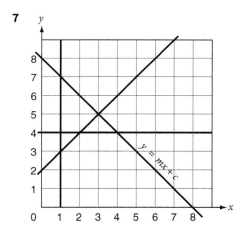

    a One of the lines in the diagram is labelled $y = mx + c$.

       Find the values of m and c.

    b Show, by shading all the unwanted regions on the graph, the region defined by the inequalities

       $x \geqslant 1$, $y \leqslant mx + c$, $y \geqslant x + 2$ and $y \geqslant 4$.

       Write the letter **R** in the region required.

       (0580 paper 02 Q20 June 2006)

8 **a** Make k the subject of the formula $\sqrt{\dfrac{h}{k}}$.

    b The matrix Y satisfies the equation

$$4\mathbf{Y} - 2\begin{pmatrix} 12 & 6 \\ -9 & 0 \end{pmatrix} = \mathbf{Y}$$

       Find **Y**, expressing it in the form $\begin{pmatrix} a & b \\ c & d \end{pmatrix}$.   *(4024 paper 02 Q2(part) June 2004)*

9 a $f(x) = x^3 - 4$

Find

i $f(-2)$,

ii $f^{-1}(x)$.

b $g(y) = y^2 - 3y + 1$

Write down and simplify an expression for $g(a - 2)$.　　　(4024 paper 12 Q19 June 2012)

10 a In the diagram, the unshaded region, **R**, is defined by three inequalities.

Two of these are

$y \leq 2x + 2$ and $y \leq 5 - x$.

Write down the third inequality.

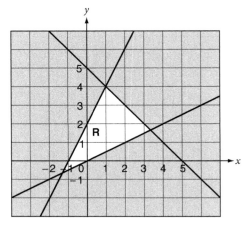

b Find the integer values of x which satisfy the following:

$4 \leq 2x + 13 < 9$　　　(4024 paper 01 Q14 November 2005)

11

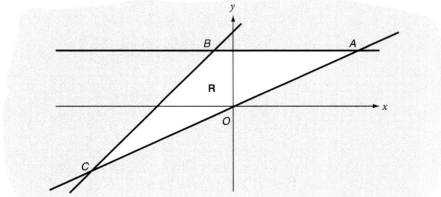

In the diagram, A is the point $(6, 3)$ and C is the point $(-8, -4)$.

The equation of AB is $y = 3$, and the equation of CB is $y = x + 4$.

a Find the coordinates of B.

b The unshaded region **R** inside triangle ABC is defined by three inequalities.

One of these is $y < x + 4$.
Write down the other two inequalities.

(4024 paper 01 Q10 June 2007)

12 Given that $f(x) = \dfrac{5x - 4}{3}$, find

a $f\left(1\dfrac{1}{5}\right)$, **b** $f^{-1}(x)$.

(4024 paper 01 Q16 June 2007)

13 John works in a shop.

The matrix below shows the number of hours he worked on Monday to Friday, Saturday, and Sunday during two different weeks.

	Monday to Friday	Saturday	Sunday
Week 1	30	5	0
Week 2	35	6	2

The matrix below shows the pay that he received per hour on Monday to Friday, Saturday, and Sunday.

$/hr

9	Monday to Friday
12	Saturday
15	Sunday

a $P = \begin{pmatrix} 30 & 5 & 0 \\ 35 & 6 & 2 \end{pmatrix} \begin{pmatrix} 9 \\ 12 \\ 15 \end{pmatrix}$

Find **P**.

b Explain the meaning of the information given by matrix **P**.

(4024 paper 11 Q11 November 2014)

14 Given that $f(x) = \dfrac{2x + 3}{5x}$, find $f^{-1}(x)$.

(4024 paper 11 Q5 November 2011)

15 $A = (5\,-8)$ $B = \begin{pmatrix} 2 & 6 \\ 5 & -4 \end{pmatrix}$ $C = \begin{pmatrix} 4 & 6 \\ 5 & -2 \end{pmatrix}$ $D = \begin{pmatrix} 4 \\ -2 \end{pmatrix}$

a Which one of the following matrix calculations is **not** possible?
  i AB   **ii** AD   **iii** BA   **iv** DA

b Calculate **BC**.

c Use your answer to part (b) to write down $\mathbf{B}^{-1}$, the inverse of **B**.

(0580 paper 02 Q22 June 2004)

16 $A = (1\,2\,3)$ $B = \begin{pmatrix} 2 & 0 \\ 1 & 4 \\ -1 & -3 \end{pmatrix}$ $C = \begin{pmatrix} 2 & -1 \\ 2 & 2 \\ -1 & 0 \end{pmatrix}$

Find

a $B - C$ **b** AB.

(4024 paper 01 Q15 November 2005)

17 a Evaluate $\begin{pmatrix} 4 & 2 \\ 1 & 1 \end{pmatrix} \begin{pmatrix} 1 & -2 \\ -1 & 4 \end{pmatrix}$.

   b **Write down** the inverse of $\begin{pmatrix} 1 & -2 \\ -1 & 4 \end{pmatrix}$.

   (4024 paper 01 Q3 June 2005)

18 Work out $\begin{pmatrix} 2 & 1 & 2 \\ 1 & 5 & 0 \\ 3 & -2 & 4 \end{pmatrix} \begin{pmatrix} 4 \\ -3 \\ -8 \end{pmatrix}$.

   (0580 paper 21 Q15 June 2008)

19 $\mathbf{A} = \begin{pmatrix} 1 & 2 \\ 1 & 1 \end{pmatrix}$ $\mathbf{I} = \begin{pmatrix} 1 & 0 \\ 0 & 1 \end{pmatrix}$

   a The matrix $\mathbf{B} = \mathbf{A}^2 - 2\mathbf{A} - \mathbf{I}$.
      Calculate $\mathbf{B}$. Show all your working.

   b Simplify $\mathbf{AA}^{-1}$.

   (0580 paper 02 Q22 November 2007)

20 $\mathbf{A} = \begin{pmatrix} x & 8 \\ 2 & x \end{pmatrix}$

   a Find $|\mathbf{A}|$, the determinant of $\mathbf{A}$, in terms of x.
   b Find the values of x when $|\mathbf{A}| = 9$.

   (0580 paper 02 Q11 June 2007)

21 $f(x) = x^3 - 3x^2 + 6x - 4$ and $g(x) = 2x - 1$.
   Find:
   a $f(-1)$ **b** $g-1(x)$

   (0580 paper 21 Q18a, c June 2008)

22 $\begin{pmatrix} 1 & -2 \\ 0 & 1 \\ 5 & 6 \end{pmatrix} \begin{pmatrix} 3 & 4 & 8 & 7 \\ 1 & 1 & 3 & 3 \end{pmatrix}$

   The answer to this matrix multiplication is of order $a \times b$.
   Find the values of a and b.

   (0580 paper 21 Q2 November 2008

23 $\mathbf{A} = \begin{pmatrix} -2 & 3 \\ -4 & 5 \end{pmatrix}$

   Find $\mathbf{A}^{-1}$, the inverse of $\mathbf{A}$.

   (0580 paper 21 Q21 June 2009

24 $\mathbf{A} = \begin{pmatrix} x & 6 \\ 4 & 3 \end{pmatrix}$ $\mathbf{B} = \begin{pmatrix} 2 & 3 \\ 2 & 1 \end{pmatrix}$

   a Find $\mathbf{AB}$.
   b When $\mathbf{AB} = \mathbf{BA}$, find the value of x.

   (0580 paper 21 Q21 June 2009)

25 $\mathbf{M} = \begin{pmatrix} 1 & 1 \\ 1 & 2 \end{pmatrix}$ $\mathbf{M}^2 = \begin{pmatrix} 2 & 3 \\ 3 & 5 \end{pmatrix}$ $\mathbf{M}^3 = \begin{pmatrix} 5 & 8 \\ 8 & 13 \end{pmatrix}$

   Find $\mathbf{M}^4$.

   (0580/02 May/June 2007 q7)s

26 A function f is defined by $f : x \rightarrow \dfrac{x+5}{3}$.

   a Given that $f : 1 \rightarrow k$, find the value of k.
   b Given also that $f^{-1} : x \rightarrow cx + d$, find the value of c and the value of d.

   (4024 paper 01 Q11 June 2004)

27

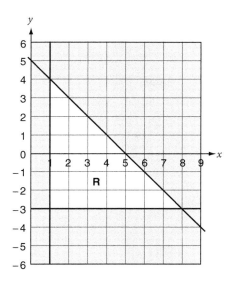

The unshaded region **R** is defined by 3 inequalities.
One of these is x > 1.
Write down the other two inequalities.

(4024 paper 01 Q16 November 2004)

28 a Given that $f(x) = 3x + 5$, find $f(3)$.
   b The function g is defined by $g(x) = (2x - 3)(x + k)$.
   Given that $g(0) = -5$, find
      i k   **ii** x such that $g(x) = 0$.   (4024 paper 01 Q17 November 2004)

29 It is given that $f(x) = 3x - 5$.
   Find:
      a $f(-4)$ **b** the value of t, given that $f(t) = 10$ **c** $f^{-1}(x)$ **d** $f^{-1}(4)$.
(4024 paper 01 Q16 November 2005)

30 a $f(x) = (x + 2)(2x - 1)$
   Evaluate $f(5.5)$.
   b $g(x) = -\dfrac{1}{3}(2x - 1)$
   Find $g^{-1}(5)$.   (4024 paper 01 Q14 June 2006)

31 a The matrix **M** satisfies the equation $3\mathbf{M} + 4\begin{pmatrix} 2 & -1 \\ 3 & 0 \end{pmatrix} = \mathbf{M}$.
   Find **M**, expressing it in the form $\begin{pmatrix} a & b \\ c & d \end{pmatrix}$.
   b Find the inverse of the matrix $\begin{pmatrix} 5 & -3 \\ -4 & 2 \end{pmatrix}$.   (4024 paper 01 Q15 November 2006)

32 a Given that $f(x) = x^2 - 2px + 3$, find
      i $f(-2)$, giving your answer in terms of p,   **ii** the value of p when $f(-2) = f(0)$.
   b Given that $g(y) = y^2 - 1$, find $g(a - 1)$.
   Given your answer in its simplest form.   (4024 paper 01 Q16 November 2006)

33 a Evaluate $\begin{pmatrix} 12 \\ 4 \\ 6 \end{pmatrix} - 3\begin{pmatrix} 3 \\ -1 \\ 2 \end{pmatrix}$.

   b A business makes toy buses and toy lorries.
   The following table is used in calculating the cost of making each toy.

	Labour (hours)	Wood (blocks)	Paint (tins)
Bus	2	3	1
Lorry	1	w	2

Labour costs \$10 per hour, wood costs \$1 per block and paint costs \$$p$ per tin.
The information above can be summarised in the matrices **A** and **B**,

where $\mathbf{A} = \begin{pmatrix} 2 & 3 & 1 \\ 1 & w & 2 \end{pmatrix}$ and $\mathbf{B} = \begin{pmatrix} 10 \\ 1 \\ p \end{pmatrix}$.

  i Given that $\mathbf{AB} = \begin{pmatrix} 28 \\ 24 \end{pmatrix}$, find

    a p **b** w.

  ii Evaluate $\begin{pmatrix} 100 & 200 \end{pmatrix} \begin{pmatrix} 28 \\ 24 \end{pmatrix}$.

  iii Explain what your answer to (ii) represents.   (4024 paper 01 Q24 June 2007)

34 The shaded region **inside** the triangle ABC is defined by three inequalities.
One of these is $x + y < 5\frac{1}{2}$.

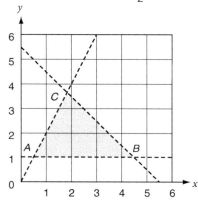

  a Write down the other two inequalities.
  b How many points with integer coordinates lie in the shaded region?
                                        (4024 paper 01 Q8 November 2007)

35 Given that $f(x) = \frac{4x + 3}{2x}$, find

  a $f(3)$,   **b** $f^{-1}(x)$.   (4024 paper 01 Q12 November 2008)

36 $\mathbf{A} = \begin{pmatrix} 2 & -1 \\ 1 & 3 \end{pmatrix}$ and $\mathbf{B} = \begin{pmatrix} 4 & -3 \\ 1 & 0 \end{pmatrix}$.

  Find:
  a **AB,**   **b** **B⁻¹.**   (4024 paper 01 Q15 November 2008)

37 Given that $f(x) = 4x - 7$, find

  a $f\left(\frac{1}{2}\right)$ **b** the value of p when $f(p) = p$.
                                 (4024 paper 01 Q12 November 2009)

38 The diagram below shows triangle *LMN*.

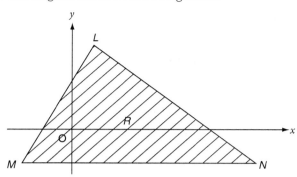

The equations of the lines *LM* and *LN* are $2y = 3x + 5$ and $x + 4y = 24$ respectively.

a Solve the simultaneous equations $x + 4y = 24$
$$2y = 3x + 5.$$
Hence write down the coordinates of L.

b *M* is $(-3, -2)$ and *MN* is parallel to the *x*-axis.
The shaded region, *R*, **inside** triangle *LMN*, is defined by three inequalities.
One of these is $2y < 3x + 5$.
Write down the other two inequalities.   (4024 paper 12 Q11 November 2009)

39 Ann went on a car journey that was split into three stages.
Two relevant matrices are shown below.
The first matrix shows the average speed, in kilometres per hour, of the car during each stage.
The second matrix shows the time, in hours, taken for each stage.

$$\begin{array}{ccc} \text{First} & \text{Second} & \text{Third} \qquad \text{Time} \\ \text{Stage} & \text{Stage} & \text{Stage} \end{array}$$

Average speed $(40 \quad 30 \quad 50) \begin{pmatrix} 1\frac{1}{2} \\ 1 \\ 2\frac{1}{2} \end{pmatrix} \begin{array}{l} \text{First Stage} \\ \text{Second Stage} \\ \text{Third Stage} \end{array}$

i Find $(40 \quad 30 \quad 50) \begin{pmatrix} 1\frac{1}{2} \\ 1 \\ 2\frac{1}{2} \end{pmatrix}$.

ii What information is given by the matrix obtained in part (i)?

iii Calculate the average speed for the whole journey.   (4024 paper 02 Q5c June 2008)

21 Trigonometry II

Learning Objectives Syllabus section 36

In this chapter you will
- extend trigonometry to cover angles between 90° and 180° (obtuse angles)
- use the sine and cosine rules to calculate acute and obtuse angles in non-right-angled triangles
- calculate the areas of non-right-angled triangles
- use trigonometry and Pythagoras' theorem in three-dimensional shapes.

21.1 Introduction

We now extend the use of trigonometry to cover triangles which do not have right angles. We look at angles greater than 90°, and use trigonometry in three dimensions.

21.2 Essential Skills

1 Use the sine, cosine and tangent ratios and Pythagoras' theorem to find the sides and angles marked with letters in the following diagrams. All lengths are in centimetres.

a

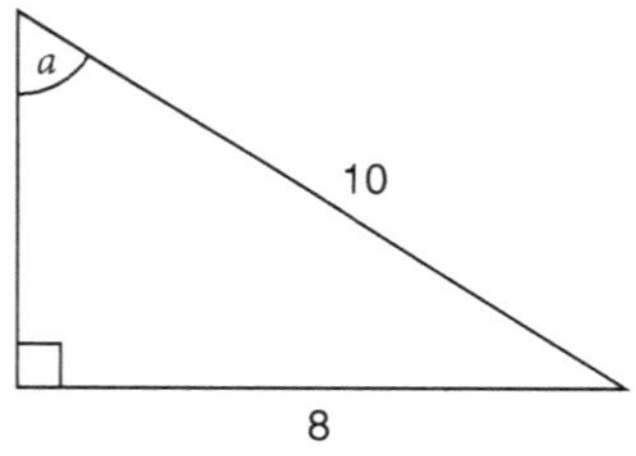

b

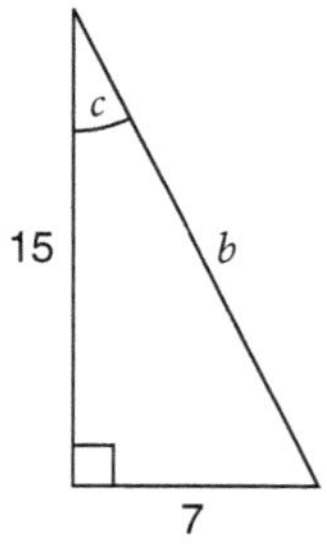

c

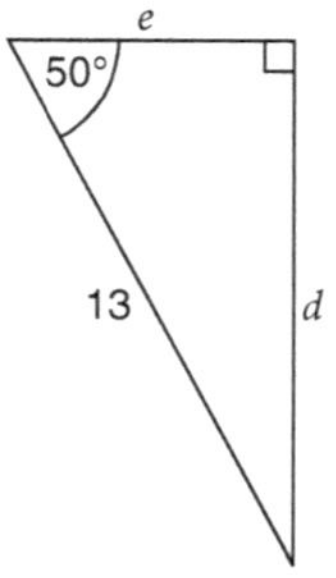

d

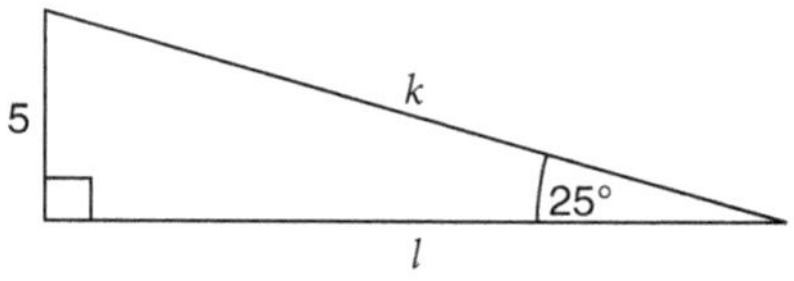

e

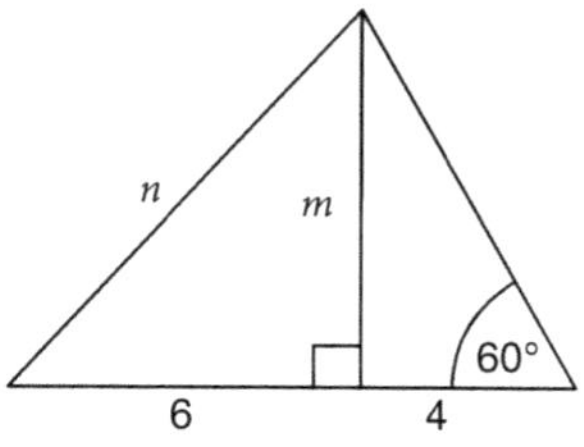

2 The bearing of *A* from *B* is 065°. Find the bearing of *B* from *A*.

3 The bearing of *C* from *D* is 200°. Find the bearing of *D* from *C*.

4 Write the following as three-figure bearings:
   a SE   b NNW.

21.3 Trigonometry with Angles between 0° and 180°

Figure 21.1 shows an angle, α. This is the Greek letter alpha, which is often used in mathematics. The angle is made by the positive *x*-axis and a line, *OP*, which can rotate *anticlockwise* through 180° about the origin. The line is 1 unit long (measured by the scale on the axes). A semicircle with the same radius is drawn with its centre at the origin.

The diagram shows two **quadrants**, (quarter circles) of the complete circle. You will go on to study the other two quadrants if you take mathematics beyond O Level. The quadrant in which both the *x*- and the *y*-coordinates are positive is always called the first quadrant, and the quadrant with negative *x*-coordinates and positive y-coordinates is always called the *second quadrant*.

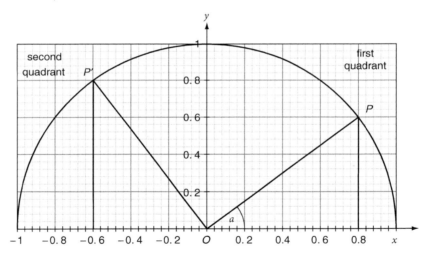

Figure 21.1 First and second quadrants

In Chapter 9 we defined the sine ratio in a right-angled triangle as $\frac{\text{opposite}}{\text{hypotenuse}}$. In Figure 21.1, using the same definition, we see that

$$\sin \angle XOP = \sin \alpha = \frac{y}{OP},$$

where *y* is the *y*-coordinate of the point *P*. But we have made *OP* to be of unit length, so $\sin \alpha = \frac{y}{1}$, which is the same as $\sin \alpha = y$.

Now we have a new definition: $\sin \alpha = y$ when α is the angle the line *OP* makes with the positive direction of the *x*-axis and *P* is the point (x, y).

Measure the angle *XOP* in the diagram. It should be about 37°. The *y*-coordinate of *P* is 0.6. The calculator value for sin 37° is 0.60 to two decimal places, so allowing for experimental error and the limitations of the printing process, this is a good agreement.

All this is no different from the earlier work you did on the trigonometric ratios, except that it gives us a method for extending the angles to include obtuse angles.

P' is in the second quadrant in Figure 21.1, so $\angle XOP'$ is obtuse. According to the new definition, sin $\angle XOP' = y$, where y is the y-coordinate of the point P'. Measure the angle XOP' in the diagram. It should be about 127°. The y-coordinate is 0.8. The calculator value for sin 127° is 0.80 to two decimal places, so again there is a good agreement.

By the same argument, $\cos\alpha = \dfrac{\text{adjacent}}{\text{hypotenuse}} = \dfrac{x}{OP} = \dfrac{x}{1} = x.$

In Figure 21.1, $\angle XOP$ is about 37°, and the x-coordinate of P is 0.8. The calculator value for cos 37° is 0.80 to two decimal places, which is a good agreement as we would expect.

Now look at the x-coordinate of P'. It is −0.6, and angle XOP' is about 127°.The calculator value of cos 127° is −0.60 to two decimal places, so our new definition of cosine works for obtuse angles too. Remember that the cosines of angles between 90° and 180° are negative because the x-coordinates of points in the second quadrant are negative.

Practical Investigation

Copy Figure 21.1, and draw a few more angles of your own. Complete Table 21.1 with your extra examples. Add the calculator values of the sines and cosines of your angles to your table. You should find quite a good agreement between your experimental values and the calculator values.

angle	35°	118°							
sine (y-coordinate)	0.58	0.88							
cosine (x-coordinate)	0.81	−0.48							
calculator value for sine	0.57	0.88							
calculator value for cosine	0.82	−0.47							

Table 21.1 Sines and cosines in the first and second quadrants

Investigation of Sine and Cosine Curves

Copy and complete Table 21.2, using your calculator and giving the sines and cosines to 2 decimal places.

$\alpha°$	0	20	40	60	80	90	100	120	140	160	180
sin α	0		0.64						0.64		
cos α	1		0.77						−0.77		

Table 21.2 Sine and cosine values

Using the values in Table 21.2 copy and complete the graphs in Figures 21.2 and 21.3, drawing a smooth continuous curve through all the points.

If you have drawn these graphs correctly they should look something like Figures 21.4 and 21.5.

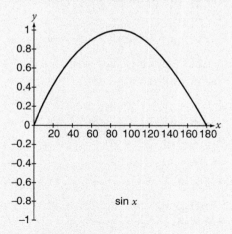

Figure 21.2 Sine curve

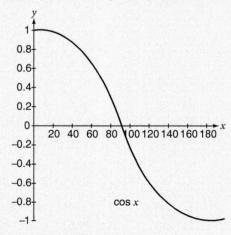

Figure 21.3 Cosine curve

You can now use your graphs to find angles when given their sines or cosines. To find the angle whose sine is 0.5 draw a horizontal line through 0.5 on the y-axis. Mark the point where the line meets the curve, and read off the x-coordinates of those points. You should find that the two points are $(30, 0.5)$ and $(150, 0.5)$.

Use your calculator to find $\sin^{-1}(0.5)$. It will give you 30°, which, as you see, is only one of the answers.

Your calculator will always give you the acute angle when you enter $\sin^{-1}$. In a right-angled triangle this is no problem, because if one angle is 90° both the others must be acute. However, in other triangles it is possible to have an obtuse angle, and you should always be aware that there might be two possible solutions when you enter $\sin^{-1} x$ into your calculator. The second solution (the obtuse angle) is found by subtracting the acute angle from 180°.

If you look at the cosine curve you will see that there is no problem: $\cos^{-1} 0.5 = 60°$ and $\cos^{-1}(-0.5) = 120°$.

Now that you have drawn these graphs of the sine and cosine curves you will see that we should think of sines and cosines of x as *functions* of x rather than ratios.

If you continue your study of mathematics beyond this course you will find that we can work out the sine, cosine and tangent of any angle, no matter how large. You might like to continue your sine and cosine curves, using your calculator, to angles up to 360°. If you are also studying physics or science you might recognise these curves as waves.

Finding Acute and Obtuse Angles from their Sines and Cosines

The signs of sines and cosines in the first two quadrants are summarised in Figure 21.4.

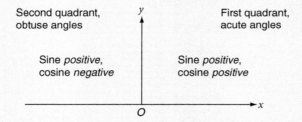

Figure 21.4 Sines and cosines in the first and second quadrants

Using your calculator to find angles:

- Your calculator will automatically give you an acute angle if you enter, for example, $\cos^{-1}(0.4)$, and an obtuse angle if you include a negative sign, for example $\cos^{-1}(-0.4)$.

- Your calculator will give you an acute angle if, for example, you enter $\sin^{-1}(0.4)$. To find the obtuse angle you need to subtract the acute angle from 180°.

You might try entering $\sin^{-1}(-0.4)$ into your calculator. Your calculator will probably give you a negative angle. Check this with your own calculator. Negative angles are not required in your O Level course and are beyond the scope of this book.

Exercise 21.1

1 Find the following:

a sin 40°	**b** sin 140°	**c** sin 150°	**d** sin 75°
e cos 40°	**f** cos 140°	**g** cos 150°	**h** cos 75°

2 Find x in the following given that x lies between 0° and 180°:

a $\cos x = 0.27$	**b** $\cos x = 0.59$	**c** $\cos x = -0.27$	**d** $\cos x = -0.59$

3 Find x given that x is obtuse:

a $\sin x = 0.28$ **b** $\sin x = 0.83$ **c** $\sin x = 0.57$ **d** $\sin x = 0.77$

4 For the following find two possible values of x, given that x lies between 0° and 180°:

a $\sin x = 0.5643$ **b** $\sin x = 0.1254$ **c** $\sin x = 0.8432$ **d** $\sin x = 0.5333$

21.4 The Sine Rule

In the triangle ABC shown in Figure 21.5, AD is drawn perpendicular to BC. The lengths of the sides are represented by letters, and all the measurements are in centimetres.

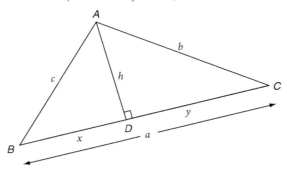

Figure 21.5 Deriving the sine rule

In triangle ADC, $\sin \angle ACD = \dfrac{h}{b}$

$$h = b \times \sin \angle ACD \qquad \ldots(i)$$

In triangle ABD, $\sin \angle ABD = \dfrac{h}{c}$

$$h = c \times \sin \angle ABD \qquad \ldots(ii)$$

Since the right-hand sides of both equations (i) and (ii) are equal to h, they must be equal to each other.

$$b \times \sin\angle ACD = c \times \sin\angle ABD$$

$$b = \frac{c \times \sin\angle ABD}{\sin \angle ACD}$$

$$\frac{b}{\sin \angle ABD} = \frac{c}{\sin \angle ACD}$$

Rewriting $\sin \angle ACD$ as $\sin C$, and $\sin \angle ABD$ as $\sin B$, the equation becomes:

$$\frac{b}{\sin B} = \frac{c}{\sin C}$$

In the same way it can be shown that:

$$\frac{a}{\sin A} = \frac{b}{\sin B} = \frac{c}{\sin C}$$

This is known as the **sine rule**, and can be written in two ways:

$$\frac{a}{\sin A} = \frac{b}{\sin B} = \frac{c}{\sin C}$$

or

$$\frac{\sin A}{a} = \frac{\sin B}{b} = \frac{\sin C}{c}$$

For convenience, if you need to calculate the length of a side you will use the first arrangement, but to calculate an angle use the second.

You can pick any pair of ratios for the calculation. For example, $\dfrac{a}{\sin A} = \dfrac{c}{\sin C}$.

Example 1

Using the measurements shown in the diagram of triangle *ABC* calculate the length of side *AC*.

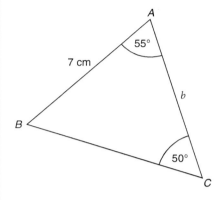

Answer 1

To use the sine rule we need pairs of opposite sides and angles, so to find *b* we need angle *ABC*.

Angle $ABC = 180 - 50 - 55 = 75°$

Using $\dfrac{b}{\sin B} = \dfrac{c}{\sin C}$

$$\dfrac{b}{\sin 75} = \dfrac{c}{\sin 50}$$

$$b = \dfrac{7 \times \sin 75}{\sin 50}$$

$$b = 8.826\,48\ldots$$

The side $AC = 8.83$ cm

The Ambiguous Case of the Sine Rule

Example 2

In triangle *DEF*, angle $EDF = 20°$, $ED = 10$ cm and $EF = 4$ cm.
Calculate angle *EFD*.

Answer 2

Using the sine rule,

$$\dfrac{\sin F}{f} = \dfrac{\sin D}{d}$$

$$\dfrac{\sin F}{10} = \dfrac{\sin 20}{4}$$

$$\sin F = \dfrac{10 \times \sin 20}{4}$$

$\sin F = 0.855\,05\ldots$

$F = \sin^{-1} 0.855\,05\ldots$

$F = 58.7652\ldots$

Angle $EFD = 58.8°$

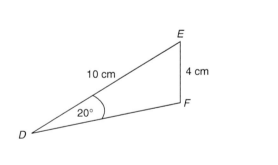

The answer to the above example appears to be 58.8°. But is this right?

In the diagram above angle *EFD* looks obtuse, although this could be because it is not drawn to scale.

Look at the diagram in Figure 21.6.

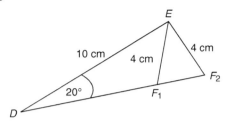

Figure 21.6 Ambiguous sine rule

There are two possible triangles that can be drawn with the given measurements. They are shown as triangles EDF_1 and EDF_2 in Figure 21.6.

Angle $EF_2D = 58.8°$ and angle $EF_1D = 180° − 58.8° = 121.2°$.

This is called the ambiguous case and unless further measurements are available it is not possible to say which is the required answer, so both should be given.

Notice that $20° + 58.8° = 78.8°$, and $20° + 121.2° = 141.2°$; both pairs of angles add up to less than $180°$ so both are possible as two of the angles in a triangle.

In each of the two triangles there is one obtuse angle.

Example 3

In triangle PQR, $PQ = 8.4$ cm, $QR = 6.7$ cm and angle $PRQ = 71°$.
Calculate angle QPR.

Answer 3

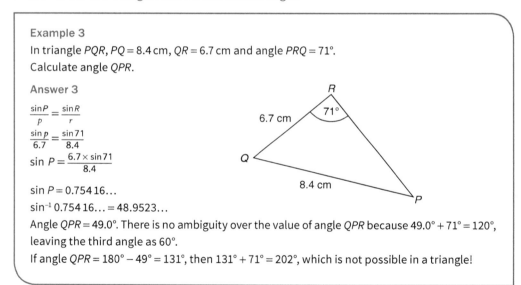

$\dfrac{\sin P}{p} = \dfrac{\sin R}{r}$

$\dfrac{\sin p}{6.7} = \dfrac{\sin 71}{8.4}$

$\sin P = \dfrac{6.7 \times \sin 71}{8.4}$

$\sin P = 0.754\,16...$

$\sin^{-1} 0.754\,16... = 48.9523...$

Angle $QPR = 49.0°$. There is no ambiguity over the value of angle QPR because $49.0° + 71° = 120°$, leaving the third angle as $60°$.

If angle $QPR = 180° − 49° = 131°$, then $131° + 71° = 202°$, which is not possible in a triangle!

Using the Sine Rule in a Practical Situation

How can you find the height of a mountain if you cannot get directly under its peak? One solution to this problem is shown in Figure 21.7.

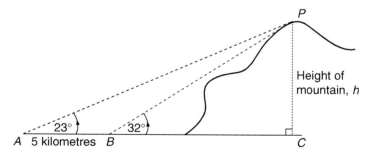

Figure 21.7 Measuring the height of a mountain

The angle of elevation is measured from a point A, and then a second angle of elevation is measured from a point B, 5 kilometres closer to the mountain. The height of the mountain is found by using the sine rule as shown below.

In triangle ABP, $\angle ABP = 180° - 32° = 148°$,

$\angle APB = 180° - 23° - 148° = 9°$

Using the sine rule, $\dfrac{AP}{\sin 148°} = \dfrac{5}{\sin 9°}$

$$AP = \dfrac{5 \times \sin 148°}{\sin 9°}$$

$$AP = 16.93\,74\ldots$$

In triangle ACP, $\sin 23° = \dfrac{PC}{AP}$

$$PC = AP \times \sin 23°$$

$$PC = 16.9374\ldots \times \sin 23°$$

$$PC = 6.617\,97\ldots$$

The height of the mountain is 6.62 kilometres to 3 significant figures.

Exercise 21.2

Find the value represented by the letter in each diagram. The diagrams are not to scale.

1

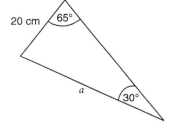

2

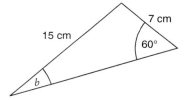

NOTE:
In question find the remaining angle first.

3

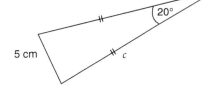

4

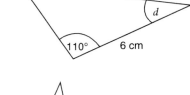

5

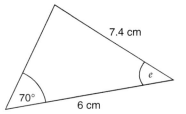

6

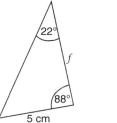

7

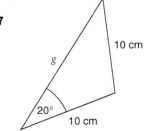

8 In triangle ABC, $AB = 4.2\,$cm, $BC = 5\,$cm and angle $ACB = 50°$. Calculate the two possible values of angle BAC.

21.5 The Cosine Rule

The sine rule involves pairs of opposite sides and angles. For example, look at Figure 21.8.

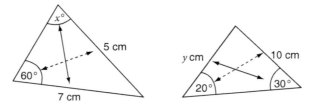

Figure 21.8 Using the sine rule

If, however, we are given either of the triangles in Figure 21.9 we cannot use the sine rule. (Try if you are not sure. In each case you will find you need another angle.)

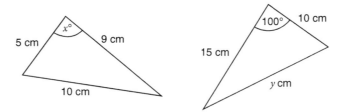

Figure 21.9 Using the cosine rule

The alternative method uses the cosine rule.

This is slightly more complicated to derive, so it will just be stated here. It involves three sides and one angle (see Figure 21.10).

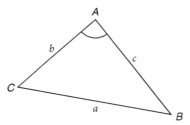

Figure 21.10 The cosine rule

- To find an angle use: $\cos A = \dfrac{b^2 + c^2 - a^2}{2bc}$
- To find a side use: $a^2 = b^2 + c^2 - 2bc \cos A$

These are both the same formula, but arranged differently.

It is worth studying these two formulae carefully. You will see some symmetry in the way they are used. The two sides (lengths b and c) which include the angle (angle A) are always squared and added. Each letter (either in capital or lower case) appears twice. The second arrangement reminds us of Pythagoras' theorem, but includes a 'correction term' ($2bc \cos A$) to allow for the fact that angle A is not a right angle.

Using the Cosine Rule and Avoiding the Very Common Errors

Practise the cosine rule using your calculator.

To find the angle, use brackets as shown here:

$$\cos A = \frac{(b^2 + c^2 - a^2)}{(2bc)}$$

To find the side, enter the terms into your calculator exactly as shown in the formula. You will have to enter the multiplication symbol in between each number in the final term, but your calculator will deal with the plus and minus signs correctly. One of the most common mistakes is to calculate the $2bc \cos A$ first and then get confused with the signs.

There is no ambiguity in the answers using the cosine rule because the calculator will distinguish between acute and obtuse angles according to whether the cosine is positive or negative.

Before going any further try these two questions to make sure that you understand the correct use of the calculator, and to check that you understand the logic your calculator uses.

1 Using your calculator find angle A, given that

$$\cos A = \frac{6^2 + 5^2 - 3^2}{2 \times 6 \times 5}$$

The correct answer is $A = 29.9°$.

- If you were correct try the next question.
- If you got 0.866 666… you have found the cosine of the angle. Press ⌊shift⌋ ⌊cos⌋ ⌊Ans⌋ to get the angle.
- If you got 0.52 your calculator is set in radians. Change to degrees and recalculate.
- If you got 780, or 60.85 or any other impossible result you have probably not followed the advice above to put brackets round the numerator and denominator.

2 Using your calculator find side a, given that

$$a^2 = 7^2 + 5^2 - 2 \times 5 \times 7 \times \cos 150°$$

The correct answer is $a = 11.6$.

- If you were correct you are ready to proceed with the rest of the chapter!
- If you got 134.62… you have found a^2 not a. Find the square root to finish the question.
- If you got 5.01 or 25.05 your calculator is in radians. Change to degrees.
- If you got −3.46, or any other impossible answer, you have not followed the advice to enter the values into your calculator exactly as they appear in the question. Do not work out part of the calculation first or put brackets into the calculator.

Example 4

With reference to the triangle PQR shown,

a if $p = 7\,\text{cm}$, $q = 8\,\text{cm}$ and $r = 11\,\text{cm}$, calculate $\angle PRQ$;

b if $p = 6\,\text{cm}$, $r = 4\,\text{cm}$ and $\angle Q = 100°$, calculate PR.

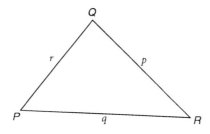

Answer 4

a $\cos R = \dfrac{p^2 + q^2 - r^2}{2pq}$

$\cos R = \dfrac{(7^2 + 8^2 - 11^2)}{(2 \times 7 \times 8)}$

$\cos R = -0.071428\ldots$

$R = 94.0960\ldots$

Angle $PRQ = 94.1°$ to 1 decimal place.

b $q^2 = p^2 + r^2 - 2pr \cos Q$

$q^2 = 6^2 + 4^2 - 2 \times 6 \times 4 \times \cos 100°$

$q^2 = 60.335\,11\ldots$

$q = 7.767\,56\ldots$

$PR = 7.77\,\text{cm}$ to 3 significant figures.

NOTE:
In both 4 **a** and **b** the calculator has dealt with the obtuse angle without any further input.

NOTE:
Remember to take square root to get the length of the side.

Exercise 21.3

Calculate the values represented by letters in the following triangles. All lengths are in centimetres.

1
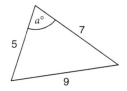

2
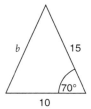

3
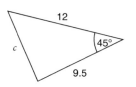

4
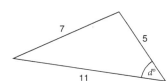

5
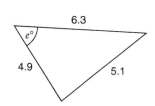

6
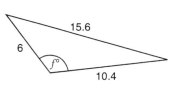

7 In triangle ABC, $AC = 15\,\text{cm}$, $BC = 12\,\text{cm}$ and angle $ACB = 30°$. Calculate the length of AB.

8 In triangle DEF, $DF = 5\,\text{cm}$, $EF = 11\,\text{cm}$ and angle $DFE = 112°$. Calculate the length of DE.

9 In triangle GHJ, $GH = 3.1\,\text{cm}$, $GJ = 6.7\,\text{cm}$ and $HJ = 4.9\,\text{cm}$. Calculate angle GHJ.

10 In triangle KLM, $KM = 35\,\text{cm}$, $KL = 15.1\,\text{cm}$ and angle $LKM = 130°$. Calculate the length of LM.

The next exercise mixes sine rule and cosine rule so that you get practice in deciding which to use, and also provides some examples in which you will have to use both.

Exercise 21.4

1 Calculate the values represented by letters in these questions. You may not have to use all the information in the questions. All the lengths are in centimetres.

a

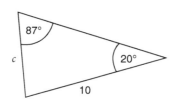

b

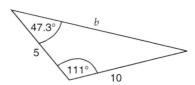

c

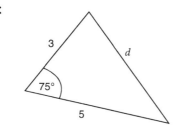

d

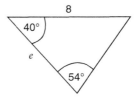

> **NOTE:**
> In shape f, work out the other side first.

e

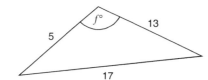

f

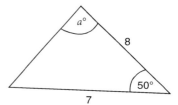

g

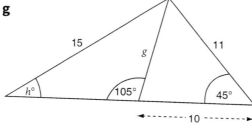

2 A ship leaves a port *P* and sails for 21 kilometres on a bearing of 073°. It then alters course to a bearing 125° and sails 13 kilometres.

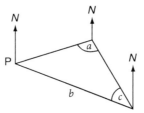

Copy the diagram and fill in the information given.
a Find the angle *a*.
b Calculate the distance *b*.
c Find the angle *c*.
d Find the bearing on which the ship must sail to return to port *P*.

21.6 Area of a Triangle

You already know how to calculate the area of a triangle if you are given, or can find, the base and the height.

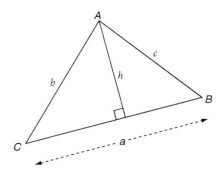

However, there is another useful formula which can be used if you know two sides and the included angle. The *included* angle is the angle between the two known sides.

Look at Figure 21.11.

Suppose you are given the lengths of AC (b) and CB (a), and the size of angle C.

Figure 21.11 Finding the area of a triangle

Drop a perpendicular line from A to BC. If BC is the base of the triangle then this perpendicular is the height.

$$\sin C = \frac{\text{opp}}{\text{hyp}} = \frac{h}{b}$$
$$h = b \times \sin C$$

The area of triangle $ABC = \frac{1}{2} \times BC \times h$
$$= \frac{1}{2} \times a \times b \times \sin C$$

The area of triangle $ABC = \frac{1}{2}ab \sin C$

This formula is often used and does not have to be derived each time.

Remember, the area is 'half the product of the two sides times the sine of the angle between them'.

It does not matter if the angle is obtuse, the area will still be correct.

Example 5

Calculate the area of triangle PQR, where $PQ = 15.1$ cm, $QR = 17.2$ cm and angle $PQR = 50°$.

Answer 5

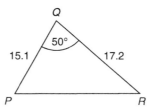

Area of triangle $PQR = \frac{1}{2}pr \sin Q = \frac{1}{2} \times 17.5 \times 15.1 \times \sin 50°$
$$= 99.4785\ldots$$
Area of triangle $PQR = 99.5$ cm² to 3 significant figures.

Exercise 21.5

1 Calculate the areas of the following triangles.

a

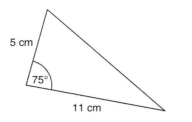

b

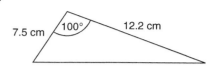

c

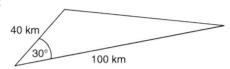

d

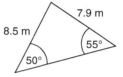

e In triangle ABC, $AB = AC = 10\,cm$, $\angle ABC = 60°$.

Calculate the area of triangle ABC.

2 Using the following triangles, calculate
  i the angle marked x
  ii the angle marked y
  iii the area of the triangle.

a

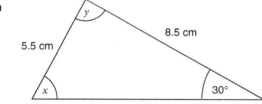

b

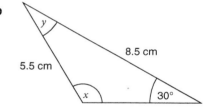

21.7 Three-dimensional Trigonometry

You need to be able to apply Pythagoras' theorem, sine, cosine and tangent ratios and the sine and cosine rules to three-dimensional objects such as pyramids.

Example 6

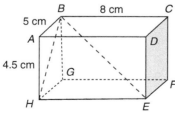

$ABCDEFGH$ is a cuboid.
$AB = 5\,cm$, $BC = 8\,cm$ and $AH = 4.5\,cm$.
Calculate

a BH **b** GE **c** BE
d angle GBE **e** angle HBE.

Answer 6

a *BH* is the diagonal of the rectangle *ABGH*:

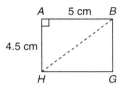

Using Pythagoras' theorem,

$BH^2 = 5^2 + 4.5^2$

$BH^2 = 45.25$

$BH = 6.726\,81\ldots$

$BH = 6.73\,cm$

b *GE* is the diagonal of rectangle *EFGH*.

Using Pythagoras' theorem,

$GE^2 = 8^2 + 5^2$

$GE^2 = 89$

$GE = 9.433\,98\ldots$

$GE = 9.43\,cm$

c *BE* is the hypotenuse of triangle *BEG*.

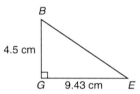

$BE^2 = 4.5^2 + 9.433\,98^2$

$BE^2 = 109.249\,97\ldots$

$BE = 10.452\,27\ldots$

$BE = 10.5\,cm$

d $\tan \angle GBE = \dfrac{GE}{BG} = \dfrac{9.43}{4.5}$

$\tan \angle GBE = 2.095\,555\,55\ldots$

$\angle GBE = 64.4895\ldots$

angle *GBE* = 64.5°

e Angle *HBE* is in triangle *BEH*.

EH is perpendicular to *ABGH* so it is perpendicular to *BH*.

We now know all the sides of triangle *BEH* so any of the ratios can be used to find ∠*HBE*.

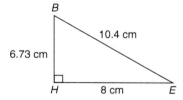

$\tan \angle HBE = \dfrac{HE}{BH} = \dfrac{8}{6.73}$

$\tan \angle HBE = 1.188\,70\ldots$

$\angle HBE = 49.927\,77\ldots$

angle *HBE* = 49.9°

NOTE:
It is not good practice to carry a rounded answer through to a subsequent part of your working. You should use the memory facility on your calculator to obtain the best accuracy. In part (c) if *GE* = 9.43 had been used instead of *GE* = 9.43 398… the answer obtained would have been *BE* = 10.4 cm.

Make sure that you have worked through this example carefully and understood it. You should see that it can be a help to draw diagrams as you go along.

The questions you will be asked will not be as long as this, but this example should have helped you understand what is required.

Exercise 21.6

1

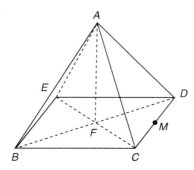

ABCDE is a square-based pyramid. *F* is the point of intersection of the diagonals of the base. *M* is the midpoint of the side *CD*.
BC = 5 centimetres, *AF* = 6 centimetres.

a Calculate *EC*.   **b** Calculate *AC*.
c Calculate angle   **d** Calculate angle
    ACF.   *AMF*.

2

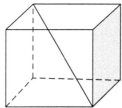

The diagram shows a cube with each side of length 8 centimetres.
Calculate the length of the diagonal shown.

3

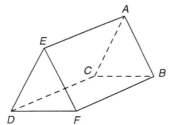

ABCDEF is an isosceles triangular prism with
DE = *EF* = *AC* = *AB* = 7 centimetres.
The length of the prism is 15 centimetres.
Angle *DEF* is 40°.

a Calculate the length of *DF*.
b Calculate the length of *DB*.
c Calculate the length of *EB*.
d Use the cosine rule in triangle *BDE* to calculate the angle *EBD*.

Exercise 21.7

Mixed exercise

1

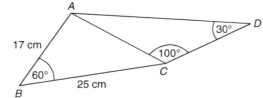

Using the diagram, calculate
a *AC*   **b** *AD*
c the area of *ABCD*   **d** angle *BAD*.

NOTE:

Draw in the radius *OA*.

2

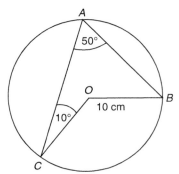

The diagram shows a circle, centre *O*, and radius 10 centimetres. Angle *CAB* = 50°.

a Find angle *BOC*.

b Calculate the length of the chord *BC*.

c Calculate the area of the quadrilateral *ABCO*.

3

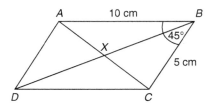

ABCD is a parallelogram, and *X* is the point of intersection of the diagonals.
Angle *ABC* is 45°.
Calculate

a *AC* **b** *DB*

c angle *AXB* **d** the area of triangle *ACD*.

4

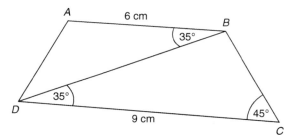

Using the diagram above calculate

a *BD* **b** *AD*

c angle *DAB* **d** the area of the quadrilateral *ABCD*.

5

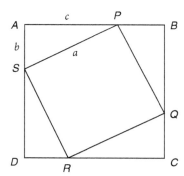

ABCD is a square, with sides of length (*b* + *c*) centimetres.
PQRS is another square with sides of length *a* centimetres.

a Write down the area of the square *ABCD* in terms of *b* and *c*.

b Write down the area of the square *PQRS*.

c Write down the area of triangle *APS* in terms of *b* and *c*.

d The area of triangle $ASP = \dfrac{ABCD - PQRS}{4}$.

Write $\dfrac{ABCD - PQRS}{4}$ in terms of *a*, *b*, and *c*.

e Put these two expressions for the area of the triangle *ASP* equal to each other. By multiplying out the brackets and simplifying show that $a^2 = b^2 + c^2$.

f What have you just proved by algebraic means?

Exam-style questions

6

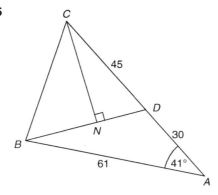

Diagram I

In Diagram I, the point *D* lies on *AC* and *N* is the foot of the perpendicular from *C* to *BD*.
$AB = 61\,\text{m}$, $AD = 30\,\text{m}$ and $DC = 45\,\text{m}$.
Angle $BAC = 41°$.

a Calculate *BD*.

b Show that, correct to the nearest square metre, the area of triangle *BDA* is $600\,\text{m}^2$.

c Explain why $\dfrac{\text{area of } \triangle BCD}{\text{area of } \triangle BDA} = \dfrac{3}{2}$.

d Calculate the area of triangle *BCD*.

e Hence calculate *CN*.

f

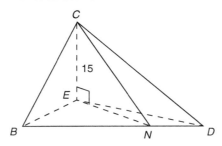

Diagram II

The same points *B*, *C*, *D* and *N* lie on a sloping plane.
The point *E* is 15 m vertically below *C*.
The points *B*, *E*, *D* and *N* lie on a horizontal plane.
Diagram II represents this information.
Calculate the angle of elevation of *C* from *N*.   (4024 paper 02 Q9 June 2007)

7

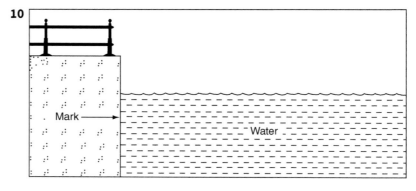

NOT TO SCALE

A, B, C and *D* lie on a circle.
AC and *BD* intersect at *X*.
Angle *ABX* = 55° and angle *AXB* = 92°.
BX = 26.8 cm, *AX* = 40.3 cm and *XC* = 20.1 cm.
  a Calculate the area of triangle *AXB*. **You must show your working**.
  b Calculate the length of *AB*. **You must show your working**.
  c Write down the size of angle *ACD*. Give a reason for your answer.
  d Find the size of angle *BDC*.
  e Write down the geometrical word which completes the statement
    'Triangle *AXB* is _____ to triangle *DXC*.'
  f Calculate the length of *XD*. **You must show your working**.   (0580 paper 04 Q3a June 2007)

8 **a** Use your calculator to work out
    $$\frac{1-(\tan 40°)^2}{2(\tan 40°)}.$$
  b Write your answer to part (a) in standard form.   (0580 paper 02 Q2 June 2007)

9 Calculate the value of $(\cos 40°)^2 + (\sin 40°)^2$.   (0580 paper 02 Q4 June 2005)

10

The height, *h* metres, of the water, above a mark on a harbour wall, changes with the tide.
It is given by the equation
$h = 3\sin (30t)°$
where *t* is the time in hours after midday.

a Calculate the value of *h* at midday.

b Calculate the value of *h* at 1900.

c Explain the meaning of the negative sign in your answer.   (0580 paper 02 Q17 June 2005)

11

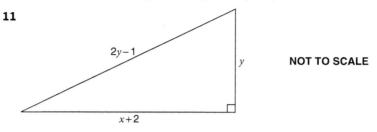

The diagram shows a right-angled triangle.

The lengths of the sides are given in terms of *y*.

i Show that $2y^2 - 8y - 3 = 0$.

ii Solve the equation $2y^2 - 8y - 3 = 0$, giving your answers to 2 decimal places.

iii Calculate the area of the triangle.   (0580 paper 04 Q8b June 2006)

12

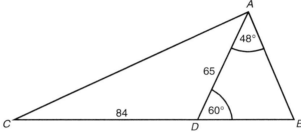

A, *B*, *C* and *D* are four points on horizontal ground.

CBD is a straight line.

AD = 65 m and *CD* = 84 m.

$D\hat{A}B = 48°$ and $A\hat{D}B = 60°$.

a Calculate *AB*.

b Calculate the area of triangle *ACD*.

c Calculate *AC*.

d A vertical tree of height 35 m stands at *A*.

  P is the point on the line *BC* such that the angle of elevation from the line *BC* to the top of the tree is greatest.

  Calculate this angle of elevation.   (4024 paper 21 Q9 November 2012)

13

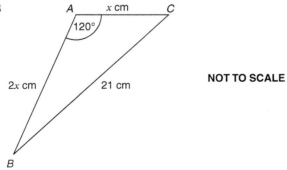

NOT TO SCALE

In triangle *ABC*, *AB* = 2*x* cm, *AC* = *x* cm, *BC* = 21 cm and angle *BAC* = 120°.

Calculate the value of *x*.   (0580 paper 21 Q11 June 2008)

14 $\sin x° = 0.866\,03$ and $0 \leqslant x \leqslant 180$.
  Find the two values of x.   (0580 paper 21 Q6 November 2008)

15

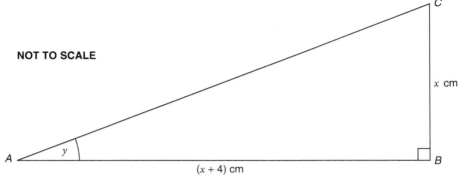

NOT TO SCALE

  a When the area of triangle *ABC* is 48 cm²,
     i   show that $x^2 + 4x - 96 = 0$,
     ii solve the equation $x^2 + 4x - 96 = 0$,
     iii write down the length of *AB*.
  b When $\tan y = \frac{1}{6}$, find the value of x.
  c When the length of *AC* is 9 cm,
     i   show that $2x^2 + 8x - 65 = 0$,
     ii solve the equation $2x^2 + 8x - 65 = 0$,
        (**Show your working** and give your answers correct to 2 decimal places.)
     iii calculate the perimeter of triangle *ABC*.   (0580 paper 04 Q2 November 2008)

16

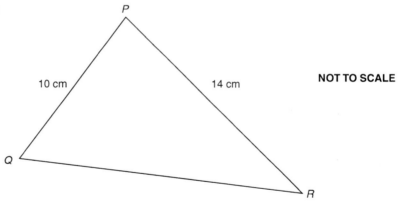

NOT TO SCALE

In triangle *PQR*, angle *QPR* is acute, *PQ* = 10 cm and *PR* = 14 cm.
  a The area of triangle *PQR* is 48 cm².
     Calculate angle *QPR* and show that it rounds to 43.3°, correct to 1 decimal place. You
     must show all your working.
  b Calculate the length of the side *QR*.   (0580 paper 04 Q3 June 2009)

17

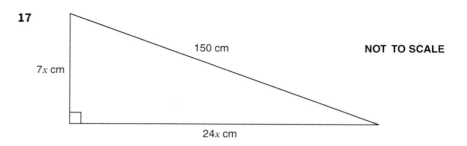

NOT TO SCALE

The right-angled triangle shown in the diagram has sides of length $7x$ cm, $24x$ cm and 150 cm.

a Show that $x^2 = 36$.

b Calculate the perimeter of the triangle.   (0580 paper 02 Q10 November 2006)

18

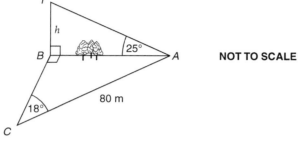

NOT TO SCALE

Mahmoud is working out the height, h metres, of a tower BT which stands on level ground.
He measures the angle TAB as 25°.
He cannot measure the distance AB and so he walks 80 m from A to BT, where angle $ACB =$ 18° and angle $ABC = 90°$.
Calculate

a the distance AB,

b the height of the tower, BT.   (0580 paper 21 Q15 June 2009)

19

North

L

1400 km

1600 km

13°

H

NOT TO SCALE

W

36°

95°

J

The diagram shows the positions of four cities in Africa, Windhoek (W), Johannesburg (J), Harari (H) and Lusaka (L).

$WL = 1400$ km and $WH = 1600$ km.

Angle $LWH = 13°$, angle $HWJ = 36°$ and angle $WJH = 95°$.

a Calculate the distance LH.

b Calculate the distance WJ.

c Calculate the area of quadrilateral $WJHL$.

d The bearing of Lusaka from Windhoek is 060°.
    Calculate the bearing of
    i Harari from Windhoek,   **ii** Windhoek from Johannesburg.

e On a map the distance between Windhoek and Harari is 8 cm.
    Calculate the scale of the map in the form $1 : n$.   (0580 paper 04 Q2 November 2006)

20 The base of a pyramid is a square with diagonals of length 6 cm.
The sloping faces are isosceles triangles with equal sides of length 7 cm.
The height of the pyramid is $\sqrt{l}$ cm.
Calculate l.

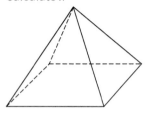

(4024 paper 01 Q18 June 2004)

21

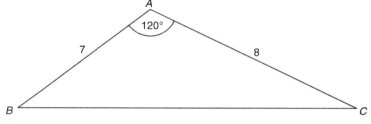

Diagram I

Diagram I shows a triangle ABC in which $AB = 7$ cm, $AC = 8$ cm and $B\hat{A}C = 120°$.

a Show that $BC = 13$ cm.

b Calculate the area of triangle ABC.

c

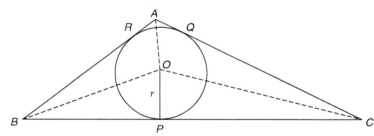

Diagram II

The sides of the triangle ABC, shown in Diagram I, are tangents to a circle with centre O and radius r centimetres.

The circle touches the sides *BC*, *CA* and *AB* at *P*, *Q* and *R* respectively, as shown in Diagram II.

    i   Find an expression, in terms of *r*, for the area of triangle *OBC*.

    ii By similarly considering the areas of triangles *OAB* and *OAC*, find an expression, in terms of *r*, for the area of triangle *ABC*.

    iii Hence find the value of *r*.

d Calculate the percentage of the area of triangle *ABC* that is **not** occupied by the circle.

(4024 paper 02 Q9 June 2004)

22

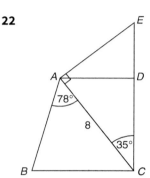

The diagram represents some beams which support part of a roof.

AD and *BC* are horizontal and *CDE* is vertical.

$AC = 8$ metres, $B\hat{A}C = 78°$, $A\hat{C}D = 35°$ and $C\hat{A}E = 90°$.

Calculate the length of the beam

a *AD*,

b *CE*,

c *AB*.   (4024 paper 02 Q1 November 2004)

23

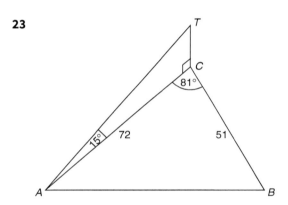

Three paths, *AB*, *BC* and *CA*, run along the edges of a horizontal triangular field *ABC*.

$BC = 51$ m, $AC = 72$ m and angle $ACB = 81°$.

a Calculate the length of *AB*.

b Calculate the area of the field *ABC*.

c Calculate the shortest distance from *C* to *AB*.

d A vertical tree, *CT*, has its base at *C*.

    The angle of elevation of the top of the tree from *A* is 15°.

    Calculate the height of the tree.

e John measured the largest angle of elevation of the top of the tree as seen from the path *AB*.

    Calculate this angle of elevation.   (4024 paper 02 Q7 November 2004)

24

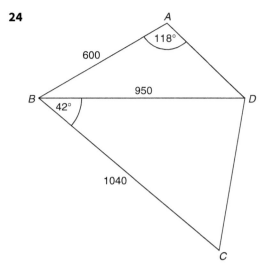

In the diagram, the quadrilateral *ABCD* represents a level park with a path *BD*.
$AB = 600$ m, $BC = 1040$ m, $BD = 950$ m, $C\hat{B}D = 42°$ and $B\hat{A}D = 118°$.

a Calculate

   i angle *ABD*,

   ii the length of *CD*,

   iii the shortest distance from *C* to *BD*.

b A helicopter flew directly above the path *BD* at a constant height of 500 m.
Calculate the greatest angle of depression of the point *C* as seen by a passenger on the helicopter.

(4024 paper 02 Q9 June 2005)

25

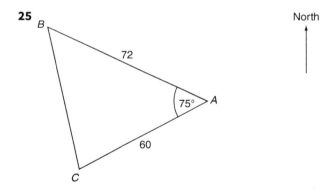

Three points, *A*, *B* and *C*, lie on a horizontal field.
Angle *BAC* = 75° and the bearing of *C* from *A* is 217°.
AB = 72 m and *AC* = 60 m.

a Calculate
   i the bearing of B from A,   **ii** BC,
   iii angle ABC,   **iv** the bearing of C from B.
b A girl standing at B is flying a kite.
   The kite, K, is vertically above A.
   The string, BK, attached to the kite is at 24° to the horizontal.
   Calculate the angle of elevation of the kite when
   viewed from C.   (4024 paper 02 Q8 November 2005)

26

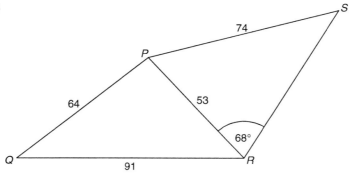

The diagram shows a footpath PR across a park PQRS.
PQ = 64 m, PR = 53 m, PS = 74 m and QR = 91 m.
Angle PRS = 68°.
Calculate
a $Q\hat{P}R$,
b $R\hat{P}S$,
c the area of triangle PRS.   (4024 paper 02 Q3 November 2006)

27 A vertical flagpole, BF, stands at the top of a hill.
AB is the steepest path up the hill.
N lies vertically below B and $A\hat{N}B = 90°$.
AN = 100 m and AB = 104 m.

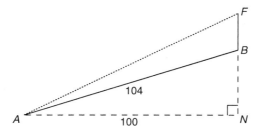

a Show that BN = 28.6 m.
b It is given that $F\hat{A}N = 25°$.
   i Write down the size of the angle of depression of A from F.
   ii Calculate the height, BF, of the flagpole.

c

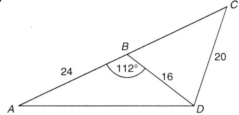

The diagram shows three other straight paths (*CB*, *DB* and *ACD*) on the hill.
The path *ACD* is horizontal and $B\hat{A}C = N\hat{A}C = 90°$.
CN and *DN* are horizontal lines.

i Given that *AC* = 60 m, calculate $B\hat{C}N$.

ii Given that $B\hat{D}N = 10°$, calculate $D\hat{B}A$. (4024 paper 02 Q9 November 2006)

28

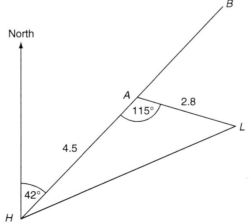

The points *A*, *B*, *C* and *D* represent four towns on a map.
ABC is a straight line.
AB = 24 cm, *BD* = 16 cm and *CD* = 20 cm.
Angle *ABD* = 112°.

a Calculate
  i *AD*,
  ii angle *BCD*,
  iii the area of triangle *ABD*.

b The scale of the map is 1 : 250 000.
  Calculate the actual distance, in kilometres, from town *A* to town *B*.

(4024 paper 02 Q5 November 2007)

29

The diagram shows the positions of a harbour, H, a lighthouse, L, and two buoys A and B.
HAB is a straight line.
The bearing of A from H is 042°.
HA = 4.5 km, AL = 2.8 km and $H\hat{A}L = 115°$.

a Find the bearing of
i H from A, **ii** L from A.
b Calculate
i HL, **ii** the area of triangle HAL.
c A boat sailed from the harbour along the line HAB.
i Calculate the shortest distance between the boat and the lighthouse.
ii The boat sailed at a constant speed of 3 m/s.
Given that the boat reached A at 0715, find at what time it left the harbour.

(4024 paper 02 Q9 June 2008)

Learning Objectives

Syllabus sections 37, 38 and 39

In this chapter you will find out about:
- the magnitude of a vector
- combining vectors
- dividing a line in a given ratio
- parallel vectors
- position vectors
- matrices and transformations
- performing successive transformations.

22.1 Introduction

We now look further at vectors and transformations. We will study how matrices can be used to describe transformations.

22.2 Essential Skills

1 Describe fully each of the following single transformations. In each case *A* is mapped to *B*.

a
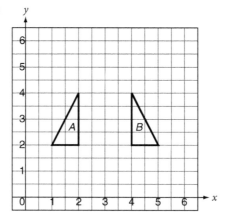

b
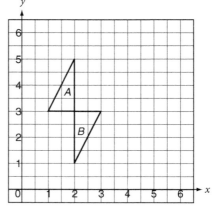

c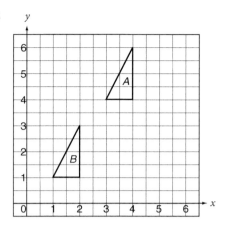

d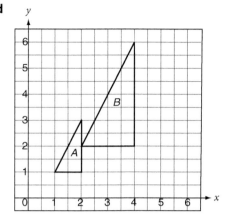

2 Simplify the following vectors.

a $4\begin{pmatrix} -1 \\ 0 \end{pmatrix} + \begin{pmatrix} 3 \\ 5 \end{pmatrix}$

b $3\begin{pmatrix} 1 \\ -4 \end{pmatrix} - 2\begin{pmatrix} 1 \\ -6 \end{pmatrix}$

3 Find x and y.

a $\begin{pmatrix} x \\ 3y \end{pmatrix} + \begin{pmatrix} 5 \\ 7 \end{pmatrix} = \begin{pmatrix} -1 \\ -2 \end{pmatrix}$

b $\begin{pmatrix} 2x \\ -5y \end{pmatrix} + \begin{pmatrix} 2y \\ x \end{pmatrix} = \begin{pmatrix} 10 \\ -7 \end{pmatrix}$

4 Which of these vectors are parallel?

$a = \begin{pmatrix} -3 \\ 4 \end{pmatrix}$
$\qquad b = \begin{pmatrix} -3 \\ -4 \end{pmatrix}$
$\qquad c = \begin{pmatrix} 3 \\ 4 \end{pmatrix}$

$d = \begin{pmatrix} 4 \\ 3 \end{pmatrix}$
$\qquad e = \begin{pmatrix} -6 \\ -8 \end{pmatrix}$
$\qquad f = \begin{pmatrix} -4 \\ 3 \end{pmatrix}$

5 What three things can you say about the relationship between these two vectors?

$v = \begin{pmatrix} 6 \\ -15 \end{pmatrix}$
$\qquad w = \begin{pmatrix} -2 \\ 5 \end{pmatrix}$

22.3 More About Vectors
Magnitude of a Vector

Vectors have a direction and a magnitude. Figure 22.1 shows two vectors, a and b, that have the same magnitude but different directions, and two vectors c and d which have the same direction but different magnitudes.

Figure 22.1 Vectors have magnitude and direction

Each of these vectors would produce an image in a different place when applied to an object.

The length of a vector is easy to calculate using Pythagoras' theorem.

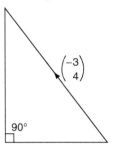

Figure 22.2 Length of a vector

Figure 22.2 shows how the vector can be part of a right-angled triangle. The two parts of the vector make up two sides of the triangle, and the vector itself is the hypotenuse.

The length of the vector $\begin{pmatrix} -3 \\ 4 \end{pmatrix}$ as shown in Figure 22.2 is $\sqrt{(-3)^2 + 4^2} = \sqrt{9 + 16} = 5$.

Notice how the fact that the x-component is negative 3 makes no difference when we are calculating length and not direction, since −3 becomes +9 when squared.

The vectors in Figure 22.3 all have different directions but the same lengths (5 units).

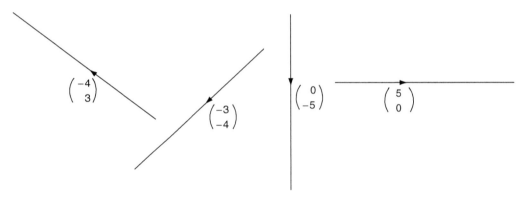

Figure 22.3 Vectors with the same length

The shorthand notation for the length of the vector $\boldsymbol{a}$ is $|\boldsymbol{a}|$, which is read 'the **modulus** of $\boldsymbol{a}$', or simply 'mod $\boldsymbol{a}$'. The length of a vector may also be referred to as the *magnitude* of the vector.

So if $\boldsymbol{a} = \begin{pmatrix} x \\ y \end{pmatrix}$, then $|\boldsymbol{a}| = \sqrt{x^2 + y^2}$.

The particular vector which joins the point A to the point B is written $\overrightarrow{AB}$, and is called a **directed line segment** (Figure 22.4). 'Directed' means it has a *direction*, that is from A to B (shown by the arrow), and 'line segment' means that it is only part of a line, that is, the part between A and B. The line itself can go on indefinitely.

The length (or magnitude) of $\overrightarrow{AB}$, or the modulus of $\overrightarrow{AB}$, is written $|\overrightarrow{AB}|$, and $|\overrightarrow{AB}| = |\overrightarrow{BA}|$.

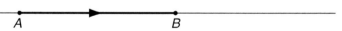

Figure 22.4 The directed line segment from A to B

Combining Vectors

In Chapter 10 we saw that vectors can be added to produce a new vector which has the same effect as applying the original vectors one after another. We also saw that vectors which have the same direction and magnitude are equivalent.

This means that vectors may be drawn anywhere on your diagram and will always have the same effect as long as they are pointing in the same direction and have the same magnitude.

The first diagram in Figure 22.5 shows two vectors a and b drawn on two edges of a rectangle $PQRS$. The second diagram shows that these two vectors may also be represented on the other sides of the rectangle, because the opposite sides are parallel and of equal length. Notice that the corresponding arrows must point in the same direction in the two diagrams.

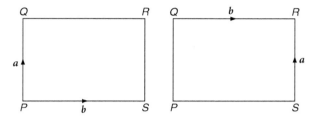

Figure 22.5 Vectors have the same effect everywhere

Suppose we wanted to get from P to R on the rectangle. We could go from:

- P to Q and then from Q to R,
- from P to S and then from S to R, or
- directly from P to R.

In terms of directed line segments:

$$\overrightarrow{PQ} + \overrightarrow{QR} = \overrightarrow{PS} + \overrightarrow{SR} = \overrightarrow{PR}$$

and in terms of vectors:

$$a + b = b + a = \overrightarrow{PR}$$

This shows that vectors may be combined to give a single vector if they are joined 'head to tail', that is, if the arrows follow round, without a break.

It is convenient to think of combining vectors as going on a journey. There are often several routes, but the start and the end of the journey are the same.

Figure 22.6 shows that the vectors may be joined in any order as long as the 'head to tail' rule is followed. The double arrow shows in each case the single vector which is equivalent to the addition. This is often called the **resultant vector**.

You will see that the resultant is the same regardless of the order in which the vectors are added.

In each case S is the start and F the finish.

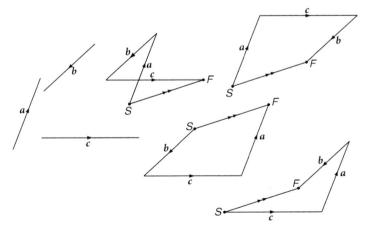

Figure 22.6 Resultant vectors

In terms of column vectors, if $\boldsymbol{a} = \begin{pmatrix} 1 \\ 3 \end{pmatrix}$, $\boldsymbol{b} = \begin{pmatrix} -2 \\ -2 \end{pmatrix}$ and $\boldsymbol{c} = \begin{pmatrix} 4 \\ 0 \end{pmatrix}$ then

$$\boldsymbol{a} + \boldsymbol{b} + \boldsymbol{c} = \begin{pmatrix} 1 & -2 & +4 \\ 3 & -2 & +0 \end{pmatrix} = \begin{pmatrix} 3 \\ 1 \end{pmatrix}, \quad \boldsymbol{b} + \boldsymbol{c} + \boldsymbol{a} = \begin{pmatrix} -2 & +4 & +1 \\ -2 & +0 & +3 \end{pmatrix} = \begin{pmatrix} 3 \\ 1 \end{pmatrix}$$

and so on.

Example 1

ABCDEF is a regular hexagon.

Copy the diagram.

a Find x in terms of $\boldsymbol{p}$ and/or $\boldsymbol{q}$.

b Find y in terms of $\boldsymbol{p}$ and/or $\boldsymbol{q}$ and/or $\boldsymbol{r}$.

c Find z in terms of $\boldsymbol{p}$ and/or $\boldsymbol{q}$ and/or $\boldsymbol{r}$.

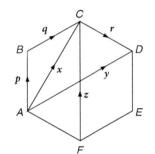

NOT TO SCALE

Answer 1

a $\overrightarrow{AC} = \overrightarrow{AB} + \overrightarrow{BC}$

$x = \boldsymbol{p} + \boldsymbol{q}$

NOTE:

x goes from A to C. In terms of a journey you could also go from A to B and then on to C. So $\overrightarrow{AC} = \overrightarrow{AB} + \overrightarrow{BC}$.

b $\overrightarrow{AD} = \overrightarrow{AB} + \overrightarrow{BC} + \overrightarrow{CD}$

$y = \boldsymbol{p} + \boldsymbol{q} + \boldsymbol{r}$

NOTE:

Notice that when you join head to tail, $\overrightarrow{AB} + \overrightarrow{BC} + \overrightarrow{CD} = \overrightarrow{AD}$.

c $z = \overrightarrow{FC} = \overrightarrow{FA} + \overrightarrow{AB} + \overrightarrow{BC}$

$z = -\boldsymbol{r} + \boldsymbol{p} + \boldsymbol{q}$

NOTE:

$\overrightarrow{FA} = \overrightarrow{DC} = -\boldsymbol{r}$

You should be aware that, while we can directly add vectors when they are pointing in different directions, and joined head to tail, the same does not apply to lengths of lines.

For example, look at the triangle in Figure 22.7, where $\boldsymbol{a}$ is the vector $\overrightarrow{PQ}$ and $\boldsymbol{b}$ is the vector $\overrightarrow{QR}$.

Subtraction of one vector from another is dealt with by adding the negative of the vector to be subtracted.

For example, look at the two diagrams in Figure 22.8.

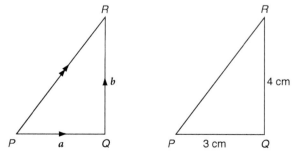

Figure 22.7 Adding vectors is not the same as adding lengths

In the first, $x = a + b$, and in the second, $y = a - b$.

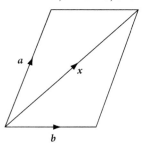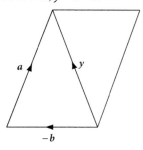

Figure 22.8 Vector subtraction: $x = a + b$; $y = -b + a = a - b$

Multiplying a Vector by a Number

Multiplying a vector by a positive number alters its length but not its direction. The first line drawn in Figure 22.9 shows the directed line segment $\overrightarrow{AB}$, which is representative of the vector $\boldsymbol{v}$. The second line drawn shows M, the midpoint of the line AB. It can be seen that the directed line segment $\overrightarrow{AM}$ is equal to the directed line segment $\overrightarrow{MA}$, which is equal to $\frac{1}{2}\boldsymbol{v}$.

The third line shows the line extended to C, where $AB = BC$. It can be seen that $\overrightarrow{AC} = 2\boldsymbol{v}$.

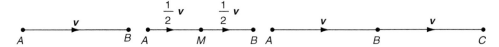

Figure 22.9 Multiplying a vector by a number

Example 2

Draw a parallelogram $ABCD$.

Mark M, the midpoint of BD.

$\overrightarrow{AD} = p$, $\overrightarrow{AB} = q$.

Find the following directed line segments in terms of p and q.

  a $\overrightarrow{BD}$ **b** $\overrightarrow{AC}$

  c $\overrightarrow{AB} + \overrightarrow{BM}$ **d** $\overrightarrow{AM}$

  e What can you say about $\overrightarrow{AM}$ and $\overrightarrow{AC}$ and hence about the diagonals of a parallelogram?

Answer 2

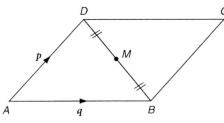

  a $\overrightarrow{BD} = \overrightarrow{BA} + \overrightarrow{AD} = -q + p = p - q$

  b $\overrightarrow{AC} = \overrightarrow{AB} + \overrightarrow{BC} = q + p$

  c $\overrightarrow{AB} + \overrightarrow{BM} = \overrightarrow{AB} + \frac{1}{2}\overrightarrow{BD} = q + \frac{1}{2}(p - q) = \frac{1}{2}(p + q)$

  d $\overrightarrow{AM} = \overrightarrow{AB} + \overrightarrow{BM} = \frac{1}{2}(p + q)$

  e $\overrightarrow{AM} = \frac{1}{2}\overrightarrow{AC} = \frac{1}{2}(p + q)$

> **NOTE:**
> $\overrightarrow{BC} = \overrightarrow{AD} = p$

Therefore M is also the midpoint of AC, and hence the diagonals of a parallelogram bisect each other.

Dividing a Line in a Given Ratio

The line AB is to be divided in the ratio $2:3$ by the point C.

Just as in ordinary ratio questions we think of dividing the line into 5 equal parts, (because $2+3=5$). See Figure 22.10.

Then $AC = 2$ parts and $CB = 3$ parts,

$AC = \frac{2}{5} AB$ and also $\overrightarrow{AC} = \frac{2}{5}\overrightarrow{AB}$.

It is important to notice that dividing the line BA in the same ratio would move C nearer to B. The order of the letters specifying the line segment matters.

Figure 22.10 Dividing a line in a ratio

Example 3

a Draw a triangle ABC. Mark the point D which divides BC in the ratio $3:2$.
$\overrightarrow{AB} = p$ and $\overrightarrow{AC} = q$.

b Find $\overrightarrow{AD}$ in terms of p and q.

Answer 3

a

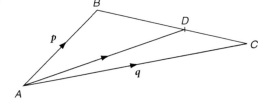

b $\overrightarrow{AD} = \overrightarrow{AB} + \overrightarrow{BD}$

To find $\overrightarrow{BD}$:

$\overrightarrow{BD} = \frac{3}{5}\overrightarrow{BC}$

$\overrightarrow{BD} = \frac{3}{5}(-p + q)$

so $\overrightarrow{AD} = p + \frac{3}{5}(-p + q)$

$\overrightarrow{AD} = \frac{2}{5}p + \frac{3}{5}q$

Parallel Vectors

As seen in Chapter 10, if one vector is a multiple of another, either positive or negative, then the two vectors are parallel to each other.

However, they could also be in the same straight line, as in Figure 22.11, for example.

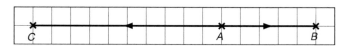

Figure 22.11 $\overrightarrow{AC} = \begin{pmatrix} -10 \\ 0 \end{pmatrix} = -2\begin{pmatrix} 5 \\ 0 \end{pmatrix}$ so $\overrightarrow{AC} = -2\overrightarrow{AB}$

In Figure 22.11, $\overrightarrow{AB}$ and $\overrightarrow{AC}$ are parallel (have the same direction, but in opposite senses), but they have the point A in common, so this can only be true if they are in the same straight line. We say that 'A is common to both', meaning that A belongs to both. The factor –2 shows that they are pointing in opposite senses, and that $\overrightarrow{AC}$ is twice as long as $\overrightarrow{AB}$.

Example 4

a Show that the vectors $u = \begin{pmatrix} 2 \\ 6 \end{pmatrix}$, $v = \begin{pmatrix} -6 \\ -18 \end{pmatrix}$ and $w = \begin{pmatrix} 1 \\ 3 \end{pmatrix}$ are all parallel to each other.

b What else can you say about these three vectors?

Answer 4

a $u = \begin{pmatrix} 2 \\ 6 \end{pmatrix} = 2\begin{pmatrix} 1 \\ 3 \end{pmatrix} = 2w$ $v = \begin{pmatrix} -6 \\ -18 \end{pmatrix} = -6\begin{pmatrix} 1 \\ 3 \end{pmatrix} = -6w$

$\dfrac{1}{2}u = -\dfrac{1}{6}v = w$

Therefore the vectors are all parallel.

b u is twice as long as w.

  v is six times as long as w.

  v is in the opposite direction (sense) to u and w.

  v is three times as long as u.

  $u = 2w$, $v = -6w$, $v = -3u$.

Exercise 22.1

1 Find the lengths of these vectors. Leave your answers in surd (square root) form, simplified where possible.

   a $\begin{pmatrix} 3 \\ 9 \end{pmatrix}$ **b** $\begin{pmatrix} -5 \\ -5 \end{pmatrix}$ **c** $\begin{pmatrix} 6 \\ -4 \end{pmatrix}$ **d** $\begin{pmatrix} -2 \\ 5 \end{pmatrix}$

2 $u = \begin{pmatrix} 7 \\ 1 \end{pmatrix}$, $v = \begin{pmatrix} 3 \\ 9 \end{pmatrix}$, $w = \begin{pmatrix} -2 \\ -5 \end{pmatrix}$

  a Find

    i $u + v + w$ **ii** $2u - 3w$ **iii** $u - v - w$

  b Find

    i $|u + v|$ **ii** $|u - v|$ **iii** $|u - v - w|$

3 $ABCD$ is a parallelogram.

  $\overrightarrow{AB} = u$ and $\overrightarrow{AD} = v$.

  a Find $\overrightarrow{AC}$ in terms of u and v.   **b** Find $\overrightarrow{BD}$ in terms of u and v.

4 $PQRS$ is a kite.

  M is the midpoint of QS.

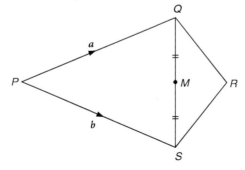

a Why is $\overrightarrow{PR}$ not equal to $a + b$?

b Write $\overrightarrow{QS}$ in terms of a and b.

c Write $\overrightarrow{PM}$ in terms of a and b.

5 *ABCDEF* is a regular hexagon.

M is the centre of the hexagon, and p, q and r are vectors as shown.

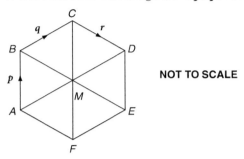

NOT TO SCALE

a Copy the figure and mark all the other representatives of p, q and r. Remember that the figure is a regular hexagon. For example, $\overrightarrow{MC} = p$.

Find, in terms of p and/or q and/or r the following directed line segments, simplifying where necessary.

b **i** $\overrightarrow{BA}$ **ii** $\overrightarrow{BD}$ **iii** $\overrightarrow{AD}$ **iv** $\overrightarrow{FM}$

  v $\overrightarrow{ME} + \overrightarrow{CB}$ **vi** $\overrightarrow{CF} - \overrightarrow{AB}$ **vii** $\overrightarrow{ED} + \overrightarrow{MA} + \overrightarrow{FM}$

Position Vectors

Key term

A position vector, p, is the vector which joins the origin to the point *P*.

The position vectors of points on a plane are the vectors drawn from a common origin to the points. It is convenient to label the position vectors with the same letters as the corresponding points, but with the vectors in lower case, and in **bold** (underline if handwritten).

Figure 22.12 shows the points *A*, *B* and *C* and their position vectors a, b and c.

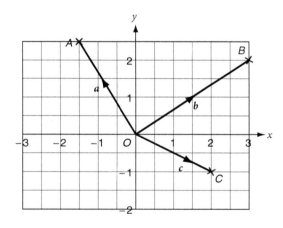

Figure 22.12 Position vectors

These position vectors are on a graph, so the vector for each point is the same as the coordinates of the point, expressed as a column vector in each case.

However, the position vectors do not have to be on a graph, and any point on the diagram can be taken as the origin. It should be labelled *O* to avoid any confusion.

For example, Figure 22.13 shows a parallelogram, *OABC*.

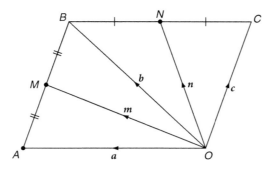

Figure 22.13 $\overrightarrow{OA} = a$, $\overrightarrow{OB} = b$ and $\overrightarrow{OC} = c$

M is the midpoint of *AB*, and *N* is the midpoint of *BC*.

m is the position vector of *M* and *n* is the position vector of *N*.

Vectors provide a powerful tool for proving geometrical facts. For example, using the above diagram we can prove that *MN* is parallel to *AC*, and that $MN = \frac{1}{2} AC$, as you will see in the worked example.

Example 5

Using the diagram of parallelogram *OABC* in Figure 22.13, find the relationship between the lines *AC* and *MN*.

Answer 5

$\overrightarrow{AC} = -a + c = c - a$

$\overrightarrow{MN} = -m + n + n - m$

> **NOTE:**
> Remember that $\overrightarrow{AB} = \overrightarrow{OC}$ and $\overrightarrow{CB} = \overrightarrow{OA}$

$m = a + \frac{1}{2} c,$

$n = c + \frac{1}{2} a$

$\overrightarrow{MN} = c + \frac{1}{2} a - (a + \frac{1}{2} c) = c + \frac{1}{2} a - a - \frac{1}{2} c = \frac{1}{2} c = \frac{1}{2} a = \frac{1}{2} (c - a)$

so $\overrightarrow{MN} = \frac{1}{2} \overrightarrow{AC}$.

Hence *MN* is parallel to *AC* and $MN = \frac{1}{2} AC$.

Exercise 22.2

1 *ABC* is a triangle. The position vectors relative to an origin *O* and the vectors *p*, *q* and *r* are shown on the diagram.

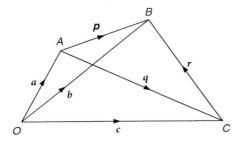

Express in terms of *a*, *b* and/or *c*:

a *p*
b *p* + *q*
c *r* − *q*
d *p* + *r*

2 a and b are the position vectors of A and B as shown on the diagram.
M is the midpoint of the line AB.

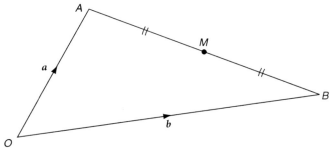

Express, in terms of a and b,

a $\overrightarrow{AB}$ **b** $\overrightarrow{AM}$ **c** $\overrightarrow{OM}$

3 PQ is a straight line.
N divides PQ in the ratio $2:1$.
Draw a diagram, showing P, Q and N, and their position vectors, p, q and n, relative to an origin, O.
Express, in terms of p and q the following directed line segments and vectors:

a $\overrightarrow{PQ}$ **b** $\overrightarrow{PN}$ **c** n **d** $\overrightarrow{NQ}$

4 ABC is a triangle.
The side BC is extended to D, where $BC = CD$, as shown in the diagram.

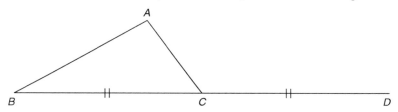

Copy the diagram, draw an origin, O, and show the position vectors of the points A, B, C and D.
Express the following in terms of a, b and c:

a $\overrightarrow{BA}$ **b** $\overrightarrow{BD}$ **c** $\overrightarrow{CD}$ **d** $\overrightarrow{DA}$

5 ABC is a triangle.

$$\overrightarrow{AB} = \begin{pmatrix} 3 \\ 3 \end{pmatrix}, \overrightarrow{BC} = \begin{pmatrix} 4 \\ -4 \end{pmatrix}$$

a Find $\overrightarrow{AC}$.

b Calculate $|\overrightarrow{AB}|, |\overrightarrow{BC}|$ and $|\overrightarrow{AC}|$ as simplified surds.

c Using $|\overrightarrow{AB}|^2, |\overrightarrow{BC}|^2$ and $|\overrightarrow{AC}|^2$ show that angle $ABC = 90°$.

6 Draw x- and y-axes from -5 to $+5$ with 1 centimetre per unit.
Plot the following points
$A(-1, -4)$, $B(0, 5)$ and $C(-4, 5)$.

a Find as column vectors

  i $\overrightarrow{CB}$ **ii** $\overrightarrow{BA}$ **iii** $\overrightarrow{CA}$
  iv $\overrightarrow{BC} - \overrightarrow{CA}$ **v** $\overrightarrow{BC} - \overrightarrow{AC} - \overrightarrow{BA}$

b Calculate

  i $|\overrightarrow{AC}|$ **iii** $|\overrightarrow{BC}|$

  ii $|\overrightarrow{BA}|$

22.4 More about Transformations
Translation

As we know, translations are defined by column vectors. The abbreviation **T** is used to represent a translation.

Example 6

T represents the translation $\begin{pmatrix} 3 \\ -5 \end{pmatrix}$, and A is the point $(1, 4)$, as in the diagram.

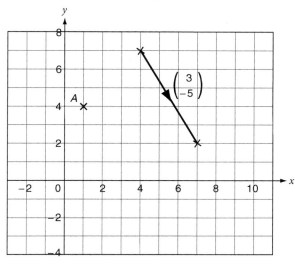

Find the image A' of A under the translation **T**.

Answer 6

You can use the diagram as shown below.

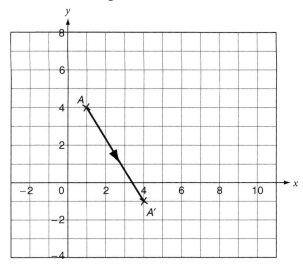

Alternatively, A' can be calculated:

$A' = \mathbf{T}(A) = \begin{pmatrix} 3 \\ -5 \end{pmatrix}(1, 4) = (3 + 1, -5 + 4) = (4, -1)$

Either way, **T** maps $A(1, 4)$ to $A'(4, -1)$, as in the diagram.

It is important that you should understand that the vector notation **T**$(1, 4)$, or $\binom{3}{-5}(1,4)$, does **not** represent matrix multiplication. The $(1, 4)$ represents a pair of coordinates, not a matrix. The translation is calculated by addition, not multiplication. If you are in any doubt draw a diagram.

Exercise 22.3

1 If $\mathbf{T}_1 = \binom{3}{-1}$ and $\mathbf{T}_2 = \binom{-5}{-1}$, find the images of the following points after the translations indicated:

    a $\mathbf{T}_1(-1, 0)$ **b** $\mathbf{T}_2(-1, 0)$ **c** $\mathbf{T}_2(16, 7)$ **d** $\mathbf{T}_1(5, 1)$

2 Find the column vectors associated with the following translations:

    a $A(4, 12)$ maps to $B(3, -8)$
    b $P(-6, 7)$ maps to $Q(-15, 0)$
    c $Y(5, 4)$ maps to $Z(-7, 4)$

> **NOTE:**
> Remember that you can write down each vector by asking yourself, for example, 'How do I get from A to B?'
>
> The answer is 'back $(-)$ 1 and down $(-)$ 20' $\binom{-1}{-20}$.

Enlargement

What happens if the scale factor for an enlargement is negative?

Figure 22.14 shows the enlargement of triangle ABC, scale factor -2 and centre $(1, -1)$. The image of triangle ABC under the enlargement is triangle $A'B'C'$.

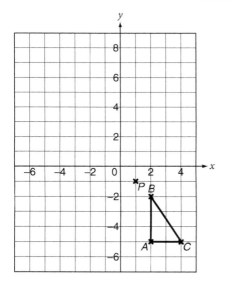 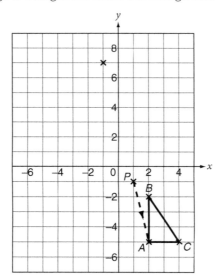 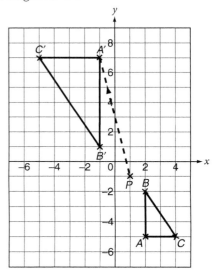

Figure 22.14 The process of enlarging triangle ABC, centre $P(1, -1)$, scale factor -2

It is convenient to plot the points for the enlargement by using vectors.

In Figure 22.14 the point $P(1, -1)$ is the centre of the enlargement. The vector $\overrightarrow{PA}$ is $\binom{1}{-4}$, so

multiplying by the scale factor -2 gives $-2\binom{1}{-4} = \binom{-2}{8}$.

Hence vector $\overrightarrow{PA'} = \binom{-2}{8}$ and A' is the point $(-1, 7)$, and so on.

Rotation

The sense, or direction, of the rotation may be described as *clockwise* or *anticlockwise*, or an alternative notation may be used. Anticlockwise rotations may be taken as positive and clockwise directions as negative. So, for example, a rotation of −90° is 90° clockwise. However, this is slightly risky as a rotation of 90° could be ambiguous: it may not be recognised as a rotation of +90°.

The centre of the rotation can be found with a tracing as described in Chapter 6, or by a geometric method which you can practise in the first question of the next exercise.

Exercise 22.4

1

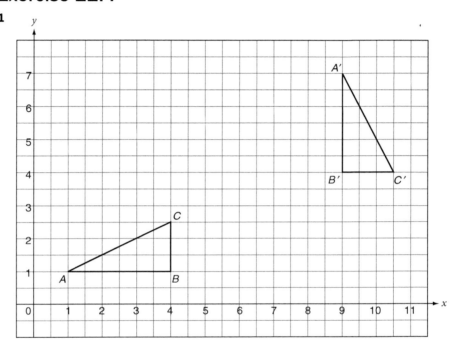

Copy the diagram showing the object, triangle *ABC*, and its image, triangle *A'B'C'* after a single transformation.

a Accurately join a pair of corresponding vertices on the object and image, such as *A* and *A'*.

b Using the method learned in Chapter 6 with straight edge and compasses only construct the perpendicular bisector of the line *AA'*.

c Repeat (a) and (b) for another pair of vertices such as *C* and *C'*.
Mark, and label with the letter *P*, the point where the two bisectors cross.

d With centre *P* and radius *PA* draw an arc from *A* to *A'*.

e With centre *P* and radius *PB* draw an arc from *B* to *B'*.

f What is special about the point *P*, and why?

> **NOTE:**
> Think back to your work on circles in Chapter 6.

g Describe fully the single transformation that maps triangle *ABC* to triangle *A'B'C'*.

2 On 5 millimetre squared paper, or graph paper, draw a rectangle 15 centimetres by 6 centimetres as shown in the diagram. The diagram here is reduced to fit on the page. Mark a point *X* in the centre of the rectangle. Copy triangle *A*.

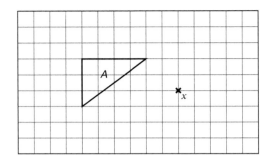

a With centre X and the scale factors below, enlarge triangle A.

   i Scale factor 2. Label the image A_1.

   ii Scale factor $\frac{1}{2}$. Label the image A_2.

   iii Scale factor −2. Label the image A_3.

   iv Scale factor $-\frac{1}{2}$. Label the image A_4.

b Describe the single transformation which would map triangle A_3 onto triangle A_2.

3 **a** $f(x) = \dfrac{6x}{x+2}$

   i Find $f^{-1}(x)$.

   ii Draw a set of axes with $0 \leqslant x \leqslant 6$ and also $0 \leqslant y \leqslant 6$.

   iii Draw accurately the line $y = x$.

   iv Plot the curves $y = f(x)$ (domain $0 \leqslant x \leqslant 6$) and $y = f^{-1}(x)$ (domain $0 \leqslant x \leqslant 4.5$) on the same graph.

   v What single transformation would map $y = f(x)$ onto $y = f^{-1}(x)$?

b Repeat questions (a) (i) to (a) (v) with $f(x) = \frac{2}{3}x + 1$, domain $0 \leqslant x \leqslant 6$, and $f^{-1}(x)$, domain $1 \leqslant x \leqslant 5$.

4 Describe fully the single transformation which maps $A(2, 4)$ to $A'(-1, -2)$ and $B(-4, 2)$ to $B'(2, 1)$.

> **NOTE:**
> Plot the points and join AB and $A'B'$.

22.5 Matrices and Transformations

Figure 22.15 shows the reflection of $A(3, 2)$ and $B(2, 1)$ in the y-axis to $A'(-3, 2)$ and $B'(-2, 1)$.

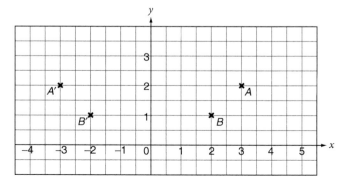

Figure 22.15 Reflection in the y-axis

The points $A(3, 2)$ and $B(2, 1)$ can be represented by entering their *position vectors* $\boldsymbol{a} = \begin{pmatrix} 3 \\ 2 \end{pmatrix}$ and $\boldsymbol{b} = \begin{pmatrix} 2 \\ 1 \end{pmatrix}$ into a matrix: $\begin{pmatrix} 3 & 2 \\ 2 & 1 \end{pmatrix}$.

In the same way, A' and B' can be written $\begin{pmatrix} -3 & -2 \\ 2 & 1 \end{pmatrix}$.

These matrices give us a powerful tool when working with transformation as we will see. Is there a matrix which could perform the reflection of A and B in the y-axis as shown above? We will look at three methods for finding a suitable matrix for this task.

First Method for Finding a Matrix

Look at the following matrix equation:

$$\begin{pmatrix} a & b \\ c & d \end{pmatrix}\begin{pmatrix} 3 & 2 \\ 2 & 1 \end{pmatrix} = \begin{pmatrix} -3 & -2 \\ 2 & 1 \end{pmatrix}$$

and multiply out the left-hand side according to the matrix rules (see Chapter 15).

$$\begin{pmatrix} 3a+2b & 2a+b \\ 3c+2d & 2c+d \end{pmatrix} = \begin{pmatrix} -3 & -2 \\ 2 & 1 \end{pmatrix}$$

$3a + 2b = -3$ ... (i)
$2a + b = 2$ ... (ii)
$3c + 2d = 2$ ... (iii)
$2c + d = 1$ ... (iv)

NOTE:
Compare the elements in the matrices.

Solving (i) and (ii) simultaneously gives $a = -1$ and $b = 0$,

and solving (iii) and (iv) simultaneously gives $c = 0$ and $d = 1$.

So $\begin{pmatrix} a & b \\ c & d \end{pmatrix} = \begin{pmatrix} -1 & 0 \\ 0 & 1 \end{pmatrix}$ which is the matrix which maps A to A' and B to B' under reflection in the y-axis.

In general, $\begin{pmatrix} -1 & 0 \\ 0 & 1 \end{pmatrix}\begin{pmatrix} x \\ y \end{pmatrix} = \begin{pmatrix} -x \\ y \end{pmatrix}$.

Check this yourself.

NOTE:
We have confirmed in Section 20.5 of Chapter 20 that the order of matrix multiplication matters. When the matrix $\begin{pmatrix} -1 & 0 \\ 0 & 1 \end{pmatrix}$ is used to perform a reflection in the y-axis it must *pre*-multiply (that is: be written in front of) the matrix of points, as shown here. This applies to all the matrices we will use for transformations.

Second Method for Finding a Matrix

Another method for finding the required matrix is to use an inverse matrix.

If $\mathbf{A} = \begin{pmatrix} 3 & 2 \\ 2 & 1 \end{pmatrix}$, $\mathbf{A}' = \begin{pmatrix} -3 & -2 \\ 2 & 1 \end{pmatrix}$ and $\mathbf{M}$ is the required matrix,

then $\mathbf{MA} = \mathbf{A}'$,   and multiplying both sides by $\mathbf{A}^{-1}$ gives

$\mathbf{MAA}^{-1} = \mathbf{A}'\mathbf{A}^{-1}$

$\mathbf{AA}^{-1} = \mathbf{I}$,   the identity matrix, so

$\mathbf{M} = \mathbf{A}'\mathbf{A}^{-1}$.

Since $\mathbf{A} = \begin{pmatrix} 3 & 2 \\ 2 & 1 \end{pmatrix}$, $|\mathbf{A}$ or det $\mathbf{A} = -1$, and $\mathbf{A}^{-1} = \begin{pmatrix} -1 & 2 \\ 2 & -3 \end{pmatrix}$.

$\mathbf{A}' = \begin{pmatrix} -3 & -2 \\ 2 & 1 \end{pmatrix}$, so $\mathbf{A}'\mathbf{A}^{-1} = \begin{pmatrix} -3 & -2 \\ 2 & 1 \end{pmatrix}\begin{pmatrix} -1 & 2 \\ 2 & -3 \end{pmatrix} = \begin{pmatrix} -1 & 0 \\ 0 & -1 \end{pmatrix}$, which again gives the matrix representing reflection in the y-axis.

Again, you are advised to work through this to practise the method.

NOTE:
Do not try this with more than two points because you only know how to find the inverse of a two by two matrix.

Third Method for Finding a Matrix

The final, and quickest, method for basic transformations is shown in Figure 22.16.

The first diagram shows two unit vectors, one along the **x**-axis and one along the **y**-axis, which form two sides of a unit square. A unit vector is a vector with a magnitude of 1 unit.

The vector in the **x**-direction is marked with a double arrow, because it is important to be able to distinguish the two vectors after the transformation. The second diagram shows what happens to these two vectors after reflection in the **y**-axis.

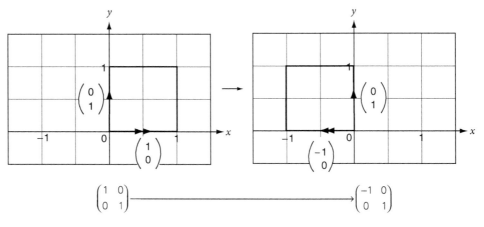

Figure 22.16 Reflection of unit vectors in the y-axis

Underneath each diagram the two vectors are shown in matrix form, with the double-arrowed vector first.

You will see that the first matrix is the unit matrix, and the second matrix represents reflection in the **y**-axis, as proved above.

Hence, for any point (x, y), $\begin{pmatrix} -1 & 0 \\ 0 & 1 \end{pmatrix}\begin{pmatrix} x \\ y \end{pmatrix} = \begin{pmatrix} -x \\ y \end{pmatrix}$.

Example 7

a Derive the matrices for

   i reflection in the line $y = x$,

   ii enlargement, scale factor 3, centre the origin.

b Describe fully the transformation represented by $\begin{pmatrix} -1 & 0 \\ 0 & -1 \end{pmatrix}$.

c **R** = rotation 90° clockwise about the origin.

   i Find the matrix representing **R**.

   ii Find the matrix **R**⁻¹.

   iii Describe fully the transformation represented by **R**⁻¹.

Answer 7

a **i**

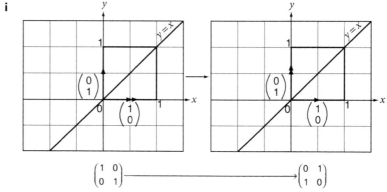

ii

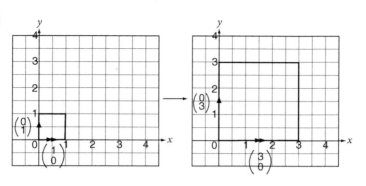

$$\begin{pmatrix} 1 & 0 \\ 0 & 1 \end{pmatrix} \longrightarrow \begin{pmatrix} 3 & 0 \\ 0 & 3 \end{pmatrix}$$

Enlargement, scale factor 3, centre the origin is represented by the matrix $\begin{pmatrix} 3 & 0 \\ 0 & 3 \end{pmatrix}$.

b

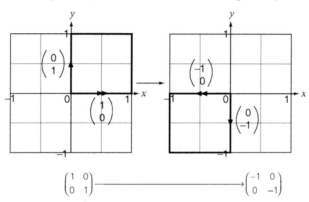

$$\begin{pmatrix} 1 & 0 \\ 0 & 1 \end{pmatrix} \longrightarrow \begin{pmatrix} -1 & 0 \\ 0 & -1 \end{pmatrix}$$

The transformation $\begin{pmatrix} -1 & 0 \\ 0 & -1 \end{pmatrix}$ is rotation about the origin 180°.

c i

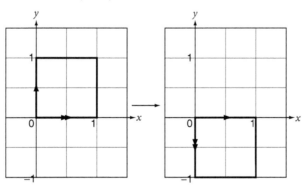

$$\begin{pmatrix} 1 & 0 \\ 0 & 1 \end{pmatrix} \longrightarrow \begin{pmatrix} 0 & 1 \\ -1 & 0 \end{pmatrix}$$

$$\mathbf{R} = \begin{pmatrix} 0 & 1 \\ -1 & 0 \end{pmatrix}$$

ii $\mathbf{R}^{-1} = \dfrac{1}{0-1}\begin{pmatrix} 0 & -1 \\ 1 & 0 \end{pmatrix} = \begin{pmatrix} 0 & -1 \\ 1 & 0 \end{pmatrix}$

$\mathbf{R}^{-1} = \begin{pmatrix} 0 & -1 \\ 1 & 0 \end{pmatrix}$

iii $\mathbf{R}^{-1}$ is rotation about the origin, 90° anticlockwise.

Example 8

a Find the coordinates of the image of the triangle ABC where A is the point $(-1, -2)$, B is

$(3, 5)$ and C is $(4, -1)$ under the transformation represented by the matrix $\begin{pmatrix} 0 & 1 \\ -1 & 0 \end{pmatrix}$.

b Describe the transformation represented by this matrix.

Answer 8

a $\begin{pmatrix} 0 & 1 \\ -1 & 0 \end{pmatrix}\begin{pmatrix} -1 & 3 & 4 \\ -2 & 5 & -1 \end{pmatrix} = \begin{pmatrix} -2 & 5 & -1 \\ 1 & -3 & -4 \end{pmatrix}$

b Clockwise rotation of $90°$ about the origin.

Exercise 22.5

1 Derive matrices for the following transformations:
   a reflection in the line $y = -x$
   b enlargement, scale factor -2, centre the origin.

2 A transformation maps triangle A to triangle $\boldsymbol{A'}$, as shown in the diagram.
   a Find the matrix associated with this transformation.
   b Describe the transformation fully.

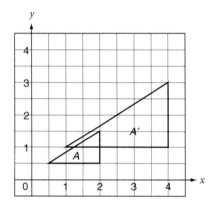

3 A transformation maps $A(2, 2)$ and $B(5, 3)$ to $\boldsymbol{A'}(-2, -2)$ and $B'(-3, -5)$.
   a Find the matrix associated with this transformation.
   b Describe the transformation fully.
   c Use the matrix to find the image of $C(-1, 6)$ and $D(0, -4)$ under the transformation.

4 Find the vectors which produce the following translations:
   a $(0, 2)$ to $(2, 0)$
   b $(1, 5)$ to $(-1, 5)$
   c $(-7, -3)$ to $(-4, -6)$.

5 Find triangle $A'B'C'$ after reflection of triangle ABC in the y-axis, where $A = (-1, -3)$, $B = (5, 7)$ and $C = (0, 1)$.

Notation

The following abbreviations are commonly used in transformation work.

- **M** Reflection
- **R** Rotation
- **E** Enlargement
- **T** Translation

> **NOTE:**
> For Reflection think of <u>M</u>irror

Any capital letter *may* be used as long as the transformation is defined in some way.

Successive Transformations

You may be asked to do more than one transformation on an object, for example reflection in the *x*-axis followed by a rotation of 90° clockwise about the origin. Under these transformations triangle *A* maps to triangle A_1, and this then maps to triangle A_2, as shown in Figure 22.17.

If $\mathbf{M}_x$ represents reflection in the *x*-axis, then $\mathbf{M}_x(A) = A_1$.

If $\mathbf{R}_{-90}$ represents rotation 90° clockwise about the origin, then $\mathbf{R}_{-90}(A_1) = A_2$.

The combined transformation of reflection ($\mathbf{M}_x$) first then rotation ($\mathbf{R}_{-90}$) on triangle *A* to give triangle A_2 is written $\mathbf{R}_{-90}\mathbf{M}_x(A) = A_2$.

The order in which this is written is important, as performing successive transformations in a different order will not necessarily give the same result.

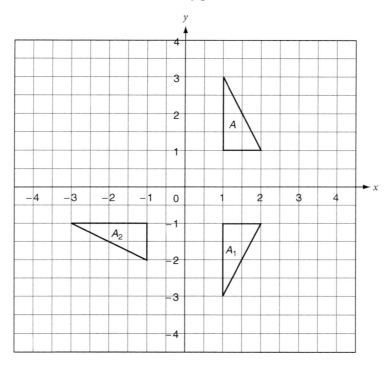

Figure 22.17 Successive transformations

It might help to read $\mathbf{R}_{-90}\mathbf{M}_x(A)$ as rotation ($\mathbf{R}_{-90}$) *after* reflection ($\mathbf{M}_x$).

Looking at Figure 22.17, is there a single transformation that would map *A* directly to A_2?

You should see that reflection in the line $y = -x$ would map *A* to A_2.

So sometimes there is a single transformation which will perform the same operation as a succession of two or more transformations.

We can check this result with the matrices for the two transformations.

$$\mathbf{M}_x = \begin{pmatrix} 1 & 0 \\ 0 & -1 \end{pmatrix} \text{ and } \mathbf{R}_{-90} = \begin{pmatrix} 0 & 1 \\ -1 & 0 \end{pmatrix}.$$

M first and then **R** would be performed by the following matrix multiplication:

$$\mathbf{R}_{-90}\mathbf{M}_x = \begin{pmatrix} 0 & 1 \\ -1 & 0 \end{pmatrix}\begin{pmatrix} 1 & 0 \\ 0 & -1 \end{pmatrix} = \begin{pmatrix} 0 & -1 \\ -1 & 0 \end{pmatrix}$$

The matrix for reflection in the line $y=-x$ is $\begin{pmatrix} 0 & -1 \\ -1 & 0 \end{pmatrix}$, so we have proved the result. Use the above methods to check the result for the transformations in the opposite order, that is, for $\mathbf{R}_{-90}$ followed by $\mathbf{M}_x$.

You should find that the combined transformation is the same as reflection in the line $y=x$, not $y=-x$ as before.

This is further proof that the order of transformations can make a difference to the outcome.

Example 9

a $\mathbf{M}_y$ = reflection in the y-axis, $\mathbf{R}_{180}$ = rotation of 180° about the origin and
$\mathbf{M}_{x=1}$ = reflection in the line $x=1$.
Find, either by drawing a sketch or by matrix multiplication where possible, single transformations to represent the following:
  i $\mathbf{R}_{180}\mathbf{M}_y$ **ii** $\mathbf{M}_y\mathbf{M}_{x=1}$

b   **i**   Find by matrix multiplication $\mathbf{M}_y^2$, where $\mathbf{M}_y$ = reflection in the y-axis as above.
  ii   Explain this result.
  iii   Hence write down $\mathbf{M}_y^{-1}$, the inverse of $\mathbf{M}_y$.

c $\mathbf{T}_1 = \begin{pmatrix} 1 \\ 3 \end{pmatrix}$, $\mathbf{T}_2 = \begin{pmatrix} -4 \\ -3 \end{pmatrix}$ and $\mathbf{T}_3 = \begin{pmatrix} 6 \\ 0 \end{pmatrix}$.

Find, by vector addition, single transformations to represent the following:
  i $\mathbf{T}_1\mathbf{T}_3$ **ii** $\mathbf{T}_3\mathbf{T}_1$ **iii** $\mathbf{T}_1\mathbf{T}_2\mathbf{T}_3$

d $\mathbf{M}_1$ = reflection in $x=y$, $\mathbf{M}_2$ = reflection in the x-axis, $\mathbf{R}$ = rotation 90° clockwise. A is the point (1, 4). Find
  i $\mathbf{M}_1\mathbf{M}_2(A)$ **ii** $\mathbf{M}_2\mathbf{M}_1(A)$ **iii** $\mathbf{M}_1\mathbf{R}(A)$ **iv** $\mathbf{R}\mathbf{M}_1(A)$.

Answer 9

a   **i** $\mathbf{R}_{180} = \begin{pmatrix} -1 & 0 \\ 0 & -1 \end{pmatrix}$ $\mathbf{M}_y = \begin{pmatrix} -1 & 0 \\ 0 & 1 \end{pmatrix}$

$\mathbf{R}_{180}\mathbf{M}_y = \begin{pmatrix} -1 & 0 \\ 0 & -1 \end{pmatrix}\begin{pmatrix} -1 & 0 \\ 0 & 1 \end{pmatrix} = \begin{pmatrix} 1 & 0 \\ 0 & -1 \end{pmatrix}$

$\mathbf{R}_{180}\mathbf{M}_y$ = reflection in the x-axis.

  ii

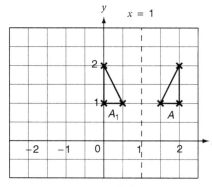
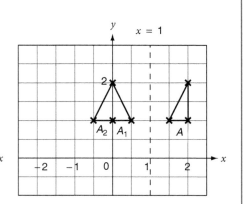

$\mathbf{M}_y\mathbf{M}_{x=1}$ = translation $\begin{pmatrix} -2 \\ 0 \end{pmatrix}$

b   **i** $\mathbf{M}_y \begin{pmatrix} -1 & 0 \\ 0 & 1 \end{pmatrix}$ $\mathbf{M}_y^2 = \begin{pmatrix} -1 & 0 \\ 0 & 1 \end{pmatrix}\begin{pmatrix} -1 & 0 \\ 0 & 1 \end{pmatrix} = \begin{pmatrix} -1 & 0 \\ 0 & 1 \end{pmatrix} = \mathbf{I}$

  ii $\mathbf{M}_y^2$ maps the object to the image and then back to the object.

  iii $\mathbf{M}_y^{-1} = \begin{pmatrix} -1 & 0 \\ 0 & 1 \end{pmatrix}$

c **i** $T_1T_2 = \begin{pmatrix} 7 \\ 3 \end{pmatrix}$ **ii** $T_3T_1 = \begin{pmatrix} 7 \\ 3 \end{pmatrix}$ **iii** $T_1T_2T_3 = \begin{pmatrix} 3 \\ 0 \end{pmatrix}$

d $M_1 = \begin{pmatrix} 0 & 1 \\ 1 & 0 \end{pmatrix}$ $M_2 = \begin{pmatrix} 1 & 0 \\ 0 & -1 \end{pmatrix}$ $R = \begin{pmatrix} 0 & 1 \\ -1 & 0 \end{pmatrix}$

i $M_1M_2(A) = \begin{pmatrix} 0 & 1 \\ 1 & 0 \end{pmatrix}\begin{pmatrix} 1 & 0 \\ 0 & -1 \end{pmatrix}\begin{pmatrix} 1 \\ 4 \end{pmatrix} = \begin{pmatrix} 0 & -1 \\ 1 & 0 \end{pmatrix}\begin{pmatrix} 1 \\ 4 \end{pmatrix} = \begin{pmatrix} -4 \\ 1 \end{pmatrix}$

$M_1M_2(A) = (-4, 1)$

Alternative method:

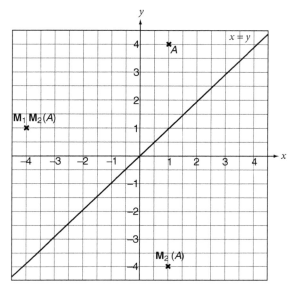

ii $M_2M_1(A) = \begin{pmatrix} 1 & 0 \\ 0 & -1 \end{pmatrix}\begin{pmatrix} 0 & 1 \\ 1 & 0 \end{pmatrix}\begin{pmatrix} 1 \\ 4 \end{pmatrix} = \begin{pmatrix} 0 & 1 \\ -1 & 0 \end{pmatrix}\begin{pmatrix} 1 \\ 4 \end{pmatrix} = \begin{pmatrix} 4 \\ -1 \end{pmatrix}$

$M_2M_1(A) = (4, -1)$

iii $M_1R(A) = \begin{pmatrix} 0 & 1 \\ 1 & 0 \end{pmatrix}\begin{pmatrix} 0 & 1 \\ -1 & 0 \end{pmatrix}\begin{pmatrix} 1 \\ 4 \end{pmatrix} = \begin{pmatrix} -1 & 0 \\ 0 & 1 \end{pmatrix}\begin{pmatrix} 1 \\ 4 \end{pmatrix} = \begin{pmatrix} -1 \\ 4 \end{pmatrix}$

$M_1R(A) = (-1, 4)$

iv $RM_1(A) = \begin{pmatrix} 0 & 1 \\ -1 & 0 \end{pmatrix}\begin{pmatrix} 0 & 1 \\ 1 & 0 \end{pmatrix}\begin{pmatrix} 1 \\ 4 \end{pmatrix} = \begin{pmatrix} 1 & 0 \\ 0 & -1 \end{pmatrix}\begin{pmatrix} 1 \\ 4 \end{pmatrix} = \begin{pmatrix} 1 \\ -4 \end{pmatrix}$

$RM_1(A) = (1, -4)$

Exercise 22.6

In this exercise the 'unit square' refers to the square with coordinates (0, 0), (1, 0), (1, 1) and (0, 1).

1 The transformation of the unit square shown in the diagrams consists of two separate transformations, a reflection and an enlargement.

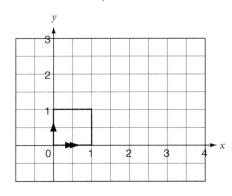 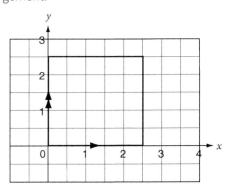

i   Describe both transformations fully.

ii Write down the matrices representing the reflection, the enlargement and the combined transformation shown in the diagram.

iii Does the order in which the two transformations are carried out make any difference to the outcome?
    Explain how you know this, either by diagrams or by matrix multiplication.

2   a   A transformation **X** maps (1, 3) to (5, 11) and (2, 1) to (5, 7).
        Find the matrix of this transformation.

    b   Draw the image, **A'**, of the unit square, A, under the transformation **X**.

    c   This image, A', is reflected in the x-axis to give A".
        Find the matrix which will transform A directly onto A".

3   a   A is the point (1, 2), B is (1, 4) and C is (2, 2). Draw triangle ABC.

    b   Draw triangle $A_2B_2C_2$, which is the image of triangle ABC after a reflection in the x-axis followed by a rotation of 90° clockwise about the origin.

    c   What single transformation will map $A_2B_2C_2$ back to ABC?

4   List the matrices representing the following transformations. Use the unit square to find the matrices where necessary.

    a   Identity, **I**

    b   Rotation 90° clockwise about O, $\mathbf{R}_1$

    c   Rotation 180° about O, $\mathbf{R}_2$

    d   Reflection in x-axis, $\mathbf{M}_1$

    e   Reflection in y-axis, $\mathbf{M}_2$

    f   Reflection in x = y, $\mathbf{M}_3$

    g   Reflection in y = −x, $\mathbf{M}_4$

5   Using $\mathbf{R}_1$ = rotation 90° clockwise about O as in question 4, find $\mathbf{R}_1^{-1}$ (the inverse of $\mathbf{R}_1$).
    What does $\mathbf{R}_1^{-1}$ represent?

6   Using the notation in questions 4 and 5 copy and complete this table showing the effects of two successive transformations.

		Second transformation					
		$\mathbf{R}_1$	$\mathbf{R}_2$	$\mathbf{M}_1$	$\mathbf{M}_2$	$\mathbf{M}_3$	$\mathbf{M}_4$
First transformation	$\mathbf{R}_1$	$\mathbf{R}_2$	$\mathbf{R}_1^{-1}$				
	$\mathbf{R}_2$		**I**				
	$\mathbf{M}_1$			**I**			
	$\mathbf{M}_2$						
	$\mathbf{M}_3$						
	$\mathbf{M}_4$						

Exercise 22.7
Mixed exercise

1   Solve this vector equation for x and y.

$$\frac{1}{2}\begin{pmatrix} x \\ y \end{pmatrix} + \begin{pmatrix} -1 \\ 3 \end{pmatrix} = \begin{pmatrix} -1 \\ 7 \end{pmatrix}$$

2 Draw a triangle *OAB* where *A* is (7, 2) and *B* is (2, 5).

    a Draw triangle *OA'B'*, under an enlargement, centre the origin and scale factor 1.5.

    b What can you say about triangles *OAB* and *OA'B'*?

    c If the area of triangle *OAB* is 32 square units, calculate the area of the trapezium *ABB'A'*.

3 Copy the diagram.

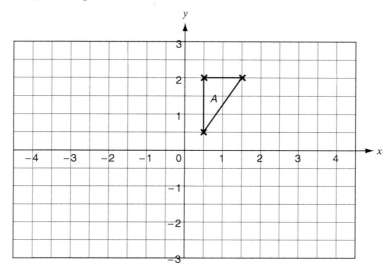

    a Draw the image of triangle *A* after reflection in the line $y = x - 1$. Label the image *B*.

    b Draw the image of triangle *A* after reflection in the line $x = -1$. Label the image *C*.

    c Describe fully the single transformation which will map *B* onto *C*.

4

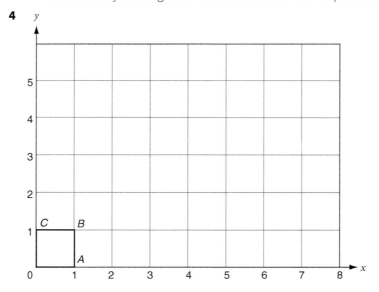

Copy the diagram.

    a *OABC* is a unit square. By carrying out the matrix multiplication below find the image *OA'B'C'* of *OABC* under the transformation given by the matrix

    $\mathbf{M} = \begin{pmatrix} 5 & 2 \\ 1 & 4 \end{pmatrix}$.

     O A B C O A' B' C'

    $\begin{pmatrix} 5 & 2 \\ 1 & 4 \end{pmatrix}\begin{pmatrix} 0 & 1 & 1 & 0 \\ 0 & 0 & 1 & 1 \end{pmatrix} = \begin{pmatrix} \dots & \dots & \dots & \dots \\ \dots & \dots & \dots & \dots \end{pmatrix}$

    b **i** Draw *OA'B'C'* on your copy of the diagram.

        ii What is the shape of *OA'B'C'*?

    c By drawing a rectangle round *OA'B'C'*, and removing triangles, or otherwise, calculate the area of *OA'B'C'*.

    d **i** Find the determinant of **M**.

        ii What do you notice about your answers to (c) and (d) (i)?

Exam-style questions

5 **a** The diagrams show triangles *A*, *B*, *C* and *D*.

    i The single transformation **P** maps Δ*A* onto Δ*B*. Describe, fully, the transformation **P**.

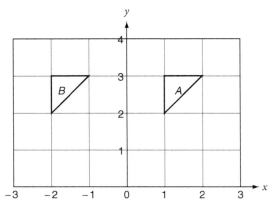

    ii The single transformation **Q** maps Δ*A* onto Δ*C*. Describe, fully, the transformation **Q**.

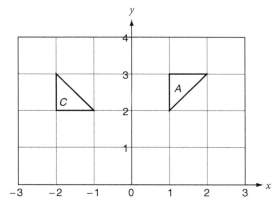

    iii The reflection **R** maps Δ*A* onto Δ*D*. Find the matrix that represents the reflection **R**.

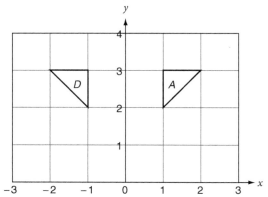

b The diagram shows the points $E(1, 3)$, $F(2, 3)$ and $G(-1, 3)$. An enlargement, centre E, maps F onto G.

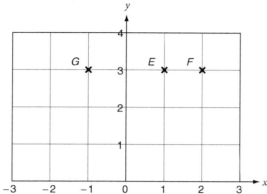

Write down
i the scale factor,
ii the coordinates of the image of $(0, 4)$.

c $M = \begin{pmatrix} -1 & 3 \\ -2 & 4 \end{pmatrix}$

i Find the determinant of **M**.
ii Write down the inverse of **M**.
iii Find the matrix **X**, where $MX = \begin{pmatrix} 4 \\ -2 \end{pmatrix}$.

(4024 paper 02 Q11 June 2007)

6

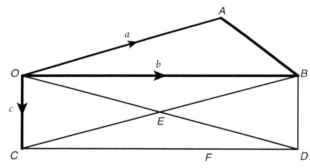

E, F, G and H are the midpoints of AB, BC, CD and DA respectively.

$\overrightarrow{AB} = \mathbf{p}$, $\overrightarrow{AD} = \mathbf{q}$ and $\overrightarrow{BC} = \mathbf{r}$.

i Find, in terms of **p**, **q** and **r** as appropriate
  a $\overrightarrow{EF}$,
  b $\overrightarrow{DC}$,
  c $\overrightarrow{HG}$, expressing the vector as simply as possible.
ii What conclusions can be drawn about the lines EF and HG?

(4024 paper 021 Q11a November 2012)

7 $OABC$ is a parallelogram. $\overrightarrow{OA} = \mathbf{a}$ and $\overrightarrow{OC} = \mathbf{c}$.
M is the midpoint of OB.
Find $\overrightarrow{MA}$ in terms of $\mathbf{a}$ and $\mathbf{c}$.

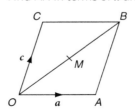

(0580 paper 02 Q8 November 2005)

8 *OAB* is a triangle and *ODBC* is a rectangle where *OD* and *BC* intersect at *E*.
F is the point on *CD* such that $CF = \frac{3}{4} CD$.
$\overrightarrow{OA} = \mathbf{a}$, $\overrightarrow{OB} = \mathbf{b}$ and $\overrightarrow{OC} = \mathbf{c}$.

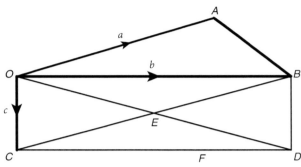

a Express, as simply as possible, in terms of one or more of the vectors **a**, **b** and **c**,
i $\overrightarrow{AB}$, **ii** $\overrightarrow{OE}$, **iii** $\overrightarrow{EF}$.

b *G* is the point on *AB* such that $\overrightarrow{OG} \frac{3}{5}\mathbf{a} + \frac{2}{5}\mathbf{b}$.
i Express $\overrightarrow{AG}$ in terms of **a** and **b**.
Give your answer as simply as possible.
ii Find *AG* : *GB*.
iii Express $\overrightarrow{FG}$ in terms of **a**, **b** and **c**.
Give your answer as simply as possible. *(4024 paper 22 Q7 June 2012)*

9 Transformation **T** is translation by the vector $\begin{pmatrix} 3 \\ 2 \end{pmatrix}$.

Transformation **M** is reflection in the line $y = x$.
a The point *A* has coordinates (2, 1).
Find the coordinates of
i **T**(*A*),
ii **MT**(*A*).

b Find the 2 by 2 matrix **M**, which represents the transformation **M**.
c Show that, for any value of *k*, the point $Q(k - 2, k - 3)$ maps onto a point on the line $y = x$ following the transformation **TM**(*Q*).
d Find **M**⁻¹, the inverse of the matrix **M**.
e **N** is the matrix such that $\mathbf{N} + \begin{pmatrix} 0 & 3 \\ 1 & 0 \end{pmatrix} = \begin{pmatrix} 0 & 4 \\ 0 & 0 \end{pmatrix}$.

i Write down the matrix **N**.
ii Describe completely the single transformation represented by **N**.
(0580 paper 04 Q7 June 2006)

10 a

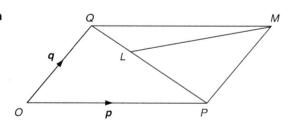

NOT TO SCALE

OPMQ is a parallelogram and *O* is the origin.
$\overrightarrow{OP} = \mathbf{p}$ and $\overrightarrow{OQ} = \mathbf{q}$.
L is on *PQ* so that $PL : LQ = 2 : 1$.
Find the following vectors in terms of **p** and **q**. Write your answers in their simplest form.
i $\overrightarrow{PQ}$ **ii** $\overrightarrow{PL}$ **iii** $\overrightarrow{ML}$
iv the position vector of *L*.

b R is the point $(1, 2)$. It is translated onto the point S by the vector $\begin{pmatrix} 3 \\ -4 \end{pmatrix}$.

   i Write down the coordinates of S.

   ii Write down the vector which translates S onto R.

c The matrix $\begin{pmatrix} 0 & 1 \\ -1 & 0 \end{pmatrix}$ represents a **single** transformation.

   i Describe fully this transformation.

   ii Find the coordinates of the image of the point $(5, 3)$ after this transformation.

d Find the matrix which represents a reflection in the line $y = x$.

(0580 paper 04 Q6 November 2006)

11

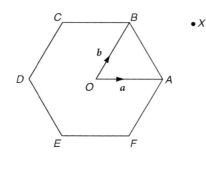

A regular hexagon, $ABCDEF$, has centre O.

$\overrightarrow{OA} = \boldsymbol{a}$ and $\overrightarrow{OB} = \boldsymbol{b}$.

a Express, as simply as possible, in terms of $\boldsymbol{a}$ and/or $\boldsymbol{b}$:

   i $\overrightarrow{DO}$ **ii** $\overrightarrow{AB}$ **iii** $\overrightarrow{DB}$.

b Explain why $|\boldsymbol{a}| = |\boldsymbol{b}| = |\boldsymbol{b} - \boldsymbol{a}|$.

c The points X, Y and Z are such that

   $\overrightarrow{OX} = \boldsymbol{a} + \boldsymbol{b}$, $\overrightarrow{OY} = \boldsymbol{a} - 2\boldsymbol{b}$ and $\overrightarrow{OZ} = \boldsymbol{b} - 2\boldsymbol{a}$.

   i Express, as simply as possible, in terms of $\boldsymbol{a}$ and/or $\boldsymbol{b}$,

      a $\overrightarrow{AX}$ **b** $\overrightarrow{YX}$.

   ii What can be deduced about Y, A and X?

d Express, as simply as possible, in terms of $\boldsymbol{a}$ and/or $\boldsymbol{b}$, the vector $\overrightarrow{XZ}$.

e Show that triangle XYZ is equilateral.

f Calculate $\dfrac{\text{Area of triangle } OAB}{\text{Area of triangle } XYZ}$.

(4024 paper 02 Q11 November 2005)

12 The diagram below shows the point P and triangles A, B and C.

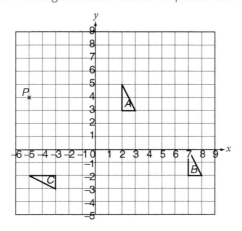

a The translation **T** maps $\triangle A$ onto $\triangle B$.

   Given that $\mathbf{T}(P) = Q$, write down the coordinates of Q.

b Describe fully the single transformation which maps Δ*A* onto Δ*C*.

c Δ*A* is mapped onto Δ*E* by a rotation of 90° clockwise about the point (4, 2).
Draw and label Δ*E* on the diagram above.

(4024 paper 01 Q25a, b and d November 2004)

13 $\mathbf{p} = \begin{pmatrix} 1 \\ -3 \end{pmatrix}$ $\mathbf{q} = \begin{pmatrix} -2 \\ 0 \end{pmatrix}$

   i   Find |**p**|.

   ii   On a copy of the unit grid below, draw and label the vector **p − q**.

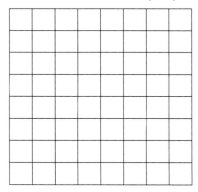

   iii   The vector **r** is shown on the unit grid below.

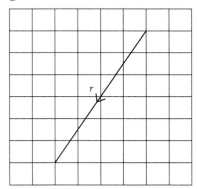

It is given that $\mathbf{r} = a\mathbf{p} + b\mathbf{q}$.
Find the values of *a* and *b*.

(4024 paper 21 Q10a June 2014)

14 *ABCD* is a parallelogram.

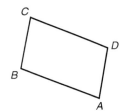

$\overrightarrow{AB} = \begin{pmatrix} -4 \\ 2 \end{pmatrix}$ and $\overrightarrow{BC} = \begin{pmatrix} 1 \\ 4 \end{pmatrix}$.

   i   Find $\overrightarrow{BD}$.

   ii   Calculate $|\overrightarrow{AC}|$.

   iii   The parallelogram *ABCD* is mapped onto the parallelogram *PBQR*.
$PB = \begin{pmatrix} -12 \\ 6 \end{pmatrix}$ and $BQ = \begin{pmatrix} 3 \\ 12 \end{pmatrix}$.

   a   Describe fully the single transformation that maps the parallelogram *ABCD* onto the parallelogram *PBQR*.

   b   *S* is the midpoint of *PQ*.
Find $\overrightarrow{SR}$.

(4024 paper 22 Q9a June 2013)

15

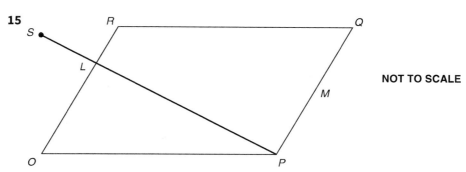

OPQR is a parallelogram.

O is the origin.

$\overrightarrow{OP} = \boldsymbol{p}$ and $\overrightarrow{OR} = \boldsymbol{r}$.

M is the midpoint of *PQ* and *L* is on *OR* such that $OL : LR = 2 : 1$.

The line *PL* is extended to the point *S*.

a Find, in terms of $\boldsymbol{p}$ and $\boldsymbol{r}$, in their simplest forms,

    i $\overrightarrow{OQ}$ **ii** $\overrightarrow{PR}$

    iii $\overrightarrow{PL}$ **iv** the position vector of *M*.

b *PLS* is a straight line and $PS = \frac{3}{2}PL$.

    Find, in terms of $\boldsymbol{p}$ and/or $\boldsymbol{r}$, in their simplest forms,

    i $\overrightarrow{PS}$ **ii** $\overrightarrow{QS}$.

c What can you say about the points *Q*, *R* and *S*?   (0580 paper 04 Q9 June 2008)

16

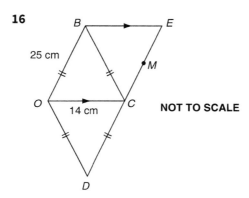

OBCD is a rhombus with sides of 25 cm. The length of the diagonal *OC* is 14 cm.

a Show, **by calculation**, that the length of the diagonal *BD* is 48 cm.

b Calculate, correct to the nearest degree,

    i angle *BCD*,   **ii** angle *OBC*.

c $\overrightarrow{DB} = 2\boldsymbol{p}$ and $\overrightarrow{OC} = 2\boldsymbol{q}$.

    Find, in terms of $\boldsymbol{p}$ and $\boldsymbol{q}$,

    i $\overrightarrow{OB}$ **ii** $\overrightarrow{OD}$.

d *BE* is parallel to *OC* and *DCE* is a straight line.

    Find, in its simplest form, $\overrightarrow{OE}$ in terms of $\boldsymbol{p}$ and $\boldsymbol{q}$.

e *M* is the midpoint of *CE*.

    Find, in its simplest form, $\overrightarrow{OM}$ in terms of $\boldsymbol{p}$ and $\boldsymbol{q}$.

f *O* is the origin of a coordinate grid, *OC* lies along the *x*-axis and $\boldsymbol{q} = \begin{pmatrix} 7 \\ 0 \end{pmatrix}$.

    ($\overrightarrow{DE}$ is vertical and $|\overrightarrow{DB}| = 48$.)

    Write down as column vectors

    i $\boldsymbol{p}$,   **ii** $\overrightarrow{BC}$.

g Write down the value of $|\overrightarrow{DE}|$.   (0580 paper 04 Q5 June 2007)

17

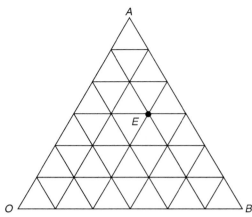

O is the origin, $\overrightarrow{OA} = \boldsymbol{a}$ and $\overrightarrow{OB} = \boldsymbol{b}$.

a C has position vector $\frac{1}{3}\boldsymbol{a} + \frac{2}{3}\boldsymbol{b}$.
Mark the point C on the diagram.

b Write down, in terms of $\boldsymbol{a}$ and $\boldsymbol{b}$, the position vector of the point E.

c Find, in terms of $\boldsymbol{a}$ and $\boldsymbol{b}$, the vector $\overrightarrow{EB}$. (0580 paper 02 Q15 November 2007)

18 a

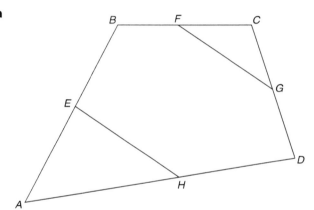

i $\overrightarrow{AD} = \begin{pmatrix} 6 \\ 1 \end{pmatrix}$

Calculate $|\overrightarrow{AD}|$.

ii $\overrightarrow{AD} = \begin{pmatrix} 1 \\ 2 \end{pmatrix}$

H is the midpoint of AD.
Find $\overrightarrow{EH}$.

iii $\overrightarrow{BF} = \begin{pmatrix} 1.5 \\ 0 \end{pmatrix}$ $\overrightarrow{CG} = \begin{pmatrix} 0.5 \\ -1.5 \end{pmatrix}$

F is the midpoint of BC.
Find $\overrightarrow{FG}$.

iv Use your answers to parts (ii) and (iii) to complete the following statement.
The lines EH and FG are .... and ....

v Given that E is the midpoint of AB, show that G is the midpoint of CD.

b

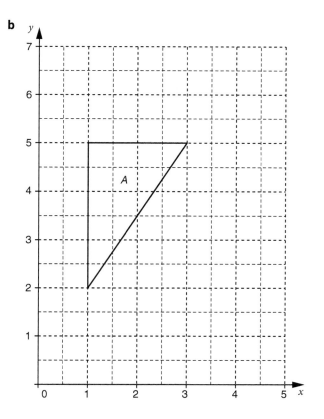

Triangle *A* has vertices (1, 2), (1, 5) and (3, 5).

i   An enlargement, centre (1, 2), scale factor −1.5, maps triangle *A* onto triangle *B*.
Draw triangle *B*.

ii An enlargement, centre (1, 2), scale factor −0.5, maps triangle *A* onto triangle *C*.
Draw triangle *C*.

iii Find the ratio   area of triangle *C* : area of triangle *B*.

(4024 paper 22 Q12 November 2013)

19

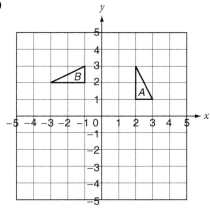

a   A transformation is represented by the matrix $\begin{pmatrix} 0 & -1 \\ -1 & 0 \end{pmatrix}$.

i   On a copy of the grid above, draw the image of triangle *A* after this transformation.

ii Describe fully this transformation.

b   Find the 2 by 2 matrix representing the transformation which maps triangle *A* onto
triangle *B*.

(0580 paper 21 Q19 June 2008)

20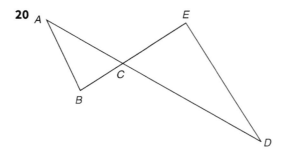

In the diagram, *ACD* and *BCE* are straight lines.

$$\frac{CB}{CE} = \frac{CA}{CD} = \frac{1}{2}.$$

a Describe fully the single transformation that maps Δ*CAB* onto Δ*CDE*.

b It is given that $\overrightarrow{EF} = \begin{pmatrix} 6 \\ -8 \end{pmatrix}$ and $\overrightarrow{BE} = \begin{pmatrix} 3 \\ 1 \end{pmatrix}$.

Calculate $\overrightarrow{AE}$.   (4024 paper 01 Q21 June 2005)

21

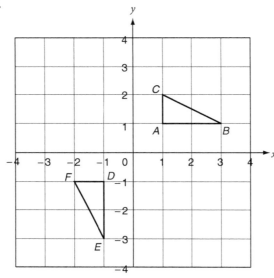

Triangle *ABC* has vertices *A*(1, 1), *B*(3, 1) and *C*(1, 2).
Triangle *DEF* has vertices *D*(−1, −1), *E*(−1, −3) and *F*(−2, −1).
The matrix **P** represents the **single** transformation, **T**, that maps triangle *ABC* onto triangle *DEF*.

a **i** Describe **T fully**.   **ii** Write down the matrix **P**.

b Another transformation is represented by the matrix **Q**, where $Q = \begin{pmatrix} 0 & -1 \\ 1 & 0 \end{pmatrix}$.

  i This transformation maps *B* onto *Y*.
   Find the coordinates of *Y*.

  ii This transformation maps *K* onto *C*.
   Find the coordinates of *K*.

  iii Describe, **fully**, the **single** transformation which is represented by **Q**.

  iv The matrix R is given by **Q = RP**.
   By considering the effects of transformations on triangle *ABC*, or otherwise, find **R**.

c The point *H* lies on *DC* produced, where $\overrightarrow{DH} = \begin{pmatrix} 18 \\ h \end{pmatrix}$.

  Calculate

  i the ratio DC : DH,

  ii the value of *h*.   (4024 paper 02 Q11 June 2005)

22 a *P* is the point (2, 9) and *Q* is the point (4, 6).

Find

   i   the length of PQ,   **ii**   the equation of the line PQ.

b

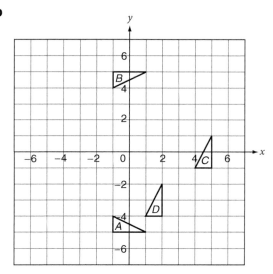

The diagram shows triangles *A*, *B*, *C* and *D*.

   i   Find the matrix representing the transformation that maps triangle *A* onto triangle *B*.

   ii   Describe fully the **single** transformation that maps triangle *B* onto triangle *C*.

   iii   Triangle *C* is mapped onto triangle *D* by the translation **T**.

  a Write down the column vector that represents **T**.

  b The transformation **R** that maps triangle *A* onto triangle *C* is represented by the matrix $\begin{pmatrix} 0 & -1 \\ 1 & 0 \end{pmatrix}$.

Show that the transformation **R** followed by **T** maps (h, k) onto $(-k - 3, h - 3)$.

  c Find the value of h and the value of k for which the transformation **R** followed by **T** maps (h, k) onto itself.

  d The single transformation that is equivalent to **R** followed by **T** is a rotation.

Write down the coordinates of the centre of this rotation.

(4024 paper 02 Q11 November 2007)

23 a The diagram shows triangles *A*, *B*, *C* and *D*.

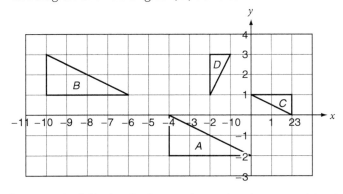

   i   Describe fully the **single** transformation that maps Δ*A* onto Δ*B*.

   ii   Describe fully the **single** transformation that maps Δ*B* onto Δ*C*.

   iii   Describe fully the **single** transformation that maps Δ*C* onto Δ*D*.

   iv   Write down the matrix that represents the transformation which maps Δ*C* onto Δ*A*.

b In the diagram,
$OT = 3OP$, $RS = \frac{1}{6}RT$ and Q is the midpoint of PR.
$\overrightarrow{OP} = \mathbf{p}$ and $\overrightarrow{PQ} = \mathbf{q}$.

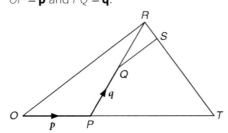

i Express, as simply as possible, in terms of **p** and **q**,

   a $\overrightarrow{OR}$,   **b** $\overrightarrow{RT}$,   **c** $\overrightarrow{QS}$.

ii Write down the value of $\frac{QS}{OR}$.   (4024 paper 02 Q11 June 2008)

24 a $\overrightarrow{PQ} = \begin{pmatrix} 12 \\ -35 \end{pmatrix}$ and $\overrightarrow{QR} = \begin{pmatrix} 4 \\ 14 \end{pmatrix}$.

i Find

   a $\overrightarrow{PQ}$,   **b** $\overrightarrow{PR}$.

ii Given that T is the midpoint of QR, find $\overrightarrow{PT}$.

iii $PQRS$ is a parallelogram.
The coordinates of R are (6, 16).
Find the coordinates of S.

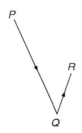

b

The diagram shows triangle ABC.

i Find the area of triangle ABC.

ii An enlargement, scale factor 4, maps triangle ABC onto triangle LMN. The point A
maps onto the point $L(10, 3)$.

   a Find the coordinates of the centre of enlargement.

   b Write down the area of triangle LMN.   (4024 paper 02 Q11 November 2008)

25 $\mathbf{a} = \begin{pmatrix} 3 \\ -4 \end{pmatrix}$ $\mathbf{b} = \begin{pmatrix} -1 \\ 7 \end{pmatrix}$

    a   Express $\mathbf{a} + 2\mathbf{b}$ as a column vector.

    b **i** Find $|\mathbf{a}|$.

         ii Given that $\dfrac{|\mathbf{b}|}{|\mathbf{a}|} = \sqrt{n}$, where n is an integer, find the value of n.

(4024 paper 01 Q15 November 2009)

23 Statistics II

Learning objectives Syllabus sections 41 and 42

In this chapter you will
- work with histograms with unequal class widths
- find the mean from a grouped frequency table

- use cumulative frequency
- find quartiles, interquartile range and percentiles.

23.1 Introduction

This chapter introduces some more statistical diagrams, and more measures of spread.

23.2 Essential Skills

1
6	5	7	9	1	3	5	8	1	2	6
5	4	3	3	3	2	9	8	4	6	7
1	5	6	5	9	8	7	2	1	9	7
5	3	4	2	8	1					

   a Construct a frequency table for the above data.
   b Find the mean, the median, the mode and the range for this data.

2 The table below shows some data for a pie chart. Find the missing values (a), (b) and (c).

Colour	Frequency	Angle
red	10	(a)
blue	(b)	72°
green	5	(c)
yellow	9	108°

3 The table shows the heights of some students rounded to the nearest centimetre. Copy and complete the table by adding the class boundaries.

Heights of students (h cm)	Lower class boundary	Upper class boundary
141 to 150		
151 to 160		
161 to 170		

23.3 More Histograms

You will have seen in Chapter 11 how to draw simple histograms. We will now look further at histograms.

Sometimes a set of data will be grouped into classes of different widths. In this case using the height of the bars as a measure of the frequency would be misleading. Instead we use the *area* of the bar to represent the frequency.

To work out the height to draw each bar we need to include the *class width* in the table. The height of each bar can now be calculated by dividing the frequency (area) by the class width (width). The height of the bar is called the **frequency density**.

- Frequency density $= \dfrac{\text{frequency}}{\text{class width}}$
- This is the same as:

  $$\text{Height of bar} = \dfrac{\text{area of bar}}{\text{width of bar}}$$

The following examples will show the method. The frequency table includes a new column to show class width, and another to show the frequency density.

You should notice that both bar charts and simple histograms also have the area of each bar proportional to the frequency, but in those cases we do not have to calculate the frequency density because the bars are all of the same width.

You need to know that the **modal class** of a grouped frequency distribution is the *class* with the highest *frequency density*, which is not necessarily the one with the highest frequency.

Key terms

Frequency density of a class is the ratio of the frequency to the class width.

The **modal class** of a grouped frequency distribution is the class with the highest frequency density.

Example 1

a Use the frequency table to draw a histogram.

Time (t minutes)	Frequency
$70 < t \leqslant 90$	8
$90 < t \leqslant 100$	7
$100 < t \leqslant 110$	28
$110 < t \leqslant 120$	11
$120 < t \leqslant 160$	16

b Write down the modal class.

Answer 1

Time (t minutes)	Class width	Frequency (area)	Frequency density (2 dp) (height = area ÷ class width)
$70 < t \leqslant 90$	20	8	0.4
$90 < t \leqslant 100$	10	7	0.7
$100 < t \leqslant 110$	10	28	2.8
$110 < t \leqslant 120$	10	11	1.1
$120 < t \leqslant 160$	40	16	0.4

a

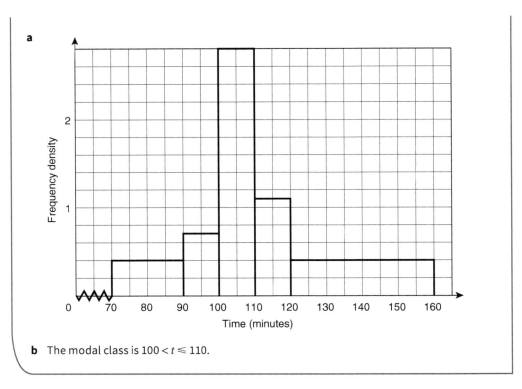

b The modal class is $100 < t \le 110$.

The scale of the histogram may be shown by labelling the vertical axis with the frequency density, or by showing a key as in the next example.

Example 2

The table and the histogram show the heights of some seedlings measured to the nearest centimetre.

a Use the table to complete the histogram.

b Use the histogram to complete the table.

Height (h cm)	Frequency (f)	Class width (w)	Frequency density ($f \div w$)
1–3	3	3	1
6–7	5	2	2.5
8–9	4	2	2
10–12	2	3	0.67

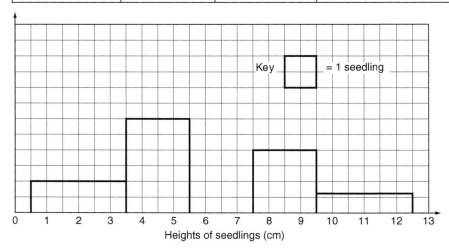

Answer 2

It may help to add the class boundaries to the table.

Height (h cm)	Frequency (f)	Class width (w)	Frequency density ($f \div w$)	Class boundaries	
1–3	3	3	1	0.5	3.5
6–7	5	2	2.5	5.5	7.5
8–9	4	2	2	7.5	9.5
10–12	2	3	0.67	9.5	12.5

> **NOTE:**
> The class boundaries in, for example, the first class, are $0.5 \leqslant h < 3.5$ because the rounding of the heights of the seedlings to the nearest centimetre means that a seedling of height 3.5 centimetres rounds to 4 centimetres and goes into the next class.

a The missing bar is the class 6–7. From the table we see that the frequency is 5 and the class width is 2. The key shows that $5\,cm^2$ will represent 5 seedlings. The height of the bar will be $5\,cm^2 \div 2\,cm = 2.5\,cm$. We can now draw the bar and complete the scale on the vertical axis

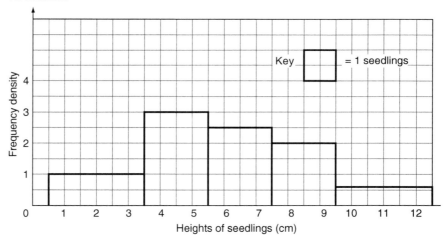

b The missing data in the table is for the class 4–5, which has a class width of 2 cm, and an area of $6\,cm^2$. The frequency density $= 6 \div 2 = 3$.

Height (h cm)	Frequency (f)	Class width (w)	Frequency density ($f \div w$)
1–3	3	3	1
4–5	6	2	3
6–7	5	2	2.5
8–9	4	2	2
10–12	2	3	0.67

Some questions may give neither a key nor a scale on the frequency density axis. However, they will tell you the frequency that one of the bars represents, so that, knowing the corresponding class width, you can calculate the scale of the frequency density from that bar.

It is important to be able to work out the class width in every case. The class width is the distance between the class boundaries.

In the case of the heights of the seedlings in Example 2 above, which were measured to the nearest centimetre, we know where each one belongs in the table but the rounding disguises the fact that the data is continuous, so we must remember the class boundaries when drawing the histogram.

Example 3

Complete each of these tables:

a   **Masses of oranges**

Class (m grams)	Class boundaries		Class width
$160 < m \leqslant 170$			
$170 < m \leqslant 190$			
$190 < m \leqslant 250$			

b   **Numbers of passengers in a coach**

Class	10–12	13–16	17–30
Class boundaries			
Class width			

c   Ages of people at a family celebration, given as a whole number of years. (Remember that ages are usually given to a whole number of years but not rounded up, so 9 years and 11 months would still be shown as 9, which is why the class is shown as $5 \leqslant age < 10$.)

Class age	Class boundaries		Class width
$5 \leqslant age < 10$			
$10 \leqslant age < 40$			
$40 \leqslant age < 60$			
$60 \leqslant age < 100$			

Answer 3

a

Class (m grams)	Class boundaries		Class width
$160 < m \leqslant 170$	160	170	10
$170 < m \leqslant 190$	170	190	20
$190 < m \leqslant 250$	190	250	60

b In this example, the *numbers* of passengers, the data is discrete. If we are to draw a histogram, which always has the bars touching, we have to use class boundaries as *if* the data was continuous.

Class	10–12	13–16	17–30
Class boundaries	9.5	12.5	16.5
	12.5	16.5	30.5
Class width	3	4	14

The class width may be found by the difference between the boundaries ($12.5 - 9.5 = 3$ in the first class above) or by counting the data values represented (10, 11, 12 = 3 in this case). However, the class boundaries are still needed when drawing the histogram, as we have seen.

c

Class *age*	Class boundaries		Class width
$5 \leqslant age < 10$	5	10	5
$10 \leqslant age < 40$	10	40	30
$40 \leqslant age < 60$	40	60	20
$60 \leqslant age < 100$	60	100	40

Exercise 23.1

1 Complete the following tables, and write down the modal classes.

a The lengths of some grass leaves

Class (l cm)	Frequency (f)	Class boundaries		Class width (w)	Frequency density ($f \div w$)
$20 < l \leqslant 30$	1				
$30 < l \leqslant 50$	10				
$50 < l \leqslant 70$	15				
$70 < l \leqslant 100$	20				
$100 < l \leqslant 150$	3				

b Numbers of letters posted each day in one letter box over 140 days

Class	Frequency (f)	Class boundaries		Class width (w)	Frequency density ($f \div w$)
0–30	5	0	30.5		
31–50	25				
51–70	41				
71–100	50				
101–150	7				
151–250	2				

NOTE:
The lower class boundary of the first class could be −0.5, which makes little sense. However, the class width is still 31 if you count the days with no envelopes as the first number in the class. Also, of course the numbers of letters are discrete.

2 Draw the histograms for the data sets in Question 1. Label the vertical axes with the frequency density.

3 Draw up a frequency table for each of these histograms. Each table should include 5 columns showing Class, Class boundaries, Class width, Frequency density and Frequency.

a

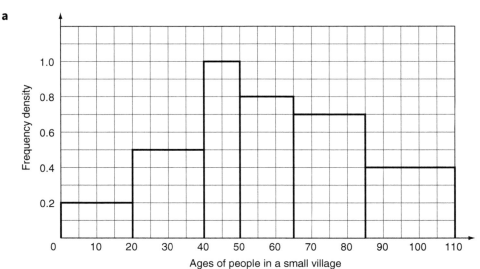

b

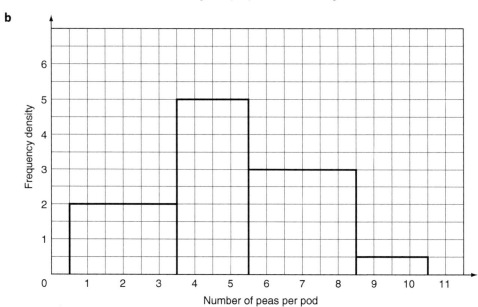

4 Using the table and histogram below,
   a calculate and add the scale of the frequency density to the vertical axis,
   b complete the histogram,
   c complete the table,
   d identify and write down the modal class.

Number of steps (s) taken in one day by some students on a fitness course

Class	$0 < s \leqslant 1000$	$1000 < s \leqslant 5000$	$5000 < s \leqslant 10\,000$	$10\,000 < s \leqslant 20\,000$
Frequency	20	100	105	

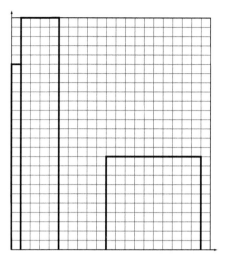

23.4 The Mean from a Grouped Frequency Table

In an ungrouped frequency table the mean can be calculated by multiplying each item of data by its frequency and then dividing by the total frequency, as we have seen in Chapter 11. However, we do not know where each data value lies within the class intervals of a grouped frequency distribution, so we can only *estimate* the mean. This is done by using the class midpoint, on the assumption that the values in the class will be scattered approximately evenly throughout the class.

The class midpoint is the number at the centre of each class, and is obtained by taking the mean of the class boundaries.

Example 4

Estimate the mean of the following distribution

Class	5–9	10–14	15–24	25–30
Frequency	3	5	7	3

Answer 4

Class	5–9	10–14	15–24	25–30	TOTAL
Frequency	3	5	7	3	18
Class midpoint	7	12	19.5	27.5	
Frequency × midpoint	21	60	136.5	82.5	300

The mean $= \dfrac{\text{total (frequency} \times \text{midpoint)}}{\text{total frequency}} = \dfrac{300}{18} = 16.7$ to 3 significant figures.

NOTE:
Copy the table and add two more columns, one for Class midpoint and one for Frequency × midpoint.

Exercise 23.2

Estimate the mean of each of these data sets

1

Class	Frequency
$10 < x \leq 15$	10
$15 < x \leq 25$	20
$25 < x \leq 40$	32
$40 < x \leq 60$	15

2

Class	1–2	3–4	5–6	7–8	9–10
Frequency	5	6	3	8	2

3

Class	0.5–0.9	0.9–1.3	1.3–2.5	2.5–6.5
Frequency	5	6	3	8

23.5 Cumulative Frequency

Key terms

Cumulative frequency is the running total of the frequencies in a grouped frequency distribution.

Data that is presented as a grouped frequency distribution loses its original individual data values. We have seen in Chapter 11 how to construct a grouped frequency table, and find the mean, median and mode from an ungrouped frequency table. Example 4 and Exercise 23.2 have shown how to estimate the mean from a grouped frequency table, and we can identify the modal class. We will now look at estimating the median from a grouped frequency distribution.

To do this we plot a **cumulative frequency curve**. Cumulative frequency is a *running total* of the frequencies (add them up as you go along), starting from the lowest values, as is shown in Table 23.1.

Class (%)	Frequency
$0 < mark \leq 15$	3
$15 < mark \leq 20$	2
$20 < mark \leq 25$	5
$25 < mark \leq 35$	10
$35 < mark \leq 45$	10
$45 < mark \leq 60$	13
$60 < mark \leq 80$	2

Mark	Cumulative frequency	
≤ 15	3	
≤ 20	5	$(3 + 2)$
≤ 25	10	$(5 + 5)$
≤ 35	20	$(10 + 10)$
≤ 45	30	$(20 + 20)$
≤ 60	43	$(30 + 13)$
≤ 80	45	$(42 + 2)$

Table 23.1 Marks of 45 students in an examination

The first thing to notice is that the cumulative frequencies in the cumulative frequency table show the number of data values in the corresponding class *and* all the previous classes. This means that the cumulative frequency is plotted against the *upper* class boundary as shown in the curve in Figure 23.1. (For example, there are 10 students who scored 25 *or less*). When drawing a cumulative frequency curve:

- The cumulative frequency is always shown on the vertical axis.
- The points are plotted against the upper class boundaries.
- The curve is always increasing, or possibly horizontal, but never decreases.
- The top of the cumulative frequency curve represents the total frequency (100% of the data set).

- It is usual to draw a smooth curve connecting the data points unless you are asked to construct a **cumulative frequency polygon**, in which case the points are joined by straight lines.

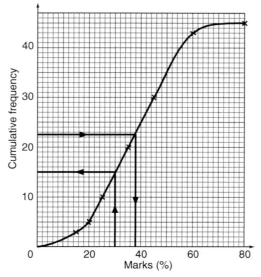

Figure 23.1 Cumulative frequency curve

The curve can now be used to estimate the median of the data.

The median is the data value that divides the data set into two equal parts when the data values are arranged in order.

Since the table has already arranged the values into increasing order we read the data value that corresponds to 50% of the cumulative frequency, that is, half way to the highest plotted point up the cumulative frequency axis. From the axis, rule a horizontal line to the curve, and then rule a vertical line down to the horizontal axis. Read the median from the scale on the horizontal axis.

Example 5

Use the curve in Figure 23.1 to estimate

a   the median of the data set,

b   how many students scored 30 or less.

Answer 5

a   The median = 38.

b   15 students scored 30 or less.

23.6 Quartiles, Interquartile Range and Percentiles

In Chapter 11 we looked at three sets of examination marks, and found that the mean was affected by the extreme, non-typical data values. These also affect the range, which is used as a rough measure of the spread of the data.

The **interquartile** range is another measure of spread which is not so affected by extreme values.

The median divides the data into two equal groups, so is a measure of the middle of the data. The **quartiles** divide each of these two equal groups again into two equal parts. So the median and quartiles divide the data into four equal parts.

Consider the following ordered data set:

2   4   4   5   5   5   6   7   8   8   8   9

There are 12 data values so the median is half way between the 6th and 7th values.

The median is $\frac{5+6}{2} = 5.5$

2   4   4   5   5   5   ...   6   7   8   8   8   9

The **lower quartile** divides the lower half into two equal parts. There are 6 data values so the lower quartile is between the 3rd and 4th.

The lower quartile is 4.5.

Similarly, the **upper quartile** is between the 9th and 10th values, so the upper quartile is 8.

These are shown in Figure 23.2.

2   4   4   ...   5   5   5   ...   6   7   8   ...   8   8   9
                ↑   ↑   ↑
            4.5   5.5   8

Figure 23.2 Data set split into quartiles

NOTE:

There are other methods of estimating the median and quartiles which may give slightly different results from those shown in this chapter, both here and in Chapter 11, but this method is perfectly adequate and easy to visualise and understand.

The median and quartiles are often abbreviated as:
Lower quartile $= q_1$ or Q_1
Median $= q_2$ or Q_2
Upper quartile $= q_3$ or Q_3
So in this example, $Q_1 = 4.5$ $Q_2 = 5.5$ $Q_3 = 8$
The interquartile range is the distance between the upper and lower quartiles.
In this case the interquartile range $= Q_3 - Q_1 = 8 - 4.5 = 3.5$.

When we need to estimate the interquartile range from a grouped frequency distribution we use the cumulative frequency curve. The typical curve in Figure 23.3 will illustrate this.

The highest point on the cumulative frequency curve (which represents the total frequency) is 100%. The lower quartile is one quarter (25%) of the way up to 100% on the cumulative frequency axis, and the upper quartile is three quarters of the way up (75%).

Be aware that the cumulative frequency scale could go higher than the highest point on the curve, but that part should be ignored, as Figure 23.3 shows.

NOTE:

When you are using your cumulative frequency curve in this way, ruled pencil lines are part of your working. Do not leave them out. It is also helpful to use arrows on these lines to show the direction of the working.

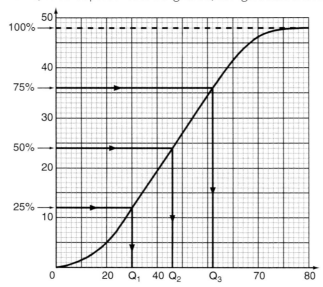

Figure 23.3 Quartiles on a cumulative frequency curve

Example 6

Use the curve in Example 5 to estimate the interquartile range of the data.

Answer 6

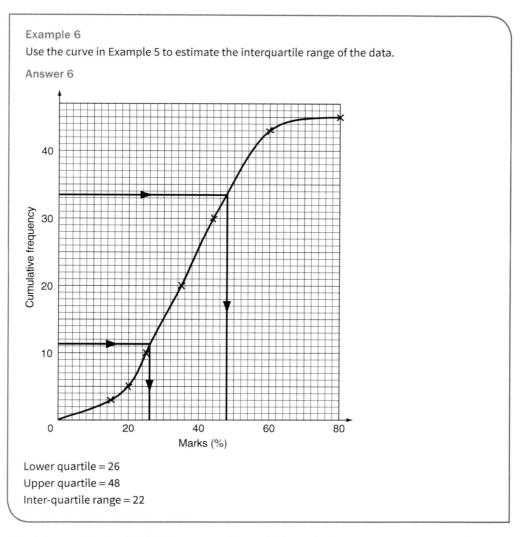

Lower quartile = 26
Upper quartile = 48
Inter-quartile range = 22

The data can also be divided into **percentiles**, which, as their name suggests, are each one hundredth of the way through the data set.

For example, to find the 30th percentile you go 30% up the vertical (cumulative frequency) axis and read across to the curve, and then down to the horizontal axis.

The last thing you have to know about the use of cumulative frequency curves is shown in the example below.

Example 7

Use the cumulative frequency curve of some students' percentage marks in a test (Example 5) to estimate:

a how many students have marks of 60% or more,
b how many students have marks between 40% and 50%,
c the range of marks between the 40th and 60th percentiles.

NOTE:
Think carefully where these data items lie! This question is often answered incorrectly in examinations.

Answer 7

We copy the curve and rule lines to show our working:

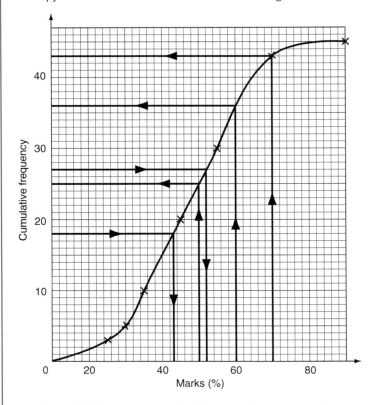

a The mark of 60% corresponds with 43 students, so 45 − 43 = 2 students have marks of 60% or more.

b 36 − 25 = 11

11 students have marks between 40% and 50%.

c 40% of 45 = 18, 60% of 45 = 27

The 40th and 60th percentiles are at 18 and 27 on the cumulative frequency axis.

The range of marks between 40th and 60th percentiles = 42 − 33 = 9 marks.

> **NOTE:**
>
> This is a very important hint, and if ignored may well lead to a common error! Make sure that you know which axis you are reading from and to. The quartiles and percentiles are not found by dividing the **horizontal** axis into equal parts! The **horizontal** axis represents the value of the data item, and the vertical axis represents its position in the ordered set of data. Think carefully every time you use a cumulative frequency curve.

Example 8

Use this cumulative frequency curve showing some more examination marks to find

    a the 45th percentile mark,

    b the number of candidates passing the examination if the pass mark is 60%.

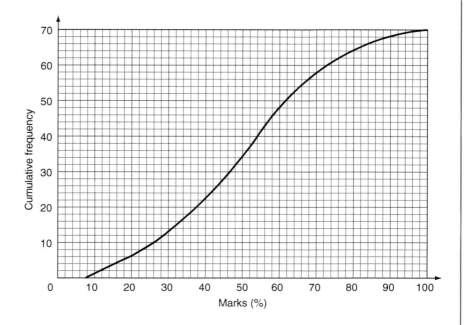

Answer 8

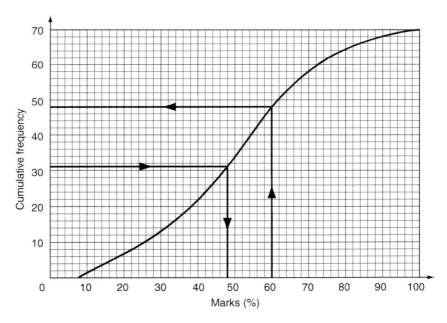

a   45% of 70 = 31.5

So the 45th percentile lies between the 31st and 32nd items on the ordered list originally used to draw the curve. We find that 31.5 on the cumulative frequency axis corresponds with a mark of 48%.

The 45th percentile is the mark 48%.

b   70 − 48 = 22

22 students passed the examination.

Example 9

a The tables below record the times, to the nearest minute, taken for students from two forms (classes) at a school to complete a memory test. Draw two cumulative frequency curves on the same grid to illustrate the two sets of data.

b Use the two curves to compare the performance of the two sets of students.

Form 3A

Time (t minutes)	Frequency
$10 < t \leqslant 15$	2
$15 < t \leqslant 20$	6
$20 < t \leqslant 25$	10
$25 < t \leqslant 35$	11
$35 < t \leqslant 45$	1

Form 3B

Time (t minutes)	Frequency
$10 < t \leqslant 20$	4
$20 < t \leqslant 25$	5
$25 < t \leqslant 30$	8
$30 < t\ 40$	10
$40 < t \leqslant 60$	3

Answer 9

a

Form 3A

Time (t minutes)	Frequency	Cumulative frequency
$10 < t \leqslant 15$	2	2
$15 < t \leqslant 20$	6	8
$20 < t \leqslant 25$	10	18
$25 < t \leqslant 35$	11	29
$35 < t \leqslant 45$	1	30

Form 3B

Time (t minutes)	Frequency	Cumulative frequency
$10 < t \leqslant 20$	4	4
$20 < t \leqslant 25$	5	9
$25 < t \leqslant 30$	8	17
$30 < t \leqslant 40$	10	27
$40 < t \leqslant 60$	3	30

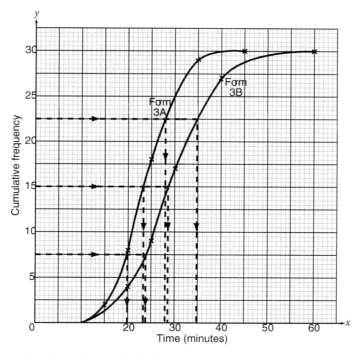
Time (minutes)

b From the cumulative frequency curves:

Form 3A
$$Q_1 = 20$$
$$Q_2 = 23.5$$
$$Q_3 = 28$$
Interquartile range $= 28 - 20 = 8$

Form 3B
$$Q_1 = 24$$
$$Q_2 = 28.5$$
$$Q_3 = 35$$
Interquartile range $= 35 - 24 = 11$

On average Form 3A completed the test quicker than Form 3B. The spread of Form 3A's marks was less than that of Form 3B.

Exercise 23.3

1 **a** Draw a cumulative frequency curve to illustrate the data given in the table.
  b Estimate the median, quartiles and interquartile range.
  c Estimate the 65th percentile.

Class	Frequency
$10 < x \leqslant 20$	9
$20 < x \leqslant 30$	16
$30 < x \leqslant 40$	27
$40 < x \leqslant 50$	13

2 Masses of 28 adults, (m kg).

74.8	74.9	90	83.3	94.5	68.7	70.1
84.5	88.0	78.5	69.1	70.5	72.9	69.4
75.7	79.9	81.4	92.5	88.5	76.8	83.4
82.8	79.8	90.5	88.8	83.1	82.5	78.5

a Use the data given above to complete the grouped frequency distribution below.

Class	$65 < m \leqslant 70$	$70 < m \leqslant 75$	$75 < m \leqslant 80$	$80 < m \leqslant 85$	$85 < m \leqslant 90$	$90 < m \leqslant 100$
Frequency						

b Draw a cumulative frequency curve.

c Estimate   **i** the median mass,   **ii** the interquartile range,   **iii** the 40th percentile.

Exercise 23.4
Mixed exercise

1 The table below shows the times some half-marathon runners took to complete the course. The times are in minutes.

74.2	75.2	77.6	79.4	80.1	80.2	84.4	86.0
88.0	93.6	94.1	95.5	98.4	98.9	99.0	99.9
100.0	100.0	101.5	102.9	103.0	103.5	104.7	105.6
105.8	106.0	106.2	106.9	107.1	107.4	107.7	107.9
108.4	108.5	108.7	108.9	109.1	109.1	109.3	109.4
109.6	109.6	109.9	109.9	110.6	111.2	111.8	115.2
116.1	117.0	117.0	117.8	118.1	118.9	119.3	120.0
134.6	135.2	135.9	141.4	143.9	146.8	149.9	153.1

a Draw a grouped frequency table with the times grouped into classes
$70 < t \leqslant 80$, $80 < t \leqslant 90$, $90 < t \leqslant 100$, $100 < t \leqslant 120$ and $120 < t \leqslant 160$.
Include in your table, Class boundaries, Class width, Class midpoint, Frequency density and Cumulative frequency.

b Draw a histogram.

c Estimate the mean.

d Identify the modal class.

e Draw a cumulative frequency curve.

f Use the cumulative frequency curve to estimate the median, quartiles and 70th percentile.

2 The following histogram shows the results of another half-marathon run.

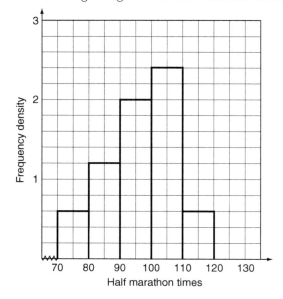

Half marathon times

   a Use the histogram to draw a grouped frequency table, including Class width, Frequency density, Class midpoint, Frequency and Cumulative frequency, with the times grouped as in question 1.

   b Estimate the mean.

   c Draw a cumulative frequency curve.

   d Estimate the median and quartiles.

   e How many people completed this marathon in less than 100 minutes?

   f Estimate the number of runners who took more than 108 minutes to complete this course.

3 A girls' school and a boys' school are to merge to form one school.

The mean number of girls per class in the girls' school is 25.4 (to 3 significant figures) and there are 12 classes all together. In the boys' school the mean number of boys per class is 23.8, and there are 15 classes. The new school will have 22 classes.

Calculate the mean number of students per class in the new school, giving your answer to 3 significant figures. Show all your working.

4 A group of 20 students have a mean mark of 72% in their maths exam. A new student joins the group. He had scored 68% in the same examination. What is the new mean mark of the enlarged group?

5 In another school the classes were being reorganised according to the marks the students had gained in their end of year examination. The top set of 25 students had a mean mark of 75% before the reorganisation. Three students with a mean mark of 61% were moved down to the second set, and two students with a mean mark of 80% were moved up into the top set.

   a How many students are there now in the top set?

   b What is the new mean mark of the top set?

Exam-style questions

6 The heights of 40 children were measured.
The results are summarised in the table below.

Height (h cm)	$105 < h \leqslant 115$	$115 < h \leqslant 125$	$125 < h \leqslant 135$	$135 < h \leqslant 145$
Frequency	5	10	20	5

   a i Identify the modal class.

     ii Calculate an estimate of the mean height.

   b The cumulative frequency curve representing this information is shown below.

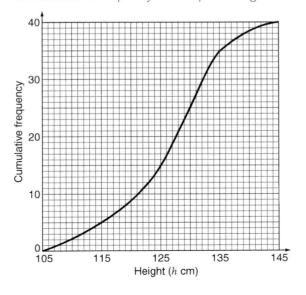

Use the curve to find
  i the interquartile range,
  ii the number of children whose heights are in the range 120 cm to 130 cm.

(4024 paper 01 Q25 June 2007)

7 Kristina asked 200 people how much water they drink in one day.
The table shows her results.

Amount of water (x litres)	Number of people
$0 < x \leqslant 0.5$	8
$0.5 < x \leqslant 1$	27
$1 < x \leqslant 1.5$	45
$1.5 < x \leqslant 2$	50
$2 < x \leqslant 2.5$	39
$2.5 < x \leqslant 3$	21
$3 < x \leqslant 3.5$	7
$3.5 < x \leqslant 4$	3

  a Write down the modal interval.
  b Calculate an estimate of the mean.
  c Make a cumulative frequency table for this data.
  d Using a scale of 4 cm to 1 litre of water on the horizontal axis and 1 cm to 10 people on the vertical axis, draw the cumulative frequency graph.
  e Use your cumulative frequency graph to find
    i the median,
    ii the 40th percentile,
    iii the number of people who drink at least 2.6 litres of water.
  f A doctor recommends that a person drinks at least 1.8 litres of water each day.
What percentage of these 200 people do not drink enough water?

(0580 paper 04 Q6 June 2007)

8 a The numbers 0, 1, 1, 1, 2, k, m, 6, 9, 9 are in order ($k \neq m$).
Their median is 2.5 and their mean is 3.6.
    i Write down the mode.
    ii Find the value of k.
    iii Find the value of m.
  b 100 students are given a question to answer.
The time taken (t seconds) by each student is recorded and the results are shown in the table.

t	$0 < t \leqslant 20$	$20 < t \leqslant 30$	$30 < t \leqslant 35$	$35 < t \leqslant 40$	$40 < t \leqslant 50$	$50 < t \leqslant 60$	$60 < t \leqslant 80$
Frequency	10	10	15	28	22	7	8

Calculate an estimate of the mean time taken.

  c The data in part b is regrouped to give the following table.

T	$0 < t \leqslant 0$	$30 < t \leqslant 0$	$60 < t \leqslant 0$
Frequency	p	q	8

i Write down the values of p and q.

ii Draw an accurate histogram to show these results.
Use a scale of 1 cm to represent 5 seconds on the horizontal time axis.
Use a scale of 1 cm to 0.2 units of frequency density (so that 1 cm² on your histogram represents 1 student). (0580 paper 04 Q9 (part) June 2006)

9 The journey times of 80 drivers are summarised in the table.

Time (t minutes)	$60 < t \leqslant 80$	$80 < t \leqslant 90$	$90 < t \leqslant 95$	$95 < t \leqslant 100$	$100 < t \leqslant 110$	$110 < t \leqslant 130$
Number of drivers	4	10	14	20	24	8

a Calculate an estimate of the mean journey time.

b Copy the diagram and complete the histogram to represent the information in the table.

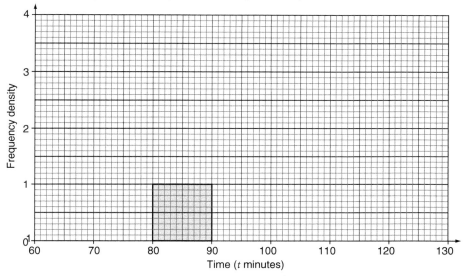

(4024 paper 21 Q6a, c November 2012)

10 The cumulative frequency curve shows the distribution of the masses of 100 people.

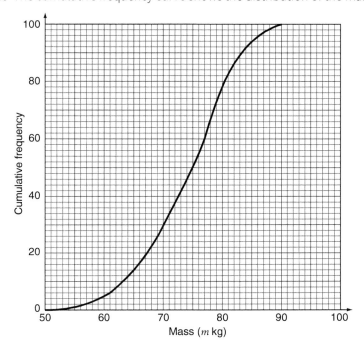

Find
a the median,
b the upper quartile,
c the number of people with masses in the range $65 < m \leqslant 72$.

(4024 paper 01 Q17 June 2005)

11

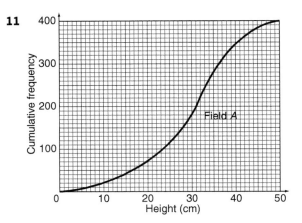

The diagram above is the cumulative frequency curve for the heights of 400 plants which were grown in Field *A*.
Use the graph to find
a the number of plants that grew to a height of **more** than 30 cm,
b the interquartile range.
c Another 400 plants were grown in Field *B*.
The cumulative frequency distribution of the heights of these plants is shown in the table.

Height (h cm)	$h \leqslant 10$	$h \leqslant 15$	$h \leqslant 20$	$h \leqslant 25$	$h \leqslant 30$	$h \leqslant 35$	$h \leqslant 40$	$h \leqslant 50$
Cumulative frequency	35	75	130	200	280	330	370	400

Copy the graph and **on the same axes as for Field *A***, draw the cumulative frequency curve for the plants grown in Field *B*.
d By comparing the two curves, state, with a reason, which field produced the taller plants.

(4024 paper 01 Q19 November 2005)

12 One hundred children were asked how far they could swim.
The results are summarised in the table.

Distance (d metres)	$0 < d \leqslant 100$	$100 < d \leqslant 200$	$200 < d \leqslant 400$
Number of children	30	50	20

a The histogram below represents part of this information.
Complete the histogram.

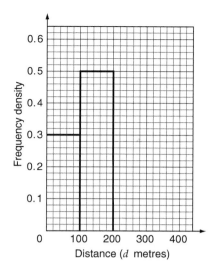

b A pie chart is drawn to represent the three groups of children.
Calculate the angle of the sector that represents the group of 20 children.

(4024 paper 01 Q11 November 2005)

13 On a certain stretch of road, the speeds of some cars were recorded.
The results are summarised in the table.
Part of the corresponding histogram is shown alongside.

Speed (x km/h)	Frequency
$25 < x \leqslant 45$	q
$45 < x \leqslant 55$	30
$55 < x \leqslant 65$	p
$65 < x \leqslant 95$	12

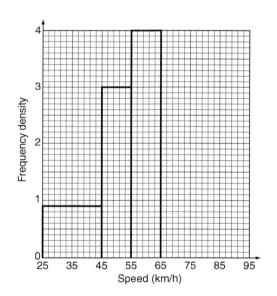

a Find the value of
i p,   **ii** q.
b Complete the histogram.

(4024 paper 01 Q11 November 2007)

14 a Each student in a class is given a bag of sweets.
The students note the number of sweets in their bag.
The results are shown in the table, where $0 \leqslant x < 10$.

Number of sweets	30	31	32
Frequency (number of bags)	10	7	x

     i   State the mode.

     ii Find the possible values of the median.

     iii The mean number of sweets is 30.65.
         Find the value of x.

  b The mass, m grams, of each of 200 chocolates is noted and the results are shown in the table.

Mass (m grams)	$10 < m \leqslant 20$	$20 < m \leqslant 22$	$22 < m \leqslant 24$	$24 < m \leqslant 30$
Frequency	35	115	26	24

     i   Calculate an estimate of the mean mass of a chocolate.

     ii On a histogram, the height of the column for the $20 < m \leqslant 22$ interval is 11.5 cm.
         Calculate the heights of the other three columns.
         Do not draw the histogram.   (0580 paper 04 Q6 November 2008)

15 The mass of each of 200 tea bags was checked by an inspector in a factory.
     The results are shown by the cumulative frequency curve.

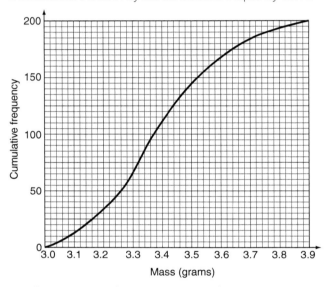

Use the cumulative frequency curve to find

  a the median mass,

  b the interquartile range,

  c the number of tea bags with a mass greater than 3.5 grams.

                                             (0580 paper 02 Q19 November 2007)

16 a The distribution of the times spent by 200 customers at a restaurant one evening is shown in the table.

Time (t minutes)	$30 \leqslant t < 60$	$60 \leqslant t < 80$	$80 \leqslant t < 90$	$90 \leqslant t < 100$	$100 \leqslant t < 120$
Frequency	24	p	q	58	28

    The diagram shows part of the histogram that represents this data.

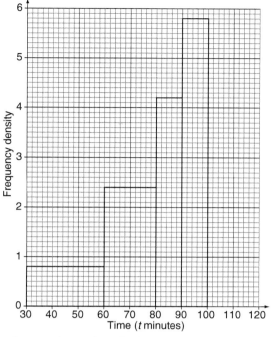

i   Copy and complete the histogram.

ii   Find p and q.

iii   Estimate the probability that a customer, chosen at random, spent more than 95 minutes in the restaurant.

b   The table below shows the distribution of the ages of these customers.

Age (y years)	$0 < y \leqslant 20$	$20 < y \leqslant 40$	$40 < y \leqslant 60$	$60 < y \leqslant 80$
Frequency	34	57	85	24

i   State the modal class.

ii   Calculate an estimate of the mean age of these customers.

(4024 paper 22 Q7 June 2013)

17 A normal die, numbered 1 to 6, is rolled 50 times.

The results are shown in the frequency table.

Score	1	2	3	4	5	6
Frequency	15	10	7	5	6	7

a   Write down the modal score.

b   Find the median score.

c   Calculate the mean score.

d   The die is then rolled another 10 times.
   The mean score for the 60 rolls is 2.95.
   Calculate the mean score for the extra 10 rolls.

(0580 paper 04 Q2 June 2009)

18 The lengths of 40 nails were measured.
Their lengths, in centimetres, are summarised in the table below.

Length (l cm)	Frequency
$0 < l \le 4$	14
$4 < l \le 8$	18
$8 < l \le 16$	8

a On a copy of the axes below in the answer space, draw the histogram which represents this information.

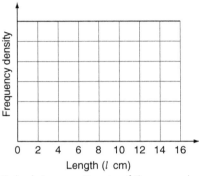

b Calculate an estimate of the mean length of the nails.

(4024 paper 01 Q19 November 2004)

19 a The lengths of 120 leaves were measured.
The cumulative frequency graph shows the distribution of their lengths.

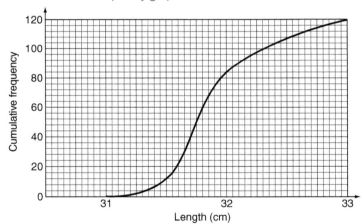

Use this graph to estimate
i the median,
ii the interquartile range,
iii the number of leaves whose length is more than 31.5 cm.

(4024 paper 02 Q10a June 2006)

20 Paul and Sam are two athletes who have training sessions together.
On 80 sessions during 2007 they ran the same route, and their times were recorded.

a The cumulative frequency curve shows the distribution of Paul's times.

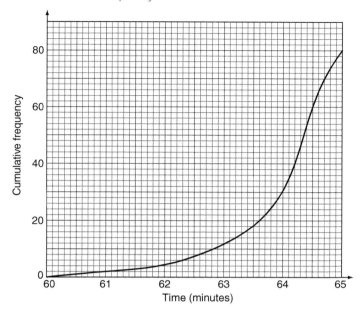

Use the curve to estimate
i the median,
ii the interquartile range,
iii how often Paul took more than 64 minutes.

b Sam's times had a lower quartile of 62.5 minutes, a median of 63 minutes and an upper quartile of 64 minutes.
State which athlete was the more consistent runner, giving a reason for your answer.

(4024 paper 02 Q6 June 2008)

21 a The graph shows the cumulative frequency curve for the playing times of the individual tracks on Andrew's MP3 player.
Use the graph to find
i the median, **ii** the interquartile range.

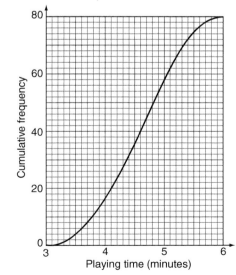

b The table summarises the playing times of each of the 100 tracks on Tom's MP3 player.

Playing time (t minutes)	Frequency
$2.5 < t \leqslant 3.5$	5
$3.5 < t \leqslant 4.5$	30
$4.5 < t \leqslant 5.5$	50
$5.5 < t \leqslant 6.5$	15

Calculate an estimate of the mean playing time of the individual tracks.

(4024 paper 01 Q23 November 2008)

22

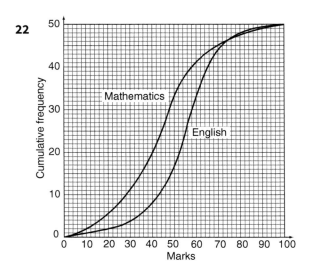

Fifty students each took a mathematics and an English test. The distributions of their marks are shown in the cumulative frequency graph.

a Use the graph
   i to estimate the median mark in the English test,
   ii to estimate the 20th percentile mark in the mathematics test.
b State, **with a reason**, which test the students found more difficult.

(4024 paper 01 Q9 June 2009)

Further Probability

Learning Objectives

Syllabus sections 2 and 40

In this chapter you will
- use tree diagrams
- learn about dependent and independent events
- use Venn diagrams
- use more set notation.

24.1 Introduction

This chapter completes your course for O Level Mathematics.

We will look at using tree diagrams and Venn diagrams to solve probability problems.

24.2 Essential Skills

1. A bag contains 10 beads coloured red, blue and green.

   a. If a bead is chosen at random it is known that the probability of it being red is $\frac{2}{5}$. How many red beads are in the bag?

   b. There are three green beads in the bag. What is the probability of choosing a blue bead?

   c. What is the probability of choosing a yellow bead?

2. A manufacturing company tests 50 components selected at random from a batch of 1500, and finds that 3 of them are faulty.

   a. What percentage of the components is faulty?

   b. How many components could be expected to be faulty in the whole batch?

3. Using a probability space diagram work out the probability of throwing two even numbers with two dice.

24.3 Tree Diagrams

In Chapter 12, we looked at combined events using probability space diagrams. We will now study another useful diagram called a **tree diagram**.

A simple example of a tree diagram is the toy train set shown in Figure 24.1.

When this train comes to a junction (marked with a dot) there is a probability of $\frac{3}{4}$ that it will go straight on. This means that there is a probability of $\frac{1}{4}$ that it will turn.

Figure 24.1 shows the layout, with the probabilities marked on each branch.

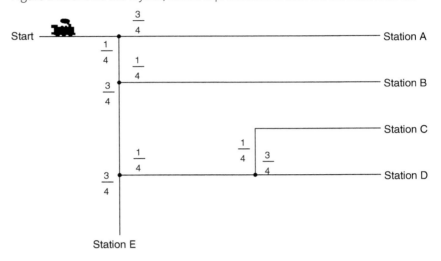

Figure 24.1 Tree diagram for train set

The probability of the train arriving at station A is $\frac{3}{4}$.

The probability of the train arriving at station B is found by *multiplying* the probabilities at each junction along the route from the start to station B: $\frac{1}{4} \times \frac{1}{4} = \frac{1}{16}$.

If you are not sure about this remember that this means that the train turns at the first junction *and* turns at the second junction. Look back to Section 12.6 in Chapter 12, where we multiplied the probabilities when we wanted two outcomes together.

The probability of the train arriving at A *or* B (we do not mind which) is found by *adding* the probability of it arriving at station A and the probability of it arriving at station B. So:

$$P(A \text{ or } B) = P(B) = \frac{3}{4} + \frac{1}{16}$$
$$= \frac{12}{16} + \frac{1}{16}$$
$$= \frac{13}{16}$$

Example 1

Use the diagram of the toy train layout to answer the following questions.

  a What is the probability of the train arriving at station C?
  b What is the probability of the train arriving at station D?
  c What is the probability of the train arriving at stations C, D *or* E?
  d What is the total of all the probabilities?
  e What is the probability of the train *not* arriving at A?

Answer 1

  a $P(C) = \frac{1}{4} \times \frac{3}{4} \times \frac{1}{4} \times \frac{1}{4} = \frac{3}{256}$ b $P(D) = \frac{1}{4} \times \frac{3}{4} \times \frac{1}{4} \times \frac{3}{4} = \frac{9}{256}$

c   P(C,D or E) = P(C) + P(D) + P(E)

$$= \frac{3}{256} + \frac{9}{256} + \left(\frac{1}{4} \times \frac{3}{4} \times \frac{3}{4}\right)$$

$$= \frac{3}{256} + \frac{9}{256} + \frac{9}{64}$$

$$= \frac{3}{256} + \frac{9}{256} + \frac{36}{256} = \frac{48}{256}$$

d   P(A) + P(B) + P(C) + P(D) + P(E) = 1

e   P(*not* A) = 1 − P(A)

$$= 1 - \frac{3}{4}$$

$$= \frac{1}{4}$$

Key terms

Two events are **independent** if the result of the first has no effect on the probability of the second.

Two events are **dependent** if the probability of the second depends on the result of the first.

A tree diagram will help you distinguish between **dependent and independent events**.

For example, suppose you are going to choose two coloured discs at random from a box containing five red and six blue discs, that is 11 discs altogether.

The first time you do this experiment you will *not* replace the first disc before choosing the second disc. This is called **selection without replacement**.

For the first choice P(R) = $\frac{5}{11}$, and P(B) = $\frac{6}{11}$. These probabilities are shown on the tree diagram in Figure 24.2.

For the second choice the probabilities depend on what happened first.

If a red was picked the first time there are now only four reds, but still six blues in the box, making ten discs altogether. So now P(R) = $\frac{4}{10}$ and P(B) = $\frac{6}{10}$. The second choice is *dependent* on the first.

Figure 24.2 shows these probabilities.

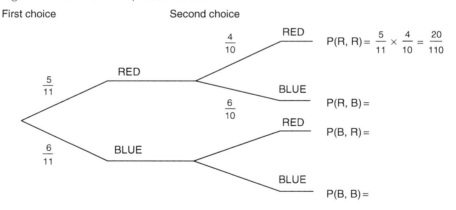

Figure 24.2 Tree diagram for choice of discs

Important points about tree diagrams:

- Read the diagram from left to right.
- Every time a choice is made the diagram splits into branches.
- The outcome of each choice is shown at the end of the branch.
- The probability of that outcome is shown on the branch.
- Every time there is a choice the probabilities on the branches at that point *add* up to 1.
- The probability of, for example, two reds in Figure 24.2 (Red *and* Red), is found by *multiplying* the probabilities along the branches that lead to P(R, R).

- The probability of getting one of each colour in the example above is found by *adding* the probabilities P(R, B) and P(B, R).
- The probabilities of all the possible outcomes are shown at the ends of the branches. They all add up to 1, because they cover all possibilities.
- It is useful to remember that if you travel along the branches from left to right you multiply the probabilities, and if you want to combine probabilities vertically you add them.

Example 2

    a Copy the diagram above and fill in the rest of the probabilities.

    b What is the probability of getting one of each colour?

Answer 2

    a

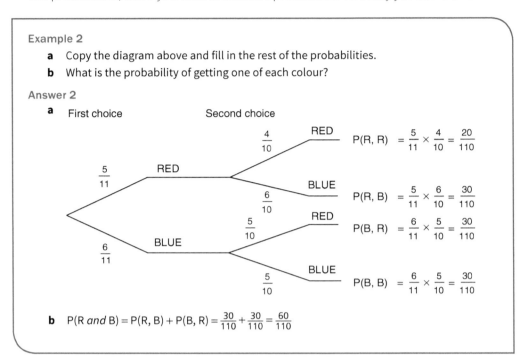

    b $P(R \text{ and } B) = P(R, B) + P(B, R) = \frac{30}{110} + \frac{30}{110} = \frac{60}{110}$

Now, if this experiment were to be repeated *with* replacement the second choice will not be dependent on the first. The outcomes of the first and second choices are *independent* of each other.

The tree diagram in Figure 24.3 shows this situation.

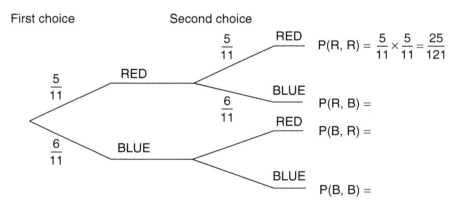

Figure 24.3 Tree diagram for choice with replacement

Exercise 24.1

1 **a** Copy and complete the diagram above showing the probabilities of the remaining outcomes of selection *with* replacement.

    b What is the probability of getting one of each colour?

2 The average number of wet days in Mumbai in September is 13.
  The average number of wet days in New Delhi in September is 4.
  a What is the probability that any day chosen at random in Mumbai in September will be
    i wet,   ii dry.
  b Draw a tree diagram to show the probabilities of wet and dry days in Mumbai and New Delhi in September.
  c Find the probability that on September 5th next year it will be
    i wet in Mumbai *and* in New Delhi,
    ii wet in Mumbai and dry in New Delhi,
    iii both cities will be dry.
  d What is the probability that it will be dry in New Delhi?

3 The probability of Sukatai passing her maths exam at the first attempt is $\frac{3}{5}$.

  If she fails it and resits the probability of her passing the second time is $\frac{3}{4}$.

  Draw a tree diagram to show this. Remember that if she passes first time she does not have to take the exam again so there is no need for another branch in this part of the tree diagram.

24.4 Venn Diagrams

Venn diagrams and set notation are also useful tools in the study of probability.

You may want to have a quick look back at Chapter 13 to remind yourself about Venn diagrams before continuing.

The Venn diagram might show the numbers in each set or it can show the probabilities in each set.

Example 3
In a class of 40 students 20 play football, 24 play cricket and 9 play both cricket and football.
Draw a Venn diagram to show the numbers of students who play each game.
If a student is picked at random, what is the probability that he or she plays

a neither football nor cricket?   b cricket but not football?

Answer 3
The Venn diagram shows the numbers of students who play each game.

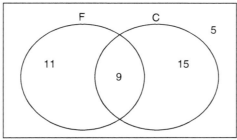

a There are 5 students who play neither football nor cricket, so the probability that the student plays neither is $\frac{5}{40}$.
b There are 15 students who play cricket but not football, so the probability is $\frac{15}{40}$.

24.5 Using Set Notation

Set notation provides a neat method for discussing probabilities.

Remember that:

$$P(A \cup B) = P(A \text{ or } B \text{ or both})$$
$$P(A \cap B) = P(\text{both } A \text{ and } B)$$
$$P(A') = P(\text{not } A) = 1 - P(A)$$
$$P(A \cup B)' = P(\text{neither } A \text{ nor } B)$$

NOTE:
Remember that the total probability is 1.

If the events are **mutually exclusive** then $P(A \cap B) = 0$.

The Venn diagram for the example above could have been drawn to show the probabilities in each set, as in the example below.

Example 4

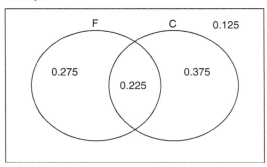

The Venn diagram from the example above has been redrawn to show the probabilities in each set.

a   Are F and C mutually exclusive?
Find the following probabilities:

b   P(F)   **c**   P(C)
d   P(neither F nor C)   **e**   P(both F and C)
f   P(F or C or both).   **g**   If a student plays football, calculate the probability that he or she also plays cricket.

Answer 4
First it is worth checking that the total probability is 1:

   $0.275 + 0.225 + 0.375 + 0.125 = 1$.

So there should be no probabilities missing, and each probability is correct.

a   F and C are not mutually exclusive because a student may play both football and cricket.
b   Using the previous Venn diagram we can calculate P(F) by finding the total number who play football and dividing by the number in the class.
    $P(F) = (11 + 9) \div 40 = 2040 = 0.5$
    It is perhaps easier to use the second Venn diagram and add the probabilities in F. So
    $P(F) = 0.275 + 0.225 = 0.5$
c $P(C) = 0.225 + 0.375 = 0.6$
d $P(\text{neither F nor C}) = P(F \cup C)' = 0.125$
e $P(\text{both F and C}) = P(F \cap C) = 0.225$
f $P(F \text{ or C or both}) = P(F \cup C) = 0.275 + 0.225 + 0.375 = 0.875$
g   Using the Venn diagram we can calculate the probability of students who play football:
    $P(F) = 0.5$
    Probability of students who play both football and cricket $= P(F \cap C) = 0.225$
    Now the probability that the student plays cricket given that he or she also plays football
    $= 0.225 \div 0.5$
    $= 0.45$

Example 5
The Venn diagram shows the probabilities of two events represented by the sets A and B.

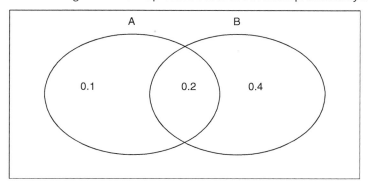

a Find P(A ∪ B)′.
b Find P(A).
c Find P(A *or* B *or* both).
d Find P(A *and* B).
e Find P(A or B but not both).

Answer 5
a P(A ∪ B)′ = 1 − (0.1 + 0.2 + 0.4) = 1 − 0.7 = 0.3
b P(A) = 0.1 + 0.2 = 0.3
c P(A *or* B *or* both) = P(A ∪ B) = 0.1 + 0.2 + 0.4 = 0.7
d P(A *and* B) = P(A ∩ B) = 0.2
e P(A or B but not both) = 0.1 + 0.4 = 0.5

Exercise 24.2

1 The Venn diagram shows two sets, D and E, and some probabilities.

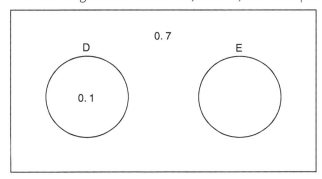

a Are the events D and E mutually exclusive?
b Find P(E).
c Write down P(D ∩ E).
d Find P(D ∪ E).
e Find P(D′).

2 In a class of 35 students, 20 wear glasses (G), 10 are tall for their age (T) and 2 are tall and wear glasses.
a Draw two Venn diagrams, one showing the numbers in the sets G and T, and one showing the probabilities.
b Find P(G ∪ T)′.
c A student who wears glasses is picked at random. What is the probability that he or she is also tall?

Using set Notation With Tree Diagrams

Example 6

Peter drives to work. His journey takes him through two sets of traffic lights which can be either red (stop) or green (go).

The probability that the first set is red when he reaches it is 0.4, and the probability that the second set is red is 0.7.

a Draw a tree diagram to show these probabilities.

b Do you think that the events that the first set is red and the second set is green are independent?

c Are the events that the first set is red and the second set is red mutually exclusive?

d Are the events that the first set of lights is red and the first set of lights is green mutually exclusive?

e Find $P(R_1 \cap R_2)$, where R_1 is the event that the first set is red, and R_2 is the event that the second set is red.

f Find the probability that either both sets are red or both sets are green.

g Find the probability that the two sets show different colours.

Answer 6

a

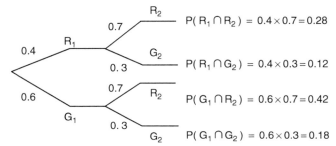

$$P(R_1 \cap R_2) = 0.4 \times 0.7 = 0.28$$
$$P(R_1 \cap G_2) = 0.4 \times 0.3 = 0.12$$
$$P(G_1 \cap R_2) = 0.6 \times 0.7 = 0.42$$
$$P(G_1 \cap G_2) = 0.6 \times 0.3 = 0.18$$

b They could be dependent if the signals are linked together to improve traffic flow. If they are not linked they are independent. These are independent because the probabilities of the second set being red or green are the same regardless of whether the first set was red or green. So the second set does not depend on what colour the first set was showing.

c These events are not mutually exclusive because they can both happen at once.

d These events are mutually exclusive because they cannot both happen at once.

e $P(R_1 \cap R_2) = 0.28$

f $P((R_1 \cap R_2) \cup (G_1 \cap G_2)) = 0.28 + 0.18 = 0.46$

g $P(\text{sets are different}) = 1 - P(\text{sets are the same}) = 1 - 0.46 = 0.54$

Exercise 24.3

Mixed exercise

1 There are two classes in a school both with girls and boys.

There are 10 girls in Class 5, and 13 boys.

There are 24 girls altogether, and a total of 49 pupils in the two classes.

Copy and complete the diagram below to show the numbers of boys and girls in each class.

	Girls (G)	Boys (B)	Totals
Class Five (F)	10	13	
Class Six (S)			
Totals	24	49	

a If a pupil is picked at random from the two classes what is the probability that it will be a girl?

b Find P(G ∩ S).

c Find P(F).

d A pupil is picked at random from Class Six. What is the probability that it is a boy?

2 A bag contains 8 coloured discs, 3 red (R) and 5 yellow (Y). Two discs are selected without replacement.

a Draw a tree diagram to show these events.

b Is P(R) for the first and second selection the same or different?

c Are the events of selecting the first and second discs independent?

d What is the probability that the second disc is yellow given that the first disc was red?

e Find $P(R_1 \cap Y_2)$ where R_1 is the event that the first disc was red, and Y_2 is the event that the second disc was yellow.

f Calculate the probability that both discs are different colours.

3

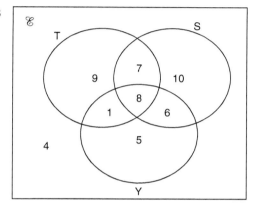

A packet of mixed flower seeds contains 50 seeds of various flowers. Some of the flowers will be tall (T), some will be yellow (Y) and some will be spring flowers (S). Some will have more than one of these characteristics.

The Venn diagram shows the distribution of these characteristics.

a If a seed is picked at random find the probability that it will be of a yellow flower.

b Find P(S').

c Write down n(S ∩ T ∩ Y).

d Find the probability that a seed picked at random is of a tall yellow flower.

e Given that a seed picked at random was of a tall flower find the probability that it was also yellow.

4

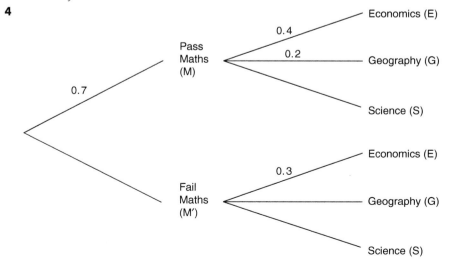

Ashna is about to take a maths examination. When she gets her results she will decide whether to study economics (E), geography (G) or science (S). If she passes her maths examination (M) the probability that she will study economics is 0.4. If she fails her maths examination (M') the probability that she will study geography (G) is 0.6.

a Copy and complete the tree diagram above, and use it to answer the following questions.

b What is the probability that she will pass her maths examination and study economics?

c Calculate P(M' ∩ E).

d Calculate the probability that she will study science.

Exam-style questions

5 An ordinary unbiased die has faces numbered 1, 2, 3, 4, 5 and 6.
Sarah and Terry each threw this die once.
Expressing each answer as a fraction **in its lowest terms**, find the probability that

i Sarah threw a 7,   **ii** they both threw a 6,

iii neither threw an even number,   **iv** Sarah threw exactly four more than Terry.

(4024 paper 02 Q5b June 2003)

6 Two unbiased spinners are used in a game.
One spinner is numbered from 1 to 6 and the other is numbered from 1 to 3.
The scores on each spinner are multiplied together. The table below shows the possible outcomes.

		First Spinner					
		1	2	3	4	5	6
	1	1	2	3	4	5	6
Second	2	2	4	6	8	10	12
Spinner	3	3	6	9	12	15	18

a Find the probability that the outcome is even.

b When the outcome is even, find the probability that it is also greater than 11.

(0580 paper 02 Q15 June 2007)

7

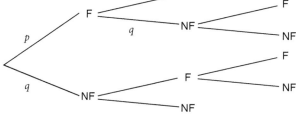

First calculator   Second calculator   Third calculator

F = faulty   NF = not faulty

The tree diagram shows a testing procedure on calculators, taken from a large batch.

Each time a calculator is chosen at random, the probability that it is faulty (F) is $\frac{1}{20}$.

a Write down the values of p and q.

b Two calculators are chosen at random.
Calculate the probability that
i both are faulty,
ii exactly one is faulty.

c If **exactly one** out of two calculators tested is faulty, then a third calculator is chosen at random. Calculate the probability that exactly one of the first two calculators is faulty **and** the third one is faulty.

d The whole batch of calculators is rejected
either if the first two chosen are both faulty
or if a third one needs to be chosen and if is faulty.
Calculate the probability that the whole batch is rejected.

e In one month, 1000 batches of calculators are tested in this way.
How many batches are expected to be rejected? (0580 paper 04 Q8 June 2009)

9 In a survey, 100 students are asked if they like basketball (*B*), football (*F*) and swimming (*S*). The Venn diagram shows the results.

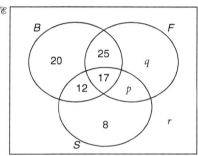

42 students like swimming.
40 students like exactly one sport.

a Find the values of *p*, *q* and *r*.

b How many students like
i all three sports, **ii** basketball and swimming but not football?

c Find
i $n(B')$, **ii** $n((B \cup F) \cap S')$.

d One student is chosen at random from the 100 students. Find the probability that the student
i only likes swimming, **ii** likes basketball but not swimming.

e Two students are chosen at random from those who like basketball. Find the probability that they each like exactly one other sport.
(0580 paper 04 Q9 November 2008)

10 a

Grade	1	2	3	4	5	6	7
Number of students	1	2	4	7	4	8	2

The table shows the grades gained by 28 students in a history test.
i Write down the mode.
ii Find the median.
iii Calculate the mean.
iv Two students are chosen at random.
Calculate the probability that they both gained grade 5.

    v From all the students who gained grades 4 or 5 or 6 or 7, two are chosen at random.
      Calculate the probability that they both gained grade 5.

    vi Students are chosen at random, one by one, from the original 28, until a student chosen has a grade 5.
      Calculate the probability that this is the third student chosen.

  b Claude goes to school by bus.
    The probability that the bus is late is 0.1.
    If the bus is late, the probability that Claude is late to school is 0.8.
    If the bus is not late, the probability that Claude is late to school is 0.05.
    i Calculate the probability that the bus is late and Claude is late to school.
    ii Calculate the probability that Claude is late to school.
    iii The school term lasts 56 days.
     How many days would Claude expect to be late?   (0580 paper 04 Q2 November 2007)

11

| 1 | 1 | 6 | 7 | 11 | 12 |

Six cards are numbered 1, 1, 6, 7, 11 and 12.
In this question, give all probabilities as fractions.

  a One of the six cards is chosen at random.
    i Which number has a probability of being chosen of $\frac{1}{3}$?
    ii What is the probability of choosing a card with a number which is smaller than **at least three of the other numbers**?

  b Two of the six cards are chosen at random, without replacement.
    Find the probability that
    i they are both numbered 1,
    ii the total of the two numbers is 18,
    iii the first number **is not** a 1 and the second number is a 1.

  c Cards are chosen, without replacement, until a card numbered 1 is chosen.
    Find the probability that this happens before the third card is chosen.

  d A seventh card is added to the six cards shown in the diagram.
    The mean value of the seven numbers on the cards is 6.
    Find the number on the seventh card.   (0580 paper 04 Q3 November 2009)

12 a Nadia must choose a ball from Bag A or from Bag B.
    The probability that she chooses Bag A is $\frac{2}{3}$.
    Bag A contains 5 white and 3 black balls.
    Bag B contains 6 white and 2 black balls.
    The tree diagram below shows some
    of this information.

Bag A   Bag B

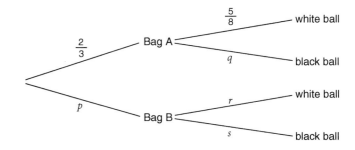

    i   Find the values of p, q, r and s.

    ii   Find the probability that Nadia chooses Bag A and then a white ball.

    iii   Find the probability that Nadia chooses a white ball.

  b   Another bag contains 7 green balls and 3 yellow balls.

      Sani takes three balls out of the bag, without replacement.

    i   Find the probability that all three balls he chooses are yellow.

    ii   Find the probability that at least one of the three balls he chooses is green.

(0580 paper 04 Q3 June 2008)

13 a   There are 30 students in a class.

     20 study Physics, 15 study Chemistry and 3 study neither physics nor chemistry.

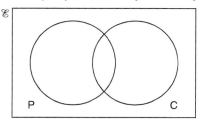

    i   Copy and complete the Venn diagram to show this information.

    ii   Find the number of students who study both physics and chemistry.

    iii   A student is chosen at random. Find the probability that the student studies physics but not chemistry.

    iv   A student who studies physics is chosen at random. Find the probability that this student does not study chemistry.

  b   Bag A contains 6 white beads and 3 black beads.

     Bag B contains 6 white beads and 4 black beads.

     One bead is chosen at random from each bag.

     Find the probability that

    i   both beads are black,

    ii   at least one of the two beads is white.

     The beads are not replaced.

     A second bead is chosen at random from each bag.

     Find the probability that

    iii   all four beads are white,

    iv   the beads are not all the same colour.

(0580 paper 04 Q7 June 2004)

14 The ages of a sample of 40 students were recorded.

    The results are given in the table below.

Age (x years)	$8 < x \leqslant 10$	$10 < x \leqslant 11$	$11 < x \leqslant 12$	$12 < x \leqslant 14$	$14 < x \leqslant 16$	$16 < x \leqslant 19$
Frequency	7	8	6	10	3	6

  a   Using a scale of 1 cm to represent 1 year, draw a horizontal axis for ages from 8 to 19 years.

     Using a scale of 1 cm to represent 1 unit, draw a vertical axis for frequency densities from 0 to 8 units.

     On your axes, draw a histogram to illustrate the distribution of ages.

  b   In which interval does the median lie?

  c   Calculate an estimate of the mean age of the students.

  d   Calculate an estimate of the number of students who were under 13 years old.

e One student is chosen at random from this sample of 40 students.
   Write down the probability that this student is
   i   under 8,
   ii over 16.
f A second student is now chosen at random from the remaining 39 students. Calculate the probability that one student is over 16 and the other is not over 16.
   Give your answer as a fraction in its lowest terms.

   (4024 paper 02 Q10 June 2004)

15 A bag contained 5 Red and 2 Blue beads.
   Chris took 3 beads, at random, and without replacement, from the bag. The probability tree shows the possible outcomes and their probabilities.

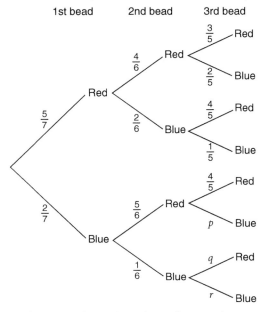

1st bead   2nd bead   3rd bead

   i   Write down the values of p, q and r.
   ii Expressing each answer as a fraction in its lowest terms, find the probability that
      a   three Red beads were taken,
      b   the first bead was Red, the second Blue and the third Red,
      c   two of the beads were Red and one was Blue.   (4024 paper 02 Q5b June 2005)

16 Each member of a group of 16 children solved a puzzle.
   The times they took are summarised in the table below.

Times (*t* minutes)	$5 < t \leqslant 10$	$10 < t \leqslant 12$	$12 < t \leqslant 14$	$14 < t \leqslant 16$	$16 < t \leqslant 20$
Frequency	2	4	6	3	1

   i   Write down an estimate of the number of children who took less than 13 minutes.
   ii   Calculate an estimate of the mean time taken to solve the puzzle.
   iii Two children are chosen at random.
       Calculate, as a fraction in its simplest form, the probability that one of these children took more than 10 minutes and the other took 10 minutes or less.
   iv   A histogram is drawn to illustrate this information.
       The height of the rectangle representing the number of children in the interval $10 < t \leqslant 12$ is 8 cm.
       Calculate the height of the rectangle representing the number of children in the interval $5 < t \leqslant 10$.   (4024 paper 02 Q10b June 2006)

17 Emma noted the number of letters in each of the 25 words in an examination question.
The results are given in the table below.

Number of letters	2	3	4	5	6	7	8
Frequency	2	6	5	5	4	0	3

  a For this distribution,
     i write down the mode,
    ii find the median,
   iii calculate the mean.

  b Emma chose one word, at random, from the 25 words.
    Find the probability that this word had
     i 5 or 6 letters,
    ii fewer than 9 letters.

  c Peter chose one word, at random, from the 25 words.
    He then chose a second word, at random, from the remaining words.
    Expressing each answer as a fraction in its lowest terms, find the probability that
     i both words had 6 letters,
    ii one word had 2 letters and the other had 4 letters.   (4024 paper 02 Q5 June 2007)

18 a Mary has 50 counters.
    Some of the counters are square, the remainder are round.
    There are 11 square counters that are green.
    There are 15 square counters that are not green.
    Of the round counters, the number that are not green is double the number that
    are green.
    By drawing a Venn diagram, or otherwise, find the number of counters that are
     i round,
    ii round and green,
   iii not green.

  b Tina has two fair, normal 6-sided dice. One is red and the other is blue.
    She throws both of them once.
    You may find it helpful to draw a possibility diagram to answer the following questions.
    Find, as a fraction in its lowest terms, the probability that
     i the red die shows a 2 and the blue die does **not** show a 2,
    ii the sum of the two numbers shown is equal to 5,
   iii one die shows a 3 and the other shows an even number.

             (4024 paper 02 Q5a and b June 2008)

19 The heights of 120 children were measured.
The results are summarised in the table below.

Height (h cm)	$135 < h \leqslant 140$	$140 < h \leqslant 145$	$145 < h \leqslant 150$	$150 < h \leqslant 155$	$155 < h \leqslant 160$	$160 < h \leqslant 180$
Frequency	15	20	25	30	20	10

  a Using a scale of 1 cm to represent 5 cm, draw a horizontal axis for heights from 135 cm
    to 180 cm.
    Using a scale of 2 cm to represent 1 unit, draw a vertical axis for frequency densities
    from 0 to 6 units.
    On your axes, draw a histogram to represent the information in the table.

  b Estimate how many children have heights greater than 170 cm.

   c One child was chosen at random.
Find the probability that the height of this child was less than or equal to 140 cm.
Give your answer as a fraction in its lowest terms.

   d Two children were chosen at random.
Find the probability that they both had heights in the range $150 < h \leqslant 155$.

(4024 paper 02 Q4 November 2008)

20 The waiting times of 50 people at a supermarket checkout were recorded.
The results are summarised in the table below.

Times (t minutes)	$1 < t \leqslant 3$	$3 < t \leqslant 4$	$4 < t \leqslant 5$	$5 < t \leqslant 7$	$7 < t \leqslant 9$	$9 < t \leqslant 12$
Number of people	4	10	8	14	8	6

   a Using a scale of 1 cm to represent 1 minute, draw a horizontal axis for waiting times between 0 and 12 minutes.
Using a scale of 1 cm to represent 1 unit, draw a vertical axis for frequency densities from 0 to 10 units.
On your axes, draw a histogram to illustrate the distribution of waiting times.

   b In which class does the upper quartile lie?

   c Calculate an estimate of the mean waiting time.

   d One person is chosen, at random, from the 50 people.
Write down the probability that this person waited
     i less than 1 minute,   **ii** more than 5 minutes.

   e A second person is now chosen, at random, from the remaining 49 people.
Expressing each answer as a fraction in its lowest terms, calculate the probability that
     i both people waited more than 5 minutes,
     ii one person waited more than 5 minutes and the other waited 5 minutes or less.

(4024 paper 02 Q10 June 2009)

21 In a group of 8 students there are 5 boys and 3 girls.
Two students are chosen at random.
The tree diagram shows the possible outcomes and their probabilities.

   a Copy and complete the tree diagram.

   b Expressing each answer as a fraction in its lowest terms, find the probability that
     i two boys are chosen,
     ii at least one boy is chosen.

First student   Second student

$\frac{5}{8}$ Boy $\frac{4}{7}$ Boy $\frac{3}{7}$ Girl

$\frac{3}{8}$ Girl   ...... Boy   ...... Girl

(4024 paper 01 Q21 November 2009)

22 A bag contains 1 red, 1 blue and 3 green balls.
Two balls are taken from the bag, at random, without replacement.
The tree diagram that represents these events is drawn below.

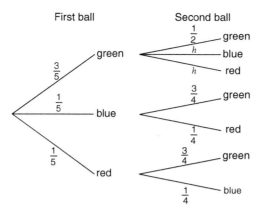

First ball   Second ball

a   Write down the value of h.

b   Expressing each answer in its simplest form, calculate the probability that

   i   both balls are green,   **ii**   both balls are blue,

  iii neither ball is green.   (4024 paper 01 Q21 November 2007)

Revision and Examination Technique

Now that you have worked through the whole book, how can you maximize your chances of success? Read through the suggestions and hints below and make a note of any that might help you.

Revision

Give yourself time to do some systematic revision before your examination. The points outlined here should give you some ideas for a routine you could follow.

- Have a special notebook for revision, some coloured pencils and a highlighter or two. Make sure that you have some tracing paper, a protractor, compasses and a ruler ready before you start.

- Make sure that you have a suitable calculator, which has a fully charged battery and you can use it for all your revision. You must know exactly how it works. You should already be very practiced in working without a calculator.

- Read each chapter through carefully, noting down in your revision notebook anything you think you might not remember. In particular, write down any formulae that you will need to learn. It is helpful to underline things in different colours, or use different coloured pens to write them down. Make your notebook as visually attractive as you can.

- Try the examination questions at the end of each chapter, *checking each answer as you go along*. It does not matter if you have already done these questions because you are unlikely to remember them all! If you need to look anything up in your revision notebook highlight it, so that you can learn it later.

- Get someone to test you on the formulae that you need to know. You *must* know the formulae or you will not be able to answer the questions! Do not just hope that you will remember them, LEARN them, and keep checking that you know them.

Method marks

- Look at the marks available for each part of the question: if there is more than one mark available you must *earn* the extra marks. This means that you *must show your working*, or you are in danger of getting no marks for that part of the question.

- In some questions you will be asked to show that some statement or result is correct. In these questions you will have to show your working. This means that you must write down the steps in the working in a way that someone can understand. Pretend that the answer is not given, and work it out. The reason that some questions are worded in this way is that the result is needed in the rest of the question. This gives you a chance to finish the question even if you get the first step wrong, but do use the result given in the question even if you have not been able to prove it!

Accuracy marks

- Some accuracy marks are awarded for getting exactly the right answer, and some for giving the answer rounded to a required degree of accuracy. In the general instructions on the front of the paper you are usually told to give answers to three significant figures if they are not exact, or unless the question specifies otherwise, so read each question carefully to see if a required degree of accuracy is specified. Angles should be given correct to one decimal place. Answers should be rounded, not truncated (for example, 12.36 should be given as 12.4, not 12.3), and you should not round in a stepwise way, (for example, 14.345 should be given as 14.3, not rounded to 14.35 and then 14.4.)

- However, you must not round in the middle of your working or you will lose the accuracy in the final answer. When you use your calculator write down most of the figures on your calculator display for each step of your working, and try to keep the answer in your calculator ready for the next step (for example, in a trigonometry question, $\sin x = 0.64571\ldots$ should not be rounded before entering *shift* $\sin 0.64571\ldots$, to obtain the answer $x = 40.2189\ldots$, which is then given as $x = 40.2°$). In this way you should not lose accuracy as you work through the question.

General points

- Write your answers clearly in ink. If you make a mistake cross through the work which is wrong and replace it. Do not use correcting fluid. If the work is crossed out, is still readable, and has not been replaced, it may be marked.

- Graphs and accurate drawings should be done in pencil. They must be recognisable, which means that the pencil marks must not be too faint.

- Make sure that your writing is readable.

- Remember to check that your answer seems reasonable. Do you expect the hypotenuse in a right-angled triangle to be larger or smaller than the other sides? If money is earning interest in the bank should you end up with more or less than when you started? Is it reasonable for your journey to school to be 200 km? Could the mean age of the students in your class possibly be 3 years 5 months?

- Remember that there are 60 minutes in one hour, not 100. So 6.5 hours is 6 hours and 30 minutes, not 6 hours and 50 minutes.

- Leave in your construction lines when you are drawing accurately.

- You will already have been told many times to *read the question carefully*. This means that you should make sure that you are answering the question that has been set, and also giving the answer in the form required.

- It is easy in the stress of an examination to make errors when copying numbers, both from the question to your working, and then from your working to the answers space. So take extra care.

- Make sure that your calculator is set in degrees, not 'rads' or 'grads'.

- Remember that to obtain an answer correct to a certain accuracy you must not approximate until the last stage of the working. (Rounding too early in the working is known as 'premature approximation' and can lead to an inaccurate answer).

- Learn to use your calculator memory.

- Read the question carefully to make sure that you are giving your answer in the required form. For example, note which units are required, or what degree of accuracy is expected.

- Look out for questions where, for example, some measurements are given in centimetres and some in metres.

- In questions which require you to 'show that' some statement or result is true make sure that you write down sufficient working to show that you know the method that is required, and give your answer in a clear and logical order.

- Be careful how you write fractions. A quarter of x should be written $\frac{1}{4}x$, or with the x level with the 1 in the numerator, *not* level with the 4 in the denominator. Careless use of fractions can all too easily lead to wrong working, thus losing marks unnecessarily. Remember that, in an examination, 'follow through' marks might be available for subsequent working, however, it can happen that the subsequent working is not actually possible if a fundamental mistake has been made.

- Remember to indicate vectors by underlining the lower case letter you are using to represent the vector (for example, u), and directed line segments by using an arrow over the capital letters (for example, $\overrightarrow{AB}$).

- Do not waste time using the Sine and Cosine Rules in a right-angled triangle; the sine, cosine and tangent ratios are quicker and simpler.

Answers

Chapter 1

Essential Skills

a 24	**b** 21	**c** 40	**d** 72	**e** 14
f 54	**g** 64	**h** 45	**i** 49	**j** 18
k 13	**l** 13	**m** 16	**n** 17	**o** 17
p 20	**q** 19	**r** 12	**s** 21	**t** 21
u 5	**v** 4	**w** 6	**x** 3	**y** 2
z 4				

Exercise 1.1

1 a $5, -100, -3.67, \pi, 0, 1507, \frac{99}{7}, \frac{6}{1}$

b $5, -100, -3.67, 0, 1507, \frac{99}{7}, \frac{6}{1}$

c $5, -100, 0, 1507, \frac{6}{1}$ **d** $5, 1507, \frac{6}{1}$ **e** π

2 a 1, 2, 3, 5, 6, 10, 15, 30   **b** 2, 3, 5
c $30 = 2 \times 3 \times 5$ **d** for example, 60, 90, 120
3 a 30, 45, 15, 1500   **b** 1, 5, 15, 3
4 a 2, 3, 5
b $2 \times 2 \times 2 \times 2 \times 3 \times 5$ or $2^4 \times 3 \times 5$
5 23, 29, 31, 37
6 37, 53, 101
7 a 83, 89   **b** 80, 85, 90   **c** 87

Exercise 1.2

1 a {1, 2, 4, 8} {1, 2, 3, 4, 6, 12}   **b** 4
2 21
3 a i 1, 3, 5, 15   **ii** 1, 5, 7, 35   **iii** 1, 2, 4, 5, 10, 20
b 5
4 a 12, 24, 36, 48, 60, 72
   8, 16, 24, 32, 40, 48
b 24
5 60
6 21603:
   does not divide by 2 (not even)
   does divide by 3 (digital root is 3)
   does not divide by 5 (does not end in 5 or 0)
   does not divide by 9 (digital root is not 9)
7 515196:
   does divide by 2 (even number)
   does divide by 3 (digital root is 9)
   does not divide by 5 (does not end in 5 or 0)
   does divide by 6 (even and divides by 3)
   does divide by 9 (digital root is 9)

Exercise 1.3

1 a divide   **b** add
   c square root   **d** cube
2 a 36   **b** 3   **c** 8
   d 5   **e** 100   **f** 1000
3 a 27.04   **b** 9.1
   c 10   **d** 10
4 a $\sqrt{256}, \sqrt{841}, \sqrt{449.44}$ **b** $\sqrt{6.1}, \sqrt{7}$
5 1, 4, 9, 16, 25, 36, 49   **6** 27, 125
7 1   **8** for example, 64
9

Natural numbers	1 2 3 4 5 6 7 8 9 1 11
Prime numbers	2 3 5 7 11
Even numbers	2 4 6 8 10
Multiples of 3	3 6 9
Square numbers	1 4 9
Cube numbers	1 8
Factors of 20	1 2 4 5 10

Exercise 1.4

1 a −5   **b** −5   **c** −3
   d −7   **e** 5
2 a 2.5m   **b** −3.6m   **c** 5.6m
3 85m
4 a $287   **b** yes   **c** $3

Exercise 1.5

1 a π **b** $\sqrt{\ }$ **c** $\sqrt[3]{\ }$
   d $\neq$ **e** $<$ **f** $\geq$
2 a $2 < 4$ **b** $-2 > -5$
   c $-10 < 4$ **d** $-1 < 0$
3 −100, −89, −76, −62, −1, 0, 61, 75, 100, 101

Exercise 1.6

1 a 1.2×10^4 **b** 3.65×10^2
   c 5.9103×10^4 **d** 6×10^3
   e 7.0104×10^6
2 a 3.5×10^{-3} **b** 1.56×10^{-1} **c** 5×10^{-4}
   d 4.3×10^{-6} **e** 1.02×10^{-2}
3 a 3.45×10^{-3} **b** 5.2016×10^5
   c 1.12×10^2 **d** 1×10^{-3}
   e 1.001×10^{-1} **f** 2×10^6
4 a 5600   **b** 0.00027   **c** 0.0116
   d 600000   **e** 0.002

5 a 18   **b** 14   **c** 0   **d** 3

6 a 5   **b** 41   **c** 19

7 a $(5 - 3) \times 4 = 8$

  b $9 + (50 - 24) \div 2 = 22$

  c $(31 - 15) \div (10 - 2) = 2$

Exercise 1.7

1 a   i true   **ii** true   **iii** false   **iv** true

  b   i $-4 < 3$ **ii** $0 > -2$ **iii** $5 > -5$ **iv** $3 > -2$

  c   i $\{2, 3, 5, 7\}$

    ii $\{1, 3, 5, 9, 15, 45\}$

    iii $\{3, 6, 9, 12, 15, 18\}$

2 a 60   **b** 90

3 a 4   **b** 4

4 a 4.41   **b** 27   **c** 5.3

  d 9   **e** 5

5 $2^3 \times 3 \times 5^2$

6 1, 2, 4, 5, 8, 10, 16, 20, 32, 40, 80, 160

7 a 42   **b** 4

8 $1 + 72 \div (4 \times 2) = 10$

9 39

10 842 m

11 a $2 \times 7 \times 11$ **b** 1078

12 $(10 - 5) \times (9 + 3) = 60$

13 28

14 3.62×10^{-3}

15 a $2^2 \times 3^3$ **b** $2^3 \times 3^3 \times 5$ or 1080   **c** $k = 75$

16 a 27, 64   **b** 31, 37

17 a 1, 2, 3, 6, 9, 18   **b** $2^3 \times 7^2$

18 a 98   **b** 28

Chapter 2

Essential Skills

1 a 10   **b** 14   **c** 24   **d** 60

2 a 12   **b** 6   **c** 50   **d** 8

Exercise 2.1

1 a $3\frac{4}{5}$ **b** $20\frac{1}{10}$ **c** $16\frac{1}{2}$

2 a $\frac{31}{8}$ **b** $\frac{201}{2}$ **c** $\frac{47}{12}$

3 $\frac{5}{15} = \frac{10}{30} = \frac{1}{3} = \frac{7}{21} = \frac{21}{63}$

4 a $\frac{70}{100}$ **b** $\frac{16}{100}$ **c** $\frac{95}{100}$

  d $\frac{26}{100}$ **e** $\frac{9}{100}$

5 a $\frac{5}{7}$ **b** $\frac{1}{5}$ **c** $\frac{5}{12}$ **d** $\frac{35}{36}$

  e $3\frac{19}{20}$ **f** $1\frac{9}{10}$ **g** $\frac{1}{7}$ **h** $\frac{7}{12}$

6 a $\frac{2}{7}$ **b** $\frac{5}{6}$ **c** $\frac{3}{4}$ **d** $\frac{1}{8}$

7 21

8 15

Exercise 2.2

1 a $\frac{3}{5}$ **b** $1\frac{1}{5}$ **c** $7\frac{1}{2}$

2 a $\frac{1}{18}$ **b** $\frac{3}{28}$ **c** $\frac{15}{32}$

3 a $\frac{1}{14}$ **b** $\frac{7}{20}$ **c** $\frac{1}{6}$

4 a $8\frac{1}{8}$ **b** $11\frac{9}{10}$ **c** $3\frac{1}{9}$

5 a $7\frac{1}{2}$ **b** $\frac{4}{9}$ **c** $\frac{1}{14}$

6 a $1\frac{1}{6}$ **b** $\frac{6}{7}$ **c** $\frac{35}{54}$

7 a $\frac{1}{3}$ **b** 3   **c** $1\frac{2}{3}$

8 a $1\frac{5}{6}$ **b** $7\frac{1}{3}$ **c** $2\frac{4}{25}$

9 a 6   **b** $\frac{18}{25}$ **c** $5\frac{4}{9}$

Exercise 2.3

1 13.86   **2** 502.97   **3** 16.55

4 4.109   **5** 13410   **6** 16.9

7 0.06017   **8** 31.62   **9** 15.8

Exercise 2.4

	Fraction	Decimal	Percentage
1	$\frac{1}{2}$	0.5	50%
2	$\frac{1}{4}$	0.25	25%
3	$\frac{3}{4}$	0.75	75%
4	$\frac{1}{10}$	0.1	10%
5	$\frac{3}{10}$	0.3	30%
6	$\frac{1}{5}$	0.2	20%
7	$\frac{1}{8}$	0.125	12.5%

Exercise 2.5

Example methods

1 75% of $64 = \frac{3}{4}$ of $64 = 3 \times \frac{1}{4} \times 64 = 3 \times 16 = 48$

2 30% of $1550 = 0.3 \times 1550 = 465$

3 9% of $3400 = 9 \times \frac{1}{100} \times 3400 = 9 \times 34 = 306$

4 55.5% of $680 = 50\%$ of $680 + 5\%$ of $680 + 0.5\%$ of 680
         $= 340 + 34 + 3.4 = 377.4$

5 3% of $73 = 3 \times \frac{1}{100} \times 73 = 3 \times 0.73 = 2.19$

Exercise 2.6

1 25% **2** 12%

3 46% **4** 32%

5 6.8% **6** 50%

7 200% **8** 2.9%

Exercise 2.7

1 $\frac{7}{10}$ **2** 4.098, 4.105, 4.51, 4.579

3 $\frac{2}{3}, \frac{3}{4}, \frac{4}{5}, \frac{17}{20}$ **4** $\frac{3}{50}, \frac{3}{25}, \frac{33}{100}, 33\frac{1}{3}\%, \frac{67}{200}$

Exercise 2.8

1 a $\frac{13}{15}$ **b** $\frac{4}{7}$

2 a $4 + 6 \times (7 - 5) = 16$ **b** 0.054

3 a 0.65 **b** 80%

4 a $\frac{8}{21}$ **b** $\frac{24}{35}$

5 a 52.7% **b** 70

6 a $\frac{11}{21}$ **b** $\frac{8}{45}$

7 80%, $62\frac{1}{2}\%$

8 a $\frac{1}{14}$ **b** $4\frac{2}{3}$

9 a 6.7 **b** 0.051

10 a 0.0035 **b** 0.8

11 0.39 $\frac{2}{5}$ $\frac{9}{20}$ 46%

12 a $15\frac{1}{2}$ **b** 0.175

13 a $\frac{11}{28}$ **b** 10

14 $d = 12$ $n = 26$

15 a $\frac{3}{10}$ **b** 82

16 a 2.44 **b** 0.021

17 a 11 **b** 0.014

18 a 1 **b** $\frac{8}{15}$

19 a $\frac{66}{100}$ $\frac{666}{1000}$ $0.\dot{6}$ 0.67

 b 1.507×10^9

Chapter 3

Essential Skills

1 a $2 \times 6 + 3 \times 5$ **b** $3 \times (6 - 4)$
  $= 12 + 15 = 27$ $= 3 \times 2 = 6$
 c $1 + 2 \times 3 - 4 \div 2 + 5 \times (6 - 3)$
  $= 1 + 2 \times 3 - 4 \div 2 + 5 \times 3$
  $= 1 + 6 - 2 + 15$
  $= 20$

2 i $5 + 6 = 11$ **ii** $5 \times 6 = 30$

3 i Factors of 20 = {1, 2, 4, 5, 10, 20}
  Factors of 45 = {1, 3, 5, 9, 15, 45}
  Factors of 15 = {1, 3, 5, 15}
  HCF of 20, 45 and 15 is 5

Exercise 3.1

a i $3x$ **ii** 90

b i y **ii** 154

c i z^3 **ii** 27

d i $3x - y$ **ii** 8

e i $2x + 2y$ **ii** 22

f i 0 **ii** 0

g i $x^2 + y^2$ **ii** 25

h i $8x - 2y$ **ii** 392

Exercise 3.2

1 $2m + n$

2 $6.5 - m$

3 a $T = 10 + t$ **b** $T = 25$

4 a $x = 21$ **b** $x = 17$ **c** $x = 51$

5 a $L = 2a + 3$ **b** $L = 23$

 c i and **ii** would not make triangles

6 a $C = \frac{e}{2} + b + \frac{t}{2}$ **b** $C = 75$

7 a 6 **b** 1 **c** 5 **d** 33

Exercise 3.3

1 $13x$ **2** $11x$ **3** $7x - 4y$

4 $4a + 6b$ **5** $3x + y$ **6** $3x + 3$

7 $4z + 3w$ **8** $6c - 3$ **9** $3 + 2a$

10 x **11** $x^2 + 2y^2$

12 $3x^2 + 3x$ **13** $5x^2 + 3xy$

14 $3x^2 + y^2 - xy$ **15** $3x^2 + xy - 4y^2$

16 $3x^2 - 5x^3 + 3x^2y$ **17** $4x^2y^2 - 2x^2y$

Exercise 3.4

1 $15ab$ **2** $24yz$ **3** $6x^2$

4 $60x^2$ **5** $6xyz$ **6** a

7 $60abd^2$ **8** $\frac{4}{x}$ **9** $2d$

10 $2x$ **11** $\frac{1}{2d}$ **12** $\frac{3}{2}$

13 $20abcd$ **14** 12

Exercise 3.5

1 -7 **2** 7 **3** 0

4 0 **5** 0 **6** 0

7 -6 **8** 7 **9** 1

10 5

Exercise 3.6

1 **a** 5   **b** 1   **c** −1
   d −5   **e** 1   **f** 1
   g −5   **h** −5
2 **a** 6   **b** −6   **c** 6
   d −6   **e** −6
3 **a** 2   **b** −2   **c** 2   **d** −2
4 **a** $\frac{1}{2}$ **b** $-\frac{1}{2}$ **c** $\frac{1}{2}$ **d** $-\frac{1}{2}$
5 10   6 −2   7 10
8 10   9 −9
10 **a** 1   **b** −2   **c** 1
   d −1   **e** 1
11 14

Exercise 3.7

1 $-2xy$ 2 $2xy$ 3 $-x-2y$
4 $-x+2y$ 5 $\frac{a^2}{2}$ 6 $-\frac{a}{2b}$
7 $8xy$ 8 $\frac{x}{2y}$ 9 $-3x^2y$
10 $xy-3x$ 11 $-\frac{y}{3}$ 12 $-6x^2y$
13 $-6z+3x^2$ 14 $2a+3b$

Exercise 3.8

1 **a** 1024   **b** 25   **c** 32
   d 4   **e** 512
2 **a** x^9 **b** x^4+x^5 **c** $2x^3$
   d x^6 **e** x^4 **f** $6x^{11}$
   g $5x^5$ **h** $4x^2$ **i** $4x^2$
   j $4x^6$ **k** $4x^6$ **l** x^{45}
3 **a** $6x^{10}$ **b** $2x^{13}y^3$ **c** $9x^6$
   d $24x^5y$

Exercise 3.9

1 **a** 16   **b** $\frac{1}{16}$ **c** 4
   d $\frac{1}{16}$ **e** $\frac{1}{25}$ **f** $\frac{2}{5}$
   g $\frac{1}{10}$ **h** $\frac{4}{25}$ **i** 8
   j $\frac{4}{25}$ **k** $\frac{49}{4}$ or $12\frac{1}{4}$ **l** $\frac{64}{343}$
2 **a** $\frac{y}{x^2}$ **b** $\frac{y^4}{x^8}$ **c** 1
   d 1   **e** $x^2y^3z^4$ **f** x^7y^8
3 **a** $n=3$ **b** $n=-4$ **c** $n=-1$
   d $n=2$ **e** $n=3$ **f** $n=-3$
   g $n=-3$ **h** $n=1$ **i** $n=0$
   j $n=-3$ **k** $n=-2$ **l** $n=1$
   m $n=2$ **n** $n=3$ **o** $n=1$
   p $n=4$ **q** $n=k+1$ **r** $n=k-2$
4 **a** $3x^2+2x^3$ **b** $\frac{6}{x^5}$ **c** $\frac{1}{3}x^2$
   d $9x^2$ **e** 18   **f** 24

Exercise 3.10

1 $2a+2b$ 2 $18+6x$
3 $3x-3y$ 4 $30-5b$
5 $12x-8$ 6 $7-21c$
7 $30x+25y$ 8 $8x-8y+32z$
9 $5x^2+20$ 10 $14x^2-21y^2$
11 $12xy+20z$ 12 $2x-3xy$
13 a^2+2a 14 x^2-xy
15 $2c^2+2cd$ 16 $6m^2-3mn$
17 $8x^2y-36xy^2$ 18 $21x^2-14x^2y+28x^2z$

Exercise 3.11

1 $6+8x$ 2 $-6-8x$ 3 $3x^2+4xy$
4 $-3x^2-4xy$ 5 $-3x^2+4xy$
6 $-14x^2+12x$ 7 $-x-y$
8 $-2+z$ 9 $6pq+18pr-6ps$
10 $-6pq-18pr+6ps$
11 $x^2y^2-5x^2y$ 12 $-6x^2y+9x^2$
13 $-8a-12a^2$ 14 $8a+12a^2$
15 $2y$ 16 $5a+12b$
17 $-22x-23y$ 18 $7x-y$
19 $-3x+7y$ 20 $xy-y$

Exercise 3.12

1 $4(2x+y)$ 2 $5(3a-5b)$ 3 $4(x-5)$
4 $x(y+2)$ 5 $x(x-2)$ 6 $x(x-1)$
7 $3x(y+3)$ 8 $3x^2(x-3y)$
9 $3a(a-2b)$ 10 $yz(x+4)$
11 $10y(1+10y)$ 12 $fg(5+6h)$
13 $3x(b-2y)$ 14 $3bx(b-2)$
15 $2b(2b-1)$ 16 $b(4b-1)$
17 $xy(xy-1)$ 18 $7cd^2(c-3)$

Exercise 3.13

1 $-24x^2z$ 2 $-3x+3y$
3 **a** 35   **b** −7   **c** 33
   d −1   **e** −10   **f** 0
   g −80   **h** −12
4 $2x^2-y-5$
5 **a** 1   **b** 1   **c** 1
   d 0   **e** x **f** 0
   g $4x$ **h** 1   **i** 1
   j x^4 **k** 1   **l** x^2
   m $-x^3$ **n** $-x^2$
6 for example,
   a $x=1, y=3$ **b** $x=2, y=-3$
   c $x=2, y=1$ **d** $x=5, y=7$
   e $x=3, y=2$ **f** $x=3, y=-1$
   g $x=4, y=3$ **h** $x=9, y=4$
   i $x=12, y=13$

7 a $\frac{16}{9}$ **b** $\frac{9}{19}$ **c** 1

    d $\frac{1}{4}$ **e** $\frac{121}{25}$ or $4\frac{21}{25}$

8 a $6x + 4y$ **b** $-3x^5$ **c** $6xy$

    d $\frac{1}{x}$ **e** x^4 **f** x^5

9 a $n = 4$ **b** $n = -2$ **c** $n = 1$

    d $n = 2$ **e** $n = -1$

10 a $a^2b - abc$ **b** $5x + 8y + 2xy$

    c $6ab + 8ac$ **d** $-3x^2 - 6x$

11 a $ab(b - a)$ **b** $2x(x - 3y + 2)$

    c $2xyz\,(z + 2xy)$ **d** $2abc(1 - 2abc)$

12 a x^2 **b** ab **c** $2x^5$

    d ab^3c^5 **e** a^6 **f** x^2

13 a $f = 10 - \frac{b}{2}$ **b** $f = 7$ **c** $b = 12$

14 a 2 **b** -9 **c** $-x + 2$

    d $2y$ **e** $\frac{1}{3}$ **f** $\frac{2}{x}$

15 $2x(2y - 3z)$

16 $y = 13$

17 a 100 **b** 400

18 a a^7 **b** b

19 a i $8t + 17$ **ii** $2p + 13q$

    b $5x^2y\,(5xy - 3)$

20 a $n = 3$ **b** $n = -4$

    c $n = 0$ **d** $n = -2$

21 $\frac{4}{9}$

22 a $y = -30$ **b** $v(4u - 3)$

23 $\frac{1}{64}$

24 -9

25 a $3r - 3s$ **b** q **c** p^4

26 a p^5 **b** q^7 **c** r^6

27 a $7a(c + 2)$ **b** $6ax(2x + 3a^2)$

28 a $p = 10$ **b** $q = 3$ **c** $r = -2$

29 a $4a^5$ **b** $3x^2 + 13x + 6$

30 $(-1)^3$ 3^{-1} 3^0 3^1

31 $9x^6$

32 $5x^6$

Chapter 4

Essential Skills

1 a 1.2345×10^4 **b** 3.4×10^{-4}

2 a $3\,450\,000$ **b** $0.005\,123$

3 a 137.7 **b** 6%

4 a i 64.5 **ii** $830\,000$

    b i 25.9 **ii** $0.007\,015$

Exercise 4.1

1 a 6 km²   **b** 45000 m²
    c 48 cm²   **d** 20 m²

2 a 343 m³   **b** 1000 cm³
    c 12 m³   **d** 200 cm³

3 a 32 cm   **b** 24 m

Exercise 4.2

1 33 cm   **2** 63 g   **3** 706 kg
4 611 m   **5** 500 km   **6** 91 cm
7 90 kg   **8** 61 m   **9** 60 m
10 800   **11** 10   **12** 100

Exercise 4.3

1 240   **2** 520   **3** 7400
4 600   **5** 3990   **6** 8000
7 1000   **8** 56.1   **9** 56.14
10 56.136   **11** 3.1   **12** 3.10

Exercise 4.4

1 216   **2** 220   **3** 350
4 400   **5** 6010   **6** 6000
7 81.0   **8** 0.199   **9** 0.20
10 1.00   **11** 0.000395   **12** 0.0004
13 10.1   **14** 657000   **15** 700000

Exercise 4.5

1 23720   **2** 8.18 to 3 sf
3 5.6° to 1 dp   **4** 56.23

Exercise 4.6

1 156.5 cm
2 a $9.5 \le w < 10.5$ **b** $18.5 \le h < 19.5$
3 a 14.5 cm $\le$ 15 cm < 15.5 cm
    b 23.55 cm $\le$ 23.6 cm < 23.65 cm
    c $3055 \le 3060 < 3065$
    d $99.65 \le 99.7 < 99.75$
    e $678.85 \le 678.9 < 678.95$
    f $55000 \le 60000 < 65000$
    g $250 \le 300 < 350$
    h $99.85 \le 99.9 < 99.95$
4 a 8.5 g   **b** 9.5 g

Exercise 4.7

1 a 350 cm   **b** 58.1 cm
    c 0.04096 km   **d** 570000 mm
    e 812 g   **f** 300 mm²
    g 0.050681 km²   **h** 6700 cm³
    i 0.21 litres
2 a 195 cm²
    b 1977 mm² or 19.77 cm²
3 a 3.038 m³   **b** 10.44 cm³

Exercise 4.8

1. a $2000 + 1000 + 2000 + 2000 = 7000$ km
   b 35 days
2. a $200000 + 500 \times 1000 = 700000$
   b $(4+1)^2 \div (7-2) = 5$
   c $\frac{4000}{200} + \frac{4000}{50} = 100$
3. a 8.2×10^8 b 2.05×10^2
   c 4.272×10^7 d 9.0109×10^5
4. a 30 b 300 c 7
   d 20 e 70
5. a 1320 b 100 c 14700
   d 10761 e 2.4 f 35
6. a 3 b 1000
7. a 1.89 b 6.75
   c 0.028 d 1890

Exercise 4.9

1. Estimate: $30 + 400 \times 0.03 = 42$
   Calculator: 45.2569
2. Estimate: $7 \times 3 - 20 + 20 \times 30 \approx 600$
   Calculator: 480 to 3 sf
3. Estimate: $\frac{30+3}{10} + 30 \approx 33$
   Calculator: 31.2 to 3 sf
4. Estimate: $\sqrt{\frac{20+20}{20-6}} \approx 2$
   Calculator: 1.94 to 3 sf
5. Estimate: $1 \times 10^4 - 6 \times 10^3 = 4 \times 10^3$
   Calculator: 6.52×10^3
6. Estimate: $4 \times 10^5 \times 8 \times 10^3 \approx 3 \times 10^9$
   Calculator: 3.03×10^9

Exercise 4.10

1. a $1 : 16$ b $2 : 3 : 5$
   c $1 : 8$ d $5 : 1$
   e $5 : 1$ f $1 : 200000$
   g $6 : 7$ h $55 : 28$
2. $1 : 30$
3. $1 : 4$
4. a $0.9 : 1$ b $200000 : 1$
5. a $1 : 0.25$ b $1 : 12$
6. $1 : 150$
7. a $1 : 9$ b $0.111 : 1$

Exercise 4.11

1. 84 Hydrogen, 42 Oxygen
2. a Rs 484 : Rs 121 b 138.6 g : 693 g
   c 3.75 m : 0.75 m d $30 : $75 : $195
   e $14.4 : 57.6 : 144$ f $0.735 : 0.245$
3. 10 cm
4. $1 : 500$
5. 315
6. a 6 b 33

7. $25
8. 1 tonne cement, 4 tonnes sand
9. 10 km
10. a 120 m³
    b i 96 m³ ii 24 m³

Exercise 4.12

1. a direct b neither
   c inverse d direct
2. 10 tins 3 $170
4. 31 minutes 5 63 minutes
6. a 2 days b 9 painters

Exercise 4.13

1. $2
2. a 5 hours 20 minutes b 90°
3. 1200000 kg 4 1 hour 45 minutes
5. 82.4 km/h 6 0615
7. 35000 kg/m³ 8 1.25 g/cm³

Exercise 4.14

1. a i loss ii $5 iii 10%
   b i profit ii $5 iii 10%
   c i profit ii Rs 91.25 iii 25%
   d i profit ii Rs 6.4 on each one
      iii 8.14%
   e i profit ii £0.05 on each one
      iii 10%
2. a i $33.33 ii $50 b 2 years 6 months
3. a €5500 b €11406.25 c €4350
4. a 12.5 miles b 56 km
5. a 1.53 m/s b 96 km/h
6. a 0.628 kg b 0.572 kg The iron one is heavier.
7. 3 km
8. 41%
9. Large: £1.80 per litre, small: £1.76 per litre. The small one is the better buy.
10. Penti: 9 km/litre, Quadri: 12 km/litre. The Quadri is more economical.
11. Maths: 60%, Science: 69%. Science is his better subject.
12. $15309
13. $59.13
14. 1813
15. $5615.77

Exercise 4.15

1. a 72 b 144
2. a 120 m³ b 0.036 m³
3. a 687.5 g and 625 g b 2
4. a 18 hours 5 minutes b 444 miles per hour
   c 21 40
5. a 163 minutes b 7 hours 9 minutes
   c 3.6 hours d 0.45 hours
6. 7.37×10^{22} kg

7 **a** 3.844×10^5 **b** 3.844×10^8

8 4.5 m

9 **a** 0.95   **b** 2.8

10 For example,
A costs \$0.001625 per ml
B costs \$0.001533 per ml
B is better value for money

11 **a** \$4.50   **b** 56.3%

12 **a** 3 hours 19 minutes   **b** 1550 g

13 1250, 1350

14 **a** 9   **b** \$144

15 **a** 88   **b** 85.5 cm, 86.5 cm

16 40%

17 35 : 8

18 \$900

19 **a** **i** $\frac{9-3\times2}{3}$ **ii** 1

20 64 km/h

21 11.5 km

22 **a** 1.515 m   **b** 3.96 km

23 \$20

24 **a** \$12.32   **b** 10 hours

25 23 35

26 **a** \$336   **b** £80

27 **a** 20 30   **b** 4 hours

28 **a** 16.66 m   **b** 0.04 km²

29 **a** 6.8×10^{-24} g   **b** 0.612 g

30 **a** \$14 000   **b** 25%

31 100 or 120

32 **a** 160.27   **b** 6820

33 **a** 259 g   **b** 20%

34 **a** 9.19×10^7 km   **b** 0.15 terametres

35 **a** 800 000 mm   **b** 7×10^3

36 **a** 14 00   **b** 14 40

37 **a** 375 euros   **b** \$27

38 **a** 40   **b** 30 km/h

39 **a** 08 45   **b** \$775

40 **a** **i** 102.50 euros   **ii** 70%

41 **a** $\frac{3}{8}$ **b** 30 litres

42 **a** $x=0$ $y=-2$ **b** **i** 13200 yen   **ii** \$500

43 **a** 1.77 kg   **b** 147 minutes

44 **a** $\frac{13}{18}$ **b** 70   **c** 8

45 **a** $88 \times 132 = N + 132$, $87 \times 131 = N - 87$
   b 219

46 **a** 8 hours 20 minutes
   b **i** 120 km/h   **ii** 4 hours 24 minutes

Chapter 5

Essential Skills

1 **a** 1   **b** −10   **c** 0
   d −18   **e** 25   **f** $-2x+2y$
   g $-3-a$

2 **a** 3   **b** 0   **c** 0   **d** 3   **e** 2
   f 0   **g** 3   **h** $-\frac{2}{3}$ **i** $\frac{2}{3}$ **j** 0
   k 1   **l** 1   **m** 1   **n** 0   **o** $-a$
   p 2   **q** 9   **r** 0

3 Expressions: (a) and (d)
   Equations: (b) and (c)

4 **a** $-5y$ **b** $2x$ and $-3x$ **c** x, y, z, w
   d 2   **e** +

5 square, square root;   divide, multiply;   add, subtract

NOTE:
Unless the question states otherwise, answers to algebraic questions which are fractions greater than 1, may be given as improper (top heavy) fractions, mixed numbers or, if they are exact, decimals. They should not be given as rounded decimals. The fractions must be simplified.

Exercise 5.1

1 $x=2$ 2 $x=4$

3 $x=8$ 4 $x=3$

5 $x=-\frac{1}{2}$ 6 $x=4$

7 $x=2$ 8 $x=\frac{1}{4}$

9 $x=5$ 10 $x=-6$

11 $x=-9$ 12 $x=7$

13 $x=-3$ 14 $x=-22$

15 $x=7\frac{1}{2}$ 16 $x=-\frac{5}{3}$

Exercise 5.2

1 $x=\frac{4}{5}$ 2 $x=-4$

3 $x=-\frac{2}{7}$ 4 $x=\frac{17}{5}$

5 $x=\frac{1}{4}$ 6 $x=-3$

7 $x=-\frac{50}{27}$ 8 $x=\frac{1}{2}$

9 $x=0$ 10 $a=-\frac{23}{6}$

11 $x=\frac{5}{4}$ 12 $a=\frac{8}{17}$

13 $y=8$ 14 $b=\frac{7}{5}$

Exercise 5.3

1 $x=-\frac{31}{9}$ 2 $x=\frac{11}{3}$

3 $x=\frac{9}{10}$ 4 $x=-\frac{14}{5}$

5 $x=-3.5$ 6 $x=\frac{27}{14}$

7 $x=-\frac{14}{9}$ 8 $x=-\frac{22}{15}$

9 $x=\frac{5}{3}$ 10 $a=-\frac{25}{34}$

Exercise 5.4

1 $x = -\frac{10}{3}$ **2** $x = 3$

3 $x = \frac{7}{2}$ **4** $x = -\frac{3}{4}$

5 $x = \frac{9}{4}$ **6** $a = -44$

7 $y = -\frac{2}{7}$ **8** $b = \frac{1}{5}$

9 $x = 1$ **10** $x = -\frac{2}{3}$

11 $c = -19$ **12** $x = 2$

13 $x = 0$ **14** $x = -1$

15 $x = \frac{1}{3}$

16 **a** $3x + 3x + (2x + 5) = 33$
     b $x = 3.5$ **c** 10.5, 10.5 and 12 cm

17 **a** blue $= \frac{x}{2}$, green $= x - 2$
     b $x + \frac{x}{2} + (x - 2) = 23$ **c** $x = 10$
     d 10 red, 5 blue and 8 green

18 **a** algebra $= x + 4$, shape $= 2x$
     b $x + x + 4 + 2x = 20$
     c $x = 4$ **d** 8

19 $x + (x + 1) + (x + 2) = 114$ $x = 37$
                                       37, 38 and 39

20 $x + (x + 2) + (x + 4) = 135$ 43, 45 and 47

> **NOTE:**
> Remember that the fraction line acts like a bracket, so that brackets in the denominator or numerator may be optional. (See question 3. (b)). Either form may be given here.

Exercise 5.5

1 **a** $x = 3$ **b** $x = d - b$
2 **a** $x = 18$ **b** $x = yz$

3 **a** $x = 6$ **b** $x = \frac{(c + b)}{a}$ or $\frac{c + b}{a}$

4 **a** $x = \frac{3}{2}$ **b** $x = \frac{c}{(a + b)}$

5 **a** $x = \frac{2}{3}$ **b** $x = \frac{2}{(a - b)}$

6 **a** $x = 1$ **b** $x = \frac{3}{(a - 1)}$ or $\frac{-3}{(1 - a)}$

7 **a** $x = -\frac{3}{2}$ **b** $x = \frac{a}{(c - b)}$ or $\frac{-a}{(b - c)}$

8 **a** $x = 6$ **b** $x = ab$

9 **a** $x = \frac{15}{7}$ **b** $x = \frac{3}{y}$

10 **a** $x = 20$ **b** $x = ab$

Exercise 5.6

1 $M = \frac{Fd^2}{Gm}$ **2** $d = \sqrt{\frac{GmM}{F}}$

3 $d = \frac{u - a}{n - 1}$ **4** $n = \frac{u - a}{d} + 1$

5 $a = ch$ **6** $h = \frac{a}{c}$

7 $d = st$ **8** $t = \frac{d}{s}$

9 $A = \frac{F}{P}$ **10** $C = \frac{5}{9}(F - 32)$

11 $a = \frac{2(s - ut)}{t^2}$

12 **a** $a = \frac{bc}{d}$ **b** $c = \frac{ad}{b}$
     c $b = \frac{ad}{c}$ **d** $d = \frac{bc}{a}$

13 **a** $y = \frac{5 - 3x}{2}$ **b** $y = -\frac{13}{2}$

14 **a** $r = \sqrt{\frac{A}{\pi}}$ **b** $r = 2.52$

15 **a** $l = \frac{5}{3}$ **b** $c = \frac{b}{l}$ $c = 13\frac{1}{3}$

16 **a** $h = \frac{2A}{a + b}$ **b** $h = \frac{10}{7}$

Exercise 5.7

1 **a** 53   **b** nth term $= n + 3$
2 **a** 56   **b** nth term $= n + 6$
3 **a** 12, 15   **b** nth term $= 3n - 9$ **c** 300
4 **a** 64, 81   **b** nth term $= (n + 3)^2$ **c** 3364
5 **a** 51, 66   **b** nth term $= n^2 + 2$ **c** 363
6 **a** 8, 14, 20   **b** 52
     c nth term $= n + 2$ **d** 1274

Exercise 5.8

1 $x = -4$ $y = 2$
2 $x = 2$ $y = 2$
3 $x = 0$ $y = 1$
4 $x = 2$ $y = -\frac{6}{5}$

Exercise 5.9

1 $x = 7$ $y = -8$
2 $x = 2$ $y = 2$
3 $x = -\frac{1}{2}$ $y = -1$
4 $x = 2$ $y = -\frac{1}{2}$
5 $x = 2$ $y = 1$
6 $p = 2$ $q = 0$
7 $x = -3$ $y = -1$
8 $x = 2$ $y = 2$
9 $x = 3$ $y = -1$
10 $x = 1$ $y = 6$

Exercise 5.10

1 **a** $x = 1$ **b** $x = -\frac{3}{2}$
     c $x = -\frac{9}{10}$ **d** $x = 2$
     e $x = \frac{23}{9}$ **f** $x = \frac{3}{4}$
     g $x = -6$ **h** $x = 0$
     i $a = -6$ **j** $b = 2$

2 **a** $r = \sqrt{\dfrac{A}{\pi}}$ **b** $h = \dfrac{2V}{bl}$ **c** $t = \dfrac{d}{V}$

d $t = \dfrac{2A}{a+b}$ **e** $V = \dfrac{M}{D}$

f $b = \sqrt{a^2 - c^2}$ **g** $S = \dfrac{q+r}{p}$

h $x = \dfrac{A - Bc}{B}$ or $x = \dfrac{A}{B} - c$

i $b = \dfrac{x}{a} - c$ **j** $x = \sqrt{b^2 - 3a^2}$

k $h = \dfrac{V}{a}$ **l** $b = ad - c$

m $a = \dfrac{2A}{l} - b$ or $\dfrac{2A - bl}{l}$

3 **b** nth term $= 2n + 1$ **c** 199

4 **a** nth term $= 4n - 2$
b nth term $= 3n - 6$
c nth term $= -2n + 6$

5 **a** $x = -1$ $y = 2$
b $x = 0$ $y = 3$
c $x = \dfrac{1}{2}$ $y = 3\dfrac{1}{2}$

6 **a** $x + y = 57$ $x - y = 15$
b $x = 36$ $y = 21$

7 $x = 3$ $y = 9$

8 **a** $P = \dfrac{I}{rT}$
b **i** $16.25
ii $375
iii 6%
iv 5 years

9 $s = \dfrac{p+q}{t}$

10 $x = 3$

11 **a** 55   **b** $\dfrac{ma - b}{m}$ or $a\dfrac{-b}{m}$

12 **a** 14   41   **b** 149
c **i** 2   5   10   17   **ii** $n^2 - 1$

13 **a** **i** $x = 6$
ii $y = 9$
iii $z = 1.5$
b **i** $p + q = 12$
ii $25p + 40q = 375$
iii $p = 7$ $q = 5$

14 **a** 930   **b** $\dfrac{2s - an}{n}$ or $\dfrac{2s}{n} - a$

15 $x = 33$ $y = -4$

16 **a** -20
b $F = \dfrac{9C + 160}{5}$

17 **a** $2\dfrac{1}{2}, -1$
b nth term $= 3n - 2$

18 **a** $4, 1, \dfrac{4}{9}$ **b** $k = 20$

19 $x = 7$ $y = -2$
20 **a** $F = 800$
b $m = \dfrac{Ft}{v - u}$
21 **a** 8, 16, 12
b $x = 2n$ $y = n^2$ $z = n^2 - n$

Chapter 6

Essential Skills

1 **a** 30°   **b** 130°
2 **a** 5.2 cm   **b** 3.8 cm

Exercise 6.1

> **NOTE:**
> The answers to questions involving measuring line and angles are given as a range of values (for example, 5.5 to 5.6 cm). If your work is sufficiently accurate you should get an answers in this range. If you do not, try again.

1 32 to 33°   **2** 90°   **3** 116 to 117°
4 180°   **5** 337 to 338°   **6** 360°

Exercise 6.2

1 **a** $x = \angle BAC, y = BC$
b $x = \angle EDH, y = \angle GFH, z = GH$
c $x = \angle JMK, y = \angle KML$
d $x = \angle QPR, y = \angle NPQ, z = NQ$

2 **a** 24 to 26°
b **i** 54 to 56°   **ii** 124 to 126°
c **i** 4.9 to 5.1   **ii** 39 to 41°
iii 82 to 84°
d **i** 89 to 91°   **ii** 167 to 169°

3 **a** acute   **b** reflex
c acute   **d** obtuse
e reflex   **f** reflex
g obtuse   **h** right angle
i acute   **j** reflex
k obtuse

4 **a** $x = 50$ **b** $x = 35$
c $x = 36$ **d** $x = 45$
e $x = 20$ **f** $x = 90$

Exercise 6.3

1 parallel   **2** vertical
3 vertical   **4** perpendicular, horizontal, vertical

5 intersecting   **6** intersecting
7 vertical   **8** parallel, horizontal

Exercise 6.4

1 **a i** 7.6 to 7.8 cm   **ii** asa
   b This is not a triangle: the third angle
     would be 0°
   c This is not a triangle: 2 + 7 <10
   d i 8.6 to 8.8 cm   **ii** sas
   e i 6.3 to 6.5 cm   **ii** asa

2 **a** $\angle A$ = 52 to 54°, $\angle B$ = 36 to 38°,
     $\angle C$ = 89 to 91°
   b $\angle D$ = 66 to 68°, $\angle E$ = 89 to 91°,
     $\angle F$ = 22 to 24°
   c GH = 3.9 to 4.1 cm, $\angle G$ = 89 to 91°,
     $\angle H$ = 59 to 61°
   d $\angle J$ = 79 to 81°, JK = 5.8 to 6.0 cm,
     JL = 7.8 to 8.0 cm
   e $\angle M$ = 59 to 61°, $\angle N$ = 59 to 61°,
     $\angle P$ = 59 to 61°

3 **a** x = 36   **b** x = 65
   c x = 36   **d** x = 45
   e x = 60   **f** x = 60, y = 55

Exercise 6.5

1 a = 145° b = 35° c = 35°
   d = 145° e = 145°
2 a = 70° b = 30° c = 70°
   d = 110° e = 150°
3 a = 70° b = 35°
   c = 145° d = 145°
4 a = 110° b = 30°
   c = 40° d = 110°

Exercise 6.6

1 5 lines, order 5
2 1 line, no rotational (or order 1)
3 2 lines, order 2
4 2 lines, order 2
5 1 line, no rotational (or order 1)
6 8 lines, order 8
7 4 lines, order 4
8 no lines, order 2
9 4 lines, order 4

Exercise 6.7

a all 90°
b opposite angles equal
c no angles equal

d equal lengths, bisect each other but not
   at right angles
e

f different lengths, bisect each other at right angles
g 2   **h** 2   **i** 0   **j** 1
k 4   **l** 2   **m** 2

Exercise 6.8

1 a = 110 b = 70
   c = 110 d = 70
2 a = 20 b = 70 c = 40
3 a = 130 b = 120
4 a = 70 b = 20 c = 20
   d = 70 e = 40
5 30, 60, y = 60
6 x = 80 y = 160 z = 20
7 $\angle TSR$ = 60° (equilateral triangle)
   $\angle SPQ$ = 60° (angles on a straight line)
   PQ is parallel to RS (corresponding angles)

Exercise 6.9

1 2340°   **2** 30°   **3** 30°
4 **a** 72°   **b** 108°   **c** 54°
   d 54°   **e** 144°   **f** 18°
   g 72°
   $\angle CAE = \angle AEF$ = 72°
   AC and DE are parallel (alternate angles)
5 n = 18
6 **a** 16   **b** 157.5°

Exercise 6.10

1 135
2 b = 70, c = 40
3 d = 60, e = 30, f = 30
4 g = 40, h = 50
5 j = 20
6 k = 50, l = 50, m = 40, n = 50

Exercise 6.11

a 12   **b** 8   **c** 5
d 9   **e** 6   **f** 4
g 6   **h** 4   **i** 5
j 8   **k** 5   **l** 1
m 1

Exercise 6.12

2 cone

Exercise 6.13

1 *a, h*;   *b, f*;   *c, g*;   *d, i*
2 *b, d*;   *c, e*

Exercise 6.14

1 **b** 11.9 to 12.1 cm   **c** 59.5 to 60.5 km
2 **b** 5.3 to 5.5 km

Exercise 6.15

NOTE:
For reasons of space some of the answers to this exercise have been reduced in size. Yours should be full size.

1
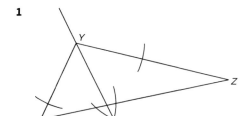

2
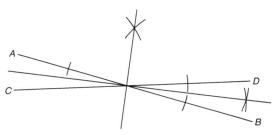

3 **a** to **c**
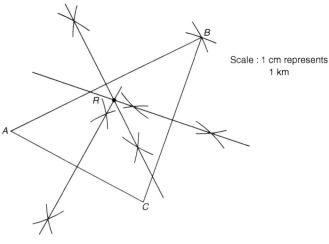

Scale : 1 cm represents 1 km

d 3.5 to 3.7 km
4 3.2 to 3.5 km

Exercise 6.16

NOTE:
For reasons of space some of the answers to this exercise have been reduced in size. Yours should be full size.

1 **a** to **e**
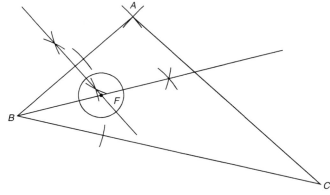

f i 6.4 to 6.8 m
  ii 22.4 to 22.8 m
2 **a** 1 line, no rotational (order 1)
    b 1 line, no rotational (order 1)
    c 4 lines, order 4
    d 4 lines, order 4
    e 2 lines, order 2
    f 1 line, no rotational (order 1)
3 **a** $a = b = 15$ cm, $c = 60°$ (equilateral triangle)
    b $a = 60°$ $\angle PST = 30°$ (angles on a straight line)
           $\angle PQT = 30°$ (symmetry of kite)
           $\angle PTQ = 90°$ (diagonals cross at right angles)
       $a = 180 - 90 - 30$ (angle sum of triangle)
       $b = 65°$ $\angle SRQ = 50°$ (angles on a straight line)
       $\angle TRQ = 25°$ (symmetry of kite)
       $b = 180 - 90 - 25$ (angle sum of triangle)
    c $a = 40°$ (angle between tangent and radius = 90°)
       $b = 90°$ (angle in a semicircle = 90°)
       $c = 50°$ (angle sum of a triangle)
    d $a = 70°$ $\angle YZX = 110°$ (alternate angles)
       $a = 70°$ (angles on a straight line)
       $b = 40°$ (angle sum of triangle)
    e $a = 90°$ (angle in a semicircle)
       $b = 40°$ (angle sum of triangle)
       $c = 60°$ (isosceles triangle)
       $d = 60°$ (angle sum of triangle)
       $e = 120°$ (angles on a straight line)

       $f = \frac{1}{2}(180 - 120) = 30°$ (isosceles triangle)

       $g = 30°$ (isosceles triangle)
4 The locus will be a hollow sphere, inner radius 10 cm, outer radius 10.5 cm, centred on point A.
5 **a** square   **b** trapezium   **c** kite

6 a 72°   **b** 36°

7 a ii 54 to 58°
  b

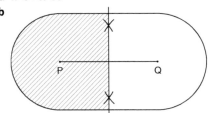

8

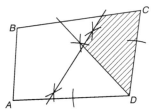

9

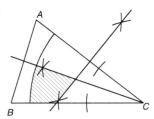

10 110°

11 a 90°   **b** 65°   **c** 25°

12 $x = 120$ $y = 150$

13 a 120   **b** 70
  c i 130   **ii** 100   **iii** 70, 30

14 a rectangle rhombus   **b** parallelogram rectangle rhombus
  c rectangle square

15 a

Shape A   Shape B

  b 2

16 a 51.4°
  b i isosceles
    ii $p = 50, q = 80, r = 50, s = 50, t = 80$
  c 25

17 75°

18 a 22° (tangent and diameter meet at 90°)
  b 90° (angle in a semicircle)
  c 68° (angle sum of triangle)
  d 68° (alternate angles)

19 a $x = 64$ **b** $y = 58$

20 a 18   **b i** $x = 70$ **ii** $y = 105$

21 a 75°   **b** 24

22 a

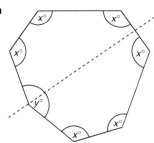

  b $x = 129$

23 a 140°   **b** 105°   **c** 75°

24 a equilateral triangle
  b rectangle   **c** kite

25 a 24   **b** $x = 45$

26 a A and E **b** B, D and F

Chapter 7

Essential Skills

1 a

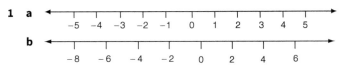

  b

2 a −7   **b** −6   **c** 9
  d −9   **e** −2   **f** 7

3 a $\frac{1}{7}$
  b 3
  c $-\frac{1}{5}$
  d $\frac{3}{7}$
  e −6

4 $\{-3, -2, -1, 0, 1, 2, 3\}$

Exercise 7.1

1

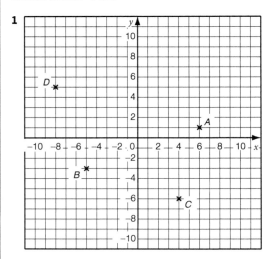

2

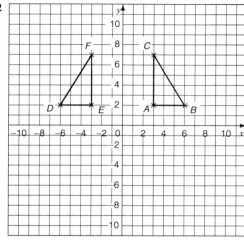

e The triangles are the same shape and size
f The triangles are facing in different directions

3 A: (8, 9)   B: (0, 8)   C: (−6, 8)   D: (−3, 3)
E: (3, 3)   F: (−7, 0)   G: (9, 0)   H: (0, 0)
J: (0, −3)   K: (9, −3)   L: (−6, −5)   M: (5, −7)

Exercise 7.2

1

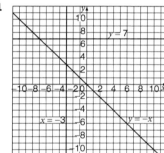

2 l : x = 10   m : y = −5

Exercise 7.3

1 a July   **b** 9

2 a

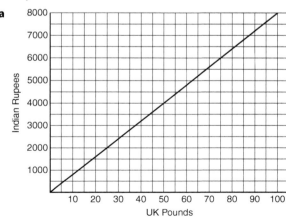

b i 6000 rupees   **ii** £37.50

3

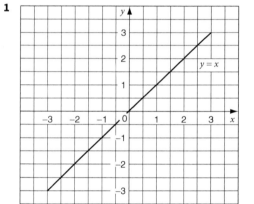

c $92.50   **d** 7.5 hours

4 a 1 hour   **b** 1.5 hours   **c** 1.5 km
d 1 kilometre per hour   **e** Anton

Exercise 7.4

1

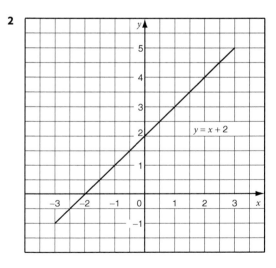

2

3

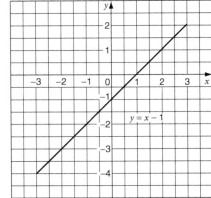

4

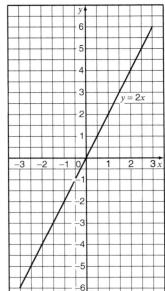

5

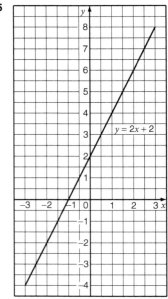

6

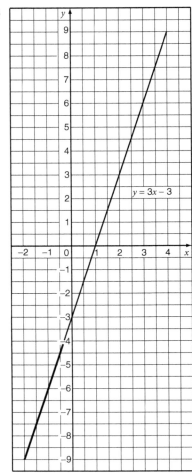

7

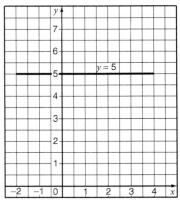

8 In each graph the constant term in the equation shows where the line cuts the y-axis

Exercise 7.5

1 a $\frac{4}{5}$ **b** $\frac{4}{3}$ **c** $-\frac{8}{9}$ **d** $-\frac{5}{2}$

2 a   **b**   **c**

d   **e**   **f**

g

3 a (ii)   **b** (iv)   **c** (i)   **d** (iii)

4

angle made with x-axis	less than 45°	exactly 45°	between 45° and 90°
gradient	$\frac{1}{2}, \frac{1}{5}, \frac{3}{5}$	$\frac{2}{2}$	$5, \frac{4}{3}$

Exercise 7.6

1 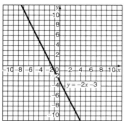   **2**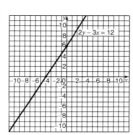

3 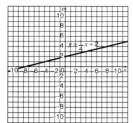   **4**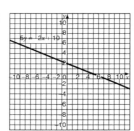

5 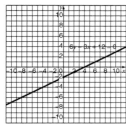   **6**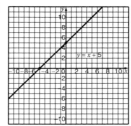

Exercise 7.7

1 $m = \frac{1}{2}, c = -5$ **2** $m = -\frac{1}{2}, c = \frac{3}{2}$ **3** $m = -\frac{2}{5}, c = \frac{4}{5}$

4 $m = -1, c = -1$ **5** $m = \frac{5}{4}, c = -5$ **6** $m = \frac{1}{2}, c = \frac{1}{2}$

7 $m = -\frac{2}{3}, c = \frac{4}{3}$ **8** $m = \frac{1}{2}, c = 3$ **9** $m = 0, c = 6$

10 $m = 1, c = 0$ **11** $m = 0, c = -10$ **12** $m = 2, c = 0$

13 $m = -1, c = 0$ **14** $m = -1, c = 4$

Exercise 7.8

1 $y = -2x + 2$ **2** $y = 2x - 2$ **3** $y = \frac{1}{2}x + 1$

4 $y = -x + 3$ **5** $\frac{1}{8}$ **6** -3

Exercise 7.9

1 **a** and **c**

2 for example, $y = \frac{1}{4}x + 5$

3 a $\frac{1}{2}$ **b** $\frac{2}{1} = 2$ **c** $\frac{2}{1} = 2$

b and **c** are parallel

Exercise 7.10

1 a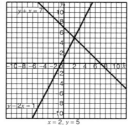

b $x = 2, y = 5$

2 a 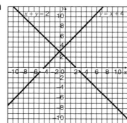   **b**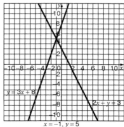

Exercise 7.11

1

x	−3	−2	−1	0	1	2	3
y	9	4	1	0	1	4	9

2

x	−3	−2	−1	0	1	2	3
y	−27	−8	−1	0	1	8	27

3

x	−3	−2	−1	0	1	2	3
y	−1	$-\frac{3}{2}$	−3	...	3	$\frac{3}{2}$	1

4

x	−3	−2	−1	0	1	2	3
y	6	2	0	0	2	6	12

5

x	−3	−2	−1	0	1	2	3
y	12	6	2	0	0	2	6

6

x	−3	−2	−1	0	1	2	3
y	−25	−6	1	2	3	10	29

7

x	−3	−2	−1	0	1	2	3
y	−9	−4	−1	0	−1	−4	−9

8

x	−3	−2	−1	0	1	2	3
y	27	8	1	0	−1	−8	−27

9

x	−3	−2	−1	0	1	2	3
y	7	1	−3	−5	−5	−3	1

10

x	−3	−2	−1	0	1	2	3
y	−2	1	2	1	−2	−7	−14

Exercise 7.12

1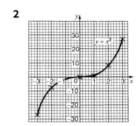

2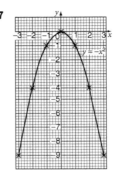

3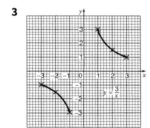

4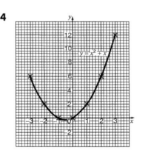

5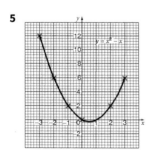

6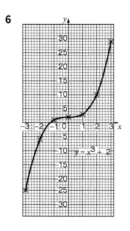

7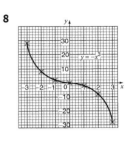

8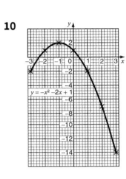

9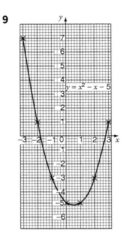

10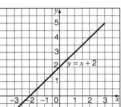

Exercise 7.13

1 a $9\,m$ **b** $2.5\,m$ **c** no

2 a $y = x$ **b** $y = -x$ **c** $x = 5$ **d** $y = -2$

3 a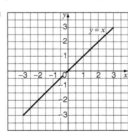

b

c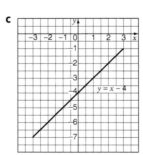

d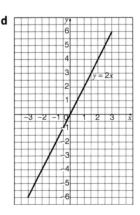

e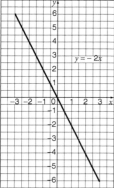

4 a 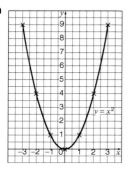 **b**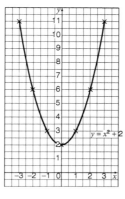

c 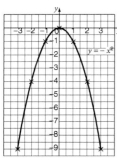 **d**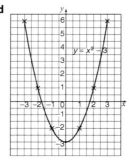

5 a This should be a continuous smooth curve, not flat at the base
   b This should be a smooth curve, not made up of straight line segments
   c One point is out of line because it has been incorrectly plotted

6 a (ii)   **b** (iv)   **c** (i)
   d (vi)   **e** (v)   **f** (iii)

7 a 1   **b** $\frac{1}{2}$ **c** 2

8 a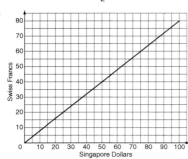

   b 55 Singapore Dollars

9 a i −10, −20, −60, 30, 20, 15
   ii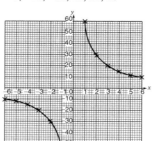

   b 2
   c i 0 between 2.4 and 2.5
   ii between −5 and −6

10 a 15 km/h   **b** 36   **c** 36 km
   d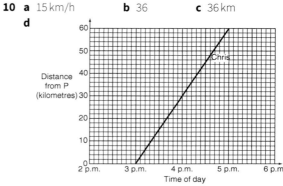

11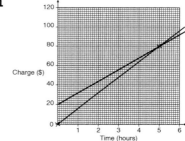

   a $62
   b 2.5 hours
   c 5 hours

12 $y = 2x - 3$

13 a i Minimum temp on Sunday = −3, Maximum temp on Sunday = 9
   ii 9 °C
   b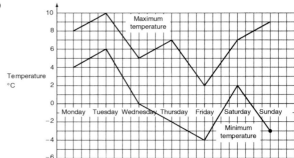

   c i 3 days
   ii Sunday
   d 42.8

14 a

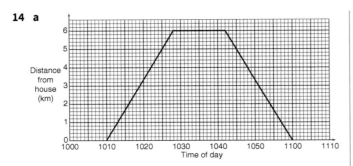

b i 10 48   **ii** 4 km

15 a

x	−4	−3	−2	−1	0	1	2	3
y	9	3	−1	−3	−3	−1	3	9

b

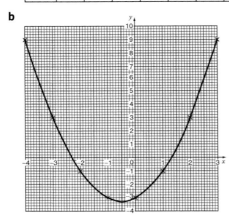

   c $x = −0.5$, $y = −3.2$ or $−3.3$ **d ii** $x = −0.5$
16 a 1.9 minutes   **b** 420 m
   c 0 m/minute   **d** 500 m/minute

Chapter 8

Essential Skills

1

Measurement	Unit	Equivalent	Working
Length	1 cm	10 mm	
	1 m	100 cm	
Area	1 cm²	100 mm²	10 mm × 10 mm
	1 m²	10 000 cm²	100 cm × 100 cm
Volume	1 cm³	1000 mm³	10 mm × 10 mm × 10 mm
	1 m³	1 000 000 cm³	100 cm × 100 cm × 100 cm
Capacity	1 millilitre	1 cm³	
	1 litre	1000 ml	
	1 litre	1000 cm³	
	1 m³	1000 litres	

2 a Square root
   b Finding the cube root
   c i 169   **ii** 3.61
     iii 2197   **iv** 2.35

Exercise 8.1

1 a 28 cm   **b** 22 cm   **c** 24 cm
   d 29 cm   **e** 32 cm
2 a 31.4 cm   **b** 15.7 cm
   c 44.9 m   **d** 330 cm
3 a 20.6 cm   **b** 26.7 cm   **c** 41.1 cm
   d 23.7 cm   **e** 30.3 cm
4 a $x = 2.6$ **b** $x = 4.77$
   c $x = 1.75$ **d** $x = 3$
5 a 2 cm   **b** 9 cm

Exercise 8.2

1 a 12 cm²   **b** 15 cm²   **c** 25 cm²
   d 12 cm²   **e** 15 cm²   **f** 21 cm²
2 a $x = 3.16$ cm   **b** $x = 1.75$ cm

Exercise 8.3

1 a 113 cm²   **b** 32.2 m²   **c** 50.3 cm²
   d 56.5 cm²   **e** 25.8 cm²
2 a 25.1 cm²   **b** 41.9 cm²   **c** 113 cm²
   d 26.5 cm²   **e** 14.1 cm²
3 a $x = 2.33$ **b** $x = 3.91$ **c** $x = 1.78$
   d $x = 3.91$
4 37.1 cm²

Exercise 8.4

1 15 cm²   **2** 54 cm²   **3** 31.5 cm²
4 163 cm²   **5** 33 cm²   **6** 36 cm²

Exercise 8.5

1 56 cm²   **2** 283 cm²
3 96 cm²   **4** 540 cm³

Exercise 8.6

1 32 ml   **2** 339 ml
3 42 cm³   **4** 648 cm³
5 a 240 cm³   **b** 860 cm³
6 2 cm   **7** 2.25 cm²
8 1.20 cm
9 a 1180 cm²   **b** 118000 cm³   **c** 7850 ml

Exercise 8.7

1 a $7\pi + 6$ cm   **b** 10.5π cm²
2 length $= \frac{V}{10.5\pi}$ cm or length $= \frac{2V}{21\pi}$ cm

3 a $2l + 2b + 2\pi r$ cm
  b $lb - \pi r^2$ cm²

Exercise 8.8

1. a Surface area: *A*: 28000 cm² *B*: 39500 cm²
            C: 35000 cm²
  b Volume: *A*: 442000 cm³ *B*: 518000 cm³
            C: 500000 cm³
  c Volume ÷ surface area: *A* : 15.8 *B* : 13.1
            C : 14.3
  d *A* is the best value
2 $h = 12.7$
3 a 1.26 cm   **b** 5.09 cm
4 b $2a + 2b = 16$ or $a + b = 8$
  c $a = 2$ $b = 6$ **d** 8 cm, 2 cm
5 7 cm and 4 cm
6 a 54 m   **b** 9.15 m
7 b 5 cm²
8 2.71
9 a 160 m   **b** 50.9 m
10 a 2830 cm²   **b** 226 litres
11 24500 litres
12 a diameter
  b i 30.8 cm   **ii** 56.5 cm²
13 a i 10.8 m   **ii** 32400 litres   **iii** 36 litres
  b i 61 hours and 30 minutes
    ii 13500 gallons **iii** 3.38 litres   **iv** 4
14 6.5 cm
15 a i 43.0 cm²   **ii** 10.0
  b i 22.2 cm, 14.8 cm, 20 cm
    ii 6570cm³   **iii** 78.5%
16 a 120 cm³   **b** 184 cm²
17 a 100 cm   **b** 475 cm²
18 a $6\pi x$ cm   **b** $3\pi x^2$ cm²
19 a $32x + 120$
  b $32x + 120 = 376$
    $x = 8$,   height = 8 cm
20 a $DE^2 = 13^2 - 5^2$
    $DE = \sqrt{144}$
  b i 116 cm   **ii** 690 cm²
21 a 4 minutes
  b

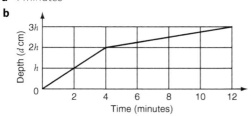

22 For example,

Width (m)	2	3	6	and so on
Length (m)	35	33	27	
Area (m²)	70	99	162	

  length = 19 m   area = 190 m²
23 a 12 cm²   **b** 344 cm²

Chapter 9

1 a 56.2   **b** 7.95   **c** 6.14
2 a 60.2   **b** 73.0   **c** 14.6
3 a $x = 2$ **b** $x = 2.24$ **c** $x = 3.22$
4 a $x = 0.739$ **b** $x = 33.58$ **c** $x = 0.859$
5 a $x = \dfrac{b}{a}$ **b** $x = ab$ **c** $x = \dfrac{b}{a}$
6 a Area = 15.21 cm²   **b** Length of side = 2.39 cm

Exercise 9.1

1 a 1.4826   **b** 3.7321   **c** 0.5122
  d 0.5774   **e** 1.7321   **f** 1.1667
2 a 9.4°   **b** 38.7°   **c** 58.9°
  d 80.5°   **e** 86.1°   **f** 26.6°

Exercise 9.2

1 20.6°   **2** 71.6°   **3** 27.4°   **4** 45°
5 71.0°   **6** 35.0°   **7** 66.1°

Exercise 9.3

1 a 3.57 cm   **b** 4.11 cm   **c** 2.29 cm
  d 2.84 cm   **e** 17.3 cm   **f** 9.18 cm
2 a 27.5°   **b** 9.60 cm   **c** 4.43 cm
  d 13.5 cm   **e** 65.3°

Exercise 9.4

1 52.4°   **2** 2.96 metres   **3** 66.4°
4 5.44 cm   **5** 20.6 cm   **6** 57.2°
7 11.7 cm   **8** 42.8 metres   **9** 62.8°
10 9.05 m

Exercise 9.5

1 5.50 cm
2 5.71 cm
3 12.5 m
4 3.85 cm

Exercise 9.6

1 110 cm   **2** 88.8 cm   **3** 49.6 m
4 9.05 cm   **5** 128 mm   **6** 68.3 mm

Exercise 9.7

1 10.2 cm   **2** 12.8 cm   **3** 9.40 cm
4 4.68 m   **5** 4.46 cm   **6** 5.80 m
7 41.8°   **8** 31.7°   **9** 53.0°

Exercise 9.8

1 a i 12   **ii** 10   **iii** 7
  b Cut the 7 m length into two pieces, 3 m and 4 m long. Join all three lengths to form a triangle with sides 3 m, 4 m and 5 m long
2 5.66 cm
3 8.66 cm
4 8.06 m
5 a 5.32 cm   **b** 48.8°   **c** 131°
6 15.1 cm or 15.2 cm
7 a 12 cm   **b** 9 cm   **c** 36.9°

Exercise 9.9

1 a 240°   **b** 280°   **c** 50°
  d 120°
2 240°   **3** 015°
4 a answer between 18.5 and 19 km
  b 282° to 284°
5 16.2 nautical miles, 158°
6 16.4 km
7 a i SE   **ii** NW
  b i 090°   **ii** 225°

Exercise 9.10

1 4 cm
2 8.10 cm
3 a 7.14 cm
  b i 0.7   **ii** 0.714   **iii** 1.02

Exercise 9.11

1 31.5 m
2 a 32.6 m   **b** 73.1 m

Exercise 9.12

1 a 32.6°, 6.11 cm   **b** 3.36 cm, 42.1°
  c 53.1°, 36.9°   **d** 7.28 cm, 74.1°
2 2.90 m
3 6.54 cm
4 a Bearing of D from W is 300° so the angle between the North line and the line DW is 60°. 60° + 30° is 90°
  b $a = 110$, $b = 30$, $c = 40$, $d = 50$
  c 6.43 km   **d** 7.66 km
5 $a = 11.3°$
6 a i 105m³   **ii** 197m²
  b i 0.845   **ii** 0.280
7 325°
8 a 1500 m   **b** 36.9°
9 a 270°   **b** 045°

10 a i $\angle COB = \frac{1}{2}(180 - 56) = 62$
    ii 2.82 m   **iii** 5.63 or 5.64 m   **iv** 5.30 m
  b i 29.8 or 29.9 m²   **ii** 12.5 m²
    iii 42.3 or 42.4 m²
  c i 21100 or 21200 m³   **ii** 30

11 a 208 cm²   **b** 192 cm³
  c ii 12.8 cm   **iii** 51.3 or 51.4°

12 26 cm

13 a 348°   **b** 218°

14 a C   **b** 40°

15 31 m

16 a 56°   **b** 2 cm

Chapter 10

Essential Skills

1 a D   **b** F   **c** E   **d** C   **e** A   **f** B

Exercise 10.1

1 a   **b**

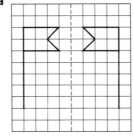

c   **d**

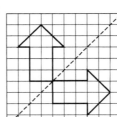
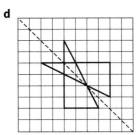

2

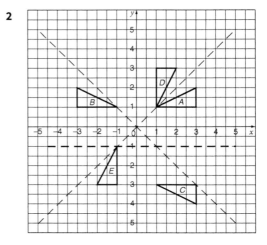

Exercise 10.2

1 Reflection in the y-axis (or the line $x = 0$)
2 Reflection in the x-axis (or the line $y = 0$)
3 Reflection in the line $y = x$
4 Reflection in the line $y = -x + 1$
5 Reflection in the line $x = -1$
6 Reflection in the line $y = -x$

Exercise 10.3

1 a 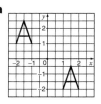 b

c

2 For example,

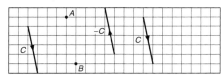

3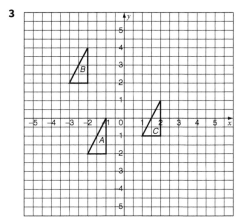

c Translation $\begin{pmatrix} 4 \\ -3 \end{pmatrix}$

4 a i Translation $\begin{pmatrix} 5 \\ 0 \end{pmatrix}$ ii Translation $\begin{pmatrix} 0 \\ -4.5 \end{pmatrix}$

iii Translation $\begin{pmatrix} -5 \\ -4.5 \end{pmatrix}$

b i Translation $\begin{pmatrix} 4 \\ -0.5 \end{pmatrix}$ ii Translation $\begin{pmatrix} 2 \\ 3.5 \end{pmatrix}$

iii Translation $\begin{pmatrix} -2 \\ -3.5 \end{pmatrix}$

Exercise 10.4

1 a 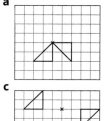 b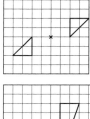

c 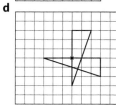 d

e

2 a Rotation 90° clockwise about (0,0)
   b Rotation 90° anticlockwise about (0, −1)
   c Rotation 90° clockwise about (1, 3)
   d Rotation 180° about (0, 0)
   e Rotation 90° clockwise about (2, 1)
   f Rotation 180° about (1.5, 1.5)
   g Rotation 90° anticlockwise about (0, 0)

Exercise 10.5

1 a 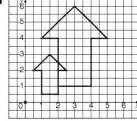 b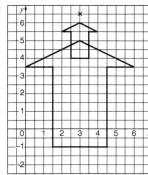

2 a Enlargement, centre (0,0), scale factor 2
   b Enlargement, centre (−1, −1), scale factor $\frac{1}{3}$

Exercise 10.6

1 a $\begin{pmatrix} \frac{3}{2} \\ 1 \end{pmatrix}$ b $\begin{pmatrix} -10 \\ 0 \end{pmatrix}$ c $\begin{pmatrix} 2 \\ 9 \end{pmatrix}$ d $\begin{pmatrix} 60 \\ 28 \end{pmatrix}$

2 $a = 4$ 3 $x = 2$, $y = 3$
4 a, b and f are parallel
5 $\begin{pmatrix} 3 \\ 12 \end{pmatrix} = 3\begin{pmatrix} 1 \\ 4 \end{pmatrix}$

6 They are parallel and the second is twice as long as the first

Exercise 10.7

1 a 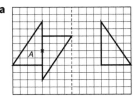 **b**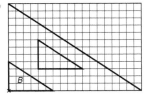

2 a i Reflector in the line $y = x$ **ii** Reflection in the line $y = -1$

b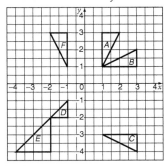

3 a $\begin{pmatrix} 2 \\ -4 \end{pmatrix}$

b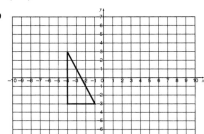

4 b i 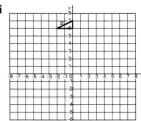 **ii**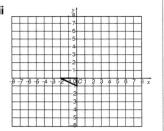

iii rotation 90° anticlockwise about (0, 3)

5 a $\begin{pmatrix} -3 \\ 12 \end{pmatrix}$ **b** AB and CD are parallel.
CD is three times the length of AB

6 a $\begin{pmatrix} -1 \\ 3 \end{pmatrix}$ **b** (−2, −1)

7 a Trapezium

b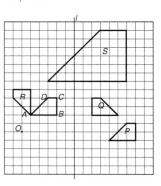

8 a i $\begin{pmatrix} 3 \\ -1 \end{pmatrix}$ **b i** $\begin{pmatrix} -2 \\ 2 \end{pmatrix}$

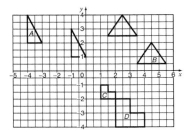

c Enlargement, centre (0, 0), scale factor 2
d i 1 **ii** 1 **iii**

iv Reflection in the x-axis.

9 a $\begin{pmatrix} 5 \\ -2 \end{pmatrix}$ **b**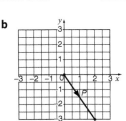

10 a i (−3, −2)

ii $\overrightarrow{AB} = \begin{pmatrix} 4 \\ 2 \end{pmatrix}$ $\overrightarrow{BC} = \begin{pmatrix} -3 \\ 2 \end{pmatrix}$

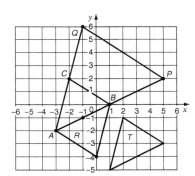

c ii Enlargement, centre (−3, −2), scale factor 2

11 a $\begin{pmatrix} 14 \\ 0 \end{pmatrix}$ **b** $5\frac{1}{2}$ and 2

12 a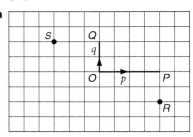

b -0.75 or $-\frac{3}{4}$

13 **a** and **b**

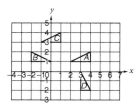

c Reflection in the line $x = 1$

14 **a** **i** $\begin{pmatrix} -8 \\ 2 \end{pmatrix}$ **ii** 3

    b **i** Reflection in $y = -x$ **ii** $(-1, 1)$

Chapter 11

Essential Skills

1 **a** $20 \times 18 = 360$ **b** $360 \times 0.05 = 18$ **c** $360 \div 20 = 18$

    d $18 \div 0.05 = 360$ **e** $20 \times 0.05 = 1$

2 **a** $360 \times 0.08\dot{3} = 30$ **b** $360 \div 12 = 30$ **c** $360 \times 0.0\dot{3} = 12$

    d $360 \div 30 = 12$ **e** $10 \times 36 = 360$ **f** $360 \times 0.02\dot{7} = 10$

    g $360 \div 36 = 10$ **h** $360 \times 2 = 720$ **i** $360 \div 0.\dot{6} = 540$

    j $1440 \times 0.25 = 360$

3 **a** $100 \times 3.6 = 360$ **b** $72 \times 0.75 = 54$ **c** $690 \div 30 = 23$

    d $690 \times 0.0\dot{3} = 23$ **e** $72 \div 3 = 24$ **f** $42 \div 1.5 = 28$

    g $55 \times 1.8 = 99$ **h** $81 \div 2.25 = 36$ **i** $81 \times 0.\dot{4} = 36$

    j $90 \times 0.8 = 72$ **k** $90 \div 1.25 = 72$

Exercise 11.1

1 **a**

Score	1	2	3	4	5	6
Frequency	6	8	10	6	10	4

    b

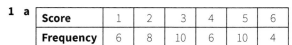

2 **a**

Class	1–10	11–20	21–30	31–40	41–50
Frequency	15	10	7	12	11

    b

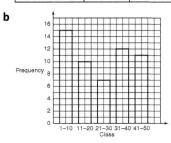

3 **a**

Class	Frequency
$0 \le x < 10$	15
$10 \le x < 20$	5
$20 \le x < 30$	2
$30 \le x < 40$	3
$40 \le x < 50$	5
$50 \le x < 60$	13
$60 \le x < 70$	1

    b

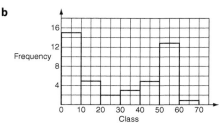

4 **a**

Height h	Frequency
$120 \le h < 130$	3
$130 \le h < 140$	4
$140 \le h < 150$	6
$150 \le h < 160$	8
$160 \le h < 170$	4

    b

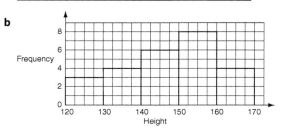

5 **a** and **b**

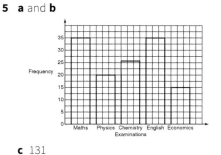

    c 131

6

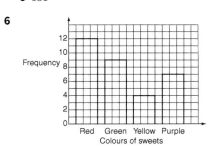

7 **a**

Box ticked	0	1	2	3	4	5
Frequency	6	7	8	11	8	4

b

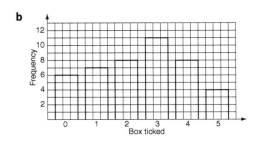

Exercise 11.2

1 **a** 360 **b** 18 **c** 20 **d** 0.05 **e** 0.05

2 **a** $\frac{1}{12}$ **b** 1 **c** $\frac{1}{30}$ **d** 30 **e** 36

  f $\frac{1}{36}$ **g** 36 **h** 2 **i** $\frac{2}{3}$ **j** $\frac{1}{4}$

3 **a** 3.6 **b** 0.75 **c** 30 **d** $\frac{1}{30}$ **e** 3

  f 1.5 **g** $\frac{9}{5}$ **h** $\frac{9}{4}$ **i** $\frac{4}{9}$ **j** 0.8

  k 1.25

Exercise 11.3

1 **a** and **b**

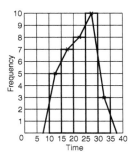

c $25 \le t < 30$

2 **a**

height (h) m	frequency
$2 \le h < 4$	7
$4 \le h < 6$	10
$6 \le h < 8$	8
$8 \le h < 10$	5
$10 \le h < 12$	3

b

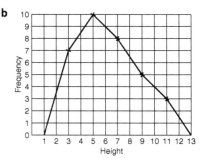

c $4 \le h < 6$

Exercise 11.4

1 **a** and **c**

Category	Fresh produce	Groceries	Household products	Magazines and stationery	Frozen goods	TOTAL
Number of items	351	183	66	315	165	1080
Angle	117°	61°	22°	105°	55°	360°
Floor space (m²)	32.5	16.9	6.1	29.2	15.3	100

b

Goods sold in a village store

2 **a**

Quarter	Units used	Angle
First quarter	23	69°
Second quarter	11	33°
Third quarter	21	63°
Fourth quarter	65	195°
TOTAL	120	360°

b

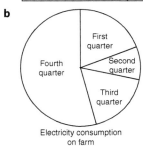

Electricity consumption on farm

3 **a**

	Percentage of total stock	Angle on pie chart
Newspapers	35	126°
Magazines	50	180°
Snacks	15	54°
TOTAL	100	360°

b

Items stocked by a newsagent

4 a

	Number of students	Angle on pie chart
Psychology	14	70°
Sociology	20	100°
Economics	22	110°
History	16	80°
TOTAL	72	360°

b

Subjects studied by a group of students

Exercise 11.5

1 a i 5.875   **ii** 5.5   **iii** 9   **iv** 9
  b i 4.93   **ii** 6   **iii** 7   **iv** 8
  c i 3.98   **ii** 4.2   **iii** 2.6   **iv** 3.1

2 a 800 cm   **b** 159 cm

3 a 28.5   **b** 5 new classrooms   **c** 24.5

4 a 1500   **b** 100 bags

Exercise 11.6

1

Data value	Frequency	Value × frequency
100	7	700
110	10	1100
120	15	1800
130	2	260
140	6	840
150	3	450
160	7	1120
TOTALS	50	6270

a 125.4   **b** 120   **c** 120

2

Data value	25	26	27	28	29	30	31	TOTALS
Frequency	51	70	69	32	15	43	15	295
Value × frequency	1275	1820	1863	896	435	1290	465	8044

a 27.3   **b** 27   **c** 26

3

Data value	Frequency	Value × frequency
12.4	3	37.2
12.5	5	62.5
12.6	2	25.2
12.7	1	12.7
12.8	0	0
12.9	5	64.5
13.0	0	0
13.1	2	26.2
TOTAL	18	228.3

a 12.7   **b** 12.6   **c** 12.5 and 12.9

Exercise 11.7

1 a mode = 8, range = 25

b

Days absent	Frequency
0 to 4	10
5 to 9	10
10 to 14	7
15 to 19	3
20 to 24	2
25 to 30	1
Total frequency	33

c

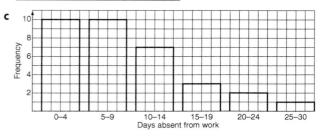

2 a 840

  b The mode might give an indication of the possible results for the whole school, but the median only refers to the data for the 100 students.

3 $a = 3$, $b = 6$, $c = 7$

4

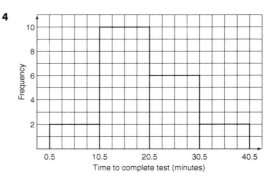

5 Mean = 3.41. Median = 3. There are two modes: 3 and 5

6 Mean = 4.9. Median = 4.5. Mode = 4

7 1.38

8 a and **c**

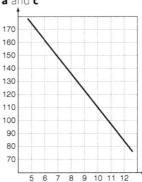

  b i 122 km/h   **ii** 9 km/l

  d Negative   **e** 9.4 to 9.6 km/l   **f** 141 to 143 km/h

9 a i 163.4 cm   **ii** 24 cm

b i, ii

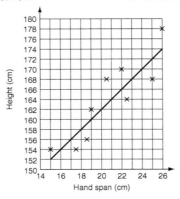

iii 163.5 to 164 cm

iv Positive

v It indicates that hand span and height are related

10 Negative

11 Negative

12 a 126   **b** 40%

13

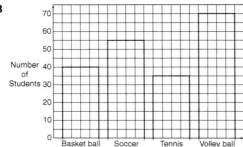

14 a

Grade	Number of students	Angle on pie chart
A	5	20°
B	15	60°
C	40	160°
D	20	80°
E	10	40°
TOTALS	90	360°

b

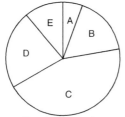

Examination grades

15 a 590 °C   **b** Neptune

16 a i 50   **ii** 43.9   **iii** 47

b Two of the estimates (20 and 24 cm) were much lower that the others and have too great an influence on the mean

17 a

Sport	Volleyball	Football	Hockey	Cricket
Number of students	6	9	7	2
Angle on pie chart	90°	135°	105°	30°

b

c football

18 a

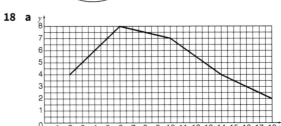

b $4 < t \le 8$ **c** 13

d There were 2 people in the class $16 < t \le 20$ but they did not necessarily take 20 min.

19 a Frequencies: 4, 7, 6, 4, 4, 2, 3

b 1   **c** 2   **d** 2.5   **e** 40

20 a i

Number of people in a car	Tally	Number of cars
1	ЖЖ	6
2	ЖЖ ЖЖ ЖЖ ||	17
3	ЖЖ |||	8
4	ЖЖ ||||	9
5	ЖЖ ЖЖ		11
6	ЖЖ ||||	9

ii

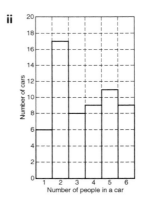

iii 2   **iv** 3   **v** 3.48

b 66°

21 a 60   **b** 13

22 a 1   **b** 2.9

23 a 9 mintues 20 seconds   **b** 2 mintues 20 seconds

c 2 mintues 45 seconds

24 a 10   **b** 8

25 a 23 35   **b** 4 mintues 1.5 seconds

26 a 2.6 m   **b** −0.5 m   **c** −0.8 m

27

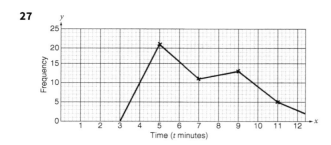

Chapter 12

Essential Skills

1 a $\frac{5}{6}$ **b** $\frac{9}{40}$ **c** $\frac{19}{20}$ **d** $\frac{2}{5}$ **e** $\frac{23}{40}$

2 a $\frac{2}{3}$ **b** $\frac{1}{3}$ **c** $\frac{1}{3}$

3 a 0.6   **b** 0.75   **c** 0.17   **d** 0.625   **e** 0.24

4 a 20%   **b** 37.5%   **c** 39%   **d** 16.5%

5 a $\frac{1}{3}$ **b** $\frac{3}{10}$ **c** $\frac{1}{4}$ **d** $\frac{12}{35}$ **e** $\frac{16}{35}$

Exercise 12.1

1 a iii   **b** i   **c** iv
   d v   **e** ii

2 a biased   **b** mutually exclusive
   c mutually exclusive   **d** random, outcome

3 a and d

4 60% or 0.6

5 a $\frac{5}{12}$ **b** $\frac{4}{12}$ or $\frac{1}{3}$ **c** 0   **d** $\frac{8}{12}$ or $\frac{2}{3}$

6 $\frac{2}{5}$ **7** $\frac{1}{5}$

8 a $\frac{3}{10}$ **b** $\frac{6}{10}$ or $\frac{3}{5}$ **c** $\frac{3}{10}$ **d** 0

9 $\frac{1}{6}$ **10** $\frac{5}{18}$

11 Because the areas are not all equal in size. The larger the area the higher the probability that the counter will land on it.

12 a Because the numbers of each car sold and awaiting collection are different so the outcomes are not all equally likely. The probability that the next car to be collected will be blue is $\frac{140}{360} = \frac{7}{18}$.

   b $\frac{60}{360}$ or $\frac{1}{6}$ **c** 0   **d** $\frac{200}{360}$ or $\frac{5}{9}$

Exercise 12.2

1 a 25   **b** $\frac{3}{25}$ **c** $\frac{10}{25}$ **d** $\frac{5}{25}$ **e** 10   **f** 6

2 a

	R	B	G	P	W
R	RR	RB	RG	RP	RW
B	BR	BB	BG	BP	BW
G	GR	GB	GG	GP	GW
Y	YR	YB	YG	YP	YW

   b $\frac{3}{20}$

3 a $\frac{3}{12}$ **b** $\frac{2}{12}$ **b** $\frac{1}{12}$ **d** 0

Exercise 12.3

1 a 0.95   **b i** 50   **ii** No

2 49% or 0.49

3 a $\frac{1}{5}$ **b** 5   **c** 20%

4 3880

5 a $\frac{20}{47}$ **b** $\frac{35}{47}$

6 a $\frac{3}{7}$ **b** $\frac{6}{7}$

7 $\frac{14}{30}$

8 a 10   **b** $\frac{4}{35}$

9 a 20, 60, 160, 80, 40
   b

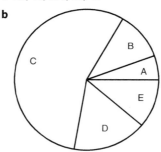

   c i $\frac{4}{9}$ **ii** $\frac{3}{9}$ or $\frac{1}{3}$

10 a i $\frac{7}{30}$ **ii** $\frac{9}{30}$ **b** 40

11 a 15% or 0.15
   b i $\frac{4}{15}$ **ii** $\frac{10}{15}$ **iii** 0

12 a i $\frac{10}{24}$ **ii** $\frac{15}{24}$ **iii** $\frac{19}{24}$
   b

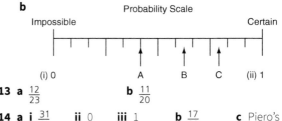

13 a $\frac{12}{23}$ **b** $\frac{11}{20}$

14 a i $\frac{31}{36}$ **ii** 0   **iii** 1   **b** $\frac{17}{99}$ **c** Piero's

15 a i

+	2	3	5	7	11
2	4	5	7	9	13
3	5	6	8	10	14
5	7	8	10	12	16
7	9	10	12	14	18
11	13	14	16	18	22

   ii a $\frac{6}{25}$ **b** $\frac{5}{25}$

NOTE: In some of these answers a range of values has been given. Answers within these ranges should obtain full marks. They represent the different values that might be obtained in the following ways. Some of the questions in some exercises require proofs or explanations. In these cases brief explanations have been given to help you, but alternatives are possible.

- Correct working, but using either rounded or calculator values from previous (numbered) parts of the question. (Remember never to round **within** the working for part of a question.)
- Using different values for π. (The calculator value is best.)
- Reading from graphs.
- Measurements from accurate drawings.

The graphs and diagrams in these answers are here to guide you, but they may have been reduced in scale for reasons of space. Yours should be full size. Where working has to be shown some of the key steps are sometimes included in the given answer.

Chapter 13

Essential Skills

1 a $100, 1, 9, 18, 24, 6, \frac{1}{2}, 2, 49$
  b $100, 1, 9, 18, 24, 6, 0, \sqrt{x}, 2, 49$
  c $100, 22.5, 1, 9, 18, 24, 6, 0, \sqrt{25}, 2, \frac{2}{7}, 49$
  d $\pi, \sqrt{2}$ e $\sqrt{25}, 2$ f $1, 9, \sqrt{25}$
  g $18, 24, 6$ h 2 i 49 j 9

2 a $\{1, 2, 3, 4, 6, 8, 9, 12, 16, 18, 24, 36, 48, 72, 144\}$
  b $\{2, 3\}$ c $144 = 2^4 \times 3^2$

3 $\sqrt{64} = 2^3$ $\sqrt{64} < 3^2$ $19 > 18$

4 $\{23, 29, 31, 37\}$

5 a $1\frac{5}{7}$ b $1\frac{15}{49}$ c 4

6 8.64

7 44.4% to 3 s.f.   8 $\frac{9}{14}$

Exercise 13.1

1 a $\{16, 25, 36\}$ b $\{March, May\}$ c $\{1, 2, 3, 4, 5, 6, 7, 8, 9, 10\}$
2 a The set of odd numbers less than 10
  b The set of days of the week.
  c The set of letters of the English alphabet.
3 a and d are empty sets
4 a $1 \notin \{prime\ numbers\}$ b $1000 \in \{even\ numbers\}$
5 a $\{a, c, e, h, i, m, s, t\}$ b 8

Exercise 13.2

1 a $\{3, 5, 7\}$ b $\{5\}$ c $\{3, 4, 5, 6, 7\}$ d $\{3, 7, 8, 9\}$
  e $\{4, 6, 8, 9\}$ f $\{3, 7\}$ g $\{8, 9\}$
2 $\varnothing$ 3 $\{4, 5, 6, 9\}$
4 2 5 4 6 4

Exercise 13.3

1 a 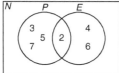   b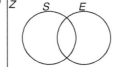

2 a 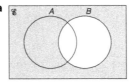   b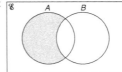

c 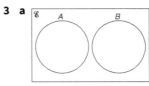   d

3 a   b

4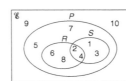

5 a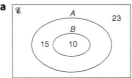

  b i 15 ii 23

6 a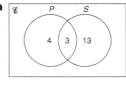

  b 3

Exercise 13.4

1 a $\sqrt{784} = \sqrt{4 \times 4 \times 49} = 4 \times 7 = 28$
  b $\sqrt{1600} = \sqrt{16 \times 100} = 4 \times 10 = 40$
  c $\sqrt{625} = \sqrt{5 \times 5 \times 25} = 5 \times 5 = 25$
2 a $\sqrt{180} = \sqrt{9 \times 20} = \sqrt{9 \times 4 \times 5} = 6\sqrt{5}$
  b $\sqrt{98} = \sqrt{2 \times 49} = 7\sqrt{2}$
  c $\sqrt{192} = \sqrt{2 \times 96} = \sqrt{2 \times 2 \times 48} = \sqrt{4 \times 3 \times 16} = 2 \times 4 \times \sqrt{3} = 8\sqrt{3}$

3 a $\sqrt{50} = \sqrt{2 \times 25} = 5\sqrt{2}$ irrational

  b $\sqrt{144} = 12$ rational

  c $\sqrt{45} = \sqrt{5 \times 9} = 3\sqrt{5}$ irrational

Exercise 13.5

1 a $2\frac{23}{100}$ **b** $\frac{223}{100}$

2 2×10^{-3} 0.21% $\frac{1}{250}$ $\frac{21}{500}$

3 a 130% **b** 95.5% **c** 0.5%

4 $\frac{9}{20}, \frac{19}{40}, \frac{77}{160}, \frac{1}{2}, \frac{9}{16}$

5 a $\frac{7}{8}$ **b** $\frac{49}{60}$

Exercise 13.6

1 a

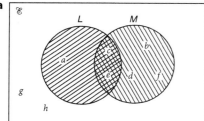

  b i {c, e} **ii** {a, b, c, d, e, f} **iii** {b, d, f, g, h}
  iv {a, g, h} **v** {a, b, d, f, g, h}

  c

  d i {a} **ii** {a, c, e, g, h}

2 {−2, −1, 0, 1, 2}

3 a The set of the first four cube numbers
  b The set of the first five square numbers

4 a $\sqrt{4096} = \sqrt{4 \times 1024} = \sqrt{4 \times 4 \times 256} = \sqrt{16 \times 4 \times 64}$
  $= 4 \times 2 \times 8 = 64$

  b $\sqrt{2450} = \sqrt{2 \times 1225} = \sqrt{2 \times 5 \times 245} = \sqrt{2 \times 5 \times 5 \times 49}$
  $= 5 \times 7 \times \sqrt{2} = 35\sqrt{2}$

5 a is irrational

6

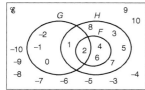

  a 1 **b** 7 **c** 1 **d** 11 **e** 10

7 a $\sqrt{16}$ or $\frac{65}{13}$ **b** π or $\sqrt{14}$

8 a i {4, 8, 10, 14} **ii** 1 **iii** {2, 5, 7, 11, 13}

  b

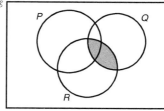

  c 16

9 a $-1, \sqrt{36}$ **b** $\sqrt{2}, \sqrt{30}$

10 a $P \cap Q \cap R'$ **b** 47

11 a 8 **b** 18

12 $\frac{3}{2500}, \frac{1}{8}\%, 0.00216$

13 $\frac{1}{125000}, 8 \times 10^{-5}, 0.0008, 0.8\%$

14 97

15 a

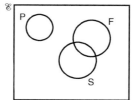

  b for example 10 or 26 or 58

16 a

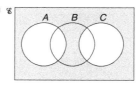

  b

17 a i $\varnothing$ **ii** {7, 8, 11, 13, 14} **iii** $\frac{6}{11}$ **iv** {5}

  b i 3 **ii** 11 **iii** 18

18 a $\varnothing$ **b** $\mathscr{E}$ **c** A

19 $1\frac{22}{37}$ or $\frac{59}{37}$

20 a $n(S \cup F)'$ or $n(S' \cap F')$ **b** $y = x - 15$

  c i 15 **ii** 20

21 i a 8 **b** 4 **c** 21 **d** 19

  ii For example, students who study Mathematics but
  not Physics

22 a

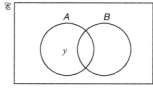

  b i 6 **ii** 4, 5

23 a $B \cap C \cap A'$ **b i** 31 **ii** 9

24 a ∅ 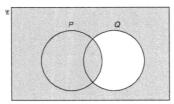 **b** 9

25 a i 1, 2, 3, 4 **ii** 1, 2 **b** 22

Chapter 14

Essential Skills

1 a $a^2 = b^2 + c^2$ **b** $y = 2x + 3$ **c** $2x + 5y - x - 1$
2 a $2x$ **b** -6 **c** -1 **d** $3xy$ and $-4xy$
3 a a^5 **b** x^9 **c** b^3
  d c^{10} **e** a^3b^6
4 a $x^2 - x^3$ **b** $\dfrac{3x}{y}$ **c** $xy + x^2y^2$ **d** b
5 a x^7y^7 **b** $6x^6$ **c** x^{12} **d** $x^{12}y^{30}$
6 a $-3x - 2y$ **b** $2a + 2c$ **c** 0 **d** $-ab + 4a$
7 a $\dfrac{1}{3}$ **b** $\dfrac{1}{16}$ **c** 4 **d** $\dfrac{4}{25}$
8 a $n = 0$ **b** $n = -1$ **c** $n = -2$ **d** $n = 1$
9 a $-4y$ **b** $-pq$ **c** $a^3 + 2a^2b^2 + b^3$ **d** $1 - x^2 - y^2$
10 a $5xy(z + 2x)$ **b** $7xy(2x - 3y)$ **c** $3a^2(1 - 2a)$ **d** $x(2x - 1)$

Exercise 14.1

1 $a^2 + 2a + 1$ **2** $x^2 + 9x + 20$
3 $x^2 - x - 20$ **4** $x^2 + x - 20$
5 $x^2 - 9x + 20$ **6** $2b^2 + 3b + 1$
7 $5c^2 - 12c + 4$ **8** $12x^2 + 28x + 15$
9 $x^2 + 2xy + y^2$ **10** $x^2 - 2xy + y^2$
11 $x^2 - y^2$ **12** $4d^2 - 9e^2$
13 $14z^2 - 5z - 1$ **14** $8 + 6x + x^2$
15 $4 - x^2$ **16** $a^3 + a^2b + ab + b^2$
17 $x^3 + x^2 - x - 1$ **18** $2b^2 + 4bc + b + 2c^2 + c$
19 $x^3 - 1$ **20** $x^4 - 1$
21 $4x^2 + 12x + 9$ **22** $4x^2 - 9$
23 $4x^2 - 12x + 9$ **24** $9x^2 - 16$
25 $4b^2 - 1$ **26** $2ac + 2ad + 3bc + 3bd$

Exercise 14.2

1 $(x + 1)(x + 3)$ **2** $(x + 1)(x + 5)$
3 $(x + 1)(x + 12)$ **4** $(x + 2)(x + 6)$
5 $(x + 3)(x + 4)$ **6** $(x + 4)(x + 4)$ or $(x + 4)^2$
7 $(x + 1)(x + 16)$ **8** $(x + 2)(x + 8)$
9 $(x + 1)(x + 17)$ **10** $(x + 1)(x + 1)$ or $(x + 1)^2$

Exercise 14.3

1 $(x + 1)(x + 5)$ **2** $(x - 1)(x + 5)$
3 $(x + 1)(x - 5)$ **4** $(x - 1)(x - 5)$
5 $(x + 1)(x - 8)$ **6** $(x - 2)(x - 4)$
7 $(x - 2)(x + 4)$ **8** $(x - 1)(x + 36)$
9 $(x + 2)(x - 18)$ **10** $(x - 4)(x - 9)$

Exercise 14.4

1 $(x + 1)(3x + 1)$ **2** $(2x + 1)(3x + 1)$
3 $(x + 1)(3x + 2)$ **4** $(x + 2)(3x + 1)$
5 $(x - 1)(3x + 1)$ **6** $(x + 1)(3x - 1)$
7 $(x - 1)(3x - 1)$ **8** $(x + 1)(6x + 1)$
9 $(4x + 1)(x - 2)$ **10** $(2x + 1)(2x + 3)$
11 $(4x + 1)(x + 3)$ **12** $(2x + 1)(2x - 3)$
13 $(2x - 1)(2x + 3)$ **14** $(2x - 1)(2x - 3)$
15 $(4x + 1)(2x + 3)$ **16** $(4x - 1)(2x + 3)$
17 $(4x + 1)(2x + 3)$ **18** $(2x - 1)(4x + 3)$
19 $(2x + 5)(4x + 3)$ **20** $(3x + 5)(3x + 5)$
21 $(3x - 5)(2x - 5)$ **22** $(2x + 5y)(4x + 3y)$
23 $(3x + 5y)(3x + 5y)$ **24** $(3xy - 5)(2xy - 5)$

Exercise 14.5

1 $(x - y)(x + y)$ **2** $(a - 1)(a + 1)$
3 $(x - 3)(x + 3)$ **4** $(2y - 3)(2y + 3)$
5 $(5 - a)(5 + a)$ **6** $(6a - 7b)(6a + 7b)$
7 $(ab - xy)(ab + xy)$ **8** $(1 - 2c)(1 + 2c)$

Exercise 14.6

1 $3(3a + 5b)$ **2** $(1 - x)(1 + x)$
3 $2(3 - x)(3 + x)$ **4** $(2x + 1)(x - 1)$
5 $6x(x - 3)$ **6** $2(x - 3)(x - 3)$
7 $5x(2x - 1)(2x + 1)$ **8** $3(x + 2)(x - 1)$
9 $2y(y - 1)(y - 1)$ **10** $4xy(4y - x)$
11 $4xy(2y - x)(2y + x)$ **12** $3(2a + x)(2b + y)$

Exercise 14.7

1 3 **2** $\dfrac{1}{3}$ **3** $\dfrac{1}{27}$
4 $7x^{\frac{2}{5}}$ **5** $10x^{\frac{4}{5}}$ **6** $\dfrac{2}{5}$
7 10 **8** $\dfrac{10}{x^{\frac{4}{5}}}$ **9** $\dfrac{2}{5}x^{\frac{4}{5}}$
10 $2y^{\frac{5}{4}}$ **11** $\dfrac{2}{y^{\frac{1}{4}}}$ **12** $x - 1$
13 $\dfrac{1}{x^{\frac{1}{2}}y}$ **14** $2 + 2x^{\frac{1}{2}}$ **15** $4x^{\frac{4}{3}}$
16 $x - 2x^{\frac{1}{2}} + 1$ **17** $x - 2 + \dfrac{1}{x}$
18 a $x = \dfrac{1}{5}$ **b** $x = \dfrac{1}{4}$ **c** $x = \dfrac{1}{3}$

Exercise 14.8

1 $\frac{1}{7}$ **2** $\frac{20}{11}$ **3** $\frac{17}{32}$

4 $2x - 4$ **5** $\frac{1}{2x+3}$ **6** $y + z$

7 $\frac{x}{2}$ **8** $\frac{1}{3y+5z}$ **9** $\frac{3x+2}{5x-4}$

10 $\frac{3yz}{y-4z}$ **11** $\frac{1}{x-y}$ **12** $2x+3$

13 $\frac{1}{y+1}$ **14** $\frac{x+1}{x-1}$ **15** $\frac{x-1}{x+1}$

16 $\frac{1}{9}$ **17** $\frac{y+x^2}{x+y^2}$ **18** a^2+b^2

Exercise 14.9

1 $\frac{8}{27}$ **2** $\frac{2}{3}$ **3** $\frac{xy}{x^2+y^2}$

4 $\frac{x+1}{y(x-1)}$ **5** $\frac{x^2 y}{(x-1)(x+1)}$ **6** $\frac{1}{x^2+y^2}$

7 $\frac{x+y}{xyz}$ **8** $\frac{1}{x}$

Exercise 14.10

1 $\frac{19}{15}$ **2** $\frac{x+1}{x}$ **3** $\frac{7x}{12}$

4 $\frac{x^2-y^2}{xy}$ **5** $\frac{2a}{(a-b)(a+b)}$ **6** $\frac{2b}{(a-b)(a+b)}$

7 $\frac{6x-3}{x(x-1)}$ **8** $\frac{3}{x(x-1)}$ **9** $\frac{-x-6}{12}$

10 $\frac{17x-18}{12}$ **11** $\frac{x+5y}{(x+y)(x+2y)}$ **12** $\frac{x^2+y^2}{(x-y)(x+y)}$

13 $\frac{x^2+2xy-y^2}{(x-y)(x+y)}$ **14** $\frac{2(a^2+b^2)}{(a-b)(a+b)}$ **15** $\frac{4ab}{(a-b)(a+b)}$

16 $\frac{-3x^2+5xy-y^2}{(2x-y)(x+y)}$ **17** $\frac{x^2-1}{xy}$ **18** $\frac{2x-1}{x(x+1)(x-1)}$

Exercise 14.11

1 a $\frac{1}{3}$ **b** 2 **c** $\frac{1}{81}$

    d 6 **e** 65 **f** 16

    g $\frac{7}{6}$ **h** $\frac{1}{42}$ **i** 42

2 a $\frac{1}{y^2}$ **b** $\frac{1}{y^{\frac{1}{3}}}$ **c** $4x^{\frac{5}{2}}$ **d** $24a^{\frac{7}{2}}b^{\frac{17}{6}}$ **e** $\frac{x^{\frac{1}{2}}}{y^2}$

3 a $6x^2 - 7x - 49$ **b** $x^2 - 2x + 1$

    c $x^4 - 2x^2y^2 + y^4$ **d** $x^2y^2 - 1$

    e $xy + xb + ay + ab$ **f** $6ac - 10bc + 9ad - 15bd$

4 a $(3x-2)(x+1)$ **b** $(x+5)(x-10)$

    c $(2x-7)(x-7)$ **d** $2(5x-3)(5x+3)$

    e $xy(x-1)(x+1)$ **f** $3(2x+3)(x-4)$

    g $(a+b)(2c+d)$ **h** $(2c-d)(a-b)$

    i $2ab(2a-3b)(2a+3b)$

5 a $\frac{1}{ax-1}$ **b** $\frac{x+1}{x+6}$ **c** $\frac{2}{x}$

    d $\frac{2+x}{2-x}$ **e** $\frac{3x^2}{2}$ **f** $\frac{y+x^2}{x(y+x)}$

6 a $\frac{2a^2}{(a+b)(a-b)}$ **b** $\frac{4x}{(x-1)(x+1)}$

    c $\frac{(x+1)^2}{(x-1)^2}$ **d** 1

7 a $\frac{c^2+cd-1}{c^2-d^2}$ **b** $\frac{c(c+d+1)}{c^2-d^2}$

8 7

9 a -1 **b** $5k$

10 a $5xy(2x+3y)$ **b** $(5a-b)(5a+b)$

    c $\frac{1-2x}{(x+1)^2}$ **d** $\frac{ab}{6}$

11 $\frac{x+11}{(x-3)(x+4)}$

12 a $(a-2b)(1-3c)$ **b** $5t^2+6$

13 $\frac{x+7}{(x-3)(x+2)}$

14 a 8 **b** $\frac{1}{3}$ **c** -3

15 a 2 **b** $\frac{1}{3}$

16 a $x^3 - 1$ **b** $(a-b)(x-3y)$

17 $\frac{4(x+1)}{x(x+2)}$

18 a $\frac{x^{18}}{9}$ **b** 2^x

19 a $(2x-3)(2x+3)$ **b** $x(4x-9)$ **c** $(4x-1)(x-2)$

20 a $(2x+3)(x-5)$ **b** $(2y-z)(t-4s)$

21 a i $3x^2 - 4$ **ii** $\frac{x^2(a-1)}{x(a-1)} = x$

    b $7(x-3)(x+3)$

22 $\frac{x^2-6x+25}{4(x-3)}$

23 a $\frac{5}{2}$ or 2.5 **b** -1

24 $\frac{11x}{18}$ **25** $9x^2$ **26** $\frac{-18}{(2x+3)(x-3)}$

27 a 0 **b** 0.2 or $\frac{1}{5}$ **c** 0.6 or $\frac{3}{5}$

28 a $3x^2$ **b** -6

29 $\frac{2}{c}$

30 a i $9 - 5p$ **ii** $3q^2 + 5qr - 2r^2$

    b $2(3t+1)(3t-1)$

    c i $y = 30$ **ii** $x = -5$ or $x = 5$ **iii** $x = \sqrt{\frac{y-18}{3}}$

31 a i $5(x+2)(x-2)$ **ii** $\frac{x-2}{2(x-1)}$

    b $\frac{y+29}{(y-3)(y+5)}$

32 a $3a^2(5+4a)$ **b** $(1-4b)(1+4b)$ **c** $(3c-d)(2x-y)$

33 $\frac{8-t}{2(t-1)(t+2)}$

34 **a** **i** $5x(3x+2)$ **ii** $(t+3)(t-5)$
    b $x=0.6$

35 **a** 1 **b** 32 **c** 25

36 **a** 1 **b** $\frac{1}{81}$ **c** 27

37 **a** 26 **b** **i** x^2 **ii** x^3

Chapter 15

Essential Skills

1 **a** 10500 cm² or 1.05 m² **b** 3014 cm or 30.14 m
2 **a** 4.67 **b** 501 **c** 0.01
    d 0.0106 **e** 516cm **f** 100 kilograms
    g 9200 **h** 1000
3 **a** $438.5 \leq 439 < 439.5$ **b** $5665 \leq 5670 < 5675$
4 **a** 2×10^{10} mm³ **b** 2×10^7 cm³ **c** 2×10^1 m³
5 **a** 0.5 cm² **b** 0.5 litres **c** 12000 g
6 **a** $700 \times 0.7 = 500$ **b** $\frac{80}{80} \div \frac{200}{400} = 2$ **c** $\frac{1000}{500} + \frac{400}{30} \approx 15$
7 **a** 1.425×10^{-2} **b** 2.49×10^{12} to 3 s.f.
    c 1.107×10^3 **d** 6.002×10^{-5}
8 **a** 1.93 **b** 4.07 **c** 6.32
    d 2.82 **e** 2.02
9 **a** 2 : 25 **b** 1 : 400 **c** 4 : 1
    d 48 : 85 **e** 2 : 1 : 10 **f** 37 : 500
10 **a** 1 : 0.0002 **b** 5000 : 1

Exercise 15.1

1 **a** **i** 1.0 **ii** 3.0
    b **i** 26 **ii** 78
    c **i** 155.25 **ii** 181.25
    d **i** 1.08 **ii** 1.26 to 3 s.f.
2 **a** **i** 702.4 **ii** 728.8
    b **i** 20.88 **ii** 21.67
    c **i** 69.2875 **ii** 71.0775

Exercise 15.2

1 $90 **2** $12.50 **3** $1388
4 **a** Rs 480 **b** Rs 408

Exercise 15.3

1 **a** 19.8 cm **b** 22.2525 cm²
2 **a** upper bound of short pieces = 10.5 cm
    lower bound of large piece = 99.5 cm
    $\frac{99.5}{10.5} = 9.476$ so it may only be possible to cut 9 whole lengths.
    b upper bound of large piece = 100.5 cm
    lower bound of short pieces = 9.5 cm
    lower bound of 10 short pieces = 95 cm
    maximum left over = 100.5 − 95 = 5.5 cm

3 **a** $3.495 \leq l < 3.505$ **b** 0.055 m or 5.5 cm
4 **a** $20493 **b** $5508
5 **a** €34 **b** €40
6 **a** 1 : 13 or 13 : 15 **b** 12600 **c** 41.0%
    d 20000 **e** 14000
7 **a** 115 125 **b** 2400 m²
8 3 h 20 min
9 50.1225 cm² **10** **a** 6.5 mm **b** 6 cm
11 38 **12** $231.13
13 **a** 1045.28 **b** 1000
14 **a** $450 **b** **i** $120 **ii** $80
15 20 **16** £3000
17 62225000 or 6.2225×10^7 or 62.225 million
18 50.1225 cm²
19 **a** **i** $6000 **ii** 15%
    b $11200 **c** **i** $7500 **ii** $\frac{9}{80}$ **d** $8640
20 **a** 06 41 **b** $204
21 **a** **i** $250 **ii** $2600 **iii** 6.12%
    b **i** 12 m **ii** 7 h 12 min **iii** 2.78 km/h **iv** 16 07
    c 25000 or 2.5×10^4
22 237.5 242.5
23 **a** $\frac{0.003 \times 3000}{(10 + 20)^2}$ **b** 0.01 or $\frac{1}{100}$
24 **a** 0.701 **b** £190
25 135 165

26 **a**

	Lower Bound	Upper Bound
x	65	75
y	875	925

    b $1175
27 **a** 5000 **b** 20 cm
28 **a** **i** 150 g **ii** 9 : 11 **iii** 48%
    b **i** $3.60 **ii** $7.75
29 **a** 340 cm **b** 9 m
30 **a** $\frac{3}{5}(x-15000)=3000$ **b** **i** 9% **ii** $17720
    c $27500 **d** **i** $\frac{3}{5}(x-15000)$ **ii** $45000
31 **a** $0.7^2, \frac{7}{11}, 0.7, \frac{7}{9}$ **b** 400
32 **a** **i** $825 **ii** £625 **iii** €691.20
    b **i** $16200 **ii** $18895.68 **iii** 126% **c** $41500

33 **a**

	Lower bound	Upper bound
Mass of 1 marble	5.35g	5.45g
Mass of the box	82.5g	87.5g

    b 189.5 g
34 **a** **i** 31.2 to 31.3% **ii** 1.76
    b **i** $5.60 **ii** $0.28 or 28 cents **iii** 16

35 a i $31.25   **ii** 150%   **iii** 2 : 5   **b** 16
36 a 9 : 250   **b i** 9.45 g   **ii a** 0.3%
  ii b 0.9%   **iii** 2.205 g   **c** 2000

Chapter 16

Essential Skills

1 a $x = sh$ **b** $x = \frac{A}{l}$ **c** $x = \frac{V-c}{y}$

  d $x = \frac{u^2 - v^2}{2a}$ **e** $x = \frac{2A}{a+b}$ **f** $x = \frac{b}{c}$

2 a $5n - 3$ **b** $5n - 15$ **c** $n^2 + 1$
  d $-2n + 12$ **e** n^2

3 a i $\frac{9}{2}$ or 4.5   **ii** 5202   **b i** −9   **ii** 9000

  c i −9   **iii** −801

4 a $x = 11, y = -4$ **b** $x = 2, y = 3$
  c $x = 0, y = 2$ **d** $x = 5, y = 4$

Exercise 16.1

1 $x = 3$ **2** $x = 6$ **3** $x = 14$ **4** $x = 2$

5 $x = -21$ **6** $x = \frac{5}{8}$ **7** $x = -\frac{1}{2}$ **8** $x = -1$

Exercise 16.2

1 $x = -2$ or −3   **2** $x = -2$ or 1   **3** $x = 5$ or 1

4 $x = -\frac{1}{2}$ or 1   **5** $x = -1$ or 1   **6** $x = 1$ or $\frac{5}{2}$

7 $x = -1$ or $\frac{4}{3}$ **8** $x = \frac{1}{2}$ or $x = \frac{3}{2}$ **9** $x = -\frac{3}{2}$ or $\frac{3}{2}$

10 $x = 3$ or 5   **11** $x = -2$ or 2   **12** $x = -1$

13 $x = 1$ **14** $x = 1$ or $\frac{8}{3}$

Exercise 16.3

1 $x = -6.14$ or 1.14   **2** $x = -1.14$ or 6.14
3 $x = -3.12$ or −0.214   **4** $x = -0.618$ or 1.62
5 $x = -1.56$ or 2.56   **6** $x = 0.314$ or 3.19

Exercise 16.4

1 $(x-3)^2 - 8$ **2** $\left(x + \frac{5}{2}\right)^2 - \frac{17}{4}$ **3** $\left(x - \frac{3}{2}\right)^2 - \frac{21}{4}$

4 $2(x+1)^2 - 7$ **5** $3(x-1)^2 - 7$ **6** $2\left(x - \frac{3}{4}\right)^2 + \frac{7}{8}$

7 $2\left(x + \frac{5}{4}\right)^2 - \frac{65}{8}$

Exercise 16.5

1 $x = -1 \pm \sqrt{2}$ **2** $x = \frac{1 \pm \sqrt{33}}{4}$

3 $x = 5$ or −1   **4** $x = \frac{-2 \pm \sqrt{5}}{2}$ or $-1 \pm \frac{\sqrt{5}}{2}$

5 $x = \frac{7 \pm \sqrt{41}}{2}$ **6** $x = \frac{1}{2}$ or 1

Exercise 16.6

1 $x = -0.618$ or 1.62   **2** $x = -7.87$ or −0.127
3 $x = 1$ **4** $x = -2$ or $\frac{3}{2}$
5 $x = 1.31$ or −0.306   **6** 0.382 or 2.62
7 $x = -0.303$ or 3.30   **8** $x = -1$ or $-\frac{1}{3}$
9 $x = -0.215$ or 1.55   **10** $x = 1$
11 $x = -42.6$ or −0.103   **12** $x = -\frac{5}{6}$ or 3

Exercise 16.7

1 $x = -1$ or −2   **2** $x = \frac{1}{2}$ or 2
3 $x = \frac{1}{2}$ or 2   **4** $x = -3$ or 2
5 $x = -2$ or 1   **6** $x = \frac{1}{2}$ or 1
7 $x = 1$ **8** $x = -\frac{1}{3}$ or 1
9 $x = 2$ or $-\frac{1}{2}$ **10** $x = 1$ or 4
11 a $(x-4)(x-5) = 12$ **b** $x = 1$ or 8   **c** 4 cm by 3 cm
12 8, 9
13 12, 14
14 a $x(x+3) = 40$
    $x^2 + 3x - 40 = 0$
  b $x = -8$ or 5
  c length 8 cm, breadth 5 cm

Exercise 16.8

1 a 1, 4, 9, 16   **b** −1, 2, 7, 14   **c** −1, 0, 3, 8
  d −3, −2, 1, 6   **e** $\frac{1}{2}, \frac{2}{3}, \frac{3}{4}, \frac{4}{5}$ **f** $\frac{1}{2}, \frac{1}{5}, \frac{1}{10}, \frac{1}{17}$
  g 0, 1, 4, 9   **h** 1, 8, 27, 64   **i** 3, 11, 30, 67
  j 0, 6, 24, 60   **k** 3, 6, 9, 12
2 a $n(n+1)$ **b** $n^2 - n$ **c** $(n+1)^2$
  d $2n^2$ **e** $\frac{n^2}{n+1}$ **f** $\frac{3n}{n+3}$
3 a 19, 99, 201   **b i** $n = 4$ **ii** $n = 11$
4 a 24, 63, 10200
  b i 1   **ii** 9   **iii** 10   **iv** 16

Exercise 16.9

1 $y = 2, x = -1$ **2** $y = \frac{1}{2}, x = \frac{1}{2}$

3 $y = -\frac{1}{6}, x = \frac{5}{6}$ **4** $y = 2, x = 2$

Exercise 16.10

1 $x = 1, y = 3$ **2** $x = -1, y = -1$ **3** $x = \frac{29}{3}, y = \frac{5}{3}$

4 $x = -2, y = 10$ **5** $x = \frac{3}{10}, y = \frac{9}{10}$ **6** $x = \frac{9}{14}, y = \frac{5}{7}$

Exercise 16.11

1 $x = 0, y = 4$ **2** $x = 10, y = -1$
3 $x = 3, y = 3$ **4** $x = -10, y = -5$

5 $x = 18, y = -1$

6 $x = 5, y = -\frac{2}{13}$

7 $x = -\frac{3}{5}, y = \frac{19}{5}$

8 $x = 7, y = -2$

9 $x = -4, y = 2$

10 $x = -\frac{9}{7}, y = \frac{52}{7}$

Exercise 16.12

1 a $x > -\frac{1}{2}$

b $x > 1$

c $x \leq -\frac{5}{2}$

d $x \geq 3$

e $x > -6.4$

f $-\frac{7}{2} < x < 2$

g $2 \leq x < 7$

h $-5 < x < -3$

2 a $x < -2$ $\{..... -5, -4, -3\}$

   b $x \leq -2$ $\{.... -5, -4, -3, -2\}$

   c $x < \frac{3}{2}$ $\{.... -2, -1, 0, 1\}$

   d $-3 < x < \frac{1}{2}$ $\{-2, -1, 0\}$

   e $-1 \leq x < 4$ $\{-1, 0, 1, 2, 3\}$

   f $-4 \leq x \leq -1$ $\{-4, -3, -2, -1\}$

   g $-3 < x < 1$ $\{-2, -1, 0\}$

3 a $\{-6, -5, -4\}$ **b** $-6 \leq x < -3$

Exercise 16.13

1 a $T = 33N$ **b** the cost of one item

2 $y = \frac{4}{9}x^2$ **3 a** $\frac{10}{7}$ **b** $D = \frac{21}{V}$

4 a $a = \frac{4}{3}\sqrt{b}$ **b** $\frac{16}{3}$ **c** 3.52

5 a $m = 3l^3$ **b** 648 g

6 a $F = \frac{10^{38}}{d^2}$ **b** $F = 10^8$ Newtons

Exercise 16.14

1 $b = \sqrt{12V} + a$

2 $r = \frac{S-a}{S}$ or $r = 1 - \frac{a}{S}$

3 $z = \sqrt{x^2 + y^2 - 2xyC}$

4 $a = \frac{y}{4x}$

5 $a = \frac{1}{2}\left(\frac{2s}{n} - (n-1)d\right)$

6 $V = \sqrt{\frac{2E}{m} + u^2}$

7 a $w = \frac{W(1-e)}{e}$ **b** $W = \frac{ew}{1-e}$

8 $u = \sqrt{v^2 - 2as}$ **9** $l = \frac{t^2 g}{4\pi^2}$ **10** $A = \frac{b^2 + c^2 - a^2}{2bc}$

Exercise 16.15

1 a $x = \frac{10}{7}$ **b** $x = -7$

2 a $x = -\frac{5}{3}$ or $\frac{5}{3}$ **b** $x = -4.5$ or 3   **c** $x = -3.10$ or 0.431

3 $(x-1)^2 - \frac{21}{4}$ **4 a** nth term $= \frac{2n-1}{3n}$ **b** nth term $= \frac{(n-1)^2}{n^2}$

5 a $y = \frac{30}{\sqrt{x}}$ **b i** $y = 4.74$ **ii** $x = 2.25$

6 a $B = A - Dc$ **b** $b = \frac{aB}{A}$

7 $-2.5 < x \leq 1$

8 a $x = 4, y = -1$ **b** $x = -\frac{44}{3}, \quad y = \frac{1}{3}$

9 $\frac{1}{9}, 0, \frac{1}{25}, \frac{1}{9}, \frac{9}{49}$

10 a i $-1 < x \leq 4$

   ii

b (1, 3), (1, 5), (3, 5), (5, 3)

11 a p is inversely proportional to the square root of q

   b $q = 9$

12 a $5x(x - 2)$ **b** $x = 4$ **c** $p = -2$ or 0

13 a 190   **b** $\frac{1}{2}(n + 1)(n + 2)$

14 $x = -7$ $y = -3$

15 a $k = -12$ **b** $y = -\frac{1}{2}$ or 2

16 a $-1 \leq x < 2$ **b** $-1, 0, 1$

17 a 120 Newtons   **b** $y = 8$

18 a $x = 28$ **b** $y = \frac{2}{3}$

19 a $t < -1.5$ **b** 58

20 a -39

   b i $3n + 1$ **ii a** $\frac{19}{36}$ **b** $\frac{3n+1}{n^2}$

21 a $y = 4x^2$ **b** $x = -\frac{3}{2}$ or $\frac{3}{2}$

22 a $T = \frac{36}{l^2}$ **b** $L = -\frac{6}{5}$ or $\frac{6}{5}$

23 a $x > -1$ **b** $y = 10$

24 a $y = 2\sqrt{x}$ **b** $x = 25$

25 a $\frac{3m}{20}$ **b** $x > 10$

26 $y = 12.5$

27 a i $k > 2$ **ii** $t = 30$
   b $x = 18\frac{1}{2}, y = 10\frac{1}{2}$

28 $x = 8, y = 6$

29 a -3 **b** $a = \dfrac{b^2}{b-c}$

30 a i $\dfrac{40}{x}$ **ii** $\dfrac{40}{x+2} = \dfrac{40}{x} - 1$

   iii $-10, 8$ **iv** $8

   b i $m = n + 2.55, 2m = 5n$

   ii $m = 4.25, n = 1.7$

31 b i $p = 25, q = 40$

   ii $x = n^2, y = (n+1)^2, z = (n+1)^2 + n^2 - 1,$ or $z = 2n(n+1)$

   c i $\dfrac{2}{3} + f + g = 4$

   ii $\dfrac{2}{3} \times 2^3 + f \times 2^2 + g \times 2 = 12$

   iii $f = 2, g = \dfrac{4}{3}$ **iv** 880

32 $x > -\dfrac{4}{7}$ or $x > -0.571$

33 a $y = \dfrac{k}{x^2}, k = 4.8 \times 5^2 = 120$ **b** $y = 30$

   c $x = 3.46$ **d** $x = 4.93$

   e y is divided by 4 **f** x increased by 25%

   g $x = \sqrt{\dfrac{120}{y}}$

34 $c = \dfrac{b^2 + 5}{3}$

35 $d = \sqrt[3]{2(c-5)}$

36 5×10^4

37 a $x = 13.5$ **b** $x = -1$ or 4

38 $x < -23.5$

39 a 3×10^{11} **b** 5×10^6

40 a i $(x+4)(x-5)$ **ii** $x = -4$ or 5

   b $x = -0.55$ or 1.22

   c i $(m - 2n)(m + 2n)$ **ii** -12

   iii $y = 20x + 5$ **iv** $n = \sqrt{\dfrac{m^2 - y}{4}}$

   d i $k = 4$ or -4

   ii $n(m-2n)(m+2n)(m^2 + 4n^2)$

41 $\sqrt{\left(\dfrac{6}{T}\right)^2 - 1}$ or $\sqrt{\dfrac{36}{T^2} - 1}$

42 a $x^2(a+b)$ **b** $x = \sqrt{\dfrac{p^2 + d^2}{a+b}}$

43 1.25 **45** $y = (9(1-x))^2$ **46** $x = 2, y = -6$

44 a $m = -13$

   b i $y = 0.5$

   ii $\dfrac{x + 11}{(x-1)(x+3)}$ **iii** $x = -\dfrac{1}{3}$

   c $q = \dfrac{p + t}{p}$

45 a $y = 3$ **b** $x = -2$ or 2

   c i $y = 3$ **ii** $y = -\dfrac{12}{5}$

   d $x = \sqrt{\dfrac{5y + 12}{3}}$

e i $\dfrac{t-3}{2} = \dfrac{3t^2 - 12}{5}$

   $5(t - 3) = 2(3t^2 - 12)$

   $5t - 15 = 6t^2 - 24$

   $6t^2 - 5t - 9 = 0$

   ii $t = -0.88$ or 1.7

46 a $a = -2.38$ or 0.66

   b i $4x + 6y = 816$ **ii** $3x + 5y = 654$

   iii $x = 78, y = 84$

47 a $x = -0.79$ or 2.12

   b $9a^2 - 24ab + 16b^2$

   c $(4 - y)(3 + 2t)$

48 a $\dfrac{24}{x}$ **b** $\dfrac{24}{x + 0.5}$

   c $\dfrac{24}{x} - \dfrac{24}{x + 0.5} = 2$

   $24(x + 0.5) - 24x = 2x(x + 0.5)$

   $24x + 12 - 24x = 2x^2 + x$

   $0 = 2x^2 + x - 12$

   d $x = -2.712$ or 2.212

   e 10 minutes 51 to 52 seconds

49 a $t = 2\dfrac{1}{3}$ **b** $x = -2\dfrac{1}{2}, y = 17$

   c $\dfrac{3y + 2}{y - 2}$ **d** $x = \dfrac{2f - 3h}{2 + g}$

50 a $y = 3$ **b** $p = 2$

   c $q = -6$ or 6 **d** $d = -1.29$ or 1.09

51 a i $p = 19$ **ii** $q = 29$

   b i $j = 16$ **ii** $k = 25$

   iii $S_n = n^2$

   c i 3, 4 **ii** $U_n = n - 1$ **iii** $T_n = n^2 + n - 1$

52 a i $\dfrac{1080}{x}$ **ii** $\dfrac{1080}{x + 30}$

   b $\dfrac{1080}{x} - \dfrac{1080}{x + 30} = \dfrac{1}{2}$

   $2160(x + 30) - 2160x = x(x + 30)$

   $2160x + 64800 - 2160x = x^2 + 30x$

   $0 = x^2 + 30x - 64800$

   c $x = -270$ or 240

   d i $4\dfrac{1}{2}$ hours **ii** 254 km per hour

53 a $p = -5$ **b** $\dfrac{2}{v + 1}$

   c i $(10y + x) - (10x + y) = 63$

   $9y - 9x = 63$

   $y - x = 7$

   ii a $(10x + y) + (10y + x) = 99$ **b** $x = 1, y = 81$

   $11x + 11y = 99$

54 a i $x = 2.71$ **ii** $b = \sqrt{x^2 - 2ax}$

   b i $8x - 27$ **ii** $8x - 27 < 300$

   $x < 40.875$

   iii 40

Chapter 17

The answers to questions in this chapter which require drawing and measuring have been given as a range of values. You should get your answers within the given range, or very close; if you do not, sharpen your pencil and try again with more attention to accuracy! The answers to many of the questions can be arrived at by different routes.

Where reasons are required one explanation has been given to help you. Yours could be different and still be correct.

Essential Skills

1 55–56°, 41–42°, 82–83°

2 140°   **3** 1980°

4 a rectangle or parallelogram   **b** kite
   c trapezium   **d** rhombus

5 a rotational symmetry, order 2. 2 lines of symmetry
   b rotational symmetry, order 2. No lines of symmetry
   c rotational symmetry, order 5. 5 lines of symmetry
   d rotational symmetry, order 4. 4 lines of symmetry

6 (regular) tetrahedron

7 a for example, $\angle TAP$ and $\angle ABR$
   b for example, $\angle PAB$ and $\angle ABC$
   c for example, $\angle ACB$ and $\angle SCV$
   d $\angle PAB = \angle RBU = 50°$ (corresponding angles)
      $\angle BAC = 180 - 50 - 55 = 75°$ (angles on a straight line)

Exercise 17.1

1 a, c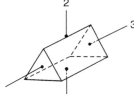

   b 4
   d 4

2 a, b and **c**

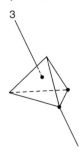

3 a One axis of rotational symmetry, order infinity.
      Infinite number of planes of symmetry.

   b One axis of rotational symmetry, order 4. 4 planes of symmetry.

   c Rotational symmetry, order 6 about one axis. 6 more axes, each with rotational symmetry order 2.
      7 planes of symmetry.

Exercise 17.2

1 $a = 20$ (isosceles triangle)
   $b = 90$ (angles between radius and tangent)
   $c = 140$ (isosceles triangle)
   $d = 40$ (angles on a straight line)
   $e = 50$ (angle sum of a triangle)

2 Let $BS = x$
   $AU = AS = 4$ cm   (tangents from a point outside the circle are equal)
   $CT = CU = 6$ cm   (tangents from a point outside the circle are equal)
   $BT = BS = x$ cm   (tangents from a point outside the circle are equal)
   $2x + 2 \times 4 + 2 \times 6 = 29$
   $x = 4.5$ $a = 10.5$

3 $a = 35$ (isosceles triangle)
   $b = 110$ (angle sum of a triangle)
   $c = 55$ ($\angle ABC = 90°$, angle in a semicircle)
   $d = 55$ (isosceles triangle)
   $e = 25$ (isosceles triangle)
   $f = 25$ (alternate angles)
   $g = 45$ (angle sum of a triangle)

Exercise 17.3

1 a $\angle BAO = 40°$ (isosceles triangle)
      $\angle AOB = 100°$ (angle sum of a triangle)
      $x = 80°$ (angles on a straight line)
   b $\angle OAB = \angle OCB = 90°$ (angle between radius and tangent)
      $\angle AOC = 130°$ (angle sum of a quadrilateral)
      $x = 65°$ (the angle at the centre is twice the angle at the circumference)

2 $a = 70°$ (cyclic quadrilateral)
   $b = 70°$ (angles in the same segment)
   $c = 20°$ (angle sum of a triangle)
   $d = 20°$ (angle sum of a triangle)

3 $a = 20°$ (isosceles triangle)
   $b = 20°$ (alternate angles)
   $c = 180° - (180° - 2 \times 20°)$ (angle sum of an
   $c = 40°$ isosceles triangle and angles on a straight line)
   $d = 40°$ (angles in the same segment)
   $e = 180° - (20° + 40°)$ (angle sum of a
   $e = 120°$ triangle and vertically opposite angles)
   $f = 20°$ (angles in the same segment)

4 $a = 35°$ (corresponding angles)
$b = 90°$ (angle in a semicircle)
$c = 55°$ (angle sum of a triangle)
$d = 90°$ (angle in a semicircle)
$e = 45°$ (isosceles triangle)
$f = 45°$ (alternate angles)

5 $\angle ADC = 50°$ (angles on a straight line)
$\angle ABC = 130°$ (angles on a straight line)
$\angle ADC + \angle ABC = 180°$
therefore $ABCD$ is a cyclic quadrilateral (opposite angles add up to 180°)

Exercise 17.4

1 13 **2** $x = 74$ **3** $a = 20, b = 70$

Exercise 17.5

1 $x = 60$ $y = 65$
2 $w = 30$
$x = 75$
$y = 60$
$z = 50$
3 **a** $a = 70°$
$b = 140°$
$c = 70°$
$d = 40°$
b $b + d = 180°$
therefore $AOCT$ is a cyclic quadrilateral (opposite angles of a cyclic quadrilateral are supplementary)
c On the midpoint of OT
4 One axis of symmetry, order 6.
6 planes of symmetry
5 **a** $AE = BD$ (equidistant from centre of circle)
b All equal and half AE and BD (perpendicular bisector of a chord passes through centre of circle)
6 $\angle OCB = 50°$ (vertically opposite angles)
$\angle CBO = 90°$ (angle between tangent and radius)
$\angle COB = 40°$ (angle sum of a triangle)
$\angle AOB = 140°$ (angles on a straight line)
$x = 20$ (isosceles triangle)
7 $a = 55°$ (isosceles triangle)
$b = 70°$ (angle sum of a triangle)
$c = 125°$ (cyclic quadrilateral)
$d = 110°$ (cyclic quadrilateral)
$e = 27.5°$ (isosceles triangle)
8 **a** $x = 78$ (alternate angles)
$y = 144$ (opposite angles of a cyclic quadrilateral)
$z = 102$ (opposite angles of a cyclic quadrilateral)
b Draw DE produced to F.
$\angle AEF = 78°$ (angles on a straight line)
$\angle AEF \neq \angle EAC$, therefore ED and AC are not parallel
c Reflex angle $EOC = 2 \times 144 = 288$ (angle at the centre is twice the angle at the circumference)
Therefore $\angle EOC = 72°$ (angles round a point)
d 51°

9 **a** 44° **b** 158°
10 **a** 90° The radius is perpendicular to the tangent at the point of contact
b $x = 75$
11 **a** 54° **b** 42° **c** 78°
12 **a** **i** 69 **ii** 57 **iii** 72 **iv** 15
b 135
13 **a** 65° **b** 25°
c 58° **d** 206°
14 Circle, centre B, radius BD
15 **a** 58° **b** 32°
c 58° **d** 24°
16 **a** **i** 107° **ii** 34°
b For example,
Let X be the point on the minor arc AC of circle II such that $AX = CX$.
Then angle $AXC = 146°$ (angles in the same segment)
Angle $AXC = 2 \times$ angle ABC
So X is the centre of circle I
(angle at the centre is twice angle at the circumference)
17 **a** **i** 23°
ii 90° $\angle ABC = 90°$ (angle in a semicircle), $AFBE$ is a straight line (given)
iii $\angle DFE = \angle CBE = 90°$ (corresponding angles in parallel lines)
b Perimeter $= PX + XY + YZ + PZ$
$\angle XYQ = \angle YQR$ (alternate angles), $\angle XQY = \angle XYQ$ (angle bisector)
so $XQ = XY$ (isosceles triangle)
$PX + XY = PQ$
The same argument for $YZ + ZP = PR$
10 72
18 **a** **i** 90° (angle in a semicircle)
ii 34° (angle sum of triangle)
iii 124° (opposite angles of a cyclic quadrilateral)
iv 28° (angles in the same segment)
b For example, $E\hat{B}D = 28°$ (alternate angles)
$A\hat{D}B = 28°$ (given that DE bisects $A\hat{D}C$)
So triangle BDX is isosceles.
c 62°
d For example, $B\hat{A}E = 90°$ (angle sum of triangle)
So BE is a diameter
AD and BE are both diameters which cross at X
So X is the centre of the circle.
Or AD is a diameter and triangle BDX is isosceles
$BX = DX$ (radii)
So X is the centre of the circle
19 **a** 9 **b** 80°
20 **a** 36° **b** 18° **c** 108° **d** 72°
21 **i** **a** 3 **b** 3
ii **a** For example, 9 sides means 7 triangles may be drawn from one vertex. Then: $7 \times 180 = 1260°$
b $y = 420 - 2x$ **c** $x = 136$
22 **a** 35° **b** **i** 55° **ii** 125°

681

Chapter 18

Essential Skills

1 a gradient = 1, y-intercept = 1
  b gradient = −1, y-intercept = −3
  c gradient = $\frac{1}{2}$, y-intercept = 0
  d gradient = 0, y-intercept = 5
  e gradient = −2, y-intercept = 1

2 y-intercept = $\frac{3}{5}$, gradient = $-\frac{2}{5}$

3

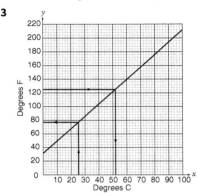

  b i 76° to 78°F   **ii** 51° to 53°C

4 a

x	−3	−2	−1	0	1	2	3	4
y	10	4	0	−2	−2	0	4	10

  b $x = -\frac{1}{2}$

Exercise 18.1

1 a 7.75 cm²   **b** 9 cm²

2 a 45 minutes   **b** $2\frac{2}{3}$ km/h
  c before visit: 9 km/h
     after visit: 7.5 km/h
  d approximately 7 27 am   **e** 1.7 km/h
  f approximately 7 12 am and 7 51 am

3 a 1050 km/h²   **b** 890 km

Exercise 18.2

1

Question	Function	x	−3	−2	−1	0	1	2	3
a	$y = x^2$	y	9	4	1	0	1	4	9
b	$y = -x^2$	y	−9	−4	−1	0	−1	−4	−9
c	$y = (x+1)^2$	y	4	1	0	1	4	9	16
d	$y = x^2 - 4$	y	5	0	−3	−4	−3	0	5
e	$y = x^2 - 2x - 8$	y	7	0	−5	−8	−9	−8	−5

a ii

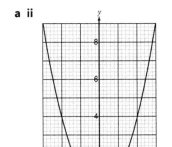

b ii

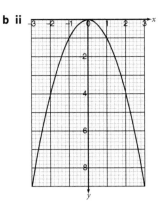

c ii

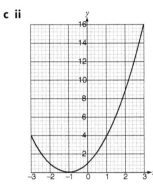

d ii

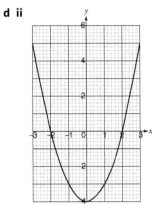

e ii

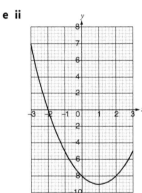

2

Question	Function	x	−3	−2	−1	0	1	2	3
a	$y = x^3$	y	−27	−8	−1	0	1	8	27
b	$y = -x^3$	y	27	8	1	0	−1	−8	−27
c	$y = (x+1)^3$	y	−8	−1	0	1	8	27	
d	$y = x^3 - 4$	y	−31	−12	−5	−4	−3	4	23

a ii

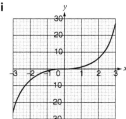

b ii

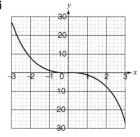

ii

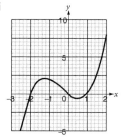

c ii

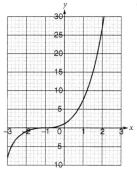

d ii

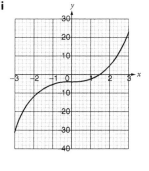

c i

x	−2.5	−2	−1.5	−1	−0.5	0	0.5	1
$y = x^2(x + 2)$	−3.1	0	1.1	1	0.4	0	0.6	3

ii

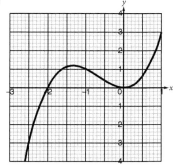

3 a i

x	−4.5	−4	−3	−2.5	−2	−1.5	−1	−0.5	0	0.5	1
$y = x^3 + 4x^2 + 1$	−9.1	1	10	10.4	9	6.6	4	1.9	1	2.1	6

ii

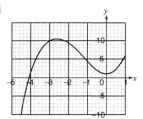

d i

x	−2.5	−2	−1.5	−1	−0.5	0	0.5	1
$y = -x^2(x + 2)$	3.1	0	−1.1	−1	−0.4	0	−0.6	−3

ii

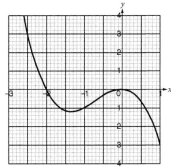

b i

x	−2.5	−2	−1.5	−1	−0.5	0	0.5	1	2
$y = x^3 + x^2 - 2x$	−4.4	0	1.9	2	1.1	0	−0.6	0	8

4

Question	Function	x	−3	−2.5	−2	−1.5	−1	−0.5	0.5	1	1.5	2	2.5	3
a	$y = \dfrac{3}{x}$	y	−1	−1.2	−1.5	−2	−3	−6	6	3	2	1.5	1.2	1
b	$y = \dfrac{9}{x^2}$	y	1	1.4	2.3	4	9	36	36	9	4	2.3	1.4	1
c	$y = x^2 + \dfrac{3}{x}$	y	8	5.1	2.5	0.3	−2	−5.8	6.3	4	4.3	5.5	7.5	10

a ii
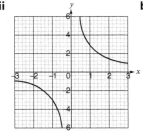

b ii
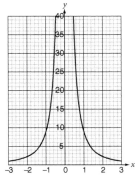

c
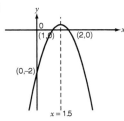

d
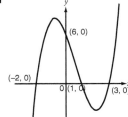

c ii
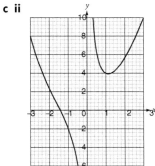

2 a iii   **b v**   **c vi**

3 a

x	0	1	2	3	3.5	4
y	0	2.5	2.2	1.9	1.7	1.6

b
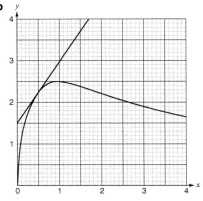

c 1.4 to 1.5

5 i

Function	x	−0.5	−0.25	0	0.25	0.5	0.75	1
y = 10ˣ	y	0.3	0.6	1	1.8	3.2	5.6	10

ii
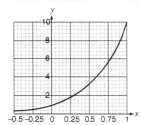

Exercise 18.4

1 a 4.12	**b** 4	**c** (0.5, 4)	**d** $-\frac{1}{4}$
2 a 1.41	**b** 1	**c** (−1.5, −1.5)	**d** −1
3 a 22.4	**b** 2	**c** (0, 0)	**d** $-\frac{1}{2}$
4 a 24.1	**b** $\frac{9}{8}$	**c** (5, 5)	**d** $-\frac{8}{9}$
5 a 10.6	**b** $-\frac{8}{7}$	**c** (0.5, −3)	**d** $\frac{7}{8}$
6 a 5.66	**b** −1	**c** (1, 1)	**d** 1
7 a 9.22	**b** $-\frac{9}{2}$	**c** (−2, 0.5)	**d** $\frac{2}{9}$
8 a 6.40	**b** $\frac{5}{4}$	**c** (3, 0.5)	**d** $-\frac{4}{5}$

Exercise 18.3

1 a
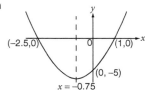

b
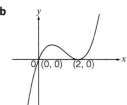

Exercise 18.5

1 a

t (seconds)	0	0.25	0.5	0.75	1	1.25	1.5	1.75	2	2.25	2.5	2.75	3
h (metres)	0	3.4	6.3	8.4	10	10.9	11.3	10.9	10	8.4	6.3	3.4	0

b

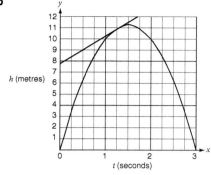

h (metres)

t (seconds)

NOTE:
This graph is reduced in size to show you the general shape. Yours should be to the scale stated in the question.

c 11.1 to 11.5 metres
d 2 to 3 m/s
e It stops momentarily before changing direction
f −16 to −14 m/s

2 a

t (seconds)	0	0.25	0.5	0.75	1	1.25	1.5
speed (m/s)	15	12.5	10	7.5	5	2.5	0

b

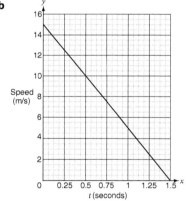

Speed (m/s)

t (seconds)

c i The graph would continue in a straight line downwards so that the speed would correspond to negative numbers on the vertical axis
ii The ball has reached its maximum height, where the speed is momentarily zero, and then is coming back down, so travelling in the opposite direction
d 10 metres
e $-\frac{15}{1.5} = -10$ m/s²

NOTE:
The acceleration is negative because the ball is slowing down as it travels upwards.

3 $\sqrt{52}$ or $2\sqrt{13}$ or 7.21 units

4 a

x	0.1	0.2	0.4	0.6	0.8	1	1.5	2	2.5	3
y	10	5.0	2.7	2.0	1.9	2	2.9	4.5	6.7	9.3

b, c

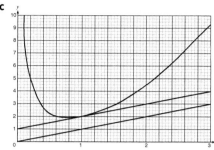

d (1, 2)
e $y = x + 1$

5

x	−3	−2	−1	0	1	2	3	4
$y = x^2 - x - 6$	6	0	−4	−6	−6	−4	0	6
$y = -x^2 - x + 6$	0	4	6	6	4	0	−6	−14

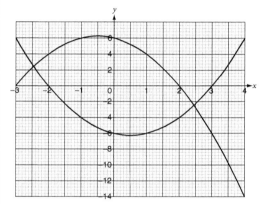

$x = -2.4$ to -2.5, $\quad y = 2.2$ to 2.4
$x = 2.4$ to 2.5, $\quad y = -2.2$ to -2.4

6 a i $\frac{3}{2}$ **ii** −4
  b $2y = 3x + 2$
  c $3y = -2x + 1$

7 a CD and GH are parallel: both have gradient $-\frac{1}{2}$
  b $\frac{1}{3} \times -3 = -1$, so AB and JK are perpendicular

8 a (−) 5 ms⁻² **b** 3400 m

9 a A (2, 0) B (0, −6)
  b AB = 6.325 **c** M (1, −3)

10 a (5, 0.5)
  b i

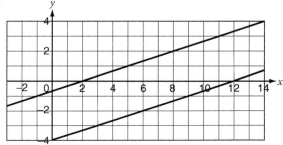

  ii $k = 12$

11 c $k = +/-1.73$

12 a $p = 2.5$

b, d, e

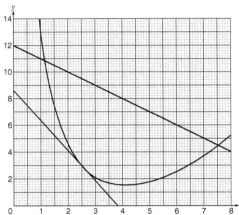

c i 1.4 to 1.5 **ii** 6.4 to 6.5

d 2.0 to 2.5

f $A = 8$ $B = -136$

13 a i $p = 12, q = 1.5, r = 1.2$

ii, iii, b

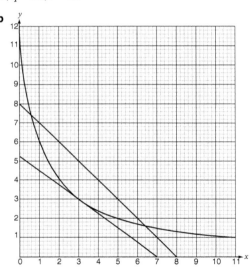

gradient: -0.6 to -1.0

c i $\dfrac{12}{x+1} = 8 - x$

$12 = (8 - x)(x + 1)$

$x^2 - 7x + 4 = 0$

ii 0.5 to 0.8, 6.2 to 6.5

14 a i $y = 5$ **ii** K: $(-1, 0)$, L: $(3, 0)$ **iii** $(1, -4)$

b i The graph would be the other way up, with a maximum point

ii The minimum point would be $(0, 0)$

c i $c = 0$ **ii** $a = 2, b = -6$

15 i 2 **ii** 1.1 to 1.3

16 a 0.6 m/s^2 **b** 1170 m

17 a, b, c i, d ii

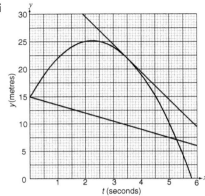

b 5.7 to 5.9

c i −6 to −4

ii speed (or velocity)

d i a 15 m **b** 9 m

iii 7 to 7.4 m

18 a i $k = 1$ **ii** $m = -1$ **iii** $n = \dfrac{3}{2}$

b i $r = 0.25$ $s = 1$ $t = 8$

c i, ii, iii

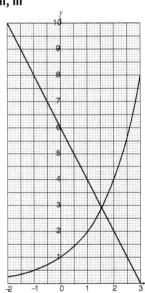

d ii 1.52 to 1.57 **iii** 1

19 a $p = 0.89$ $q = -10.1$

b, d, f i

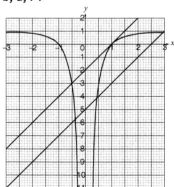

c for example, $k = 2$

e i −0.45 to −0.3, 0.4 to 0.49, 2.9 to 2.99

ii $2x^3 - 6x^2 + 1 = 0$

f ii $y = 2x - 2$

20 a, b i, c ii

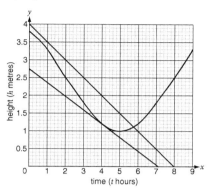

b i −0.45 to −0.32

ii This is the rate at which the water level is changing

c i 4 m   **iii** 75 to 85 cm   **iv** 5.7 to 5.9 hours

21 a (2.5, 4)   **b** 5   **c** $\frac{4}{3}$

d $3y = 4x + 2$ **e** (7, 2)

22 a figure 6   **b** figure 4   **c** figure 2

23 $y = \frac{1}{2}x + 5$

24 (4, 2)

25 a i 1.5, 3.75, −1.5

ii

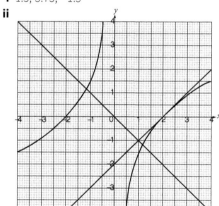

b −1.4 to −1.1 and 3.1 to 3.4

c i 0.8 to 1.2   **ii** 0.8 to 1.2

d ii −1.3 to −1.05 and 1.05 to 1.3

e for example, $y = x$ or $y = x - 1$

26 a $k = -12$ **b i** $l = -4$ **ii** $m = 3$

27 a i $-\frac{4}{3}$ **ii** $4x + 3y = 10$

b i 5 units   **ii** 10 units

c For example, $AC^2 = 5^2 + 10^2 = 125$, $AB^2 = 25$, $BC^2 = 100$
So $AC^2 = AB^2 + BC^2$, angle $ABC = 90°$ (Pythagoras)

d 25 square units

28 a 13 to 14 ms^{-1} **b** $\frac{2}{3}$ ms^{-2}

c i 500 m   **ii** 700 m

d

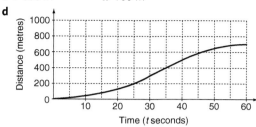

29 a (4, 4)   **b** (2.5, 2)   **c** $y = 4$

d $y = \frac{1}{2}x - \frac{1}{2}$ **e** 20 square units

30 a i (9, 6)   **ii** $\frac{3}{4}$ **iii** 10 units

b i (−12, 2)   **ii** trapezium

31 a 40 seconds   **b** 0.12 to 0.24 ms^{-2}

32 a 3.75 ms^{-2} **b** 270 m

33 a (3, −6)   **b** −4   **c** $y = -4x + 6$

34 a 1.7 to 1.71

b i

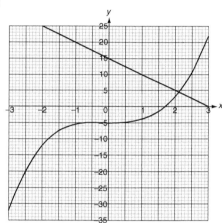

ii (2.1, 4.5)   **iii** $a = 20$, $b = -5$

35 a 3   **b** 2   **c** 1

36 a i a 0.02 ms^{-2} **b** 1200 m   **c** 5 ms^{-1}

ii 6.5 ms^{-1}

b i 195 m   **ii** 7.64 to 7.65 ms^{-1}

Chapter 19

Essential Skills

1 a 0.25 m   **b** 0.00002 m^3 or 2×10^{-5} m^3

c 150000 cm^2 **d** 1700 ml

2 a 56.5 cm   **b** 254 cm^2

3 i a 19 cm   **b** 20 cm^2

ii a 15.6 cm   **b** 13.5 cm^2

4 a 460 cm^2 **b** 600 cm^3

5 a 471 cm^2 **b** 785 cm^3

6 707 ml

Exercise 19.1

a 5.24 cm   **b** 26.2 cm²
c 19.5 cm   **d** 78.2 cm²
e 17.5 cm   **f** 43.6 cm²
g 191.0°   **h** 15 cm²
i 11.5 cm   **j** 68.8 cm²
k 15.3°   **l** 4 cm
m 15.1 cm   **n** 5.28 cm
p 35.4°   **q** 5.56 cm
r 8.29 cm   **s** 14.5 cm

Exercise 19.2

1 a 113 cm²   **b** 113 cm³
    c 84.8 cm²   **d** 56.5 cm²
    e 616 cm²   **f** 1440 cm³
    g 462 cm²   **h** 718 cm³
    i 1.26 cm   **j** 8.41 cm³
    k 15 cm²   **l** 4.21 cm³
    m 1.93 cm   **n** 46.7 cm²
    p 35.0 cm²   **q** 15 cm³
    r 2.88 cm   **s** 104 cm²
    t 100 cm³   **u** 78.1 cm²
2. a 47.1 cm²   **b** 264 cm³
    c 1.91 cm   **d** 30.6 cm³
    e 1.20 cm   **f** 48.9 cm²
3. a 339 cm²   **b** 467 cm²   **c** 75.6 cm³
4. a 3.00 cm   **b** 245 cm²

Exercise 19.3

1 a i 1:25   **ii** 1:5
    b i 0.4 cm   **ii** 424 cm²
      iii 100 cm   **iv** 10000 cm³
2 1.26 cm
3 a 2:3   **b** 4:9   **c** 45 cm²
4 a 125:343   **b** 2000 ml, or 2.00 litres
5 3.125×10^5 m²
6 95 cm³

Exercise 19.4

1 a In triangle *ABC*
    $\angle ABC = 53.1°$ (angles on a straight line)
    $\angle BAD = 36.9°$ (angle sum of a triangle)
    $\angle DAC = 45°$ (isosceles triangle)
    $\angle BAC = 36.9 + 45 = 81.9°$
    In triangle *PQR*
    $\angle PQR = 53.1°$ (angle sum of a triangle)
    $\angle SPR = 45°$ (isosceles triangle)
    $\angle QPR = 36.9 + 45 = 81.9°$

In triangles *ABC* and *PQR*
    $\angle ABC = \angle PQR = 53.1°$
    $\angle BAC = \angle QPR = 81.9°$
    $\angle ACB = \angle PRQ = 45°$
    the triangles are similar   (equiangular)
b i 5.6 cm   **ii** 27.44 cm²
2 a In triangles *ABC* and *CDE*
    $\angle ABC = \angle CDE$ (alternate angles)
    $\angle BAC = \angle DCE$ (alternate angles)
    $\angle ACB = \angle DCE$ (vertically opposite angles)
    the triangles are similar (equiangular)
b 5.71 cm   **c** 18.375 cm²
3 a In triangles *PRT* and *QRS*
    $\angle PTR = \angle SQR$ (cyclic quadrilateral and angles on a
                      straight line)
    $\angle RPT = \angle RSQ$ (cyclic quadrilateral and angles on a
                      straight line)
    $\angle R$ is common to both
    The triangles are similar   (equiangular)
b 30 cm

Exercise 19.5

1. For example,
    $X\hat{Y}Z = A\hat{B}C = 90°$ (angles in a semicircle)
    $YZ = BC$ (given)
    $AC = XZ$ (diameters)
    $AB = XY$ (by Pythagoras)
    So the triangles are congruent (SSS)
2. For example,
    $AP = AB$ (sides of square)
    $AR = AC$ (sides of square)
    $C\hat{A}P = B\hat{A}R = 90 + 50 = 140°$
    So the triangles are congruent (SAS)
3. For example,
    $A\hat{C}B = D\hat{C}E$ (vertically opposite)
    $BC = CE$ (given)
    $A\hat{B}C = C\hat{E}D$ (alternate angles)
    So the triangles are congruent (ASA)

Exercise 19.6

1 144°
2 1250 m²
3 a $AB:DF = 3:4.5 = 1:1.5$
     $BC:EF = 8:12 = 1:1.5$
     $AC:DE = 6:9 = 1:1.5$
     The triangles are similar (sides in the same ratio)
b $w = 121.9°, x = 39.5°, y = 18.6°, z = 39.5°$
c 1:2.25

4 square, side 6 cm
rectangle, length 9 cm, breadth 4 cm

5 a $\frac{1}{3}\pi x^3$ **b** $\frac{2}{3}\pi x^3$

    c The conical bowl has twice as much wood as the hemispherical bowl

6 a i 462 cm³   **ii** 216 cm²

      iii a 118 cm²   **b** 81.2 cm²

    b i 71 to 72 cm³   **ii** 15.7 to 16.4 cm

7 i $\dfrac{y}{y+2} = \dfrac{y+1}{2y-1}$

$$y(2y-1) = (y+1)(y+2)$$
$$2y^2 - y = y^2 + 3y + 2$$
$$y^2 - 4y - 2 = 0$$

    ii $y = \dfrac{4 \pm \sqrt{16+8}}{2}$

$$y = -0.45 \text{ or } y = 4.45$$

    iii 7.90 cm

8 a 64.8 m³   **b** 1230%

    c 22.1 m   **d** 150 m

9 18 cm

10 a 74.8 to 74.9 cm

    b 365 cm²

    c 14600 cm³

    d 3720 to 3730 cm²

11 i $(x^2 - 40) + (x + 2) + (2x + 4) + x = 62$

$$x^2 + 4x - 96 = 0$$

    ii $x = -12$ or 8   **iii** 8

    iv 176 square units

12 a i 60.3 cm³

      ii a 6.4 cm × 9.6 cm

         b 98.9 cm³

    b i 224.5375 cm²

      ii No, the photo might not fit in the frame. The lower bound of the frame is smaller than the lower bound of the photo.

13 radius = 18 cm   height = 42 cm

14 a 45498 km   **b** 7240 km

15 a 320 cm³   **b** 567 cm²

16 a 40 cm³   **b** 0.00004 m³

17 a 440 cm²   **b** $h = \dfrac{A - 2\pi r^2}{2\pi r}$

    c 3.99 to 4.01 cm²   **d** 9.77 to 9.78 cm

18 a i 2400 km   **ii** 520000 km²

    b i 1 : 5000000   **ii** 738 to 742 km/h

19 28.2, 28.6

20 314 cm²

21 a i For example,

      $AB = BC$ (square)

      $AP = BQ$ (given)

      So $PB = QC$

     ii For example,

$BP = QC$ (proved)

$BQ = CR$ (given)

$P\hat{B}Q = Q\hat{C}R = 90°$ (square)

so the triangles are congruent (SAS)

     iii For example,

Let $B\hat{Q}P = x°$

then $B\hat{P}Q = 90 - x = R\hat{Q}C$ (congruent triangles)

$P\hat{Q}R + x + (90 - x) = 180$ (angles on a straight line)

So $P\hat{Q}R = 90°$

    b For example,

$PQ = QR$ (corresponding sides in congruent triangles)

by extension

$PQ = QR = RS = SP$

Also $P\hat{Q}R = 90°$

22 a i $t = 69$ **ii** $u = 57$

      iii $x = 72$ **iv** $y = 15$

    b $z = 135$

    c i 12 cm   **ii** 15 cm

23 i 78.2 cm²   **ii** 46.7 cm

24 a 3 : 5   **b** 9 : 25   **c** 27 : 98

25 a 21700 cm² to 3 s.f.

    b i 254 litres   **ii** 1 minute 25 seconds

      iii 1.690 to 1.700 m

26 a i 25 litres

      ii For example, cost per litre for the three bags: 40, 35, 36 cents per litre.

So 25 litre bag is best value.

    b i 2.20 litres   **ii** 34   **iii** 272

27 a i 9.82 m

      ii a $OE = EB$.

AB and CD are perpendicular

∴ $CE = ED$, ∴ OCBD is a rhombus

$C\hat{Q}D = C\hat{B}D$

Let $C\hat{A}D = x$

$x = 60°$, $C\hat{O}D = 120°$

$E\hat{O}D = 60°$

     b 0.497 m²

     c 4880 to 4890 litres

    b 5 m

Chapter 20

Essential Skills

1 a $x = 14, y = -3$ **b** $x = 1, y = -2$

2 a $-\dfrac{7}{8}$ **b** $\dfrac{5}{2}$ **c** $\dfrac{1}{16}$

3 a $y > 7$ **b** $y > -1$ **c** $x > -10$

Exercise 20.1

1 a

	Black	White
Laptops	10	20
Desktops	4	15

$\begin{pmatrix} 10 & 20 \\ 4 & 15 \end{pmatrix}$

b

	Win	Draw	Lose
Reds	3	2	1
Blues	4	0	2
Greens	0	5	1
Yellows	0	3	3

$\begin{pmatrix} 3 & 2 & 1 \\ 4 & 0 & 2 \\ 0 & 5 & 1 \\ 0 & 3 & 3 \end{pmatrix}$

2 a $\begin{pmatrix} 3 & 10 \\ -8 & 3 \end{pmatrix}$ **b** $\begin{pmatrix} -1 & 1 \\ 1 & -7 \end{pmatrix}$

c $\begin{pmatrix} 2 & 0 \\ 6 & -16 \end{pmatrix}$ **d** $\begin{pmatrix} 2 & -5 \\ 0 & -1 \end{pmatrix}$

3 a A 2×3 **B** 2×2 **C** 2×3
     D 2×2 **E** 3×2 **F** 1×3

b $\mathbf{A}' = \begin{pmatrix} 5 & 4 \\ 1 & 5 \\ -3 & 2 \end{pmatrix}$ $\mathbf{B}' = \begin{pmatrix} 3 & 7 \\ 9 & 1 \end{pmatrix}$

   $\mathbf{C}' = \begin{pmatrix} 1 & 4 \\ 2 & 9 \\ 5 & 3 \end{pmatrix}$ $\mathbf{D}' = \begin{pmatrix} 7 & 3 \\ 0 & 1 \end{pmatrix}$

   $\mathbf{E}' = \begin{pmatrix} 5 & 4 & 9 \\ 1 & 6 & 3 \end{pmatrix}$ $\mathbf{F}' = \begin{pmatrix} -1 \\ 2 \\ 6 \end{pmatrix}$

c i $\mathbf{D}'$ 2×2 **ii** $\mathbf{E}'$ 2×3 **iii** $\mathbf{F}'$ 3×1

d i $\begin{pmatrix} 6 & 3 & 2 \\ 8 & 14 & 5 \end{pmatrix}$ **ii** $\begin{pmatrix} 4 & -9 \\ -4 & 0 \end{pmatrix}$ **iii** $(-4 \quad 8 \quad 24)$

Exercise 20.2

1 FG not   **2 GH** not   **3 HK** 2×2 **4 KH** 4×4

5 LG not   **6 GL** 3×2 **7 LF** 3×2 **8 FL** not

Exercise 20.3

1 $a = 34$ **2** $b = -8$ $c = 8$

3 a not possible   **b** $\begin{pmatrix} 5 & 3 & 5 \\ 15 & 7 & 9 \end{pmatrix}$ **c** $(12 \quad 25)$ **d** $\begin{pmatrix} 30 & 13 & 15 \\ 20 & 6 & 2 \\ -5 & 2 & 10 \end{pmatrix}$

4 $x = 2$ $y = 0$ $z = 2$

5 a $\begin{pmatrix} -3 & 9 \\ 0 & -6 \end{pmatrix}$ **b** $\begin{pmatrix} 1 & -3 \\ 0 & 2 \end{pmatrix}$ **c** $\begin{pmatrix} 1 & -9 \\ 0 & 4 \end{pmatrix}$

d $\begin{pmatrix} -2 & 0 \\ 0 & -2 \end{pmatrix}$ **e** $\begin{pmatrix} -2 & 3 \\ 3 & -4 \end{pmatrix}$

Exercise 20.4

1 det $\mathbf{P} = 5$ **2** det $\mathbf{Q} = 2$ **3** det $\mathbf{R} = 18$ **4** det $\mathbf{S} = -19$

Exercise 20.5

1 $\mathbf{A}^{-1} = -\frac{1}{2}\begin{pmatrix} 10 & -8 \\ -9 & 7 \end{pmatrix}$ **2** $\mathbf{B}^{-1} = -\frac{1}{3}\begin{pmatrix} -2 & -1 \\ 1 & 2 \end{pmatrix}$

3 $\mathbf{C}^{-1} = \frac{1}{8}\begin{pmatrix} 10 & 6 \\ -3 & -1 \end{pmatrix}$ **4** $\mathbf{D}^{-1} = -\begin{pmatrix} 0 & -1 \\ -1 & 0 \end{pmatrix} = \mathbf{D}$

5 $\mathbf{I}^{-1} = \begin{pmatrix} 1 & 0 \\ 0 & 1 \end{pmatrix} = \mathbf{I}$

Exercise 20.6

1 $\mathbf{E}: 2\times 2$ $\mathbf{F}: 2\times 3$ $\mathbf{G}: 2\times 2$
    $\mathbf{H}: 2\times 1$ $\mathbf{J}: 1\times 2$ $\mathbf{K}: 3\times 2$

2 a 2×2 **b** 3×3 **c** 2×2
   d 1×1 **e** 3×1

3 $\mathbf{F}' = \begin{pmatrix} 7 & 3 \\ 1 & 5 \\ 6 & 2 \end{pmatrix}$ $\mathbf{F}': 3\times 2$

4 a $\begin{pmatrix} 7 & 1 & 6 \\ 10 & 6 & 4 \end{pmatrix}$ **b** $\begin{pmatrix} 6 & 10 & 4 \\ 14 & 2 & 12 \end{pmatrix}$

   c $\begin{pmatrix} 4 & 6 \\ 8 & 12 \end{pmatrix}$ **d** (16)

5 $\begin{pmatrix} 1 & 0 \\ 0 & 1 \end{pmatrix}$

6 a $\frac{1}{2}\begin{pmatrix} 2 & 0 \\ 0 & 1 \end{pmatrix}$ **b** $-\frac{1}{4}\begin{pmatrix} 0 & -2 \\ -2 & 0 \end{pmatrix}$

   c $\begin{pmatrix} 1 & 0 \\ 0 & 1 \end{pmatrix}$ **d** $\begin{pmatrix} 1 & 0 \\ 0 & 2 \end{pmatrix}$ **e** $\begin{pmatrix} 0 & 2 \\ 2 & 0 \end{pmatrix}$

7 a $\begin{pmatrix} a \\ b \end{pmatrix} = \begin{pmatrix} 5 \\ -7 \end{pmatrix}$ **b** $a = 5$, $b = -7$

8 a $\begin{pmatrix} p & q \\ r & s \end{pmatrix} = \begin{pmatrix} -3 & 4 \\ -2 & 4 \end{pmatrix}$ **b** $p = -3$, $q = 4$, $r = -2$, $s = 4$

9 a $\begin{pmatrix} 17 \\ 10 \\ 18 \end{pmatrix}$ **b** $\begin{pmatrix} x \\ 10x \\ 5x \end{pmatrix}$

10 a $a = 1.5$, $b = 1$, $c = -2.5$, $d = 2$
   b $x = 4, b = 6$ **c** $y = \frac{1}{3}$
   d $p = \frac{1}{4}$, $q = 3$, $r = 7$

11 a

	Reliables	Gofasters
Retail Value	$5000	$6000

	Blue	Red	Black
Reliables	10	5	2
Gofasters	5	16	3

b $R = (5000 \quad 6000)$ $N = \begin{pmatrix} 10 & 5 & 2 \\ 5 & 16 & 3 \end{pmatrix}$

c $RN = (8000 \quad 121000 \quad 28000)$ **d** 229000

e The total value of the cars sold by the salesperson

12 **A** is 2×3 **B** is 1×4

They are not conformable for multiplication either as **AB** or **BA**

13 The determinant is zero. The inverse does not exist

Exercise 20.7

1 a $\frac{1}{3}$ **b** $-\frac{1}{3}$ **c** $\frac{2}{7}$ **d** 0

2 $x = -5$ or $x = -1$

3 a $\frac{1}{5}$ **b** 0.25 **c** $\frac{11}{13}$

4 $x = -3$

5 a 0 **b** 0 **c** 0.5

  d -1 or 3 **e** -2 or 2 **f** -1

Exercise 20.8

1 $f^{-1}(x) = \frac{x-1}{3}$ **2** $f^{-1}(x) = \frac{2-x}{5}$

3 $f^{-1}(x) = 2(x-1)$ **4** $f^{-1}(x) = \frac{4}{3}x - 2$

5 $f^{-1}(x) = 5 - 2x$ **6** $g^{-1}(x) = x^2 + 3$

7 $g^{-1}(x) = (x+1)^{\frac{1}{3}}$ **8** $g^{-1}(x) = \frac{1-x}{x}$

9 $f^{-1}(x) = \frac{x}{1-x}$ **10** $f^{-1}(x) = \frac{x}{3} + \frac{1}{2}$

Exercise 20.9

1 a -1 **b** -2 **c** $-\frac{1}{2}$ or -1

2 a 2 **b** $\frac{1}{2}$ **c** $\frac{2}{3}$ **d** $\frac{1}{y} - 1$ or $\frac{1-y}{y}$

  e $x = -2$ or 2

3 a $\frac{5}{7}$ **b** $\frac{13}{18}$ **c** $h^{-1}(x) = \frac{3x-2}{1-x}$

  d $x = -2$ **e** $-\frac{8}{3}$ **f** -2 **g** $-\frac{8}{3}$

Exercise 20.10

1 a $x + y \leq 5, y > x + 3, x \geq 0$

  b $x + y \leq 5, x \geq 3, y \geq 0$

  c $y \geq 0, x \geq 0, x + y \leq 5, y < x + 3, x \leq 3$

  d $y \leq 0, x \geq 3, x + y \leq 5$

  e $x \geq 3, x + y \geq 5, y < x + 3$

  f $x + y \geq 5, y > x + 3$

  g $x + y \leq 5, y > x + 3, x \leq 0$

2 a

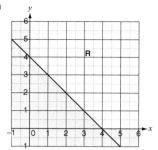

b

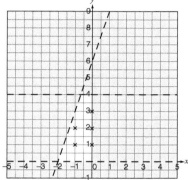

3 a, b

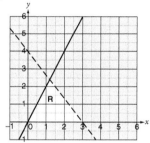

c $(-1, 2), (-1, 1), (0, 1), (0, 2), (0, 3)$

4 a $\begin{pmatrix} 9000 & 7200 \\ 10500 & 5400 \\ 12000 & 3600 \\ 13500 & 1800 \end{pmatrix}$

b The profit from each possible combination of cars

c 6 Reliables and 4 Gofasters. Total profit: $16200

Exercise 20.11

1 a **A**: 2×2 **B**: 2×2 **C**: 2×3 **D**: 1×2

  E: 3×2 **F**: 2×1

  b **i** 2×2 **ii** 3×3

  iii 1×1 **iv** 2×2

c $\mathbf{C'} = \begin{pmatrix} 1 & 2 \\ 3 & 0 \\ -5 & 4 \end{pmatrix}$

d i det $\mathbf{A} = 1$ **ii** $\begin{pmatrix} 2 & 1 \\ 3 & -1 \end{pmatrix}$

iii $\begin{pmatrix} 2 & 1 \\ 3 & -1 \end{pmatrix}$ **iv** $\begin{pmatrix} 1 & 0 \\ 0 & 1 \end{pmatrix}$

v $\mathbf{B}^{-1} = -\frac{1}{5}\begin{pmatrix} -1 & -1 \\ -3 & 2 \end{pmatrix}$

2 a i 1 **ii** 1 **iii** $x = 4$
   iv $g^{-1}(x) = \frac{1}{x}$ **v** 4
   b i $x = -\frac{1}{2}$ or $\frac{1}{2}$ **ii** $x = 0$ **iii** $x = -1$ or 2

3 a $f^{-1}(x) = \frac{1 - 3x}{2x}$
   b $g^{-1}(x) = \frac{3x}{1 - 2x}$

4 a

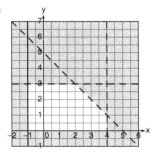

b $(-1, 0)$, $(-1, 1)$, $(-1, 2)$, $(0, 0)$, $(0, 1)$, $(0, 2)$, $(1, 0)$, $(1, 1)$, $(1, 2)$, $(2, 0)$, $(2, 1)$, $(2, 2)$, $(3, 0)$, $(3, 1)$

5 a $4\frac{1}{2}$ **b** $\frac{1}{2}\begin{pmatrix} 2 & 1 \\ 4 & 3 \end{pmatrix}$

6 a $\begin{pmatrix} 10 & 17 & 4 \\ -6 & -9 & 0 \end{pmatrix}$ **b** $\frac{1}{2}\begin{pmatrix} -2 & -4 \\ 3 & 5 \end{pmatrix}$ **c** $\begin{pmatrix} 0.4 & 0.1 \\ 0.2 & 0.3 \end{pmatrix}$

7 a $m = -1$ $c = 8$
   b

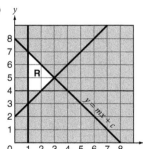

8 a $k = \frac{h}{9}$ **b** $\begin{pmatrix} 8 & 4 \\ -6 & 0 \end{pmatrix}$

9 a 13 **b** -4

10 a $y \geq \frac{1}{2}x$ **b** $x = -4$ or -3

11 a $(-1, 3)$ **b** $y < 3$, $y > \frac{1}{2}x$

12 a $\frac{2}{3}$ **b** $g^{-1}(x) = \frac{3x + 4}{5}$

13 a $\begin{pmatrix} 330 \\ 417 \end{pmatrix}$
   b P shows John's total earnings in Week 1 and Week 2.

14 $f^{-1}(x) = \frac{3}{5x - 2}$

15 a BA **b** $\begin{pmatrix} 38 & 0 \\ 0 & 38 \end{pmatrix}$ **c** $\frac{1}{38}\begin{pmatrix} 4 & 6 \\ 5 & -2 \end{pmatrix}$

16 a $\begin{pmatrix} 0 & 1 \\ -1 & 2 \\ 0 & -3 \end{pmatrix}$ **b** $(1\ -1)$

17 a $\begin{pmatrix} 2 & 0 \\ 0 & 2 \end{pmatrix}$ **b** $\frac{1}{2}\begin{pmatrix} 4 & 2 \\ 1 & 1 \end{pmatrix}$

18 $\begin{pmatrix} -11 \\ -11 \\ -14 \end{pmatrix}$ **19 a** $\begin{pmatrix} 0 & 0 \\ 0 & 0 \end{pmatrix}$ **b** I

20 a $|\mathbf{A}| = x^2 - 16$ **b** $x = -5$ or 5

21 a -14 **b** $g^{-1}(x) = \frac{x + 1}{2}$
22 $a = 3$, $b = 4$

23 $\frac{1}{2}\begin{pmatrix} 5 & -3 \\ 4 & -2 \end{pmatrix}$ **24 a** $\begin{pmatrix} 2x + 12 & 3x + 6 \\ 14 & 15 \end{pmatrix}$ **b** $x = 5$

25 $\begin{pmatrix} 13 & 21 \\ 21 & 34 \end{pmatrix}$ **26 a** $k = 2$ **b** $c = 3$, $d = -5$

27 $y \geq 3$ $x + y \leq 5$
28 a 14 **b i** $k = 5$ **ii** $x = -5$ or $11\frac{1}{2}$

29 a -17 **b** $t = 5$ **c** $\frac{1}{3}x + 7$ **d** 3
30 a 75 **b** 8

31 a $\begin{pmatrix} -4 & 2 \\ -6 & 0 \end{pmatrix}$ **b** $-\frac{1}{2}\begin{pmatrix} 2 & 3 \\ 4 & 5 \end{pmatrix}$

32 a i $4p + 7$ **ii** 3 **b** $a(a - 2)$

33 a $y > 1$ and $y < 2x$ **b** 3

34 a 2.5 **b** $\frac{3}{2x - 4}$

35 a $\begin{pmatrix} 7 & -6 \\ 7 & -3 \end{pmatrix}$ **b** $\begin{pmatrix} 0 & 1 \\ -\frac{1}{3} & \frac{4}{3} \end{pmatrix}$

36 a -5 **b** $p = \frac{7}{3}$

37 a $(2, 5.5)$ **b** $y > -2$ $x + 4y < 24$

38 i (215) **ii** Total distance travelled
   iii 43 km/h

Chapter 21

Essential Skills

1 a $a = 53.1°$
  b $b = 16.6$ cm, $c = 25.0°$
  c $d = 9.96$ cm, $e = 8.36$ cm
  d $k = 11.8$ cm, $l = 10.7$ cm
  e $m = 6.93$ cm, $n = 9.17$ cm
2 245°
3 020°
4 a 135°　　　　**b** 337.5°

Exercise 21.1

1 a 0.643　　**b** 0.643　　**c** 0.5
  d 0.966　　**e** 0.766　　**f** −0.766
  g −0.866　**h** 0.259
2 a 74.3°　　**b** 53.8°
  c 105.7°　　**d** 126.2°
3 a 163.7°　　**b** 123.9°
  c 145.2°　　**d** 129.6°
4 a 34.3°, 145.6°　**b** 7.2°, 172.8°
  c 57.5°, 122.5°　**d** 32.2°, 147.8°

Exercise 21.2

1 $a = 36.3$ cm　　**2** $b = 23.8°$
3 $c = 14.4$ cm　　**4** $d = 20.4°$
5 $e = 60.4°$　　　**6** $f = 12.5$ cm
7 $g = 18.8$ cm　　**8** $j = 65.8°$ or $114.2°$

Exercise 21.3

1 $a = 95.7°$　　　**2** $b = 14.9$ cm
3 $c = 8.55$ cm　　**4** $d = 28.1°$
5 $e = 52.4°$　　　**6** $f = 142.6°$
7 $g = 7.57$ cm　　**8** $h = 13.7$ cm
9 $i = 111.8°$　　　**10** $j = 46.2$ cm

Exercise 21.4

1 a $c = 3.42$ cm　　**b** $b = 12.7$ cm
  c $d = 5.12$ cm　　**d** $e = 9.86$ cm
  e $f = 137.0°$　　　**f** $a = 56.9°$
  g $g = 8.09$ cm, $h = 31.4°$
2 a $a = 128°$　　　**b** $b = 30.8$ km
  c $c = 32.5°$　　　**d** 273° or 272.5°

Exercise 21.5

1 a 26.6 cm²　　**b** 45.1 cm²　　**c** 1000 km²
  d 32.4 m²　　**e** 43.3 cm²
2 a i 50.6°　　**ii** 99.4°　　**iii** 23.1 cm²
  b i 129.4°　　**ii** 20.6°　　**iii** 8.22 cm²

Exercise 21.6

1 a 7.07 cm　　**b** 6.96 cm
  c 59.5°　　　**d** 67.4°
2 13.9 cm
3 a 4.79 cm　　**b** 15.7 cm
  c 16.6 cm　　**d** 24.9°

Exercise 21.7

1 a 22.1 cm　　**b** 43.6 cm
  c 553 cm²　　**d** 128.4°
2 a 100°　　**b** 15.3 cm　　**c** 66.3 cm²
3 a 7.37 cm　　**b** 14.0 cm
  c 136.8°　　**d** 17.7 cm²
4 a 6.46 cm　　**b** 3.77 cm
  c 79.2°　　　**d** 27.8 cm²
5 a $(b + c)^2$　　**b** a^2
  c $\frac{1}{2}bc$　　**d** $\frac{(b+c)^2 - a^2}{4}$
  e $(b + c)^2 - a^2 = 2bc$
    $b^2 + 2bc + c^2 - a^2 = 2bc$
    $b^2 + c^2 = a^2$
  f Pythagoras' Theorem
6 a 43.1 cm
  b $\frac{1}{2} \times 61 \times 30 \times \sin 41 = 600$
  c The two triangles have the same height, and bases in the ratio
    $45 : 30 = 3 : 2$.

> **NOTE:**
> Drop a perpendicular from B to the line CA. This is the height of both triangles.

  d 900 m²　　**e** 41.7 to 41.9 m　　**f** 21.0 to 21.1°
8 a $\frac{1}{2} \times 40.3 \times 26.8 \times \sin 92 = 540 \text{cm}^2$
  b $\frac{AB}{\sin 92} = \frac{40.3}{\sin 55}$
    $AB = \frac{40.3 \times \sin 92}{\sin 55} = 49.2 \text{cm}$
  c 55° (angles in the same segment)
  d 33°
  e similar
  f $\frac{XD}{40.3} = \frac{20.1}{26.8}$
    $XD = 30.2$ cm
9 a 0.176　　**b** 1.76×10^{-1}
10 1
11 a 0　　　**b** −1.5
  c It is below the height at midday
12 i $(2y - 1)^2 = y^2 + (y + 2)^2$
    $4y^2 - 4y + 1 = y^2 + y^2 - 4y + 4$
    $2y^2 - 8y - 3 = 0$
  ii −0.35 or 4.35　　**iii** 13.8

13 **a** 59.2 m **b** 2360 m² **c** 129 m² **d** 31.9°
14 7.94
15 60, 120
16 **a** **i** $\frac{1}{2}x(x+4)=48$
    ii −12 or 8   **iii** 12 cm
  b $\frac{4}{5}$ or 0.8
  c **i** $(x+4)^2+x^2=9^2$
      $x^2+8x+16+x^2=81$

    ii $x=\dfrac{-8\pm\sqrt{64+4\times2\times65}}{4}$
      $x=-8.04$ or 4.04
    iii 21.1 cm

17 **a** $\frac{1}{2}\times10\times14\times\sin P=48$
    $\sin P=\frac{48}{70}$, $P=43.29=43.3°$ to 1 dp
  b 9.60 cm
18 **a** $(7x)^2+(24x)^2=150^2$
    $625x^2=22500$, $x^2=36$
  b 336 cm
19 **a** 24.7 m   **b** 11.5 m
20 **a** 393 to 393.5 km   **b** 1210 km
  c 820900 to 822000 km²
  d **i** 073°   **ii** 289°
  e 1 : 20 000 000
21 $l=40$
22 **a** Hint: use the Cosine Rule
  b 24.2 cm²
  c **i**   **ii** $14r$ **iii** $r=1.73$
  d 61.1%
23 **a** 4.59 m   **b** 9.77 m   **c** 8.96 m
24 **a** 81.5 m   **b** 1810 m²   **c** 44.5 m
  d 19.3 m   **e** 23.4°
25 **a** **i** 28.1°   **ii** 718 m   **iii** 696 m
  b 35.7°
26 **a** **i** 292°   **ii** 80.9 m   **iii** 45.70 to 45.80°
    iv 157.70 to 158°
  b 28.1°
27 **a** 101.7°   **b** 70.4°   **c** 1850 m²
28 **a** Hint: use Pythagoras
  b **i** 25°   **ii** 18.00 to 18.10 m
  c **i** 13.70 to 13.80   **ii** 50.75 to 50.85
29 **a** **i** 33.5 cm   **ii** 47.9°   **iii** 178 cm²
  b 60 km
30 **a** **i** 222°   **ii** 107°
  b **i** 6.22 km   **ii** 5.71 km²
  c **i** 2.54 km   **ii** 0650

Chapter 22

NOTE:
Diagrams have been drawn for some of the answers in this chapter. For others, enough information has been given for you to check your own diagrams.

1 **a** Reflection in the line $x=3$
  b Rotation 180° about the point (2, 3)
  c Translation $\begin{pmatrix}-2\\-3\end{pmatrix}$
  d Enlargement, centre the origin, scale factor 2
2 **a** $\begin{pmatrix}-1\\5\end{pmatrix}$ **b** $\begin{pmatrix}1\\0\end{pmatrix}$
3 **a** $x=-6, y=-3$
  b $x=3, y=2$
4 b and c and e
5 They are parallel, but pointing in opposite directions, and v is 3 times longer than w.

Exercise 22.1

1 **a** $\sqrt{90}=3\sqrt{10}$ **b** $\sqrt{50}=5\sqrt{2}$
  c $\sqrt{52}=2\sqrt{13}$ **d** $\sqrt{29}$
2 **a** **i** $\begin{pmatrix}8\\2\end{pmatrix}$ **ii** $\begin{pmatrix}20\\-17\end{pmatrix}$ **iii** $\begin{pmatrix}6\\0\end{pmatrix}$
  b **i** $\sqrt{149}$ **ii** $\sqrt{41}$
    iii $\sqrt{104}=2\sqrt{26}$
3 **a** $\overrightarrow{AC}=v+u$ **b** $\overrightarrow{BD}=-u+v$ or $v-u$
4 **a** Because PQRS is not a parallelogram
    (or $\overrightarrow{QR}\neq b$)
  b $\overrightarrow{QS}=-a+b$ or $b-a$ **c** $\overrightarrow{PM}=\frac{1}{2}(a+b)$

5 **b** **i** $\overrightarrow{BA}=-p$
    ii $\overrightarrow{BD}=q+r$
    iii $\overrightarrow{AD}=p+q+r$ or $2q$
    iv $\overrightarrow{FM}=p$
    v $\overrightarrow{ME}+\overrightarrow{CB}=\overrightarrow{CD}+\overrightarrow{CB}=r-q$
    vi $\overrightarrow{CF}-\overrightarrow{AB}=\overrightarrow{CF}+\overrightarrow{BA}=2p-p=p$
    vii $\overrightarrow{ED}+\overrightarrow{MA}+\overrightarrow{FM}=p-q+p=2p-q$

Exercise 22.2

1 **a** $-a+b$ or $b-a$ **b** $-2a+b+c$
  c $a+b-2c$ **d** $-a+2b-c$
2 **a** $-a+b$ or $b-a$ **b** $\frac{1}{2}(b-a)$
  c $\frac{1}{2}(a+b)$
3

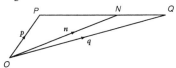

NOTE:
Your diagram may not look like this because it depends on where you put O.

a $q - p$ **b** $\frac{2}{3}(q - p)$

c $\frac{1}{3}(p + 2q)$ **d** $\frac{1}{3}(q - p)$

4

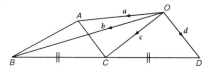

NOTE:

As in question 3, the diagram depends on where you put O.

a $-b + a$ **b** $2(-b + c)$
c $-b + c$ **d** $a + b - 2c$

5 a $\begin{pmatrix} 7 \\ -1 \end{pmatrix}$

b $|\overrightarrow{AB}| = 3\sqrt{2}$, $|\overrightarrow{BC}| = 4\sqrt{2}$, $|\overrightarrow{AC}| = 5\sqrt{2}$

c $|\overrightarrow{AB}|^2 = 18$, $|\overrightarrow{BC}|^2 = 32$, $|\overrightarrow{AC}|^2 = 50$

so $|\overrightarrow{AC}|^2 = |\overrightarrow{BC}|^2 + |\overrightarrow{AB}|^2$, $\angle ABC = 90°$,

(by Pythagoras)

6 a i $\begin{pmatrix} 4 \\ 0 \end{pmatrix}$ **ii** $\begin{pmatrix} -1 \\ -9 \end{pmatrix}$ **iii** $\begin{pmatrix} 3 \\ -9 \end{pmatrix}$

iv $\begin{pmatrix} -7 \\ -9 \end{pmatrix}$ **v** $\begin{pmatrix} 0 \\ 0 \end{pmatrix}$

b i $3\sqrt{10}$ **ii** $\sqrt{82}$ **iii** 4

Exercise 22.3

1 a $(2, -1)$ **b** $(-6, -1)$
  c $(11, 6)$ **d** $(8, 0)$

2 a $\begin{pmatrix} -1 \\ -20 \end{pmatrix}$ **b** $\begin{pmatrix} -9 \\ -7 \end{pmatrix}$ **c** $\begin{pmatrix} -2 \\ 8 \end{pmatrix}$

Exercise 22.4

1 a, b, c, d, e

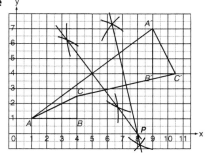

f P is the centre of the rotation which maps triangle ABC on to triangle $A'B'C'$. AA' and CC' are chords of two circles which have the same centre. The perpendicular bisectors of the chords pass through the centre of the circles, so where the bisectors meet is the centre of rotation.

g rotation, 90° clockwise, centre $(8, 0)$.

2 a

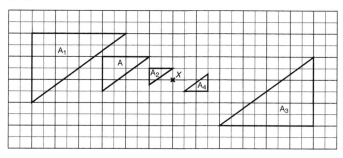

b Enlargement, scale factor $-\frac{1}{4}$

3 a i $f^{-1}(x) = \frac{2x}{6 - x}$

ii, iii, iv

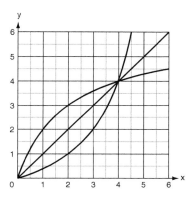

v reflection in the line $y = x$

b i $f^{-1}(x) = \frac{3}{2}(x - 1)$

ii, iii, iv

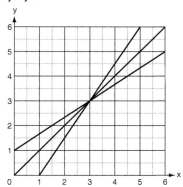

v reflection in the line $y = x$

4 a The sides of triangles A and A' produced should meet on the line $x = 1.5$.

Stretch, factor 3, invariant line $x = 1.5$

b The diagonals of rectangles B and B' produced meet on the y-axis.

Stretch, factor 2, invariant line y-axis

Exercise 22.5

1 a $\begin{pmatrix} 0 & -1 \\ -1 & 0 \end{pmatrix}$ **b** $\begin{pmatrix} 1 & 0 \\ 2 & 1 \end{pmatrix}$

2 a $\begin{pmatrix} 2 & 0 \\ 0 & 2 \end{pmatrix}$ **b** enlargement, centre (0, 0), scale factor 2

3 a $\begin{pmatrix} 0 & -1 \\ -1 & 0 \end{pmatrix}$ **b** reflection in the line $y = -x$

c $\begin{pmatrix} 0 & -1 \\ -1 & 0 \end{pmatrix}\begin{pmatrix} -1 & 0 \\ 6 & -4 \end{pmatrix} = \begin{pmatrix} -6 & 4 \\ 1 & 0 \end{pmatrix}$

4 a $\begin{pmatrix} 2 \\ -2 \end{pmatrix}$ **b** $\begin{pmatrix} -2 \\ 0 \end{pmatrix}$ **c** $\begin{pmatrix} 3 \\ -3 \end{pmatrix}$

5 $A' = (1, -3), B' = (-5, 7), C' = (0, 1)$

Exercise 22.6

1 i reflection in the line $y = x$
Enlargement, centre (0, 0), scale factor 2.5

ii $\begin{pmatrix} 0 & 0 \\ 1 & 0 \end{pmatrix}, \begin{pmatrix} 2.5 & 0 \\ 0 & 2.5 \end{pmatrix}, \begin{pmatrix} 0 & 2.5 \\ 2.5 & 0 \end{pmatrix}$

iii No. $\begin{pmatrix} 0 & 1 \\ 1 & 0 \end{pmatrix}\begin{pmatrix} 2.5 & 0 \\ 0 & 2.5 \end{pmatrix} = \begin{pmatrix} 2.5 & 0 \\ 0 & 2.5 \end{pmatrix}\begin{pmatrix} 0 & 1 \\ 1 & 0 \end{pmatrix}$
$= \begin{pmatrix} 0 & 2.5 \\ 2.5 & 0 \end{pmatrix}$

2 a $\begin{pmatrix} 2 & 1 \\ 2 & 3 \end{pmatrix}$

b vertices at (0, 0), (2, 2), (1, 3), (3, 5)

c $-\frac{1}{4}\begin{pmatrix} 3 & 1 \\ -2 & -2 \end{pmatrix}$

3 b $A_2(-2, -1), B_2(-4, -1), C_2(-2, -2)$

c reflection in $y = x$

4 a $I = \begin{pmatrix} 1 & 0 \\ 0 & 1 \end{pmatrix}$ **b** $R_1 = \begin{pmatrix} 0 & 1 \\ -1 & 0 \end{pmatrix}$

c $R_2 = \begin{pmatrix} -1 & 0 \\ 0 & -1 \end{pmatrix}$ **d** $M_1 = \begin{pmatrix} 1 & 0 \\ 0 & -1 \end{pmatrix}$

e $M_2 = \begin{pmatrix} -1 & 0 \\ 0 & 1 \end{pmatrix}$ **f** $M_3 = \begin{pmatrix} 0 & 1 \\ 1 & 0 \end{pmatrix}$

g $M_4 = \begin{pmatrix} 0 & -1 \\ -1 & 0 \end{pmatrix}$

5 $R_1^{-1} = \begin{pmatrix} 0 & -1 \\ 1 & 0 \end{pmatrix}$ Rotation 90 anticlockwise about (0, 0)

6

Second transformation

		R_1	R_2	M_1	M_2	M_3	M_4
First transformation	R_1	R_2	R_1^{-1}	M_3	M_4	M_2	M_1
	R_2	R_1^{-1}	I	M_2	M_1	M_4	M_3
	M_1	M_4	M_2	I	R_2	R_1^{-1}	R_1
	M_2	M_3	M_1	R_2	I	R_1	R_1^{-1}
	M_3	M_1	M_4	R_1	R_1^{-1}	I	R_2
	M_4	M_2	M_3	R_1^{-1}	R_1	R_2	I

Exercise 22.7

1 $x = 0, y = 8$

2 a $A'(10.5, 3), B'(3, 7.5)$
b similar
c 40 square units

3 a, b

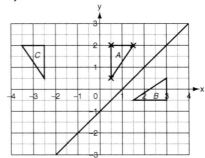

c Rotation, 90° anticlockwise, centre $(-1, -2)$

4 a $\begin{pmatrix} 0 & 5 & 7 & 2 \\ 0 & 1 & 5 & 4 \end{pmatrix}$
b ii rhombus
c 18 square units
d i det **M** = 18 **ii** They are the same

5 a i translation $\begin{pmatrix} 3 \\ 0 \end{pmatrix}$

ii rotation, 90° anticlockwise, centre (0, 1)
iii $\begin{pmatrix} -1 & 0 \\ 0 & 1 \end{pmatrix}$

b i -2 **ii** (3, 1)

c i 2 **ii** $\frac{1}{2}\begin{pmatrix} 4 & -3 \\ 2 & -1 \end{pmatrix}$

iii $\begin{pmatrix} -1 & 3 \\ -2 & 4 \end{pmatrix}\begin{pmatrix} x \\ y \end{pmatrix} = \begin{pmatrix} 4 \\ -2 \end{pmatrix}$, $x = 11, y = -2$

$X = \begin{pmatrix} 11 \\ 5 \end{pmatrix}$

6 a i a $\frac{1}{2}p + \frac{1}{2}r$ **b** $r + p - q$ **C** $\frac{1}{2}p + \frac{1}{2}r$
   ii they are equal and parallel

7 $\frac{1}{2}a - \frac{1}{2}c$

8 a i $b - a$ **ii** $\frac{1}{2}(b + c)$ **iii** $\frac{1}{4}b + \frac{1}{2}c$

 b i $\frac{2}{5}b - \frac{2}{5}a$ **ii** $2:3$ **iii** $\frac{3}{5}a - \frac{7}{20}b - c$

 e reflection in the y-axis

 f i $A_3 = (2, -1)$, $B_3 = (3, 0)$, $C_3 = (5, -4)$
   ii shear, y-axis invariant, factor 1

 iii $\begin{pmatrix} 1 & 0 \\ 1 & 1 \end{pmatrix}$

9 a i $(5, 3)$ **ii** $(3, 5)$

 b $\begin{pmatrix} 0 & 1 \\ 1 & 0 \end{pmatrix}$

 c $\mathbf{M}(Q) = (k - 3, k - 2)$
   $\mathbf{TM}(Q) = (k - 3 + 3, k - 2 + 2) = (k, k)$
   this point lies on the line $y = x$

 d $\begin{pmatrix} 0 & 1 \\ 1 & 0 \end{pmatrix}$

 e i $\begin{pmatrix} 0 & 1 \\ -1 & 0 \end{pmatrix}$ **ii** rotation, centre $(0, 0)$,
                  90° clockwise

10 a i $-p + q$ **ii** $\frac{2}{3}(-p + q)$

  iii $-\frac{2}{3}p - \frac{1}{3}q$ **iv** $\frac{1}{3}p + \frac{2}{3}q$

 b i $(4, -2)$ **ii** $\begin{pmatrix} -3 \\ 4 \end{pmatrix}$

 c i rotation, 90° clockwise about $(0, 0)$
  ii $(3, -5)$

 d $\begin{pmatrix} 0 & 1 \\ 1 & 0 \end{pmatrix}$

11 a i a **ii** $-a + b$ **iii** $a + b$
 b triangle OAB is equilateral, so the lengths of OA, OB and AB
   are equal
 c i a b **b** $3b$
  ii Y, A and X lie on a straight line
 d $3a$
 e $\overrightarrow{XZ} = -3a$, $\overrightarrow{YX} = 3b$, $\overrightarrow{YZ} = 3(b - a)$,

   since $|a| = |b| = |b - a|$, then $|\overrightarrow{XZ}| = |\overrightarrow{YX}| = |\overrightarrow{YZ}|$

   The triangle is equilateral

 f $\frac{1}{9}$

12 a $(0, -1)$ **b** reflection in $y = -x$
 c $(2, 1)$, $(2, -1)$, $(3, -3)$

13   **i** $\sqrt{10}$ or 3.16   **ii** $\begin{pmatrix} 3 \\ -3 \end{pmatrix}$

  iii $a = 2$ $b = 3$
  iv shear, x-axis invariant, factor 0.5

14 a i $\begin{pmatrix} 5 \\ 2 \end{pmatrix}$

  ii $\sqrt{45}$ or 6.7

  iii a enlargement scale factor 3 centre B   **b** $\begin{pmatrix} 7.5 \\ 3 \end{pmatrix}$

15 a i $p + r$ **ii** $-p + r$

  iii $-p + \frac{2}{3}r$ **iv** $p + \frac{1}{2}r$

 b i $-\frac{3}{2}p + r$ **ii** $-\frac{3}{2}p$

 c Q, R and S lie on a straight line

16 a $2\sqrt{25^2 + 7^2} = 48$
 b i 147°   **ii** 33°
 c i $p + q$ **ii** $-p + q$
 d $p + 3q$ **e** $0.5p + 2.5q$
 f i $\begin{pmatrix} 0 \\ 24 \end{pmatrix}$ **ii** $\begin{pmatrix} 7 \\ -24 \end{pmatrix}$
 g 50

17

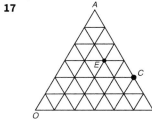

 b $\frac{1}{2}a + \frac{1}{3}b$ **c** $-\frac{1}{2}a + \frac{2}{3}b$

18 a i 6.08   **ii** $\begin{pmatrix} 2 \\ -1.5 \end{pmatrix}$ **iii** $\begin{pmatrix} 2 \\ -1.5 \end{pmatrix}$
  iii reflection in $y = -x$
  iv equal and parallel G is the mid-point of CD
  v

$$\overrightarrow{GD} = -\begin{pmatrix} 2 \\ -1.5 \end{pmatrix} - \begin{pmatrix} 1.5 \\ 0 \end{pmatrix} - \begin{pmatrix} 1 \\ 2 \end{pmatrix} + \begin{pmatrix} 2 \\ -1.5 \end{pmatrix} + \begin{pmatrix} 3 \\ 0.5 \end{pmatrix} = \begin{pmatrix} 0.5 \\ -1.5 \end{pmatrix} = \overrightarrow{CG}$$

 b i $\begin{pmatrix} 0 & -1 \\ -1 & 0 \end{pmatrix}$ **ii** $\begin{pmatrix} 1 & 0 \\ 0 & 2 \end{pmatrix}$

19 a i $(-1, -2)$, $(-1, -3)$, $(-3, -2)$
  ii reflection in $y = -x$

 b $\begin{pmatrix} 0 & -1 \\ 1 & 0 \end{pmatrix}$

20 a Enlargement, scale factor -2, centre C
 b $\begin{pmatrix} 12 \\ -1 \end{pmatrix}$

21 a i Reflection in $y = -x$ **ii** $\begin{pmatrix} 0 & -1 \\ -1 & 0 \end{pmatrix}$
 b i $(-1, 3)$ **ii** $(2, -1)$
  iii Rotation, 90° anticlockwise, centre of the origin

  iv $\begin{pmatrix} 1 & 0 \\ 0 & -1 \end{pmatrix}$

 c i $1:9$ **ii** $h = 27$

22 a i 3.61 units   **ii** $3x + 2y = 24$

   b i $\begin{pmatrix} 1 & 0 \\ 0 & -1 \end{pmatrix}$ **ii** Reflection in $y = x$

     iii a $\begin{pmatrix} -3 \\ -3 \end{pmatrix}$

       b $\begin{pmatrix} 0 & -1 \\ 1 & 0 \end{pmatrix}\begin{pmatrix} h \\ k \end{pmatrix} + \begin{pmatrix} -3 \\ -3 \end{pmatrix} = \begin{pmatrix} -k & -3 \\ h & -3 \end{pmatrix}$

        c $h = 0$ $k = -3$ **d** $(0, -3)$

23 a i Translation $\begin{pmatrix} -6 \\ 3 \end{pmatrix}$

     ii Enlargement, scale factor $-\frac{1}{2}$, centre $(-2, 1)$

     iii Rotation 90° anticlockwise, centre $(-1, 0)$

     iv $\begin{pmatrix} -2 & 0 \\ 0 & -2 \end{pmatrix}$

   b i a $p + 2q$ **b** $2p - 2q$ **c** $\frac{1}{3}p + \frac{2}{3}q$

     ii $\frac{1}{3}$

24 a i a 37   **b** $\begin{pmatrix} 16 \\ -21 \end{pmatrix}$

     ii $\begin{pmatrix} 14 \\ -28 \end{pmatrix}$ **iii** $(-6, 51)$

   b i 2 units²   **ii a** $(-2, 3)$ **b** 32 units²

   iii a $(3, 1)$ **b** 2 units²

25 a $\begin{pmatrix} 1 \\ 10 \end{pmatrix}$ **b i** 5 units   **ii** $n = 2$

Chapter 23

Essential Skills

1 a

Data item	1	2	3	4	5	6	7	8	9
Frequency	5	4	5	3	6	4	4	4	4

   b mean = 4.87
     median = 5
     mode = 5
     range = 8

2 $a = 120°$ $b = 6$ $c = 60°$

3

Heights of students (h cm)	Lower class boundary	Upper class boundary
141 to 150	140.5	150.5
151 to 160	150.5	160.5
161 to 170	160.5	170.5

Exercise 23.1

1 a

Class (l cm)	Frequency (f)	Class boundaries		Class width (w)	Frequency density ($f \div w$)
$20 < l \le 30$	1	20	30	10	0.1
$30 < l \le 50$	10	30	50	20	0.5
$50 < l \le 70$	15	50	70	20	0.75
$70 < l \le 100$	20	70	100	30	0.67
$100 < l \le 150$	3	100	150	50	0.06

   Modal class = $50 < l \le 70$

b

Class	Frequency (f)	Class boundaries		Class width (w)	Frequency density ($f \div w$)
0–30	5	0	30.5	31	0.16
31–50	25	30.5	50.5	20	1.25
51–70	41	50.5	70.5	20	2.05
71–100	50	70.5	100.5	30	1.67
101–150	7	100.5	150.5	50	0.14
151–250	2	150.5	250.5	100	0.02

   Modal class = 51–70

2 a

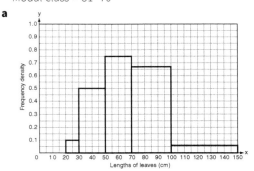

b

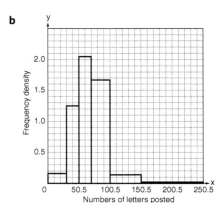

3 a

Age (*a*)	Class boundaries		Class width	Frequency density	Frequency
$0 \leq a < 20$	0	20	20	0.2	4
$20 \leq a < 40$	20	40	20	0.5	10
$40 \leq a < 50$	40	50	10	1.0	10
$50 \leq a < 65$	50	65	15	0.8	12
$65 \leq a < 85$	65	85	20	0.7	14
$85 \leq a < 110$	85	110	25	0.4	10

b

Number of peas	Class boundaries		Class width	Frequency density	Frequency
1–3	0.5	3.5	3	2	6
4–5	3.5	5.5	2	5	10
6–8	5.5	8.5	3	3	9
9–10	8.5	10.5	2	0.5	1

4 a, c

Class	$0 < s \leq 1000$	$1000 < s \leq 5000$	$5000 < s \leq 10000$	$10000 < s \leq 20000$
Frequency	20	100	105	100
Class width	1000	4000	5000	10000
Frequency density	0.02	0.025	0.021	0.01

b

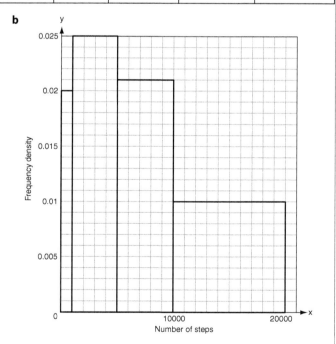

d $1000 < s \leq 5000$

Exercise 23.2

1 30.1   **2** 5.17   **3** 1.70

Exercise 23.3

1 a

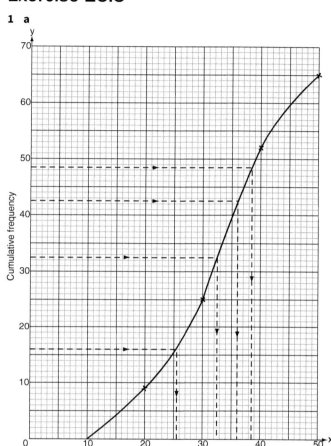

b median = 31.5 to 33.5

Q_1 = 24.5 to 26.5 Q_2 = 37.5 to 39.5

Inter-quartile range = 11 to 15

c 65th percentile = 35 to 37

2 a

Class	$65 < m \leq 70$	$70 < m \leq 75$	$75 < m \leq 80$	$80 < m \leq 85$	$85 < m \leq 90$	$90 < m \leq 100$
Frequency	3	5	6	7	4	3
Cumulative frequency	3	8	14	21	25	28

b

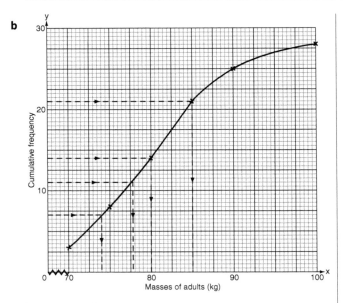

c i 79.5 to 80.5 kg

ii 10 to 12 kg

iii 77 to 78 kg

Exercise 23.4

1

Time	Class boundaries		Midpoint	Class width	Frequency	Cumulative frequency	Frequency density
$70 < t \leq 80$	70	80	75	10	4	4	0.4
$80 < t \leq 90$	80	90	85	10	5	9	0.5
$90 < t \leq 100$	90	100	95	10	9	18	0.9
$100 < t \leq 120$	100	120	110	20	38	56	1.9
$120 < t \leq 160$	120	160	140	40	8	64	0.2

b

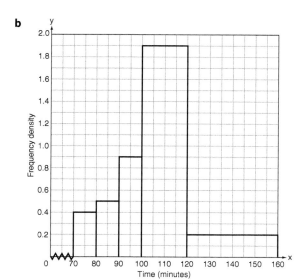

c 108 min

d $100 < t \le 120$

e

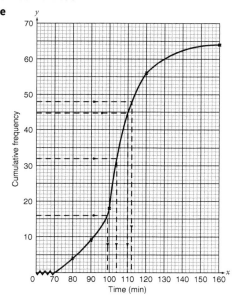

f median = 102 to 106　　　lower quartile = 97 to 101
upper quartile = 110 to 114　　70th percentile = 108 to 112

c

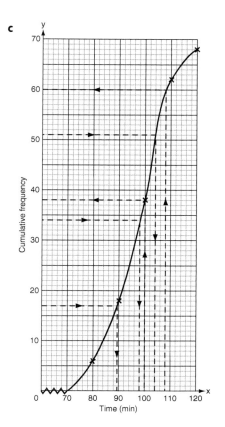

d median = 96 to 100　　Q_1 = 88 to 92　　Q_2 = 102 to 106
e one of 37, 38 or 39　　**f** one of 7, 8 or 9

3 Total girls = 25.4 × 12 = 305 to 3 s.f.
Total boys = 23.8 × 15 = 357
Total students = 662
Total classes = 22
Mean number of students per class = $\frac{662}{22}$ = 30.1

4 71.8%

5 a 24　　　　　　　　　**b** 77.2%

6 a i $125 < h \le 135$　　**ii** 126.25 cm
　　b i 11 cm　　　　　　　**ii** 16

2 a

Class	Class width	Midpoint	Frequency	Cumulative frequency	Frequency density
$70 < t \le 80$	10	75	6	6	0.6
$80 < t \le 90$	10	85	12	18	1.2
$90 < t \le 100$	10	95	20	38	2.0
$100 < t \le 110$	10	105	24	62	2.4
$110 < t \le 120$	10	115	6	68	0.6

b 96.8 minutes

7 a $1.5 < x \leq 2$ **b** 1.73 litres

c

Amount of water (x litres)	Number of people	Cumulative frequency
$0 < x \leq 0.5$	8	8
$0.5 < x \leq 1$	27	35
$1 < x \leq 1.5$	45	80
$1.5 < x \leq 2$	50	130
$2 < x \leq 2.5$	39	169
$2.5 < x \leq 3$	21	190
$3 < x \leq 3.5$	7	197
$3.5 < x \leq 4$	3	200

d

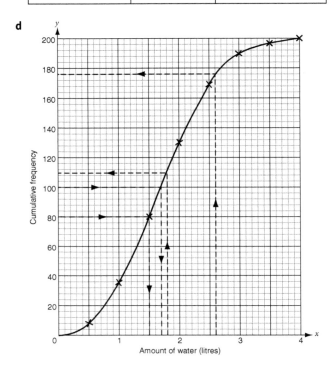

NOTE:

Shown half-scale. Yours should be twice this scale.

e i 1.65 to 1.75 litres
ii 1.5 litres
iii one of 23, 24, 25, 26, 27, 28 or 29
f 54 to 56.5%

8 a i 1
ii 3
iii 4
b 38.2 seconds
c i $p = 20$, $q = 72$

ii

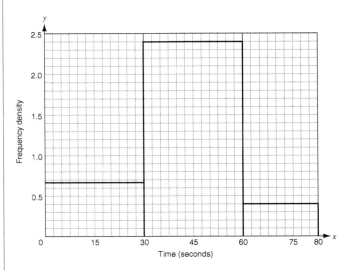

9 a 98.2

c

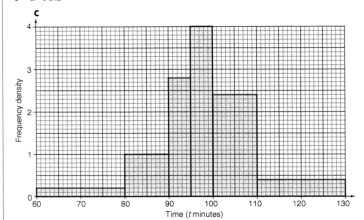

10 a 74.4 to 74.7 kg
b 79.1 to 79.4 kg
c one of 23, 24 or 25

11 a one of 219, 220 or 221 plants
b 13

c

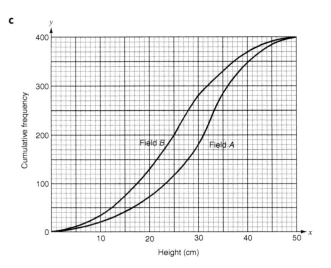

d For example, we can see that Field *A* produced the taller plants because the whole of curve for Field *A* is to the right of the curve for Field *B*. The median for Field *A* is 31 cm. The median for Field *B* is 25 cm

13 a

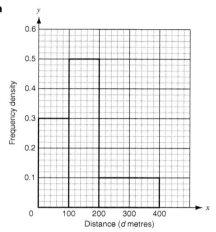

b 72°

14 a i 40 ii 18

b

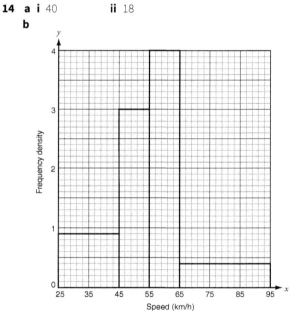

15 a i 30 ii 30, 30.5, 31 iii 3
b i 20.9 grams ii 2.6, 0.7, 0.8
16 a 3.365 to 3.375 grams
b 0.26 to 0.27 grams
c one of 55, 56 or 57

17 a i

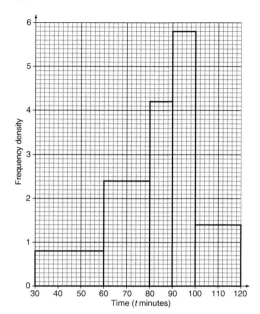

ii $p = 48$ $q = 42$
iii $\frac{57}{200}$ or 0.285

b i $40 < y \le 60$ ii 39.9
18 a 1 **b** 2.5 **c** 2.96 **d** 2.9
19 a

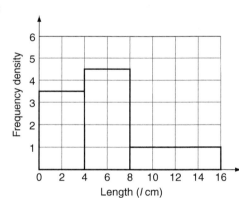

b 5.8 cm
20 a i 31.8 cm ii 0.42 to 0.48 cm
iii 108
21 a i 64.2 minutes ii 0.9 minutes
iii 50
b Paul, because his interquartile range is smaller.
22 a i 4.55 to 4.65 minutes ii 0.9 to 1 minutes
b 4.75 minutes
23 a i 55 ii 28
b Mathematics. For example, because the median is lower.

Chapter 24

Essential Skills

1 **a** 4   **b** $\frac{3}{10}$ **c** 0

2 **a** 6%   **b** 90

Exercise 24.1

1 **a**

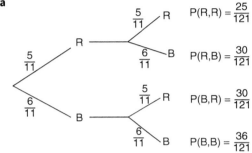

b $\frac{60}{121}$

2 **a i** $\frac{13}{30}$ **ii** $\frac{17}{30}$

b

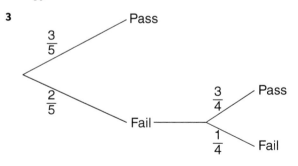

c i $\frac{52}{900}$ **ii** $\frac{338}{900}$ **iii** $\frac{442}{900}$

d $\frac{26}{30}$

3

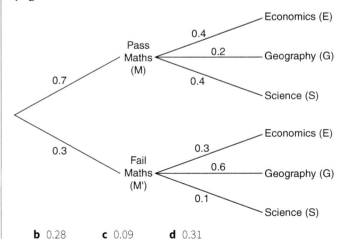

Exercise 24.2

1 **a** Yes   **b** 0.2   **c** 0   **d** 0.3   **e** 0.9

2 **a**

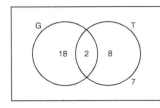 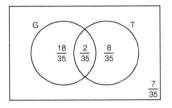

b $\frac{7}{35}$ **c** $\frac{2}{20}$

Exercise 24.3

1

	Girls (G)	Boys (B)	Totals
Year Five (F)	10	13	23
Year Six (S)	14	12	26
Totals	24	25	49

a $\frac{24}{49}$ **b** $\frac{14}{49}$ **c** $\frac{23}{49}$ **d** $\frac{12}{26}$

2 **a**

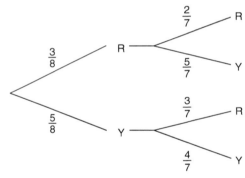

b different   **c** No   **d** $\frac{5}{7}$

e $\frac{3}{8} \times \frac{5}{7} = \frac{15}{56}$ **f** $\frac{15}{56} + \frac{15}{56} = \frac{30}{56}$

3 **a** $\frac{20}{50}$ **b** $\frac{19}{50}$ **c** 8   **d** $\frac{9}{50}$ **e** $\frac{9}{25}$

4 **a**

b 0.28   **c** 0.09   **d** 0.31

5 i 0 **ii** $\frac{1}{36}$ **iii** $\frac{1}{4}$ **iv** $\frac{1}{18}$

6 a $\frac{12}{18}$ **b** $\frac{3}{12}$

7 a $p = \frac{1}{20}$ $q = \frac{19}{20}$

  b i $\frac{1}{400}$ **ii** $\frac{38}{400}$

  c $\frac{38}{8000}$ **d** $\frac{58}{8000}$

  e 7 or 7.25 or 8

8 a $p = 5, q = 12, r = 1$

  b i 17 **ii** 12

  c i 26 **ii** 57

  d i $\frac{8}{100}$ **ii** $\frac{45}{100}$

  e $\frac{37}{74} \times \frac{36}{73} = \frac{18}{73}$

9 a i 6 **ii** 4.5 **iii** 4.54

  iv $\frac{1}{63}$ **v** $\frac{1}{35}$ **vi** $\frac{92}{819}$

  b i 0.08 **ii** 0.125 **iii** 7

10 a i 1 **ii** $\frac{3}{6}$

  b i $\frac{2}{30}$ **ii** $\frac{4}{30}$ **iii** $\frac{8}{30}$

  c $\frac{18}{30}$ **d** 4

11 a i $p = \frac{1}{3}, q = \frac{3}{8}, r = \frac{6}{8}, s = \frac{2}{8}$

  ii $\frac{5}{12}$ **iii** $\frac{2}{3}$

  b i $\frac{1}{120}$ **ii** $\frac{119}{120}$

12 a i

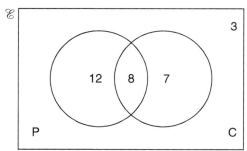

  ii 8 **iii** $\frac{12}{30}$ **iv** $\frac{12}{20}$

  b i $\frac{12}{90}$ **ii** $\frac{78}{90}$ **iii** $\frac{900}{6480}$ **iv** $\frac{5508}{6480}$

13 a

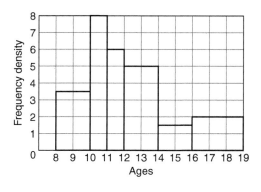

b $11 < x \le 12$ **c** 12.4 **d** 26

e i 0 **ii** $\begin{pmatrix} -2 \\ 0 \end{pmatrix}$ **f** $\begin{pmatrix} 3 \\ -3 \end{pmatrix}$

14 i $p = \frac{1}{5}$ $q = 1$ $r = 0$

  ii a $\frac{2}{7}$ **b** $\frac{4}{21}$ **c** $\frac{4}{7}$

15 iii $\frac{7}{30}$ **iv** 1.6 cm

16 a i 3 **ii** 4 **iii** 4.6

  b i $\frac{9}{25}$ **ii** 1

  c i $\frac{1}{50}$ **ii** $\frac{1}{30}$

17 a i 24 **ii** 8 **iii** 31

  b i $\frac{5}{36}$ **ii** $\frac{1}{9}$ **iii** $\frac{1}{6}$

18 a

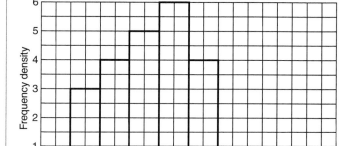

b 5 **c** $\frac{1}{8}$

d $\frac{870}{14280}$ or $\frac{29}{476}$ or 0.061

19 a

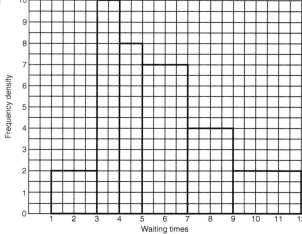

b $7 < t \leq 9$ **c** 5.8
d i 0   **ii** $\frac{14}{25}$
e i $\frac{54}{175}$ **ii** $\frac{88}{175}$

20 a

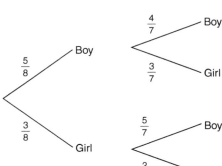

First student   Second student

b i $\frac{5}{14}$ **ii** $\frac{25}{28}$

21 a $\frac{1}{4}$

b i $\frac{3}{10}$ **ii** 0   **iii** $\frac{1}{10}$

Glossary

Acceleration is rate of change of speed.

Alternate angles are between the transversal and the parallel lines on alternate sides of the transversal.

Angle of depression measures the angle between the line of sight of an object *below* the observer and the horizontal.

Angle of elevation measures the angle between the line of sight of an object *above* an observer and the horizontal.

Approximation is expressing a measurement or other value to a convenient or sensible degree of accuracy.

Area is a measurement in two dimensions.

Axes on a graph are two lines which cross at right angles and are used to locate the positions of points.

Bar chart is a graph in which *separated* bars are drawn to illustrate the frequency of categorical or discrete data.

Bearing gives the direction of one place from another relative to due north.

Bias describes how fair a supposedly random event is.

Biased means that one result is more likely than another.

Calculate means find a numerical answer.

Cancelling down is writing a fraction in a simpler form by dividing the numerator and denominator by the same number.

Capacity is the amount of liquid a container can hold.

Categorical data is usually non-numerical data such as people's names.

Central tendency is a measure of the middle or most representative value of a set of data.

The middle is assessed by finding the mean, the median or the mode.

Class boundaries are used to decide into which class rounded continuous data should be entered.

Coefficient of a term is the number in front of it, for example the coefficient of $3x$ is 3.

Common factors are factors that are in more than one term; for example, in $3xy$ and $9x^3$, 3 and x are common factors.

Common or vulgar fractions are ordinary fractions, for example $\frac{2}{3}$. Here, 2 is the numerator and 3 is the denominator. Usually just abbreviated to 'fractions'.

Complement of a set is all the elements that are not in the set, but that *are* in the universal set.

Completing the square is a method used to solve quadratic equations. The quadratic formula is derived using this method.

Compound interest is calculated on the original amount plus all the interest to date.

Conformable: Two matrices are conformable for multiplication if the number of columns in the first is the same as the number of rows in the second.

Congruent shapes have exactly the same size and exactly the same angles.

Continuous data is measured data such as length. It has to be divided into suitable groups by rounding, such as 'to the nearest metre'.

Correlation is a measure of how strongly two sets of data appear to be connected.

Corresponding angles are equal angles on the same side of the transversal.

Corresponding sides in two or more similar triangles are the sides opposite the equal angles in each triangle.

Cosine of an angle in a right-angled triangle is the ratio of the length of the adjacent side to the length of the hypotenuse.

Cosine rule extends Pythagoras' theorem so that it can be used in any triangle. It has a 'correction term' which allows for the fact that the triangle is not right angled.

Cumulative frequency is the running total of the frequencies in a grouped frequency distribution.

Data is the set of pieces of information, usually numbers, which will be examined statistically.

Decimal fractions are usually abbreviated to 'decimals'.

Denominator is the number under the line of a fraction.

Density is the weight per unit volume of a material.

Dependent events: Two events are **dependent** if the probability of the second depends on the result of the first.

Depreciation is the loss of value of goods as they age.

Determinant of a 2×2 matrix $\begin{pmatrix} a & b \\ c & d \end{pmatrix}$ is the number obtained from the difference of the products of the diagonals: $ad \times bc$.

Difference of squares is an expression with two terms, both perfect squares, in which one term is subtracted from the other.

Direct proportion: Two items, or amounts, are in **direct proportion** when the rate at which they increase or decrease is always the same for both.

Directed line segment, $\overline{AB}$, is the particular vector which joins the point A to the point B.

Directed numbers are numbers that can be positive as well as negative. The sign indicates a direction, for example $-10\,°C$ is $10\,°C$ *below* freezing.

Discrete data is data that takes individual values such as shoe sizes.

Domain is the set of numbers that a function maps from.

Elements: The members of a set are also called the **elements** of the set.

Elimination is a method used to solve simultaneous equations.

Empty set has no members.

Enlargement makes an object larger or smaller according to a given scale factor.

Equation has an equals sign and can often be solved.

Equivalent fractions represent the same number, for example $\frac{3}{5}, \frac{6}{10}, \frac{90}{150}$ all represent $\frac{3}{5}$ of the whole.

Estimation is a method of making an informed guess at the size of a measurement or other value.

Event is any collection of outcomes of an experiment.

Expressions are groups of terms to be added or subtracted. They do not have an equals sign. They cannot be solved, but may be simplified.

Factors of a number can be multiplied together to make that number, for example 1, 2, 3 and 6 are factors of 6.

Formula (plural **formulae**) is used to calculate quantities, for example speed $= \frac{distance}{time}$.

Frequency density of a class is the ratio of the frequency to the class width.

Frequency distribution or **frequency table** shows how often each item in the data set occurs.

Frequency polygon is formed when the midpoints of the tops of the bars of a simple histogram are joined by straight lines.

Frustum is the part of a cone left when the pointed part (vertex) of the cone is removed.

Function is a mapping from one set of numbers to another.

Gradient is a measure of the steepness of a line on a graph.

Grouped frequency table is where the data set is collected into groups or classes.

Highest Common Factor (HCF) of two or more given numbers is the highest number which will divide into both or all of the given numbers without leaving a remainder, for example 3 is the HCF of 9, 12 and 15.

Horizontal lines are parallel to the surface of the Earth.

Hypotenuse: In a right-angled triangle the side opposite the right angle is the longest side and is called the **hypotenuse**.

Identity matrix: A 2×2 matrix multiplied by the 2×2 **identity matrix** is unchanged.

Improper fractions are 'top heavy' fractions, for example $\frac{9}{5}$.

Independent events: Two events are **independent** if the result of the first has no effect on the probability of the second.

Independent: Two results are **independent** if one does not affect the other.

Index (plural **indices**) or **power** shows how many of a certain number or variable are to be multiplied together, for example $n^4 = n \times n \times n \times n$.

Inequality is like an equation, but its solution is a range of values rather than discrete values.

Integers (Z) are the counting numbers and also zero and negative whole numbers, for example $-50, -2, 0, 11, 251$.

Interest is the amount you pay for borrowing money, or the amount you are paid for lending money. It is calculated as a percentage or **interest rate**.

Interquartile range is the difference between upper and lower quartiles.

Intersection of two or more sets contains all the elements that are present in both or all of the sets.

Inverse of a function maps the members of the range back to the domain.

Inverse matrix: A 2×2 matrix multiplied by its **inverse matrix** gives the identity matrix.

Inverse operation reverses the effect of another operation. For example, divide and multiply are inverses of each other, or square and square root.

Inverse proportion: Two items are in **inverse proportion** when while one increases the other decreases always at the same rate.

Irrational numbers are numbers which cannot be written as fractions, for example $\pi, \sqrt{2}, \sqrt{51}$.

Irregular polygon does not have all its sides or all its angles equal.

Length is a measurement in one dimension.

Like terms have the same letters, for example $4z$ and $10z$.

Limits of accuracy are the smallest and largest values a measurement might take and still be within the stated accuracy.

Line symmetry: A shape has **line symmetry** if it fits exactly on itself when it is folded along its **line of symmetry**.

Linear equation is an equation in two variables which will produce a straight line when it is drawn on a graph (see Chapter 7), for example $y = 2x - 1$.

Locus (plural **loci**) of points is the possible positions of those points defined by some rule. The positions may be in one (a line), two (an area) or three (a volume) dimensions.

Lower bound or **limit** is the lowest value a measurement might take.

Lowest Common Multiple (LCM) of two or more given numbers is the lowest number which is a multiple of both or all of the given numbers, for example 18 is the LCM of 2, 6 and 9.

Mariner's compass expresses a bearing direction with reference to the four main directions, N, S, E and W.

Matrix (plural **matrices**) is a rectangular arrangement of elements, usually numbers.

Mean is calculated by adding all the values together and dividing by the number of values used.

Median is the middle value when all the values are arranged in order of size.

Mixed numbers combine integers and fractions, for example $3\frac{2}{5}$. Here, 3 is the whole number part and $\frac{2}{5}$ is the fraction part.

Modal class is the class with the highest frequency in a grouped frequency distribution.

Mode is the most frequent value.

Modulus of a vector is the same as the length or magnitude of the vector.

Multiples of a number are the result of multiplying that number by any of the natural numbers for example 6, 12, 36 and 600 are multiples of 6.

Mutually exclusive results cannot possibly happen at the same time.

Natural (or Counting) numbers (N) are the whole numbers you need to count individual items, for example 1, 5, 72, 1000.

Negative correlation is seen if as one set of data increases the other set decreases. For example, the more builders you employ to build a house the less time it should take.

Net of a solid is a two-dimensional shape which can be cut and folded to make the three-dimensional solid.

nth term in a sequence provides the rule for working out every term in the sequence, for example if the nth term $= 3n + 1$ then the *second* term is $3 \times 2 + 1 = 7$.

Numerator is the number above the line of a fraction.

Order of a matrix is given as the number of rows by the number of columns.

Order of symmetry: The number of times a shape will fit on itself before a complete rotation is its **order of symmetry**.

Origin on a graph is the point where the two axes cross.

Outcome is the result of an experiment or other situation involving uncertainty.

Parallel lines never meet.
Percentages are fractions with a denominator of 100. Think of the % sign as 'out of 100'.
Percentiles divide a set of data into one hundred equal parts.
Perimeter of a shape is the sum of all its sides. It is a length measurement.
Perpendicular lines are at 90° to each other.
Pictogram is a simple method of illustrating the frequency of usually categorical data.
Pie chart is a circle divided into sectors to represent categories with angles at the centre proportional to the frequency of each category.
Polygons have three or more straight sides.
Population is the entire set of data from which a sample is taken.
Position vector, *p*, is the vector which joins the origin to the point *P*.
Positive correlation is seen if as one set of data increases in value the other also increases. For example, as the population of a city increases more schools are needed.
Possibility or **probability space** diagram illustrates all the possible outcomes of combined events.
Prime numbers can be divided only by themselves and 1 without leaving a remainder, for example 2, 11, 37, 101.
Prism is a solid which has the same cross-section all the way throughout its length.
Probability measures how likely it is that something will happen.
Probability scale is a fraction lying between 0 (impossible) and 1 (certain to happen).
Proper subset does not contain *all* of the elements of the larger set.
Pythagoras' theorem defines the relationship between the lengths of the three sides in a right-angled triangle.

Quadrant is a quarter of a circle.
Quadratic expression is a sum of terms usually involving a single variable in which the highest power of that variable is 2. There may also be a term with the variable to the power 1, and a constant term.

Quadrilateral shape has four straight sides.
Quartiles together with the median divide a set of data into four equal parts.

Random means completely without order.
Range is the difference between the highest and lowest values. It is a measure of the spread of the data.
Range is the set of numbers that a function maps to.
Rate is a measure of how one quantity changes as another changes.
Ratio compares the sizes of two or more quantities that are in proportion.
Rational numbers (Q) are the counting numbers, integers and also numbers which can be written as fractions (or ratios), for example $-20, -\frac{3}{4}, 0, 1, 50\frac{1}{2}$.
Real numbers (R) include natural numbers, integers, rational numbers and also irrational numbers.
Reflection is the image of an object in a mirror.
Regular polygon has all of its angles equal, and all of its sides equal.
Relative frequency is a measure of how often a particular result occurs in a repeated experiment.
Rotation is the turning of an object about a given point through a given angle.
Rotational symmetry: A shape has **rotational symmetry** about a point if it fits exactly on itself when rotated about that point through an angle less than 360°.
Rounding is the process of writing the number to a stated degree of accuracy according to a rule. Degrees of accuracy could be, for example, to the nearest whole number, to the nearest metre, to a stated number of decimal places, or to a stated number of significant figures.

Sample is taken when the entire set of data is too large to be conveniently used.
Scale factor is the ratio of a length of the image to the corresponding length of the object.
Scatter diagram or **scatter graph** is a method for showing the connection between two sets of data. For example, shoe sizes and ages of children.
Sequence is a list of numbers or terms which vary according to some rule. Each term is related to the previous term, or to its place in the sequence.

Set: A collection of objects, ideas or numbers that can be clearly defined.

Significant figures are literally the figures in a number which are significant. For example, 5.01 has three significant figures, but 0.12 has only two.

Similar shapes have exactly the same angles, but are different sizes.

Simple histogram is similar to a bar chart, but is used to represent continuous data that has been grouped into classes of equal size. The bars are not separate but must be of equal width.

Simple interest is calculated on the original amount only, at the same rate year after year.

Simplify means write in its simplest form.

Simplifying fractions means expressing them in their lowest terms, for example $\frac{20}{35}$ simplifies to $\frac{4}{7}$.

Simultaneous equations are two equations, each with two variables, which have a solution which satisfies both equations. When drawn on a graph the lines cross at this solution.

Sine of an angle in a right-angled triangle is the ratio of the length of the opposite side to the length of the hypotenuse.

Sine rule equates the ratios of the lengths of sides of a non-right-angled triangle and the sines of the opposite angles.

Solve usually means find a numerical solution to a problem or equation.

Speed is rate of change of distance.

Straight line segment is part of a straight line.

Subject of a formula is the quantity the formula is designed to find; for example, in $s = ut + \frac{1}{2}at^2$, s is the subject.

Subset is a smaller set entirely contained within another set. It may also be *all* the elements of the larger set.

Substitution is replacing an unknown variable by a number so that a formula or expression may be evaluated. It can be used to solve simultaneous equations.

Subtended The angle at the centre of a circle standing on an arc of that circle is called the angle **subtended** at the centre by the arc.

Supplementary angles add up to 180°.

Surd An irrational square root of a natural number.

Survey is a collection of information.

Tally chart is a convenient method of recording data before it is organised further.

Tangent ratio is usually shortened to **tangent**. The tangent of an angle in a right-angled triangle is the ratio of the length of the opposite side to the length of the adjacent side.

Terms in algebra are numbers and letters that are added or subtracted for example, in $3x + 5y$, $3x$ and $5y$ are terms. $3x$ is a **term in x** and $5y$ is a **term in y**.

Three-figure bearings express the direction as an angle measured clockwise starting with 000° at due north.

Total surface area of a three-dimensional object is the sum of the areas of each of its faces.

Transformation is the collective name for a group of movements or changes of shape or size of a two-dimensional object on a plane according to certain rules.

Transforming a formula means rearranging it to change the subject of the formula.

Translation is the movement of a two-dimensional object in a plane without turning it or changing its shape or size.

Transposed A matrix is transposed by turning the columns into rows and the rows into columns.

Transversal is a line which cuts a pair of parallel lines.

Trapezium (plural trapezia) is a quadrilateral with two parallel sides.

Tree diagram displays all possible results of two or more events.

Unbiased means that each result is equally likely.

Union of two or more sets is all the elements of both or all of the sets.

Universal set in a particular context contains all the elements from which the other sets are drawn.

Upper bound or **limit** is the highest value a measurement might take.

Variables are usually letters which represent numbers or amounts that can change or be given different values.

Variation relates two or more variables which are in direct or inverse proportion in an algebraic way.

Vector specifies the exact translation of an object or point on a graph from one place to another.

Venn diagram shows the relationship between the sets in the universal set.

Vertical lines are perpendicular to the surface of the Earth.

Vertically opposite angles are made when two straight lines cross. They are opposite at the vertex or point of intersection.

Volume is a measurement in three dimensions.

x- and y-coordinates of a point on a graph locate the exact position of that point relative to a pair of axes.

y-intercept is the point where a line cuts the y-axis.

Zero correlation means that there is no correlation between the two sets of data.

Zero matrix: All the elements of a zero matrix are zero.

Index